The History of Wales

HISTORY

OF

WALES.

WRITTEN ORIGINALLY IN BRITISH,

BY CARADOC OF LHANCARVAN,

ENGLISHED BY DR. POWELL,

AND AUGMENTED

W. WYNNE, Fellow of Jesus College, OXON.

TO WHICH IS ADDED,

A DESCRIPTION OF WALES,

BY SIR JOHN PRICE.

NEW EDITION, GREATLY IMPROVED AND ENLARGED,

WITH PEDIGREES OF FAMILIES.

The Chief Druid.

LONDON:

INTE
S7

M DCC LXXIV.

T O

S<small>IR</small> WATKIN WILLIAMS WYNNE, B<small>ART</small>.

K<small>NIGHT</small> OF THE SHIRE FOR THE COUNTY OF SALOP,

THIS NEW AND IMPROVED EDITION

OF THE HISTORY OF WALES,

A COUNTRY IN WHICH HIMSELF

AND FAMILY,

ARE UNIVERSALLY, AND DESERVEDLY RESPECTED,

IS INSCRIBED,

BY HIS MOST OBEDIENT

HUMBLE SERVANT,

Strand, N<small>c</small>
March   S.

THE

PREFACE.

THE hiſtory of the Britains, may not improperly be diſtinguiſhed into two periods; the former comprehending the interval from Brute to Cadwalader, whilſt the Britains are thought to have enjoyed a general poſſeſſion of the whole iſland; the other containing the memoirs and tranſactions of the Britains under their ſeveral princes, after their receſſion to that part of the iſland, ſince called Wales. The former of theſe has been generally accounted of late, abſolutely falſe and unhiſtorical; and it is undoubtedly concluded that all the paſſages in Geoffrey of Monmouth, (the only remaining monument of the affairs of the ancient Britains) which are not conſonant to, and agreeable with the Roman hiſtorians that ſpeak of Britain, are abſolutely fabulous and inſincere. The hiſtory of the Princes of Wales, has indeed met with better fortune, and the author Caradoc of Lhancarvan is accounted juſt and authentick; ſo that there need no other apology for the following work, than that it is for the beſt part the genuine hiſtory of that author. But becauſe the hiſtory of Wales has no ſmall dependence upon, and relation to the hiſtory of the ancient Britains publiſhed by Geoffrey, I think it neceſſary to make ſome general reflection, in relation to the truth and authority of that copy.

And here in the firſt place, I muſt take notice of two ſorts of opinions, moſt widely repugnant, and as I may ſay, diametrically oppoſite to each

b   other;

other; and both in my opinion, equally deviating from the right apprehenfion of the matter in debate. The one, perfectly rejecting the whole foundation and procefs of Geoffrey's hiftory, will not believe fo much as one paffage relating to the ancient Britains, but what is delivered by Roman writers; as if nothing remarkable could happen in Britain, but what muft needs fall un-, der their fpecial cognizance and obfervation. The other, without any allowance to the age when thefe Britifh affairs were tranfacted, (not to mention the utmoft antiquity of fome part of this hiftory, cotemporary with which, nothing is certain among the more civilized Greeks and Romans) will believe the whole frame, and all the circumftances of Geoffrey's hiftory, be they never fo ridiculous and extravagant. But not to infift on fo bigotted an opinion, as to think that the Britifh hiftory is univerfally true, and altogether authentick; I will confine myfelf to the examination of the other extream, to fee whether that hiftory publifhed by Geoffrey, be fo abfolutely fabulous as is frequently reprefented and generally believed. Now they who difcredit this hiftory, either wholly attribute the frame and invention of it to Geoffrey, or elfe granting him to be a faithful tranflator, affure themfelves that the copy he received was fictitious, and perfectly owing to the unwarrantable forgeries of the fabulous monks. So that the fubject of my prefent enquiries, will naturally fall under thefe two difquifitions; firft, Whether Geoffrey be the real contriver and compofer of this hiftory? and fecondly, Suppofing him to be innocent of this fufpicion, Whether the hiftory publifhed by him, be perfectly fabulous, and in all refpects a monkifh legend?

Firft.

THE PREFACE.

First, As to what relates to Geoffrey, though methinks there need no greater argument to evidence his innocency from so suspected an imposture, as his being the contriver of this history, than that he professedly owns the receipt of the British manuscript from Walter, archdeacon of Oxford; yet because the prejudice of some men oftentimes obscures their understanding, in things otherwise very clear and open, it will be requisite to dwell somewhat more particularly upon that subject: or if the world be once persuaded, that the whole invention is owing to Geoffrey, and that there was no such account of the Britains in being, before he published his history, the whole series of British affairs not mentioned in the writings of the Roman authors, and all that long continued succession of British kings for so many ages, must of necessity be accounted fabulous, and a perfect legend. But before that Geoffrey should be so unreasonably attainted of such notorious forgery, and his history be so generally condemned; one might expect that such evident proofs could be produced to evince so absolute a position, as to render it past all dispute and contradiction. For to charge any one with insincerity, for no other reason, than because it is the common vogue and sentiment of the world, is in my opinion a greater argument of partiality and prejudice, than of solid and judicious reasoning.

Now the greatest reason that I can think of, why the British history is attributed to the invention of Geoffrey, is, that almost upon its first appearance in the world, William of Newbo-

rough

rough and Geraldus Cambrensis exclaim against it, and seem to lay the whole imposture to the charge of Geoffrey. The words of Newborough are these : *At contra quidem* (speaking before of Gildas) *nostris temporibus pro expiandis his Britonum maculis scriptor emersit, ridicula de iisdem figmenta contexens, eosque longe supra virtutem Macedonum et Romanorum impudenti vanitate attollens. Gaufridus hic dictus est, agnomen habens Arturi, pro eo quod fabulas de Arturo ex priscis Britonum figmentis sumptas, et ex proprio auctas per superductum Latini sermonis colorem, honesto historiæ nomine palliavit. Qui etiam majori ausu, cujusdam Merlini divinationes fallacissimas, quibus utique de proprio plurimum adjecit, dum eas in Latinum transfunderet, tanquam authenticas, et immobili veritate subnixas prophetias vulgavit.*

From this passage it is apprehended, that Newborough thought that the British history was solely owing to the contrivance and invention of Geoffrey; whereas nothing is more evident than that the only thing he lays to Geoffrey's charge, is, that he augmented, and of his own head made additions to the copy he received. And seeing that Newborough expresly mentions Geoffrey's translating into Latin, some ancient figments of the Britains concerning King Arthur, and unwarrantably adding to the same; it is manifestly apparent that he never took Geoffrey to be the contriver of the whole of what he had published, otherwise it is hardly conceivable, that such an inveterate enemy of that history, would conceal any thing that might derogate from the truth and authority of it. Besides, Newborough throughout his whole

preface

preface, wherein he endeavours to invalidate, and render the Britifh hiftory fabulous, chiefly infifts upon the life of King Arthur, and the prophecies of Merlyn; not a word of Brutus and his Trojans, which, though fince accounted as notorious a piece of romance as any at all; it feems he had faith to fwallow. Indeed, the paffages in King Arthur's life, and the prophecies of Merlyn tending much to the fame purpofe, were too great and extravagant to be credited by him, (who by his character of them, feems to have bore but very flender affection towards the Welch,) by reafon that they derogated much from the fame and valour of the Saxons; fo that I am afraid, that the odium which Newborough bore to Geoffrey and his hiftory, depended more upon national honour and reputation, than the truth and fincerity of hiftory. For furely he could never be fo warmly exafperated againft a fabulous hiftory, had he but the candour to confult his own, unlefs there had been fome other motive to raife and foment his paffion. As to the fcurrilous language he cafts upon the Britifh hiftory, and his umannerly treatment of the tranflator; he therein expreffes his ignorance and malice, rather than any love and regard to truth and ingenuity. For who but an ignorant and an unfkilful pretender, would confidently affert the Britains never had any metropolitans or archbifhops, and would produce this as an invincible argument for the falfity of the Britifh hiftory; whereas it is notorioufly manifeft, that the Britains had their archbifhops long before the arrival of Auguftine the monk, whom Newborough pretends to have been the firft who underwent that dignity in

b 3   this

this ifland. But as his arguments againft Geoffrey's hiftory are weak and invalid, and his
whole preface more an invective than a confu-
tation, fo his credit fhould be rejected and undervalued, for charging another hiftory with
falfhood, when his own feems wholly inter-
woven with ridiculous legends and monkifh fictions.

But be the occafion of Newborough's diflike
of the Britifh hiftory what it will, it is evident,
that nothing can be concluded from the above-
quoted paffage, more than that Geoffrey made
additions to the Britifh copy he received of the
archdeacon of Oxford. And this is no more
than what may eafily and fafely be granted ; for
the life of King Arthur, and the prophecies of
Merlyn, the main fubjects of Newborough's
difcontent, may probably be inferted into the
hiftory by Geoffrey, at leaft they were augmented,
and feveral traditions were added by him. Bale,
affures us, that he writ the life of King Arthur
in a diftinct treatife; and himfelf owns in the preface to his fourth book, which comprehends the
prophecies of Merlyn, that upon the requeft of
Alexander bifhop of Lincoln, he had tranflated
Merlyn's propecies out of Britifh into Latin, before the Britifh copy came to his hands. Now,
when Geoffrey had received the manufcript from
the archdeacon, and was engaged in tranflating
it into Latin, it is no ftrange matter to imagine, that as occafion required, he might ampli-
fy, and add to it, out of his former tracts. For it
is obvious to fuppofe, that the feveral things concerning Arthur and Merlyn, might be preferved
in the ifland of Great Britain, which were long
ago obfolete among the Britains of Armorica;

from

from whence the Britifh copy is faid to have been brought over.

But fuppofing that Newborough had attributed the whole frame of the Britifh hiftory to Geoffrey, which is evident he does not, his authority cannot balance with far more authentic hiftorians, fuch as H. Huntington, R. Hovedon, Matthew of Weftminfter and others, but more particularly Matthew Paris, who in exprefs terms, calls Geoffrey, the faithful tranflator of the Britifh hiftory. And feeing then, that it was in thofe times apprehended to be an antient manufcript, and none of Geoffrey's contrivance, when the cheat might be beft difcovered, and there wanted not good inclinations to detect fo notorious a forgery; how in thefe latter times, it could be fo luckily found out, that Geoffrey was the fole inventor and compofer of the hiftory, I cannot poffibly divine.

Ad Ann. 1151.

The other reafon, why Geoffrey is thought to be the author of the Britifh hiftory, is grounded upon a paffage in Giraldus Cambrenfis, who fpeaking of the etymology of Wales, rejects the denomination of it from either duke Wallo, or queen Wendolen, *Sicut fabulofa Galfredi Arturi mentitur hiftoria*. Now this is thought an invincible argument againft Geoffrey, and a palpable detection of his infincerity, fince Giraldus, his own countryman, ftrikes at him, and accufes him of forgery; whereas upon nicer examination, we may eafily difcover how that Giraldus quarrels only with the hiftory which Geoffrey publifhed, and which upon that account bore his name. For had Giraldus thought it to be only a contrivance of Geoffrey's, had he fufpected that Geoffrey falfly pretended to have received an

Camb. Defcrip. Cap. 7.

antient

antient British manufcript, and by that means
to have impofed upon the world; can it be fuppofed that upon fo plain conviction of falfhood,
he would believe and give credit to an hiftory,
which he was fatisfied was altogether a fable? But
on the contrary, we find him affenting to the ftory
of Brutus, and the divifion of the ifland betwixt
his three fons; and in fhort, excepting in this
one place, he expreffes himfelf to be an abfolute
votary of the Britifh hiftory, whence 'tis evident,
he apprehended Geoffrey to be no more than a
faithful tranflator of an antient Britifh copy.

I need not take notice of William of Malmfbury, becaufe that by the beft account, he is fuppofed to have been dead before Geoffery publifhed
his hiftory, and confequently he could never fee
Lib. I. it; fo that this expreffion in him, *Hic eft Arthurus
de quo Britonum nugæ hodieque delirunt*, muft likely
refer to the then prefent traditions and accounts
of the Welch concerning king Arthur, which
probably might be too great and extravagant.
For 'tis certain that a traditional account of any
perfon or action, the farther it recedes from the
fpring and original, the more corrupt and imperfect it ftill proceeds; and like a ball of fnow, it
gathers and augments in its journey; fo that it
may be reafonably fuppofed, that the vulgar account which the Welch in Malmfbury's time delivered of king Arthur, was too far incredible and
furprifing.

But fince the reafons produced for proving Geoffrey to be the author of the Britifh hiftory, feem
not to be fatisfactory and evincing; let us fee
whether the contrary affertion can be more reafonably maintained. And firft, 'tis manifeft that Geoffrey could not be the total inventor of the Britifh
hiftory,

The PREFACE.

hiftory; by reafon that feveral things, and fome of the moft material paffages therein contained, are agreeable with the hiftories of the Gildas and Nen- Notes upon Bede. nius, the poetical fragments of Talieffyn, not to mention the Saxon Manufcript, quoted by Mr. Wheelock, and other authors far more antient than Geoffrey. 'Tis owned indeed Geoffrey might borrow the ground and plat-form of his romance from Merlyn or Talieffyn, or rather from Nennius, in whofe writings there is fome flight account of the Britains being defcended from the Trojans ; but the fuperftructure is all his own, who living in an ignorant age, and well knowing he could not well be difproved, took the liberty to make what invention he pleafed, and then recommended it to the world, for a true, undoubted hiftory. But notwithftanding all this conceffion, I think there is as little reafon to attribute the frame and compofition of this hiftory to Geoffrey as there can be, to think him contriver of the ground and plot of it. For it feems to me very unaccountable, that if Geoffrey was to invent and compofe this hiftory, why in this account of the tranfactions betwixt the Britains and Romans, he fhould fo widely difagree with, and deviate from the writings of the Roman hiftorians. For certainly, nothing could add more authority to a fable, than exactly to follow the fteps of creditable authors, in thofe things they both had occafion to treat of. This in all probability, would not only render that part of the hiftory unfufpicious, but likewife credit and authorize the reft, of which there was no account in Roman authors. And this difagreement betwixt the Britifh hiftory, and the writings of the Roman hiftorians, though frequently produced to overthrow the authority of it, induces me to believe,

lieve, not only that Geoffrey was not the author, but likewise that the macuſcript was ancient, and much older than the time, in which it was firſt made public.

But beſides, Geoffrey dedicates his tranſlation to Robert earl of Gloceſter, ſon to king Henry I. which in all likelihood he would never have ventured to do, had the original been of his own contrivance, for fear leaſt that the cheat being diſcovered, he ſhould be found, to put upon a perſon of eminent quality, with whom the Britiſh hiſtory was then in great eſteem. For to him it is that Geoffrey owns the receipt of this manuſcript from the archdeacon of Oxford, which he affirms to be very antient, and by his requeſt was perſuaded to tranſlate it into the Latin tongue. It was a very eaſy matter for the earl of Gloceſter to find out Geoffrey's integrity, by enquiring of the archdeacon (who by all accounts is reckoned his co-temporary) whether he had delivered ſuch an antient Britiſh copy into Geoffrey's hands, and whether the tranſlation juſtly anſwered the original. Theſe enquiries were natural, upon the publication of any new hiſtory, which made ſuch conſiderable noiſe and clamour in the world, and which gave ſuch an account of the antient Britains, as was never before thought or heard of among the Engliſh nation. And ſuppoſing the earl of Gloceſter to have omitted theſe enquiries, yet it is ſcarce conceivable, but that in caſe of ſo open a forgery, the archdeacon would diſcover the cheat, unleſs it can be thought that he was privy to, and had a hand in the contrivance. But he was ſo far from detecting Geoffrey's impoſture, that he himſelf owns too, to have tranſlated the Britiſh hiſtory firſt into Latin, and then in his

latter

latter days, to Britifh again from the Latin, as may. be ftill feen in the Archives of Jefus-College library. Now if there be any heed to, or dependance upon this, if it be true, that the archdeacon did tranflate, and confequently allow of this hiftory, it appears very evident to me, that Geoffrey can be in no wife the author or contriver of it.

But that Robert of Glocefter took a fancy to Geoffrey's tranflation, more upon the account that his father had lately fubdued the Welch, and therefore feemed to add to his father's glory, than that he did credit and believe the hiftory, does not feem to be fo true and evincing. For wherein could the publication of this hiftory contribute to the advancement of his father's name? Was it becaufe he had conquered a people whofe anceftors appeared by this hiftory to be formerly valiant and warlike? this was performed by others before him, and I can conceive no great addition to any man's fame, to conquer a handful of people, with a numerous army, tho' their forefathers had been ftout and victorious. This is furely too flight a pretence for the reception of the Britifh hiftory by the earl of Glocefter, and too weak an argument to deftroy the truth and authority of it. It is certain, that it took exceeding well in the world at that time, nor was it oppofed till after Robert's death, when William of Newborough more out of malice and difcontent than any love he bore to truth, began to charge both the original and tranflator with infincerity. I cannot fee upon the whole, the leaft reafon, why the contrivance and invention of this hiftory fhould be attributed to Geoffrey, or that the authority of it depends any way upon him, more than the fidelity of his

tranf-

tranflation. I fhall therefore conclude this fubject with the character beftowed upon Geoffrey,
and the hiftory by him publifhed by Ponticus
Virunnius, who flourifhed in the year 1290, a
man of great reading, and excellent learning of
his time, who did not think it loft labour to draw
an epitome of the Britifh hiftory: *Giraldus*
(fays he) *hiftoricus egregius et cardinalis, magnæ vir auctoritatis apud Robertum Claudiocef-
triæ ducem, Henrici regis filium, ac patriæ fuæ
curiofiffimus fautor, ex fumma philofophia atque
archivis, hiftoriam antiquiffimam continua ferie
ab ipfis Trojanis collectam tranftulit. Veriffimas
Britannorum hiftorias arguit regum occidentalium
confuetudo; quæ erat, fecum femper habere eos,
qui veritate præcipua eorum gefta notarent.*

Secondly, But fuppofing Geoffrey to be innocent from this fufpected impofture, and that he
did no more than faithfully tranflate a Britifh manufcript he received of the archdeacon; it may
be farther objected, that feeing it abounds with
fo many unwarrantable matters of fact, and fo extravagant fables and prodigies, it appears extremely fufpicious, and fenfibly fmells of a monkifh
production. For how is it poffible, you will
fay, that any account, excepting what is found
in the Roman hiftories, could be had of the Britains, and that not only before, but even after
their fubjection to the Romans; fince there is fo
much reafon to doubt, whether the Britains, as
well as other unlettered nations, had any means
to convey any knowledge to pefterity, for want
of the art of writing? for if the affairs and
tranfactions of the Britains were only handed
down by tradition, and they had no other way

or

or method to preferve their memories, then certainly all pretences to ancient records, and confequently to this Britifh manufcript, fuppofed to have been tranflated by Geoffrey, muft of neceffity be vain and groundlefs.

And thus it is fuppofed, that the Britains had no writing among them, neither before nor after the Roman conqueft; whence it follows, that there is no true nor certain account of any matter tranflated among them, but what is recorded in Roman hiftories. But tho' this be frequently infinuated, yet I think, the contrary can with greater eafe and perfpicuity, be made to appear. As to the Britains having no writing among them, during their fubjection to the Roman empire, the contrary is fo evident and notorious, that I conceive it loft time to go about to difprove it. It is fufficient to lay down the words of Tacitus, an author of unfhaken reputation; *Jam vero* Vita Agric. *principum filios liberalibus artibus erudire, et ingenia Britannorum ftudiis Gallorum anteferre, et qui modo linguam Romanorum abnuebant, eloquentiam concupifcerent. Inde etiam habitus noftri honor, et frequens toga; paulatimque difceffum ad deliniamenta vitiorum, porticus et balnea, et conviviorum elegantiam.* Now, can any one fuppofe, that when the Britifh youths were inftructed in all the arts and fciences of the Romans, when they began to ape and imitate them in their habits, buildings, and other neceffary fooleries, they fhould neglect fo neceffary a qualification, as that of writing? and can we imagine, that among fo many able and learned perfons, as the Britains muft in reafon be, when educated in the Roman way, and owned to be very tractable in their education, not one fhould prove

fo

so affectionate to his country, as to note down the
state and transactions of it? certainly, if they learnt
all the civilites and sciences of the Romans, history was not so slight and trivial a subject of their
industry, as to be undervalued; and I know not
where they could better employ their skill, than
in writing the history of their native country.
It was natural for them being once civilized, to
enquire into the origin and antiquity of their nation, the state and condition of their conntry
before the Roman conquest; and having made
the best search they could, whether by oral or
written tradition into these enquiries, they would
in all reason, according to the custom and manner of the Romans, commit all to writing.

But allowing the Britains to have learnt the
art of writing from the Romans, after their subjection to the empire, yet it is certain they had
no such thing among them, before the discovery
of this island by Julius Cæsar, and consequently,
that all the former part of the British history
which precedes that epoch, must be false and
fictitious. And that this is no precarious objection, a passage out of Cæsar's Commentaries
is produced to strengthen it, which in my opinion, evidently proves the contrary. The words
of Cæsar are these: *Magnum ibi numerum* (speaking of the Druids) *versuum ediscere dicuntur, itaque annos nonulli vicenos in disciplina permanent;
neque fas esse existimant ea literis mandare, cum in
reliquis fere rebus, publicis privatisque rationibus,
Græcis literis utuntur.* Why any one from hence
should conclude, that the superstition of those
ancient philosophers the Druids, forbad the Britains to commit to writing the transactions of
their country, much more that they had no writ-

De Bell.
Gal. lib. vi.

ing at all among them, does I confess, very far
exceed my comprehension. Cæsar, truly does
intimate, that the doctrine and mysteries of their
religion, the Druids did not think fit to commit
to writing; but in all matters besides, whether
private or publick (among which, history may
be reasonably accounted) they used the Greek
characters: for so I understand these words, *Græcis literis utuntur.* For it may not be supposed
that all publick and private affairs of the Britains
were translated in Greek, when they had a different language of their own, and which in all
reason must be the common tongue of the country; but only that when the Britains had occasion to put any thing in writing, they used the
Grecian character, which probably was the only
letter, they then were acquainted with. But to
confirm this matter the more, Cæsar makes mention of the like custom among the Gauls; *In ca-* Lib. I.
stris Helvetiorum tabulæ repertæ sunt literis Græcis
confectæ. Now if he concluded from hence, that
the Gauls (for the Helvetians were a Gaulish
people) made use of the Greek language, rather
than the Grecian characters; I would fain be informed, why Cæsar should write in Greek to
Quintus Cicero, *Ne intercepta epistola sua, a Gal-* Lib. V.
lis consilia noscerentur; lest that his letter being
intercepted, all his measures and martial intrigues
be discovered by the Gauls. Certainly, if he
had known (as well he might, in case the Helvetians understood and writ in Greek) that the
Gauls were not ignorant of the Greek language,
he would not make use of so mean a stratagem
to conceal his counsels. But suppose it be acknowledged that the Gauls and Britains used,
not only the Greek characters, but the language
4   too

too (one of which muſt be allowed) it is evident that they had the art and uſe of writing before Cæſar made an invaſion to either country, and conſequently the Britains might have ſome written memorials of their country, which might be afterwards eaſily handed down to poſterity. For it ſeems to me very ſtrange, that men of ſuch reputed learning and knowledge, and ſo well verſed in the myſteries of philoſophy, as the Druids are acknowledged to have been, ſhould be ignorant of ſo neceſſary and uſeful a qualification as writing. And ſince it is affirmed, that their religious ſuperſtitions were interdicted to be committed to writing, we may rationally conclude, by the rule of contrariety, that all other things beſides their religion, were allowed to be written, and conſequently, that they had the art and uſe of writing among them.

But ſuppoſing the Britains to have recorded the tranſactions of their country, both before and after the Roman conqueſt, yet when the Saxons prevailed in the iſland, all the monuments and writings of the ancient Britains were utterly loſt; ſo that this pretended hiſtory of the Britains, muſt be modern and fabulous, built upon vulgar and uncertain traditions. For how was it poſſible that any one could write a true and faithful account of the ancient Britains, and be ſo particular in the tranſactions of thoſe times, whereas there was not the leaſt light to guide him to the knowledge of thoſe obſcure ages. This is expreſly acknowledged by Gildas, who lived long before Geoffrey, and openly declares, that all the records and monuments of his country were loſt in his time; and that in writing thoſe ſmall fragments of the hiſtory of Britain, he was forced

to

to abstract his materials out of the writings of foreigners. *Illa tantum proferre conabor in me-* Excid. Brit. *dium, quæ temporibus Romanorum Imperatorum et passa est, et aliis intulit civibus, et longe positis mala : quantum tamen potuero, non tam ex scriptis patriæ scriptorum monimentis ; quippe quæ vel si fuerint, aut ignibus hostium exusta, aut civium exulum classe longius deportata non compareant ; quam transmarina relatione, quæ crebris interrupta intercapedinibus non satis claret.*

I shall here by the by, observe the levity of Aylet Sames's objection against the history of Britan. p. Brute ; namely, because Gildas makes no mention 150. of Brute and his Trojans, he concludes that the British history must be a real fiction ; whereas Gildas in this place manifestly declares his design only of writing the history of the Britains, during their subjection to the Roman empire. But as to this passage in Gildas, if in his time, there were no remains of his ancestors left in writing ; I would fain learn upon what ground and authority, he could so positively assert that the Britains from their first plantation in this island, were proud and irreligious, and their kings cruel and tyrannical. For a little before the above quoted passage, he says of Britain, *Hæc erecta cervice et mente ex quo inhabitata est, nunc Deo, interdum Civibus, nonnunquam etiam transmarinis regibus ingrata consurgit.* And a little after, *Tacens vetustos immanium tyrannorum annos, qui in aliis positis regionibus vulgati sunt.* Here he passes his judgment very liberally upon the state and condition of Britain from all antiquity ; and yet by and by, he confesses, that he had no guide to direct him to the knowledge of those times he so freely censures ; so that if he had not the light of other historians, he may falter in his conjectures, or elfe he was guided by fome Britifh light, of which he was not willing to own the perufal.

But allowing that Gildas, in compofing that fmall fragment of the Britifh hiftory, received no light from any Britifh record, but was con-ftrained to borrow out of the writings of fore-igners; it concludes no farther, than that he had not the good fortune to meet with Britifh manufcripts, not that there were none really re-maining in Britain. And farther, fuppofing that in Gildas his time, there were no remains of the antient Britains left in this ifland, but were all utterly loft; yet according to Gildas his own acknowledgment, and upon the Saxons prevail-ing in the country, they might be carried over by the exuled Britains to Armorica, from whence the archdeacon of Oxford is faid to have brought over the Britifh copy he delivered to Geoffrey. But if there was no written account of the for-mer ftate of Britain, in the age of Gildas, how comes it to pafs, that any fuch thing fhould be difcovered and brought to light in fucceeding ages? And not to infift upon the authority of the Britifh manufcript tranflated by Geoffrey, we have good reafon to prefume, that the antient Britains before Gildas had both ecclefiaftical and civil hiftories of their country.

As to the former, Bede, whofe authority, I prefume, will not be queftioned, exprefly affirms it. For in his preface to his ecclefiaftical hiftory, he fays, *A principio itaque voluminis hujus, ufque ad tempus quo Gens Anglorum fidem Chrifti percepit, ex priorum maxime fcriptis hinc inde collectis, ea quæ promemoramus, didifcimus.* Here Bede plain-ly declares, that in writing a church hiftory of

Britain, he extracted all his matter, before the
conversion of the Saxons to Christianity, out of
antient authors. But who can these former
writers be? Surely they were not Saxons, for
we read of no Saxon writer before Bede; besides, that several things contained in this history,
were translated before the landing of the Saxons;
and as to the ecclesiastical part, betwixt the
arrival, and the conversion of the Saxons to
Christianity that cannot be extracted out of their
writings. For in the first place they were no
Christians, and it is very unreasonable to suppose,
that they would write the history of a church,
of which they were at that time very fatal and
implacable enemies; not to question whether the
Saxons before their conversion had any writing
or learning at all among them. For though it
be pretended, that the Irish, who use the same
manner of writing, borrowed their characters
from the Saxons; yet 'tis extremely suspitious,
that these received them from the Irish, if not
rather from the Britains. As to the former, it is
well known, that during the disturbances betwixt
the Britains and Saxons here in Britain, the incursions of the Goths, Vandals, and other northern nations into other countries; all the learning of these western parts of the world, fled into
Ireland, which for a considerable time remained
to be the nursery of learning and learned men.

And that the Saxons, long after their conversion to Christianity, retired to Ireland for this purpose, we have the testimony of their antient and
most authentick historian; so that, I think, 'tis
no presumption to suspect, that as the Saxons
borrowed their learning from the Irish, they might
for the same reason, re... ... their ... ...

C 2   ic.. 1

Bed. Hist.
Eccl. lib. 3.
chap. 27.

form of writing from them. But 'tis again to be doubted, whether both the Saxons and the Irish did not primarily derive their characters from the Britains : for though the British language be now writ in a different character from the Irish and Saxon, yet upon antient British monuments and inscriptions, most of the Saxon letters, different from the present Roman alphabet, are plainly to be seen. Nor was this character originally British, the same being used in the first age of the Roman empire, if we can lay any stress on Julius Cesar's will and testament, represented by Mabillon. But farther yet ; if the Irish character be originally Saxon, the Saxons must either bring it along with them from Germany, or else they must have invented it after their arrival and settlement in Britain : if the first, it may seem wonderful, how it came to be quite lost and forgotten in all parts of Germany ; unless we can suppose, that it was limited only to the Saxons, and that they to a man came and settled in this island : for no body can be ignorant, that not only the Germans, but the Swedes and Danes too, use the Latin character; which, if we suppose them to have but lately borrowed, yet in all probability, their former letter was Gothick or Runick, to which the Saxon bears no great resemblance. But if it be said, that the Saxons invented this character after their coming to Britain ; I cannot well conceive, why they should put themselves to such unnecessary trouble, when with far greater ease and facility they might copy and borrow from the Britains ; unless the odium betwixt both nations made them scorn to ape and imitate an enemy. But be it so, that the Saxons invented this character in

De Re Diplo p. 345.

Britain; it will follow, that they had no letters nor learning before they came over; and consequently, that thefe authors which Bede mentions to have tranfcribed out of, could not be Saxons.

As to the civil part of the Britifh hiftory, that the tranfactions of ftate were recorded, and that copies thereof came to the hands of pofterity, we have the exprefs teftimony of Nennius, who flourifhed about three hundred years after Gildas. For in his preface to the hiftory of the Britains. he openly declares, that he compofed his hiftory, *Partim majorum traditionibus, partim fcriptis, partim etiam monumentis veterum Britanniæ incolarum.* Here Nennius fays, that he partly extracted his hiftory out of the writings of the antient Britains. And what could thefe writings be? Certainly, they were not the works of Gildas, the only Britifh author we read of before Nennius; upon the account that the hiftory of Nennius is much larger, and far more complete than that of Gildas; this latter, befides the names of a few Britifh kings, having left nothing hiftorical to pofterity; the main, it feems, of his defign being to rail, and to inveigh againft his country, to which he had taken fome difpleafure. From whence then elfe could Nennius extract the materials of his hiftory? Why, 'tis reafonable to fuppofe, that from fome Britifh records, which poffibly might be recovered fince the time of Gildas; and if then, why might not more be difcovered fince Nennius, and that delivered to Geoffrey by the arch-deacon of Oxon, be one?

But befides, that the Britains kept memorials of their tranfactions, we may rationally gather from the conftitution and profeffion of the bards.

c 3

The PREFACE.

Diodorus Siculus says, Οὗ τοι ᾗ μετ' Ὀργαίνων ταῖς λύραις ὁμοίων, ὅς μὴ ὑμνῶσιν, ὡς βλασφημῶσι; The bards singing to an instrument like a harp, repeat the praises and commendations of some, the faults and dispraises of others. And in like manner

Lib. 15. Marcellinus; *Bardi quidem fortia virorum illuf- trium facta heroicis compofita verfibus, cum dulcibus lyræ modulis cantitarunt.* And above the reft

Pharfal. lib 1. Lucan;

> Vos quoque qui fortes Animas, belloque peremptas
> Laudibus in longum vates emittitis ævum,
> Plurima fecuri fudiftis Carmina Bardi.

But that the Bards did not only commit to me- mory the famous deeds of their princes and heroes, and fo recite and repeat them upon occafions; but also that they wrote down and recorded what they repeated, we have the ample teftimony

Cambr. Defcrip. cap. 3. of Giraldus Cambrenfis. *Hoc etiam mihi notan- dum videtur, quod Bardi Cambrenfes, et Canta- tores feu recitatores, genealogiam habent prædic- torum principum in libris eorum antiquis et au- thenticis, fed tamen Cambrice fcriptam, eandemque memoriter tenent a Roderico magno ufque ad Belinum magnum, et inde ufque ad Silvium, Afcanium, et Æneam; et ab Ænea ufque ad Adam, generationem linealiter producunt.*

Now that the genealogies here mentioned by Giraldus, were not only a bare account of the feveral defcents and fucceffions of the British kings, but also fome memorials of their lives and actions, may be eafily gathered from the above faid manners and cuftoms of the Bards. And feeing thefe Bards did preferve not only in memory but in writing too, the lineal fucceffion and moft famous tranfactions of their kings; I

. . . . .ey may
not,

not, as to a great part of it, pretend to greater
authority than is generally attributed to it. And
if it be objected, that the Bards, by a poetical
liberty outdid the truth of hiftory, in the praifes
of thofe princes they were to celebrate ; yet thus
far it may reafonably be acknowledged, that the
names and fucceffion of the feveral kings are real,
and confequently that Geoffrey could never be
the inventer of fo large a lift of nick-names, as
he is generally thought to be. For it is very probable, that the hiftory of the Britains tranflated by
Geoffrey, was compofed partly out of thefe genealogies peculiar to the Bards, and partly out of
any other records and monuments of the Britains ;
both which I have fhewn to have been preferved,
and ufed among them antiently.

But to defcend to the particulars of this hiftory,
the firft and moft fufpicious relation, is that of
the landing of Brute with a colony of Trojans,
the feveral croffes and encounters he fuftained in
his voyage ; and then of this ifland receiving
its name from him. Should we indeed reflect
upon the particular circumftances of this ftory,
we might upon good reafon be fatisfied of the
vanity and falfenefs of them ; but therefore to
conclude, that becaufe the building is fufpicious,
the foundation confequently muft be fabulous,
and a perfect contrivance; does, I think, deferve
fome better examination : for if we do but reflect
upon the contemporary hiftories of the Greeks and
Romans, thofe more polite and literate nations,
we may with equal pretence of reafon affirm,
that there is no foundation for any matter of fact
before the Olympids; or that the relation of
Æneas coming to Italy, and all that hiftory, to
the building of Rome, are altogether ....

c 2

and impertinent, becauſe they are intermixt with fables and impoſſibilities. Livy aſſures us, that all the tranſactions, before the building of Rome, are rather owing to poetical fancy and extravagancies, than to any true and certain matter of fact; and therefore he declined to give either his aſſent or diſſent, to any thing related of thoſe times: *Quæ ante conditam condendamve Urbem, poeticis magis decora fabulis, quam incorruptis rerum geſtarum monumentis traduntur, ea nec affirmare, nec refellere in animo eſt.* And Plutarch goes farther, and tells us, that the original and etymology of Rome, that famous city, ſo well known afterwards over all the world, could not be agreed upon among the diverſity of authors, and conſequently muſt be very obſcure and uncertain. *Τὸ μέγα τῆς Ῥώμης ὄνομα ϗ δόξη διὰ πάντων ἀνθρώπων κεχωρηκὸς ἀφ' ὅτου ϗ δι' ἣν αἰτίαν τῇ πόλει γέγονεν, οὐχ ὡμολόγηται παρὰ τοῖς συγγράφουσιν.*

Præfat.

Vita Rom.

But for all their own hiſtorians do allow that the hiſtory of thoſe times are fabulous and uncertain; yet there are none that queſtion the being of Æneas, and that the Romans were deſcended from him. The like may be urged for the hiſtory of Brutus, and the landing of the Trojans in this iſland; that though many particular circumſtances are fabulous, and entirely poetical, yet it does not thence neceſſarily follow, that there is no manner of ground or foundation for ſuch a relation. Neither is it ſufficient conviction, to urge, that the very being of Brute is all a fiction, by reaſon that the Roman hiſtorians make no mention of ſuch a perſon to be the ſon of Silvius; becauſe, that through the whole Succeſſion from Æneas to Romulus, the Hiſtories of thoſe times take notice only of the ſon that was to ſuc-

ceed;

ceed; it being unreasonable to suppose, that all the kings of Latium during that period, should beget each of them, but one son. And therefore, what by the obscurity of those ages, and what by bearing regard to the line of succession, many collateral princes escaped the cognizance of future historians. Nor is it enough to affirm, that the history of Brute is but lately known and discovered to the world; whereas the fabulous Roman history has been recorded from antiquity; because, that though we are not certain that the British history has been handed down to posterity in writing; yet we are sure, that it was an antient tradition, long before Geoffrey's publishing of it; and one should think, that an ancient national tradition, might require a stricter examination, than hastily to throw it aside, as fabulous and one of no consequence.

But the question is not, whether the British history, as related by Geoffrey, be, as to all the circumstances of it, true and real matter of fact; for that, no man, I presume, can reasonably maintain; but whether there be any ground or foundation of truth couched under these poetical and fabulous narratives. Now the first thing we meet with in the British history, is, an account of Brutus his pedigree, how he was descended from the Trojans, and having accidentally slain his father Silvius, how he was forced to flee into Greece, whence, after several scuffles with Pendrasus, a petty prince of that country, he thought fit to retire, and to seek his fortune by sea. But he had not wandered long, when he met with Corinæus, with another party of desolate Trojans, with whom having joined his for... he ...... the .... of the Oracle,

Oracle, and at laft arrives in this Ifland, from him afterwards called Britain. Now as to the particular circumftances related in the life of Brutus, they may properly be placed in the fame clafs with Homer's account of the travels of Ulyffes, or Virgil's defcription of Æneas, his adventure to Italy; that is to fay, that they are poetical fictions, and perfectly confonant to the humour of that fabulous age. But the queftion in hand will be, whether there be any probability for the ground of this ftory, that Brute fhould bring over a colony of Trojans, and feat himfelf in this ifland. Now what is moft materially urged againft it, is the novelty of this difcourfe, that none of the Roman hiftorians make the leaft mention of fuch a perfon as Brutus; and that Cæfar and Tacitus, who feem to have enquired more narrowly into the original of the Britains, found no fuch tradition in their time; otherwife in giving their opinion whence the Britains were derived, they would never have omitted fuch an ancient national tradition, of their being defcended from the Trojans. Befides, that Gildas, who was a Briton, takes no notice of fuch a tradition, which in all probability he would never have omitted, had there been fuch an account of their origin in his time.

As to what is objected againft the antiquity of this tradition, is certainly very erroneous; for it is fo far from being firft known to the world, at the publication of Geoffrey's hiftory, that Nennius, long before that time, and Merlyn much antienter than he, fpeak of the Britains being defcended from Troy. Nay the ſ....ᴏ ...., were not

unac-

unacquainted with this tradition, as plainly appears from the antient Saxon poet, mentioned
by Mr. Wheelock, whom he thus tranflates:

——*Hæc unica fœmina prima*
Ante omnes fœvit Trojani femina belli,
Hanc Britones dixere Helenam, fed Dardanus ille
Excelfus Bruti pater extitit, unde Britanni
Heroum fumpfere genus; fortiffimis idem
Hunc orbem primus regere, & dominarier aufus.

And again:

Infula dicta fuit Britannia nomine Bruti.

That Gildas fhould make no mention of this
Britifh tradition, is no great wonder, and as little to the purpofe, to invalidate the antiquity of
it; for we muft not regard the intent and pur-
port of Gildas's writing, which was not to give
an account of the hiftory and antiquity of the
Britains, as much as to inveigh againft the pro-
phanenefs and licentioufnefs of the age; wherein
his zeal and paffion carried him fo far, that he
did not fpare either princes or the greateft perfons; and therefore he might well omit to give
an account of the origin of the Britains, feeing
it was remote from, and exclufive of his purpofe. Cæfar indeed feems to have been fomewhat more inquifitive about the antient ftate and
defcent of thofe people he invaded; but his ftay
in Britain was fo fhort, and his knowledge of
the country fo defective, being he had no communication with the inland Britains, whom he
owns himfelf to be the antient inhabitants,
that it was but great wonder he fhould be
ignorant of the thing: for if this curious
perfon

perfon had had the opportunity of a free converfation with the Britains, he would in all
likelihood have left a large difcovery of their
manners and cuftoms, and given a more perfect
defcription of Britain ; which at that time would
have been a very acceptable performance, to all
the perfons of learning and curiofity in Rome,
who as yet had but very fhallow knowledge of
the ifland. Or if we fuppofe that he made the
ftricteft enquiry about the ftate of the Britains,
which he might probably have learnt from
Mandubratius the fon of Imanuentius, king of
the Trinobantes, who, for fear of Caffibelan,
had come over to him to Gaul, and fided with
him during the Britifh wars, it is very poffible
he might be ignorant that the Britains were
defcended from the Trojans, and that to be an
antient and a current tradition among them.

Tacitus was never in Britain, but from the
relation of his father-in-law, Julius Agricola,
and others, he made a guefs, that from the different fhapes and colour, they were defcended
from different nations ; fome from Germany,
fome from Gaul, and others from Spain ; but yet,
as to the primitive Britains, thofe who feemed
to be the ancient inhabitants of the ifland, he
concludes after the ufual pagan manner, *Britan-*
In vita *niam qui mortales initio coluerint, indigenæ an ad-*
Agric. *vecti, ut inter Barbaros parum compertum.* The
Britains, indeed, in Tacitus's time, were well
known to the Romans, and confequently thefe
latter might have been eafily inftructed, as to
what knowledge the Britains had of their antiquity ; but it does not therefore neceffarily follow, that becaufe this hiftorian does not mention
a ꞏ ꞏ ꞏ ꞏ ꞏ ꞏ ꞏ ꞏ ꞏ ꞏ ꞏ ꞏ nong
ꞏ nem ;

them; becaufe poffibly he might never have heard of it; or if he did, he might have omitted inferting of it in his hiftory : for what he has delivered relating to the antiquity of the Britains, was but contingent to his purpofe, the whole fcope of his defign being to defcribe the actions of his father-in-law, during his lieutenancy in this ifland; and therefore it is not at all wonderful, that he has given but a flight and an imperfect account of what he never defigned to make a narrow infpection into. Befides, if we fuppofe him to have made a diligent enquiry into the matter, and to have mind to know the ancient ftate and origin of the Britains; yet fince he wonted the opportunity of converfing with them, having been never in Britain ; and none of the Britains that we know of, being at Rome, except thofe who from their youth were educated there, and conefquently were in all probability ignorant of the traditions of their own country ; he might very well at fuch a diftance have been never acquainted with fuch a national tradition, which for all that, might have been current and prevailing among the Britains themfelves. As to other Roman hiftorians, who have writ of the antiquity and primitive ftate of Rome, that they have made no mention of any fuch perfon as Brutus the fon of Sylvius ; I have already obferved, is not of that force as to overthrow this tradition, by reafon that, from Æneas down to Romulus, there is regard only had to the line of fucceffion, and thofe only recorded who fucceeded in the throne.

Let us confider now, in the next place, what probable reafons may be affigned to vindicate this fuppof   the   d it; and whether

whether the history of Brutus have any probable dependance upon some real foundation. And not to insist on the antiquity of this tradition, nor the authority of the British history published by Geoffrey, nothing gives greater confirmation to assert some real foundation for this supposed fable, than the near alliance and affinity betwixt the Britains and the Grecians. All learned men allow that the Greek was the ancient language of the Trojans, and that their customs were not much different; and whoever will compare the manners, religion and customs of the Britains with those of the Grecians will easily discover a palpable conformity betwixt both nations, but more especially in the language; in which, as Mr. Camden says, *Maximum est disputationis firmamentum et certissimum originis gentium argumentum. Qui enim* (as he goes on) *linguæ societatæ conjuncti sunt, originis etiam communione fuisse conjunctos, homo opinor nemo inficiabitur.*

I shall not at present trouble the reader with a particular enumeration of that affinity; but will refer him to Sir John Price's *Defensio Historiæ Britannicæ,* and Mr. Sheringham's treatise *De Gentis Anglorum Origine.* Now, since there is such demonstrable affinity betwixt the Britains and the Grecians in all these respects; we must either suppose, with Mr. Camden, that they are of the same origin, at least that a colony of either Greeks or Trojans came over to this island; or else, that the Britains had correspondence, traffick and communication with the Grecians. Now, that the Grecians had no knowledge of the Britains till very late, may be gathered from hence, that even the name of Britain is not so much as mentioned by any Greek author

author before Polybius, who lived lefs than two hundred years before the Roman invafion, and by him but juft named, as betokening a very remote and diftant country, wherein indeed it was reported that there was plenty of tin. Nay, Britain was fo far unknown to the eaftern parts of the world, long after this, that even Cæfar himfelf, when he intended an invafion, was perfectly ignorant of the ftate of the ifland; and tho' he made what enquiry he could of the Britifh merchants in Gaul, yet for all that, he fays himfelf, *Neq; quanta effet infula magnitudo, neq; quæ aut quantæ nationes incolerent, neq; quem ufum belli haberent, aut quibus inftitutis uterentur, neq; qui effent ad majorum navium idonei portus reperire poterat :* and therefore he was forced to fend Caius Volufenus before him to fearch into the ftate and condition of the ifland. Such ftrangers were the Romans at this time to the ifle of Britain. And can it be fuppofed, that the Grecians had a better knowledge of it, fince, in all probability, if they had had a commerce with the Britains, the Romans, who were mafters of the fea long before this, would have quickly difcovered their merchandizing; which, if as profitable as is imagined, they were no fuch enemies to gain but they would fhare in the booty. At leaft, had the Grecians had any correfpondence with the Britains, the Romans would in all probability have known it, and confequently they muft needs have received better intelligence of the Ifland than what they feem to have had at Cæfar's landing. But Dion Caffius feems to put this matter out of difpute, and gives us a very plain account of what knowledge the Greeks . .d Rcr.... in ... thi. Ifland, which I vil!

Bell. Gall. Lib. 4.

THE PREFACE.

Lib 39. I will fet down in the Latin tranflation, *Primis Græcorum Romanorumque ne effe quidem Britanniam compertum fuit, pofteriores in controverfiam adduxerunt, continens ea terra, an verò infula effet : multaque de utraque opinione confcripta funt ab iis, qui certi quidem nil noverant (quippe qui nec vidiffent, nec ab indigenis qualis effet accepiffent) fed conjecturis tantum, quantum vel otii vel ftudii fingulis aderat uterentur.* And the antient poet, in Euftathius upon Dionyfius, reckoning up the greateft iflands of the world in his time, makes no mention of Britain, which fhews it was not then known. And that Britain was the antient Caffiterides of the Grecians, from whence they received their tin, is altogether uncertain ; for Herodotus, making mention of thofe iflands of Caffiterides, fairly declares he knew not where they were; which cannot well be fuppofed, if the Grecian merchants traded thither in his time ; it being rational to imagine that, in treating of any country, fuch a learned hiftorian would endeavour to get the beft intelligence he poffibly could; and learning being at the higheft pitch in Greece at this time, it is very ftrange we had not a better account of this ifland, which is fuppofed to be fo well known to thofe who had a conftant traffick here. But indeed, all authors who have mentioned thefe Caffiterides do not feem to have known where they were fituated, only Dionyfius, in his περιήγησις, makes them plainly to be the fame with the Hefperides, thofe Iflands lying in the Atlantick Ocean, far enough from Britain, concerning which the poets have invented fo many fables.

— Αὐτά'ς

THE PREFACE.

——— Αὐτὰρ ὑπ' ἄκρην,
Ἴρην ἣν ἐνέπουσι κάρην ἐμῆν Εὐρωπείης,
Νήσους δ' Ἑσπερίδας τόθι χρυσιτέροιο γενέθλη,
Ἀργυροὶ ναίουσιν ἀγαυῶν παῖδες Ἰβήρων.

But admitting the Grecians to have been ignorant of any such place as Britain, and that
there never was any traffic or communication
betwixt thefe two nations; yet fince the Gauls
fpoke Greek, it is not very improbable but that
the Britains might borrow from them. That
the Gauls ufed the Greek tongue, we have the
teftimony of Cæfar; and it is very certain, that
all the Grecian learning flourifhed at Marfeils,
which was an ancient and and famous univerfity,
and is very much celebrated by all almoft, both
Greek and Latin writers. And by this means,
it may be reafonably concluded, how the Britifh
and Gaulifh Druids became acquainted with the
Grecian philofophy, which being as to all the
different fects and opinions of it, taught at Marfeils, the Druids more particularly adhered to
the Pythagorean, to which the Druid philofophy bears a very near refemblance, both as to
the doctrine of the Μετεμψύχωσις, or the tranf-
migration of the foul, and the reft of their my-
ftical Cabala, which they fo fuperftitioufly kept
fecret and clofe from the people.

But in oppofition to this, it may be with
greater certainty urged, that neither the Gaulifh
nor Britifh Druids had any correfpondence with
the Grecians, and confequently could not borrow their philofophical myfteries from them.
For if Cæfar may be believed, The art and
learning of the Druids was firft found out in Lib VI.
Britain, and from thence is thought to be
brought into Gaul; and at this time, as he goes
on, fuch a will attain to the perf t knowlage

d   of

of that difcipline, do for the moft part travel
thither to learn it. Now if this be true, that
the Britifh Druids were the inventors of this
kind of learning, and that the Gauls came over
hither to be inftructed in the way and method
of it; I can fee no reafon, why they fhould
have any communication with the Grecian aca-
demy at Marfeils, much lefs that they borrowed
it from the difciples of Pythagoras, efpecially
fince they accounted their myfteries fo facred,
that they would communicate them to none,
befides thofe of their own order. Nay, it may
be better queftioned, whether Druidifm be not
much antienter than Pythagoras, and antecedent
to that æra, when the Grecians began to philo-
fophife. And for the fame reafon, that the
Druids of Britain did not derive their philofophy
from Marfeils, it will follow, that they could
not borrow their language; for if we fuppofe,
which is the moft we can, that the Gauls had
fome communication with thofe Grecians, and
upon that account that their language was in
fome meafure mingled with the Greek; yet in
their travel to Britain, they came not to communicate, but to borrow; and it is not likely
that the Britains fhould be effected with the
language of thofe who came to learn of them.
Befides, of all the number of Gaulifh words
collected by Cambden, which agree with the
Britifh, few or none feem to be of Greek deri-
vation; fo it is highly improbable, as far as we
can fee into this matter, that the Gauls fhould
ever communicate the Greek tongue to the Britains. And therefore, fince this difficulty cannot be removed by any other way, it is not unreafonable to fufpect, that there is fome real
foundation lodged in the ruins of the ftory of
Brutus,

Brutus; and that the truth is disfigured by the boundless acceffion of poetical invention.

. I fhould tire the reader, and exceed the juft bounds of what I at firft propofed, if I fhould take a particular view of the Britifh hiftory, publifhed by Geoffrey, and therefore I fhall now only take notice of the life of King Cadwalader, where the hiftory of Wales begins, and where a palpable miftake, I may call it forgery, has been committed by one fide or another. For the very fame things, which the Britifh hiftory relate of Cadwalader, the Saxon writers attribute to Ceadwalla King of the Weft Saxons, how he was driven by a famine out of his dominions, came afterwards to Rome, and was received by Pope Sergius, with other particulars here too tedious to relate. But that which feems to charge the fault upon Geoffrey, or whoever elfe was the author of the Britifh hiftory, is, that Bede an author of eftablifhed credit, and one who lived near thofe times, fays that it was the Weft Saxon King Ceadwalla that went to Rome in Pope Sergius's time. But then on the other fide, it is hardly conceivable, fuppofing the Britifh hiftory a perfect contrivance, that Geoffrey or any other fhould be fo grofly over-feen, as to borrow the tranfaction of a real king, and one fo well known, to make up the life of a fictitious one cotemporary with him. Bede's reputation was too firm, to be fhaken by an upftart hiftory, and therefore it cannot well be fuppofed that the author of the Britifh hiftory was fo unwary, in cafe he defigned a cheat, as to let himfelf open to fo eafy a detection of forgery. All then that can be faid, is, that the agreeablenefs of the names and time that thefe two princes lived in, and poffibly their both

d 2 going

going to Rome, which was not unufual in thofe
days, might without any defign of putting upon
the world, make a confufion in ther hiftories.
But whether the life of Cadwalader be a fable,
the reader is at his own liberty to judge ; it.be-
ing prefixed to the hiftory of Wales, not as it is
more authentic, or any way of greater certainty
than the reft of Geoffrey's hiftory, but only becaufe the author, Caradoc of Lhangarfan, began his continuance of the Britifh hiftory with it.

This Caradoc of Lhangarfan, an author of
undoubted integrity, was cotemporary with
Geoffrey, who taking his rife from the place
where the Britifh hiftory concluded, made a
continuation of it through the reigns of feveral
of the princes of Wales, till the year 1157, about
which time he flourifhed. After him, all things
of moment that happened in Wales, were kept
and recorded in the abbies of Conwey in North-
Wales, and Yftratflur in South-Wales, where
the princes and noblemen of Wales were buried,
as appears by the teftimony of Gutryn Owen,
who lived in the time of Edward IV. and writ
the moft exact and perfect copy of the fame. All
the moft notable occurrences being thus regiftered in thefe abbies, were moft generally com-
pared together every third year, when the
Beirdh or Bards belonging to thefe two houfes
went their ordinary vifitations, which was called
Clera. And this continued until the year 1270,
a little before the death of the laft Prince Lhewelyn, who was flain at Buelht. Humphrey
Lloyd, Gent. who flourifhed in the reign of
Henry VIII. and one greatly fkilled in the Britifh antiquities, continued this hiftory to the
death of Prince Lhewelyn ; and afterwards having tranflated the whole into Englifh language,
had

had defigned to commit it to the prefs. But his death prevented what he purpofed, and ftopped the publication of this hiftory for a long time after, until David Powel, D. D. in the time of Queen Elizabeth, having met with Humphrey Lloyd's tranflation, collected what he could out of Englifh hiftorians, which he added by way of annotations, and fo publifhed it in the year 1584. This being the fole hiftory of the princes of Wales, and the only edition of this hiftory, I was moved to prepare it for another impreffion, by a new modelling the language, making the body of the hiftory intire, without troubling the reader to fee the fame thing by way of annotation, Dr. Powel's notes being for the greateft part but a repetition of the fame matter of fact out of the Englifh hiftorians, with what other improvements could be made. The additions which I made to the former hiftory, I chiefly took out of the notes of that late great antiquarian Mr. Robert Vaughan of Hengwrt; by whofe help alfo I have corrected, fupplied, and continued the chronology. Sir John Price's defcription of Wales will pretty well anfwer the geographical part of this hiftory, till we fhall be able to recover and fix feveral of thofe places whofe names are only left to us at prefent, which we have great hopes, will be fuccefsfully perfected, by the unwearied labours of my ingenious friend Mr. Edward Lhwyd, in his intended Etymological Dictionary. I have added by way of appendix, the feveral records belonging to this hiftory, and chofe rather to infert the articles of peace betwixt Prince Lhewelyn and John Peckam Archbifhop of Canterbury, in the original, with reference thereunto, than to infert all the grievances which the Welch then made in the Englifh language, which do not fo handfomely bear a tranflation.   d 3   A

A

DESCRIPTION

OF

CAMBRIA,

NOW CALLED

WALES,

Drawn firft by Sir John Price, Knight, and afterward augmented and made perfect by Humphry Lloyd, Gentleman.

THE three fons of Brutus having divided the whole ifle of Britain into three parts; that part contained within the French feas, with the rivers of Severn (called in Britifh, Hafren) Dee and Humber, fell to the eldeft fon Locrinus, which was after his name called Lhoyger, which name it hath in the Britifh tongue to this day, and in Englifh now it is called England, and is augmented northward to the river Tweed. The fecond fon Albanactus, had all the land northward from Humber to the fea Orkney, called in the Britifh tongue Mor Werydh, and in the Latin Mare Caledonicum. The third fon Camber had to his part, all that which remained undivided, lying within the Spanifh and Irifh feas, and feparated from England, with the rivers Severn and Dee; and this

Cambria. part was after his name called Cambria, and the inhabitants thereof Cambryi and their language Cambe-raec, and fo they are at this day. So that they have kept the fame country and language this 2700 and odd years, without commixtion with any other nation,

efpecially

especially in North-Wales, as it shall hereafter appear.

And because the name of this country is changed, or rather mistaken by the inhabitants of England, and not by them called Cambry, but Wales : I think it necessary to declare the occasion thereof, which is, that where the Saxons a people of Germany were the first that after the Britains inhabited and ruled the greatest part of this isle, and drove the Britains to that corner, which according to the manner of their country they called Wales, and the people Welch-men, and the tongue Welch, that is to say, Strange, or not of them understood. For at this day the inhabitants of the Low Countries call their next neighbours language of Henegaw, or other that speak French, Walsh, as a language to them unknown. Likewise the dwellers of Tyroll and other the higher countries of Germany do name the Italian their next neighbour a Welchman, and his language Welsh. And this is an evident proof, that they which harped upon a Queen Gwalaes, and of a Prince Wala (of whom neither British, Latin, nor English maketh mention) were foully deceived ; and so likewise was a great historiographer of late days, which saith, that it was called Wallia, quasi Italia, because the rest of the Romans which remained in the isle were driven thither. Neither is this any new invention, although Polydore Virgil with an Italian brag doth glorify himself to be the first that espied it out, for divers antient writers do alledge the same cause of the name of Wales, of whom Sylvester Giraldus is one, who wrote in the time of Henry the second, after the conquest, before 380 years passed ; which is an evident token, that the said Polydore did either never see nor read the antient histories of this realm, or dissembleth the same to the advancement and praise of himself and his country ; which to the learned and indifferent reader shall appear to be the only occasion he took that work in hand, for all his book redoundeth only to the praise and honour of the Romans, as well spiritual as temporal, and to blase

for

for their acts and deeds within this realm: and upon the other part doth either openly flander, or elfe privily extenuuate, or fhamely deny the martial prowefs and noble acts, as well of Saxons, Danes, and Normans, as of the Britains, all inhabiters of this ifle. Which thing he that lift to prove, let him read and confer Cæfar's Commentaries, Cornelius Tacitus, Herodianus, and other antient writers, as well in Latin as in Greek, with his work. As for the antient writers of the Britifh hiftory, as the Britifh chronicle, the hiftory of Gildas, Ponticus Verunnius, yea the golden work of Matthew Paris, monk of St. Alban, which wrote from William Baftard, to the laft years of Henry the third; I dare well fay he never faw them, they be in divers places to be had, fo that the truth may be eafily proved. To make an end I fay, that he being firft a ftranger born, and alfo ignorant as well in the hiftories of this realm, as of thofe tongues and languages wherein the fame were written, could never fet forth the true and perfect chronicle of the fame. But he having a good grace, and a pleafant ftile in the Latin tongue, and finding himfelf in a country where every man either lacked knowledge or fpirit to fet forth the hiftory of their own country, took this enterprife in hand, to their great fhame, and no lefs difpraife, becaufe he a blind leader fhall draw a great number of undifcreet and rafh followers, as well geographers and cofmographers, as chroniclers and hiftoriographers, to the dark pit of ignorance, where I leave them at this time, remitting the reader to the apology of Sir John Price, Knt. and his Britifh hiftory, written by him of purpofe, againft the envious reports, and flanderous taints of the faid Polydore, where he fhall fee a great number of his errors confuted at large. And to return to my former matter of the name of Wales, which name to be given of late by a ftrange nation may be otherwife proved: for the Welchmen themfelves do not underftand what thefe words WALES and WELCH do fignify, nor know any other name of their country or themfelves but Cambry, nor

Wales.

of

of their language but Cambraec, which is as much as to fay, as Camber's language or fpeech. So likewife they know not what England or Englifh meaneth, but commonly they call the country Lhoyger, the Englifh men, Saifon, and the Englifh tongue, Saifonaec. Which is an evident token that this is the fame language which the Britains fpake at the beginning; for the works of Merdhyn and of Talieffin, who wrote above 1000 years paft, are almoft the fame words which they ufe at this day, or at the leaft-eafy to be underftood of every one which knoweth perfectly the Welch tongue, efpecially in North Wales.

A Locrino

A Saxon.

Befide this, where at this day, there do remain three remnants of the Britains, divided every one from other with the feas, which are in Wales, Cornwail (called in Britifh Cerniw) and little Britain, yet almoft all the particular words of thefe three people are all one, although in pronunciation and writing of the fentences they differ fomewhat, which is no marvel, feeing that the pronunciation in one realm is often fo diverfe, that the one can fcarce underftand the other. But it is rather a wonder, that the Welchmen being feparated from the Cornifh, well nigh thefe 900 years, and the Britains from either of them 290 years before that, and having fmall traffic or concourfe together fince that time, have ftill kept their own Britifh tongue. They are not therefore to be credited, which deny the Welch to be the old Britifh tongue. And here I cannot pafs over what one of thefe fine Chronicler's wrote of late, of the name of Britain, affirming that it fhould be fo called of Britanie in France, as the elder of that name. But furely he had either never feen Ptolomy nor Cæfar, nor any other antient writer, or read them with fmall judgment and memory. For there he might have learned, that when this land was called Britain, the other was called Armorica, and how in Maximus's time, Conan Meriadoc was the firft that gave it that name, and inhabited it with Britains out of this ifle. Other derivations of thefe words,

Rob. Cæ-
nal, lib 2.
Pei. 2.

I

P'ir pri

Britannia and Albion, out of Greek and Latin, I am
aſhamed to rehearſe; for unto ſuch errors do they
commonly fall, that either puffed up with vain-glory
of their own wits, or pinched with deſpite and envy
at other men's works, or blinded with ignorance, do
go about to write and ſet forth any hiſtory or chro‑
nicle. But paſſing over this matter until another time,
I will return to the deſcription of Wales, which (as
I ſaid) was of old time compaſſed almoſt about with
the Iriſh ſeas, and the rivers Dee and Severn, al‑
though afterwards the Saxons won by force from the
Britains all the plain and champion country over the
rivers, and ſpecially Offa King of Mercia, who made
a ditch of great breadth and depth, to be a mear be‑
twixt his kingdom and Wales, which ditch began at
the river Dee, by Baſſingwerk, between Cheſter and
Ruthlan,‑ and ran along the hills ſides to the South
ſea, a little below Briſtol, reaching above a hundred
miles in length, and is in many places to be ſeen at
this day, bearing the name of Clawdh Offa, that is
to ſay, Offa's ditch, and the country between it and
England is commonly called in Welch, Y Mars, al‑
though the greateſt part of it be now inhabited by
Welchmen, namely in North Wales, which yet
keepeth the antient limits to the river Dee, and in
ſome places over it. Other (as Sylveſter Giraldus)
make the river Wy, called in Welch Gwy, to be
the mear between England and Wales, on the ſouth
part, called South Wales, who meaſureth the breadth
of Wales, from Salow or Willoweford, called Rhyd
yr helig upon Wy, to St. David's in Menevia 100
miles, and the length from Caerlheon upon Yſc in
Gwentland, to Holyhead, called Caergybi in Angle‑
ſey, in Welch, called Môn, above 100 miles, and
theſe be the common mears at this day, although the
Welch tongue is commonly uſed and ſpoken in
England, beyond theſe old mears a great way, as in
Herefordſhire, Glouceſterſhire, and a part of Shrop‑
ſhire. And thus for the general deſcription of Wales,
which afterward, about the year of Chriſt 870. Ro‑

dericus Magnus, King of Wales, divided into three
territories which they called kingdoms, which remained until of late days.

Thefe three were Gwynedh, in Englifh North
Wales, Deheubarth, in Englifh South Wales, and
Powys Land; in every of the which he ordained a
princely feat or court for the prince to remain at, moft
commonly; as in Gwynedh (which fome old writers
call Venedotia for Gwynethia) Aberffraw in the ifle of Aberffraw.
Môn or Anglefey. In Deheubarth, called in Latin
Demetia, Caermardyn, from whence it was afterward
removed to Dynefowr, eight miles thence. In Powys, Dynefowr.
Pengwern, called Y Mwythic, and in Englifh Shrewfbury, from whence it was removed to Mathrafal in Mathrafal.
Powys Land. And becaufe this hiftory doth as well
treat of wars betwixt thefe three provinces, as betwixt
them and the Saxons, Normans and Flemings, I think
it good to fet forth the particular defcription of every
part by itfelf. And firft of North Wales as the North
chiefeft part, which he gave his eldeft fon, ordaining Wales.
that either of the other two fhould pay him yearly
200l. of tribute, as it appeareth in the laws of Howel
Dha, which are to be had in Welch, and alfo in Latin.
Therefore Gwynedh (called North Wales) had upon
the north fide the Sea, from the river Dee at Bafing-
werke to Aberdyfi, and upon the Weft and South
Weft the river Dyfi, which divideth it from South
Wales, and in fome places from Powys Land. And
on the South and Eaft, it is divided from Powys,
fometimes with mountains, and fometimes with rivers,
till it come to the river Dee again. This land was of
old time divided to four parts, of which the chiefeft
was Môn, in Englifh called Anglefey, where the Mon.
prince's chief houfe was at Aberffraw, which is an
ifland feparated from the main land, with an arm of
the fea called Mænai, and had in itfelf three cantreds
or hundreds, which were fubdivided to fix comots,
as cantref Aberffraw to comot Lhion, and comot
Malhtraeth, cantref Cemais, to the comots Talibolion
and Twr Celyn; cantref Roffyr to the comots Tyn-
deth vy

daethwy and Mænai. And at this day there is a fine town in that isle called Bewmoris, and a common passage to Ireland at Caergybi, called in English Holyhead. But here I cannot wink at that notable error of Polydore, which (after his accustomed fashion) denieth this isle to be called Móna, but Anglesia, or Anglorum Insula, because it is called in English Anglesey, and gives this name Móna to Man, and so hath lost the names of both isles: which ignorance and forgetfulness might be forgiven him, if he had not drawn a great number to this error with him, which in their charters do daily wrong name these isles, which may be easily proved. First, because the inhabitants of the isle do know none other name but Món; and it is called through all Wales, Tîr Món, that is to say, the land of Món, unto this day. So that neither by memory of man, neither by any monument in writing in the British tongue can it appear, that ever it had any other name but Món, yet there be manifest monuments for these 1000 years. It is also grown to a proverb through Wales, for the fertility of the ground, Món mam Gymry, that is to say, Món mother of Wales.

The antient history of Cornelius Tacitus (which belike age had beaten out of Polydore's head) saith, that the soldiers of Paulinus Suetonius, and afterward of Julius Agricola, after they had passed through North Wales, then came over against Móna, where they did swim over an arm of the sea of 200 paces, and so by force won the isle. Now whether it is more reasonable thus to swim over 200 paces, or 20 miles? I know there is no man that believeth Polydore in this point; let all men therefore judge the rest. As for that which he saith of the great woods, it is nothing; for both the Romans, and after when the christian faith took place in this realm, the christians did fall and root them out, for the idolatry and absurd religion which was used there; that the King of Man sent for timber to Món; read the life of Hugh Earl of Chester, which also is evident by the great beeches and other

other trees found in the earth at thefe days. His other reafon is, becaufe it is called Anglefey in the Englifh tongue : fo is Lhoyger England, and Cambry Wales; Are thofe therefore the old names ? No furely. And what if the inhabitants called it fo ? (as they did not) had it not a name before the Angles won it ? Yes, I warrant you, but he had forgotten that. Now to the name of Man, it was ever, or at leaft thefe 1000 years named in Britifh Manow, of which cometh the Englifh name Man. The inhabitants thereof call it fo, and no nation about it did ever call it Môn, no nor any writer but Polydore, which was too young a godfather to name fo old a child. For Gildas who wrote above 900 years paffed, whofe writings Polydore never faw, but untruly fathers upon him his own device; Giraldus in his defcription of Ireland to Henry the Second, and Henry Huntington, do plainly call Man in Latin Eubonia, adding thereto either Manaw or Man, for the better underftanding of the name; Will you believe them or Polydore ? Other arguments there are which I will pafs over, till I have more leifure and occafion to write of this matter.

The fecond part of North Wales was called Arfon, _{Arfon.} which is as much as to fay, over againft Môn; and had in it four cantreds, and ten comots.

Cantref Aber had in it three comots, Y Lhechwedhuchaf, Y Lhechwedh-ifaf and Nant-Conwey.

Cantref Arfon had two comots, Ywch Gwyrfai, and Ifgwyrfai.

Cantref Dunodic had two comots, Ardudwy and Efionyth.

Cantref Lhyn containeth three comots, Cymytmayn, Tinlhayn and Canologion. This is now called Caernarvonfhire, as Môn is called Anglefeyfhire, and have the fame divifion at this day. In this fhire are Snowden-hills, called Eryri, neither in height, fertility of the ground, wood, cattle, fifh and fowl, giving place to the famous Alps, and without controverfy the ftrongeft country within Britain.

He e

Here is the town of Caernarvan, called in the old time Caerſegonce; and there is alſo Conwey called Caergyffyn. And the ſee of Bangor, with divers other antient caſtles and places of memory, and was the laſt part of Wales that came under the dominion of the kings of England. It hath on the north the ſea and Mænai, upon the eaſt and ſouth eaſt, the river Conwey, which divideth it from Denbighſhire, although it now paſs the river in one place by the ſea ſhore. And on the ſouth weſt and weſt, it is ſeparated from Merionyth by high mountains and rivers, and other mears.

Merionyth. The third part of Gwynedh was Merionyth containing three cantreds, and every cantred three comots.

As cantref Meyreon hath three comots, Talybont, Pennal and Yſtumaner.

Cantref Aruſtly had theſe, Vwchcoed, Iſcoed, and Gwarthrenium.

Cantref Penlhyn had theſe, Vwchmeloch, Iſmeloch, and Micnaint, and this keepeth the ſaid name till this day, but not within the ſame mears, and is full of hills and rocks, and hath upon the north the ſea, notable at this day for the great reſort and number of people that repair thither to take herrings. It hath upon the eaſt, Arfon and Denbigh-land, upon the ſouth, Powys, and upon the weſt, Dyfi and Cardiganſhire.

Tegyd. In this country ſtandeth the town of Harlech, and a great lake called Lhyn-Tegyd, through which the river Dee runneth, and mingleth not with the water of the lake, which is three miles long, and alſo the ſalmons, which are commonly taken in the river hard by the lake, are never ſeen to enter the lake. Likewiſe a kind of fiſh called Gwyniaid, which are like to whitings, and are full in the lake, are never taken in the river. Not far from this lake is a place called Caergay, which was the houſe of Gay, Arthur's foſter-brother. This ſhire, as well as Arfon, is full of cattle, fowl and fiſh, with great number of red deer and roes; but there is great ſcarcity of corn.

The

The fourth part of Gwynedh, was called y Berfedh- wlad, which may be englished, the in-land or middle country, which contained five cantreds and thirteen comots, as cantref Rhyfonioc had in it thefe comots, Uwchalet and Ifalet.

Cantref Yftrad had Hiraethoc and Cynmeirch.

Cantref Rhos thefe, Uwchdulas, Ifdulas and Creu- thyn, all which are in the lordfhip of Denbigh, faving the Creuthyn which is in Caernarvonfhire, wherein the caftle of Dyganwy did ftand, which was the earls of Chefter, and is commonly called in the Latin and Eng- lifh chronicle, Gannoc.

The fourth cantref was Dyffryn Clwyd, which may be englifhed the valley of Clwyd, and now is called the lordfhip of Rhuthyn, and hath thefe comots, Co- leigion, Lhannerch and Dogueilvn.

The fifth cantref is Tegengl, and now is a part of Flintfhire, having thefe comots, Counfylht, Preftatyn, and Ruthlan. And in this part is one of the faireft vallies within this ifle, containing 18 miles in length, and 4, 5, 6 or 7 in breadth, as rhe hills either draw inward together, or backward afunder, which high hills do inclofe it on the eaft, weft, and fouth parts, and northward the fea. It is plentiful of cattle, fifh and fowl, corn, hay, grafs, and wood, and divided along in the midft with the river Clwyd, to whom runneth Clywedoc, Yftrat, Whilar, Elwy, and a great number of other rivers from the hills. In this valley, two miles from the fea, is the town and caftle of Ruthlan, where fometimes a parliament hath been kept. And two miles above it is the fee of St. Afaph, between the rivers Clwyd and Elwy, called in the old time the bifhop's fee of Lhan Elwy. Four miles thence, and two miles from the river, is fituate upon a rock the town and caftle of Denbigh, where is one of the greateft markets in the marches of Wales, and one of the faireft and ftrongeft caftles within this realm, which being the houfe of David brother to Lhewelyn, the laft prince of the Welch blood, was enlarged and ftrengthened by Henry Lacy, Earl of

Linco'r,

Lincoln, to whom King Edward gave the same lordship; it is also the shire-town of that shire. Five miles above this, is the town of Ruthyn with a fair castle, which sometimes belonged to the lords Gray earls of Kent. This part of North-Wales, hath upon the north the river Dee, and the sea. Upon the west, Arfon, and the river Conwey. South and east, Merionyth, and the country then called Powys. And these be the mears and bounds of Gwynedh or Venedotia for the name of North-Wales containeth, besides this, all Powys, at these days. So there was under the territory of Aberffraw fifteen cantreds, and in them thirty-eight comots.

Mathrafal or Powys. The second kingdom was Mathrafal, which in right order was the third, which came to the third brother, yet for the better understanding of the history following, I have placed it here. To this kingdom belonged the country of Powys, and the land between Wy and Severn. Which part had upon the south and west, South-Wales, with the rivers Hy and Tywy, and other mears. Upon the north, Gwynedh, and upon the east the marches of England, from Chester to Wy, a little above Hereford; and therefore it was most troubled with wars, as well of the Saxons, as afterwards of the Normans, lords marches, who daily won some part thereof, and by that means it was the first part that served the Kings of England, and therefore less esteemed of all the rest. This part called Powys, was divided again into Powys Fadoc, and Powys Wenwynwyn. Powys Fadoc contained in itself five cantreds and fifteen comots.

Cantreff Y Barwn, which had three comots, Dynmael, Edeyrneon, and Glyndourdwy, which are now in Merionythshire (saving Dinmael which is in Denbighshire)

Cantref Y Rhiw, whose comots were these, Yal now in Denbighshire; Ystratalyn and Hop in Flintshire.

Cantref Uwchnant hath thee comots, Merfforth in Flintshire; Maelor Gymraeg, in English Bromfield,

now

now in Denbighſhire, and Maelor Saeſneg in Flint-
ſhire.

Cantref Trefred containeth theſe comots, Croesfain,
Tref y Wayn, in Engliſh Chirke, and in Denbigh-
ſhire. Croeſoſwallt, in Engliſh Oſweſtrey, and in
Shropſhire.

Cantref Rhaiyder with his comots Mochnant Iſraiy-
der, Cynlhaeth and Nanheudwy all in Chirke-land,
and in Denbighſhire. Alſo the lordſhip of Whyting-
ton, now in Shropſhire, was in this part of Powys,
which part at this day, hath loſt the name of Powys,
and is ſituated in divers ſhires, as it appeareth by the
diſcourſe before paſſed. In this part is the caſtle of
Holt in Bromfield, and the caſtle of Chirke in Chirke-
land. Likewiſe the lordſhip and caſtle of Whyting-
ton, which came by marriage to Foulk Fitz-Warren.
There is beſide theſe, the lordſhip of Oſweſtry, of the
which the Fitz-Alans have been lords theſe 300 and
odd years, and of divers other lordſhips in thoſe
marches, as Shrarden, the eleven towns, Clun and
many others, which are all now in Shropſhire.

The ſecond part called Powys Wenwynwyn, had
likewiſe five cantreds, and twelve comots.

Cantryf Y Fyrnwy had theſe comots, Mochnant
uwch Rayader, Mechain Iſcoed and Lhannerch Hudol.

Cantref Yſtlyc had theſe, Deuthwr, Corthwr Iſaf,
and Yſtrat Marchelb.

Cantref Lhyſwynaf had theſe, Caerneon, and Mechain Uwchcoed.

Cantref Cydewen had comot Conan and Comot
Hauren.

Cantref Gonan had Cyfeilioc and Mouthwy, which
is in Merionythſhire. Of all theſe, the three firſt cantreds do only at this day bear the name of Powys,
which are upon the north-ſide of Severn, and are all
five (ſaving the comot of Mowthwy) in Montgomeryſhire.

This is a country full of woods, hills, and rivers,
and hath in it theſe towns, the Poole, New-Town and
Machylhaeth. Aruſtly was in old time in this part,
but afterwards it came to the princes of Gwynedh.

e　　　　　Theſe

These lordships came by just descent from the princes thereof, to a woman named Hawys, the daughter of Owen ap Gruffydh. Aruftly and Cyfeilioc came to the baron of Dudley, and afterwards it was sold to the king.

The third part belonging to Mathrafal, was the land between Wy and Severn, containing four cantreds, and thirteen comots.

Cantref Melienyeth hath these comots, Ceri, Swydhygre Rhiwalalht, and Glyn Iiethon.

Cantref Elfel hath these, Uwchmynydh, Ismynydh, and Lhechdhyfnog.

Cantref y Clawdh these, Dyffryn Teyfediat, Swydhynogen, and Pennwelht.

Cantref Buelht hath these, Swydh y Fam, Dreulys, and Isyrwon. Of this part there is at this day some in Montgomeryshire, some in Radnorshire, and some in Brecknockshire. In this part, and in the lordships marching to it, which although at the time of this division, which was in the time of the last prince, were not in his subjection, yet to this day speak Welch, and are called Wales, and in these comots are these towns and castles. Montgomery called in Welch Trefaldwyn, a pretty town and a fair castle. The castle of Clun, called Colunwy, which is the earls of Arundel. The town Knighton, in Welch Trefyclawd. The castle of Cymaron. Presteyn in Welch Lhanandras. The town and castle of Radnor, in Welch Maesyfed, at this day the shire town. The town of Kington and the castle of Huntingdon, called in Welch Y Castelh Mayn, which were the Bohuns earls of Hereford, and after the dukes of Buckingham. Castle Payne, Haye, Lhanfair in Buelht. These lordships with Brecknock and Abergefenny, were belonging to the Bruces lords of Brecknock, and after came divers times, and by sundry means to the Bohuns, Nevils, and Mortimers. And so (as I have rehearsed) in this territory or kingdom were found fourteen cantreds, and forty comots. Two of these parts, which are Powys and Gywnedh, are at this day called North-Wales, and divided into six shires, Mon called Anglesey, Caernarvon, Merionyth, Denbigh, Flint,

Flint, and Montgomeryſhire, and are all on the north-ſide Severn, ſaving a piece of Montgomeryſhire.

. And here I think it good to let the reader underſtand what the Britiſh chronicle ſaith of North-Wales, which affirmeth that three times it came by inheritance to women. Firſt to Stradwen, daughter to Cadfan ap Conan ap Endaf, and wife to Coel Godeboc, mother to Genaw, Dyfyr and Gwawl. The ſecond time to the ſame Gwawl wife to Edeyrn ap Padarn, and mother to Cunetha Wledic; which Cunetha inhabiting in the north parts of England, about the year 540, after the incarnation of Chriſt, and hearing how the mingled nations of Iriſh-Scots, and Piſts, had over-run the ſea-ſhore of Cardigan, which was part of his inheritance, ſent his ſons thither to enjoy their inheritance, of whom Tibiaon his eldeſt ſon died in Man, which land the ſaid Iriſh-Scots had won. For Gildas ſaith, that the children of Glam Heſtor, which peopled a great part of Ireland, Yſcroeth with his people inhabited Dalrieuda, which is a part of Scotland: Builke with his people came to Man. But I think it good to put in Gildas's words which ſaith; *Builke cum filiis ſuis inhabitavit Euboniam inſulam vulgo Manaw, quæ eſt in meditullio maris inter Hyberniam & Britanniam*; that is to ſay, Builke with his children inhabited the iſle Eubonia, commonly Manaw (for ſo it was and is named in Britiſh) which lieth in the middle of the ſea, between Ireland and Britain. This was not called Môna, as Polydore faineth. The children of Bethoun inhabited Demetia, which is South-Wales, with Gwyr and Cydweli, till they were chaſed thence by the children of Cunetha. Thus far Gildas. Therefore the ſons of Cunetha, being arrived in North-Wales (as well I think being driven by the Saxons, as for their inheritance) divided the country betwixt them. And firſt Meiredon the ſon of Tibiaon, the ſon of Cunetha, had cantref Meireaon. to his part. Aruſtel ap Cunetha had cantref Aruſtly. Caredic ap Cunetha, had Caerdigion, now called Cardiganſhire. Donod had cantref Dunodic. Edeyrn had Edeyrnion. Mael had D.. ... Col had Coleyon. Doguael had D-guailyn. k. fan had Rhyfoniuc

Maelor the Rhyfonioc, now Denbighland. Eineon Yrch had
son of Caereneon in Powys. Uſſa had Maeſuſwalht near Oſ-
Gwran, ſon
to Cunedha wſtry. For ſurely that they ſay commonly of Oſwald
had Maelo- King of Northumberland, to be ſlain there, and of the
ron, that is
the two well that ſprung where his arm was carried, nothing ſo.
Maelors, For Beda and all other writers teſtify that Peanda ſlew Oſ-
Maelor
Gymbraeg, wald at Maſerfelt, in the kingdom of Northumberland,
called Br.
and Maelor and his body was buried in the abby of Bradney, in the
Saeſneg. province of Lhyndeſey. But to my former matter. Theſe
names given by the ſons of Cunetha, remain to this day.
After the Iriſh-Picts or Scots, which which the Britains
called Y Gwydhyl Phictiaid, which is to ſay, the
Iriſh-Picts, did over-run the iſle of Môn, and were
driven thence by Caſwalhon Lhawhîr, that is Caſwalhon with the long hand, the ſon of Eineon Yrch ap
Cunedha, who ſlew Scrigi their king with his own
hands, at Lhan y Gwydhyl, which is the Iriſh church
at Holyhead. This Caſwalhon was father to Maelgon
Gwynedh, whom the Latins call Maglocunus, Prince
and King of Britain.

In his time was the famous clerk and great wiſe
man Talieſſyn Ben Beirdh, that is to ſay, the chiefeſt
of the Beirdh or wiſemen ; for this word Bardh in
Cæſar's time, ſignified (as Lucan beareth witneſs) ſuch
as had knowledge of things to come, and ſo it ſignificth
at this day. This Maelgon had a ſon called Run, in
whoſe time the Saxons invited Gurmond into Britain
from Ireland, who had come thither from Afric, who
with the Saxons was the utter deſtruction of the Britains, and ſlew all that profeſſed Chriſt, and was the
firſt that drove them over Severn. This Run was father to Beli, who was father to Iago, (for ſo the Britains call James) who was father to Cadfan, and not
Brochwel called Brecyfal (as the Engliſh chronicle
ſaith) for this Brochwel called Yſgithroc, that is, long
toothed, was choſen leader of ſuch as met with Adelred alias Ethelbertus Rex Cantiæ, and other Angles
and Saxons, whom Auguſtine had moved to make
war againſt the chriſtian Britains, and theſe put Brochwel twice to flight, not far from Cheſter, and cruelly
ſlew

flew 1000 priefts and monks of Bangor, with a great number of lay-brethren of the fame houfe, which lived by the labour of their hands, and were come bare-footed and woolward to crave mercy and peace at the Saxons hands. And here you fhall underftand that this was not Auguftine Bifhop of Hippona the great clerk, but Auguftine the monk, called the apoftle of England.

Then this Brochwell retired over Dee, hard by Bangor, and defended the Saxons the paffage, till Cadfan King of North Wales, Meredyth King of South Wales, and Bledrus or Bletius Prince of Cornwal, came to fuccour him, and gave the Saxons a fore battle, and flew of them the number of 1066, and put the reft to flight. After the which battle, Cadfan was chofen King of Britain, and was chief ruler within the ifle; after whom his fon Cadwalhon, who was father to Cadwalader, the laft of the Britifh blood, that bare the name of King of Britain, was king.

The third time that North Wales came to a woman, was to Efylht the daughter of Conan Tindaythwy, the fon of Edwal Ywrch, the fon of Cadwalader. She was wife to Merfyn Frych, and mother to Rhoderic the Great, as fhall be hereafter declared. By this you may underftand, that North Wales hath been a great while the chiefeft feat of the laft kings of Britain, becaufe it was, and is the ftrongeft country within this ifle, full of high mountains, craggy rocks, great woods, and deep vallies, ftrait and dangerous places, deep and fwift rivers, as Dyfi, which fpringeth in the hills of Merionyth, and runneth north weft through Mowthwy, and by Machynlaeth, and fo to the fea at Aberdyfi, dividing North and South Wales afunder. Dee, called in Welch Dourdwy, fpringing alfo on the other fide of the fame hills, runneth eaft through Penlhyn, and the lake Tegyd, Corwan and Lhangolhen, between Chirkeland and Bromfield, where it boweth northward toward Bangor, to the Holt, and to Chefter, and thence north weft to Flint-caftle, and fo to the fea.

c 3   There

There is alfo Conwey, rifing likewife in Merionyth-
fhire, and dividing Caernarvon from Denbighfhire,
runeth under Snowden north eaft, by the town of
Aberconwey to the fea.

Alfo Clwyd, which rifing in Denbigh Land, runneth down to Ruthyn, and plain north, not far from
Denbigh to St. Afaph, and fo by Ruthlan and to the
fea. There be many other fair rivers, of which fome
run to the fea, as Mawr at Traethmawr, and Afon y
Saint at Caernarvon, and other that run to Severn, as
Murnwy in Powys, and to Murnwy, Tanat; fome
other to Dee, as Ceirioc betwixt the lordfhips of Chirke
and Whittington; Alyn through Yal and Moldfdale,
and Hopedale, and fo to Dee, a little above Chefter.
And this fhall fuffice for the perfeà defcription of that
which in old time was called Gwynedh and Powys,
and at thefe days the fix fhires of North Wales.

Dynefawr.   Now remaineth the laft kingdom of Wales, called
Dynefawr, which although it was the greateft, yet was
it not the beft, as Giraldus witneffeth, chiefly becaufe
it was much molefted with Flemings and Normans,
and alfo that in divers parts thereof, the lords would
not obey their prince, as in Gwent and in Morganwc,
which was their own confufion, as fhall hereafter appear. This was divided into fix parts, of the which
Caredigion. Caredigion was the firft, and contained four cantreds
and ten comots, as cantref Penwedic had in it thefe
comots, Geneurglyn, Perfedh and Creuthyn.

Cantref Canawl had thefe, Mefenyth, Anhunoc,
and Pennarth.

Cantref Caftelh had thefe comots, Mabwynion and
Caerwedros.

Cantref Syrwen had thefe, Gwenionyth and Ifcoed;
and this part is at this day called in Englifh Cardiganfhire, and in Welch Swydh Aberteifi. This is a champion country without much wood, and hath been divers times overcome with Flemings and Normans,
which builded many caftles in it, and at the laft were
beaten out of them all. It hath on the eaft North
Wales with the river Dyfi and part of Powys, upon
the

the south Caermardhynshire, upon the west Pembrokeshire, with the river Teifi, and upon the north the Irish sea. In this part is the town of Cardigan upon Teifi, not far from the sea. The town of Aberystwyth upon the river Ystwyth, by the sea, and Lhanbadarn Fawr, which was a great sanctuary, and a place of religious and learned men in times past. And in this shire were a great number of castles, as the castle of Ystratmeyric, of Walter, of Lhanrysted, of Dynerth, of the sons of Wyneaon, of Aber-Reidol, and a great number more, with the town of Tregaron and Lhandhewibrefi.

The second part was called Dyfed, and at this day Dyfed, Pembrokeshire, and had in it eight cantreds, and twenty-three comots, which were these. Cantref Emlyn had these comots, Uwchcuch, Iscuch and Lefethyr.

Cantref Arberth had these, Penrhyn ar Elays, Esterolef and Talacharn.

Cantref Daugledheu had these, Amgoed, Pennant and Efelfre.

Cantref Y Coed had these, Lhanhayaden and Castelh Gwys.

Cantref Penfro hath these, Coed yr haf, Maenor byrr, and Penfro,

Cantref Rhos hath these, Hulfforth Castelh Gwalchmai and Ygarn.

Cantref Pubidioc hath these, Mynyw, Pencaer and Pebidioc.

Cantref Cemais hath these, Uwchnefer, Isnefer and Trefdraeth.

In this part are divers towns and havens at this day, as Pembroke, Tenby, in Welch Dynbegh-y-pyscot, Hereford-West, in Welch Hulfforth, with the fair haven of Milford, called in Welch Aberdaugledheu, St. David's or Menevia, called in Welch Mynyw, the chiefest see in all Wales. Then Fiscard called Abergwayn; and Newport, named Trefdraeth; these be along the sea coast, or not very far off. Besides these there be divers castles, as Cilgerran, Arberth, Gwys,

Lhanhayaden, Walwyn, and divers others. This part was won firſt by the Montgomery's earls of Shrewſbury, and after given to the Marſhalls, and ſo to Valence, and from thence were the princes of Wales moſt troubled with the Normans and Flemings, who do remain and inhabit about Tenby, Pembroke and Rhos to this day, which can neither Welch nor good Engliſh as yet. Dyfed (for ſo will I call it hereafter) hath on the weſt and north the Iriſh ſea, upon the ſouth the Spaniſh ſea, and upon the eaſt Caermardhynſhire, and on the north eaſt Cardiganſhire. The third part was Caermardhynſhire, having four cantreds, and fifteen comots, as cantref Finioc with the comots of Harfryn, Derfedh, and Iſgeneny.

Caermardhyn. *(margin)*

Cantref Eginoc with theſe Gwyr, now in Glamorgonſhire, Cydweli, and Carnwilheon.

Cantref Bachan with theſe, Malhaen, Caeo, and Maenor Deilo.

Cantref Mawr with theſe, Cethineoc comot mab Elfyw, comot mab Uchdryd and Wydigada. In this ſhire are the towns and caſtles of Caermardhyn, Dynefowr, which was the prince's ſeat of the country, Newtown, Lhandeilo, Lhanymdhyfri, Emlyn, Swanſey, now in Glamorganſhire, called in Welch Abertawy upon the ſea, the caſtle of the ſons of Uchtryd, of Lhanſtephan, and others. It hath upon the weſt Dyfed or Pembrokeſhire, on the north Cardiganſhire, upon the ſouth weſt the ſea, and upon the ſouth eaſt Glamorgan, aud upon the eaſt Brecknockſhire. This is counted the ſtrongeſt part of all South Wales, as that which which is full of high mountains, great woods, and fair rivers, eſpecially Tywy. In this, and in the other two parts of South Wales, were the notableſt acts that this hiſtory treateth of, atchieved and done.

Morganwc. *(margin)*

The fourth called Morganwc, now Glamorganſhire, containing four cantreds, with fifteen comots. As cantref Croneth, with theſe comots, Rwngneth ac Afan, Tir yr Hwndrwd, and Maenor Glynogwr.

Cantref

- ᛫ Cantref Pennythen with thefe, Meyfcyn, Glyn-rhodny, Maenor Talafan, and Maenor Ruthyn.

᛫ Cantref Brenhinol with thefe, Cibowr, Senghen-nyth, Uwchcaeth,. and Ifcaeth.

Cantref Gwentlhw, which is now in Monmouth-fhire, with thefe comots, y Rhardh Ganol, and Eithaf-dylgion. In this part are thefe towns and caftles, Lhandaf the bifhop's fee, Caerdyffe, called Caerdhyf, Cowbridge, called in Welch Y bont faen, which is as much as to fay Stonebridge, Lantwyd, Caerffyli, and others, and hath divers rivers which run to the fouth fea, as Lay, Taf, Tawy, Neth, Afan, Ogwr, and Lhychwr; it hath on the fouth, the fea of Severn, which divideth it from Devonfhire and Cornwall; up-on the weft and north weft, Caermardhynfhire; upon the north eaft, Brecknockfhire; and upon the eaft, Monmouthfhire. Of this you fhall read very little, for one Ieftyn being chief of the country, and having war with his neighbours, called one Robert Fitzhamon, with a great number of ftrangers to his fuccours, which after they had atchieved the enterprife, liked fo well the country, that they found occafion to fall out with Ieftyn, and inhabited the country themfelves and their heirs to this day.

The fifth part was called Gwent and now in Mon-mouthfhire, which had three cantreds, and ten co-mots, as cantref Gwent, which hath thefe comots, Y mynyth, Ifcoed Lhefnydh, and Tref y grug.

Cantref Ifcoed thefe, Brynbuga, Uwchcoed, y Teir-tref, and Erging ac ewyas, now in Herefordfhire.

Cantref Côch was the feventh cantred of Morganwc, which is now in Gloucefterfhire, and is called the Fo-reft of Dean.

In this part was the antient city of Caerlheon upon Ufk, where was the archbifhop's fee of Wales; here are alfo divers towns and caftles, as Chepftow, Glyn, Strigul, Rhos, Tyntern upon the river Wy; there is alfo Newport, called y Caftelh Newydh, Uyfc called Brynbuga, Grofmont, Raglan, White-caftle, Aber-gefenny, and many others. This is a fair and a fer-tile

tile country,' of which likewife the gentlemen were never obedient to their prince, which was the caufe of
their own deftruction. It hath on the weft Glamorgan and Brecknockfhires, upon the north Herefordfhire, upon the eaft Gloucefterfhire, with the river
Wy, and upon the fouth and fouth eaft Severn.

Brecheinoc.   Laft of all cometh Brecheinoc, now Brecknock-
fhire, which hath three cantreds, and eight comots.
As cantref Selef which hath thefe comots, Selef and
Trahayern.

Cantref Canol thefe, Talgarth Yftradyw and Brwyn-
lhys or Eglwys Yail.

Cantref Mawr thefe, Tir Raulff, Lhywel and Cerrig-
Howel. In this part is the town of Brecknock upon
the meeting of Ufk and Honddi, and is called Aber-
honddi, and Hay called Y Gelhy, with Talgarth,
Buelht, Lhangors ; it hath weft Caermardhynfhire,
with the river Tywy, upon the north Radnorfhire with
Wy, upon the eaft Herefordfhire and Monmouth,
upon the fouth Glamorgan. This for the moft part is
full of mountains, woods and rivers, efpecially Buelht.
And the lords of this country called Bruces with the
Mortimers, moft of all others lords marches, fometimes by might, but oftener by treafon, have molefted
and grieved the princes of Wales. This land came
after the Bruces to the Bohuns earls of Hereford, and
fo to the Staffords dukes of Buckingham.

Thefe fix fhires being fubject to the territory of
Dynefawr with Radnorfhire, which was belonging to
Mathrafal, are now commonly called South Wales,
which country is both great and large, with many fair
plains and vallies for corn, high mountains and rocks
full of pafture for cattle ; great and thick woods, with
forefts and parks for red deer and fallow ; clear and
deep rivers full of fifh, of which Severn is the chiefeft,
which with Wy and Rheidol fpring out of a high
mountain called Pymlhymon, in the edge of Cardiganfhire, and are called commonly the three fifters. Severn runneth full eaft through Cydewen by the pool,
and under the caftle of Shraden to Shrewfbury, from

whence

whence it turneth fouthward and runs to Bridgenorth, Bewdley, Worcefter, Glocefter and fo to the fea by Briftol. The fecond fifter is Gwy, in Englifh Wy, which took her journey fouth eaft, by Rayader Gwy to Buelt, where Irwon meeteth her, thence to Glafbury, and fo to Hereford and Monmouth, and to the fea of Severn at Chepftow; for fo they call Môr Hafren the fea which fevereth Wales from Somerfetfhire, Devonfhire and Cornwal. The third fifter named Rheidol, ran northward to the fea being not far off, at Aberyftywth. There be other fair rivers as Ufk, which rifing in a high mountain called y Mynydh dy in the fouth part of Brecknockfhire runneth to Brecknock, and fo through Monmouthfhire to the town of Ufk, Caerlheon and Newport, and fo to the faid fouth fea. Tywy alfo rifing not far from Wy, runneth fouth to Lhanymdhyfri, and thence fouth weft by Lhandeilo and Dynefawr to Abergwily and Caermardhyn, and fo by Lhanftephan to the fea.

Teifi likewife which rifeth in the edge of Caermardhynfhire, and runneth north weft by Emlyn, Cilgerran, Cardigan, and fo to the north fea. In Teifi above all the rivers in Wales, were in Giraldus's time a great number of caftors, which may be englifhed bevers, and are called in Welch afanc, which name only remaineth in Wales at this day, but what it is very few can tell. It is a beaft not much unlike an otter, but that it is bigger, all hairy faving the tail, which is like a fifh tail, as broad as a man's hand. This beaft ufeth as well the water as the land, and hath very fharp teeth, and biteth cruelly, till he perceives the bones crack, his ftones be of great efficacy in phyfic. He that will learn what ftrong nefts they make, which Giraldus calleth caftles, which they build upon the face of the water with great boughs which they cut with their teeth, and how fome lie upon their backs, holding the wood with the fore feet, which the other draweth with a crofs ftick, the which he holdeth in his mouth to the water fide, and other particularities of their natures, let him read Giraldus in his topography

Κάςωρ Greek, Fiber, Latin, Peaver Englifh, Afanc Britifh, Giraldus in Itiner.

of

of Wales. There be befides thefe a great number of rivers, of which fome run to the fouth, and fome to the weft and north fea, as Tywy in Glamorganfhire, Taf alfo in Caermardhynfhire, which runneth to Cledheu, two rivers either called Cledheu, which do give Milford the name of Aberdaugledheu in Pembrokefhire, Arth, Aeron, and Yftwyth, in Cardigan. There be alfo divers lordfhips which be added to other fhires, and were taken heretofore for parts of Wales, and in moft part of them at this day the Welch language is fpoken, as Ofweftry, Knocking, Whittington, Elfmer, Mafbroke, Chirbury, Caurs, Clun, which are now in Shropfhire, Ewyas-Lacy, Ewyas-Haroald, Clifford Winforton, Yardley, Huntingdon, Whitney, Loghardneys in Herefordfhire. Alfo this country of South Wales as all the reft of Britain, was firft inhabited by the Britains, which remain there to this day, faving that in divers places, efpecially along the fea fhore, they have been mingled with Saxons, Normans (which the Welch hiftory calleth Frenchmen) and Flemings; fo that the princes of Wales, fince the conqueft of the Normans, could never keep quiet poffeffion thereof, but what for ftrangers, and what for difloyalty of their own people, vexation and war, were for the moft part compelled to keep themfelves in Caermardhynfhire.

The winning of the Lordfhip of *Gla-morgan* or *Morgannwc* out of the *Welfhmen*'s Hands, and firft of the Defcription of the fame Lordfhip.

Reprinted from the Edition of 1584.

IN primis, the faid lordfhip in length from *Rymny* 1
bridge on the eaft fide, to *Pwlh Conan* on the weft
fide, is 27 miles. The breadth thereof from the haven of *Aburthaw* alias *Aberdaon*, on the fouth fide, to
the confines of *Bredinockfhire*, above *Morleys* caftle,
is 22 miles.

Item the fame lordfhip, being a lordfhip marcher, 2
or a lordfhip royal, and holden of no other lordfhip,
the lords ever fince the winning of the fame, owing
their obedience only to the crown, have ufed therein
jura regalia : that is, the trial of all actions, as well real
as perfonal, with pleas of the crown, and authority to
pardon all offences, treafon only excepted.

Item there were 11 lordfhips, to wit, *Senghennyth*, 3
Myfkyn, *Ruthin*, *Lhanblethian*, *Tir Iarlh*, *Glyn Rothney*, *Auan*, *Neth*, *Coyty*, *Tulauan* and *Lhantuit*, alias,
Bouiarton, that were members of the faid lordfhip of
Clamorgan. In every of the members were the like
jura regalia ufed in all things, faving that if any
wrong judgement were given in any of the courts of
the faid members, it fhould be reverfed by a writ of
falfe judgement in the county court of *Glamorgan*, as
fuperior court to the faid members. Alfo all matters
of confcience happening in debate in any of the faid
members, fhould be heard and determined in the
chancery of *Glamorgan*, before the chancellor thereof.

Item, the body of the faid lordfhip of *Glamorgan* 4
was (before the alteration of the laws in *Wales*) a
county of itfelf, wherein the lord had two caftles and
three market towns, to wit, the caftle and town of
Kynfigs, alias *Kefnffgen*, in the weft part thereof, and
Cowbridg town, alias *Font wen*, in the middeft. And
the

the town and caftle of *Cardyff*, or *Caer-Dhydh*, in the eaft part, in which caftle of *Cardyff*, the lord did moft inhabit; and therein he had his Chancery and Exchequer, and a fair court houfe, wherein the county court was monthly kept on the Monday for all the fuiters of the fhrievalty, that is, of the body of the faid lordfhip itfelf, without the faid members.

5   Item, within the faid fhrievalty, or body of the faid lordfhip, were 18 caftles, and 36 knight's fees and an half, that held of the faid lordfhip of *Glamorgan* by knights fervice, befides a great number of freeholders.

6   Item, in eight of the faid members were ten caftles and four borough towns.

7   Item, the annual revenues of the faid lordfhip, with

The value of the feniory, before the purchafe thereof.

the members, was 1000 marks, whereof was allowed in fees 400 marks; of the which members aforefaid, *John Gamage*, Efq; occupieth one at this day, defcended unto him from the *Turberuiles* his anceftors, that is to wit, the lordfhip of *Coytie:* and the heir of *John Baffet* enjoyeth another, to wit, the lordfhip of *Talauan*, by purchafe from King *Edward* the fixth. The other nine members, with four of the aforefaid knights fees, and all the caftles, market towns, and borough towns, with the demefnes of the fame; and all the lands that were in the lords hands, parcel of the faid lordfhip and members, the earl of *Penbroke* hath pur-

The value of the feniory now.

chafed. So that there remaineth now to the fenior of the faid lordfhip of *Glamorgan* (being in the Queen's Majefty's hands) but the moity only of the manor of *Dynafpowys*, of the value of 26 pounds by the year.

The Manner of the winning of the faid Lordfhip.

1091   IN the year of our Lord 1091, and in the fourth year of the reign of King *William Rufus*, one *Ieftyn* the fon of *Gungant*, being lord of the faid lordfhip of *Glamorgan*, R : n *Theodoc*, prince of *South Wales*,

Wales, that is, of *Caermarthyneſhire* and *Cardiganſhire*, made war upon him. Whereupon the ſaid *Ieſtyn*, underſtanding himſelf unable to withſtand the ſaid *Rees* without ſome aid otherwiſe; ſent one *Eneon*, a gentleman of his, to *England*, to one *Robertuſ Fitzhamon*, a worthy man, and knight of the privy chamber with the ſaid king, to retain him for his ſuccour. The which *Robert*, being deſirous to exerciſe himſelf in the feats of war, agreed ſoon with him thereto for a ſalary to him granted for the ſame. Whereupon the ſaid *Robert Fitzhamon* retained to his ſervice for the ſaid journey, twelve knights, and a competent number of ſoldiers, and went into *Wales*, and joining there with the power of the ſaid *Ieſtyn*, fought with the ſaid *Rees ap Tewdor* and killed him, and one *Conan* his ſon. After which victory, the ſaid *Robert Fitzhamon*, minding to return home again with his company, demanded his ſalary to him due of the ſaid *Ieſtyn*, according to the covenants and promiſes agreed upon between him and the aforeſaid *Eneon*, on the behalf of the ſaid *Ieſtyn* his maſter. The which to perform in all points, the ſaid *Ieſtyn* denied; and thereupon they fell out, ſo that it came to be tried by battle. And forſomuch as the ſaid *Eneon* ſaw his maſter go from divers articles and promiſes that he had willed him to conclude with the ſaid *Robert Fitzhamon*, on his behalf, he forſook his maſter, and took part, he and his friends, with the ſaid *Robert Fitzhamon*. In the which conflict, the ſaid *Ieſtyn* with a great number of his men were ſlain, whereby the ſaid *Robert Fitzhamon* won the peaceable poſſeſſion of the whole lordſhip of *Glamorgan*, with the members, of the which he gave certain caſtles and manors, in reward of ſervice, to the ſaid twelve knights, and to other his gentlemen.

The

The Names and Sirnames of the said Twelve Knights were these.

1 *WILLIAM de Londres*, alias *London*.
2 *Richardus de Grana villa*, alias *Greenfeeld*.
3 *Paganus de Turberuile*.
4 *Robertus de S. Quintino*, alias *S. Quintine*.
5 *Richardus de Syward*.
6 *Gilbertus de Humfreuile*.
7 *Rogerus de Berkrolles*.
8 *Reginaldus de Sully*.
9 *Peter le Soore*.
10 *Johannes le Fleming*.
11 *Oliverus de S. John*, a younger brother of the Lord *S. John*, of *Basing*.
12 *William le Esterling*, whose ancestors came out of *Danske* to *England* with the *Danes*, and is now by shortness of speech called *Stradling*.

The Parcels given by the said *Robert Fitzhamon* to the said Twelve Knights and others, in Reward of Service.

1
Ogmor.

IN primis, to the said *William de Londres*, the said *Robert Fitzhamon* gave the castle and manor of *Ogmor*, being four knights fees; now parcel of the possessions of the duchy of *Lancaster*.

2
Neth.

Item, to the forenamed Sir *Richard Greenfeeld*, he gave the castle and lordship of *Neth*, being one of the members aforesaid; and now parcel of the possessions of the Right Hon. the Earl of *Penbroke*.

3
Coyty.

Item, to Sir *Paine Turberuile*, he gave the castle and lordship of *Coyty*, being another of the said members; and now parcel of the possessions of *John Gamage*, Esq.

4
Lhan Ble-
thyan.

Item, to Sir *Robert S. Quintine* he gave the castle and lordship of *Lhan Blethan*, being another of the said
members,

members; and now parcel of the poffeffions of *S. William-Herbert*, of *Swanfey*, Knt.

Item, to Sir *Richard Syward*, he gave the caftle and lordfhip of *Talauan*, being another of the faid' members; and now parcel of the poffeffions of *Anthony Maunfell*, Efq. 5 Talauan:

Item, to Sir *Gilbert Humfrevile*, he gave the caftle and manor of *Penmarke*, being three knights fees; now parcel of the poffeffions of the Right Hon. Lord St. *John*, of *Bledfo*. 6 Penmarke.

Item, to Sir *Reginald de Sully*, he gave the caftle and manor of *Sully*, fo fince called after his name, being two knights fees; now divided betwixt the Earl of *Penbroke*, and the Lord *St. John*, of *Bledfo*. 7 Sully.

Item, to Sir *Roger Berkrolles*, he gave the manor of *Eaft Orchard*, being one knight's fee; now parcel of the poffeffions of *S. William Herbert*, of *Swanfey*. 8 Eaft Orchard.

Item, to Sir *Peter le Soore*, he gave the caftle and manor of *Peterton*, fo now called after his name, being one knight's fee; now parcel of the poffeffions of the Earl of *Penbroke*. 9 Peterton.

Item, to Sir *John Fleming*, he gave the caftle and manor of *St. George*, being one knight's fee; and holden of his pofterity the *Flemings* to this day. 10 S. George.

Item, to Sir *John St. John*, he gave the caftle and manor of *Fonmon* or *Fenuon*, being one knight's fee; and now parcel of the poffeffions of the Lord *St. John*, of *Bledfo*. 11 Fonmon:

Item, to Sir *William le Efterling*, alias *Stradling*, he' gave the caftle and manor of *St. Donats*, or *St. Denwit*, being one knight's fee; now parcel of the poffeffions of Sir *Edward Stradling*, Knt. that now is. 12 S. Donat's.

Sum. Four Lordfhips Members, and Thirteen Knights Fees.

ITEM, he gave to the aforefaid *Eneon* that took his part, the lordfhip of *Senghenmyth*, being another of the faid members. 13

f   Item,

14   Item, he gave the caftle and lordfhip of *Auan*, another of the faid members, to *Caradoc Fitz Ieftyn*, the eldeft fon of the faid *Ieftyn*.

15   Item, he gave the lordfhip of *Ruthyn*, another of the faid members, to another fon of the faid *Ieftyn*.

16   Item, the reft of the forefaid knights fees, being twenty-two and an half, he diftributed part to gentlemen that ferved him, and part to the *Welfhmen*, right owners of the fame.

The Portion that the Lord kept for himfelf and his Heirs.

THE caftle of *Cardyff* and *Kenfigg*, with the forefaid three market towns of *Cardyff*, *Kenfigg*, and *Cowbrige*, and the fhrievalty, being the body of the faid lordfhip of *Glamorgan*, and all the demefnes of the fame, with the reft of the faid members; to wit, *Mifkyn*, *Glynrothney*, *Tyr Iarl*, and *Boviarton*, alias *Lentwit*: and the chief feniory of the whole, the faid *Robert Fitzhamon* kept to himfelf. And in the faid lordfhip of *Boviarton*, he had a large grange or houfe of hufbandry, with lands to the fame belonging, that ferved him for the provifion of corn to his houfe. He dwelt himfelf moft in the faid caftle or town of *Cardyff*, being a fair haven town. And becaufe he would have the aforefaid twelve knights and their heirs give attendance upon him every county day (which was always kept by the fheriff in the utter ward of the faid caftle, on the Monday monthly as is before faid) he gave every one of them a lodging within the faid utter ward, the which their heirs, or thofe that purchafed the fame of their heirs, do enjoy at this day.

Alfo the morrow after the county day, being the Tuefday, the lord's chancellor fat always in the Chancery there, for the determining of matters of confcience in ftrife, happening as well in the faid fhrievalty as in the

the members; the which day also, the said knights used to give attendance upon the lord; and the Wednesday every man drew homeward, and then began the courts of the members to be kept in order, one after another.

The Pedigree of *Robert Fitzhamon*, and of his Heirs, Lords of *Glamorgan*.

1   THE said *Robert Fitzhamon*, was son to *Hamon*, a great lord, and kinsman of *William* the *Conqueror*, who came into the realm with him. This *Robert* (as is before said) was knight of the privy chamber with King *William Rufus*; who (as it appeareth in the Chronicles) dreamed the night before the king was killed, that he saw the king torn in pieces by wolves; and therefore, by his persuasion, he willed the king to forbear to go abroad that forenoon. But the king, when he had dined, there was no man able to stay him, but that he would ride forth a hunting into the new forest, where he was slain by *Walter Tyrrell*, by the glancing of his arrow shooting at a red deer.

Some do affirm that he was lord of Aftrevile in Normandy.

Matt. West. lib 2, p 21. I. Caftor. Matt. Paris, page 22.

2   *Mawd*, the only daughter and heiress of the said *Robert*, was married to *Robert*, Earl of *Glocester*, base son to King *Henry* the first.

3   *William*, Earl of *Glocester*, son to the said *Robert* and *Mawd*, died without issue male, leaving behind him three daughters; of the which, *Isabel*, the eldest, was married to King *John*, then Earl of *Oxenford* and *Lancaster* (as some chronicles do declare) who so soon as he was made king was divorced from her. And then she was married to *Geffrey Mandevile*, Earl of *Essex*, and died without issue, as far as I can find.

4   The second daughter named *Amicia*, was married to Sir *Gilbart de Clare*, then Earl of *Clare*, by whom

he had the earldom of *Glocefter.* And *Mabile,* the third daughter was married to the Earl of *Eureux.*

5 Sir *Gilbart de Clare,* fon to the faid *Gilbart,* was the fourth Earl of *Glocefter.*

6 Sir *Richard de Clare's* fon was the fifth earl.

7 Sir *Gilbart's* fon was the fixth earl.

8 Sir *Gilbart's* fon, who married *Jane de Acres,* daughter to King *Edward* I. was the feventh earl.

9 Sir *Gilbart de Clare* their fon was the eighth earl, and he was flain by the *Scots* in King *Edward* the Second's time; and then the earldom fell between his three fifters. Of the which *Elianor* the eldeft was married to *Hugh Spenfer* the fon, in her right Earl of *Glocefter.* *Margaret* the fecond was married to *Peires Gaueston,* and after to the Lord *Awdeley.* *Elizabeth* the third was married firft to *William Lord Burgh,* Earl of *Ulfter,* and after to *Ralph Roch,* Baron of *Armoy,* in *Ireland;* fhe was married the third time to *Theobald L. Verdoun,* and laftly to Sir *Roger Damory,* and had iffue by every one of them.

10 Sir *Hugh Spencer* had to his wives purpartee the faid lordfhip of *Glamorgan.*

11 Sir *Hugh* Lord *Spencer* their fon enjoyed the fame, and died without iffue.

12 *Edward* Lord *Spencer,* fon to *Edward,* brother to the faid *Hugh,* fucceeded the faid *Hugh* therein.

13 *Thomas* Lord *Spencer,* his fon, fucceeded him.

14 *Richard* Lord *Spencer,* his fon, fucceeded him, and died in ward.

15 *Ifabell,* fifter to *Richard,* fucceeded him, and married with *Richard Beauchamp,* Earl of *Worcefter,* and Lord *Burgavenny,* who had iffue by her a daughter only, and died. The which daughter was married to *Edward,* the fon of *Dawraby,* *Ralph Neuel,* Earl of *Weftmoreland.* And after the death of the faid Earl of *Worcefter,* the faid *Ifabell* married

married with *Richard Beauchamp*, Earl of *War-wick.*

16 *Henry Beauchamp,* Earl of *Warwick,* and after Duke of *Warwick,* their son died without iſſue.

17 *Anne* his ſiſter of whole blood ſucceeded him, and married with *Richard Neuel,* after Earl of *Saliſburie,* and in her right Earl of *Warwick;* and had iſſue two daughters, *Marie,* married to the Duke *Clarence,* and *Anne,* married firſt to Prince *Edward,* ſlain at *Teuxburie,* and after his death with *Richard,* Duke of *Gloceſter,* who was afterward King of *England.*

18 The ſaid *Anne* and King *Richard* (being then Duke of *Gloceſter*) had the ſaid lordſhip given unto them by the ſaid *Anne,* Counteſs of *Warwick,* her mother:

19 King *Henry* the Seventh enjoyed the ſame after the death of King *Richard.*

20 *Iaſper,* Duke of *Bedford,* enjoyed the ſame by the gift of King *Henry* the Seventh, and died without iſſue; and by reaſon thereof it remained to the king again.

21 King *Henry* the Eighth enjoyed the ſame after his father.

22 King *Edward* the Sixth ſucceeded him therein, and ſold almoſt all the lands thereof.

23 Queen *Mary* ſucceeded him in the ſeniory.

24 Queen *Elizabeth* our moſt dread ſovereign that now is, doth ſucceed her in the ſame ſeniory, and hath ſold the lordſhip of *Neth* from it; ſo that now there remain no more lands appertaining to the ſeniory, but the moity of the manor of *Deinaſpowys* only.

The Pedigree of *Londres*, Lord of *Ogmore*, one of the said Twelve.

1 *WILLIAM Londres*, lord of the castle and manor of *Ogmore* (as is before said) won afterwards the lordships of *Kydwelbey* and *Carnewilhion*, in *Caermarthenshire*, from the *Welshmen*; and gave to Sir *Arnold Butler*, his servant, the castle and manor of *Dunreeven*, in the lordship of *Ogmore* aforesaid. The which ever since hath continued in the heirs male of the said *Arnold Butler*, until within these few years that it fell to *Walter Vaghan*, sister's son to *Arnold Butler*, the last of the *Butlers* that was owner thereof.

2 *Simon de Londres*, his son, succeeded him.

3 *William de Londres* succeeded his father *Simon*, and had issue one son.

4 *Moris de Londres*, his son, succeeded him, and had issue one only daughter.

5 The said daughter married with one *Seward*, a man of great possessions.

6 They had issue a daughter only, married to *Henrie*, Earl of *Lancaster*, brother to *Thomas*, Earl of *Lancaster*.

7 *Henrie* their son, made afterwards Duke of *Lancaster*, did succeed them; and so the said three lordships, *Ogmore*, *Kydwelbey*, and *Carnewilhion*, became parcels of the Duchy of *Lancaster* ever after.

The Pedigree of *Greenefeeld*.

SIR *Richard Greenefeeld* before said (to whom the lordship of *Neth* was given in reward) was lord of the castle and manor of *Bydyford*, in *Devonshire*, at the time he came into *Wales* with the said *Robert Fitzhamon*, and founded an abby of white monks in *Neth*, and gave the whole lordship to the maintenance of the same, and then returned back again to *Bydyford*, whereas the issue male of his body doth yet remain, and enjoyeth the same.

The

The Pedigree of *Turberuile*, Lord of *Coyty*.

1   SIR *Paine Turberuile*, Lord of *Coyty*, as is be-
     fore said.

2   Sir *Simon Turberuile* succeeded him, and died with-
     out issue.

3   Sir *Gilbart Turberuile* succeeded his brother.

4   Sir *Paine Turberuile*, his son succeeded him, and
     married *Mawd*, daughter and sole heir to *Morgan
     Gam*, one of the nephews of the aforesaid *Iestyn*.

5   Sir *Gilbart* their son quartered *Iestyn*'s arms with
     Turberuile's.

6   Sir *Gilbart*, his son, succeeded him.

7   Sir *Richard*, his son, succeeded him.

8   Sir *Paine*, his son, succeeded him, who married
     with *Wenlhian*, daughter to Sir *Richard Talbot*,
     Knt. and had issue by her, two sons, that is to
     wit, *Gilbart* and *Richard*; and four daughters,
     namely, *Catharine*, *Margaret*, *Agnes*, and *Sara*.

9   Sir *Gilbart* succeeded Sir *Paine* his father.

10   Sir *Gilbart*, his son, succeeded him, and died
     without issue

11   Sir *Richard*, his father's brother, succeeded him,
     and having no issue, entailed the lordship of *Coity*
     to the heirs male of Sir *Roger Berkerolles*, Knt.

1   Sir *Roger Berkerolles*, Knt. son to Sir *William
     Berkerolles*, Knt. and *Phelice* his wife, one of the
     daughters of *Veere*, Earl of *Oxenford*, which said
     Sir *Roger* had married *Catharine*, the eldest sister
     of the said Sir *Richard*. And for default of such
     issue, the remainder to the heirs male of Sir *Ri-*

2   *chard Stakepoole*, Knt. who married with *Margaret*,

3   second sister of the said *Richard*. And for default
     of such issue, the remainder to the heirs of Sir
     John de la Beare, Knt. and *Agnes* his wife, the

4   third sister to the said *Richard*. And for lack of
     such issue male, the remainder to the heirs male of
     William Gamage. and of *Sara* his wife, the fourth
     sister to the said Sir *Richard Turberuile*.

The said *Berkrolles*, *Stakepoole*, or *Stacpoole*, and *De la Beare*, died without issue male*, by reason whereof, after the death of Sir *Laurence Berkerolles*, Knt. son to the said Sir *Roger*, and *Catharine* his wife; the said lordship fell to Sir *William Gamage*, son to *Gilbert*, son to the foresaid *William Gamage*, and *Sara*. The said *William* was son to Sir *Robert Gamage*, Knt. son to *Paine Gamage*, lord of the manor of *Rogiade*, in the county of *Monmowth*. The foresaid Sir *William* had issue *Thomas*, *Thomas* had issue *John*, *John* had issue *Morgan*, *Morgan* had issue Sir *Thomas Gamage*, Knt. and *Margaret*, wife to *Ienkin Thomas*, and *Anne*, wife to *Robert Raglan*, and *Catharine*, wife to *Reginald ap Howel*, and *Wenlhian*, wife to *Thomas ap Meyric*.

The said Sir *Thomas Gamage* had issue *Robert Gamage*, that late was; *Catharine* his eldest daughter, wife to Sir *Thomas Stradling*, Knt. *Marie* the second daughter, wife to *Matthew Herebert*; *Margaret* the third daughter, wife to the Lord *William Howard*;

---

* *Robert*, the only brother of the said Sir *RICHARD STAC-POOLE*, married a daughter of Sir *John Sitfylt*, or *Cecill*.

Sir *William Stacpoole*, his eldest son, married a daughter of *Howel ap Ithel*, Lord of *Roos* and *Rynonioc*, now *Denbighland*. The said Sir *WILLIAM STACPOOLE* had a command in an army, raised in the reign of King *Stephen*, against *David*, King of *Scots*, but died young, leaving three sons and one daughter.

Sir *RICHARD STACPOOLE*, his eldest son, of *STAC-POOLE*, in the county of *Pembrooke*, married a daughter of Sir *Henry Vernon*, of *Haddon*, in the *Peke*.

No mention is made of the second son; but *Robert*, the youngest son, encouraged by his cousin *Robert Fitzstephen*, went over to *Ireland* with *Richard*, Earl of *Strigule*, known by the name of *Strongbow*, and was a captain of archers in that division of the army that *Fitzstephen* commanded under *Strongbow*, in the year 1168, the fourteenth year of King *Henry* the Second.

The said *ROBERT STACPOOLE* afterwards settled in *Ireland*, and his lineal descendant has a large property in the county of *Clare* in that kingdom.

The old mansion of *STACPOOLE* Court, and a large estate in *Pembrookeshire*, descended to a grand daughter of the second Sir *RICHARD STACPOOLE*, and is now the property of the son of the late *Pryse Campbell*, Esq; who was member for that county, and died in 1769.

and

and *Elizabeth* the fourth daughter, wife to *Richard Hogan*, of *Penbrookeshire*, Esq. The said *Robert Gamage* had issue *John Gamage*, that now is.

1 Sole heir general to the said Sir *Roger Berkrolles*, Knt. and *Catharine*, one of the four sisters, and heirs general to the aforesaid Sir *Richard Turberuile*, Knt. is Sir *Edward Stradling*, Knt. that now is.

2 Sole heir general to the said Sir *Richard Stakepoole*, of *Penbrookeshire*, and *Margaret* his wife, another of the four sisters, and heirs general to the said Sir *Richard Turberuile*, Knt. is Sir *George Vernon*, Knt.

3 Heirs general to the said Sir *John de la Beare*, Knt. and *Agnes* his wife, another of the four sisters, and heirs general of the said Sir *Richard Turberuile*, Knt, are *Oliuer S. John*, Lord *S. John*, of *Bledso*, and *William Basset*, of *Glamorgan*, Esq. that now is.

4 *John Gamage*, Esq. that now is, is as well heir general lineally descended from *Sara* the fourth sister, and heir to the said Sir *Richard Turberuile*, Knt. as also heir by the entail aforesaid, to the whole lordship of *Coyty*.

Robert de S. Quintine, his Pedigree.

SIR *Robert de S. Quintine*, to whom the lordship of *Lhanblethian* was given, and his issue male enjoyed the same, until King *Henry* the Third's time. And then, or in short time after, his issue male failed, of whom is descended Sir *William Parr*, late Marquiss of *Northampton*.

Richard de Syward, his Pedigree.

SIR *Richard Syward*, to whom the lordship of *Talauan* was given, and his issue male, enjoyed the same until King *Edward* the Third's time; at which time the heirs thereof having other lands in *Somersetshire*, sold the said lordship to the Lord *Spencer*, then Lord of *Glamorgan*, and went into *Somersetshire* to dwell there, where his issue male continueth yet.

Gilbert

Gilbert de Humfreuile, his Pedigree.

SIR *Gilbert Humfreuile* aforesaid, to whom the castle and manor of *Penmarke* was given, and his issue male, enjoyed the same till the said King *Edward* the Third's time; and then the inheritance of the said castle and manor descended to Sir *John S. John*, of *Fonmon*, Knt. to whom the forenamed Lord *S. John*, of *Bledso*, is sole heir.

Roger de Berkerolles, Knt. his Pedigree.

SIR *Roger Berkerolles* aforesaid knight, to whom the manor of *East Orchard* was given; and his issue male, enjoyed the same till the thirteenth year of *Henrie* the Fouth; that Sir *Laurence Berkerolles*, Knt. died, whom Sir *Edward Stradling*, Knt. as sole heir did succeed, being son to Sir *William Stradling*, Knt. son to Sir *Edward Stradling*, Knt. and *Wenlhian* sole sister and heir to the said Sir *Laurence*, of whom *Edward Stradling*, Knt. (that now is) is lineally descended.

Reginald de Sully, Knt. his Pedigree.

SIR *Reginald de Sully*, to whom the castle and manor of *Sully* was given, and his issue male, enjoyed the same until about King *Edward* the First's time. And then it fell to a daughter married to Sir *Morgan de Avan*, Lord of the lordship of *Avan* above named; whose son, Sir *John de Avan*, had but one daughter, of whom Sir *George Blunt*, of *Shropshire*, is lineally descended as sole heir, whose ancestor gave the said lordship of *Avan*, and the castle and manor of *Sully* to the Lord *Spencer*, in exchange for other lands in *England*.

Peter

Peter le Score, Knt. his Pedigree.

SIR *Peter le Score*, Knt. to whom was given the castle and manor of *Peter's Towne*, and his issue male, enjoyed the same until King *Henry* the Fourth's time, and then died without issue, and his inheritance fell between divers.

John le Fleming, Knt. his Pedigree.

SIR *John le Fleming*, Knt. to whom the castle and manor of *S. George* was given, and his issue male, enjoyed the same until King *Henry* the Fourth's time; and then it fell to *Edmond Malefant*, who had married a daughter to the last *Fleming*. And in King *Henry* the Seventh's time the *Malefants* issue by *Flemings* daughter failed; and then it fell to *John Butler*, of *Dunreeven* above named, Esq. and after the death of him and of *Arnold* his son, both the inheritances of *Fleming* and *Butler* fell to *Walter Vaghan*, of *Brodemard*, in the county of *Hereford*, Esq. now living, sister's son to the said *Arnold Butler*.

Oliuer de S. John, Knt. his Pedigree.

SIR *Oliuer S. John*, Knt. to whom the castle and manor of *Fonmon* was given, and his heirs male have ever since enjoyed the same, to whom the above named Lord *S. John*, of *Bledso*, that now is, is sole heir; whose ancestors from the winning of the said lordship or *Glamorgan* out of the *Welshmens* hands, have continually dwelt at *Fonmon* aforesaid, until the latter time of King *Edward* the Fourth. That *John S. John*, Esq. had the said lordship of *Bledso*, and many other possessions besides, by the death of dame *Margaret Beauchampe*, his mother, who was also mother to *Margaret*, Duchess of *Somerset*, mother to King *Henry* the Seventh. Since which time the said *John S. John*, and Sir *John S. John*, Knt. father to my lord that now is, have always dwelt in *Bledso*, but they do keep their lands in *Wales* still in their hands.

William le Eſterling, alias *Stradling*, his Pedigree.

1   SIR *William Eſterling*, Knt. to whom the caſtle and manor of *S. Donat*'s was given.

2   Sir *John le Eſterling*, Knt. his ſon, ſucceeded him.

3   Sir *Moris le Eſterling*, Knt. his ſon, ſucceeded him.

4   Sir *Robert le Eſterling*, Knt. (moſt commonly called *Stradling* by ſhortneſs of ſpeech and change of ſome letters) ſucceeded him.

5   Sir *Gilbert Stradling*, Knt. his ſon, ſucceeded him.

6   Sir *William Stradling*, Knt. his ſon, ſucceeded him.

7   Sir *John Stradling*, Knt. his ſon, ſucceeded him. It doth not appear in what ſtock or firname any of theſe ſeven knights above named did marry; but the names of the wives of *William* the firſt, *Robert*, and *John* the ſecond, were *Hawiſia*, *Mathilda*, and *Cicilia*.

8   Sir *Peter Stradling*, Knt. his ſon, ſucceeded him, who in the beginning of King *Edward* the Firſt's time and reign married *Iulian*, ſole daughter and heir of *Thomas Hawey*, by whom he had three manors, *Hawey* and *Combawey*, in *Somerſetſhire*, yet remaining to his heirs, and *Compton Hawey*, in *Dorcetſhire*, ſold of late years.

9   Sir *Edward Stradling*, Knt. their ſon, ſucceeded them, and he quartered the *Haweys*' arms with his, and married with *Elianor*, daughter and heir to *Gilbert Strangbow*, a younger brother, whoſe wife was daughter and heir to *Richard Garnon*, and had by her two manors in *Oxefordſhire*.

10   Sir *Edward Stradling*, Knt. his ſon, ſucceeded him, and married with *Wenlhian*, daughter to *Roger Berkrolles*, Knt. and ſole ſiſter and heir to Sir *Laurence Berkrolles*, Knt. as it happened afterward.

11   Sir *William Stradling*, Knt. his ſon, married with *Iſabel*, daughter and heir to *John S. Barbe*, of *Somerſetſhire*; but he had no lands by her, for it was entailed

entailed to the heirs male. This Sir *William*, in
King *Richard* the Second's time, went a pilgrimage
to *Ierufalem*, and received there alfo the orders of
knighthood of the fepulchre of Chrift.

12. Sir *Edward Stradling*, Knt. his fon, fucceeded
him, who, becaufe he was fole heir general to the
faid *S. Barbe*, did quarter *S. Barbe's* arms with his.
To whom alfo (in the thirteenth year of King
Henry the Fourth) fell the whole inheritance of the
Berkerolles, and the right of the fourth part of
Turberuile's inheritance, Lord of *Coyty* aforefaid;
the which, for lack of iffue male of the faid *Berkerolles*, remained to *Gamage* and to his heirs male
by the efpecial entail aforefaid. The which Sir
Edward did quarter not only the faid *Berkerolles'*
arms with his, but alfo the *Turberuiles* and *Ieftynes*
arms; of whom the *Turberuiles* had in marriage
one of the inheritors, as is before faid; becaufe
the faid Sir *Edward* was one of the four heirs general to Sir *Richard Turberuile*, to wit, fon to Sir
William Stradling, fon to *Wenlbian*, fifter and heir
to the faid *Laurence Berkerolles*, and daughter to
Catharine, eldeft fifter, and one of the four heirs
general to the aforefaid Sir *Richard Turberuile*.

The faid Sir *Edward* married with *Jane*, daughter
to *Henry Beauford*, afterwards Cardinal, begotten
(before he was prieft) upon *Alice*, one of the daughters of *Richard*, Earl of *Arundell*; and in the beginning of King *Henry* the Seventh's reign, he
went likewife on pilgrimage unto *Ierufalem*, as his
father did, and received the order of the fepulchre
there.

This Sir *Edward* had to his brother Sir *John
Stradling*, Knt. who married with the heir of
Dauncy, in *Wiltfbire*, and had iffue Sir *Edmond*,
who had iffue *John* and *Edmond*. *John* had iffue
Anne, Lady *Davers*, of whom the *Davers*, *Huger-
fordes*, *Fynes*, and *Leuet*, and a great progeny of
them are defcended; and of the faid *Edmond*
cometh *Carnyfoyes*, of *Cornewal*.

The

The said *Edward* had another brother called *William*, of whom *Stradling* of *Ruthyn* and others are descended; the same *William* had a daughter named *Wenlbian*, who, by the Earl of *Ryuers*, had a daughter, married to Sir *Robert Poynes*, of whom cometh all the *Poynes*, the *Newtons*, *Perots*, and others.

13   Sir *Harrie Stradling*, Knt. his son, succeeded him, and married with *Elizabeth*, sister of whole blood to Sir *William Herbert*, Knt. Earl of *Penbrooke*, and had issue by her one son and two daughters; one of them was married to *Myles ap Harry*, of whom Mrs. *Blanch ap Harrie* and her brethren and uncles are descended;—the other daughter was married to *Fleming*, of *Monton*, in *Wales*.

This Sir *Harrie*, in the sixteenth year of King *Edward* the Fourth, went in like manner on pilgrimage to *Ierusalem*, and received the order of the sepulchre there, as his father and grandfather did, and died in the Isle of *Cypres* in his coming home; whose book is to be seen as yet, with a letter that his man brought from him to his lady and wife. The saying is, that divers of his said ancestors made the like pilgrimage, but there remaineth no memory in writing but of these three.

This Sir *Harrie*, sailing from his house in *Somersetshire* to his house in *Wales*, was taken prisoner by a *Brytaine* pirate, named *Colyn Dolphyn*, whose redemption and charges stood him in 2000 marks; for the payment whereof he was driven to sell the castle and manor of *Besselek* and *Sutton*, in *Monmouthshire*, and the manors in *Oxfordshire*.

14   *Thomas Stradling*, Esq. his son, succeeded him, and married *Ienet*, daughter to *Thomas Matthew*, of *Rayder*, Esq. and had issue by her two sons, *Edward* and *Harrie*, and one daughter named *Jane*, and died before he was twenty-six years of age. After whose death, his wife married with Sir *Rice ap Thomas*, Knight of the Garter. *Harrie* married with the daughter and heir of *Thomas Iubb*, learned in the law, and had issue by her *Francis Stradling*,

Stradling, of *S. George*, of *Briſtow*, yet living *Iane* was married to Sir *William Gruffyth*, of *North Wales*, Knt. and had iſſue by her three ſons, *Edward*, Sir *Rice Gruffyth*, Knt. and *John*, and ſeven daughters. The eldeſt married to *Stanley*, of *Honghton*, the ſecond to Sir *Richard Buckley*, Knt. the third to *Lewys*, the fourth to *Moſton*, the fifth to *Conwey*, the ſixth to *Williams*, the ſeventh to *Pers Motton*, and after to *Simon Theloal*, Eſq. whoſe wife at this time ſhe is; the eighth to *Philips*. Of which daughters there be a wonderful number deſcended. *Edward* married *Jane*, daughter to Sir *John Puleſton*, Knt. and had iſſue by her three daughters; *Jane* married to *William Herbert*, of *S. Julian*; *Catharine* married to *William Herbert*, of *Swanſey*, and another daughter married to Sir *Nicholas Bagnoll*, Knt.

15 Sir *Edward Stradling*, Knt. ſucceeded his father, and married with *Elizabeth*, one of the three daughters of Sir *Thomas Arundell*, of *Lanbeyron*, in *Cornewall*, Knt. The other two were married to *Speke* and *S. Lowe*, and had iſſue four ſons; *Thomas*, *Robert*, *Edward*, and *John*. *Robert* married *Watkyn Lodher*'s daughter, and by her many children; *Edward* married with the daughter and heir of *Robert Baglan*, of *Lantwit*, and hath alſo divers children; and *John* is a prieſt. Alſo the ſaid Sir *Edward* had two daughters; *Jane* married to *Alexander Popham*, of *Somerſetſhire*, of whom is a great number deſcended; and *Catharine* married to Sir *Thomas Palmer*, of *Suſſex*, who hath a ſon named *William*.

16 Sir *Thomas Stradling*, Knt. his ſon, ſucceeded him, and married *Catharine*, the eldeſt daughter to Sir *Thomas Gamage*, of *Coyty*, Knt. and to dame *Margaret* his wife, daughter to Sir *John S. John*, of *Bledſo*, Knt. by whom he hath living yet two ſons, *Edward* and *David*; and five daughters, *Elizabeth*, *Damaſyn*, *Iane*, *Ioice*, and *Wenlhian*.

17   Sir *Edward Stradling*, Knt. that now is, married
Agnes, second daughter to Sir *Edward Gage*, of
Suffex, Knt. and as yet in the year 1572 hath no
issue.

Memorandum, that of the heirs male of the aforesaid twelve knights that came with Sir *Robert
Fitzhamon* to the winning of *Glamorgan*, the lordship aforesaid, there is at this day but the *Stradling*
alive, that dwelleth in *Wales*, and enjoyeth the
portion given in reward to his ancestors.

There be yet of the younger brothers of the
Turberuiles and *Flemings*.

Greenefeeld and *Syward* do yet remain, but they
dwell in *England*, and have done away their lands
in *Wales*.

The Lord *S. John*, of *Bledfo* (although he keepeth his ancient inheritance in *Wales*) yet he dwelleth in *Eugland*.

Thus far the copy of the winning of Glamorgan,
as I received the same at the hands of Mrs.
Blanch Parrie, *penned by* Sir Edward Stradling, *Knt.*

D. POWEL.

THE

THE

HISTORY

OF

WALES.

WHEN the Roman empire, under Valentinian, the younger, began to decline, and became fenfibly unable to reprefs the perpetual incurfions of the Goths, Huns, Vandals, and other barbarous invaders; it was found neceffary to abandon the remoteft Parts of that unweildly body, and to recal the Roman forces that defended them, the better to fecure the inward, and the provinces moft expofed to the depredations of the Barbarians. And in this exigency of the Roman affairs, Britain, as lying far remote from the heart of the empire, was deprived of the Roman garrifons; which, being tranfported into Gaul upon more urgent occafions, left it naked and expofed to the inveterate cruelty of the Scots and Picts: for no fooner had they underftood of the Romans departure out of Britain; and that the Britains were to expect no further help from the empire; but they defcend in greater number than formerly, and with greater courage and expectation, being now rid of the fear they entertained of the Roman legions, who always ufed to hinder their progrefs, and to prevent their incurfions into the Roman province. The Britains perceiving their antient and implacable enemies to fall upon them, and finding themfelves far too weak to repel their endlefs devafta-

B   tions;

tions; with a lamentable narrative of their own Miferies, and the cruel oppreffions of their enemies, they fent over to Gaul, imploring aid of Ætius præfect of that province; who, being moved with the deplorable condition of that province, difpatched over a legion under the command of Gallio, which unexpectedly furprifing the Picts and Scots, forced them, with great lofs and deftruction, to retire over the feas or friths to their own habitations. Then helping them to build a wall of ftone crofs the land, for a bulwark againft any future irruptions; the Romans, at their departure, told them, they could not any more undertake fuch dangerous expeditions for their defence, and therefore admonifhed them to take arms, and like Men vindicate their country, their wives, children and liberties from the injuries or their barbarous enemies.

But as foon as the Roman legion was tranfported into Gaul, back return the Picts and Scots; and having by a defperate affault paffed the wall, purfued the Britains with a more dreadful and bloody flaughter than formerly. The Britains, perceiving their condition moft defperate, once more fend their miferable complaints to Ætius in thefe tragical words: " To Ætius thrice conful the groans of the Britains: the Barbarians drive us to the fea, and the fea drives us back to them; and fo, diftracted betwixt two deaths, we are either drowned, or perifh by the fword." But they folicit to no purpofe; the Romans having already bid abfolutely farewel to Britain, and the empire being cruelly oppreffed by the Goths, and other barbarous nations, was not in a condition poffible to affift them. The Britains therefore finding themfelves abfolutely forfaken by the Romans, and conceiving it utterly impracticable to drive away the barbarians by their own ftrength; faw it urgently neceffary to call in the aid of fome foreign nation, whofe labour in repelling their enemies fhould be gratefully and fatisfactorily rewarded.

The reafon that the Britifh nation was at this time fo weak and impotent, and fo manifeftly unable to withftand thefe barbarous enemies, who were far infe-

rior

rior as to extent of country, and probably in number of people, may in great meafure be attributed to the eafe and quietnefs the Britains enjoyed under the Roman government. For whilft the Roman legions continued in Britain, they ever undertook the fecurity and prefervation of it; fo that the Britains heretofore were little concerned at the incurfions of the Scots and Picts, depending wholly upon the ftrength and valour of the Romans, infomuch, that within a while, they fell into a fit of luxury and effeminacy, and quickly forgot that martial prowefs, and military conduct which their anceftors fo famoufly excelled in. For after their entire fubjection to the Roman empire, they had little or no opportunity to experience their valour excepting in fome home bred commotions, excited by the afpiring ambition of fome male-contented general, which were quickly compofed and reduced to nothing. And after the Scots and Picts grew formidable, and durft venture to make incurfions into the Roman province, the Britains were the leaft concerned in oppofing them, leaving that to the care and vigilancy of the Roman garrifons. And this eafinefs and fupinity of the Britains, may not be untruly attributed to the policy of the Roman conftitution: for when the Britains were brought fubject to the empire, the firft thing the Romans effected towards the confirmation of their obedience, was to take the fword out of their hands. They were fenfible how bold and valorous the Britains naturally were, how unlike to fubmit their necks to a foreign yoke, and therefore they found it impracticable to obtain a quiet poffeffion of this province, as long as the Britains had power and opportunity to oppofe them. This courfe they found very effectual, and when they had once lulled them afleep, they were not over folicitous to roufe and awaken them.

The Britains alfo might poffibly be too much taken with this fedentary and unactive life; and as long as they lived fecure under the protection of the Roman empire, they little feared their country would become a prey to any barbarous nation. No one would have

imagined that that glorious empire would be fo foon
cruſhed to pieces, which could not otherwiſe be effected,
than by the infupportable preſſure of its own weight.
The apprehenſion of the greatneſs and ſtrength of the
Romans, made the Britains probably leſs folicitous.
of enabling themfelves to defend. their country, not
thinking they would ever forfake and relinquiſh the
province of Britain.   But to their forrow they experienced the contrary, the affairs of the empire elfewhere
requiring the help of the British legions, fo that they
were left expofed to the cruelties of the northern invaders, having not as yet recovered any power or conduct to oppofe them.   For had not the Scots and Picts
come on fo forcibly at firſt, but had given time to the
Britains to ſhake off that lethargy they had for many
years been buried in, and to renew their ancient difcipline and vigour, there had been no need of calling
in the Saxons, feeing they would in all probability
been able to maintain their ground againſt any oppofition, and likely had been in poſſeſſion of their whole
country to this time.   But next to the decree of heaven, the ruin of the British nation muſt be attributed
to its too much luxury and effeminacy, and to the univerfal lapfe of the nobility and people, into an averfion of all military action and martial difcipline.   For
though a continued peace be in itfelf defirable, yet oftentimes nothing tends more to the future ruin and
downfal of a nation.   For peace begets in men generally a habit of loofenefs and debauchery, is the occafion of many notorious extravagancies and vicious prac-
tifes, which weakens their hands, and cools their courage and greatnefs of mind, fo that in cafe of any open
danger, they are uncapable to defend their country,
and unfit to oppofe the common enemy.   Scarce any
kingdom or nation was fubverted, but the ruin of it
was uſhered in by theſe means; witnefs the Affyrian under
Sardnapalus, the Perfian under Darius, and the Egyp-
tian under Cleopatra ; fo that it was moſt prudently
urged by a Roman fenator, that Carthage might not be
demoliſhed ; left that for want of an enemy abroad,
the valour of the Romans might degenerate, and their.
conduct

conduct be forgotten. Had the Britains had the fortune to be continually in action, and not exchanged their courage and discipline for ease and laziness, they had no reason to dread the incursions of the Scots and Picts, nor any need of the Aid and Assistance of a foreign Nation; but the condition of their affairs then required it, and help must be had, or else their country must unavoidable become a prey to those northern invaders.

To prevent therefore and repel their violence, King Vortigern held a council of his great men and nobles, where it was concluded to be most advantageous to the Britains, to invite the Saxons out of Germany to their aid, who in all probability would gladly embrace the opportunity, by reason that their own country was grown too scanty for their superfluous numbers. This message of the Britains, however originally delivered, is by an antient Saxon Writer repeated in this manner: " Most noble Saxons, the miserable Britains, shattered and quite worn out by the frequent incursions of their enemies, upon the news of your many signal victories, have sent us to you, humbly requesting that you would assist them at this juncture. A land large and spacious, abounding with all manner of necessaries, they give up entirely to your disposal. Hitherto we have lived happily under the government and protection of the Romans: Next to the Romans we know none of greater valour than yourselves, and therefore in your arms do now seek refuge. Let but that courage and those arms make us conquerors, and we shall refuse no service you shall please to impose." To this message the Saxons returned this short answer : " Assure yourselves, the Saxons will be true friends to the Britains, and as such, shall be always ready both to relieve their necessities, and to advance their interest."

The Saxons being thus happily courted to what themselves had a thousand times wished for, arrived soon after in Britain, in three gallies, called in their own language Kiules, under the conduct of two brethren Hengist and Horsa. Being honourably received by the king, and affectionately treated by the people,

their

their faith was given of both fides; the Saxons ftipu-
lating to defend the Britains country, and the Britains
to give the Saxons a fatisfactory reward for all the
pains and dangers they fhould undergo upon their
account. At firft the Saxons fhewed themfelves very
diligent in their employment, and fuccefsfully repelled
the Scots and Piéts; who being probably ignorant of
the landing of the Saxons, and fearing no oppofition,
boldly advanced to the heart of the country. But
when the Saxons became better acquainted with the
ifland, and happily difcovered the weaknefs and inability of the Britains; under pretence that their pay was
not anfwerable to their fervice and deferts, they qua-
relled with the Britains, and inftead of fupporting them
according to oath, entered into a league with their
enemies the Scots. Moreover, Hengift perceiving with
whom he had to do, fent over to acquaint his countrymen with the beauty and fertility of the ifland, the
infirmity and effeminacy of the inhabitants; inviting
them to be fharers of his future fuccefs and expecta-
tions. To his invitation they readily comply, and
failing over in great numbers, they thought to take
poffeffion of that country, which fortune promifed
fhould be their own: but they muft fight for it firft;
the Britains being refolved to the laft to defend themfelves and their country againft thefe treacherous
practices of the Saxons; and if poffible, to drive
them to their primitive habitations. For when the
Britains became fenfible of the undermining aim of
the Saxons, how they fecretly endeavoured the total extirpation of the Britifh nation, they prefently
betook themfelves to their fwords, and in a fhort
time became fignally famous for their valour and
conduct. This the Saxons afterwards grievoufly felt,
though the total recovery of Britain proved impracticable for want of power; the Saxons having
by maffacres and other treacherous means, moft unmercifully leffened the force and number of the Britains. King Vortigern loved his eafe too well to obferve their practices; and befides, became fo foolifhly
enamoured with the daughter of Hengift, which purpofely,

pofely was laid to intrap him, that the Saxon upon the ftrength of their marriage began to carve for himfelf, and during Vortigern's reign, laid fo firm a foundation for the Saxon conqueft, that the fucceeding Britifh kings, though famoufly valiant, could never undermine it. This Scottifhnefs of his father, young Vortimer could not at length endure; to fee himfelf and his country fo openly and fhamefully impofed upon by ftrangers; and therefore he refolved to take the Britifh government upon himfelf, and to endeavour the univerfal expulfion of the Saxons. With him the Britifh nobility willingly join, and after feveral famous victories over the Saxons, he was unhappily poifoned by a Saxon lady. After him the Britains bravely defended themfelves againft the prevailing greatnefs of the Saxons, under thefe valiant princes, Aurelius Ambrofius, Uter Pendragon, Arthur, Conftantine II. Aurelius Conanus, Vortiper, and Maelgon. To him fucceeded Careticus; in whofe time the Saxons afpiring to a total conqueft of Britain, invited over one Gurmundus, a Norwegian pirate, who had lately fignalized himfelf in Ireland, and obtained a conqueft over that kingdom. Him they employ to march againft Careticus, who being overcome and vanquifhed by him, the Britains were forced, fome to retire beyond the rivers Severn and Dee, fome to Cornwal, and the reft to Little Britain in France. The Britifh affairs were now brought very low, and their government reduced within a very narrow compafs; fo that the title of the Kings of Britain, can be but fuperficially attributed to the fucceeding princes, Cadwan, Cadwallan, and Cadwalader.

C A D-

CADWALADER.

CADWALADER, furnamed Bhendiged, or the Bleffed, was the laft of Britifh race, that enjoyed the title of King of Britain ; after him, the Welch, who were the moft numerous remains of the Britains, difdaining to own any fubjection to the oppreffing Saxons, fet up a new government among themfelves, and altered the ftile of Britifh kings to that of princes of Wales. But whilft Cadwalader ruled in Britain, a very fevere famine, attended with a raging peftilence, which affuredly fprung from the continued war, which was fo eagerly carried on betwixt the Britains and Saxons, happened in the ifland, which occafioned a moft lamentable mortality among his fubjects ; infomuch that he was compelled, together with a great number of his nobility and others, to retire for refuge to his coufin Alan, King of Lhydaw, or Little Britain in France. There he was fure to meet with all civility fuitable to his quality and condition, as well, becaufe of his own near relation and confanguinity to Alan, as upon the account that their fubjects were originally one and the fame people : for the Britains of France, about the year of Chrift 384, went over out of this ifland under the command of Conan, Lord of Meriadoc, to the aid of Maximus the tyrant, againft the emperor Gratianus. For this fervice Maximus granted to Conan and his followers the country of Armorica, where the Britains having driven out the former inhabitants, feated themfelves, and erected a kingdom, which lafted for many years under feveral kings, whofe names and fucceffion are as follows :

The

The LIST of the ARMORICAN KINGS.

1. Conan Meriadoc.	13. Conobertus.
2. Gradlonus.	14. Budicus II.
3. Salomon I.	15. Theodoricus.
4. Auldranus.	16. Ruhalhonus.
5. Budicus I.	17. Daniel Dremroft, i. e.
6. Howelus Magnus.	rubicunda facie.
7. Howelus II.	18. Aregftanus.
8. Alanus I.	19. Maconus.
9. Howelus III.	20. Neomenius.
10. Gilquellus.	21. Harufpogius.
11. Salomon II.	22. Salomon III.
12. Alanus II.	

Alan II. then reigned in Little Britain, when Cad-walader was forced to forfake his own dominions, and to retire beyond the feas. He was defcended from Rune the fon of Mailgon Gwyneth, King of Great Britain, by a daughter married to Howel the fecond, King of Little Britain. This kingdom remained firm, till Salomon III. who was treacheroufly flain by his own fubjects; upon which unlucky accident, the kingdom was converted to an earldom, whereof one Alan was the firft, a valiant and warlike prince, who ftoutly refifted the Normans, and frequently vanquifhed and overcame them.

But after that Cadwalader had continued fome time with Alan, the plague being abated in Britain he pur-pofed to return, and if poffible, to recover that part of his kingdom which the Saxons were now in pof-feffion of. He received frequent intelligence of their number and increafe, how they fairly bid for the conqueft of that country, which had been governed by Britifh kings for the fpace of 1827 years. This troubled him exceedingly, and though he had little hopes of prevailing by the ftrength and number of his forces, yet he made the beft preparation that the opportunity would permit, and difpatched his fleet for the tranfportation of his army, which

confifted partly of his own fubjects, and partly of
fuch fuccours as he received from Alan. · Whilft he
vigoroufly profecuted this defign, and was ready to
ftrike fail for Britain; his voyage was prevented by
a meffage from heaven; which counfeled him to
lay afide the thoughts of recovering his kingdom,
becaufe it·was already decreed above, that the Britains fhould no longer enjoy the government of Britain, till the prophefy of Merlyn Ambrofe was fulfil-
ed. And inftead of a vóyage to Britain, he is ordered to take his journey to Rome, where he fhould
receive holy orders at the hands of Pope Sergius,
and inftead of recovering the Britifh crown, have
his own crown fhaved off, and be initiated into the
order of the monks. Whether this vifion was fig-
nified to him in a dream, or by the impofitious illu-
fions of fome wicked fpirit; or whether it may be a
fantaftical conceit of his own, being a man of a
mild and eafy temper, wearied with troubles and
miferies, is very dubious: only this is certain, that
he never returned again to Britain, after he had gone
over to Alan. But Cadwaladar had no fooner received this Vifion, but immediately he relates the whole
to his friend Alan, who prefently confults all his pro-
phetical books, chiefly the famous works of the two
Merlins, Ambrofe and Silvefter: the firft is faid to be
begotten on a fpirit, and born in the town of Carmarthen, whence he received the name of Merlin,
and to flourifh in the reign of King Vortigern. The
latter called Caledonius, from the foreft Caledon in
Scotland, and Silvefter or Merlyn Wylht, by reafon
he fell mad, and lived defolately after that he had feen
a monftrous fhape in the air, prophefied in the time
of King Arthur, and far more full and intelligible
than the former. Both thefe were in great reverence
and reputation among the Britains, and their works
very religioufly preferved, and upon any confiderable
occafion moft venerably confulted. They were of
opinion, that nothing could efcape their knowledge;
and that no accident of moment or revolution could
happen, which they did not foretel, and was to be
difco-

.difcovered in their writings. In the confultation therefore of their prophefies, and the words which an eagle is faid to have fpoken at the building of Caer Septon, now Shaftfbury; namely, that the Britains muft lofe the government of Britain till the bones of King Cadwalader were brought back from Rome. Alan found out that the time was now come, when thefe prophefies were to be accomplifbed, and the Britains forced to quit their native inheritance to ftrangers and invaders. Upon this he advifed Cadwalader to obey the commands, and follow the counfel of the vifion, and to haften his journey for Rome. This he was willing to fubmit to, being defirous to fpend the remainder of his days in peace and quietnefs, which before he had no opportunity to enjoy. To Rome therefore he haftens, where he was kindly received by Pope Sergius: and after eight years fpent there in piety and devotion, he died in the year 688, and with him the kingdom and total government of the Britains over this ifland.

King Cadwalader is faid to have been a confiderable benefactor to the abby of Clynnoc Vawr in Arvon, upon which he beftowed the Lordfhip of Giayanoc. This place was primarily founded by S. Beuno, to whom it is dedicated, who was the fon of Hywgi ap Gwynlliw ap Glywis ap Tegid ap Cadell, a prince or Lord of Glewifig, brothers fon to S. Cadoc ap Gwynlliw, fometime bifhop of Beneventum in Italy. He was by the mothers fide coufin German to Laudatus the firft abbot of Enlli, or the ifland of Bardfey; and to Kentigern bifhop of Glafgow in Scotland, and of Lhanelwey, or S. Afaph in Wales; which laft was fon to Owen Regent of Scotland, and grandfon to Urien King of Cumbria. The building of a monaftery at Glynnoc happened upon this occafion: Beuno having raifed to life, as the tradition goes, S. Wenifryd, who was beheaded by one Caradoc, a lord in North Wales, upon the account that fhe would not yield to his unchafte defires, became in very great efteem with King Cadvan, who beftowed upon him certain lands whereon to build a monaftery. Cadwallon

wallon alfo, Cadran's fon, gave him the lands of
Gwareddoc, where beginning to build a church, a
certain woman with a child in her arms, prevented
his further progrefs, affuring him, that thofe lands
were the proper inheritance of that child. Beuno
was fo exceeding troubled at this, and without
any more confideration on the matter, taking the
woman along with him, he went in all hafte to Caer
Sevant (called by the Romans Segontium, now Car-
narvon) where King Cadwallon then kept his Court;
when he was come before the king, he told him with
a great deal of zeal and concern, that he had not
done well to devote to God's fervice what was another man's inheritance, and therefore, demanded
back of him the golden fcepter he had given him in
lieu and confideration of the faid land, which the
king refufing to do, was prefently excommunicated by
Beuno, who thereupon departed and went away. But
a certain perfon called Gwyddeiant, the king's coufin-
german, hearing what had happened, immediately
purfued after Beuno; whom when he had overtaken,
he beftowed upon him (for the good of his own foul
and the kings) the townfhip of Clynncovawr, being
his undoubted inheritance, where Beuno built a
church, about the year 616, about which time King
Cadvan died, leaving his fon Cadwallon to fucceed
him. And not long before this time, Eneon Bhrenin,
or Anianus King of the Scots, a confiderable prince
in the north of Britain, leaving all his royalty in
thofe parts, came to Lhyn in Gwyneth, where he
built a church, which is ftill called from him, Lhan
Eingan Bhrenin; where he is faid to have fpent the
remainder of his days in the fear and fervice of God.
He was fon to Oven Danwyn, the fon of Eneon Yrth,
fon to Cunedha Wledig king of Cambria, and a great
prince in the north, and coufin-german to the great
Maelgwyn Gwyneth King of Britain, whofe father was
Cafwallon-law-hir, the brother of Owen Danwyn; and
his mother Medif the daughter of Voylda ap Talu
Traws of Nanconway. This Maelgwyn died about the
year 586.

                                                    Ivor

IVOR and EDWAL YWRCH.

WHEN Cadwaladar was departed for Rome, Alan began to reflect upon the state and condition of Great Britain; he imagined with himself that the recovery of it was not impracticable, but that a confiderable army might regain what the Saxons now quietly poffeffed. Therefore he was refolved to try the utmoft, and to fend over all the forces he was able to draw together; not doubting the conqueft of fome part of Britain, in cafe the whole fhould prove irrecoverable. He was the more encouraged to this expedition, by reafon that the advantage was like to be his own, and no one could challenge the government of Britain, in cafe fortune fhould deliver it to his hands. Cadwalader was gone to Rome, and in all probability never to return; his fon Edwal Ywreh, or the Roe, was young and under the tuition of Alan; fo that the event of this expedition muft of neceffity fall to himfelf, or by his conceffion to his fon Ivor, who was to be chief in the undertaking. Having raifed a confiderable army, confifting chiefly of his own fubjects, with what remained of the Britains that came over with King Cadwalader, he difpatched it for Britain, under the command of his fon Ivor, and his nephew Ynyr: they fafely landed in the weftern parts of Britain, which put the Saxons into fo great a fright, that immediately they drew up all their power to oppofe them, and to hinder their progrefs into the country. The Britains, though fomewhat fatigued with their voyage, however gave them battle, and after a very great flaughter of the Saxons, poffeffed themfelves of the countries of Cornwal, Devon, and Somerfetfhires. This proved a fortunate beginning for the Britains, and gave them great hopes of farther fuccefs in the recovery of their

country;

country; but that could not be expected without great opposition, and several hot engagements with the Saxons. This they were immediately made sensible of; for they had scarce time to breath, and to recover their spirits after the last battle, but Kentwinus, King of the West-Saxons marched against them with a powerful army, consisting of Saxons and Angles. The Britains resolved to fight them; but whilst both armies were in view of each other, they thought it more adviseable to cease from any hostility, and to enter into articles of composition. Ivor seemed already satisfied with his conquest; and willingly agreed to marry Ethelberga, Kentwyn's cousin, and peaceably to enjoy for his life so much as he was already in possession of. This he faithfully observed during the reign of Kentwyn, and his nephew Cadwal; who, after two years, resigned the kingdom of the West-Saxons to his cousin Ivor. And now Ivor was become unexpectedly powerful, being King as well of the Saxons, as Britains that inhabited the Western parts of the island. He was now able to undertake somewhat considerable, and therefore began to fall foul upon his neighbours the kings of Kent, the West-Saxons, and Mercia, whom he vanquished in several battles. But being at length tired with the weight of government, he went to Rome, after the example of Cadwaladar, and resigned the rule of the Saxons to his cousin Adelred, leaving the Britains to the care of Roderick Molwynoc, the son of Edwal Ywrch.

This Ivor founded the abby of Glastenbury, called in the British tongue Ynys Avalon; where there had been a christian church for several years before, and the first that was ever erected in Britain. For Joseph of Arimathea being sent by Philip the apostle in the days of Arviragus, An. Chr. 53. to preach the gospel in Britain, seated himself here, and built a church for the British christians. This church afterwards Ivor converted into an abby, which he endowed with very large possessions; being famous for the burying-place of Joseph of Arimathea, and King Arthur. He bestowed also some lands upon the church of Winchester.

But

But there happened feveral cafualties in his time. Brythe, a Subject to Egfride King of Northumberland, paffed over to Ireland, and wafted and deftroyed a great part of that Kingdom. In the fourth year of his reign there happened a remarkable earthquake in the Ifle of Man, which much difturbed and annoyed the Inhabitants; and the year following it rained blood both in Britain and Ireland. This occafioned the butter and milk to refemble the colour of blood; and two years after the Moon alfo appeared all bloody. Thefe accidents of nature might prefage fome tumults and difturbances in the kingdom; which were very great in his time. For he was almoft in perpetual hoftility with the Kings of Kent, Weft-Sex, and Mercia; which occafioned great bloodfhed and flaughter in Britain. His Journey to Rome put an end to all thefe commotions, from whence he never did return, but ended his days there in the practice of piety and religion.

RODERICK MOLWYNOC.

THE Government of the Britains Ivor refigned to Roderick Molwinoc the fon of Edwal Ywrch, who began his reign An. 720. But Adelred, King of the A. D. 720 Weft-Saxons, was difpleafed that Ivor had not beftowed upon him his whole kingdom; and upon that account he is refolved to trouble and plague Roderick and his Britons. He raifed immediately a powerful army, and with all his forces marched to Devonfhire. which he deftroyed with fire and fword. From thence he proceeds to Cornwal, intending to make that country, fenfible of the fame mifery; but he came far fhort of his expectation; for upon his entrance into the county, the Britains oppofed him, and gave him battel, where he was vanquifhed, and forced to retire with all fpeed to his own dominions. This victory the Britains cal-
le l

led Gwaeth Heilyn; from the place where this battle was fought. The year following, the Britains
again obtained two notable victories over the Saxons, the one at a place called Garth Maclawch in
North-Wales, the other at Pencoft in South-Wales.
But the joy and satisfaction which the Britains entertained of these succeffes, was fomewhat abated by the
death of Belin the fon of Elphin, a Man of noble birth;
and great worth among them.

A.D. 721.

About the fame time Celredus King of Mercia died;
and was fucceeded by Ethelbaldus, who being very
defirous to annex that fertile and pleafant country
lying between the rivers Severn and Wye to his
kingdom of Mercia, entred Wales with a puiffant
army. He deftroyed and ravaged the country before him, to Carno; a mountain lying not far from
Abergavenny, where he was met with by the Britains
between whom a bloody and fore battle was fought
in the year 728. but the victory proved very dubi-
table.

Not long after died venerable Bede, who was educated and brought up in the Abby of Wyrnetham or
Iarewe; a man of great learning and extenfive
knowledge; who wrote feveral books, one of which
entitled, the Eclefiaftical Hiftory of the Englifh Nation; he dedicated to Cleolwolfe King of Northumberland. The fame time Adelred King of the Weft-Saxons, and Ethelbald King of Mercia, united their forces,
and jointly marched to fight againft the Britains.
The Welch were now put to very hard ftreights, and
forced to oppofe the numerous armies of two powerful kings. However, fight they muft, or fuffer their
country to be miferably over-run by their inveterate
enemies. Both armies being engaged, a very difmal
battle enfued thereupon, and a very great flaughter happened on both fides, but the Saxons prevailing by the number of their forces, obtained a very
bloody victory over the powerlefs Britains. But
Adelred, who was fhortly followed by Edwyn King of
the Picts, did not long furvive this battle; and Cudred
took upon him the government of the Weft-Saxons.
                                                    The

A.D. 733.

The Welch found themselves unable to cope with the Saxons, and too weak to repress their endless incursions; therefore they apply themselves to Cudred and joined in league with him, who upon some occasion or other, was actually fallen out with Ethelbald King of Mercia. But Ethelbald was so proud with the success of the last engagement, that notwithstanding the league with Cudred, he must needs again fall upon the Welch. He advanced as far as Hereford, where the Britains, by the help of Cudred, gave him a signal overthrow, and caused him to repent of his rash and precipitous expedition. But shortly after, Cudred and Ethelbald were unluckily reconciled, and made friends together, and Cudred relinquishing the Welch, joined his forces to Ethelbald's. Hereupon ensued another battle, in which the Welch being greatly overpowered, were vanquished by the Saxons; after which victory, Cudred shortly died. To him succeeded Sigebert, a man of a loose and vicious inclination; who for his ill behaviour in the management of his kingdom, was in a short time expelled and deprived by his nobility, and at last miserably slain by a rascally swineherd. After him Kenulph was chosen king of the West-Saxons, Ann. 750. in whose time died Theodore the son of Belin, a man of great esteem and reputation among the Britains. And about the same time, a remarkable battle was fought between the Britains and the Piâts, at a place called Magedawc; in which the Piâts were put to a total rout, and Dalargan their king casually slain. But the Britains did not succeed so well against the Saxons; for Roderic Molwynoc was at length forced to forsake the western countries of Britain, and to claim his own inheritance in North Wales. The sons of Bletius or Bledericus Prince of Cornwal and Devonshire, who was one of them that vanquished Adelred and Ethelbert at Bangor on the river Dee, had enjoyed the government of North Wales ever since Cadfan was chose King of Britain. Roderic therefore demanded the government of this country as his right, which he was now willing to accept of, being he was forced to quit what he had hitherto poss'd in

A.D. 746

A.D. 743.

A.D. 750.

C

D..

But he did long enjoy it, but died in a short time, leaving behind him two sons Conan Tindaythwy and Howel; after that he had in all reigned over the Britains thirty years.

CONAN TINDAYTHWY.

A. D. 755. ROderic Molwynoc being dead, his son Conan Tindaythwy took upon him the government and principality of Wales, in the year 755. He was scarce settled in his throne, but the Saxons began to make in-roads into his country, to spoil and destroy what they conveniently could meet with. They were animated hereto by the bad success of Roderic; and having forced the Britains out of Cornwal and Devonshire, they thought it practicable to drive them out of Wales too, and so to reduce the possession of the whole Island to themselves. This was their aim, and this they endeavoured to put in execution; but they were met with at Hereford, where a severe battle was fought between them and the Welch, in which Dyfwal the son of Theodore a stout and valiant soldier, was slain. And shortly afterwards died Athelbert King of Northumberland, and was succeeded by Oswald.

About the same time happened a religious quarrel between the Britains and Saxons, concerning the observation of the feast of Easter, which Elbodius a learned and a pious Man, endeavoured to rectify in Wales, and to reduce it to the Roman calculation, which the Saxons always observed. The Britains did differ from the church of Rome in the celebration of this feast; and the difference was this. The church of Rome according to the order of the council of Nice, always observed Easter-day the next Sunday after the 14th day of the Moon; so that it never happened upon the 14th day itself, nor passed the 21st. The

Britains

Britains on the other hand, celebrated their Eafter upon the 14th and fo forward to the 20th, which occafioned this difference, that the Sunday obferved as
Eafter-day by the Britains; was but Palm-Sunday with
the Saxons. Upon this account the Saxons did moft
uncharitably traduce the Britains, and would fcarcely
allow them the name and title of Chriftians. Hereupon, about the year 660, a great conteft happened,
managed on the one part by Colman and Hylda, who defended the rites and celebration of the Britains; and
Gilbert and Wilfride on the part of the Saxons. Hylda
was the niece of Edwine king of Northumberland,
educated by Pauline and Aedan. She publickly oppofed Wilfride and other fuperftitious monks, as to
fuch trifles and bigotry in religion, alledging out
of Polycrates, the fact of Irenæus, who withftood
Victor bifhop of Rome upon the fame account; and
the cuftom of the churches of Afia obferved by
St. John the Evangelift, Philip the Apoftle, Polycarpus
and Melito; and likewife obferved in Britain by Jofeph of Arimathea, who firft preached the gofpel
here.

Offa was made King of Mercia, and Brichtrich of A.D. 763.
the Weft-Saxons; about which time died Fermael the
fon of Edwal and Cemoyd King of the Picts. The
Saxons did daily encroach upon the lands and territories of the Welch beyond the river Severn, but
more efpecially towards the fouth part of the country. Thefe encroachments the Welch could not endure, and therefore were refolved to recover their
own, and to drive the Saxons out of their country.
The Britains of South-Wales, as receiving the greateft A.D. 776.
injury and difadvantage from the Saxons, prefently
took up arms and entered into the country of Mercia; which they ravaged and deftroyed with fire and
fword. And fhortly after; all the Welch joined their
forces together, fell upon the Saxons, and forced them
to retire beyond the Severn, and then returned home,
with a very confiderable fpoil of Englifh cattle.
The Welch finding the advantage of this laft incur-
fion; and how that by thefe means they gauled and

C 2   read

vexed the Saxons, frequently practised the same; and entering their country by stealth, they killed and destroyed all before them; and driving their cattle beyond the river, ravaged and laid waste the whole country. Offa King of Mercia not being able to endure these daily incursions and depredations of the Welch, entered into a league with the rest of the Saxon Kings, to bend their whole force against the Welch; who having raised a very strong and numerous army, passed the Severn into Wales. The Welch being far too weak to oppose and encounter so great an army, quitted the even and plain country, lying upon the banks of Severn and Wye, and retired to the mountains and rocks, where they knew they could be most safe from the inveterate and revengeful arms of the Saxons. But as soon as the Saxons decamped, being not able to effect any thing against them in these strong and natural fortifications, the Welch still made inroads into their territories, and seldom returned without some considerable booty and advantage. The Saxons were heartily nettled at these bo-peeping ravagers, and would compliment them still to their holes, but durst not pursue them further, for fear they should be entrapped by such as defended the streights and passages into the rocks. King Offa perceiving that he could effect nothing by these measures, annexed the country about Severn and Wye to his kingdom of Mercia, and planted the same with Saxons. And for a farther security against the endless invasions of the Welch, he made a deep ditch, extending from one sea to the other, called Clawdh Offa, or Offa's dike; upon which account, the royal seat of the Princes of Powys was translated from Pengwern, now Shrewsbury, to Mathraval in Montgomeryshire.

A. D 795.   While these things are transacted in the west, the Danes began to grow powerful at sea, and durst venture to land in the north of England; but without doing any great hurt, being forced to betake themselves to their ships again. Within six years after, they landed again in a country that received much

more

more terrible; they ravaged and deftroyed a great part
of Linfey and Northumberland, over-run the beft part
of Ireland, and miferably wafted Rechreyn. At the
fame time a confiderable battle was fought at Ruth-
land between the Saxons and the Welch, wherein Caradoc King of North Wales was killed, The government of Wales was as yet green, and not firmly root-
ed, by reafon of the perpetual quarrels and difturbances between the Welch and the Saxons; fo that
the chief perfon or lord of any country affumed to
himfelf the title of king. Caradoc was a perfon of great efteem and reputation in North Wales,
and one that did very much contribute towards the fecurity of the country, againft the incurfions of the
Saxons. He was fon to Gwyn, the fon of Colhoyn,
the fon of Ednowen, fon to Blethyn, the fon of Ble-
cius or Bledericus Prince of Cornwall and Devonfhire.
Offa King of Mercia did not long furvive him, and
was fucceeded by his fon Egfert, who in a fhort time
left his kingdom alfo to Kenulphus, a year after that
Egbertus was created King of the Weft Saxons. About
the fame time died Arthen fon to Sitfylht, the fon of
Clydawc King of Cardigan; and fometime after, Run
King of Dyfed, and Cadelh King of Powys: who were
followed by Elbodius Archbifhop of North Wales, before whofe death happened a very fevere eclipfe of
the fun. The year following, the moon was like- A. D. 808.
wife eclipfed upon Chriftmas-day. Thefe fatalities
and eclipfes did portend no fuccefs to the Welch affairs; the laying of St. Davids in afhes by the Weft
Saxons being followed by a general and a very grie-
vious murrain of cattle, which was like to impoverifh
the whole country. The following year Owen the
fon of Meredith, the fon of Terudos, dyed; and the
Caftle of Deganwy was ruined and deftroyed by
thunder.

But thefe feveral loffes which the Welch fuftained
could not reconcile Prince Conan and his brother
Howel; but they muft needs quarrel and contend with
one another, w' 1 they ' d   .   .   .
embrace ard   te the . .

C 3

mon enemy. Howel claimed the iſle of Angleſey, as part of his father's inheritance, which Conan would by no means hearken to, nor conſent that his brother ſhould take poſſeſſion of it. It was the cuſtom of Wales, that a father's eſtate ſhould be equally diſtributed between all his ſons; and Howel by virtue of this cuſtom, commonly called Gavelkind from the word Gafel to hold; claimed that iſland, as his father's eſtate. The cuſtom of Gavelkind has been the occaſion of the ruin and diminution of the eſtates of all the ancient Nobility in Wales; which being endleſly divided between the ſeveral ſons of the ſame family, where at length reduced to nothing. From hence alſo proceeded ſeveral unnatural wars and diſturbances between brothers; who being either not ſatisfied with their portions, or diſpleaſed with the country they were to poſſeſs, diſputed their right by dint of the ſword. This proved very true in this preſent inſtance; for Howel would not ſuffer himſelf to be cheated out of his paternal inheritance, and therefore he would endeavour to recover it by force of arms. Both armies being engaged, the victory fell to Howel, who immediately thereupon poſſeſſed himſelf of the iſland, and valiantly maintained it againſt the power and ſtrength of his brother Conan.

The Welch being thus at variance and enmity among themſelves, and ſtriving how to deſtroy one another; had yet another diſaſter added to their misfortune. For the following year they received a very conſiderable loſs by thunder, which very much ſpoiled and annoyed the country, and laid ſeveral houſes and towns in aſhes. About the ſame time, Gruffith the ſon of Run a perſon of conſiderable quality in Wales, dyed; and Griffri the ſon of Kyngen, was treacherouſly murthered by the practices of his brother Elis.

But Conan could not reſt ſatisfied with his brother Howel's forcible poſſeſſion of the Iſland of Angleſey; and therefore he was reſolved to give him another battle, and to force him to reſtore and yield up the poſſeſſion of that Country, which he had now violently

kept

kept in his hands. Howel on the other hand, being
as refolutely bent to maintain his ground, and not to
deliver up a foot of what he was now, upon a double
refpect, *viz.* his father's legacy, and his late conqueft,
owner of; willingly met his brother, put him to flight,
and killed a great number of his forces. Conan was
cruelly enraged at this fhameful overthrow, and therefore made a firm refolution, either to recover the
Ifland from his brother, or to facrifice his life and
his crown in the quarrel. Having drawn up all the A.D. 817.
forces he could raife together, he marched to Anglefey to feek his brother Howel; who being too weak
to encounter and oppofe fo confiderable a number,
was compelled to make his efcape to the Ifle of Man,
and to leave the Ifland of Anglefey to the mercy of
his brother. But Conan did not live long to reap the
fatisfaction of this victory, but died in a fhort time,
leaving iffue behind him, one only daughter called
Efylht, married to a nobleman of Wales named Merfyn Frych. He was fon to Gwyriad or Uriet, the fon
of Elidure, who lineally defcended from Belinus the
brother of Brennus king of the Britains. His mother was Neft, the daughter of Cadelh king of Powys,
the fon of Brochwel Yfcithroc; who together with Cadfan king of Britain, Morgan king of Demetia, and
Bledericus king of Cornwall, gave that memorable
overthrow to Ethelred king of Northumberland, upon the river Dee, in the year 617. This Brochwel by
the Latin writers named Brecivallus and Brochmaelus,
was a very confiderable prince in that part of Britain,
called Powys-land; as alfo Earl of Chefter, and lived
in the town then called Pengwern Powys, now Salop;
in the houfe where fince the college of St. Chad ftands.
He was a great friend and a favourer to the monks
of Bangor, whofe part he took againft the Saxons that
were fet on by Auguftine the monk, to profecute them
with fire and fword, becaufe they would not forfake
the cuftoms of their own church, and conform to
thofe of Rome.

MERFYN FRYCH and ESYLHT.

CONAN being dead, Merfyn Frych and his wife
Efylht, who was fole heir to Conan, took upon
them the government or principality of Wales.
This Merfyn was king of Man, and fon to Gwyriat
and Neft the daughter of Cadelh ap Brochwel ap Elis
king of Powys. Howel being forcibly ejected out of
Anglefey by his brother Conan Tindaethwy, efcaping to the Ifland of Man, was honourably and kindly received by Merfyn; in return of whofe civilities
Howel ufed fuch means afterwards that Merfyn married Efylht, the daughter and heir of his brother Conan, (though others fay, that he died prefently after
his efcape to Merfyn.) Howel after that he had for a-
bout five years enjoyed the Ifle of Man, and other
lands in the north, given him by Merfyn to hold
under him, died about the year 825; after whofe
death, they again returned to Merfyn, whofe anceftors had always held the fame, under the kings
of the Britains; and fo, upon his marriage with E-
fylht, the Ifle of Man was annexed to the crown of
Wales.

In the firft year of their reign, Egbert, the powerful king of the Weft Saxons, entered with a mighty
army into Wales, deftroyed and wafted the country as far as Snowden Hills, and feized upon the
lordfhip of Rhyvonioc in Denbighland. About the
fame time a very fore battle was fought in Anglefey,
between the Saxons and the Welch, called, from the
place where this fight happened, the battle of Lhan-
vaes. Fortune feemed all this while to frown upon
the Welch, and their affairs fucceeded very ill; for
fhortly after that Egbert had advanced his colours as
far as Snowden, Kenulph king of Mercia wafted the
cou   ·ed
                                            ad

Powis-land, and greatly difturbed and incommoded the Welch nation. Soon after this, Kenulph died, and was fucceeded by Kenelm; and he in a fhort time by Ceolwulph, who, after two years reign, left the kingdom of Mercia to Bernulph.

Egbert, king of the Weft Saxons, was grown very ftrong and powerful, able to reduce all the petty king-doms in Britain, under one fingle monarchy; upon the thoughts of which, he fet upon Bernulph, king of Mercia, and vanquifhed him at Elledowne; and after-wards brought under fubjection the countries of Kent and of the Weft Angles. But the Britains could not be fo eafily fubdued; for after a long and a cruel fight at Gavelford, between them and the Weft Sax-ons of Devonfhire, in which feveral thoufands were flain on both fides, the victory remained uncertain. He had better fuccefs againft Wyhtlafe, king of Mer- A. D. 829, cia, whofe dominions he eafily added to his now increaf-ing Monarchy; and paffing the Humber, he quickly reduced that country to his fubjection. The Saxon heptarchy was now become one kingdom, and Eg-bert fole monarch of all the countries that the Saxons poffeffed in Britain; which name he ordered fhould be changed to England, his people to be called En-glifhmen, and the language Englifh.

They who came over out of Germany into this ifland to aid the Britains againft their enemies the Picts and Scots, were partly Saxons, Angles, and Juthes; from the firft of which came the people of Effex, Suffex, Middlefex, and the Weft Saxons; from the Angles, the Eaft Angles, the Mercians, and they that inhabited the north fide of the Humber; from the Juthes, the Kentifhmen, and they that fettled in the Ifle of Wight. Thefe Germans, after that they had drove the Britains beyond Severn and Dee; erected feven kingdoms called the heptarchy in the other part of the Ifland; whereof, 1. Kent. 2. Of the South-Saxons, containing Suffex and Surrey. 3. The Eaft-Angles, in Norfolk, Suffolk, and Cambridgefhire. 4. The kingdom of the Weft Saxons comprehending Berkfhire, Devonfhire, Somerfetfhire, and Cornwall. 5. Mercia,

5. Mercia, containing Glocefter, Hereford, Worcefter, Shropfhire, Stafford, Chefhire, Warwick, Leicefter, Darby, Nottingham, Lincoln, Northampton, Oxford, Buckingham, Bedford, and half Hertfordfhire. 6. The Eaft-Saxons, containing Effex, Middlefex, and the other part of Hertford. 7. Of the Northumbrians, taking in all the country beyond Humber, which was divided into two parts, Deyra and Bernicia; the firft from Humber to Tyne, the other from Tyne to the Scottifh Sea.

Egbert, king of the Weft-Saxons, having feverally conquered thefe kingdoms, annexed them together, and comprehended them under one monarchy, which was called the kingdom of England, 968 years after the coming of Brute to this Ifland; 383 years after the landing of Hengift; and 149 after the departure of Cadwalader to Rome.

Egbert having thus united under one government thefe feveral kingdoms, which ufed continually to moleft, and to incroach upon each others territories; might reafonably have expected to enjoy his new A. D. 883. kingdom quietly, and not fear any difturbance or trouble in his dominions. But no fooner was he eftablifhed king of England, but the Danes began to threaten new commotions, and landed in great numbers, and in divers places of the kingdom. Egbert fought feveral battles with them, and with various fuccefs: at length the Danes landed in Weft Wales, marched forward for England, being joined by a great number of Welch, and met Egbert upon Hengift-down, where a fevere battle was fought, and the Danes put to a total rout. The Welch fuffered feverely for this; Egbert, being highly incenfed that the Danes were fupported by them, laid fiege to Caer Lhéon ar Dhyfrdwy, or Chefter, the chief city of Venedotia, which hitherto had remained in the hands of the Welch; took the town, and, among other tokens of his indignation, he caufed the brazen effigies of Cadwalhon, king of Britain, to be pulled down and defaced, and upon pain of death forbad the erecting of fuch again. He iffued out a proclamation, by the infti-

inftigation of his wife Redburga, who always bore an
inveterate malice to the Welch; commanding all that
were any ways extracted from British blood, to depart, with all their effects, out of his kingdom, within
fix months upon pain of death. Thefe were very
fevere and infupportable terms; but he did not live
long to fee them put in execution; for dying fhortly
after the battle of Hengift-down, he was fucceeded by
his fon Ethelwulph. This King Ethelwulph married his
daughter to Berthred, who was his tributary king of
Mercia, by whofe help he fuccefsfully oppofed the
cruel incurfions of the Danes, who miferably deftroyed the fea-coafts of England with fire and fword.
Thefe Danifh commotions being indifferently well ap-
peafed, Berthred, king of Mercia, fet upon the
Welch, between whom a remarkable battle was fought
at a place called Kettell; where Merfyn Frych, king
of the Britains, was killed, leaving to fucceed him in
the government of Wales, his fon Roderic Mawr, or
the Great.

RODERIC THE GREAT,

Mᴇʀꜰʏɴ FRYCH having loft his life, and A. D. 843.
with it his kingdom, in the battle of Kettell; his fon
Roderic, furnamed the Great, without any oppofition or conteft, fucceeded in the principality of Wales.
The firft thing he effected after his advancement to
the crown, was the dividing of Wales into feveral
provinces, which he diftinguifhed into thefe three;
Aberffraw, Dinevowr, and Mathraval. Berthred, king
of Mercia, being animated by his late fuccefs againft
Merfyn Frych, purpofed to perform the like exploits
againft his fon Roderic. And having gained the aid
and affiftance of King Ethelwulph, he entered North
Wales, with a ftrong army, and advanced as far as
Anglefey, which he cruelly and miferably deftroyed.

Roderic

Roderic met him feveral times, and the Welch did at
length fo gaul and torment him, that, in fine, he had
little or nothing to boaft of; only Meyric, one of the
chiefeft princes among the Britains, was flain.

But he was foon forced to quit his expedition
againft the Welch, and to convert his forces another
way; his own dominions requiring their conftant
refidence, being feverely threatened by a foreign in-
A. D. 846. vafion. For the Danes were by this time grown fo
very powerful, that they over-ran a great part of
England, fought with Athelftan, king of Kent, brother to Ethelwulph; and obtained fo much conqueft,
that whereas before they returned to their own country when the weather grew too cold for action,
they now took up their winter-quarters in England.

The Welch, in the mean time, being fecure from
any violence, which might otherwife be expected,
from the Englifh; began to quarrel and fall out a-
mongft themfelves. Ithel, king of Gwent, or Wentland,
for what occafion not known, fell foul upon the men
of Brecknock, who were fo refolute as to fight him;
and the event proved very unfortunate to Ithel, who
was flain upon the fpot. It is the unhappinefs of a
nation that is governed by feveral petty ftates, when
it is apprehenfive of no danger from an outward enemy that it will fall at variance, and create difturbances
among itfelf.

Had the Britains, inftead of falling upon one another, taken the advantage of this opportunity, when
the Saxons were altogether employed in oppofing and
repelling the Danes, to increafe and ftrengthen their
number, and to fortify their towns; they might at
leaft fecurely have poffefled their own dominions, if
not extended their government to a great part of England. But a fort of an equality in power, begat an
emulation between the feveral princes, and this emulation for the moft part ended in blows and contention;
fo that inftead of ftrengthening themfelves whilft they
had refpite from the Englifh, they rather weakened

Longer

Kongen, king of Powys; was gone to Rome, there
to end his days peaceably and religiously, but his death
did not prove so natural as he expected, being barbarously flain, or (as some fay) choaked by his
own fervants. Shortly after died Cemoyth, king of
the Picts, and Jonathan, lord of Abergeley. It was
now become cuftomary for princes wearied with
government to go to Rome, and the Pope willingly
difpenfed with the refignation of their crowns, by
reafon that his Holinefs feldom loft by it. King
Ethelwulph paid very dear for his entertainment there,
made his kingdom tributary to the Pope, and paid
the Peter-pence to the church of Rome. The Saxon
genealogifts bring the pedigree of Ethelwulph for feveral fucceffions and generations, up to Adam, as
may be feen in Matthew of Weftminfter, who in like
manner derives the pedigree of Offa, king of Mercia.
This has been the cuftom of moft nations, both antient and modern: and is always practifed by them
whofe families are any thing antient and honourable;
fo that it is a very great miftake to fcoff at, and de-
ride the Welch becaufe they keep up this antient and
laudable cuftom.

Berthred, king of Mercia, became at length far
too weak to repel the daily increafing power of the
Danes, who fo numeroufly poured upon him, that at
laft he was forced to relinquifh his kingdom and fly
to Rome, where in a fhort time he forrowfully ended
his days. Ethelwulph fhortly followed, and left his
fons, Athelbald, king of the Weft-Saxons, and Athelbright, king of Kent, and the Eaft-Saxons. Ethelwulph
is reported to have been fo learned and devout, that the
church of Winchefter elected him in his youth bifhop
of that fee, which function he took upon him about
feven years before he was made king. He is faid
alfo to have conquered the kingdom of Demetia or
South-Wales; which together with the kingdom of
the South-Saxons he beftowed upon his fon Alfred,
upon condition he would bring a thoufand men out
of Wales to Wlithsf, to the aid of his brother
Ethelbert againft the Danes. Athelbald fucceeded

his father in the kingdom of the Weft-Saxons, kept his mother-in-law, the wife of Ethelwulph, for his concubine, and afterwards married her in the city of Chefter. But he did not live long to enjoy this unnatural conjunction, but dying without iffue after that he had reigned eight years, left his kingdom to his brother Athelbright.

About the fame time the Danes began again to beftir themfelves and fell upon the city of Winchefter and deftroyed it, which Athelbright perceiving, after a long fight forced them to quit the land, and to betake themfelves to fea again: But the Danes quickly returned to the Ifle of Thanet, where they remained for that winter, doing much mifchief upon the fea-coaft, and deftroying all places near the fhoars of England. The Englifh were very glad that they durft venture no further, and the more, becaufe the Welch began again to be troublefome, againft whom an army muft be fpeedily difpatched, otherwife they would certainly advance to the Englifh country. Both armies met at Gweythen, where a fierce battle was fought, and a great number flain on either fide, but the victory was not plainly difcoverable. But the Welch not long after, received a confiderable lofs by the death of Conan Nant Nifer, a ftout and fkilful commander, who oftentimes had valiantly repulfed the Englifh forces, and obtained many fignal victories over them.

The Danes had been for fome time quiet, being unable to venture upon any confiderable action, and therefore they thought it advifeable to fecure only what they had already won; and to expect a re-inforcement from their own country. This was quickly fent them, under the command of Hungare and Hubba; who landed in England with a very confiderable army of Danes. King Athelbright, whether terrified with a difmal apprehenfion of thefe invaders, or otherwife being indifpofed, quickly afterwards gave up the ghoft; leaving the management of his kingdom, together with that of his army againft the Danes, to his brother Ethelred. The Danes in the mean time

got

got sure footing, and advanced as far as York, which they miserably destroyed, killing Osbright and Elba two Kings of Northumberland that opposed them. From hence they proceeded, and over-run all the country as far as Nottingham, destroying and spoiling all before them, and then returned back to York. But having once tasted how sweet the Spoil of a country, much more fertile than their own was, they could not rest satisfied with what they had already obtained, but must needs make a farther progress into the country, and fall upon the kingdom of the East-Angles. Edmund king of that country being not able to endure their insolencies, endeavoured to oppose them, but in the undertaking was unfortunately slain. And now after the same manner that the Saxons had formerly attained to the conquest of Britain, the Danes proceeded to the conquest of England. For the Saxons having found out the sweetness of this island, and withal, discovered the weakness and inability of the Britains to oppose them, brought over their numbers by degrees, and in several companies, by which they wearied and tired out the British armies. For it is certain that nothing can produce more to the conquest of an island, than the landing an army at several places and at several Times, which distracts the counsels and proceedings of the inhabitants, and which at this time for want of sufficient power at sea, could not be prevented. And so the Danes being informed of the good success of Hungare and Hubba in England, sent over another army under the command of Basreck and Alding, who landed in West-Sax, and fought five battles with King Ethelred and his brother Alfred, namely at Henglefield, Eastondown, Redding, Basing and Mereton, in which two first the English overcame, and the three last the Danes got the victory.

Soon after this Ethelred died, leaving his kingdom to his brother Alfred, who no sooner had taken the government upon him but considered with himself what a heavy burthen he was to sustain, and therefore

fore he began to enquire after the wifeſt and learned-
eſt men that he could hear of, to be directed by them,
whom he worthily entertained, making uſe of their
advice as well in the publick government of the
kingdom, as in his private ſtudies and conference
of learning. He ſent for two men famouſly learned
out of Wales, the one called John de Erigena, ſurnamed
Scotus; the other Aſſerius, ſurnamed Menevenſis. De
Erigena was born at Menevia or St. Davids, and was
brought up in that college; who, for the ſake of
learning; having travelled to Athens, and beſtowed
there many years in the ſtudy of the Greek, Hebrew,
and Caldaick tongues, and the ſecret myſteries of
philoſophy, came to France; where he was well accepted of by Carolus Calvus, or Charles the Bald, and
Ludovicus Balbus, or Lewis the Stammerer: and there
tranſlated the works of Dionyſius Areopagita, De
Cœleſti Hierarchia out of the Greek into the Latin
tongue. Being returned home to Wales, he was
ſent for by this King Alfred, who was then founding
and erecting the univerſity of Oxford, of which
Erigena became the firſt profeſſor and publick reader. But King Alfred bore ſo great a reſpect to
learning, that he would ſuffer none to bear any conſiderable office in his court but ſuch as were learned; and withal, exhorted all perſons to embrace
learning, and to honour learned men. But though a
love to learning be ſeldom reconcileable with a warlike and a military life, King Alfred was alſo forced
to regard the diſcipline of war to defend his kingdom againſt the increaſing power of the Danes. For
he was ſcarce ſettled in his throne, but this reſtleſs
and ever troubleſome people began to moleſt and deſtroy his country, inſomuch that he was of neceſſity
forced to oppoſe them, which he did twice upon the
ſouth ſide of the river Thames, in which engagements he ſlew of the Danes one king, nine earls, together with an innumerable multitude of inferior ſoldiers. About the ſame time Gwgan ap Meyric ap
Dunwal ap Arthen ap Sitfylht, prince of Cardigan, died,
being at iſſue ſo, ꝓꝓꝓ ꝓꝓꝓ ꝓꝓꝓ ꝓꝓꝓ. But the

late

late victories which Alfred had obtained over the
Danes, did not so much weaken and dishearten them,
but that in a short time they recovered their spirits
and began again to look terrible and threatening. For
as soon as they could re-unite their scattered forces, they
set upon and destroyed the town of Alclyde, won
the city of London and Reading, over-ran all the
inland country, and the whole kingdom of Mercia.
Another army of Danes at the same time proved
very successful in the North and possessed themselves
of the country of Northumberland, which action did
not so much grieve the English, as trouble and vex
the Picts and Scots, who were incessantly gauled, and
frequently beat off by these Danish troops. The
next year three of the Danish captains marched from
Cambridge towards Warham in Dorsetshire, of which
expedition King Alfred being informed, presently
detached his forces to oppose them, and to offer them
battle. The Danes were so startled at this, that
they immediately desired peace, and willingly consented forthwith to depart out of the country, and
to forswear the sight of English ground. According
to which capitulation, the horse that night marched
for Exeter, and the foot being shipped off, were
all of them drowned at Sandwich. The Danes having thus abjured England, were not willing to return home empty, but thought it prudent to bend
their course against Wales. They fancied that they
were like to meet with no great opposition from the
Welch, and therefore could carve for themselves according as their fancy directed them. But having landed their army in Anglesey, they quickly experienced
the contrary; Prince Roderic opposing them, gave
them two battles, one at a place called Bengole, and
the other at Menegid in Anglesey. At the same time
another army of Danes under the command of Halden and Hungare landed in South-Wales, over-ran
the whole country, destroying all before them, nei-
their sparing churches nor religious houses. But they
received their due reward at the hands of the West
Saxons, who meeting with them on the coasts of Devonshire,

yonſhire, ſlew both Halden and Hungare, with 1200 of their men. The ſame year Einion, biſhop of St. Davids died, and was the following year ſucceeded by Hubert, who was inſtalled in his place.

A. D. 876. The Engliſh being rid of their powerful and ever reſtleſs enemies the Danes, began now to quarrel with the Welch, entering into Angleſey, with a numerous army, fought a ſore battle with Roderic, who together with his brother (or as others ſay his ſon) Gwyriad, was unhappily ſlain in the field, which battle is called by the Welch, Gwaith Duw Sul y Mon. This Roderic had iſſue by his wife Angharad, Anarawd, Cadelh and Merſyn, the laſt of which, Giraldus Cambrenſis, contrary to the vulgar and received opinion, will have to be the eldeſt ſon of Roderic, upon whom was beſtowed the principality of North-Wales. For it was unanimouſly granted that Roderic was undoubted proprietor of all the dominions of Wales, North-Wales deſcending unto him by his mother Eſylht, the daughter and ſole heir of Conan Tyndaethwy; South-Wales by his Wife Angharad, the daughter of Meyric ap Dyfnwal ap Arthen ap Sitſylht, King of Cardigan; Powis by Neſt, the ſiſter and heir of Congen ap Cadelh, King of Powis his father's mother. Theſe three dominions Roderic divided between his three ſons, appointing North-Wales for his eldeſt ſon Anarawd, South-Wales to Cadelh, who ſhortly after his father's death, forcibly ſeized upon his brother Merfyn's portion, upon whom Roderic had beſtowed Powis-Land. Wales being thus divided between theſe three princes, they were called Y Tri Tywyſoc Talaethioc, or the three crowned princes, by reaſon that each of them did wear on his helmet a coronet of gold, being a broad head band indented upward, ſet and wrought with precious ſtones, which in the Britiſh Tongue is called Taleath. To each of theſe princes Roderic built a royal ſeat, for the Prince of Gwyneth or North-Wales, at Aberffraw; of South-Wales, at Dinefawr; for the Prince of Powis, at Mathrafel. Roderic had iſſue alſo, beſides theſe three, Roderic, Meyric, Edwal or Tudwa', Gwyriad and Gwiddelic.

But

But Roderic having divided his principality betwixt his eldeft fons, namely, Aberffraw, with the fifteen cantreds thereunto belonging to Anarawd; Dinefawr with its 15 cantreds extending from the mouth of the river Dofi, to the mouth of Severn to Cadelh; and Powis with fifteen cantreds from the mouth of the river Dee, to the bridge over Severn at Glocefter to Merfyn: Ordained, " That his eldeft fon Anarawd, and his fuc-ceffors, fhould continue the payment of the ancient tribute to the Crown of England; and the other two, their heirs and fucceffors fhould acknowledge his fo-vereignty; and, that upon any foreign invafion, they fhould mutually aid and protect one another."

And he farther appointed, " That when any diffe-rence fhould arife betwixt the Princes of Aberffraw and Cardigan or Dinefawr, the three Princes fhould meet at Bwlch y Pawl, and the Prince of Powis fhould be umpire. But if the Prince of Aberffraw and Powis fell at variance, they fhould meet at Dol Rhian-edd, probably Morva Rhianedd, on the bank of the river Dee, where the King of Cardigan was to adjuft the controverfy; and if the quarrel happened betwixt the Princes of Powis and Cardigan, the meeting was appointed at Llys Wen upon the river Wye, and to be decided by the Prince of Aberffraw."

And the better to fruftrate any attempt of the Eng-lifh, he ordained moreover, " That all ftrong. holds, caftles and citadels, fhould be fortified and kept in re-pair; that all churches and religious houfes fhould be re-edified and adorned, and that in all ages the hiftory of Britain, being faithfully regiftered and tranfcribed, fhould be kept therein.

A N A R A W D.

THE Welch had often forrowfully felt the unnatural effects of inward feditions, and of being governed by feveral princes, which were now unavoidably to be renewed by reafon of Rodric's imprudent
divifion of his dominions between his three fons. For
the feveral principalities being united in him, it was
certainly the moft politic means for the prefervation of
the country fiom the inveterate fury of the Englifh,
to compofe the inward differences which would otherwife happen, by perpetuating the whole government of
Wales in one prince. For it was impoffible effectually to oppofe the common enemy by feparate armies, and where a different intereft interfered, as if
the fafety of the fame country, and the honour of the
prince were unanimoufly regarded. This was the unhappinefs of the ancient Britains, when the Romans
invaded their country ; domeftic broils and inward dif-
fentions being fown among themfelves, they could not
agree to unite their powers, and jointly to oppofe the
common enemy ; fo that Tacitus wifely concludes,
Dum finguli pugnant univerfi vincuntur.

There are few nations but have experienced the
folly of being rent into feveral portions, and the
downfal of that great body the Roman empire, may
not be abfurdly attributed to Conftantine's dividing of
it between his fons. But the Welch at this time
prefently felt the unhappinefs of it ; Cadelh, Prince
of South-Wales, being diffatisfied with his portion,
and defirous to feed his ambition with larger territories, could not fpare his brother Merfyn's country,
but muft needs forcibly difpoffefs him of his lawful
inheritance, and fo involve the Welch in a Civil
War.

But

But the fucceffion of the Princes of Wales proceeds in Anarawd, the eldeft fon of Roderic, who
began his reign over North-Wales, in the year 877.
At that time Rollo, with a numerous army of Normans defcended into France, and poffeffed themfelves
of the country of Neuftria, which from them has fince
received the name of Normandy. But the treacherous Danes in England, who had retired to the city
of Exeter, quickly violated the capitulation which
they had lately fwore to obferve, and upon that account were fo warmly purfued by King Alfred, that
they gladly delivered up hoftages for the performance
of the articles formerly agreed upon between them.
But it was not their intention to keep them long,
for the next year they again broke loose, poffeffed
themfelves of all the country upon the north fide
of Thames, and paffing the river, put the Englifh
to flight, and made themfelves mafters of Chippen-
ham in Weft-Sax. But their whole army did not
fucceed fo well, for Alfred meeting with a party
of them, flew their captain and took their ftandard,
which the Danes called RAVEN. After this he vanquifhed them again at Edendown, where after that
the Danes had given hoftages for their peaceable behaviour; Godrun, their commander, received the Chriftian faith, and fo reigned in Eaft-Angle. But this
opportunity feemed to threaten a great ftorm upon
Wales; for befides the death of Aedan, the fon of A. D 8-8.
Melht, a nobleman of the country; the articles of
compofition between the Englifh and the Danes, occafioned thefe laft to join their power with the people of Mercia to fight againft the Welch, between
whom a fevere battle was fought at Conwey, wherein
the Welch obtained a very fignal victory, which was
called " Dial Rodri, or the Revenge of the Death of
Prince Roderic."

The reafon why the Mercians were fo irreconcilably
enraged againft the Welch at this time, was this: After the death of Roderic the Great, the northern Britains of Strat-lyd and Cumberland were mightily ir
fefted and weakened throu'h the dul incurfions of the

Danes, Saxons and Scots, infomuch that as many
of them as would not fubmit their necks to the yoke
were forced to quit their country, and to feek for more
quiet habitations. Therefore towards the beginning of
Anarawd's reign, feveral of them came to Gwyneth,
under the conduct of one Hobert, whofe diftreffed ·
condition the prince commiferating, granted them all
the country betwixt Chefter and Conwey to feat themfelves in, in cafe they could drive out the Saxons who
had lately poffeffed themfelves of it.

The Britains having returned their thanks to Anarawd, prefently fell to work, and neceffity giving edge
to their valour, they eafily difpoffeffed the Saxons who
were not as yet warm in their feats. For fome time
they continued peaceably in this part of Wales; but
Eadred, Duke of Mercia, called by the Welch Edryd
Wallthir, not being able any longer to bear fuch an ig-
nominious ejection, made great preparations for the
re-gaining of the faid country. But the northern Britains, who had fettled themfelves there, having intelligence of his defign, for the better fecurity of their
cattle and other effects, removed them beyond the river
Conwey. Prince Anarawd in the mean time was not
idle, but drawing together all the ftrength he could
raife, encamped his army near the town of Conwey at a
place called Cymryt, where himfelf and his men having
made gallant refiftance againft the preffing efforts of
the Saxons, obtained a very compleat victory.

This battle was by fome called Gwaeth Cymryt Conwey, by reafon that it was fought in the townfhip of
Cymryt, near Conwey. But Prince Anarawd would
have it called Dial Rodri, becaufe he had there revenged the death of his father Rodri.

In this battle Tudwal, Rodri's fon, received a wound
in the knee, which made him be donominated Tudwal Gloff ever after; but for his fignal fervice in
this action his brethren beftowed upon him Uchelogoed
Gwynedd. But the Britains purfuing their victory,
chafed the Saxons quite out of Wales into Mercia,
where having burnt and deftroyed the borders, they
returned home much with rich fpoils, and fo took
                                    poffeffion

poffeffion of the country betwixt Chefter and Conwey, which for a long time after they peaceably enjoyed. But Anarawd to exprefs his thankfulnefs to God for this great victory, gave very confiderable lands and poffeffions to the collegiate churches of Bangor and Clynnoc Vawr in Arfon. After this, thofe Danes that lay at Fulhenham near London, croffed the fea to France, and paffing to Paris along the river Seyn, fpoiled the country thereabouts, and vanquifhed the French that came againft them; but in their return towards the fea coaft, they were met with by the Britains of Armorica, who flew the greateft part of them, and the reft confufedly endeavouring to efcape to their fhips, were all drowned.

One fhould think that the feveral misfortunes the Danes fuftained firft at Sandwich, then by King Alfred, and now in France, would have quite drained their number, and utterly have rid Britain from fo troublefome an enemy. But like ill weeds, the more you root them, the fafter they will grow; the Danes were ftill fupplied from abroad, and if an army was vanquifhed here, another was fure to come in their room. This the Welch found too true, for not long after this famous defeat by the Armorican Britains, the Danes not able to venture upon thefe, were refolved to revenge themfelves upon their friends of Wales, and therefore landing in North-Wales, they cruelly harraffed and deftroyed the country. Nor is it ftrange to confider from whence fuch a wonderful number of Danes and Normans could come. For the kingdom of Denmark had under it, not only Denmark, which is a fmall country divided by the fea into Infulas and Peninfulas, as that which joins upon Saxony and Holfatia, called Cymbrica Cherfonefus, with the iflands of Zealand and Finnen, but alfo Norway, and the large country of Sweden, reaching to Mufcovy, and almoft to the North-Pole. This country being then fcarce known to the world, did of a fudden pour out fuch a multitude of people, which like a fudden ﬧ ... over ran all Europe, with a gr.... f ... from

D 4 hence

h nce proceeded thefe Danes who annoyed England; ard the Normans, who conquered France; both nations being originally derived from the fame ftock.

A. D. 890. The Danes had not appeared in England for fome time, and therefore are now refolved to take fo fure a footing, as they cannot eafily be repulfed. Two hundred and fifty fail being landed at Lymene in Kent, hard by the great foreft of Andreflege, they built the caftle of Auldre or Apledore. The fame time Hafting with a fleet of eighty fail ventured to the Thames mouth, and built the caftle of Mydlton; having firft made an oath to King Alfred, not to moleft him or any of his fubjects: but having built the caftle of Beamfleer, he thought himfelf to have obtained fo great a ftrength, that there was no neceffity of obferving the oath lately fworn to King Alfred, and therefore invaded the country round about him. But he foon found his miftake, and was forced to betake himfelf back to his caftle, which was quickly pulled down upon his head, and his wife and two fons taken prifoners; who being chriftened, were again reftored to their father. Upon this Hafting and his Danes departed from England, and made their way for France; where laying fiege to the city of Limogis, and defpairing of a fpeedy furrender of it, betook himfelf to his ufual way of dealing finiftroufly, and devifed this trick to win the town: He feigned himfelf to be dangeroufly fick, and fent to the bifhop, and the conful of the city, defiring of them moft earneftly, that he might be admitted to the Chriftian Faith, and be baptized before his departure out of this world. The bifhop and conful fufpecting no deceit, were very glad, not only to be delivered from the prefent danger of being befieged, but alfo to win fo great a perfon to the congregation of Chrift. Whereupon a firm peace being concluded betwixt both nations, Hafting is baptized, the bifhop and conful being his godfathers; which being ended, he was carried back by his foldiers to his fhips, in a very infirm condition, as he outwardly pretended. About midnight he caufed himfelf with his arms about him to be l ' . a ', r, r   : ed his

foldiers

soldiers to carry their weapons with them under their coats, and so to be ready when he should give them the word. The next day, all things being in a readiness, he was solemnly brought by his soldiers with great clamour and conterfeit mourning, to be interred in the chief church of the city; where the bishop and consul, accompanied with all the most honourable members of the town, came to honour the funeral. but when the bishop had made himself ready to bury the body, and all the citizens being in the church, up starts Hasting with his Sword drawn, and killing first the bishop and the consul, afterwards fell in with his armed soldiers upon the naked people, putting all to the sword, and sparing neither age, sex, nor infirmity. Having ransacked the town, he sent messengers to Charles the French king, to mediate for peace, which he easily obtained, together with the town of Chartres towards the defraying of his charges.

At this time Hennith ap Bledric, a baron of Wales, A. D. 891. died; and two years after, Anarawd prince of North 893. Wales, with a confiderable number of Englifh, marched againft his brother Cadelh, and spoiled the countries of Cardigan and Yftradgwy. At the fame time the Danes laid fiege to the city of Exeter; and when Alfred had marched to oppose them, they that continued in the castle of Auldre passed over to Effex, and built another castle at Scobrith, and from thence, marched to Budington, seated upon the Severn. When Alfred came near to Exeter, the Danes presently raised the Siege, and betaking themselves to their ships, sailed towards Wales, and spoiled the sea-coft thereof, and advanced as far as Buellt.

But the Danes at Budington being informed that king Alfred marched againft them, fled back to their caftle in Effex: so that the king was fain to alter his march, and to convert his forces againft Leicefter; where a party of Danes was so warmly befieged, that at length they were reduced to that extremity, as to feed upon their horses. But the feafon of the year for ... the extremity

of

of the weather being advanced, Alfred was forced to raise the siege, and to wait the next opportunity A. D. 895. for the recovery of the town. But before he could appear before it again, the Danes fairly quitted it, and together with those in Northumberland, passed by the North Sea to Meresige, an isle in Essex. The 896. next year they entered the Thames; and built a castle twenty miles distant from London; upon the strength of which, they ventured to spoil and waste the country thereabouts; but paid very dear for their courage, being accidentally met with, they received a bloody overthrow, having four of their princes slain upon the spot, and the rest very glad to make their escape to the castle. Upon this Alfred divided the river into three streams, by which stratagem the water became so diminished in the Thames, that the Danish ships could not return back into the sea. When the Danes perceived this, and found it impracticable for them to escape in their ships, they left their wives and children and all their effects in Essex; and so passed by land to Enadbryge upon the Severn; and then passing the river, spoiled the countries of Brecknock, Gwentland, and Gwentlhwg. Some of them at the same time, passed over to France; and another company coasting about Devonshire; destroyed the maritime countries; but being met with by the English, lost six of their ships in the dispute.

897. The following summer the kingdom of Ireland suffered extremely by locusts; who consumed all the corn and all grass through the whole country; but were at length by continued prayers and fasting quite destroyed. These are common in Africk, and other hot regions, but seldom seen in colder climates; and when they happen to travel so far, they are always very pestilentious and destructive to that country they come to.

900. This year Igmond, with a great number of Danes, landed in Anglesey, and was met with by the Welch, at a place called Molerain, where Merfyn was slain: though others call it Meilen, and from the battle fought there, Maes Rhos Meilen. The same year
King

King Alfred died, who translated the antient laws
of Dyfnwall Moelmut, king of Britain, and the laws
of Queen Marfia, out of Britifh into Englifh, and
called it Marfian law, which was afterwards called
Weft-Saxon law, and obferved in part of Mercia;
with all the countries on the fouth of Thames: The
other part of the country having another law called
Dane Lex, both which remained to the time of
Edward the Confeffor, who of thefe two made one
law. It is very obfervable, what is related of King
Alfred, concerning his divifion of the natural day into three parts; the one he fet apart for devotion and
ftudy, the next for the affairs of the commonwealth, and the third for his own reft and refrefh-
ment.

Alfred being dead, Edward his eldeft fon took upon him the crown, which fo difpleafed the ambitious
fpirit of his brother Adelwulph, that prefently he raifed a cruel war againft him, and flying to Northumberland, ftirred up the Danes againft his brother
Edward. The Danes were glad of the opportunity;
having now a fair pretence to render themfelves
mafters of the whole ifland; and therefore Adelwulph is made king, as well of the Angles as of the
Danes, who by this time were grown to be one People. Marching then proudly, with a very confiderable
army at his heels, he fubdued the Eaft-Saxons, fpoiled the country of Mercia; and paffing over the Thames
at Crickland, deftroyed Brythend, and returned home
with very great booty. At the fame time Euneth
was flain in Arwyftly. But Edward being informed of
his brother's retreat, purfued him very eagerly; but
miffing of him, over-ran and deftroyed all the country betwixt Oufe and the Dike of St. Edmund, and
then returned home with his whole army; faving the
Kentifh men, who being too greedy of plunder, rafhly tarried behind. For the Danes perceiving the body of the army to be returned, and that a fmall
party ftill continued to ravage the country, prefently fet upon 'em, flew a great number of 'em, and
put the reft to a fhameful flight. Nor were the
Da...

Danes only powerful in England, but molested and A.D. 905. grew prevalent in Ireland: For this year they entered that kingdom, slew Carmot, king and bishop of all Ireland, a religious and a virtuous person, the son of Cukeman; and Kyrnalt, son of Murgan, king of La-906 gines. The year after died Asser, archbishop of St: David's, uncle to the famous and learned Asser, sur-named Menevensis, who being chancellor to his uncle the archbishop, was sent for by King Alfred to instruct his children; whose life he afterwards wrote, and was made bishop of Shireburn.

Edward, to force his brother from his country, and to revenge the death of the Kentishmen, dis-patched an army to Northumberland; which having spoiled the country, returned home: Upon which the Danes, to return their kindness, destroyed a great part of Mercia. But within a while after, Edward having raised a very considerable army, gave the Danes battle, overthrew them, and slew their kings Alden and Edelwulph, with a great number of their nobles. This added very much to his dominions; which were the more increased and strengthened by the addition of the cities of London and Oxford; which upon the death of Edelred, duke of Mercia, Edward seized into his own hands; permitting his wife Elfleda to enjoy the rest of his dukedom. 907. Shortly after, Cadelh, prince of South Wales, died; leaving behind him three sons; Howel Dha, or the Good, who succeeded his father in the kingdom of South Wales; Meyric and Clydawc. King Edward having obtained so signal a victory over the Danes, and rendered his kingdom for some time quiet, began to build places of strength, which might be serviceable against a future storm: He built a castle at Hertford, betwixt the rivers Benefic, Minier, and Lige; and also erected the borough of Wytham in Essex; and continued sometime in Wealdyne, to keep those coun-tries in awe. But in spite of all this precaution, the Danes of Leycester and Hampton, began the follow-ing year to be very troublesome, slew a great number of English at St. Edmer on, and a made towards Rome-ward,

ward, deftroyed the country of Oxford. About the fame time a confiderable fleet from Tydwike, under the command of Uther and Rahald, failed by the weftern fea to Wales, and deftroyed St. David's; where was fought the battle of Dinarth, and Mayloc, the fon of Peredur Gam, was flain. After this they en- A. D. 911, tered into Herefordfhire, where they were fought withal, and Rahald was flain, and the reft compelled to forfwear the king's land, and never to return any more to England. King Edward, to prevent any future difturbance from fuch open invaders, caufed a ftrong army to be quartered upon the fouth fide of Severn; but the Danes, for all he could do, entered twice into his country, once at Werd, and then at Portogan; but were both times overthrown by the Englifh. From thence they departed to the Ifle of Stepen, whence they were forced by hunger to fail to South Wales, intending to make a confiderable prey of that country; but failing of their aim, they were conftrained to make the beft of their way for Ireland. But the next year, a party of Danes fought a very fevere battle with the Kentifh men at Holm; but which of them obtained the victory, is not certainly reported. About the fame time Anarawd, prince of   913, North Wales, died, leaving behind him two fons, Edwal Foel, and Elis; and fome fay a third, named Meyric.

EDWAL FOEL.

AFTER the death of Anarawd, his eldeft fon Edwal Foel took upon him the government of North-Wales; Howel Dha holding the principality of South-Wales and Powis: At what time, a terrible comet appeared in the heavens. The fame year the city of Chefter, which had been deftroyed by the Danes, was, by the procurement of Elfleda, new built, and

repaired, as the ancient records of that city do te-
ftify. This in the ancient copy is called Leycefter,
by an eafy miftake for Legeceftria or Chefter, called
by the Romans, Legionum Ceftria. The next fummer the men of Dublin cruelly deftroyed the ifle of
Anglefey; and foon after, Clydawc the fon of Cadelb,
was unnaturally flain by his brother Meyric, about the
fame time that the Danes received a cruel overthrow
by the Englifh, at Tottenhale. But Elfleda did not
long furvive the rebuilding of the city of Chefter;
a woman of fingular virtues, and one that greatly
ftrengthened the kingdom of Mercia, by building
of towns and caftles againft the incurfions of the Danes;
as Strengat and Bruge, by the foreft of Morph, Tamworth, Stafford, Edelburgh, Cherenburgh, Wadeburgh,
and Runcofe. After this, fhe entered with her whole
army into Wales, won Brecknock, and took the queen,
with thirty-three of her men prifoners; which in
Welch is called " Gwaith y Ddinas Newydh, or the
battle of the new city. From hence fhe marched for
Derby, which fhe took from the Danes, lofing only
four of her chief commanders in the action.

The occafion of thefe two expeditions, according to
fome, was this: Huganus, lord of Weft Wales, perceiving King Edward to be unavoidably bufy in the
Danifh war, gathered an army of Britains, and entering into England, deftroyed the king's country.
Upon the news of this, Elfleda came to Wales with
a great army, fought with the Welch at Brecknock,
and putting Huganus to flight, took his wife and fome
of his men prifoners, whom fhe carried with her to
Mercia. Huganus being thus defeated, fled to Derby,
and being there kindly received, joined himfelf with
the king's enemies, the Danes. Elfleda being certified of that, followed him with her army; but in
ftorming the gates of the town, had four of her beft
officers killed by Huganus. But Gwyane, Lord of
the Ifle of Ely, her fteward, fetting fire to the
gates, furioufly ran upon the Britains, and entered the
town; upon which Huganus perceiving himfelf to
be overmatched, chofe rather to fall by his fword,
than

than cowardly to yield himfelf to a woman. The next year Elfleda laid fiege to the city of Leicefter, which was quickly furrendered, and the Danes therein perfectly fubdued. The fame of thefe feveral actions being noifed abroad, her neighbours became fomewhat fearful and timerous; and the Yorkfhiremen voluntarily did her homage, and proffered their fervice. She died at Tamworth, after eight years' rule over Mercia; and lies buried at Glocefter by St. Peters.

After the death of Elfleda, king Edward moft ungratefully difinherited her daughter Alfwyen; and entering into Mercia, feized all the land into his own hands; upon pretence that fhe, without his knowledge, (whom her mother had appointed her guardian) had privily promifed and contracted marriage with Raynald king of the Danes. But this unjuft and unnatural action of king Edward's, might poffibly bring upon him thofe vehement troubles, which prefently enfued upon it. For Leofred a Dane, and Gruffydh ap Madoc brother-in-law to the prince of Weft Wales, came from Ireland with a great army to Snowdon, and minding to bring all Wales and the marches thereof to their fubjection, over-ran and fubdued all the country to Chefter, before king Edward was certified of their arrival. Whereat being fore offended, and loth to trouble his fubjects for help, vowed that himfelf and his fons, with their fingle forces, would be revenged upon Leofred and Gruffydh; and thereupon marching to Chefter, forced the city from them. Then he divided his army into two battles, whereof he and his fon Athelftane led the firft, Edmund and Edred the fecond; and followed them fo clofe, that he overtook them at the foreft of Walewode (now Sherwode) where Leofred and Gruffydh fet upon them fo fiercely, that the king at firft was in fome danger; until Athelftane ftepped in and wounded the Dane in the arm in that manner, that being no longer able to hold his fpear, he was taken prifoner, and committed to the cuftody of Athelft... In the mean time Edmund and Edred encountering with Gruffydh, flew him, and brought his head to their father; and Leofred's head being like-wife cut off, they were both fet up upon the town of Chefter; and then Edward, together with his fons, 'victoriously returned home. But King Edward, ha-

A. D. 924. ving built Glademutham, foon after this died at Farandon, and his fon Alfred the fame time at Oxford, and were both buried at Winchefter.

Edward being dead, his bafe fon Athelftane, for many excellent virtues appearing in him, was pre-ferred to the crown; the worthieft prince of the Saxon blood that ever reigned. He overcame Cudfryd, the father of Raynald, King of the Danes, at York; and being invaded by Hawlaf, King of Ireland, who, with all the power of the Scots and Danes marched againft him, gave him battle at Brimeftbury, and obtained a very notorious victory; King Hawlaf, together with the King of the Scots, five Kings of the Danes and Normans being flain upon the fpot: fo that the whole country of England and Scotland became fub-ject to him, which none of his predeceffors ever at-tempted.

933. Sometime after, Owen, the fon of Gruffydh, was flain by the men of Cardigan: And then Athelftane entering with his army into Wales, forced the princes thereof to pay a yearly tribute of 20 l. in gold, 300 l. in filver, and 200 head of cattle; which notwithftand-ing was not obferved, as appears by the laws of Howel Dha, wherein it is appointed, That the Prince of Aberffraw fhould pay no more to the King of London, than 66 l. tribute; and that the Princes of Dinefawr and Powis fhould pay the like fum to the Prince of Aberf-fraw. But King Athelftane was not lefs terrible abroad, than he was awed and feared at home; the Kings of France and Norway fending him very great and coftly prefents, to obtain his favour, and to gain his good will.

936. This year Euneth, the fon of Clydawc, and Meyric, the fon of Cadelh died. The fame time King Athel-ftane removed the Britains who lived at Exeter and the neighbouring country to Cornwall; bounding them

Bri-
tains

tains of Wales, with the Wey. Not long after, the A.D. 940 noble Prince Athelftane died, to the great and inexpreffible forrow of all his fubjects, and was buried at Malmefbury; and fucceeded by his brother Edmund, not inferior to him in courage; but preferable by right of nativity, being born in wedlock. In the firft year of his reign, he gave a very confiderable blow to the Danes; took from them the cities of Leicefter, Derby, Stafford, Lincoln, and Nottingham. Then Aulafe, King of the Danes, finding it impracticable to withftand the force of King Edmund, defired peace, and withal to be initiated into the Chriftian Faith; which being granted him, and all his Danes received baptifm, King Edmund ftanding godfather at the font: after which both parties concluding a firm and a lafting peace, Edmund honourably returned to Weft-Saxony.

The fame year died Abloic, chief King of Ireland: And the year following, Cadelh, the fon of Arthual, a nobleman of Wales, was, for what reafon not difcovered, imprifoned by the Englifh. To revenge which indignity, Edwal Foel and his brother Elis, gathered their forces together, and fought againft the Englifh and Danes, but were both unhappily flain.

This Edwal Foel had fix fons, Meyric, Ievaf, Iago, Conan, Edwal, Fychan, and Roderic: and his brother Elis had iffue Conan, and a daughter, named Trawft, the mother of Conan ap Sitfylht, Gruffydh ap Sitfylht, and Blethyn ap Confyn, which two laft were afterwards Princes of Wales.

HOWEL DHA.

HOWEL DHA, had been for a confiderable time 940, Prince of South-Wales and Powis; in which government he had fo juftly and difcreetly behaved him, f that upon the death of Edwal Foel, he was worthily

J. preferred

preferred to the principality of Wales: Notwithstanding that Edwal had left behind him feveral fons, who
at firft feemed to murmur at and refent the election of
Howel Dha. The firft thing he took care of, was
to enact good and wholfom laws for the benefit of his
country; which held in force in Wales, till the time
of Edward the firft, when the Welch received the laws
of England, yet not fo generally, but that in fome
places they continued long after, and are ftill to be
feen in the Welch and Latin tongue: For Howel Dha
perceiving the laws and cuftoms of his country to
have grown to great abufe, fent for the Archbifhop of
Menevia, with the reft of the bifhops and chief clergy,
to the number of one hundred and forty, and all the
barons and nobles of Wales, and ordered that fix of
the wifeft and beft efteemed perfons in every commote
fhould be cited before him, at his palace called y Ty
Gwyn ar Taf, or the White Houfe upon the river Taf.
Thither coming himfelf, he remained with his nobles,
prelates, and fubjects for all the Lent, in prayers and
fafting, imploring the affiftance and direction of God's
holy Spirit, that he might reform the laws and cuftoms
of the country of Wales, to the honour of God, and
the peaceable government of his fubjects. Towards
the end of Lent, he chofe out of that affembly twelve
of the wifeft and graveft, and perfons of the greateft
experience, to whom he added Blegored, a man of
fingular learning, and one exquifitely verfed in the
laws. To thefe he gave commiffion to examine the
antient laws and cuftoms of Wales, and to collect out
of them what was requifite towards the government
of the country; according to which charge they retained thofe that were wholfom and profitable, ex-
pounded thofe that were doubtful and ambiguous,
and abrogated them that were fuperfluous and hurt-
ful: And fo thefe laws were diftinguifhed into three
forts; the firft concerned the order and regulation of
the king's houfhold and court, the fecond, the affairs
of the country and commonwealth; and the laft had
regard to fpecial cuftoms belonging to particular per-
claim-
ed

ed and generally allowed of, Prince Howel ordered three copies to be written ; one for his own ufe, another to be laid up at his palace of Aberffraw, and the third at Dinefawr ; fo that the three provinces of Wales might have eafy recourfe to either of them, when need required. And for the better obfervation of thefe laws, he caufed the Archbifhop of St. David's to denounce fentence of excommunication againft all fuch of his fubjects as would not obey the fame.

Within a while after, Howel, to admit nothing that might procure any countenance or authority to thefe his laws, accompanied with Lambert, Archbifhop of St. David's, Mordaf, Bifhop of Bangor, and Chebur of St. Afaph, and thirteen of the moft prudent and learned perfons in Wales, took a journey to Rome, where the faid laws being recited before the Pope, were by his holinefs ratified and confirmed : after which, Howel, with all his retinue, returned home to his country.

The particulars of thefe laws are too numerous to be here inferted ; only it is obfervable, that all matters of inheritance of land were determined and adjudged by the prince in perfon ; or if fick, by his fpecial deputy. And that upon view of the fame land, citing together the freeholders of that place, two elders of his council, the chief juftice always attending in the court, the ordinary judge of the country where the land lay, and the prieft. The method of their proceeding was in this manner :

The prince fate in his judicial-feat above the reft of the court, with an elder on each hand, next to whom the freeholders on both fides, who upon that account were probably called UCHELWYR. Below the prince, at a certain diftance, fate the chief juftice, having the prieft on his right hand, and the ordinary judge of the country concerned upon the left. The court being thus fate, the plaintiff with his advocate, champion and Rhingylh or fergeant, ftood on the left fide of the court, as did the defendant in like manner on the right. And laftly, the witneffes on both fides appeared, and ftood at the lower end of the hall, diftinct,

E 2

opposite to the chief juſtice, to teſtify the beſt of their knowledge in the matter in debate. After the taking the depoſitions of the witneſſes, and a full pleading of the cauſe in open court, upon notice given by the ſergeant, the chief juſtice, the prieſt, and the ordinary judge, withdrew themſelves for a while, to conſult of the matter; and then *ſecundum allegata & probata,* brought in their verdict. Whereupon the prince, after conſultation had with the elders that ſate next him, gave definitive ſentence; excepting the cauſe was ſo obſcure and intricate, that the juſtice of it could not appear; and then the two champions put an end to the controverſy by combat.

Whilſt Howel Dha is thus regulating the cuſtoms, and meliorating the laws and conſtitutions of Wales; Aulafe and Reginald, Kings of the Danes, forcibly entered the country of King Edmund, who being vexed with their inceſſant hoſtility, gathered his forces together, and (as ſome ſay) by the help of Lhewelyn ap Sitſylht, who was afterwards Prince of Wales, followed them to Northumberland; and having overcome them in a pitched battle, utterly chaſed them out of his kingdom, and remained a whole year in thoſe parts to regulate and bring that country to ſome quiet order. But finding it impracticable to reduce the inhabitants of Cumberland to any peaceable conſtitution, having ſpoiled and waſted the country, he gave it up to Malcolm king of Scotland, upon condition that he ſhould ſend him ſuccours in his wars whenever A. D. 942. demanded of him. In the mean time the Welch had but little occaſion to rejoice; Hubert biſhop of St. David's, Marclois biſhop of Bangor, and Uſſa the ſon of Lhafyr being dead: And ſhortly after the 944. Engliſh entering into Wales with a very ſtrong army, put the country into a great conſternation; but being ſatisfied with the deſtruction and ſpoil of Strat Clwyd, they returned home without doing any more miſchief. The ſame time Conan the ſon of Elis was like to be treacherouſly put to death by poiſon; and Everus biſhop of St. David's died. The

next

next year Edmund King of England was unluckily
flain upon St. Auguftine's day.; but the manner of his
death is varioufly delivered; fome fay, that difcover-
ing a noted thief, who was out-lawed fitting among
his guefts, being tranfported with indignation againft
fo confident a villain, ran upon him very furioufly,
who expecting nothing lefs than death, thought to
die not unrevenged, and therefore with a fhort dagger gave the king a mortal wound in the breaft.
Others report, that as the King would have refcued a
fervant of his from an officer who had arrefted him,
he was unwittingly and unhappily flain by the fame.
But however his death happened, he lies buried at
Glaftenbury; in whofe place his brother Edred was
crowned King of England, who no fooner had entered upon his government but he made an expedition
againft Scotland and Northumberland, which being
fubdued, he received fealty and homage by oath of
the Scots and Northumbrians, which they did not
long obferve. Shortly after Howel Dha, after a long A.D. 948.
and peaceable reign over Wales, died, much lamented
and bewailed of all his fubjects, being a prince of a
religious and a virtuous inclination, and one that ever
regarded the welfare and profperity of his people.
He left iffue behind him, Owen, Run, Roderic, and
Edwyn, betwixt whom and the fons of Edwal Foel,
late Prince of North Wales, great wars and commotions arofe afterwards about the chief rule and government of Wales.

But the fons of Howel Dha, as fome writers record,
were thefe, _viz._ Owen who did not long furvive his
father, Eineon, Meredyth, Dyfnwal, and Rodri, the
two laft whereof, as is conceived, were flain in the
battle fought near Lhanrwft, in the year 952, by the
fons of Edwal Foel; Run lord of Cardigan, who was
flain before the death of his father; Conan y Cwn,
who poffeffed Anglefey; Edwin, who was alfo flain, as
is fuppofed in the forementioned battle: There was
alfo another battle fought betwixt Howel and Conan ap
Edwal Foel for the Ifle of Anglefey, wherein Conan fell,
and Gruffyth his fon renewing the war, was likewife

E 3   _ever-_

overcome; and so Cyngar, a powerful person, being driven out of the island, Howel enjoyed quiet possession thereof, and of the rest of Gwynedh. It is supposed that this Howel Dha was chosen governor of Wales, during the minority of his uncle Anarawd's sons, who, at the death of their father, were too young to manage the principality; which he kept till his return from Rome, at which time Edwal Foel being come of age, he resigned to him the kingdom of Gwynedh or North Wales, together with the sovereignty of all Wales: Before which time Howel is styled Brenhin Cymry oll, that is, King of all Wales, as is seen in the preface to that body of laws compiled by him.

IEVAF and IAGO the Sons of EDWAL FOEL.

AFTER the death of Howel Dha, his sons divided betwixt them the principalities of South Wales and Powis; laying no claim to North Wales, though their father had been a general Prince of all Wales. But Ievaf and Iago the sons of Edwal Foel, having put by their elder brother Meyric, as a person uncapable of government, and being dissatisfied with the rule of North Wales only, imagined that the principality of all Wales was their right, as descending from the elder house; which the sons of Howel Dha denied them. Indeed, they had been wrongfully kept out of the government of North Wales during the reign of Howel; in whose time the recovery of their own was impracticable, by reason that for his moderation and other good qualities, he had attracted to himself the universal love of all the Welch. But now he being gone, they are resolved to avenge the injury in the worst manner they can, and made a descent on a

small

finall pretence, endeavour to reduce the whole country of Wales to their own fubjection. Ievaf and Iago were indeed defcended from the elder branch; but fince Roderic the Great conferred the principality of South Wales upon his younger fon Cadelh, the father of Howel Dha, it was but juft his fons fhould enjoy what was legally defcended to them by their father: But ambition feldom gives place to equity; and therefore, right or wrong, Ievaf and Iago muft have a touch for South Wales, which they enter with a great army; and being oppofed, they obtained a very opportune victory over Owen and his brethren the fons of Howel, at the hills of Carno. The next year A. D. 950. the two brothers entered twice into South Wales, deftroyed and wafted Dyfet, and flew Dwnwalhon lord of the country. Shortly after which, Roderic the 951. third fon of Howel Dha died. But his brethren per- 952. ceiving the folly of ftanding only upon the defenfive, muftered all their forces together, and entering North Wales, marched as far as Lhanrwft upon the river Conwy; where Ievaf and Iago met them. A very cruel battle enfued upon this, and a very great number were flain on both fides, among whom were Anarawd the fon of Gwynrad, the fon of Roderic the Great; and Edwyn the fon of Howel Dha. But the victory plainly favoured the brothers Ievaf and Iago; fo that the Princes of South Wales were obliged to retire to Cardiganfhire, whether they were warmly purfued; and that country cruelly harraffed with fire and fword. The next year Merïyn was unhappily 953. drowned; and fhortly after Congelach King of Ireland was flain.

The Scots and Northumbrians having lately fworn allegiance to King Edred, he was fcarce returned to his own country, but Aulafe, with a great army, landed in Northumberland, and was with much rejoicing received by the inhabitants. But before he could fecure himfelf in the government, he was fhamefully banifhed the country; and fo the Northumbrians elected one Hircius, the fon of Harold for their king But to fhew the inconftancy of an unfettled multitud, they

L 4   they

they foon grew weary of Hircius, and after three years fpace expelled him, and voluntarily fubmitted themfelves to Edred, who after he had reigned eight years, died, and was buried at Winchefter. To him fucceeded Edwin the fon of Edmund, a man fo immoderately given to venery, that he forcibly married another man's wife; for which, and other irregularities, his fubjects, after four years reign, fet up his brother Edgar, who was crowned in his ftead; with grief of which, he foon ended his days. The fummer, that fame year, proved fo immoderately hot, that it caufed a very difmal plague in the following fpring, which fwept away a great number of people; before which, Gwgan the fon of Gwyriad the fon of Roderic died. At this time, Ievaf and Iago forcibly managed the government of all Wales, and acted according to their own good pleafure, no one daring to confront or refift them. But for all their power, the fons of Abloic King of Ireland, ventured to land in Anglefey; and having burnt Holyhead, wafted the country of Lhyn. Alfo the fons of Edwyn the fon of Colhoyn, deftroyed and ravaged all the country to Towyn, where they were intercepted and flain. About the fame time died Meyric the fon of Cadfan, Rytherch bifhop of St. David's, and Cadwalhon ap Owen. Not long after, the country of North Wales was cruelly wafted by the army of Edgar King of England; the occafion of which invafion was the non-payment of the tribute that the king of Aberffraw, by the laws of Howel Dha, was obliged to pay to the King of London. But at length a peace was concluded upon thefe conditions, that the Prince of North Wales, inftead of money, fhould pay to the King of England the tribute of 300 wolves yearly; which creature was then very pernicious and deftructive to England and Wales. This tribute being duly performed for two years, the third year there were none to be found in any part of the Ifland; fo that afterwards the Prince of North Wales became exempt from paying any acknowledgment to the King of England. The tenor of the g . . . . g by thefe

A.D. 958

561.

965.

966.

these means vanished; there threatened another cloud from Ireland; for the Irish being animated by their late expedition, landed again in Anglesey; and having slain Roderic the son of Edwal Foel, they destroyed Aberffraw. And this danger being over, Ievaf and Iago who had jointly and agreeably, till now, managed the government of Wales from the death of Howel Dha, began to quarrel and disagree among themselves; and Iago having forcibly laid hands upon his brother Ievaf, confined him to perpetual Imprisonment. These heats and animosities between the two brothers, gave occasion and opportunity to Owen prince of South-Wales to carve for himself, who presently seized to his hands the country of Gwyr. And to augment the miseries of the Welch at this time, Mactus the son of Harold, with an army of Danes, entered the isle of Anglesey, and spoiled Penmon. King Edgar was so indulgent to these Danes, that he permitted them to inhabit through all England; insomuch that at length they became to be as numerous and as strong as the English themselves; and fell into such lewd courses of debauchery, and such horrid' drinking, that very great mischief ensued thereupon. The king to reform this immoderate sottishness, enacted a law, that every one should drink by measurre, and so stamped a mark upon every vessel, how far it should be filled. But Harold having taken Penmon, made subject to himself the whole isle of Anglesey, which however he did not keep long, being forced to quit the same, and to return home; as did the fleet of king Alfred, which he had sent to subdue Caerlheon upon Use. And now being rid of the English and Danes, the Welch begin to raise commotions among themselves. Ievaf continued still in prison, to rescue whom, his son Howel raised his power, and marched against his uncle Iago, who being vanquished in fight, was forced to quit the country, to save himself. Howel having won the day, took his eldest uncle, Meyric the son of Edwal prisoner, and pulled out both his eyes, clapt him in prison, where in a woeful condition he shortly died. leaving behind him two sons, Edval and Iorwrth;

A. D. 967.

968.

969.

970.

971.

972.

Ionafal; the firſt of which lived to be afterwards prince of Wales, and to revenge upon the poſterity of Howel, that unnatural barbarity ſhewed to his father. But though Howel delivered his father from his long and tedious impriſonment, yet he did not think fit to reſtore him to his principality; for whether by age or infirmity he was incapable, Howel took upon him the ſole government of Wales, which he kept and maintained for his lifetime, but afterwards it deſcended to his brethren. For Ievaf had iſſue beſides this Howel; Meyric, Ievaf, and Cadwalhan; all three men of great repute and eſteem.

About this time died Morgan Hen, in his younger days called Morgan Mawr, being an hundred years old, having lived fifty years after the death of his wife Elen, daughter of Roderic the great, by whom he had one ſon called Owen. Morgan was a valiant and a victorious prince, and well beloved of his ſubjects; but ſometime before his death, Owen, the ſon of prince Howel Dha, laid claim to Yſtradwy and Ewy, (called the two Sleeves of Gwent Uwchcoed) being the right of Morgan, and ſeized upon them to his own uſe. But the matter, through the mediation of the clergy and nobility, being by both parties referred to the deciſion of Edgar king of England, it was by him adjudged, that the ſaid Lands did of right belong to Morgan, and to the dioceſs of Lhandaff; and that Owen ap Howel Dha had wrongfully poſſeſſed himſelf of them. The charter of the ſaid award was made before the archbiſhops, biſhops, earls, and barons of England and Wales; as may be ſeen at Lhandaff, in an old manuſcript called y Cwtta Cyfarwydd o Forgannwg. And there is ſomewhat to the ſame purpoſe in the old book of Lhandaff; only the miſtake in both is, that they make Howel Dha the intruder into the ſaid lands, who had been dead at leaſt twenty years before king Edgar began his reign,

HOWEL ap IEVAF.

HOWEL, after that he had expelled his uncle Iago, and forced him to quit his own dominions, took upon himself the government of Wales, in right of his father, who though alive, yet by reason of his years, was willing to decline it. About the same time Dwnwalhon Prince of Stradclwyd, took his journey for Rome; and Edwalhon son of Owen Prince of South Wales died. But the English received a greater blow by the death of King Edgar, who was a prince of excellent qualities, both warlike and religious, and one that founded several monasteries and religious houses, and particularly at Bangor.

For Iago ap Edwal having fled to King Edgar, prevailed so far with him, that he brought an army into North Wales to restore him to his right. Being advanced as far as Bangor, he was honourably received by Howel, who, at his request, was contented his uncle Iago should have a share in the government, as he had in his father Ievaf's time. Then Edgar founded a new church at Bangor, on the south-side of the Cathedral, which he dedicated to the blessed Virgin Mary; and confirmed the ancient liberties of that see, and bestowed lands and gifts upon it: And then with Howel and Iago in his company, he marched towards Chester, where met him, by appointment, six kings more, viz. Kenneth King of the Scots, Malcolm King of Cumberland, Macon King of Man, and Dyfnwal, Sifrethus, and Ithel, three British kings. These eight princes having done homage, and sworn fealty to him, entered with him into his barge, and rowed him, four of each side, from his palace to the church or monastery of St. John Baptist, and divine service being ended, in like state rowed him back again. To King Edgar succeed his son Edward, known younger; who, after four years reign, was treacherously slain through the treason of his step-mother Elfrida, to make room for her own son Edelred, upon pretence of whose minority, being a child only of seven years, she might have the management of the kingdom in her own hands. But whilst the English A.D. 976. were in this waving and unsettled condition, Eineon, the son of Owen king of South Wales, the second time entered the country of Gwyr, and having spoiled and wasted it, returned home again. This, though an unsufferable affront to Howel Prince of North Wales, yet he thought it most convenient to pass by and wink at it; being then warmly engaged against the aiders and abettors of his uncle Iago; and marching against them with a numerous army, consisting of Welch and English, pursued them to Lhyyn and Kelynnoc Fawr, the very extremity of Wales; where, after cruel ravaging and miserable harrassing of the country about, Iago was at last taken prisoner; but so generously received by Howel, that he granted his uncle to enjoy his portion of the country peaceably for his life. But he did not deal so kindly with his uncle Edwal Fychan 979 the son of Edwal Foel; who, for what pretence, not discovered, was slain by him. It may be, that being in a manner secure of his uncle Iago, he was apprehensive that Edwal Fychan would put in his pretence for the principality; and therefore he judged it convenient to remove this obstacle in time, and to send him to seek for it in another world. For nothing can be the cause of greater injustice and inhumanity in princes, than the jealousy and apprehension of rivals and pretenders to their government; to prevent which, they will sacrifice any thing that is just and legal, so that the person offending be removed out of the way. But though Howel had murdered his uncle Edwal Fychan, yet he could not remove all disputes and pretences to North Wales: For at that same time that he was employed in this unnatural action, Cystenyn Dhu, or Constantine the Black, son to Iago then prisoner to Howel, having hired an army of Danes, under the command of Gothred the son of Harald, marched

against

against his coufin Howel, and entering North Wales, destroyed Anglefey and Lhyn. Whereupon Howel having drawn his forces together, set upon them at a place called Gwyath Hirbarth, where the Danes received a very shameful overthrow, and Conftantine the son of Iago was slain. But another army of Danes fared better in England, who having landed at, and spoiled Southampton, over-ran the countries of Devon and Cornwal, burnt the town of Bodman, whereby the cathedral church of St. Petrokes, with the bishop's palace, were laid in ashes; by reason of which disafter, that bishop's fee was tranflated to St. Germains, where it continued till the uniting thereof to Crediton. Within a while after, St. Dunftan archbishop of Canterbury died, a pious and religious person, who foretold of very great and unfupportable calamities, the English should endure by the cruel outrages of the Danes.

But Godfryd the son of Harold being highly difgufted at the shameful rout he received of Howel in the quarrel of Conftantine, was refolved to recover his credit, and to revenge himfelf of the Welch. And accordingly he landed with a powerful army in Weft Wales, where, after that he had spoiled the land of Dyfed, with the church of St. David's, he fought the famous battle of Lhanwanoc. But Harold being forced upon this to retire and forfake the country, the following year Duke Alfred with a confiderable number of English came to fupply his room, and to conquer the Welch. But he received as little advantage or honour as Harold in this expedition; for after that he had laid wafte and deftroyed the town of Brecnock, with fome part of South Wales, he was shamefully vanquished, and his army almoft totally cut off by the troops of Eineon the fon of Owen Prince of South Wales, and Howel Prince of North Wales, who had joined their forces againft him. And now the Welch having quite difabled the Danes and the English, began to fall to their old courfes, to make ufe of their profperity and quietnefs from abroad, for quarrelling and creating difturbances at home. The inhabitants

of

of Gwentland imagined themselves very strong and powerful, and therefore must-needs endeavour to shake off their allegiance to their prince, and to set up one of their own making. Owen Prince of South Wales, to pacify the rebellious humour of these seditious and turbulent people, sent his son Eineon to perfuade them to obedience. But a distracted multitude got loose, is not to be worked upon by arguments, which Eineon fatally experienced, who was so far from perfuading them in their allegiance by fair means, that they prefently set upon him, and thinking that they had the bird in their fist, who was next to succeed, put him to present death. And thus most ignobly fell this worthy prince, who, in his father's time was the only support of his country, being a stout and a valiant commander, and one famously experienced in the art and discipline of war. He had issue two sons, Edwyn and Tewdor Mawr, or Theodore the Great, out of whose loins several Princes of South Wales were since descended. But Howel prince of North Wales did not regard this diffention and rebellion in South Wales, and therefore took opportunity to strengthen and multiply his army, with which he marched the next year for England, intending to revenge the incursions and invasions of the English upon Wales, and to destroy and waste their country. But having entered into England, he was presently fought with, upon which, being resolved either to return victoriously, or to die couragiously, he fell in among them, but in the action was slain, leaving no issue behind him to succeed in his principality, though in some ancient genealogies he is reputed to have a son called Conan y Cwn.

984.

CADWALHON.

CADWALHON AP IEVAF.

HOWEL, the son of Ievaf, had for a long time enjoyed the principality of North-Wales, more by main force and usurpation, than any right of succession he could pretend to it. For Ionafal and Edwal the sons of Meyric, the eldest son of Edwal Foel, were living, and tho' their father had been rejected as unfit for government, yet that was no reason to deprive them of their right. Indeed, Howel could pretend to no other right or title, than that his father Ievaf had been prince of North-Wales before him, and this he thought sufficient to maintain his possession against the rightful heir, who was far unable to oppose or molest his wrongful usurpation. But he being slain in this rash expedition against the English, and leaving no issue to succeed him in the crown, his brother Cadwalhon thought he might rightfully take upon him the government of North-Wales, seeing his father and his brother had without any molestation enjoyed the same. However, to make his title secure, he thought fit to remove all manner of rubs which might create any dispute concerning his right of succession, and to that end, concluded it necessary to make away his cousins Ionafal and Edwal the lawful heirs; the first of which he executed accordingly, but Edwal being aware of his intention, privately made his escape, and so prevented his wicked design. This unnatural dealing with his cousins Ionafal and Edwal cost Cadwalhon not only his life, but the loss of his principality and the utter ruin of his father's house. For he had scarce enjoyed his government one year, but Meredith the son of Owen prince of South-Wales entered into North-Wales, slew Cadwalhon and his brother Meyric, the only remains of the house of Iva, and under the pretence of conquest, possessed himself of the whole country. Here we may observe and admire the wisdom of providence, in permitting wrong and oppression for some time to flourish and wax great, and afterwards by secret and hidden methods, in restoring the posterity of the right and lawful heir to the just and pristine estate of his ancestors. For after the death of Edwal Foel, Meyric who by right of birth was legally to succeed, was not only deprived of his just and rightful inheritance, but had his eyes most inhumanly put out, and being condemned to perpetual imprisonment, for grief of being so barbarously treated, quickly ended his days. But tho' his brothers Ievaf and Iago, and Howel and Cadwalhon the sons of the former successively enjoyed the principality of North-Wales; yet not one died naturally or free from the revenge of Meyric's ejection. For Ievaf was imprisoned by his brother Iago, and he with his son Constantine, by Howel the son of Ievaf, and afterwards Howel fell by the hands of the English, and his brethren Cadwalhon and Meyric were both slain by Meredith ap Owen. On the other side, Edwal ab Meyric who was right heir of North-Wales after the death of his brother Ionafal, escaped the snare intended by Cadwalhon; and Meredith ap Owen after some time leaving North Wales exposed to the enemies, by reason he had enough to do to preserve South-Wales, Edwal was received of the North-Wales men as their true prince.

MEREDITH AP OWEN.

486. MEREDITH having won the field and slain Cadwalhon and his brother Meyric, the only seeming pretenders to the principality of North-Wales, took upon himself the rule and government of it. But before he could be well confirmed in his dominions, Godfryd
the

the fon of Harold, third time entered into the ifle of
Anglefey, and having taken Lhyarch the fon of Owen
with 2000 men prifoners, moft cruelly put out his
eyes; which fo ftartled and ftruck fuch a terror into
Prince Meredith, that with the reft of his army, he
forthwith made his efcape and fled to Cardigan. This
lofs to the Welch was the fame year feconded by another, but of another fort; for there happened fuch a
difmal and unufual murrain, that the beft part of the
cattle of Wales perifhed. Neither were the Englifh
at this time free from adverfities and troubles, for
the Danes landed again in England with feveral armies, and at Weftport and Witeft, gave two Englifh
lords, Godan and Britchwould fuch a blow, that the
king was forced to buy his peace, with the payment
of 10,000 pound, which was termed, Dane Gelt. But
within a while after, King Edelred violated and brake
the peace himfelf, and prepared a great fleet, thinking to vanquifh the Danes at fea; But it proved far
otherwife, and much contrary to his expectation, all
his fhips being either deftroyed or taken, together
with the Admiral, Alfric earl of Mercia. The Danes
being animated with this victory failed up to the
mouth of the Humber, and landing in Yorkfhire,
fpoiled and deftroyed the cities of York and Lindfey; but in their march through Northumberland,
were routed and put to flight by Godwyn and Frid-
gift, two Englifh generals who were fent to oppofe
them. The fame time Anlaf king of Norway, and
Swane of Denmark with 94 gallies failed up the
Thames and befieged London, which the citizens fo
bravely defended, that at length the Danes thought
beft to raife and quit the fiege. But though they
could effect nothing upon the city, yet the country
was at their mercy and therefore leaving their fhips,
they landed and wafted with fire and fword all Kent,
Effex, Suffex, Surry and Hampfhire Wherefore
King Edelred inftead of manly oppofition in the field,
fends ambaffadors to treat about another payment,
and fo the Danes being fatisfied with a great fum of
money and victuals, lay quiet that winter at South-

ampton. Upon this compofition, Anlaf was invited by Adelred, and royally entertained, and being difmiffed with very many rich prefents, he promifed upon oath to depart the kingdom and never to moleft it any more, which he faithfully performed.

987   Whilft the Englifh and the Danes were thus for a time agreed, Ievaf the fon of Edwal having fpent for feveral years a retired and a private life, died: And was quickly followed by Owen the fon of Howel Dha Prince of South Wales. This Owen had three fons, Eineon who in his father's time was flain by the rebels of Gwentland, and Lhywarch who had his eyes put out by Godfryd the fon of Harold the Dane, and Prince Meredith, who had already conquered North Wales, and now upon his father's death takes poffeffion alfo of South Wales, without any regard had to Edwyn and Theodore the fons of Eineon his elder brother. But upon his advancement to his new principality, he was like to meet with no very fmall troubles; for the Danes at Hampton quickly broke the league with king Adelred, and failing towards the Weft mightily annoyed the coafts of Cornwal and Devonfhire, and at laft landed in South Wales. Having deftroyed St. David's, Lhanbadarn, Lhanrhyftyd, Lhandydoch, and feveral other religious places; the country was fo cruelly haraffed and weakened that Prince Meredith was forced to compound with them,

988. and to pay a tribute of one penny for every perfon within his dominions, which in Welch was called Glwmaem, otherwife, the tribute of the black army. And Ireland too at this time received no inconfiderable blow from the Danes, who flew Elwmaen the fon of Abloic king of the country, and fo fpoiled and ravaged that kingdom, that a great number of the natives perifhed by famine.

989. The year following Owen the fon of Dyfnwal, a man of confiderable note and reputation among the Welch, was flain; befides which, nothing remarkable happened this year. But the next year Edwin ap Eineon, who was right heir to the principality of South Wales, having

ving drawn to his help a great army of English and Danes hoftibly entered into Meredith's country, fpoiled all the land of Cardigan, Dyfed, Gwyr, Kydwely and St. David's, and received hoftages of the chief perfons of thofe countries to own him as their rightful prince. To return thefe outrages upon Edwyn, Meredith deftroyed the town of Radnor, fpoiled Glamorgan, and carried the chiefeft men therein prifoners, who paying their ranfom, were fet at liberty. But whilft Wales was in this tottering condition, and fcarce any place free from hoftility; it happily fell out, that Meredith and Edwyn were made friends, and the differences compofed between them, fo that the Englifh and Danes who came in with Edwyn, and who expected to fare beft by thefe civil difturbances of the Welch, were unexpectedly cafhiered and fent home. And foon after this agreement, Cadwalhon, the only fon of Meredith, died, which rendered the compofition between Meredith and Edwyn more firm, by reafon that this latter thought now, without any difpute to fucceed Meredith in his principality. But this fell fhort of his aim, for Meredith being very much difturbed in South Wales, had fo much work upon his hands to defend that country, that he left North Wales open and expofed to the common enemy, which the Danes were quickly acquainted with, and fo landing in Anglefey, they ravaged and laid wafte the whole ifland. The North Wales men finding themfelves thus forfaken by Meredith, and their country like to be over-run by the Danes, if not timely prevented, fet up Edwal the fon of Meyric, the indifputable heir of North Wales, though long kept from it, and owned him for their prince. But thofe inceffant wars and commotions in South Wales, occafioned a very difmal famine and fcarcity in the country, of which a very confiderable number of people perifhed; And thus Meredith who had once conquered North Wales, and for a long time had got poffeffion of South Wales; without any right or title to either, was now obliged to relinquifh the one, and was fcarce able to maintain the other.

Edwal

EDWAL AP MEYRIC.

993. EDWAL after a long and tedious expectation, being now joyfully received by the North Wales men for their prince, endeavoured the first thing to defend his subjects from the injuries and depredations they received from the Danes. And having in a measure effected that, he was accosted by another enemy ; for Meredith being resolved to revenge the indignity and disgrace put upon him by the North Wales men, in depriving him of the government of their country, gathered and mustered together all his power, intending to recover again that principality. Being advanced as far as Lhangwm, Edwal met him, and in plain battle routed his army ; in which action, Theodore or Tewdor Mawr, Meredith's nephew was slain, leaving behind him two sons, Rhys and Rytherch, and a daughter named Elen. But it is probable that it was not Tewdor Mawr, but his brother Edwyn that was slain in this battle, which also seems rather to have been fought at Hengwm in Ardudwy in Merionethshire, then at Lhangwm, for in that place there are to this day certain monuments of victory to be seen ; as heaps of stones, tomb-stones and columns, which they call Curneddi Hengwm. Edwal returning home triumphantly after this victory, thought he had now secured himself in his government, and expected to enjoy his dominions quietly, and without any molestation. But he had scarce recovered the fatigue of the last engagement, when Swane the son of Harold having lately pillaged and wasted the isle of Man, landed in North Wales, whom Edwal endeavouring to oppose, was slain in the encounter leaving one son behind him, called Iago.

Within

Within a while after the Danes returned again againſt
St. David's, and deſtroying all before them with fire
and ſword, ſlew Morgeney or Urgenev, biſhop of that
dioceſe. Prince Meredith being highly concerned at
the miſchiefs theſe barbarous people continually did
to his country, and the more, becauſe he was not able
to repel their inſolencies, out of grief and vexation
died; having iſſue one only daughter named Angharad, who was twice married; firſt to Lhewelyn
ap Sitſyhlt, and after his death to Confyn Hirdref, or
as others think, to Confyn ap Gweryſtan. She had
children by both huſbands, which occaſioned afterwards great diſturbances and civil commotions in
Wales, the iſſue of both adventures pretending a
right of ſucceſſion to the principality of South
Wales.

AEDAN ap BLEGORAD.

EDWAL Prince of North Wales being killed in
the battle againſt Swane, and having no other iſſue
than Iago, who was a minor, and too young to take
upon him the government; and Meredith Prince of
South Wales dying without any other iſſue than a
daughter, cauſed very heavy quarrels and contentions
among the Welch, ſeveral without any colour of right,
putting in their claim and pretenſions to the government. In North Wales, Conan the ſon of Howel, 1093.
and Aedan the ſon of Blegorad were the chief aſpirers
to that principality; and becauſe they could not
agree who ſhould be the man, they fairly conſented
to try the matter in open field, where Conan had
the misfortune to be ſlain; and ſo Aedan was vic-
toriouſly proclaimed Prince of North Wales. But
who this Aedan was deſcended from, or what co-

lour

lour or pretence he could lay to the principality, cannot be as much as guessed at, there being none of that name to be met with in any Welch records, excepting that Blegorad who is mentioned in the line of Howel Dha, whose estate and quality was too mean, that his posterity should lay any claim to the principality, of of Wales. But be that how it will, Aedan after his victory over Conan ap Howel, was owned Prince by the North Wales men, over whom he bore rule for the space of twelve years ; though besides his conquest of Conan ap Howel, there being nothing recorded of him, excepting his being slain, together with his four sons by Lhewelyn ap Sitfylht.

But whilst the Welch are in this inconstant and unsettled condition, the Scots in Ireland began to grow powerful, and having destroyed the town and country of Develyn, they took Gulfath and Ubiad, two Irish lords, prisoners, whose eyes they most inhumanly put out. The Danes also, who had lately made their incursions into South Wales, began now to molest the English; having landed in the West, passed through the counties of Somerset, Dorset, Hampshire and Sussex, destroying and burning all before them. Having advanced without any opposition, as far as the river Medway, they laid siege to Rochester, which the Kentish men endeavouring to preserve, assembled themselves together, and gave the Danes battle, but were vanquished in the undertaking. King Edelred was then in Cumberland, where the Danes were more numerously planted, which country he kept quiet and in subjection. But in the mean time another army of Danes landed in the West, against whom the country people of Somersetshire assembling themselves, shewed their readiness to attack them, but wanting a head to direct them, were easily put to their heels, and the Danes ruled and commanded the country at their pleasure. The King being sorely vexed at the insolencies and restless depredations of the Danes, thought convenient to strengthen himself by some powerful affinity, and to that end, sends ambassadors to Richard duke of Normandy, desiring his daughter Emma in marriage,

marriage, and fuccours to repel the Danifh incurfions. Here it is obfervable, that as the Saxons being formerly called over as friends and allies to the well-meaning Britains, violently and wrongfully poffeffed themfelves of the greateft part of the ifland; fo now the Normans being invited to aid the English againft the Danes, took fo good a liking to the country, that they never gave over their defign of gaining it, till at laft they became conquerors of the whole ifland. The mifchief of calling in the Normans, though foretold to King Adelred, he was fo far concerned about the prefent calamities received by the Danes, that he was deaf to all futurities, how dangerous and mifchievous foever they might prove. And therefore being puffed up with hopes of increafe of ftrength by this new affinity, he fent private letters to all cities and towns throughout his dominions where the Danes were quartered, requiring them all upon St Brice's night to maffacre the Danes, which was accordingly performed with much unanimity and fecrecy. This cruel difafter was fo far from difcouraging the Danes, that they now began to vow the eradication of the English nation, and to revenge that unmanly maffacre of their country-men; to which end they landed in Devonfhire, and over-running the country with fire and fword, fpared nothing that had the leaft fpark of life in it. The city of Exeter they razed to the ground, and flew Hugh the Norman, whom the Queen had recommended to the government of it. To prevent their further incurfions, Almarus Earl of Devon gathered a great army out of Hampfhire and Wiltfhire, and the country thereabouts, and marched with a refolution ftoutly to oppofe the Danes, who put Almarus to flight and purfued him to Wilton and Salifbury, which being ranfacked and plundered, they carried the pillage thereof triumphantly to their fhips,

The next year Swane, a prince of great repute in Denmark, landed upon the coaft of Norfolk and laid fiege to Norwich, and wafted the country thereabouts. But Wolfkettel duke of that country, being too weak to oppofe him, thought it moft convenient to make a peace with the Dane ; which was quickly broke ; and then Swane marched privately to Thetford, which after he had fpoiled and ranfacked, he returned with his prey to his fhips. Wolfkettel hearing this, privately drew up his forces, and ftoutly marched againft the enemy ; but being far inferior in number, the Danes got the day, and afterwards failed to their own country. Within two years after, the Danes returned again. bringing with them their ufual companions, the fire, the fword, and the fpoil, and landed at Sandwich ; which after they had burnt and pillaged, they failed to the ifle of Wight, where they took up their winter-quarters till Chriftmas : And then coming forth thence, they over-ran, by feveral parties the countries of Hampfhire and Berkfhire, as far as Reading, Wallingford and Colfey ; devouring up, for want of other plunder, all the provifions and victuals they found in the houfes, and retributed the fame with fire and fword at their departure. In their return they met with the army of the Weft Saxons near Effington, but this confifting only of a raw and unexperienced rabble, they eafily broke through, and paffing triumphantly by the gates of Winchefter, they got fafe with great booty to the ifle of Wight. King Adelred all this while lay at his manor-houfe in Shropfhire, much troubled and concerned at thefe uninterrupted devaftations of the Danes. But the nobility of England, rather to fave fome than lofe all they poffeffed, bought their peace of the Danes for the fum of 30,000 pound ; during which interval, King Adelred roufing his drooping fpirits, ordained, that every three hundred hides of land, one hide being as much as one plough can fufficiently till, through his dominions, fhould man out a fhip, and every eight hides a corflet and a helmet ; befides which the king had no i... ter bie n v fent him from Normandy. This

fleet

fleet when rendezvoused at Sandwich seemed terrible in those days, and was the greatest that ever before then rode upon the British sea. And now, one might have thought, that all things would go well with the English, when of a sudden another cloud appears; for one Wilnot, a nobleman of Suffex, being banished by King Adelred, got to sea with a small number of ships, and practised pyracy along the coasts of Britain, and mightily annoyed all merchants and passengers. Brightrych, brother to the traiterous Edric Earl of Mercia, thinking to advance his reputation by some signal exploit, promised to bring Wilnot dead or alive before him: To which end, he sets forth with a confiderable fleet; which meeting with a terrible storm, was by the tempest driven back, and wrecked upon the shores; so that a great number of the ships were drowned, and the rest burnt by Wilnot and his company. Brightrych being abashed with this unfortunate beginning, returned ingloriously by the Thames back to London; so that this great preparation against the Danes, was dashed to pieces, and came to nothing.

A.D. 1008.

The Danes were not ignorant of the misfortune the English received by this storm, and without any further enquiry, landed at Sandwich, and so passed on to Canterbury, which they intending to destroy, was by the citizens bought off for 3000 l. Passing from thence, through Kent, Suffex and Hampshire, they came to Berkshire, where King Edelred at length met with them, and purposing resolutely to set upon them, was by the cunning infinuations and subtile arguments of traytor Edric dissuaded from fighting. The Danes being thus delivered from the danger which they certainly expected, passed on joyfully by the city of London, and with great booty returned to their ships. The next year they landed again at Ipswich, upon Ascension day, where Wolfkettel entertained them with a sharp encounter; but being overpowered by number, he was forced to give back, and yield the day to the Danes. Passing from thence to Cambridge, they met with Ethelftan, King Edelred's nephew by his

1009.

sister,

fister, who with an army was come to oppofe them;
but the Danes proving too powerful, he with many
other noblemen were flain; among whom were duke
Ofwyn and the Earls Edwyn and Wolfrike. From
hence they paffed through Effex, leaving no manner of
cruelty and barbarity unpractifed, and returned laden
with booty to their fhips, which lay in the Thames.
A.D. 1010 But they could not contain themfelves long in their
veffels; and therefore fallying out, they paffed by the
river fide to Oxford, which they ranfacked over again;
adding to their prey, Buckingham, Bedford, Hartford,
and Northamptonfhire; and having accomplifhed that
year's cruelties, at Chriftmas they returned to their
fhips. Yet the prey of the country from the Trent
fouthward, would not fatisfy thefe unmerciful barba-
1011. rians; but as foon as the feafon gave them leave to
peep out of their dens, they laid fiege to the city of
Canterbury, which being delivered up by the treachery of Almarez the archdeacon, was condemned to
blood and afhes, and Alfege the archbifhop carried
prifoner to the Danifh fleet, where he was at length
1012. moft cruelly put to death. The next year Swane,
king of Denmark, came up the Humber, and landed
at Gainefborow; whether repaired to him Uthred
Earl of Northumberland, with his people, the inhabitants of Lindfey, with all the countries northward
of Watling-ftreet, being a highway croffing from the
eaft to the weft fea, and gave their oath and hoftages
to obey him. Whereupon, King Swane perceiving
his undertaking to prove fo fortunate beyond expectation, committed the care of his fleet to his fon
Cnute, and marched himfelf firft to Oxford, and
then to Winchefter; which cities, whether for fear
of further calamities, readily acknowledged him for
their king. From thence he marched for London,
where King Edelred then lay; and which was fo
ftoutly defended by the citizens, that he was like to
effect nothing againft that town; and therefore he
directed his courfe to Wallingford and Bath, where
the principal men of Weft Saxon yielded him fubjection. The Londoners too, fearing his
fury

fury and difpleafure, made their peace, and fent him hoftages; which city being received to mercy, Swane, from that time was accounted king of all England. King Edelred perceiving all his affairs in England to go againft him, and his authority and government reduced to fo narrow a compafs, having fent his queen, with his two fons Edward and Alfred, to Normandy, he thought convenient within a while after to follow himfelf. Being honourably received by his brother-in-law Richard; he had not been there long but news arrived of the death of Swane, and that he was defired by the Englifh to return to his kingdom. Being animated and comforted with this furprifing news, he fet forward with a great army for England, and landing at Lyndfey, he cruelly harraffed that province, by reafon that it had owned fubjection to Cnute the fon of Swane, whom the Danes had elected king in his father's ftead. King Cnute being at Ipfwich, and certified of the arrival of King Edelred, and the devaftation of Lyndfey; fearing that his authority was going down the wind, barbaroufly cut off the hands and nofes of all the hoftages he received from the Englifh, and prefently ftruck fail for Denmark. And whilft England was in this general confufion, there fell out no lefs a ftorm in Ireland; for Brian king of that ifland, and his fon Murcath, with other kings of the country fubject to Brian, joined their forces againft Sutric the fon of Abloic king of of Dublin, and Mailmorda king of Lagenes. Sutric being of himfelf too weak to encounter fo numerous a multitude, hired all the pyrates and rovers who cruifed upon the feas, and then gave Brian battle, who, with his fon Murcath, was flain; and on the other fide, Mailmorda, and Broderic General of the auxiliaries.

But Cnute, though he was in a manner forced to forfake England upon the recalling of King Edelred, yet he did not abandon all his pretence to the kingdom; and therefore the next year he came to renew his claim, and landed with a ftrong fleet in Weft Sex, where he exercifed very great hoftility. To A. D. 1013.

prevent

prevent his incurfions, Edric and Edmund bastard-son to Edelred, raifed their forces feparately; but when both armies were united, they durft not, whether for fear, or the diffention of the two generals, fight with the Danes. Edmund therefore paffed to the North, and joined with Uthred duke of Northumberland, and both together defcended and fpoiled Stafford, Leicefter, and Shropfhire. On the other fide, Cnute marched forcibly through Buckingham, Bedford, Huntingtonfhire, and fo by Stafford paffed toward York, whither Uthred haftened, and finding no other remedy, fubmitted himfelf, with all the Northumbrians, to Cnute, giving hoftages for the performance of what they then agreed upon. But nevertheless this fubmiffion, Uthred was treacheroufly flain, not without the permiffion of Cnute, and his dukedom beftowed upon one Egrick a Dane; whereupon Edmund left them, and went to his father, who lay fick at London. Cnute returning to his fhips prefently followed, and failed up the Thames towards London; but before he could draw nigh the city, King Edelred was dead; having prolonged a long and troublefome reign for thirty-feven years. After his deceafe, the Englifh nobility chofe his bafe fon Edmund, for his eminent ftrength and hardinefs in war, furnamed Ironfide, for their king. Upon this Cnute brought his whole fleet up the river to London, and having cut a deep trench round about the town, invefted it on all fides; but being valouroufly repulfed by the defendants, he detached the beft part of his army to fight with Edmund, who was marching to raife the fiege; and both armies coming to battle at Proman by Gillingham, Cnute with his Danes were put to flight. But as foon as time and opportunity would give him leave to increafe his forces, Cnute gave Edmund a fecond battle at Caerftane; but Edric, Almar, and Algar under hand fiding with the Danes, Edmund was hard put to it, to maintain the fight obftinately, till night and wearinefs parted them. Both armies having fufficiently foiled in this action, Edmund went to W........ to reinforce himfeif, and the

Danes

Danes returned to the fiege of London, where Edmund
quickly followed, raifed the fiege, and forced Cnute
and his Danes confufedly to betake themfelves to their
fhips, and then entered triumphantly into the city.
Two days after, paffing the Thames at Brentford, he
fell upon the enemies backs; by which lucky opportunity obtaining a confiderable victory, he returned
again to raife recruits among the Weft-Saxons. Cnute,
upon Edmund's removal, appeared again before London, and invefted it by land and water; but all in
vain; the befieged fo manfully and refolutely defending themfelves, that it was impracticable to mafter
the town before Edmund could come to the relief of
it. And this they prefently experienced; for Edmund,
after having augmented his forces, croffed again the
Thames at Brentford, and came to Kent in purfuit of
Cnute, who upon engaging, was fo fhamefully defeated at firft, and his men put to that terrible flight, that
there wanted nothing of a full and abfolute victory,
but the true loyalty of the traytor Edric, who perceiving the victory to incline to Edmund, and the
Danes like to receive their mortal and final blow,
cryed aloud, Fled Engle, Fled Engle, Edmund is dead,
and thereupon fled with that part of the army under
his command, leaving the king over-powered with
number. By this defertion the Englifh were at the
laft overthrown, and a great number flain; among
whom were Duke Edmund, Duke Alfric, Duke Godwyn, and Ulfkettel, the valiant Duke of the Eaft-Angles, together with all the Englifh cavalry, and a
great part of the nobility. After this victory, Cnute
marched triumphantly to London, and was crowned
king; but Edmund preparing to try his fortune in another field, muftered together all the forces he could,
and meeting with Cnute in Gloucefterfhire, intended
to give him battle; but confidering what cruel and
unnatural bloodfhed had already happened, both generally agreed to put an end to their tedious quarrel by
fingle combat; and the place being appointed, Edmund
and Cnute fell to it very vigourouſly, till at laſt Cnute
perceiving it impracticable to vanquifh a man of Iron-

fiꞇes,

fides, laid down his weapon, moving this compofition, to divide the kingdom fairly betwixt them:
Edmund was not difpleafed at the offer, and therefore both parties fubmitted to this decifion, that Edmund fhould rule the Weft-Saxons and the South;
Cnute in Mercia and all the North; and fo they parted
friends, Cnute, moving to London, and Edmund to
Oxford. But Edric was not pleafed, that Edmund
fhould have any fhare at all of the government, and
therefore he is refolved to confpire againft his life,
and to deliver the whole kingdom of England into
the hands of Cnute; of whom he might reafonably
expect for this, and other traiterous fervices, a very
ample and an anfwerable return. This he committed
to one of his own fons to put in execution, an imp
of the old ftock, and one early verfed in wicked and
traiterous defigns; who perceiving the king go to
ftool, thurft a fharp knife up his fundament, of
which wound he prefently died. Edric being quickly
certified of the fact, pofted it up to London, and
with great joy and loud acclamations came to Cnute,
greeting him as fole king of England, and withal,
telling him in what manner, and by whofe means his
old enemy King Edmund was affaffinated and killed at
Oxford. Cnute, though pleafed at the death of Edmund, was a perfon of greater honour than to com-
mend fo horrible a deed, though done to an enemy,
and therefore told Edric, that he would without fail
take care to reward him, as his deferts required, and
would advance him above all the nobility of England,
which was quickly performed, his head being placed
upon the higheft tower in London for a terror to
fuch villainous traitors to their king. Edric being thus
defervedly difappointed of the mighty thoughts he entertained of greatnefs, upon the advancement of King
Cnute, this generous Dane fcorned his bafenefs, and fo
having paid him a traitors reward, caufed execution to
be done upon all Edric's accomplices, and thofe that
confented to the bafe murder of that brave Prince
King Edmund.

About

About the fame time there happened no fmall difturbance and commotions in Wales; Lhewelyn ap
Sytfylht having for fome years fat ftill and quiet, began now to beftir himfelf; and having drawn all his
forces together, marched againft Aedan, who forcibly and without any legal pretence, had entered upon, and for all this time had kept himfelf in the government of North Wales, Aedan would not eafily
eject himfelf from what had been fo long in his poffeffion to maintain which, he gave Lhewelyn battle:
But the day going againft him, himfelf, with his four
fons, were flain upon the fpot; upon which, Lhewelyn, without any regard had to Iago the fon of Edwal
the right heir, took upon himfelf the title and authority of Prince of all Wales. His pretence to North-
Wales, was, as being defcended from Trawft daughter to Elis, fecond fon to Anarawd, who was the eldeft
fon of Roderic the Great; and to South Wales, as
having married Angharad the only daughter of Meredith Prince of South Wales; by virtue of which
pretenfions he affumed to himfelf the government of
all Wales.

LHEWELYN ap SITSYLHT.

LHEWELYN having, as is faid, taken upon
him the general government of Wales, managed his
charge with fuch prudence and moderation, that the
country in a fhort time became very flourifhing and
profperous; peace and tranquility being eftablifhed
produced plenty and increafe of all things neceffary to
human fubfiftence: For there was none that could
lay any claim or pretence to either of the principalities, excepting Iago the fon of Edwal, who was indeed lawful heir of North Wales; but either too weak
to withftand, or unwilling to difturb Lhewelyn's
title, he lay quiet for a time, expecting a better opportunity

portunity to recover his right. In the mean time, Cnute being crowned king of all England, marries Emma the widow of King Edelred; and for the better securing the English crown to himself and his heirs, he thought it expedient to dispatch Edmund and Edward the sons of Ironside out of the way. But lest such an execrable fact should seem too black to be done in England, he sent the two youths to Solomon King of Hungary, willing him to use some convenient opportunity to take away their lives; which seemed to Solomon so very unnatural, that instead of complying with Cnute's request, he educated and brought them up as his own children. But Cnute imagined now that his fear was over, and his business effectually finished; so that he could the more boldly demand of his subjects, what either his necessity or curiosity would prompt him to. And reflecting with himself, what excessive expence he had been at in the conquest of England, was resolved that the English should repay him; and therefore required a subsidy of seventy two thousand pounds, besides eleven thousand, which the city of London contributed. The same time Meyric the son of Arthfael, a person of quality in Wales, rebelled, and raised an army against Prince Lhewelyn, who no sooner appeared in the field to quell his male-contented General, but manfully slew him with his own hand, and easily discomfited his followers. The same time Cnute sailed over into Denmark, and made war upon the Vandals, who, for all that they had a greater army in the field, were overcome by the incomparable valour of earl Godwyn; for which famous action Cnute had the English in great esteem ever after.

A. D. 1020.

But Lhewelyn Prince of Wales, though he had lately quelled the rebels headed by Meyric, was now to encounter with another difficulty, which seemed to threaten greater disturbance and trouble to him: for a certain person of a mean quality in Scotland, coming to South Wales, assumed the name of Run, and gave out that he was the son of Mereith Prince of South-Wales; to whom joined a great number of the nobility,

bility, who had no great affection to Lhewelyn, and
proclaimed Run Prince of South Wales. Lhewelyn
being then in North Wales, and certified of this famous impoftor, drawing his army together, marched
to meet him ; who, with the whole ftrength of South
Wales, then lay at Abergwili, where he abode the arrival of Lhewelyn. When both armies were ready
to join battle, Run makes a vaunting fpeech to his
foldiers, affuring them of victory ; and fo perfuading
them courageoufly to fall on, privately himfelf retired
out of harm's way ; there one might have obferved on
the one fide a valiant army under a cowardly general,
and on the other part a valiant and a noble commander engaging with a flow and a faint-hearted army ; for Lhewelyn, like a bold and courageous prince,
ventured into the midft of his enemies, whilft Run
privately fneaked off out of all danger ; and the South
Wales men were more fierce and eager in the caufe of
a pretender than the North Wales men to maintain the
quarrel of a prince of their own blood. But after
great flaughter on both fides, the North Wales men
calling to mind the feveral victories they had obtained,
and withal being in a very great meafure animated by
the incomparable valour of their prince, fell on fo
warmly, that they put their enemies to flight, and purfued Run fo clofe, that notwithftanding his feveral
fhifts, he was at laft overtaken and flain. Lhewelyn,
after this victory, returned laden with fpoil into North
Wales, and for fome time lived peaceably and without
difturbance : But the next year Howel and Meredith,
the fons of Edwyn, confpired againft him and flew
him, leaving behind him a fon called Gruffydh ap
Lhewelyn, who afterwards, though not immediately,
afcended to the principality of North Wales.

IAGO AP EDWAL.

AFTER the death of Lhewelyn, Iago the fon
Edwal, the true heir to the principality of North
Wales, who had been all this time wrongfully kept
from it; thought this the beſt opportunity to enter
upon his right, by reaſon of the minority of Gruffydh
the fon of Lhewelyn; upon which pretence likewiſe
Rytherch the fon of Ieſtyn forcibly aſſumed the principality of South Wales. About the fame time Cnute
King of England, failed over to Denmark and Sweden, againſt Ulf and Alaf, who had moved the Fin-
landers againſt him; whom he ſubdued with the loſs
of a great part of his army, as well Engliſh as Danes.
Within a while after his return to England, he made
a very pompous and magnificent journey to Rome;
more to ſatisfy his ambitious temper, and to ſignify to
the world his greatneſs and might, which he expreſſed
by his coſtly preſents and princely behaviour, than
any way to make atonement for the oppreſſion and
bloodſhed by which he had eſtabliſhed himſelf in his
kingdom: For what holineſs and mortification he had
learnt at Rome, preſently appeared upon his return to
England; for upon no provocation he marched with
an army into Scotland, and forced Malcolm the
king thereof, together with Molbeath and Jermare,
the kings of the Orkneys and Ewiſt, to do him homage.

A.D 1031.   But the affairs of Wales were at this time very turbulent and uneaſy; for Howel and Meredith, after the
murder of Prince Lhewelyn, expected to enjoy ſome
part of his principality themſelves; but finding Iago
to have ſeized upon North Wales, and Rytherch upon
South Wales, and withal perceiving their own power
too weak to oppoſe their deſigns, they invited over
the Iriſh-Scots, to their aid againſt Rytherch ap Ieſtyn,
                                                      Prince

Prince of South Wales. By the help of thefe, Howel
and Meredith prevailed over Rytherch; who being at
length flain, they jointly took upon them the rule and
government of South Wales. But this was not a fufficient title to eftablifh them fo firmly in it, that their
ufurpation would not be called in queftion; for the A. D. 1032.
fons of Rytherch, prefently after their father's death,
gathered their forces together to fight with the brothers Howel and Meredith, who met at Irathwy, where
a cruel battle was fought, called Gwaith Irathwy; and
at laft the fons of Rytherch, were put to flight. But
though thefe victories, the one over Rytherch, and
the fecond over his fons, feemed in a great meafure to
favour Howel and Meredith's pretence to, and efta-
blifhment in the principality, yet fo unpardonable a   1033.
crime, as the murder of Lhewelyn, a prince of fo
extraordinary qualities, could not remain long unrevenged; for the fons of Conan the fon of Sitfylht,
Prince Lhewelyn's brother, were refolved to return
their uncle's murder upon the two ufurpers, which in
a fhort time they effected againft Meredith, who met
with the fame end from the fons of Conan, that he had
formerly inflicted upon Lhewelyn. But thefe civil dif-
cords in Wales were quickly difcovered by the En-   1034.
glifh, who taking advantrge of fo fair an opportunity,
entered with a great army into the land of Gwent,
where after they had committed confiderable wafte for
fome time, Caradoc the fon of Rytherch ap Ieftyn,
gave them battle, but was in that engagement unhappily flain. And fhortly afterwards died King Cnute, the   1035.
moft famous and mightieft prince then in the weftern
parts of the world; whofe dominions extended over
all Sweden, from Germany almoft to the north Pole;
together with the kingdoms of Norway and Denmark,
and the noble ifland of Britain. To him fucceeded
his fon Harold, for his fwiftnefs, furnamed Harefoot,
begotten upon Alwyn the daughter of Duke Alfelyn;
though feveral ftickled firmly for Hardycnute, his other
fon by Emma, who was then in Denmark. But Harold
being once advanced to the throne, took care to eftablifh
himfelf as firmly as he could in it; and to that end,

thought

thought it expedient to banifh out of his dominions his mother-in-law Emma, who was reftlefs to promote the intereft of her own fon Hardycnute, and to bring him to the crown of England.

A. D. 1037.   And whilft Harold was by thefe meafures fettled in his throne, Iago ap Edwal was juft upon the point of lofing his principality of North Wales: for Gruffydh the fon of Lhewelyn ap Sitfylht, fometime Prince of North Wales, having once hinted a rebellion againft Iago, was fo generally encouraged, and univerfally followed by all people, for the love they bore to his father; that in a fhort time his army mounted to an invincible number. However, Iago was not fo thoroughly affrighted, that he would deliver up his principality without drawing a fword for it; but providing for himfelf as well he could, and drawing together what forces he was able; he gave Gruffydh battle; But his number being far too weak to oppofe fo great an army as fided with Gruffydh, was prefently overpowered and put to the rout, and himfelf flain, leaving after him a fon called Conan, by his wife Afandred, daughter to Gweir the fon of Pylh.

GRUFFYDH ap LHEWELYN.

IAGO ap Edwal being killed, Gruffydh ap Lhewelyn was received with loud acclamations, and joyfully faluted Prince of North Wales; who treading in his father's fteps, behaved himfelf in his government with that prudence and conduct, that he manfully defended his country from the frequent invafions of the Englifh and Danes: for he was fcarce fettled in his throne, when thefe inveterate enemies of the Welch entered in an hoftile manner into Wales, and advanced as far as Crosford upon the Severn, where Gruffydh met them, and forced them fhamfully to fly, and retire

tire back to their own country. From thence Gruffydh paffed to Lhanbadarn Vawr in Cardiganfhire, which he laid in afhes ; and afterwards marched through all the country of South Wales, receiving of the people oaths of fidelity and fubjection to him. In the mean time, Howel ap Edwyn, Prince of South Wales, fled to Edwyn brother to Leofric Earl of Chefter, and prevailed with him to come with an army confifting of Englifh and Danes, to his aid againft Gruffydh, who meeting his enemies in the field, eafily overcame them, Edwyn being flain upon the fpot, and Howel forced to preferve his life by flight. After which victory, Gruffydh having reduced all the country of Wales to fubjection, returned again to North Wales. But Howel as foon as he could recover him- A. D. 1039. felf and recruit his army, entered again into South Wales, intending the recovery of that principality, which he was now fo well affured of, that he brought his wife with him to the field, to let her fee how eafily he could conquer and overcome Prince Gruffydh. But too great an affurance of victory feldom proves profperous; which Howel prefently experienced; for Gruffydh meeting with him at Pencadair, gave him fo warm an entertainment, that he was forced prefently to take his heels, which however could not fo well fecure him, but that he was narrowly purfued, and his wife who was to be entertained with the conqueft of Gruffydh, on the contrary, faw herfelf taken prifoner by him, and forced to comply fo far to his humour, as to be his concubine.

The fame time Harold King of England died, and was fucceeded by his brother Hardycnute, a Prince very famous for hofpitality, and a great lover of good chear, having his table covered four times a-day, with great plenty and variety of difhes, with other fuperfluities for all comers. But he likewife dying at Lambeth after two years reign, the Englifh agreed to fend for Alfred the eldeft fon of Edelred from Normandy, and to make him king. This meffage by no means pleafed Earl Godwyn, a man of great fway now in England; who knowing Alfred to be a perfon of

G 3 greater

greater spirit than to permit him to domineer as he
pleased, endeavoured all he could to diffuade the English from fending for Alfred. He shewed them how
dangerous it was to permit a warlike nation to take
root in their country, and how well Alfred was accompanied with Normans, to whom he had promised
the chief places and rule of the kingdom; by which and
other like infinuations he so disguifted the English nobility againft the Normans, that to diminish their number, they put every tenth man to death. But seeing
this was not fufficient, they acted the fame part over
again, and tythed them a second time; and being
highly enraged againft the Normans, they led Alfred,
who had brought them over, from Gilford, where this
execution was committed, to Gillingham, where having put out his eyes, they removed him to Ely, and
there at length pitifully murdered him. Then they
fent for Edward out of Normandy, and made him
king, who, according to his promife to Earl Godwyn,
married his daughter Edith, a lady much commended
not only for beauty, modefty, and other feminine qualifications, but also beyond what is requifite for a woman, learning. But King Edward did not deal so favourably with her brother Swane, fon to Earl Godwyn, who upon fome diftafte was banished England,
and thereupon forced to betake himself to Baldwyn
earl of Flanders, by whom he was very honourably
received.

A. D. 1041　　Thefe troubles and revolutions in England were fucceeded by others of no lefs confequence in Wales. For
Howel, not brooking to be kept so shamefully out of
his kingdom, returns again the third time into South
Wales, where he had not continued long, but a great
number of ftrangers landed in the weft of Wales, and
advancing farther into the country, pillaged and deftroyed all places they came to. Howel, though defirous to referve his army to fight with Prince Gruffydh,
yet could not behold his country so miferably wafted
and over-run by ftrangers; and thinking moreover,
that by so charitable an action he 'nould win the univerfal love of the South Wales men, drew up his
forces

forces againſt them, and overtaking them at Pwll
Fynach, forced them with much loſs, to retire to their
ſhips; which action was called in Welch, Gwaith Pwll
Fynach. At the ſame time Conan the ſon of Iago ap
Edwal, who was forced for fear of Prince Gruffydh
to flee to Ireland, with the forces of Alfred king of
Dublin, whoſe daughter named Ranulph he had married, landed in North Wales; and having by ſome
treacherous ſtratagem taken Gruffydh, triumphantly
carried him priſoner towards his ſhips. This unhappy accident being diſcovered, and publickly known,
the North Wales men did riſe on a ſudden, and ſo unexpectedly overtook the Iriſh, that they eaſily recovered their Prince, and drove his enemies with great
ſlaughter to their ſhips; who, without any farther conſultation, were glad to ſtrike ſail with Conan for
Ireland. And now Wales, both North and South,
is free from all foreign invaſion, and Howel, as yet
too weak to diſpute his title with Gruffydh; ſo that A. D. 1042.
the next year could be ſubject to no great action, in
which nothing happened remarkable, ſaving the death
of Howel the ſon of Owen Lord of Glamorgan, a
man of great quality and eſteem in Wales. But as 1043.
ſoon as Howel could call in his Danes, to whom he
added all the forces he could raiſe in South Wales;
he intended preſently to march againſt Prince Gruffydh.
But he being aware aforehand to what end thoſe levies
were deſigned, prepared againſt the enſuing ſtorm;
and to avert the war from his own country, marched
courageouſly to South Wales, not fearing to face an
enemy whom he had ſhamefully vanquiſhed twice already. Both armies being joined, Gruffydh eaſily
overcame, and purſued Howel as far as the ſpring-
head of the river Towy, where after a long and a
bloody fight, Howel was at laſt ſlain, and his army
ſo univerſally routed, that few eſcaped with their
lives. But though Howel was dead, yet there remained ſtill more pretenders to the principality of
South Wales; ſo that Gruffydh was in no great pro-
ſpect to enjoy the ſame peaceably: For as ſoon as it was
publiſhed that Howel's army was defeated, and himſelf

felf flain, Rytherch and Rhys the fons of Rytherch ap
Ieftyn put in their claim to South Wales in right of
their father, who had once enjoyed the fovereignty of
that country. And in order to the recovery of the
fame, they drew together a great army, confifting partly of ftrangers and partly of fuch as they could raife
in Gwentland and Glamorgan, and marched to fight
with Gruffydh. The Prince according to his ufual
manner detracted no time, but animating and folacing
his foldiers with the remembrance of their former victories and conquefts, bid the enemies battle, which
proved fo very bloody and terrible, that nothing could
part them befide the darknefs of the night. This battle fo tired and tamed both armies, that neither was
very defirous of another engagement, and fo one being unwilling to fet upon the other, they both agreed
to return to their own habitations. The fame time
Jofeph bifhop of Teilo or Llandaf died at Rome. But
both armies being feparated, Prince Gruffydh enjoyed
a quiet and unmolefted poffeffion of all Wales for
about two years; after which, the gentry of Yftrad
Towy treacheroufly flew 140 of the choice of his army,
which he took in fo high an indignation, that to revenge
their death, he deftroyed all Dyfed and Yftrad Towy.

About the fame time, Lothen and Hyrling two Danifh pirates, with a great number of Danes, landed at
Sandwich, and having plundered the town, returned
again to their fhips, and failed for Holland, where they
fold the booty they had taken, and then returned to
their own country. Shortly afterwards Earl Swayn
came out of Denmark with eight fhips, and returned to England, and coming to his father's houfe at
Pevenefe, humbly requefted of, and his brothers Harold and Toftie, to endeavour his reconciliation with
the King. Earl Beorned too promifed to intercede for
him, and going to Swayn's fleet to fail to Sandwich,
where the King then lay, he was by the way moft
treacheroufly and ungratefully murdered, and his body
caft upon the fhore, which lay there expofed, till
his friends hearing of the fact, came and carried it to
Winchef   ,   : ou.ic it by the body of King Cnute,

Beorned's uncle. Swayn having committed this moſt deteſtable murder, put himſelf again under the protection of the earl of Flanders, not daring to ſhew his face in England, till his father by earneſt mediation wrought his peace with the king.

This year Conan the ſon of Iago raiſed again an army of his friends in Ireland, and ſailed towards Wales, purpoſing to recover his inheritance in that country. But when he was come near the Welch coaſt, there ſuddenly aroſe ſuch a violent ſtorm, that his fleet was preſently ſcattered, and moſt of his ſhips drowned, which rendered this expedition ineffectual. About the ſame time, Robert archbiſhop of Canterbury impeached Earl Godwyn and his ſons Swayn and Harold of treaſon, and the queen of adultery, and upon the account of their non-appearance when cited before the the peers at Gloceſter, the queen was divorced, and Godwyn and his ſons baniſhed, who with his ſon Swayn fled to Flanders, and Harold to Ireland. But theſe unlucky claſhings, and the many troubles that enſued thereupon, happened upon this occaſion. Euſtace earl of Bologne being married to Goda the king's ſiſter, came over this year to England to pay king Edward a viſit, and in his return to Canterbury, one of his retinue forcibly demanding a lodging, provoked the maſter of the houſe ſo far, as by chance or anger to kill him. Euſtace upon this affront returns back to the king, and by the inſinuations of the archbiſhop, makes a loud complaint againſt the Kentiſh-men; to repreſs whoſe inſolencies, earl Godwyn is commanded to raiſe forces, which he refuſing to do, for the kindneſs he bore to his countrymen of Kent, the king ſummons a parliament at Gloceſter, and commands Godwyn to appear there. But he miſtruſting either his own cauſe, or the malice of his adverſaries, gathered a powerful army out of his own and his ſons earldoms, and marched towards Gloceſter, giving out that their forces were to go againſt the Welch, who intended to invade the Marſhes. But King Edward being ſatisfied by the Welch that they had no ſuch

design

deſign in hand, commanded Godwyn to diſmiſs his army, and to appear himſelf to anſwer to the articles exhibited againſt him. Godwyn refuſing to obey, the king by the advice of earl Leofrick, ſummoned an aſſembly at London, whither a great number of forces arrived from Mercia, which Godwyn perceiving, and withal, finding himſelf unable to withſtand the king's proceedings, privately retired with his ſons out of the kingdom, and fled into Flanders. Whereupon the king iſſued out an edict, proclaiming Godwyn and his ſons out-laws, and then confiſcating their eſtates, beſtowed them upon others of his nobility. And, to purſue his diſpleaſure the farther, he divorced his queen Edith, earl Godwyn's daughter, and committed her to a cloiſter, where in a mean condition ſhe ſpent ſome part of her life. In the diſtribution of the forfeited eſtates, Adonan obtained the earldoms of Devon ſand Dorſet, and Algar the ſon of Leofrick, that of Harold. But Godwyn could not patiently behold his eſtate beſtowed upon another, and therefore having hired ſome men and ſhips in Flanders, he ſailed to the Iſle of Wight, where after that he had made a ſufficient havock, he put in at Portland, which he treated after the ſame manner. The ſame time Harold having ſailed from Ireland, at length met with his father, and then with their united navy, they burnt Preveneſeny, Romney, Heath, Folkſton, Dover and Sandwich, and entering the Thames, they deſtroyed Cheppy, and burnt the king's houſe at Middletown. Then they ſailed up the river towards London, where the king's army being ready to oppoſe them, a treaty of peace was by the means of Biſhop Stigand agreed upon, which proved ſo effectual of Godwyn's ſide, that the king received him again to his favour, reſtored him and ſons to all their eſtates, recalled the queen, and baniſhed the archbiſhop, with all the Frenchmen who had been promoters of that unhappy ſuſpicion the king had entertained of them.

About this time, Rhys brother to Gruffydh Prince of Wales, who by ſeveral irruptions upon the borders,

had

had confiderably gauled and damaged the Englifh, was taken and put to death at Bulendun, whofe head being cut off, was prefented to the king, then at Glocefter. But he received better news fome time after from the North, for Siward earl of Northumberland having fent his fon againft Macbeth king of Scotland vanquifhed the fons, tho' not without the lofs of his fon, and many others, both Englifh and Danes. But Siward was not caft down at his fon's death, but enquiring whether he received his death's wound before or behind, and being affured that it was before, replied, " He was very glad of it, for he " could not wifh his fon to die otherwife." After this victory, King Edward marched in perfon to Scotland, and having again overcome Macbeth in battle, he made the whole kingdom of Scotland tributary to the crown of England. The next year, earl Godwyn fitting with the king at table, funk down dead of a fudden, being choaked, as 'tis thought, in fwallowing a morfel of bread; whofe earldom the king beftowed upon his fon Harold, and his upon Algar earl of Chefter.

To this time is referred the original of the Stewards in Scotland, which being a remarkable paffage, and in a great meafure dependant upon the affairs of the Welch, is requifite to be here recorded. Macbeth king of Scotland having caufed Bancho a nobleman of that kingdom to be inhumanly murdered; Fleance, Bancho's fon, to avoid the like cruelty to himfelf, fled to Gruffydh ap Lhewelyn prince of Wales, who taking a very great liking to his perfon, and withal commiferating his condition, fhewed him all the refpect and kindnefs poffible. But Fleance had not continued long with Gruffydh when he fell enamoured upon the prince's daughter, and having obtained her good-will, without any regard had to her father's civility towards him, abufed her fo far as to beget her with child. Gruffydh being acquainted with the matter of fact, fo heinoufly refented the affront, that he occafioned Fleance to be flain, and treated his daughter moft fervilef for j ruftrating her

chaft'ty,

chaftity, efpecially to a ftranger. However, fhe was
in a fhort time delivered of a fon, whofe name was
chriftened Walter; a child, who in his youth expreffed
very great hopes, and in all probability like to make a
very confiderable man, which happened according
to expectation. But the firft original of his future
greatnefs happened upon a very accidental occafion;
being reproached of baftardifm by one of his fellow
companions, he took it in fo unpardonable a dudgeon,
that nothing could fatisfy his revenge, but the life of
the aggreffor. Being upon this mifchance affraid to
undergo the punifhment of the law, he thought it fafe
to fly to Scotland, where falling in company with
certain Englifhmen who were come thither with
queen Margaret fifter to Edgar Edeling, he behaved
himfelf fo foberly and difcreetly, that he won the favour and good character of all that knew him. But
his fame daily increafing, he grew at length to that
height of reputation, as to be employed in the moft
inward affairs of the commonwealth, and at laft was
made Lord Steward of Scotland, from which office
his pofterity retained the furname of Steward, the
kings of Scotland of that name, with feveral other
families of quality in that kingdom being defcended
from him.

But to return to England, Siward the worthy earl
of Northumberland died about this time of the bloody-
flux, a man of a rough demeanour, and a meer
foldierly temper, as he plainly manifefted at the
point of death. For bewailing his misfortune that
had efcaped fo many dangerous engagements, and
withal difdaining to die fo effeminately in bed, he
caufed himfelf to be compleatly armed, and as it
were in defiance of death, prefently expired in a
martial bravery. But his fon being too young, the
king beftowed his earldom upon Tofty the fon of earl
Godwyn.

1054. Wales had been now a long time quiet, and void
of all troubles both abroad and at home, but it could
not be expected that fuch a life fhould prove durable,

ble, but fomething or other would create new commotions and difturbances. Gruffydh fon to Rytherch ap Ieftyn having recruited and recovered himfelf after the laft blow he received from Prince Gruffydh, muft needs venture another trial for the principality of South Wales. The Prince protracting no time, fpeedily marched againft him, and both armies being joined, Gruffydh ap Rytherch was eafily vanquifhed, and in fine, flain. But the troubles of the Welch did not end with him, for Algar Earl of Chefter being convicted of treafon, and thereupon banifhed the kingdom, fled to Gruffydh Prince of Wales, requefting his aid againft king Edward, who, repeating the frequent wrongs he had received at the hands of the Englifh, by upholding his enemies againft him, gladly embraced the opportunity, and promifed him all imaginable fupport. And thereupon affembling his forces, he entered with him into Herefordfhire, and advancing into the country, within two miles of the city of Hereford, they were oppofed by Randulph Earl of that country, who boldly gave them battle. The fight continued very dreadful and dubious for fome hours, till at laft Gruffydh fo encouraged his foldiers with the remembrance of their former victories over the Englifh, that they fell on a-main, and eafily difcomfited Randulph, and flew the beft part of his army. Afterwards they purfued their chace to the town, and having made all the wafte and havock they were able, they laid the town itfelf in afhes, and fo returned home triumphantly, laden with rich booty and plunder. King Edward receiving notice of this invafion, prefently gathered a great army at Glocefter under the conduct of Harold Earl Godwyn's fon, who courageoufly purfuing the enemies, entered into Wales, and encamped beyond Stradclwyd. But Gruffydh and Algar dreading to oppofe him, retired further into South Wales, of which Harold being certified, leaves one part of his army behind with orders to fight, if ocoafion offered, and with the other paffed to Hereford, which he fortified with a ftrong wall round the town. Gruffydh perceiving his undaunted induftry, after many meffages concluded a

peace

peace with Harold at a place called Biligelhag, by which articles Algar was pardoned by the King, and restored to his earldom of Chester. But he did not continue long in the king's favour, for about two years after, upon conviction of treason, he was again banished the land, so that he was forced to betake himself to his old friend Gruffydh Prince of Wales, by whose aid, and a fleet from Norway in spite of of the king he was restored to his earldom. But King Edward was sore offended with the Prince of Wales for harbouring traitors, and therefore to be revenged upon him, he dispatched Harold again with an army to North Wales, who, coming to Ruthlan, burnt the Prince's palace there, and his fleet, that lay in the harbour, and then returned to the king at Glocester.

This year Edward the son of Edmund Ironside, who was sent for out of Hungary, being designed successor to the crown, came to England, but in a short time after his coming, died at London, leaving behind him a son called Edgar Edeling, and a daughter named Margaret, who was afterwards queen of the Scots, and mother to Maud the wife of Henry the first. About two years after, Roderic, son to Harold king of Denmark came with a considerable army into Wales, and being kindly received by Prince Gruffydh, united his power with the Welch, and so entered into England, which they cruelly harrassed and destroyed. But before they could advance any considerable distance, Roderic was compelled to sail for Denmark, and so Gruffydh returned laden with spoils into Wales. The same time Harold Earl Godwyn's son sailing to Flanders, was driven by force of weather to land at Poytiers, where being seized upon, he was brought before William bastard duke of Normandy, to whom he declared the reason of his voyage, that it was purposely to tender him his service in the affairs of England; and so taking an oath, first to marry the duke's daughter, and after the death of Edward to secure the kingdom of England for him,

1956.

4   he

he was honourably difmiffed. Upon his return to
England, by the perfuafions of Caradoc the fon of
Gruffydh ap Rytherch, himfelf with his brother Tofty,
raifed a great army and entered into South-Wales,
which they deftroyed after that manner, that the
Welch were glad to deliver up hoftages for the payment of the antient tribute, which afore-time they
were ufed to pay. Gruffydh hearing of the infolencies
of the Englifh in South-Wales, made all poffible hafte
and preparation to oppofe them, but all to no purpofe; Harold having already treacheroufly hired fome
of Gruffydh's neareft friends to murder him, who
watching their opportunity, executed their wicked defign and brought his head to Harold. Gruffydh being
dead, Harold by King Edward's orders, appointed
Meredith fon of Owen ap Edwyn prince of South-
Wales, and the government of North-Wales to Blethyn
and Rywalhon the fons of Confyn, brothers by the
mother fide to Prince Gruffydh, and who probably
for the defire of rule, were acceffary to the murder
of that noble prince. This Gruffydh ap Lhewelyn
enjoyed the principality of Wales for the fpace of thirty
four years; a prince of incomparable virtues, both
wife and valiant, beloved of his fubjects and formidable
to his enemines, in all his actions he behaved himfelf
great and princely; and having defended his country
fo bravely againft all foreign oppofition; he was far
unworthy of that treacherous and cruel death, which
his unkind fubjects and unnatural friends beftowed
upon him. He left iffue but one daughter called Neft,
abufed firft by Fleance fon of Bancho, and afterwards
married to Trahaern ap Caradoc prince of North-
Wales.

BLETHYN

BLETHYN and RYWALHON.

AFTER the deplorable murder of Prince Gruffydh, Meredith the fon of Owen ap Edwyn, who according to fome, was fon to Howel Dha, did take upon him, as 'tis faid, the government of South-Wales, and Blethyn and Rywalhon the fons of Confyn, half brothers to Gruffydh, as defcended from Angharad daughter to Meredith fometime prince of Wales, entered upon the principality of North-Wales ; Conan the fon of Iago ap Edwal the right heir to that crown being then with his father-in-law in Ireland. This partition of Wales fell much fhort of the expectation of Caradoc ap Gruffydh ap Rytherch, who being the chief promoter of Harold's making an expedition againft Gruffydh ap Lhewelyn, made no queftion to attain to the government of South-Wales, in cafe Gruffydh got the worfe. But it happened otherwife ; Harold being fenfible of Caradoc's fubtilty and knavery, and doubting whether if he was made prince of South-Wales, he could obtain a certain lordfhip nigh Hereford, which he had a longing mind to, made a compofition with Meredith ap Owen for the faid lordfhip, and created him Prince of South Wales, and on the contrary banifhed Caradoc out of the country. Harold having obtained his requeft, built a very magnificent houfe at a place called Portafcyth in Monmouthfhire, and ftoring it with great quantity of provifion, fplendidly entertained the king, who honoured him with a vifit. This was by no means pleafing to Tofty, to fee his younger brother in greater efteem and favour with the king than himfelf, and having concealed his difpleafure for a time, could not forbear at length but difcover his grievance. For one day at Windfor, while Harold reached the cup to king Edward, Tofty ready to burft

? for

for envy that his brother was so much respected beyond himself, could not refrain to run furiously upon him, and pulling him by the hair, dragged him to the ground, for which unmannerly action, the king forbad him the court. But he with continued rancour and malice rides to Hereford, where Harold had many servants preparing an entertainment for the king, and setting upon them with his followers lopped off the hands and legs of some, the arms and heads of others, and threw them into the buts of wine and other liquors, which were put in for the king's drinking, and at his departure charged the servants to acquaint him, " That " of other fresh meats he might carry with him what " he pleased, but for sauce he should find plenty provid- " ed ready for him." For which barbarous offence the king pronounced a sentence of perpetual banishment upon him. But Caradoc ap Gruffydh gave a finishing stroke to Harold's house, and the king's entertainment at Portascyth; for coming thither shortly after Tosty's departure, to be revenged upon Harold, he killed all the workmen and labourers, with all the servants he could find, and utterly defacing the building, carried away all the costly materials, which with great charges and expence had been brought thither to beautify and adorn the structure. Soon after which, the Northumbrians (who could not endure the insolencies of the two brothers Harold and Tosty, who bearing an uncontroulable sway in the kingdom, were used to practise most hellish villainies to encompass any man's estate that displeased them,) in a tumult at York beset the palace of Tosty, and having pillaged his treasure, slew all his family, as well Englishmen as Danes. Then adjoining to themselves the people of Lincoln, Nottingham and Derbyshire, they elected Marcher the son of Earl Algar their general, to whom came his brother Edwyn with a considerable number of forces, and a great party of Welchmen. Then they marched in an hostile manner to Northampton, where Harold met them, being sent by the king to know their demands; to whom they laid open their grievances, and the cruelty of Tosty's government, and at last, with an absolute

H   refusal

refusal of admitting him again, defired that Marcher
fhould be appointed Earl over them, which the king
upon the reafonable complaints of injuries done by
Tofty, eafily granted, and willingly confirmed Marcher's title. Whereupon they peaceably returned back
to the North, and the Welch with feveral prifoners
and other booties got in this expedition, returned
to Wales.

. D. 1066　The year following, King Edward died, and was
buried at Weftminfter, being the laft king of the
Saxon blood before the conqueft that governed the
kingdom of England, which from Cerdic king of the
Weft Saxons had continued 544, and from Egbert
the firft monarch, 171 years. Edward being dead,
the next debate was about an election of a fucceffor,
Edgar Edeling being fet up by fome, as lawful heir
to the crown, which Harold as being a perfon of
greater power and authority in the kingdom, much
wealthier and better befriended, prefently thwarted,
and brought matters fo cunningly about, that himfelf was chofen king, without any regard obferved
to the oath and promife he had formerly made to
William Duke of Normandy. Duke William upon
notice of Harold's advancement, how that he had accepted of the crown of England contrary to the articles between them, convened together his nobles, and
laid before them the feveral wrongs and affronts he
had received at the hands of Harold, as the death
of his coufin Alfred, the banifhment of archbifhop
Robert, Earl Odan and all the Normans, and laftly
the breach of his oath and promife. Then he declared to them the pretence he had to claim the crown
of England, that Edward had given him formerly an
abfolute promife in Normandy, that if ever he enjoyed
the Englifh crown, William fhould be his heir; which
title, though in itfelf weak and infignificant ferved
William's purpofe well enough to make an expedition againft an intruder. Duke William's pretence
feemed plaufible enough to the Norman nobility, but
the difficulty of the undertaking and the danger of
this expedition was fomething perplexive, and made
them

them lefs inclinable to encourage fo precipitous an undertaking; which they the more difliked upon the perfuafion of William Fitzofbert the duke's fewer, whom
they pitched upon to deliver their thoughts as to the
expedition, unto the duke. But he inftead of diffuad-
ing him from this voyage, politically declared that
himfelf with all his power were ready to live and die
with him in this expedition, which the reft hearing,
could not but offer the duke their fervice in the fame
manner; and fo all things were prepared for an invafion of England. In the mean while Tofty, full of
indignation at his brother's advancement to the crown,
entered the river Humber with forty fail, but meeting
with Earl Edwyn who came to oppofe him, he was
forced after a confiderable encounter to bear off, and
fecure himfelf by flight. But meeting with Harold
king of Norway upon the coaft of Scotland, coming
for England with three hundred fail, he joined his
forces with Harold, and fo both together entering the
Humber, they landed their army and marched to
York, where the Earls Edwyn and Marcher unfuc-
cefsfully gave them battle. Having pillaged and deftroyed that city, they paffed on to Stamford-bridge,
and there met with King Harold, who with a well
difciplined army was come to ftop their farther carreer.
After a long and a terrible fight, and much bloodfhed
on both fides, the Norwegians began at laft to give
back, which the Englifh perceiving, fell on fo manfully that few or none efcaped with their lives, Harold and Tofty being alfo flain upon the fpot. One
of the Norwegians is defervedly recorded for his incomparable exploits performed in this battle, who
with incredible valour maintaining the bridge againft
the whole ftrength of the Englifh army for above an
hour with his fingle refiftance delayed their victory,
and having flain a great number of his enemies, he
feemed invincible, till in the end, no one daring to
grapple with him fairly, he was run through with a
fpear from under the bridge, and fo by his fall, a
paffage was opened for purfuit to compleat the vic-

tory. King Harold over-joyed with this fucces, triumphantly entered into York, and whilft he was
making merry with his nobles at a fumptuous feaft,
news came that Duke William of Normandy was
fafely landed at, and began to fortify himfelf in Haftings, with which tidings being no way dafhed, as
fearing nothing after his late victory, he forthwith
marched towards him, and as foon as he was arrived
in Suffex, without any confideration of the fatigue
his army had underwent in their march, bid William
battle. The Duke dividing his army into five battalions, made a long harrangue to his foldiers, wherein
he repeated and commended the noble acts of their anceftors the Danes and Norwegians, who had perpetually vanquifhed the Englifh and French, and other
nations, as many as they had to do with; how that
themfelves being well horfed and armed, were now to
engage with a people void of both, who had no other
defence to truft to, than the nimblenefs and fwiftnefs
of their heels. Both armies being joined upon the
fourteenth day of October, Duke William after fome
hours engaging ordered his army fo to retire, as if
they feemed to fly, which the Englifh perceiving,
broke their ranks in hafte of purfuing the fuppofed
chace, which falling out according to the Duke's expectation, he fent in a frefh fupply of Normans, who
falling upon the confufed battalions of the Englifh,
eafily overcame them, and Harold receiving firft a
wound by an arrow, were at length flain, and then
both the field and the victory were left to the Normans. The day being thus won, William from this
time called the Conqueror, went ftraight to London,
where he was received with all poffible formality,
and upon Chriftmas-day folemnly crowned king of
England. This change and alteration in England,
was afore prognofticated by a comet which appeared
in the fpring of this year, upon which a certain poet
made the following verfes;

Anno milleno fexageno quoque feno,
Anglorum metæ flammas cenfere comitæ.

King

King William having established himself in the A.D.1066. crown of England, passed over the next year to Normandy, so to settle affairs there, as afterwards they might have no need of his presence. In the mean while Edgar Edeling taking advantage of his absence, returned from Scotland to York, being declared king by the inhabitants of the country, who had already slain Robert, upon whom William had bestowed that earldom with nine hundred of his men. But the king upon his return from Normandy, presently marched to the North, and having sufficiently revenged himself upon the inhabitants, by wasting and destroying their country, chased Edgar to Scotland again. The like advantage Edric Sylvaticus the son of Alfric Earl of Mercia embraced, who refusing to own any submission to the conqueror, took the opportunity of his departure to Normandy to fall foul upon such as were appointed vicegerents and governors of the kingdom in his absence. Whereupon Richard Fitzscrope governor of the castle of Hereford, with the forces under his command so bitterly gauled him, by wasting and consuming his lands, and carrying off the goods of his tenants, that he was compelled to desire aid of Blethyn and Rywalhon princes of Wales, by whose help, to recompence the loss he had received, he passed into Hereford, and after that he had over-run and pillaged the country to Wyebridge, returned back with exceeding great booty. But no sooner were Blethyn and Rywalhon arrived in North Wales, but they received news of a rebellion raised against them by Meredith and Ithel the sons of Gruffydh ap Lhewelyn, who had drawn together a considerable number of men, upon pretence of recovering the principality of North Wales, which they said was fraudulently detained from them. Blethyn and Rywalhon did not delay to march to find the enemies, and meeting with them at a place called Mechain, without any farther ceremonies, set upon the rebels, who behaved themselves so gallantly, that after a fight of several hours, they wanted nothing but number to compleat the victory. There fell in this battle on the one side

Prince

Prince Rywalhon, and on the other Ithel, who being
slain, Meredith was forced to give ground, and endeavour to save himself by flight, which could not
secure him, he being narrowly pursued by Blethyn,
that in fine, he was glad to escape to the mountains,
where for want of victuals and other necessaries, he
quickly perished, leaving Blethyn ap Confyn sole
Prince of North Wales and Powis.   During these
Welch disturbances, Swane king of Denmark, and
Osburn, his brother with three hundred sail came up
the Humber, and being joined by Edgar Edeling
and Earl Waltelfe, marched to York, and taking the
castle disposed of their forces to winter-quarters, betwixt the rivers of Ouse and Trent.   The king understanding the matter, posted to the North; whose
coming so dashed the confederates, that they quickly
dispersed their power, and the Danes escaped to their
ships, and the king having taken vengeance upon the
rebellious inhabitants of the country, and upon his
submission, having pardoned Earl Waltelfe, returned
back to London.

BLETHYN ap CONFYN.

ABOUT the same time Caradoc son to Gruf-
fydh ap Rhytherch ap Iestyn all this while being fore-
ly dissatisfied that he could not attain to the principality of South Wales, invited over a great number of
Normans, to whom he joined all the forces he could
raise out of Gwentland, and other parts of Wales.
Then setting upon Prince Meredith who was far
too weak to encounter so considerable an army, gave
him an easy overthrow near the river Rymhy, where
Meredith was slain, and so Caradoc obtained the government of South Wales, which for a long time he
had endeavoured sinistriously to encompass.   He had
sometime afore procured Harold to make an invasion

upon

upon Gruffydh ap Lhewelyn, purpofely that himfelf might arrive at the principality of South Wales; and failing then of his expectation, he now invites over the Normans, not being willing to truft the Englifh any more, by reafon that he had fo ungratefully been baulked by Harold: fo that it feems he cared not by what courfe, or by whofe means he fhould gain his point; though it were by. the ruin and deftruction of his country, which hitherto he had earneftly promoted. Being at length advanced to his long expected government of South Wales, (which though not recorded, feems yet very probable, by reafon that his fon Rhytherch ap Caradoc enjoyed the fame very foon after) he did not enjoy this honour long, but dying in a fhort time after his advancement, left to fucceed him, his fon Rytherch ap Caradoc. At the fame time that Caradoc carried on this rebellion in Wales, the Earls Edwyn, Marcher, and Hereward revolted from the king of England; but Edwyn fufpecting the fuccefs of their affairs, and determining to retire to Malcolm king of Scotland in his journey thither was betrayed, and flain by his own followers. Then Marcher and Hereward betook themfelves to the Ifle of Ely, which though fufficiently fortified, was fo warmly befieged by the king, that Marcher and his accomplices were in a fhort time forced to furrender themfelves up prifoners; only Hereward made his efcape to Scotland: but the king followed him fo clofe; and after he had received homage of Malcolm king of Scotland, returned back to England; and after a fhort ftay here, paffed over to Normandy, where he received Edgar Edeling again to mercy.

The next year, the Normans having already tafted A.D. 1071. of the fweetnefs of wafting and plundering a country, came over again to Wales; and having fpoiled and deftroyed Dyfed and the country of Cardigan, returned home with very great fpoil; and the following year failed over again for more booty. About the fame time, Bleythyd bifhop of St. David's died, and was fucceeded by one Sulien. But this was not all the misfortune that befel the Welch; for Radulph Earl

H 4 of

Of the East Angles, together with Roger Earl of Hereford and Earl Waltelpe, entered into a conspiracy against King William, appointing the day of marriage between Radulph and Roger's sister, which was to be solemnized in Essex; to treat of and conclude their design. Radulph's mother was come out of Wales, and upon that account, he invited over several of her friends and relations to the wedding; meaning chiefly by this seeming affection, by their help and procurement to bring over the princes and people of Wales, to favour and assist his undertaking. But King William being acquainted with the whole plot, quickly ruined all their intrigues; unexpectedly coming from Normandy surprised the conspirators; only Radulph, who either doubted of the success of their affairs, or else had intimation given him of the king's landing, before hand took shipping at Norwich, and fled to Denmark. Waltelpe and Roger were executed, and all the other adherents; more particularly the Welch, some of whom were hanged, others had A.D. 1073. their eyes put out, and the rest were banished. Soon after, Blethyn ap Confyn Prince of Wales was basely and treacherously murdered by Rhys ap Owen ap Edwyn and the gentlemen of Ystrad Tywy, after he had reigned thirteen years: a prince of singular qualifications and virtues, and a great observer of justice and equity towards his subjects; he was very liberal and magnificent, being indeed very able, having a prodigious and almost an incredible estate, as appears by these verses made upon him;

Blethyn ap Confyn bôb Cwys
Ei bûn bioedb bên Bowis.

He had four wives, by whom he had issue, Meredith by Haer daughter of Gylhyn, his first wife; Lhywarch and Cadogan by the second; Madoc and Riryd by the third; and Iorwerth by his last.

TRAHAERN

TRAHAERN ap CARADOC.

BLETHYN being, as is said, traiterously murdered, there was no regard had to his issue, as to their
right of succession; but Trahaern ap Caradoc his
cousin-german being a person of great power and
sway in the country was unanimously elected Prince
of North Wales, and Rhys ap Owen with Rytherch
ap Caradoc did jointly govern South Wales.   Trahaern indeed had none of the least pretence to that
principality, as having married Nest the only surviv-
ing issue of that great prince, Gruffydh ap Lhewelyn;
his two sons Meredith and Ithel being lately slain in
their attempt against Blethyn and Rywalhon. But his
title could not secure him in his government as much
as his possession, since there was one still living, though
much regarded, who without any dispute, was true
heir and proprietor of the principality of North
Wales. And this was Gruffydh son to Conan, son
to Iago ap Edwal, who being informed of the death
of Blethyn ap Confyn, and the advancement of Trahaern, thought this a proper time to endeavour the
recovery of what was truly his right, and out of which
he had been all this time most wrongfully excluded.
Wherefore having obtained help in Ireland, where he
privately sojourned during the reign of Blethyn ap
Confyn, from Encumalhon king of Ultonia, Ranalht
and Mathawn two other kings of that country, he
sailed for Wales, and landed in the isle of Anglesey,
which he easily reduced and brought to subjection.
At the same time Cynwric ap Rywalhon, a nobleman of Maeler or Bromfield was slain in North Wales,
but how, or upon what account, is not known. But
whilst Gruffydh ap Conan endeavours to dispossess
Trahaern out of North Wales, Gronow and Lhewelyn
the sons of Cadwgan ap Blethyn having united their
                                              forces

forces with Caradoc ap Gruffydh ap Rytherch, intended to revenge the murder of their grandfather Blethyn ap Confyn, upon Rys ap Owen and Rytherch ap Caradoc, the joint rulers of South Wales. And then marching confidently to find them, both armies met together and fought at a place called Camdhwr; where after a fore engagement, the fons of Cadwgan at length obtained a glorious victory. In North Wales the fame time, Gruffydh ap Conan having eftablifhed his poffeffion of the ifle of Anglefey, intended to proceed farther in the continent of Wales; to which end, having tranfported his forces over the river, encamped in the neighbouring country of Carnarvonfhire, purpofing to reduce North Wales by degrees. Trahaern ap Caradoc being informed of this defcent of Gruffydh's, made all poffible fpeed to prevent his farther progrefs; and having made all neceffary preparations that the fhortnefs of the opportunity would permit, he drew up his forces to Bron yr Erw, where he gave Gruffydh battle, and in fine put him to a fhameful flight; fo that he was glad to retire back fafe to Anglefey.

A.D. 1074.   The next year Rytherch ap Caradoc Prince of South Wales died, being murdered through the unnatural villainy of his coufin-german Meyrchaon ap Rhys ap Rytherch; after whom Rhys ap Owen obtained the fole government of South Wales: but his enjoyment of the whole principality was not very lafting, and fcarce at all void of trouble and vexation of war.

1075.   For fhortly after the death of Caradoc, the fons of Cadwgan thinking they might eafily now foil and vanquifh one, feeing they had fome time ago victorioufly overcome both princes together, with all the forces they could raife, fet upon Rhys again at a place called Gwanyffyd; who not being able to endure their number, was routed and forced to flee; however the blow was not fo mortal, but that Rhys gathered together new levies, by the help of which he was emboldened ftill to maintain himfelf in his principality. But Fortune which had advanced him to the crown, feemed now to frown at and crofs all his endeavours and undertakings

ings and being reduced to a very weak condition in the late battle, he was set upon by a fresh enemy, before he could have sufficient time to recover and recruit himself. For Trahaern ap Caradoc Prince of North Wales, perceiving the weakness and inability of Rhys to make opposition against any foreign enemy that invaded his territories, thought it now very feasible to obtain the conquest of South Wales, and then to annex it to his own principality of North Wales. Being egged on by these pleasant imaginations, he dispatched his army to South Wales, to fight with Rhys, who with all the forces he could possibly levy, as laying his whole fortune upon the event of this battle, boldly met him at Pwlhgwttic; where after a tedious fight on both sides, Rhys having lost the best part of his army, was put to flight, and so warmly pursued, that after long shifting from place to place, himself with his brother Howel fell at length into the hands of Caradoc ap Gruffydh, who put them both to death, in revenge of the base murder of Blethyn ap Confyn, by them formerly transacted.   The principality of South Wales being thus vacant by the death of Rhys ap Owen; Rhys son to Theodore, ap Eineon, ap Owen, ap Howel Dha, as lawful heir to that government, put in his claim, which being very plain and evident, so prevailed with the people of the country, that they unanimously elected him for their prince; much against the expectation of Trahaern ap Caradoc Prince of North Wales.   The next year St. David's suffered greatly by strangers, who landing there in a considerable number, A. D. 1077. spoiled and destroyed the whole town; shortly after which barbarous action, Abraham bishop of that see died; and then Sulien, who the year before had relinquished and resigned up that bishoprick, was compelled to resume it.

The government of all Wales both North and   1079. South, had been now for a long time supplied by usurpers, and forcibly detained from the right and legal inheritors; but Providence would suffer injustice to reign no longer, and therefore restored the rightful heirs to their principalities. Rhys ap Theodore had

actual

actual poſſeſſion of South Wales; and there wanted no more at this time, but to bring in Gruffydh ap Conan to the principality of North Wales; both theſe princes being indiſputably right and lawful heirs to their reſpective governments, as lineally deſcended from Roderic the Great, who was legal proprietor of all Wales. Gruffydh ap Conan had already reduced the iſle of Angleſey, but not being able to levy a ſufficient army from thence to oppoſe Trahaern, he invited over a great party of Iriſh and Scots, and then with his whole army joined with Rhys ap Theodore Prince of South Wales. Trahaern in like manner aſſociating to himſelf Caradoc ap Gruffydh and Mailyr the ſons of Rywalhon ap Gwyn his couſins-german, the greateſt and moſt powerful men then in Wales, drew up his forces together, with reſolution to fight them. Both armies meeting upon the mountains of Curno, a terrible and cruel battle enſued preſently thereupon; which proved the more fierce and bloody, by reaſon that both parties reſolutely referred their whole fortune to the ſucceſs of their arms; and life would prove vain if the day was loſt. But after a diſmal fight on both ſides, the victory fell at laſt to Gruffydh and Rhys, Trahaern with his couſins being all ſlain in the field; after whoſe death Gruffydh took poſſeſſion of North Wales; and ſo the rule of all Wales, after a tedious interval, was again reſtored to the right line. About the ſame time, Urgeney ap Sitfylht, a perſon of noble quality in Wales, was treacherouſly murdered by the ſons of Rhys Sais, or the Engliſhman; by which name, the Welch were accuſtomed to denominate all perſons, as either had lived any conſiderable time in England, or could fluently and handſomely ſpeak the Engliſh tongue.

GRUFFYDH

GRUFFYDH AP CONAN.

GRUFFYDH ap Conan being confirmed in the principality of North Wales, and Rhys ap Theodore in that of South Wales; there was no body that could create them any moleftation or difturbance upon the account of right, which was unqueftionably juft; fo that they quietly enjoyed for fome time their refpective dominions, without apprehenfion of any other pretender. Indeed, it had feldom been known before, but that one of the princes was an ufurper; and particularly in North Wales, where from the time of Edwal Foel, none had legally afcended to the crown, excepting Edwal the fon of Meyric, eldeft fon to Edwal Foel, in whofe line the undoubted title of North Wales lawfully defcended. And the right line being now reftored in Gruffydh ap Conan, the fame legally continued to Lhewelyn ap Gruffydh, the laft Prince of the Britifh blood. But during thefe revolutions in Wales, fome things memorable were tranfacted in England; Malcolm king of the Scots defcending into Northumberland, ravaged and deftroyed the country without mercy, carrying away a great number of prifoners; after which the Northumbrians fell upon Walter bifhop of Durham, whom they flew, together with a hundred men, whilft he fate keeping of court, not dreaming of any fuch treacherous villainy. The fame time Robert Curthoys the Baftard's eldeft fon, being for fome reafon difgufted againft his father, and fet on by the inftigation of the king of France, entered Normandy with an army, and claimed it as his right; which King William being acquainted with, paffed over to Normandy, and meeting with his fon hand to hand in battle, was by him overthrown. But being returned from Normandy, he entered with a great army into Wales, and marching after the man
ner

ner of a pilgrimage as far as St. David's, he offered and paid his devotion to that. faint, and afterwards received homage of the kings and princes of the country. About the fame time the tomb of Walwey king Arthur's fifter's fon, a moft valiant perfon in his time, and governor of that country, from him called Walwethey, was difcovered in the country of Ros, nigh the fea-fhore, whofe body proved monftroufly prodigious, being in length about fourteen foot.

A.D. 1086. This year Madawc, Cadwgan and Riryd, the fons of Blethyn ap Confyn fome time Prince of Wales, raifed a rebellion againft Rhys ap Tewdor; and having drawn together a great number of licentious and malecontented people, thought to ejeCt him out of the principality of South Wales. Rhys had not power and forces enough to oppofe them; the rebels' army increafing daily by the addition of the difcontented multitude, who always rejoice at any new commotion or difturbance; and therefore he was compelled to retire to Ireland, where he obtained a very confiderable party of Irifh and Scots, upon promife of a fufficient reward, in cafe he was reftored again to his principality. Having by this meafure got a very fenfible increafe to his former ftrength, he landed in South Wales; the news of whofe arrival being blazed abroad, his friends from all quarters prefently retired to him; fo that in a fhort time his army became numerous, and able to confront the enemy. The rebels were fenfible how the Prince's forces daily multiplied, and therefore to prevent any farther addition, they made all poffible hafte to force him to a battle, which in a fhort time after happened at Lhech y Creu, where the rebels were vanquifhed; Madawc and Riryd being flain, and Cadwgan glad to fave his life by flight. Rhys having won fo fignal a viCtory, and fearing no farther difturbance difmiffed the Irifh and Scots with great rewards, who honourably returned to their 1087 own country. Within a while after, an unaccountable facrilege was committed at St. David's; the fhrine belonging to the cathedral, being feloniously conveyed out of the church, all the plate and other utenfils

were

were ſtolen, and only the ſhrine left empty behind.
The ſame year a civil war broke out in England,
and ſeveral armies in ſeveral parts of the kingdom
were up in arms at the ſame time, and among the reſt
the Welch, who entering into Gloceſter and Worceſter ſhires, burnt and deſtroyed all before them, to
the gate of Worceſter. The king having drawn his
army together, proceeded againſt his enemies by degrees, and falling upon their ſeparate parties, without
any great difficulty, reduced all to obedience. With-A. D.1089.
in two years after, Archbiſhop Sulien, the moſt pious
and learned perſon in Wales, died, in the eightieth
year of his age, and in the ſixteenth year of his bi-
ſhoprick; preſently after whoſe death the town of
St. David's ſuffered a more ſenſile calamity, being firſt
plundered, and afterwards burnt by a company of pyrates, who ſorely infeſted the Britiſh coaſts. About
the ſame time alſo died Cadifor the ſon of Calhoyn
Lord of Dyfed, whoſe ſons Lhewelyn and Eineon moved Gruffydh ap Meredith to take up arms againſt his
ſovereign Prince Rhys ap Tewdor, with whom they
joined all the forces they could levy among their tenants and dependants; then paſſing with their army
to Lhandydoch, boldly challenged Rhys to fight;
who thereupon gave them battle, and after a reſolute
engagement of both ſides, the rebels were at length
worſted, and put to flight, and then ſo narrowly purſued, that Gruffydh ap Meredith was taken priſoner,
and in fine executed as a traitor: but Eineon made his
eſcape, and not daring to truſt himſelf with any of
his own kindred, he fled to Ieſtyn ap Gurgant, Lord
of Morgannwc, who was then in actual rebellion
againſt Prince Rhys. And to ingratiate himſelf the
more in Ieſtyn's favour, he promiſed, upon condition
of the performance of certain articles, one of which
more eſpecially was, That he ſhould receive his daughter in matrimony; that he would bring over to his aid
a conſiderable body of Normans, with whom he was
ſingularly acquainted, as having ſerved a long time
in England. Theſe articles being agreed to and recorded, Eineon poſted to England, and in a little
time

time brought matters so about, that he prevailed with Robert Fitzhamon and twelve more knights, to levy a strong army of Normans, and to come to Wales to A.D. 1090. the protection and aid of Ieftyn. The beginning of the following year they landed in Glamorganshire; and were honourably received by Ieftyn, who joining his power to theirs, marched to Prince Rhys's dominions; where, without the leaft shew of mercy to his own countrymen, he encouraged the Normans, by his own example, to spoil and deftroy all that came before them. Prince Rhys was mightily grieved to find his country so unmercifully haraffed; and though at this time very antient, being above ninety-eight years of age, he could not refrain but meet his enemies; and having with all poffible fpeed raifed a convenient army; he met with them near Brecknock, where after a terrible fight, and a great flaughter on both fides, he was unhappily flain. With him fell the glory and grandeur of the principality of South Wales, being afterwards rent in pieces, and divided into feveral parts and piece-meals among the Norman captains, as fhall be by and by more particularly related. Prince Rhys left iffue behind him by the daughter of Rywalhon ap Confyn, two fons, Gruffydh and Grono, the latter of which was detained prifoner by the king of England; though the author of the winning of the lordfhip of Glamorgan, affirms, that he was flain, together with his father, in this battle againft the Normans.

The Normans having received a fufficient reward from Ieftyn, upon the account of their fervice againft Prince Rhys, returned to their fhips, in order to their voyage homeward. But before they could loofe anchor to fail off, Eineon recalled them, being ungratefully affronted by Ieftyn, who abfolutely refufed to make good to him the conditions which they had agreed upon, before the Normans were invited to Wales. Upon this account, Eineon was fo irreconcilably incenfed againft Ieftyn, that to be revenged upon him, he was willing to facrifice his native country into the hands of ftrangers; and therefore endeavoured to perfuade the Normans concerning the fatnefs and
fertility

fertility of the country, and how eafily they might conquer and make themfelves mafters of it. But he needed not many arguments to perfuade a people that were willing of themfelves, efpecially being encouraged thereto by a perfon of fome efteem in the country; whereupon, without any more queftions, they prefently fell to their bufinefs; and from friends became unexpectedly foes. Ieftyn was much furprifed to find the Normans, whom he had but lately honourably difmiffed from his fervice, and as he thought, with fatisfaction, fo foon become his enemies; but perceiving a ferpent in the hedge, and Eineon fo amicably great among them, he quickly gueffed at the reafon, of which there was no other remedy left but to bewail the unneceffary folly of his own knavery. The Normans eafily difpoffeffed Ieftyn of the whole lordfhip of Glamorgan; the moft pleafant and fertile part of which they divided among themfelves; leaving the more mountainous and craggy ground to the fhare of Eineon. The knights who accompanied Fitzhamon in this expedition were, William de Londres or London; Richard de Grena villa, or Greenfield; Paganus de Turberville; Robert de S. Quintino, or Quintin; Richard de Sywarde; Gilbert de Humfrevile; Roger de Berkrolles; Reginald de Sully; Peter le Soore; John le Fleming; Oliver de S. John; William de Efterling, or Stradling. Thefe perfons having diftributed that fair and pleafant lordfhip among themfelves, and confidering that they were much better provided for here than they could be at home, fettled in Glamorgan, where their pofterity have continued to this time. And here we may obferve, what a train of circumftances concurred together, in favour of the Normans, having poffeffion of this lordfhip: for had not Eineon, being vanquifhed by Prince Rhys, fled to Ieftyn, rather than to another; or had not Ieftyn been fo vain as to attempt the conqueft of South Wales, and to that end confented to the advice of Eineon; there had been no neceffity of inviting the Normans at all to Wales. And then, the Normans being arrived, had not Ieftyn ungenteely violated his promife, and refufed to perform the articles agreed upon between him and Eineon; or had not Eineon pursued so desperate revenge, but satisfied his passion upon Iestyn, without prejudice to his country; the Normans would have returned home with satisfaction, and consequently could never have been proprietors of that noble country they then forcibly possessed. And now again the Welch experienced the dangerous consequence of calling in a foreign nation to their aid; the Saxons had already dispossessed them of the best part of the island of Britain, and now the Normans seized upon a great part of that small country, which had escaped the sovereignty and conquest of the English. But here it will be necessary to lay down the state and condition of this lordship of Morgannwc or Glamorgan, and what share each particular knight obtained in the distribution of it.

The lordship of Glamorgan reaches in length twenty-seven miles, even from Rymny bridge to the east, to Pwlh Conan westward; and in breadth from Aberthaw, otherwise Aberdaon on the south part, to the confines of Brecknockshire above Morley's castle, twenty-two miles. This being a royal lordship, the lords thereof owing no other subjection than obedience only to the crown, assumed to themselves all the privileges of a regal court, excepting only the pardoning of criminals in case of treason. And not only Glamorgan, but the several petty lordships of which it consisted, namely, Sengennyth, Myscyn, Ruthin, Lhanblethian, Tir Iarlh, Glyn Rothney, Avan, Neth, Coyty, Talavan, and Lantuit or Boviarton; exercised the same privilege of Jura Regalia, with this difference only, that in case of wrong judgment in these courts, appeal might be made in the county-court of Glamorgan, which being superior to the rest, had power to reverse any judgment given in them. Within this lordship were eighteen castles, and thirty-six knight's fees; besides the town and castle of Kynfig, the town of Cowbridge or Pont Vaen, and the town and castle of Caerdaf; in the latter of which the lord of Glamorgan chiefly re-

I   sided

fided, wherein the county-court was monthly kept. The annual revenue of this lordſhip amounted to a thouſand marks; whereof four hundred was allowed for the fees and ſalary of the ſeveral officers belonging to the ſame. This lordſhip of Glamorgan Robert Fitzhamon kept to himſelf; and the others he diſtributed between his ſeveral followers; namely, to William de Londres he gave the caſtle and manor of Ogmore: to Richard Greenfield the lordſhip of Neth; to Paine Turberville that of Coyty; to Robert S. Quintine Lhan Blethyan; to Richard Syward Talavan; to Gilbert Humfrevile the caſtle and manor of Penmare; to Reginald Sully the caſtle and manor of Sully; to Roger Berkiolles that of Eaſt Orchard; to Peter le Soor that of Peterton; to John Fleming that of S. George; to John S. John that of Fonmon or Fenyon; and laſtly, to William le Eſterling or Stradling that of S. Donats. But that theſe knights ſhould have dependence upon, and might ſeem to hold their ſeveral lordſhips and eſtate from him; Robert Fitzhamon appointed them their ſeveral apartments in his caſtle of Caerdaf, where they were obliged to give their attendance at every court-day, which was monthly kept upon Monday.

But about the ſame time that Robert Fitzhamon took the lordſhip of Glamorgan, Barnard Newmarch, a nobleman likewiſe of Normandy, obtained by conqueſt the lordſhip of Brecknock; and Henry de Newburgh ſon to Roger de Bellemont, by the Conqueror made Earl of Warwick, the country of Gower. But Barnard Newmarch gave the people of Wales ſome ſmall ſatisfaction and content, by marrying Neſt, the daughter alſo of Neſt, daughter to Lhewelyn ap Gruffydh Prince of Wales, by whom he had iſſue, a ſon called Mahael. This worthy gentleman being legally to ſucceed his father in the lordſhip of Brecknock, was afterwards diſinherited by the malice and baſeneſs of his own unnatural mother. The occaſion was thus, Neſt happening to fall in admiration of a certain knight, with whom ſhe had more then ordinary familiarity, even beyond what ſhe expreſt to her own

huſband;

husband; Mahael perceiving her diffolute and loofe behaviour, counfelled her to take care of her fame and reputation, and to leave off that fcandalous liberty which fhe took : and afterwards meeting cafually her gallant coming from her, fought and grievoufly wounded him. Upon this Neft to be revenged upon her fon, went to Henry the firft, king of England, and in his prefence took her corporal oath, that her fon Mahael was illegitimate, and not begot by Barnard Newmarch her hufband, but another perfon; by virtue of which oath or rather perjury, Mahael was difinherited, and his fifter, whom her mother attefted to be legitimate, was beftowed by the king upon Milo, the fon of Walter Conftable, afterward Earl of Hereford, who in right of his wife enjoyed the whole eftate of Barnard Newmarch lord of Brecknock. Of this Milo it is reported, that telling King Henry of a ftrange accident which had occurred to him by Lhyn Savathan in Wales, where the birds upon the pond at the paffing by of Gruffydh the fon of Rhys ap Theodor, feemed by their chirping to be in a manner overjoyed; the king replied, It was not fo wonderful; for although, fays he, manifeftly we have violently and injurioufly oppreffed that nation, yet it is known, that they are the lawful and original inheritors of that country.

But whilft the Normans were thus carving for themfelves in Glamorgan and Brecknock, Cadogan ap Blethyn ap Confyn towards the end of April entered into Dyved, and having ravaged and deftroyed the country, returned back. But within eight weeks after, there fucceeded him a more fatal enemy; for the Normans landing in Dyved and Cardigan, began to fortify themfelves in caftles and other ftrong places, and to inhabit the country upon the fea-fhore, which before was not in their poffeffion. Indeed the Normans having by the connivance of the Conqueror already got into their hands all the beft eftates in England, began now to fpy out the commodities of Wales; and perceiving moreover how bravely Robert Fitzhamon and Barnard Newmarch had fped there, thought
they

they might as well expect the like fortune. Wherefore having obtained a grant from King William (who readily confented to their requeft, becaufe by this means he killed two birds with one ftone, procured to himfelf their utmoft fervice upon occafion, and withal provided for them without any charge to himfelf) they came to Wales, and fo entered upon the eftates appointed them by the king, which they held of him by knight-fervice, having firft done homage and fworn fealty for the fame. Roger Montgomery Earl of Arundel did homage for the lordfhips of Powis and Cardigan; Hugh Lupus Earl of Chefter for Tegengl and Ryfonioc, together with all the land lying upon the fea-fhore to the river Conwey; Arnulph a younger fon of Roger Montgomery for Dyved; Barnard Newmarch for Brecknock; Ralph Mortimer for Eluel; Hugh de Lacy for the land of Ewyas; Euftace Omer for Mold and Hapredale; and feveral others did the like homage for other lands. But Roger Montgomery, who by the Conqueror was created Earl of Arundel and Shrewfbury, entered in an hoftile manner into Powis-land, and having won the caftle and town of Baldwyn, fortified it in his own right, and called it Montgomery after his own name. King William of England was now in Normandy, and bufily engaged in a war againft his brother Robert; by the advantage of whofe abfence, Gruffydh ap Conan Prince of North Wales, and Cadogan ap Blethyn, who now ruled in South Wales, with joint force entered into Cardigan and flew a great number of Normans, whofe pride and exceffive cruelties towards the Welch, were altogether intolerable. But after fufficient execution there, being returned home, the Normans fent for more aid from England; which being arrived, they thought to make a private in-road into North Wales, and fo to be revenged upon the Welch. But their defign being happily difcovered to Cadogan, he drew up his forces to meet them, and then unexpectedly fetting upon them in the foreft of Yfpys, after a very warm refiftment of the Normans fide, forced them to retire by flight, and then triumphantly marching through Cardigan and

I 3 Dyved,

Dyved, he deſtroyed all the caſtles and fortifications, in the country, beſides Pembrock and Rydcors, which proved too-ſtrong, and impregnable.

A. D. 1093. The next year the Normans who inhabited the country of Glamorgan fell upon and deſtroyed the countries of Gwyr, Kidwely, and Yſtrad Tywy, which they harraſſed in ſuch a cruel manner, that they left them bare of any people to inhabit. And to increaſe as it was thought, the miſeries of the Welch, King William Rufus being informed of the great ſlaughter which Gruffydh ap Conan, and the ſons of Blethyn ap Confyn had lately committed upon the Engliſh, as well within Cheſhire, Shropſhire, Worceſterſhire, and Herefordſhire, as within Wales; entered the country at Montgomery, which place the Welch having ſome-time ſince demoliſhed, King William lately rebuilt. But the Welch kept all the paſſages through the woods and rivers, and all other ſtreights ſo cloſe, that the King could effect nothing conſiderable againſt them; and therefore when he perceived that his labour was but loſt, in continuing in thoſe parts, he forthwith de-camped, and returned with no great honour back to 1094. England. But this retreat of King William was not altogether ſo favourable to the intereſt of the Welch, as the death of William Fitz-Baldwyn, who was owner of the caſtle of Rydcors, and did the greateſt miſ-chief and hurt to the South Wales men of any other. He being dead, the garriſon of Rydcors which was wont to keep the Welch in continual awe, forſook that place, and by that means gave opportunity to the inhabitants of Gwyr, Brecknock, Gwent, and Gwentlhwc, to ſhake off that intoleraule yoke the Nor-mans forced upon them, who after they had robbed them of their lands, kept them in perpetual ſubjection. But now William Fitz Baldwyn being dead, and the garriſon of Rydcors ſcattered, they ventured to lay violent hands upon the Normans, who thought them-ſelves free from all fear; and prevailed ſo ſucceſsfully, that they drove them all out of the country, and re-covered their own antient eſtates. But the Normans liked that country ſo well, that they were reſolved not

to

.to be fo eafily befooled out of what they had with a
great deal of pains and danger once poffeffed; and
therefore having drawn a great number of Englifh and
Normans to their aid, they were defirous to venture
another touch with the Welch, and to return if poffible, to their once acquired habitations.   But the
Welch fo abhorred their pride and tyrannical dominion
over them when they were mafters, that they were refolved not to be fubject to fuch tyrants again; and
therefore they boldly met them at a place called Celly
Iarfawc, and fet upon them fo manfully, the very apprehenfion of fervitude whetting their fpirits, that they
put them to flight with great flaughter, and drove them
out of the country.   The Normans however were not
fo abfolutely routed with this overthrow: but like a
fly in the night which deftroys itfelf in the candle, they
muft needs covet their own deftruction; their greedinefs egging them on to venture with few, what was not
practicable to be effected by many.   Therefore on
they came as far as Brecknock, with this abfolute
vow and refolution not to leave one living thing remaining in that country.   But they fell fhort of their
policy, the people of the country being removed to
a narrow ftreight, to expect their paffing through;
whither the Normans being advanced, they fell upon
them, and killed a great number of them.   About the
fame time, Roger Montgomery Earl of Salop and
Arundel, William Fitzeauftace Earl of Glocefter,
Arnold de Harecourt, and Neal le Vicount, were flain
by the Welch between Caerdaf and Brecknock; and
Walter Eureux Earl of Sarum, Rofmer, and Manti-
lake; Hugh earl of Gourney, were wounded, who
afterwards died in Normandy.   The Normans finding
that they continually loft ground, thought it not advifeable to ftay any longer; and therefore having
placed fufficient garrifons in thofe caftles which they
-had formerly built, they returned with what fpeed
they could to England.   But all the hafte they did
make, could not fecure them from the fury of the
Welch; for Gruffydh and Ifor, the fons of Ednerth

ap Cadogan, expected them privately at a place called Aberlhech, where falling unexpectedly upon them; they flew the greatest part of their number, the rest narrowly escaping safe to England. But the Norman garrisons which were left behind, defended themselves with a great deal of bravery, till at last, finding no prospect of relief, they were forced for their own safety to deliver them up to the Welch, who from that time, became again proprietors of those places which the Normans had dispossed them from. And this encouraged the Welch to undertake other things against the English; for immediately after this, certain of the nobility of North-Wales, Uchthed the son of Edwyn ap Grono by name, together with Howel ap Grono, and the sons of Cadogan ap Blethyn of Powys-land, passed by Cardigan into Dyved (which country King William had given to Arnulph son to Roger Montgomery, who had built thereon the castle of Pembrock, and appointed Gerald de Windsore governour of the same) and destroying all the country with fire and sword, excepting Pembrock castle, which was impregnable, they returned home with a great deal of booty. In recompence of this, when the lords of North-Wales were returned, Gerald issued out of the castle, and spoiled all the country about S. Davids; and after he had got sufficient plunder, and taken divers prisoners returned back into the castle.

A. D. 1095.   The year following, King William returned from Normandy, and having heard how that the Welch had cut off a great number of his subjects in Wales, gathered all his power together, and with great pomp and ostentation entered the marshes, resolving utterly to eradicate the rebellious and implacable humour of the Welch nation. But after all this boast and seeming resolution, he durst venture no farther than the marshes, where having built some few castles, he returned with no greater honour than he came. But the next Spring, Hugh de Montgomery earl of Arundel and Salop, by the Welch
named

1096.

named Hugh Goch, and Hugh Fras, or the Fat, Earl of Chester, being invited by some disaffected Welch lords, came into North-Wales with a very great army. Prince Gruffydh ap Conan, and Cadogan ap Blethyn, perceiving themselves to be too weak to oppose so numerous an army, and what was worse, being very suspicious of the fidelity and honesty of their own forces, thought it their best way to take the hills and mountains for their safety, where they were like to remain most secure from the enemy. Then the English army marched towards Anglesey, and being come over against the island, they built the castle of Aberlhiennawc. But Gruffydh and Cadogan could no longer endure to see their country over-run by the English, and therefore they descended from the mountains, and came to Anglesey, thinking, with what succours they should receive from Ireland, of which they were disappointed, to be able to defend the island from any attempt that should be made upon it. And now the whole reason, and the occasion of the English coming to Wales was discovered; for Owen ap Edwyn, the Prince's chiefest counsellor, whose daughter Gruffydh had married (having himself also married Everyth the daughter of Confyn, aunt to Cadogan) upon some private grudge or other, called in the English into Wales, and at this time openly joined his forces with theirs, and led the whole army over into Anglesey. Gruffydh and Cadogan finding how they were betrayed by their dearest friend, as they thought; for fear of farther treachery, judged it prudent to sail privately for Ireland; after whose departure, the English fell cruelly to work, destroying all they could come at, without any respect to either age or sex.

And whilst the English continued in Anglesey, Magnus the son of Harold, lately King of England, came over with a great fleet, intending to lay faster hold upon that kingdom, than his father had done, and to recover the same to himself. But whilst he steered his course thitherward, he was driven by contrary winds to the coasts of Anglesey, where he would fain

have

have landed, had not the English army kept him off. But in this skirmish Magnus accidentally wounded Hugh Earl of Salop with an arrow in the face, whereof he died; and then of a sudden both armies relinquished the island, the English returning to England, appointing Owen ap Edwyn, who invited them over, prince of the country. But Owen did not enjoy the principality long; for in the beginning of the following spring, Gruffydh ap Conan and Cadogan ap Blethyn returned from Ireland, and having concluded a peace with the Normans, for some part of their lands in Wales; Gruffydh remained in Anglesey, and Cadogan had Cardigan, with part of Powis. But though Cadogan recovered his estate, yet in a little while after he lost his son Lhewelyn, who was treacherously murdered by the men of Brecnock: at which time also died Rythmarch archbishop of S. David's, the son of Sulien, being in the forty-third year of his age; a man of the greatest piety, wisdom, and learning, as had flourished a long time in Wales, excepting his father, under whose tutelage he was educated. The year following, King William Rufus, as he was hunting in the new forrest, was accidentally slain with an arrow, which one Walter Tyrrel shot at a stag; and his eldest brother being then engaged in the holy war, Henry his younger brother, whom in his life-time he had nominated his successor, was crowned in his stead. The same year, Hugh Earl of Chester, Grono ap Cadogan, and Gwyn ap Gruffydh departed this life.

About two years after, a rebellion broke out in England; Robert de Belesmo, the son of Roger de Montgomery Earl of Salop, and Arnulph his brother Earl of Pembrock, took up arms against king Henry; which he being informed of, sent them a very gracious message to come before him, and declare their grievances, and the reason of their rising up in arms against his Majesty. But the Earls instead of appearing in person, sent him slight and frivolous excuses, and in the mean while made all necessary preparations for the war, both by raising of forces, and fortifying

A. D. 1097

1098.

1100.

fortifying their castles and strong holds. And to strengthen themselves the more, they sent rich presents, and made large promises to Iorwerth, Cadogan, and Meredith, the sons of Blethyn ap Confyn; for to bring them to their side. Robert fortified four castles, namely, Arundel, Tekinhil, Shrewsbury, and Brugge; which last, by reason that Robert built it without the consent of the king, was the chief occasion of this war; and Arnulph fortified his castle at Pembrock. After this, they entered in an hostile manner into the territories of the king of England, wasting and destroying all before them. And to augment their strength, Arnulph sent Gerald his steward, to Murkart King of Ireland, desiring his daughter in wedlock; which was easily granted, with the promise too of great succours and large supplies. King Henry, to put a stop to their bold adventures, marched in person against them; and laying siege to the castle of Arundel, won it without any great opposition; and quickly afterwards the castle of Tekinhill; but that of Brugge, by reason of the situation of the place, and the depth of the ditch about it, seemed to require longer time and harder service; and therefore King Henry was advised to send privately to Iorwerth ap Blethyn, promising him great rewards if he forsook the earl's part, and came over to him; urging to him, what mischief Roger, earl Robert's father, and his brother Hugh, had continually done to the Welch-men. And to make him the more willing to accept of his proposals, he promised to give him all such lands as the earl and his brother had in Wales, without either tribute or homage; which was a part of Powys, Cardigan, and half Dyfed; the other part being in the possession of William Fitz-Baldwyn. Iorwerth receiving these offers, accepted of them very gladly, and then coming to the king, he sent all his forces to earl Robert's lands, who having received very strict orders, destroyed without mercy every thing they met with; and what made the spoil the greater, earl Robert upon his rebelling against King Henry, had caused his people to con-

vey

vey all their goods to Wales, for fear of the Englifh;
not thinking how his father's memory founded a-
mong the Welch. But when the News of Iorwerth's revolt reached the ears of the earl, Cadogan and Meredith, Iorwerth's brothers; their
fpirits began to faint, as defpairing any longer to
oppofe the king, fince Iorwerth, who was the perfon of greateft ftrength in Wales, had left and forfaken them. Arnulph was gone to Ireland to fetch
home his wife, and to bring over what fuccour his
father-in-law, King Murkart, could afford to fend
him; but he not coming in time, fome other method
was to be tried, how to get fome aid againft the
Englifh. A little before this rebellion broke out,
Magnus, Harold's fon, landed the fecond time in the
ifle of Anglefey, and being kindly received by Gruffydh ap Conan, he had leave to cut down what timber he had need for; and fo returning to the Ifle of
Man, which he had got by conqueft, he built there
three caftles, and then fent to Ireland to have the
daughter of Murkart in marriage to his fon, which
being obtained, he created him king of Man, earl
Robert hearing this, fent to Magnus for aid againft
king Henry; but receiving none, he thought it now
high time to look to his own fafety; and therefore
he fent to the king, requefting that he might quietly
depart the kingdom, in cafe he fhould lay down his
arms; which the king having granted, he failed to
Normandy. And then king Henry fent an exprefs
to his brother Arnulph, requiring him either to
follow his brother out of the kingdom, or to deliver
himfelf up to his mercy; and fo Arnulph went over
alfo for Normandy. When the king was returned
to London, Iorwerth took his brother Meredith prifoner, and committed him to the king's cuftody;
his other brother Cadogan having reconciled himfelf
beforehand, to whom Iorwerth gave Cardigan, with
a part of Powys. Then Iorwerth went to London,
to put the king in mind of his promife, and the fervice he had done him againft earl Robert; but the
king finding now all matters at quiet, was deaf to
                                          all

rall fuch remembrances, and inftead of promifing
what he had once voluntarily propofed, againft all
rules of equity and gratitude, he took away Dyfed
from Iorwerth, and gave it to a knight of his own,
called Saer; and Stratywy Cydwely, and Gwyr he
beftowed upon Howel ap Grono, and fent Iorwerth
away more empty than he came: nor was this fufficient reward for his former fervices; but the next
year King Henry muft fend fome of his counfel A. D. 1101.
to Shrewfbury, and cite Iorwerth to appear there,
under pretence of confulting about the king's bufinefs and affairs of thofe parts. But the plot was
laid deeper; and when without any fufpicion of
treachery he made his appearance, he was furprizedly
attainted of high treafon, and then contrary to all
right and juftice actually condemned to perpetual imprifonment; the true reafon of this unparalleled
feverity being, the king feared his ftrength, and
was apprehenfive that he would revenge the wrong
and affront he received at his hands. And indeed,
well had he reafon to fear that, when he fo ungratefully treated him, whofe fervice he had experienced
to be fo greatly advantageous to him. But the policy of Princes is unaccountable; and whether to
value an eminent perfon for his fervice, or to fear
him for his greatnefs, is a fubject that frequently
difturbs their moft fettled confiderations. But the
noblemen that were at this time fent by the king
to Shrewfbury, were Richard de Belmerfh, who being
chief agent about Roger Montgomery earl of Salop,
was prefered to the bifhoprick of London, and afterwards appointed by this king, to be warden of the
marfhes, and governour of the county of Salop.
With him were joined in company, Walter Conftable,
the father of Milo, earl of Hereford, and Rayner the
king's lieutenant in the county of Salop. About
this time, as Bale writes, the church of Menevia or
S. Davids, began to be fubject to the fee of Canterbury, being always afore the metropolitan church of
all Wales.

Shortly

A.D.1102. Shortly after this, Owen ap Edwyn, who had been
author of no small mischief and disturbance to the
Welch, in moving the English against his natural
prince, and son-in-law Gruffydh ap Conan, departed this life, after a tedious and miserable sickness;
of which he was so much the less pitied, by how
much he had proved an enemy and a traitor to his
native country. He was the son of Grono, by his
wife Edelflede the widow of Edmund, surnamed
Ironside, king of England; and had the title of
Iegengl; though the English, when they had compelled Gruffydh ap Conan to flee to Ireland for safety,
constituted him prince of all North Wales. After
his death, Richard Fitz-Baldwyn laid siege to, and
took the castle of Rydcors, and forcibly drove Howel
ap Grono, to whom king Henry had committed the
custody of it, out of the country. But Howel quickly returned; and with a high spirit of revenge, began to destroy and burn whatsoever he could meet
with, and then meeting a party of the Normans in
their return homewards, he fell upon the flank of them
with a very considerable slaughter; and so brought all
the country to his subjection, excepting some few
garrisons and castles which would not surrender to
him. The same time King Henry took away from
Saer the government of Dyfed, which formerly was
Iorwerth ap Blethyn's, and bestowed it upon Gerald,
who had been some time earl Arnulph's steward in
those parts; and therefore by reason of his knowledge of the country, was in all probability best able
to take upon him the management of it. But the
Normans in Rydcors castle being sensible that they
were not able to effect any thing against Howel ap
Grono in open field, after their accustomed manner,
began to put that in execution by treachery, which
they could not compass by force of arms. And
how to make Howel a sacrifice to those Normans he
had lately slain, they could find no safer way than by
corrupting one Gwgan ap Meyric, a man in great
favour and esteem with Howel, upon the account
chiefly that one of his children was nursed by Gwgan's
                                        wife.

wife. This ungrateful villain, to carry on his wicked
intrigue the more unfufpected, gave Howel a very
earneft invitation to his houfe to a merriment, where,
without any fufpicion of treachery, being come, he
was welcomed with all the feeming affection and
kindnefs imaginable. But no fooner was he fettled, A. D. 1103.
but Gwgan gave notice thereof to the Norman garrifons; and therefore by break of day they entered the
town, and coming about the houfe where Howel
lay in bed, they prefently gave a great fhout. Howel
hearing the noife, fufpected fomething of mifchief,
and therefore leaping in all hafte out of bed, he
made to his weapons, but could not find them, by
reafon that Gwgan had conveyed them away whilft
he was afleep. And now being affured of treachery
in the cafe, and finding that his men had fled for
their lives, he endeavoured all he could to make his
efcape; but Gwgan and his company were too quick
for him; and fo being fecured, they ftrangled him,
and delivered his body to the Normans, who having
cut off his head, conveyed it to the caftle of Rydcors.
This moft villainous murder, fo barbaroufly committed upon the king's lieutenant, was not in the leaft
taken notice of; for King Henry was fo unreafonably
prejudiced in favour of the Normans, that whatever
mifdemeanor, be it of never fo high a nature, was
by them committed, it was prefently winked at,
and let fall to the ground; whereas, if the Welch
trefpaffed but againft the leaft injunction of the king's
laws, they were moft feverely punifhed: which was
the caufe that they afterwards ftood up againft the
king in their own defence, being by experience
affured, that he minded nothing more than their utter
deftruction.

About this time Anfelm, archbifhop of Canterbury,
convened a fynod at London, wherein among other
injunctions then decreed, the celibacy of the clergy
was enjoined; marriage being before ever allowed
of in Britain, to them in holy orders. But this
new injunction created a great deal of heat and
animofity among the clergy, fome approving of it

as reasonable, and orthodoxical; others condemning it, as an innovation, and contrary to the plain letter of scripture. But during these disputes between the clergy, king Henry being now in the fifth year of his reign, failed over with a great army into Normandy, where his brother Robert, together with Robert de Belefmo, Arnulph, and William earl of Mortaign, gave him battle; but the king having obtained the victory, took the duke his brother, with William of Mortaign, prisoners; and carrying them into England, he caused first his brother Robert's eyes to be plucked out, and then condemned them both to perpetual imprisonment in the castle of Cardyff.

A.D. 1104. About the same time Meyric and Gruffydh, the sons of Trahaern ap Caradoc were both slain by the means of Owen ap Cadogan ap Blethyn; whose uncle Meredith ap Blethyn, who had been prisoner for a long time in England, now broke open the prison, wherein he was very narrowly confined; and returning to his own country, had his estate restored, which afterwards he quietly enjoyed.

1105. The next year a very dismal and calamitous accident happening in the Low-countries, proved very incommodious and prejudicial to the Welch; for a great part of Flanders being drowned by the overflowing of the sea, the inhabitants were compelled to seek for some other country to dwell in, their own being now covered with water. And therefore a great many being come over to England, they requested of King Henry to assign them some part of his kingdom which was empty and void of inhabitants, where they might settle and plant themselves. The king taking advantage of this charitable opportunity, and being in a manner assured, that these Flemings would be a considerable thorn in the side of the Welch, bestowed upon them very liberally what was not justly in his power to give; and appointed them the country of Ros, in Dyfed or West-Wales, where they continue to this day. But Gerald the king's lieutenant in those parts, was resolved to be afore-hand with them, and rebuilt the castle of

Pembrock,

Pembrock, in a place called Congarth Fechan; whither he removed his family and all his goods. But here a very unfortunate accident happened to him; for Cadwgan ap Blethyn having prepared a sumptuous feast in the Christmas, invited all the lords to his country-house in Dyfed, and among the rest his son Owen, who lived in Powis. This young gentleman being at his father's house, and hearing Nest the wife of Gerald universally praised for her incomparable beauty, was so smitten with the rumour that went abroad of her, that by all means he must see the lady, who was by all so much admired. And forasmuch as Gwladys, wife to Rhys ap Theodore, and mother to Nest, was the daughter of Rywalhon ap Confyn, cousin-german to Cadwgan his father; under pretence of friendship and relation, he made bold to pay her a visit. But finding the truth far to surpass the fame that went of her, he returned home so inflamed with her charms, that not being able to keep the mastery over himself, he went back again the same night, and being attended by a company of wild, head-strong youths, they privily entered into the castle, and encompassing the chamber about, where Gerald and his wife lay, they set the house on fire. Gerald hearing a noise, would fain go out to know the meaning of such unseasonable disturbance; but his wife fearing some treachery, persuaded him to make as private an escape as he could: and then pulling up a board in the privy, let him go that way. Then returning to her chamber, she would fain assure those notorious youths, that there was no body besides herself and children there; but this being not satisfactory, they forcibly broke in, and having searched every the most private corner, and not finding Gerald, they took his wife and two sons, with a son and a daughter born by a concubine, and carried them away to Powis; having first set fire to the castle, and destroyed the country as they went along, Cadwgan, Owen's father, hearing of what outrageous crime his son had committed, was exceedingly concerned and sorry, chiefly because hereby he was like to incur King Henry's great displeasure; and therefore

K   he

he went with all speed to Powis, and desired his son
with all intreaties, to send home to Gerald his wife and
children, with whatever else he had taken away from
him. But Owen was so amourously inexorable with
respect to the woman, that he would by no means part
with her ; however, upon her request, he was willing to restore Gerald his children back again, which
forthwith he performed. But when Richard bishop
of London, whom King Henry had constituted Warden of the Marches, being now at Shrewsbury, heard
of this, he sent for Ithel and Madoc the sons of Ryryd
ap Blethyn, persons of great power and interest in
Wales, promising them very considerable rewards, besides the government of the whole country, in case they
could bring Owen and his father Cadwgan, either
dead or alive, to him, that he might revenge that
heinous affront which they had done to the king of
England. With them he joined Lhywarch the son of
Trahaern ap Caradoc, whose two brethren Owen had
slain, and Uchtryd the son of Edwyn ; which four undertook to answer effectually the bishop's proposal to
them. But when they had united their forces, and began in an hostile manner to destroy the country as they
passed along ; Uchtryd sent private notice before him,
requiring all who were any way desirous of their own
safety, to come to him ; because no quarters was to be
given to any that was found in the country. The people being thus so opportunely forewarned, began to
bethink with themselves how they might best avoid so
eminent a danger; and thereupon some fled to Arustly,
others to Melienyth, some to Stradtywy, and some to
Dyfed ; but in this latter place they met with very
cold welcome ; for Gerald, who was then very busy
in exercising revenge upon that country, falling in
among them, cut off a considerable number of them.
The like fate befel them who escaped to Arustly and
Melienyth ; for Walter bishop of Hereford having
raised an army in defence of the town of Caermyrdhyn,
before he could come thither, accidentally met with
these stragling fugitives, and knowing to what country
they belonged to, without any further ceremony, he
fell

fell upon them, and put moft of them to the fword.
But they who fled to Stradtywy, were gently received
by Meredith ap Rytherch, and fuch as reforted to
Uchtryd, were kindly entertained by him; and fo he
marched with the reft of his confederates to Rydcors
caftle; it being the general opinion, that it was beft
to enter the country by night, and to take Cadwgan
and Owen his fon by furprife. But Uchtryd reflecting
upon the difficulty of the country, and how eafily they
might be entrapped by an ambufcade, diffuaded them
from any fuch nocturnal undertakings; and told them,
that it was far more advifeable to enter the country in
good order, when the light gave the foldiers opportunity to keep and obferve their ranks. But whilft they
were thus confidering of the moft effectual way to carry on their purpofe, Owen got a fhip at Aberdyfi,
bound for Ireland; and efcaping thither, avoided the
narrow fearch that was the following day made for
them. But when neither father nor fon could be found,
all the fault was laid upon Uchtryd, who had diffuaded
them from falling upon the caftle unexpectedly; and
therefore all they could do, fince their efcape, was to
burn and deftroy the country; which they did effectually, excepting the two fanctuaries of Lhanpadarn
and Lhandewi Brefi; out of which however they took
feveral perfons who had efcaped thither, and carried
them away prifoners to their feveral countries. But
Owen, with them who were acceffary to the burning
of Rydcors caftle, being fled into Ireland, defired the
umbrage and protection of King Murcart; who received him very gladly, upon the account of their former acquaintance; for Owen, during the war betwixt
the Earls of Arundel and Chefter, and the Welch, had
fled to King Murcart, and brought him very rich
prefents from Wales, Cadwgan all this while lay privately in Powis; but thinking it impoffible to continue there long undifcovered, he adjudged it his wifer
way to fend to King Henry, and to declare his innocency and abhorrence of that fact which his fon had
committed. The King was eafily perfuaded that the
old man was guiltlefs, and wholly ignorant of his

fon's crime; and therefore he gave him permiffion to
remain in the country, and to enjoy the town and
lands he received by his wife, who was the daughter
of a Norman lord, called Pygot de Say. But his
lands in Powis were otherwife diftributed; for his nephews Madoc and Ithel, finding what circumftances
their uncle Cadwgan lay under, upon the account of
his fon Owen; they divided betwixt themfelves fuch
lands as he and his fon poffeffed in Powis, though afterwards they could never agree about the equal diftribution of it. To counterbalance this, Cadwgan
made fuch friends to the King of England, that upon paying the fine of 100 l. he had a grant of all his
lands in Cardigan, and a power to recall all the inhabitants, who had rubbed off upon the publication of
the King's late order, That no Welchman or Norman
fhould dwell in Cardigan. Upon information of this
grant to Cadwgan, feveral of them that retired to Ireland returned again privately to Wales, and lurkingly
remained with their friends; but Owen durft not appear in Cardigan, by reafon that his father had received
that country from King Henry, upon condition that
he would never entertain nor receive his fon, nor by
any means fuccour him either with men or money.
Neverthelefs, Owen came to Powis, and would fain
be reconciled to the king, and make an atonement for
his late mifdemeanor; but he could find no body that
would venture to fpeak in his behalf, nor make the
king acquainted with his defire and willingnefs to fubmit. And thus being hopelefs and full of defpair, he
could not poffibly divine which way to turn himfelf; till
at laft, a very unexpected opportunity offered him
means and occafion to oppofe the Englifh. The matter
was this, there happened a difference betwixt Madoc
ap Ryryd and the bifhop of London, lieutenant of the
marches of Wales, about certain Englifh felons, who
being under the protection of Madoc, he would not
reftore at the bifhop's requeft. The bifhop being
much offended at Madawc's denial, threatened him
very feverely; and therefore to make all poffible
preparations

preparations againſt an enſuing ſtorm, Madawc ſent to Owen, who heretofore was his greateſt enemy, deſiring his help againſt the biſhop ; and by this means being reconciled, they took their mutual oaths not to betray each other, and that neither ſhould make a ſeparate agreement with the Engliſh without the knowledge and approbation of the other. And ſo uniting their power, they ſpoiled and ravaged all the country about them, deſtroying whatever they could meet with which belonged to thoſe they had no kindneſs or affection for, without the leaſt diſtinction of Engliſh or Welch.

Iorwerth ap Blethyn had been very ūnjuſtly detained A.D. 1107. in priſon all this time ; and now King Henry calling to mind what hardſhip he laboured under, and that he committed him to cuſtody upon no pretence of reaſon, ſent to know of him, what he was willing to pay for his liberty, Iorwerth being now almoſt ready to ſink under a fatigue of ſo long impriſonment, was glad to give any thing he was able, to obtain that which he had ſo long in vain hoped for; and therefore he promiſed either 300 l. in ſpecie, or to the value of it in cattle and horſes ; for the payment of which, Iorwerth and Ithel the ſons of his brother Ryryd were delivered for pledges. Then the king releaſed him out of priſon, and reſtored him all his lands which were taken from him ; and of the due for his liberty, the king beſtowed 10 l. upon Henry, Cadwgan's ſon by the daughter of Pygot de Say the Norman. Owen and Madawc all this while committed all the waſte and deſtruction poſſible, and cruelly annoyed both the Engliſh and Normans; and always withdrew and retired to Iorwerth's eſtate, which ſo troubled him, by reaſon of the king's ſtrict orders, not to permit Owen to come to his or Cadwgan's territories, that at length he ſent to them this poſitive and peremptory rebuke ;
" Since it hath pleaſed God to place us in the midſt
" of our enemies, and to deliver us into their hands ;
" and hath ſo far weakened us, as that we are not able
" to do any thing by our own ſtrength ; and your fa-
" ther Cadwgan and myſelf, are particularly com-

K 3   " manded

" manded, under penalty of forfeiting our lands and
" eftates, not to afford you any fuccour or refuge during
" thefe your rebellious practices; therefore as a friend
" I intreat you, command you as a lord, and defire
" you as a kinfman, that you come no more to mine
" or your father Cadwgan's territories."

Owen and Madawc receiving fuch a prefumptuous
meffage, were the more enraged, and in the way of a
malignant retribution, did more frequently than heretofore, fhelter themfelves in Iorwerth's country; in fo much,
that at laft, fince that they would neither by threats
nor intreaties defift from their wonted courfes, he was
forced to gather his power, and drive them out by force
of arms. Being chafed out hence, they made in-roads
into Uchtryd's country in Merionethfhire; but Uchtryd's fons, being then in Cyveilioc, hearing of it, they
fent to the people of the country, with pofitive orders
to oppofe and refift any offer they would make to enter the country. The people, though wanting a fkilful commander, were refolved to do as much as lay in
their power; and fo meeting with them by the way,
they fet upon them fo furioufly, that Owen and Madawc, though after a brave defence, were forced to bear
back, and to take the heels; Owen to Cardigan to his
father Cadwgan, and Madawc to Powis. Yet all this
misfortune could not fupprefs the reftlefs fpirit of
Owen; for as foon as he could rally together his fcattered troops, he made divers inroads into Dyfed, and
carrying away feveral perfons to the fhips, that they
came in from Ireland; he firft ranfomed them, and
then lifting them under his own command, made fuch
addition to his army, that he ventured to fet upon a
town in Dyfed belonging to the Flemings, and having
rafed it to the ground, he returned to Cardigan; having
no regard to what inconveniency might befal his father
from the king of England, upon this account: which
a little afterwards unhappily fell out. For it happened
that fome of Owen's men having had intelligence, that
a certain bifhop called William de Brabant, was upon
his journey through that country to the court of England, laid wait for his coming; who without any ap-
                                        prehenfion

prehenfion of treachery, paffing through the country was unexpectedly flain, he and all his retinue. Iorwerth and Cadwgan were then at court, to fpeak with King Henry, concerning certain bufinefs of their own; but whilft they difcourfed, the king, in comes a Fleming, that was a brother to the deceafed bifhop, and with a very loud exclamation, complained how that Owen, Cadwgan's fon had flain his brother and the reft of his company; and that he was fuccoured and entertained in Cardigan's country. King Henry hearing this, was wrathfully difpleafed at fuch cruel barbarity, that a perfon of that quality and profeffion fhould be fo treacheroufly murdered; and therefore he asked Cadwgan what he could fay to the matter; who anfwered, that what had fo unhappily fell out, was done without the leaft of his knowledge or approbation, and therefore defired his Majefty to impute all the blame and guilt of that unfortunate action to his fon Owen. But King Henry was fo far from being fatisfied with this reply, that he told Cadwgan in a violent paffion, That fince he could not keep his fon fo, but that he was aided and continually entertained in his country, he would beftow it upon another perfon, who was better able and more willing to keep him out; and would allow him a maintenance upon his own proper charges, upon thefe conditions, that he fhould not enter into Wales any more, without his farther orders; and fo granting him twenty days for the ordering his affairs, he gave him liberty to retire to any part of his dominions, excepting Wales. When Owen and Madawc were informed how Cadwgan was treated by the king of England, and that Cardigan, which was their chiefeft place of refuge, was to be given to another perfon, they thought that their condition by this time was defperate, and that they had not better ftay any longer in Britain; and therefore with all fpeed they took fhipping for Ireland, where they were fure to be honourably entertained by King Murkart. Then King Henry fent for Gilbert Strongbow, Earl of Strygill, a perfon of noted worth

K *2*　and

and valour, and one who had often fued to the king for
to grant him fome lands in Wales, and beftowed upon
him all the lands and inheritance of Cadwgan ap Blethyn, in cafe he could conquer and bring the country
under. Gilbert very thankfully accepted of the propofal, and having drawn together all the forces he
was able to raife, he paffed to Wales, and being come
to Cardigan, without the leaft trouble or oppofition,
he reduced the whole country to his fubjection. The
firft thing he did, was the beft he could to fecure
himfelf in this new-purchafed inheritance; in order
to which, he erected two caftles, one upon the frontiers of North Wales, upon the mouth of the river
Yftwyth, a mile diftant from Lhanbadarn; the other
towards Dyfed, upon the river Teifi, at a place called
Dyngerant; where, as fome think, Roger Montgomery had fome time before laid the foundation of Cilgarran caftle.

Owen and Madawc were all this while in Ireland;
but this latter being at length tired with the country,
and not willing to endure the manners and cuftoms of
the Irifh, came over for Wales, and paffed to the country of his uncle Iorwerth. Iorwerth being acquainted
with his arrival was feaful to fuffer the fame fate with
his brother Cadwgan, by winking at his being there;
and therefore without any regard to relation or confanguinity, he prefently iffued out a proclamation, forbidding any of his fubjects under a great penalty to
receive him, but that they fhould account him an
open enemy to their country, and endeavour all they
could to fecure him, and to bring him prifoner before him. When Madawc underftood this, how that
his perfon was in continual danger whilft he remained
there; having drawn to him all the out-laws and villains in the country, he kept in the rocks and mountains devifing all the ways and means he could to
be revenged upon Iorwerth; and fo made a private
league and agreement with Lhywarch ap Trahaern,
who for a long time had been a mortal enemy of
Iorwerth's. Thefe two affociates, having intelligence
that

that Iorwerth lay one night at Caereineon, gathered all
their ſtrength, and came and encompaſſed the houſe at
midnight; which when Iorwerth's ſervants perceived,
they aroſe and defended the houſe with all the might
they could; but the aſſailants at laſt putting the
houſe on fire, they were glad, as many as could, to
eſcape through the flames; the greateſt part being
forced to yield, either to the enemies ſword, or the
more conquering fire. Iorwerth ſeeing no remedy,
but that he muſt undergo the ſame fate as his men
had done, choſe rather to die in the preſence of his
enemies, with his ſword in his hand, than to commit his life to the cowardly flames; and therefore
ruſhing out with great violence, he was received upon the points of the enemies ſpears, and ſo being toſ-
ſed into the fire, he miſerably periſhed by a double
death. As ſoon as King Henry heard of his death, he
ſent for Cadwgan to him, and gave him all his brother's eſtate, being Powys-land; and promiſing his
ſon Owen his pardon, upon condition he would de-
mean himſelf quietly and loyally hereafter, willed
him to ſend for him back from Ireland. King Henry
alſo about this time, married his natural ſon Robert
to Mabil daughter and ſole heir to Robert Fitz-hamon,
lord of Glamorgan, in whoſe right this Robert became
lord of Glamorgan, being before the king created earl
of Gloceſter; by whom the caſtle of Cardaf was built.

But Madawc finding the matter nothing mended,
and that his other uncle Cadwgan, who lay under the
ſame obligation to the king of England, ruled the
country, hid himſelf in the moſt private and inac-
ceſſible places, watching only an opportunity to commit the like fact upon Cadwgan, and to murder him
by one treacherous way or another. And this he
effected in a little time; for Cadwgan having reduced
the country to ſome ſort of ſettlement and quietneſs,
and reſtored the courts of judicature, where he ſate
in perſon to adminiſter juſtice; came with the reſt of
the elders of the country to Trallwng, now Pool; and
having begun to build a caſtle, he thought to make
that the conſtant ſeat of his habitation. Madawc
under-

underſtanding his defign, laid in ambuſh for him in
his way to Trallwng; and as Cadwgan unconcernedly
paſſed by, without the leaſt fuſpicion of treachery,
he ſuddenly ſet upon him, and ſlew him, without allowing him any time either to fight or eſcape. Then
he ſent preſently a meſſage to Shrewſbury, to the biſhop
of London, the king's lieutenant in the marches, to
put him in mind of his former promiſes to him, when
he chaſed Owen out of the country; becauſe that the
biſhop bearing an inveterate enmity to Cadwgan, and
his ſon Owen, granted Madawc ſuch lands, as his
brother Ithel was poſſeſſed of. But Meredith ap Blethyn, being informed of the death of both his brothers,
went in all haſte to the king, defiring of him the lands
of Iorwerth in Powys, which he had lately granted to
Cadwgan; which the king granted him, till ſuch time
as Owen ſhould return from Ireland. Owen did not
ſtay long before he came over; and then going to
King Henry, he was honourably received, and had
all his father's eſtate reſtored to him; whereupon, in
gratitude of this ſignal favour, he voluntarily promiſed
to pay the king a confiderable fine, for the due payment of which, he gave very reſponſible pledges.
Madawc finding himſelf alone to be left in the lurch,
and that he had no ſeeming power to bear head againſt
the king, thought it alſo his wifeſt way to make what
reconciliation he could; and therefore he offered the
king a very great fine, if he ſhould peaceably enjoy
his former eſtate, promiſing withal, never to moleſt
or diſturb any one that was ſubject to the crown of
England. King Henry willing to bring all matters to
a ſettled condition, readily granted his requeſt, and
conferred upon him all he could reaſonably aſk for;
only with this proviſo, that upon his peril, he ſhould
provide for the relations of them whom he had ſo baſely
murdered.

A D. 1109.   And thus all matters being brought to a peaceable
conclufion in Wales; the next year, Robert de Belefmo,
who had been one of the chief inſtruments of theſe
Welch diſturbances, in that great rebellion, which
himſelf, with Roger de Montgomery, earl of Salop, and
his

his brother Arnulph earl of Pembroke had raifed againft the king; was taken prifoner by King Henry in Normandy, and committed to perpetual imprifonment in Warham-caftle. The year following, Mere- A.D. 1110. dith ap Blethyn detatched a confiderable party of his men, to make incurfions into the country of Lhywarch ap Trahaern ap Gwyn, who was an inveterate enemy of himfelf and Owen; by reafon that by his aid and inftigation, Madawc was encouraged to kill his uncles Iorwerth and Cadwgan. Thefe men as they paffed through Madawc's country, met a perfon in the night-time who belonged to Madawc; who being afked where his mafter was, after fome pretence of ignorance, at laft through fear confeffed, that he was not far from that place. Therefore lying quietly there all night, by break of day they arofe to look out their game; and unexpectedly furprizing Madawc, they flew a great number of his men, and took himfelf prifoner; and fo carrying him to their Lord, they delivered him up, as the greateft honour of their expedition. Meredith was not a little proud of his prifoner, and therefore to ingratiate himfelf the more with his nephew Owen, he committed him to fafe cuftody, till he was fent for; who coming thither ftreight, Meredith delivered Madawc up to him. Owen, though he had the greateft reafon for the moft cruel revenge, by reafon that both his father and uncle were bafely murdered by this Madawc, would not put him to death, remembering the intimate friendfhip and oaths that had paffed betwixt them; but however, to fecure him from any future mifchief he might practife, he pulled out his eyes, and then fet him at liberty. But leaft he fhould be capable of any revenge, by reafon of his eftate and ftrength in the country, Meredith and Owen thought fit to divide his lands betwixt them; which were Caernarvon, Aberhiw, with the third part of Deuthwfyr.

These home-bred difturbances being pretty well 1111. abated, a greater ftorm arofe from abroad; for the next year, King Henry prepared a mighty army to enter into Wales, being provoked thereto by the requeft

of

of thofe who enjoyed a great part of the Welchmens lands, but would not be fatisfied till they got all. For Gilbert Strongbow earl of Strygill, upon whom the king had beftowed Cardigan, made great complaints of Owen ap Cadwgan; declaring how that he received and entertained fuch perfons as fpoiled and robbed in his country; and Hugh earl of Chefter made the like of Gruffydh ap Conan Prince of North Wales, how that his fubjects and the men of Grono ap Owen ap Edwyn Lord of Tegengl, unreproved, wafted, and burnt the country of Chefhire; and to aggravate the matter the more, he added farther, that Gruffydh nei. ther owed any fervice, nor paid any tribute to the king. Upon thefe complaints, King Henry was fo cruelly enraged, that he fwore he would not leave one living creature remaining in North-Wales and Powys-land; but having extirpated utterly the prefent race of people, he would plant a colony of new inhabitants. And then dividing his army into three parts, he delivered one to the conduct of the Earl of Strygill, to go againft South-Wales, which comprehended the whole power of the fourth part of England and Cornwall: the next battle was defigned againft North-Wales, in which was all the ftrength of Scotland and the North, and was commanded by Alexander king of the Scots, and Hugh Earl of Chefter: the third the king led himfelf againft Powys, wherein was contained the whole ftrength of the middle part of England. Meredith ap Blethyn hearing of thefe mighty preparations, and being informed that this vaft army was defigned againft Wales, was quickly apprehenfive that the Welch were not able to make any great defence; and therefore thought it his fafeft way to provide for himfelf beforehand; and fo coming to the king, yielded himfelf up to his mercy. But Owen fearing to commit himfelf to thofe whom he knew fo greedily to covet his eftate, and whom he was affured were far more defirous to difpoffefs the Welch of their lands, than any other way to punifh them for former crimes and mifcarriages, fled to Gruffydh ap Conan to North-Wales. Upon that, king Henry converted his whole force that

way,

way, and came himself as far as Murcaftelh, and the Scotch king to Pennant Bachwy; but the people flying to the mountains, carried with them all the cattle and provifion they had; fo that the Englifh could not follow them, and as many as attempted to come at them, were either flain or wounded in the ftreights. But Alexander king of the Scots finding that nothing could poffibly be effected againft the Welch, as long as they kept the rocks and mountains, fent to Prince Gruffydh advifing him to fubmit himfelf to the king, promifing him all his intereft to obtain an honourable peace. But the prince was too well acquainted with Englifh promifes, and therefore refufed his propofals; and fo King Henry being very unwilling to return without doing fomething in this expedition, fent to Owen to forfake the prince, who was not able to defend himfelf, but was ready to ftrike a peace with the Scottifh king and the earl of Chefter. But this cunning infinuation would not take effect; for Owen was for his life as diftruftful of King Henry as Prince Gruffydh; and therefore he would hearken to no intreaties for revolting from him, who had all this while afforded him refuge, till at length his uncle Meredith, an old infinuating politician, perfuaded him, with much ado, not to forfake the king of England's propofals, who offered him all his lands without tribute, in cafe he would come to his fide; and therefore Meredith advifed him inftantly to accept of his offer, before Prince Gruffydh made a peace with the king, which if it was once done, he would be glad upon any fcore to purchafe the king's mercy. Owen being prevailed upon by fuch arguments, came to the king, who received him very gracioufly, and told him, that becaufe he believed his promife, he would not only perform that, but likewife exalt him above any of his kindred, and grant him his lands free from any payment of tribute. Prince Gruffydh perceiving how that Owen had fubmitted to the king, thought it alfo his wifeft way to fue for peace; and fo promifing the king a great fum of money, a peace was then actually agreed upon, and confirmed; which the King of England

England was the more ready to confent to, becaufe he
found it impoffible to do him any hurt, whilft he continued encamped in that place.   Some affirm, that the
fubmiffion as well of Prince Gruffydh as Owen, was
procured by the policy of Meredith ap Blethyn and the
earl of Chefter; this laft working with Gruffydh, and
affuring him that Owen had made his peace with the
king before any fuch thing was in agitation, fo that
the prince yielding fomewhat to the earl's requeft,
if Owen had gone contrary to his oath, which they
had mutually taken, not to make any peace with the
Englifh, without one anothers knowledge, feemed
to incline to a peace.   On the other hand, Meredith
going in perfon to his nephew Owen, affirmed for
truth, that the prince and the earl of Chefter were
actually agreed, and the prince was on his journey
to the king to make his fubmiffion.   And in the mean
while Meredith took efpecial care that all meffengers
betwixt the prince and Owen fhould be intercepted, and
by that means Owen wilfully fubmitted himfelf to the
king.

King Henry having thus finifhed and brought to an
end all his bufinefs in Wales, calling Owen to him,
told him, that in cafe he would go over with him to
Normandy, and there be faithful to him, he would
upon his return confirm all his promifes upon him;
and fo Owen accepting of the king's offer, went with
him to Normandy, where he behaved himfelf fo gallantly, that he was made a knight; and after his return the year following, he had all his lands and
A D. 1112. eftate confirmed unto him.   About the fame time
Griffri bifhop of St. David's died, and king Henry appointed to fucceed him one Barnard a Norman, much
againft the good-will and inclination of the Welch,
who before this time were ever ufed to elect their
own bifhop.   And this year the rumour of Gruffydh
fon to Rhys ap Theodore was fpread throughout South-
Wales, who, as the report went, for fear of the king
had been from a child brought up in Ireland, and
having come over about two years afore, paft his
time privately among his relations, particularly
with

with Gerald Steward of Pembroke his brother-in-law. And now the noise of a new prince being spread abroad, it came at last to the ears of the king of England, that a certain person appeared in Wales, who pretended to be the son of Rhys ap Theodore, late prince of South Wales, and laid claim to that principality, which was now in the king's hands. King Henry being somewhat concerned with such a report, and fearing left that this new starter should create him some greater trouble, he thought to nip him in the bud, and sent down orders to apprehend him. But Gruffydh ap Rhys being aware of the traps laid against him, sent to Gruffydh ap Conan prince of North Wales, desiring his assistance, and that he might have liberty to remain safe in his country, which Gruffydh for his father's account, readily granted, and treated him honourably. A little after, his brother Howel who was imprisoned by Ardulph Earl of Pembroke in the castle of Montgomery, where he had remained for a great while, made his escape and fled to his brother, then with Gruffydh ap Conan in North Wales. But King Henry being informed that Gruffydh ap Rhys and his brother Howel were entertained by the Prince of North Wales, sent very smooth letters to Gruffydh ap Conan, desiring to speak with him, who being come, he received him with all the tokens of honour and friendship, and bestowed upon him very rich presents, just after the Norman policy, who usually make very much of those whom they design afterwards to be serviceable to them. After some time's general discourse, King Henry came at length to the main point, and promised the prince even mountains of gold, in case he would send Gruffydh ap Rhys or his head to him, which the Prince, overcome by such fair words and large promises, promised to perform, and so returned joyfully home, big with the expectation of his future reward. But some who wished better to Gruffydh ap Rhys and his brother Howel, presently suspected the occasion of the king's message, and therefore they advised them to withdraw themselves privately for some time, till Prince Gru-

Gru's

fydh's mind be better underſtood, and whether he
had made any agreement with the king of England
to betray them to him. As ſoon as the Prince was
returned to his palace at Aberffraw, he preſently enquired for Gruffydh ap Rhys, and learning in a little
time where he was, he ſent a troop of horſe to recall
him to his court, but Gruffydh hearing of their approach, with all ſpeed made his eſcape to the church
of Aberdaron, and took ſanctuary there. But Prince
Gruffydh was ſo reſolute to make his promiſe good
to the king of England, that without any reſpect to
the religious place he had eſcaped too, he commanded the ſame meſſengers to return, and to bring
him away by force, which the clergy of the country
unanimouſly withſtood, proteſting that they would
not ſee the liberties of the church in the leaſt in-
fringed. And whilſt the clergy and the prince's officers were thus at debate, that ſame night, ſome who
had compaſſion upon the young prince, and ſeeing
how greedily his life was thirſted for, conveyed him
away out of North Wales to Straywy in South Wales.
And ſo being delivered from the treacherous and more
diſhonourable practices of the Prince of North Wales,
he was forced for the defence of his own life to bid
open defiance to the king of England, and thereupon
having raiſed all the forces which the ſhortneſs of the
opportunity would permit, he made war upon the Flemings and Normans.

A. D. 1113.   The next year, he laid ſiege to the caſtle which
ſtood over-againſt Arberth, and winning the ſame,
made it plain with the ground, and from thence
marched to Lhanymdhfry caſtle, belonging to Richard de Pwns, upon whom the King had beſtowed
Cantref Bychan, but the garriſon commanded by
Meredith ap Rytherch ap Caradoc, ſo manfully defended it, that Gruffydh after killing only ſome few
of the beſieged, and burning the out-works, was
forced to remove with no ſmall loſs of his own men.
Finding this place impregnable, he came before A-
bertawy-caſtle, which was built by Henry Beaumont
Earl

Earl of Warwick, but this proving too ftrong to be quickly furrendered, after he had burnt fome of the outward buildings, he returned to Stratywy, burning and deftroying all the country as he went along. And now his fame being fpread abroad through all the country, all the wild and head-ftrong youth, and they whofe fortunes were defperate, reforted unto him from all parts, by which means being waxed ftrong and numerous, he made in-roads into Ros and Dyfed, fpoiling and deftroying the country before him. The Normans and Flemings were cruelly enraged with thefe continual depredations, and how to remedy this mifchief, was not eafily determined ; but after a long confultation, they thought it the beft way to call together fuch Welch lords as were friends to the king of England, fuch were Owen ap Rhytherch, and Rhytherch ap Theodore, with his fons Meredith and Owen, whofe mother was Heynyth the daughter of Blethyn ap Confyn, and Owen ap Caradoc the fon of Gwenlhian another daughter of Blethyn, and Meredith ap Rhytherch. Thefe protefting their loyalty and fidelity to King Henry were defired to defend the king's caftle of Carmardhyn, and that by turns; Owen ap Caradoc the firft fortnight, and then by fucceffion by Rhytherch ap Theodore and Meredith ap Rhytherch. Owen undertook the defence of Carmardhyn caftle for the time required of him, and Blethyn ap Gadifor had committed to him the government of Abercomyn or Abercorran caftle, which appertained to Robert Courtmain. But for all thefe preparations, Gruffydh ap Rhys had a wifhful eye upon Carmardhyn, and therefore he fent out fome fpies to learn the ftrength and condition of the town, who bringing him a very kind and hopeful account, he decamped by night, and rufhing fuddenly into the town, ordered his men to make a great fhout, thereby to ftrike a great terror into thofe within. Owen ap Caradoc the governor, being furprifed with fuch an unexpected uproar, made all poffible hafte to the place where he had heard the fhouting, and thinking that his men were at his heels, fell in among the enemy ; but

L   having

having none to fupport him, his men being all fled, he was after a manful defence cut in pieces, and fo the town being taken, Gruffydh burnt every thing to the ground, excepting the caftle, which was alfo fore defaced. And then returning with a great deal of fpoil and booty to his ufual refidence at Stratywy; his forces were confiderably increafed by the acceffion of many young men, who came to him from all quarters, and thought that fortune fo profpered his arms, that no body was able to ftand before him. After this he marched to Gwyr, but William de Londres thinking it impoffible to ftand before him, forfook the caftle with all his men in all hafte, fo that when Gruffydh was come thither, he found a great deal of cattle and fpoil, and none to own them, and therefore having burnt down the caftle, he carried away every thing of value in the country. When the Cardiganfhire men heard how fortunately he fucceeded in all his attempts, and being extremely fearful, left his next expedition fhould be againft them, fent to him, defiring him, as being their near relation and countryman, to take upon him the rule and government over them. Gruffydh willingly accepted of their offer, and coming thither, was joyfully received by the chief men in the country, who were Cadifor ap Grono, Howel ap Dinerth, and Trahaern ap Ithel, which three perfons had forfaken Dyfed, by reafon that it was fo thwacked with Normans, Flemings and Englifh men. Nor was Cardigan free from ftrangers, who pretended to fway and rule the country, but the people bearing in mind the continual wrong and oppreffion they received from them, bore an inveterate hatred to them, and were very glad to be delivered from their infolent and imperious oppreffors. For King Henry what by force and banifhment of thofe that ftood up ftiff for their liberty, and what by corrupting of thofe that were wavering, had brought all that country to his fubjection, and beftowed what lands he thought fit upon his Englifh or Norman favourites. But notwithftanding the ftrength of the Englifh in this country, Gruffydh was not a whit caft

3   down,

down, but boldly coming on to Cardigan Ifcoed, he laid fiege to a fort that Earl Gilbert and the Flemings had built at a place called Blaen Porth Gwythan. After divers affaults, and the killing of feveral of the befieged, with the lofs only of one of his men, Gruffydh took the place, and razing it to the ground, brought all the country thereabouts to fubjection. This action proved very fatal to the Englifh, for immediately upon this, they began to forfake their houfes and habitations, as thinking it too hot for them to ftay any longer in the country, and fo the Welch burnt and deftroyed as far as Penwedie all the houfes of thofe ftrangers whom Earl Gilbert had brought with him. Then Gruffydh befieged the caftle of Stradpythylh which belonged to Ralph Earl Gilbert's fteward, and having made himfelf mafter of it, he put all the garrifon to the fword. Removing from thence, he incamped at Glafgryg a mile from Lhanbadarn, purpofing to befiege Aberyftwith caftle next morning, but for want of provifion neceffary for his army, he was forced to make bold with fome cattle which grazed within the limits of the fanctuary. And here it may be obferved, that not only men enjoyed the privilege of thefe fanctuaries, but alfo cattle and horfes, and whatever elfe lived within the liberties of them. But the day following, Gruffydh marched diforderly towards the caftle, being apprehenfive of no great oppofition, by reafon that he was ignorant of the number of the garrifon, and fo encamping upon an oppofite hill, which was divided from the caftle by a river, with a bridge over it, he called a council to determine with what engines they might with beft fuccefs play againft it, and fo make a general affault. The Normans obferving their diforder, very cunningly fent out fome of their archers to fkirmifh with them, and fo by little and little to entice them to the bridge, where fome of the beft armed horfemen were ready to iffue out upon them. The Welch not thinking the garrifon to be fo ftrong approached near the bridge, ftill fkirmifhing with the Normans, who pretended to give ground; but when they came very near, out fal-

lies

lies one on horſeback, who would fain paſs the bridge; but being received upon the points of their ſpears, he began to flag, and as he endeavoured to return, he fell off his horſe, and ſo the Welch purſued him over the bridge. The Engliſhmen ſeeing this, fled towards the caſtle, and the Welch with all ſpeed followed them to the top of the hill; but whilſt they thought that the day was their own, up riſes a party of horſe which lay in ambuſcade under the hill, and ſtanding betwixt the Welch and the bridge, prevented any ſuccour to come to them. And the Welch being thus hemmed in betwixt both parties, the former recoiling with greater ſtrength, were ſo unmercifully cut off, that ſcarce one man was left living. When the reſt of the Welch army, that ſtaid on the other ſide of the river, ſaw what number the garriſon contained, and that they were ſtrong beyond their expectation, preſently decamped, and with all ſpeed departed out of the country.

When King Henry was informed of all the miſchief and cruelties that Gruffydh ap Rhys had committed among his ſubjects in Wales, he ſent for Owen ap Cadwgan, deſiring him and Lhywarch ap Trahaern to uſe all the effectual methods poſſible to take or kill the arch-rebel Gruffydh, promiſing very ſpeedily to ſend his ſon Robert with an army to Wales for that purpoſe. Owen being very proud that the king put ſuch confidence in him, encouraged his men to be now ſo induſtrious to merit the king's favour, as they had been formerly to deſerve his diſpleaſure; and ſo joining his forces with Lhywarch, they both marched to meet Prince Robert at Stratywy, where they ſuppoſed Gruffydh ap Rhys had hid himſelf in the woods. When they were come to the frontiers of the country, they made a vow, that they would let neither man, woman, or child eſcape alive; which ſo affrighted the people of the country, that all made what ſhift they could to ſave their lives, ſome by fleeing to the woods and mountains, and ſome by getting into the king's caſtles, from whence they had come but a little before. Then Owen and Lhywarch

ſeparated

feparated with diftinct parties to fcour the woods, which about Stratywy are very defertous; and Owen having entered with an hundred men, prefently difcovered the tract of men and cattle, and followed their footfteps fo clofe, that within a little while he overtook them; and having flain a great many of them, and put the reft to flight, he carried away all their cattle back to his army.

But whilft Owen was bufy in fearching the woods, Gerald fteward of Pembrock, who with a great power of Flemings was upon his march to join the king's fon, met with them who fled from Owen; who defiring help of Gerald, declared how Owen had forcibly drove them out, flain a great many of their companions, and fpoiled them of all their goods. Gerald and his Flemings underftanding that Owen was fo nigh with fuch a fmall number of men, thought he had now very convenient opportunity to be revenged of him upon the account of his wife; and therefore to make fure work with him, he purfued him clofe into the woods. Owen being forewarned by his men that a great number followed him, and advifed to make all fpeed to get away, was deaf to all fuch counfels, as thinking that they of whom his men were fo much afraid of, were the king's friends, and therefore their integrity need not be queftioned, fince they had all refpect to the fame common caufe. But he found, that a private quarrel is fometime more regarded than the publick good; and therefore when Gerald was advanced within bowfhot, he greeted him with a volley of arrows, to fhew how great a friend he was; but Owen, though perfuaded to flee, was fo little terrified at fuch an unwelcome falutation, that though the enemy were feven to one, yet he told them, that they were but Flemings, and fuch as always trembled at the hearing of his name. And then falling on with a great deal of courage, he was at the firft onfet ftruck with an arrow into the heart, of which wound he prefently died; which when his men faw they all fled, and brought word to Lhywarch and the reft o. their feilows of what had happened; and fo fufpecting the

king's

king's army, seeing they could not be trusted in their service, they all returned to their respective countries.

Owen being in this manner unhappily slain, his brethren divided his lands betwixt them; excepting Caereneon, which properly belonged to Madawc ap Ryryd ap Blethyn; and which he had forcibly taken away from his uncle Meredith. His father Cadwgan had several children by different women; and besides himself, he had issue Madawc by Gwenlhian the daughter of Gruffydh ap Conan; Eineon by Sanna the daughter of Dyfnwal; Morgan, by Efelhiw or Elhiw the daughter of Cadifor ap Colhoyn lord of Dyfed; Henry and Gruffydh were by the daughter of the lord Pigot his wedded wife; Meredith by Euroron Hoodliw; and himself by Inerth the daughter of Edwyn. But a while afterwards, Eineon ap Cadwgan and Gruffydh ap Meredith ap Blethyn, besieged the castle of Cynimer in Merionethshire, which was lately built by Uchtryd ap Edwyn; for Cadwgan had bestowed upon Uchtryd his cousin-german Merioneth and Cyfeilioc, upon condition, that in all cases he should appear his friend, and his sons after him; contrary to which promise he bore no manner of regard to Cadwgan's children after Owen's death; but to strengthen himself the better, he erected this castle of Cymmer, which very much displeased many of Cadwgan's sons. And therefore Eineon and Gruffydh, to make Uchtryd sensible of his error in despising of them, furiously set upon Cymmer castle, and having slain divers of the garrison, the rest surrendered themselves; and so taking possession of it, they divided the country betwixt them; Mowdhwy Cyfeilioc and half Penlhyn to Gruffydh ap Meredith; and the other half of Penlhyn with all Merioneth to Eineon.

The next year King Henry sailed with a great army into Normandy, against the French king, who with the Earl of Flanders and others, went about to make William the son of Robert Curthoise duke

of

of Normandy ; but at the appearance of the king of England, they all scattered, and laid aside their intended design. About the same time Gilbert Strongbow Earl of Strigill, to whom King Henry had given all Cardigan, departed this life, after a long fit of a consumption ; much to the joy and satisfaction of the Welch, who were in great measure displeased, that they should be deprived of their own natural lord Cadwgan, from whom this country was taken away, and be forced to serve and be subject to a stranger, whose kindness they had no great reason to expect. But the year following, an irreconcileable quarrel A. D. 1115, happened betwixt Howel ap Ithel lord of Ros and Ryfonioc, now Denbigh-land, and Riryd and Lhywarch the sons of Owen ap Edwyn. And when they could not otherwise agree, they broke out into open war; and thereupon Howel sent to Meredith ap Blethyn, and to Eineon and Madawc, Cadwgan's sons; who came down from Merioneth with a party of four hundred well-disciplined men, and encamped in Dyffryn Clwyd. Riryd and Lhywarch on the other hand, desired the assistance of their cousins the sons of Uchtryd; and so both armies meeting in the vale of Clwyd, they fell to blows with a great deal of spirit and alacrity, and after a tedious and a bloody fight, Lhywarch, Owen ap Edwyn's son, was at last slain, and with him Iorwerth the son of Nudh, a noble and a valorous person; and Riryd was forced to make his escape by flight. But though Howel obtained the victory, yet he did not long survive his slain enemies; for having received a desperate wound in the action, died of it within forty days ; and then Meredith ap Blethyn, and the sons of Cadwgan finding it dangerous to stay longer there, for fear of some French, who lay garrisoned in Chester, returned home with all speed.

King Henry was still in Normandy, and about this time, a very great battle was fought betwixt him, and the French king, who was shamefully vanquished and overthrown, and had a great number of his nobles taken prisoners. But as King Henry returned the following year for England, one of the ships happened,

by the negligence of the pilot, to be caft away, wherein perifhed the king's two fons, William who was legitimate and heir apparent to the crown, and Richard
his bafe fon; together with his daughter and niece,
and feveral others of his nobility, to the number in
all of one hundred and fifty perfons. This unparallelled lofs of fo many kindred and friends did not per-
plex his mind fo long, but that within a fhort time,
he began to folace and raife his drooping fpirits with
A. D. 1118. the thoughts of a new wife ; and having married A-
delice the daughter of the duke of Lovain, he purpofed to go againft Wales, and having prepared his
forces, he led them in perfon to Powis-land.

When Meredith ap Blethyn and Eineon, Madawc
and Morgan, the fons of Cadwgan and lords of the
country heard of it, they fent to Gruffydh ap Conan
Prince of North Wales, defiring fome help at his
hands; who flatly refufed, affuring them, that becaufe
he was at peace with the king of England, he could
neither with honour nor fafety fend them any fuccour,
nor permit them to come within his dominions. The
lords of Powis receiving this unwelcome anfwer, and
having now no manner of hopes of any aid, were refolved however to defend themfelves as well as they
could ; and therefore they thought it the moft effectual
means to annoy the enemy, and to keep them from
entering into the country, was to obferve and defend
the ftreights, by which the enemy muft of neceffity
pafs. Neither were they out in their policy ; for it
happened that the king himfelf, with a fmall number,
advanced to one of thefe narrow paffages, the reft
of the army, by reafon of their carriages, having
taken fome compafs about; which the Welch perceiving, prefently poured a fhower of arrows upon
them, and the advantage of the ground giving help
to their execution, they flew and wounded a great
many of the Englifh. The king himfelf was ftruck in
the breaft, but for all that the arrow could not hurt
him, by reafon of his armour; yet he was fo terrified with this unexpected conflict, and confidering with
himfelf, that he muft receive feveral fuch brufhes before
he

he could advance to the plain country; and what was above all, being fenfible that by fuch a rafh misfortune he might lofe all the 'honour and fame which he had before obtained, fent a meffage to parly with them who kept the paffage, and with all affurance of fafety, to defire them to come to the king. The Welch being come, and queftioned how they had fuch confidence to oppofe the king, and to put his life in fo much danger; made anfwer, that they belonged to Meredith ap Blethyn, and according to their mafter's orders they were refolved to keep the paffage, or to die upon the fpot. The king finding them fo refolute, defired them to go to Meredith, and propofe to him an agreement of peace, which he and his coufins the fons of Cadwgan accepted of; and promifed to pay the king 10,000 head of cattle, in retribution for former offences. And fo King Henry leaving all things in a peaceable and quiet pofture in Wales, and appointing the Lord Fitz-Warren warden or lieutenant of the Marches, returned to England.

But when a foreign enemy was removed out of the A. D. 1120. country, the Welch could never forbear quarrelling with each other; for Gruffydh ap Rhys ap Theodore, who had been now for fome time quiet, fell upon Gruffydh ap Sulhaern, and for what reafon not difcovered, treacheroufly flew him. But the next year there 1121. happened another occafion of difturbances and falling out among the Welch; for Eineon the fon of Cadwgan dying, left all his fhare of Powis and Merioneth to his brother Meredith. But his uncle Meredith ap Blethyn, thinking that thefe lands more properly belonged to him, ejected his nephew Meredith to whom his brother Eineon had left them, and took poffeffion of them himfelf. And what augmented thefe differences, King Henry fet now at liberty Ithel ap Riryd ap Blethyn, Meredith's nephew, who had been for a long time detained in prifon; who coming to his own country, was in expectation to enjoy his eftate, which, upon his being put in cuftody, his relations had divided betwixt them; of which, the greateft fhare fell

to

to his uncle Meredith. But when Gruffydh ap Conan was informed, how that Meredith ap Blethyn,
contrary to all juftice, had taken away by force the
lands of his nephew Meredith ap Cadwgan, he fent
his fons Cadwalhon and Owen with an army into Merioneth, who conquering and bringing to fubjection all
the country, carried away the chief of the people, and
all the cattle to Lhyn. And at the fame time the
fons of Cadwgan entered into the lands of Lhywarch
ap Trahaern, and cruelly wafted and deftroyed it, by
reafon that he had countenanced the doings of their
uncle Meredith ap Blethyn. But thefe inward clafhings and animofities concerning eftates and titles, were
feconded by moft unnatural bloodfhed and unparallelled cruelties; for Meredith ap Blethyn, when he found
that his nephew Meredith ap Cadwgan was affifted by
the Prince of North Wales, and that it was impracticable to keep Merioneth from him, he was refolved
to practife that upon his nephew, which he had failed
A.D. 1122. to effect upon another. And therefore left his other
nephew Ithel ap Riryd fhould meet with the like help
and encouragement to recover thofe lands, which during his imprifonment were taken away from him, of
which his uncle actually enjoyed a confiderable fhare;
Meredith thought it his wifeft way to prevent all manner of difputes, by fending Ithel out of the world,
which upon mature deliberation he treacheroufly effected. Nor was this the only murder committed at
this time; for Cadwalhon the fon of Gruffydh ap Conan exceeded him far, and flew his three uncles, Grono, Ryryd, and Meilyr the fons of Owen ap Edwyn;
but which was moft unnatural of all, Morgan ap Cadwgan with his own hands killed his brother Meredith;
a crime moft execrable, though he did afterwards repent of it.

1125.   Not long after this, Gruffydh ap Rhys, by the falfe
and invidious accufations of the Normans, was difpoffeffed of all the lands which King Henry had formerly granted him, and which he had for a confiderable time peaceably enjoyed. And towards the
end of the fame year died Daniel ap Sulgien bifhop
                                                    of

of St. David's, and archdeacon of Powis, a man of extraordinary piety and learning, and one who made it his continual employment to endeavour to work a reconciliation betwixt North Wales and Powis, which in his time were at perpetual variance and enmity with one another. The next year died likewife Gruf-A.D. 1125, fydh the fon of Meredith ap Blethyn ; and about the fame time Owen ap Cadwgan having got into his hands Meredith ap Lhywarch, delivered him to Pain Fitz-John, to be kept fafe prifoner in the caftle of Bridgnorth. The reafon of this was, becaufe Meredith had flain Meyric his coufin-german, and very barbaroufly had pulled out the eyes of two more of his coufins the fons of Griffri. This cruel and in-human cuftom of plucking out the eyes of fuch as they hated or feared, was too frequently practifed in Wales ; for the following year Ievaf the fon of Owen 1126, ferved two of his brethren after this unnatural man-ner, and thinking that too little, paffed a fentence of perpetual banifhment upon them. A little after, his brother Lhewelyn ap Owen flew Iorwerth ap Lhywarch ; but all this mifchief practifed by thefe two brothers Ievaf and Lhewelyn, turned at laft up-on themfelves ; for their uncle Meredith ap Blethyn being apprehenfive that his two nephews were a con-fiderable rub in his way, and if they trooped off, that all their eftate would of right fall to him ; flew Ievaf outright, and having plucked out Lhewelyn's eyes, caftrated him, for fear he fhould beget any children to inherit his lands after him. Thefe no doubt were implacable times, when for the leaft offence, nay fome-time fufpicion, murder was fo openly and incorrigibly committed ; which muft of neceffity be attributed to this one principle, That fo many petty ftates having equal power and authority in their own territories, and being fubject to none but the king of England, ftill endeavoured to outvie and overtop each other. And fo, nearnefs of relation giving way to ambition, they never regarded thofe of the fame blood, fo that themfelves might add to their ftrength, and increafe their eftate by their fall ; and for this reafon Mey-

ric

ric flew Lhywarch, and his fon Madawc, his own
coufins ; but before he could make any advantage
of their death, he was himfelf ferved after the fame
manner. But the only perfon who afterwards repented of fuch a foul crime, was Morgan ap Cadwgan, who being feverely troubled in mind for the
murder he had lately committed upon his brother
Meredith, took a journey to Jerufalem to expiate for
his crime, and in his return from thence, died in the
ifle of Cyprus. But this treacherous way of private
murdering thofe by whom they were offended, could
A. D. 1129. not be forgot among the Welch; for Eineon the fon
of Owen ap Edwyn calling to mind how that Cadwalhon the fon of Gruffydh ap Conan had bafely flain
three of his brothers, and taking the opportunity of
his being at Nanhewdwy, affifted by Cadwgan ap Grono ap Edwyn, fet upon him, and flew him. About
the fame time, that great ufurper Meredith ap Blethyn
ap Confyn, who by moft unnatural and moft hellifh
practices, had got the lands of all his brothers and nephews, and by that means was become a man of the
greateft ftrength and fway in Powis, died of a fevere
fit of ficknefs, which reduced him to that apprehenfion of his former mifcarriages, that he endured penance for the expiation of former guilt.

1134.   In the year 1134, till which time nothing of moment was tranfacted in Wales, Henry, the firft of that
name, king of England, died in Normandy in the
month of October; after whom Stephen Earl of Bu-
loign fon to the Earl of Blois, his fifter's fon, by the
means of Hugh Bygod, was crowned king by the
archbifhop of Canterbury, all the nobility of England
confenting thereunto; though contrary to a former
oath they had taken to Maud the Emprefs. The firft
thing that employed his thoughts after his acceffion to
the government, was againft David king of the Scots;
who taking advantage of this new revolution in England, by fome treacherous means or other, got the
towns of Carlifle and Newcaftle into his hands. But
King Stephen, though fcarcely fettled in his throne,
pretently marched to oppofe the Scots; or whofe coming

ing David being affured, and fearing to meet.him, voluntarily reftored Newcaftle, and compounded for Carlifle; but would not fwear to him by reafon of his oath to Maud; which, however, his fon Henry did not ftick at; and thereupon was by King Stephen created Earl of Huntington. This change and alteration of affairs in England made alfo the Welch beftir themfelves; for Morgan ap Owen, a man of con-A. D. 1135; fiderable quality and eftate in Wales, remembering the wrong and injury he had received at the hands of Richard Fitz-Gilbert, flew him, together with his fon Gilbert. And fhortly after, Cadwalader and Owen Gwyneth the fons of Gruffydh ap Conan Prince of North Wales, having raifed a mighty army, marched againft the Normans and Flemings, and coming to Cardigan, committed very confiderable wafte and havock in the country, and took two of the ftrongeft places, one belonging to Walter Efpec, and the caftle of Aberyftwyth. In this laft place they were joined by Howel ap Meredith, and Rhys ap Madawc ap Ednerth; who marching forward, took the caftle of Richard de la Mare, together with thofe of Dinerth and Caerwedros, and then returned with very valuable booty. But having fucceeded fo well in this expedition, they could not reft fatisfied, till they had rid the whole country from the intolerable pride and oppreffion of the Normans and Flemings; and therefore returning the fame year to Cardigan with 6000 foot, and 2000 horfe, well difciplined and experienced foldiers; and being joined by Gruffydh ap Rhys and Howel ap Meredith of Brecknock with his fons, and Madawc ap Ednerth; they over-ran the country, as far as Aberteifi, reftoring all the former inhabitants to their proper inheritances, and difcarding all fuch ftrangers as the late Earl of Strygil had placed in the country. But when Stephen, who was governor of Aberteifi, faw that, he called to him Robert Fitz-Martyn, the fons of Gerald, and William Fitz-John, with.all the ftrength of the Normans, Flemings, and Englifh in Wales, or the Marches; and meeting with the Welch berwixt Aber Ned and Aber Dyfi, gave them battle; in

after a very fore and bloody encounter, the Englifh began to give ground, and according to their ufual manner, trufting too much to the ftrength of their towns and fortifications, began to look how to fave themfelves that way. But the Welch preffed upon them fo hard, that they killed above 3000 men, befides feveral that were drowned and taken prifoners. This victory being fo happily obtained, Cadwalader and Owen over-ran the whole country, forcing all the Normans and Flemings to depart the country with all fpeed, and placing in their room thofe miferable Welch, who had been fo long deprived and kept from their own eftates; and after they had weeded the country of thofe infatiable caterpillars, they returned to North Wales, laden with very rich fpoils and acceptable plunder. The king of England was not in a condition to take notice to what extremities his fubjects were reduced to in Wales, by reafon that his own nobles of England were rifen in arms againft him; the reafon of which tumult among the nobility was occafioned by a fallacious report that went about of the king's death, who then lay fick of a lethargy. They that bore him no good will, verified the rumour as much as they could, and ftirred up the common people in behalf of the Emprefs; whereas on the other hand the king's friends betook themfelves to caftles and ftrong holds for fear of the Emprefs, and among others Hugh Bygod fecured the caftle of Norwich, and after that he was affured that the king was well again, he was loth to deliver the fame out of his
A D. 1136. poffeffion, unlefs it were to the king's own hands. But during thefe commotions and troubles in England, Gruffydh ap Rhys, fon to Rhys ap Theodore, the right heir to the principality of South Wales, died, leaving iffue behind him a fon called Rhys, commonly known by the name of Lord Rhys, by Gwenlhian the daughter of Gruffydh ap Conan, who by fome is faid to have poifoned her hufband. Towards the end of the fame year died likewife Gruffydh ap Conan Prince of North Wales, after he had reigned 57 years; to the great grief and difcontent of all his fubjects, as being a Prince of incomparable qualities, and one who after

divers

divers victories obtained over the English, had thoroughly purged North Wales from all strangers and foreigners.
He had issue by Angharad the daughter of Owen ap
Edwyn, three sons, namely, Owen, Cadwalader, and
Cadwalhon, and five daughters, Marret, Susanna,
Ranulht, Agnes, and Gwenlhian; and by a concubine, Iago, Ascain, Edwal abbot of Penmon, Dolhing,
and Elen, who was married to Hova ap Ithel Felyn of
Yal. There were several good and wholsome laws
and statutes enacted in his time; and among the rest,
he reformed the great disorders of the Welch minstrels,
which were then grown to great abuse. Of these there
were three sorts in Wales; the first were called Beirdh,
who composed several songs and odes of various measures, wherein the poet's skill was not only required,
but also a natural endowment, or a vein which the Latins term *furor poeticus.* These likewise kept the records of all gentlemen's arms and pedigrees, and were
principally esteemed among all the degrees of the
Welch poets. The next were such as played upon
musical instruments, chiefly the harp and the crowd;
which musick Gruffydh ap Conan first brought over into
Wales; who being born in Ireland, and descended by
his mother's side of Irish parents, brought with him
from thence several skilful musicians, who invented
almost all the instruments as were afterwards played
upon in Wales. The last sort were called Atcaneaid,
whose business it was to sing to the instruments played
upon by another. Each of these, by the same statute,
had their several reward and encouragement alloted to
them; their life and behaviour was to be spotless and
unblameable, otherwise their punishment was very severe and rigid, every one having authority to punish
and correct them, even to the deprivation of all they
had. They were also interdicted and forbidden to enter any man's house, or to compose any song of any
one, without the special leave and warrant of the party
concerned; with many other ordinances relating to the
like purpose.

OWEN

OWEN GWYNEDH.

AFTER the death of Gruffydh ap Conan, his eldest son Owen, surnamed Gwynedh, succeeded in the principality of North Wales; who no sooner had entered upon the government, but together with the rest of his brethren, he made an expedition into South Wales; and having demolished and overthrown the castles of Stradmeyric, Stephan, and Humffreys, and laid in ashes the town of Caermardhyn, he returned home with no less honour than booty and plunder. About the same time, John archdeacon of Lhanbaran departed this life, a man of singular piety and strictness of life, who for his rigid zeal in religion and virtue, was thought worthy to be canonized, and to be counted among the number of the saints. This year likewise King Stephen passed over to Normandy, and having concluded a peace with the French king, and the duke of Anjou, returned back to England without any further delay. But the following Spring gave opportunity for greater undertakings; David king of Scots, upon the king of England's going to France last summer, had entered the borders of England, and continued to make considerable waste and havock in that part of the country. Whereupon King Stephen, to rid his country and his subjects from so dangerous an enemy, marched with an army towards the North, whose coming the king of Scots hearing of, he relinquished the borders of England, and retired to his own country. But that would not satisfy King Stephen, who desired to be further revenged for the unpardonable hostilities committed by the Scots in his country; and therefore pursuing the Scots to their own country, he harassed and laid waste all the south part of the
kingdom

kingdom of Scotland. But the king's abfence animated feveral of the Englifh nobility to rebel; to
which purpofe they fortified every one their caftles
and ftrong holds; William Earl of Glocefter thofe of
Leeds and Briftol; Ralph Lunel, Cari; William Fitz-
Allen, Shrewfbury; Paganellus, Ludlow; William de
Moyun, Dunefter; Robert de Nichol, Warham; Euftace Fitz-John, Merton; and Walklyn, Dover. But
for all thefe mighty preparations, the king in a fhort
time became mafter of them all; fome he won by affault, others upon fair promifes and advantageous conditions were furrendered up, and fome he got by treacherous and under-hand contrivances. The Scots
thought to make good advantage of thefe commotions
in England; and thereupon, as foon as they heard that
fome of the nobility were in actual rebellion againft
the king, they entered into the borders, and began,
as they thought, without any apprehenfion of oppofition, to ravage and lay wafte the country before them.
But William, Earl of Albemarle; William Pyppell,
Earl of Nottingham; Walter Efpec and Gilbert Lacy, gathered together all the forces they could raife in
the North; and being animated and encouraged by the
eloquent and preffing oration of Ralph bifhop of Orkneys, which he delivered in the audience of the whole
army, they fet upon the Scots at Almerton with fuch
unanimous courage, that after a very great flaughter
of his men, King David was glad to efcape with his
life by flight. After this, King Stephen feized to his
own ufe the caftles of Ludlow and Leeds, and preffed
the bifhops of Salifbury and Lincoln, fo hard, that to
prevent their perifhing by famine, they were conftrained to furrender; the former the caftles of Vifes
and Shirburn; the latter thofe of Newark upon Trent
and Sleeford. This did not a little augment the king's
ftrength againft the enfuing ftorm; for in the fummer
this year, Maud the Emprefs, daughter and heir to King
Henry, to whom King Stephen, with all the nobility
of England, had fworn allegiance, landed at Arundel,
with her brother Robert Earl of Glocefter, and was
there honourably received by William de Albineto,

M   who

who was lately married to Queen Adeliz, King Henry's widow, with whom he received the earldom of Arundel in dowry. But as foon as King Stephen heard of her landing, he marched with all poffible fpeed to Arundel, and laid fiege to the caftle; but finding it upon trial impregnable, he raifed the fiege, and by that means fuffered the Emprefs and her brother to efcape to Briftol.

A.D. 1138. The next year an unlucky accident fell out in Wales; Cynric, one of Prince Owen's fons, having by fome means or other difgufted Madawc ap Meredith ap Blethyn ap Confyn, a perfon of confiderable efteem and eftate in the country, was, with his connivance fet upon and flain by his men. But the affairs of England this year, afforded greater rarity of action; King Stephen with a formidable army laid fiege to the city of Lincoln, to the relief of which, Ranulph Earl of Chefter, and Robert Earl of Glocefter, marched with their forces. But before they could arrive, the town was taken; whereupon they drew up their forces in order to give the king battle, who on the other fide, was as ready to receive them. King Stephen drew up his forces in three battles, the firft being led by the Earls of Britain, Mellent, Norfolk, Hampton, and Warren; the fecond by the Earl of Albemarle, and William of Ypres; and the third by the king himfelf, affifted by Baldwyn Fitz-Gilbert, with feveral others of his nobility. Of the enemy's fide, the difinherited barons had the firft place; the Earl of Chefter, with a confiderable party of Welchmen, far better couraged than armed, led the fecond; and the Earl of Glocefter the third battle. After a hot and bloody difpute of both fides, the victory at length favoured the barons, King Stephen being firft taken prifoner, and a little after the queen, together with William of Ypres, and Bryan Fitz-Count. But within a while after, William Martell and Geffrey de Mandeville gathered together fome frefh forces, and fought the Emprefs and her brother at Winchefter, and having put the Emprefs to flight, took Earl Robert prifoner, for exchange of whom, the king was fet at liberty.

berty. The next year King Stephen would try the other adventure, and received a second overthrow at Wilton; which, however, did not so much discourage him, but that he laid so close a siege to the Empress at Oxford, that she was glad to make her escape to Wallingford. The same year died Madawc ap Ednerth, a person of great quality and note in Wales; and Meredith ap Howel, a man of no mean esteem, was slain by the sons of Blethyn ap Gwyn.

For the two succeeding years nothing remarkable passed in Wales; excepting that this year Howel ap Meredith ap Rhytherch of Cantref Bychan, and Rhys ap Howel were cowardly slain by the treachery and perfidious practices of the Flemings; and the next year Howel ap Meredith ap Blethyn was basely murdered by his own men; at which time, Howel and Cadwgan the sons of Madawc ap Ednerth, upon some unhappy quarrel, did kill each other. But shortly af- ter this, an irreconcileable difference fell out betwixt Anarawd son to Gruffydh ap Rhys Prince of South Wales, and his father-in-law Cadwalader the son of Gruffydh ap Conan, and brother to Prince Owen Gwynedh; which from words quickly proceeded to blows. In this scuffle Anarawd was unhappily slain; which so exasperated Prince Owen against his brother Cadwalader, that together with his son Howel, he marched with an army into his brother's country, and after a considerable waste and destruction, burnt to the ground the castle of Aberystwyth. Cadwalader, upon the news of Prince Owen's approach, withdrew himself and fled to Ireland; where having hired a great number of Irish and Scots for two thousand marks, under the command of Octer, and the sons of Turkel and Cherulf, he struck sail for Wales, and landed at Abermeny in Carnarvonshire. The Prince, to protract no time, marched with all speed to prevent their farther progress into the country; and both armies being come in view of each other, a peace was happily concluded betwixt the two brothers. The Irish understanding this, and how that their coming over was

M 2   like

like to prove but a fool's errand to them, they surprised and secured Cadwalader, till their wages and arrears were paid; who, to obtain his liberty, delivered to them two thousand heads of cattle, besides many prisoners, and other booty, which they had taken in the country. But as soon as the Prince was informed that his brother Cadwalader was set loose, without any farther demur upon the case, he fell in upon the Irish, and having slain a very considerable number of them, recovered all the booty they purposed to ship off, and forced as many as could escape, to return with great loss, and a greater shame back to Ireland.

But the Normans sped far better in Wales; Hugh son to Radulph Earl of Chester, having fortified his castle of Cymaron, set upon and won the country of Melienyth a second time; and the castle of Clun being fortified by another lord, all Eluel became subject to the Normans. The same time King Stephen took Geffry Mandeville prisoner at St. Albans, where the earl of Arundel, by the slip of his horse, was like to be drowned in the river. But the Earl of Mandeville, to obtain his liberty, delivered up to the king the tower of London, with the castles of Walden and Plaffey, which reduced him to that condition, that he was forced to live upon the plunder and spoil of abbies and other religious houses, till at length he was slain in a skirmish against the king, and his son banished the kingdom.

A. D. 1144. The next year a skirmish happened betwixt Hugh de Mortimer and Rhys ap Howel, wherein the latter was taken prisoner, with many others of his accomplices, who were all committed to prison by the English. But it fared much better with Howel and Conan the sons of Prince Owen, who having raised an army against the Flemings and Normans, gained a considerable victory at Abertiefi, and having placed a garrison in the town, returned home with great honour, and much booty.

About the same time, Sulien ap Rhythmarch, one of the college of Lhanbadarn, and a person of great reading and extensive learning, departed this life. Shortly after, Gilbert Earl of Clare, came with a great number
of

of forces to Dyfed, and built the caftle of Caermardhyn, and the caftle of the fons of Uchtryd. Hugh A.D. 1145.
Mortimer likewife flew Meyric ap Madawc ap Riryd
ap Bleddu, and Meredic ap Madawc ap Ednerth. And
fo far it went of the fide of the Englifh; but now
the Welch begin to gain ground; Cadelh the fon of
Gruffydh ap Rhys Prince of South Wales, laid fiege
to the caftle of Dynefowr, belonging to Earl Gilbert,
which being furrendered up, Cadelh, affifted by his
brethren Meredith and Rhys, brought his army before
the caftle of Caermardhyn, which after a fhort fiege
yielded in like manner, referving only this one condition, that the garrifon fhould not be put to the
fword.

From thence he marched to Lhanftephan, and fet
before the caftle; to the relief of which the Normans
and Flemings coming with their forces, were fhamefully vanquifhed and overcome, and fo the caftle was
eafily delivered up to the Welch. But the Normans
were fo cruelly nettled at this, that they muftered up all
the forces they could poffibly draw together out of the
neighbouring countries, and unexpectedly furrounded
the caftle, intending by all poffible means to recover
the fame. But the governor, Meredith ap Gruffydh,
a man of great years, and no lefs experience, fo animated and encouraged the befieged, that when the
Normans and Flemings ventured to fcale the walls,
they were beat back with fuch vigour, and lofs of
their fide, that at length they were compelled to
raife the fiege, and leave the Welch in poffeffion of
the caftle.

Shortly after this, Run the fon of Prince Owen of
North Wales, a youth of excellent hopes, and incomparable qualifications, died, whofe death his father
took fo much to heart, that for fome time he feemed
to be paft all comfort, being fallen into fuch a me-
lancholy difpofition, that he was diverted with nothing but retirement. But an accident fell out, which
roufed him out of this lethargical fit of forrow and
difcontent; the caftle of Mould was fo very ftrong

M 3 and

and well garrisoned by the English, that it mightily
annoyed the country thereabouts, and had been frequently besieged, but could never be taken. Prince
Owen at this time levied an army and laid close
siege to it; and the garrison for several assaults, behaved itself so manfully, that the place seemed impregnable and invincible. But the presence and example of Prince Owen so encouraged his men, that
they fell on with all possible vigour and might, and at
last forced their entrance into the castle. Having put
a great number of the garrison to the sword, and taken
the rest prisoners, the castle was razed to the ground;
and this fortunate attempt so pleased the Prince, that
he forgot all sorrow for his son, and returned to his
usual temper and accustomed merriments. At the
same time, King Stephen of England obtained a remarkable victory over his enemies at Farendon; and
although the ensuing year Rondel Earl of Chester and
he were reconciled, yet he thought it more adviseable
to detain him prisoner, though contrary to his promise,
until such time as the Earl would deliver up the castle
of Lincoln, with all the forts and places of strength
in his custody.

A. D 1146   The next year, Cadelh, Meredith, and Rhys, the
sons of Gruffydh ap Rhys ap Theodor, brought an
army before the castle of Gwys; but finding themselves
too weak to master it, they desired Howel, son to
Prince Owen Gwynedh, a person famously remarkable
for martial endowments, to come to their assistance.
Howel, who was very desirous to signalize himself,
and to evidence his valour to the world, readily consented to their request; and having drawn his forces
together, marched directly towards Gwys, where being arrived, he was joyfully received, and honourably
entertained by such lords as desired his help. Having
viewed the strength and fortification of the castle, he
found it was impracticable to take the place, without
the walls could be destroyed; and therefore he gave
orders, that certain battering engines should be provided, whilst the rest should gaul and molest the besieged,

fieged, by throwing of great ftones into the caftle. The enemies perceiving what irrefiftible preparations the befiegers contrived, thought it to no purpofe to with-ftand their fury; and therefore to do that voluntarily which muft be done by compulfion, they prefently yielded up the caftle. Shortly after this a great diffe-rence happened betwixt the fons of Prince Owen, Howel, and Conan, and their uncle Cadwalader ; whereupon the former entered with an army into the country of Merioneth, and committed great waftes and hoftilities there, infomuch that the inhabitants flocked into fanctuaries to fave their lives. But the young lords finding what fearful and unftable condi-tion the people were in, and the better to draw them to their fide, iffued out their proclamation, affuring that all who would favour their country, fhould not only enjoy their lives, but their former liberty and ac-cuftomed privileges ; upon the publication of which edict, the people returned to their own habitations. Having by this ftratagem brought all the country un-der their own pleafure and good will, they led their army before the caftle of Cynfael, belonging to Cad-walader, which he had built and ftrongly fortified. The government of this caftle Cadwalader had com-mitted to Merfyn, abbot of Tygwyn, or the White-Houfe ; who being fummoned to furrender, by the brothers Howel and Conan, did not only refufe, but defied their utmoft efforts upon the place. The lords finding they could do no good by threats and menaces, judged it more convenient to make ufe of the other extream ; and therefore promifed the abbot a very high reward, if he would deliver the caftle into their hands. But all proved to no effect, the abbot being a perfon, of more honefty and greater honour, than to be corrupted to betray his truft ; told them flatly, That he would not deceive his mafter's expectation, and therefore would choofe rather to die with honour, than to live with fhame. The lords finding him in-exorable, and withal being vexed, that a churchman fhould put fuch a ftop to their fortunate proceedings,

M 4   made

made fuch a vigorous affault upon the caftle, that after they had pulled down fome part of the walls, they
entered in by force, and ravaged fo furioufly, that
they killed and wounded the whole garrifon, the abbot only efcaping, who by the help of fome of his
friends in Howel's army, got away fafe. Towards the
clofe of this year, feveral perfons of note departed this
life, among whom were Robert Earl of Glocefter,
and Gilbert Earl of Clare, as alfo Uchthryd bifhop of
Llandaf, a man of great piety and learning, in whofe
fee fucceeded Nicholas ab Gurgant.

A D. 1147. , The following year alfo died Bernard bifhop of St.
David's, and was fucceeded by David Fitzgerald, then
1148. archdeacon of Cardigan. Sometime after, Prince Owen
Gwynedh built a caftle in Yale, called Caftelh y Rod-
wyth; and his brother Cadwalader built another at
Lhanryftid, and beftowed his part of Cardigan upon
his fon Cadwgan. Alfo Madoc the fon of Meredith
ap Blethyn founded the caftle of Ofweftry, and gave
his nephews Owen and Meyric the fons of Gruffydh
ap Meredith his fhare of Cyfeilioc.

1149. The next year Conan fon to Prince Owen Gwynedh
for certain faults and mifcarriages committed againft
his father, though the particulars are not difcovered,
was put in prifon, where for fome time he continued in
cuftody. But it fared better with his brother Howel,
who having made his uncle Cadwalader his prifoner,
reduced all his country, together with his caftle fubject to himfelf. In South Wales, fome bufinefs of moment happened this year; Cadelh the fon of Gruffydh
ap Rhys having fortified the caftle of Carmardhyn,
marched with his army towards Cydwely, wafted and
deftroyed the whole country, and being returned home,
joined his army with his brothers Meredith and Rhys,
who entering into the country of Cardigan, won that
part called Is Aeron. This was fucceeded by an action of greater importance in North Wales; fome irreconcileable difference arifing betwixt Prince Owen,
and Rondel Earl of Chefter, quickly broke out into
open war. The Earl made all the poffible preparations

tions the opportunity would permit, and drew together a confiderable army from all parts of England,
and which ftrengthened and encouraged him the more,
he was joined by Madoc ap Meredith prince of
Powys, who difdaining to hold his lands of prince
Owen Gwynedh, chofe rather to fide with, and abet
his enemies. The prince, on the other hand, was
not backward in his preparations, and perceiving the
enemy to come upon him, thought it not advifeable
to fuffer him to advance too far into the country,
but to ftop and prevent his career before he fhould
take too firm a footing in his dominions. To this
end he marched with his whole power as far as
Countylht, with full refolution to give the earl of
Chefter battle, which the Englifh were glad of, as
thinking themfelves far more numerous, and much
better armed and difciplined than the Welch. But
both armies having joined battle, they quickly fal-
tered in their expectation of undoubted fuccefs,
and finding the Welch to prefs fo irrefiftably fevere
upon them, they thought it wifer to retire, and endeavour to fave themfelves by flight. But the
Welch purfued them fo hard, that few efcaped
without being either flain or taken prifoners, and
they fome of the chief commanders, who through the
fleetnefs of their horfes, avoided the fury of their
purfuers.

The next year, the fcene of action removed to A. D. 1150.
South-Wales, Cadelh, Meredith and Rhys, the fons of
Gruffydh ap Rhys prince of South Wales, being entered with an army into Cardigan, won all the country
from Howel the prince of North-Wales's fon, excepting the caftle of Lhanfihangel in Pengwern. The
fiege of Lhanryftyd caftle proved fo difficult and
unmanageable, that the young lords of South-Wales
loft a great part of their braveft foldiers before it,
which fo troubled and vexed them, that when they
got poffeffion of the caftle, they put all the garrifon
to the fword. From thence they marched to Yftrat-
meyric caftle, which after they had won, manned
and re-fortified, they difbanded their forces, and returned

turned home. But Cadelh, the eldeſt of the brothers, was upon the point of receiving his laſt blow by treachery at home, which he had eſcaped from the enemies abroad. For ſome of the inhabitants of Tenbigh in Pembrokeſhire, having conceived ſome diſpleaſure and hatred againſt Cadelh, were reſolved to revenge themſelves, and to lay a trap for his life ; and having obſerved what pleaſure he took in hunting, were reſolved to execute their plot, whilſt he was hot and eager at his ſport. Obſerving there-fore one day how he went a hunting with only a few companions, they placed themſelves · in an ambuſcade, and when the game came that way, they unexpectedly ſet upon the unarmed ſportſmen, and having eaſily made all the reſt fly away, they wounded Cadelh ſo cruelly, that he narrowly eſcaped their hands alive ; who making ſhift to get home, lay for a long time dangerouſly ill, and with great difficulty at length recovered his life. Upon this, his brothers Meredith and Rhys paſſed with an army into Gwyr, and having burnt and deſtroyed the country thereabouts, they beſieged and took the caſtle of Aberlhychwr, but finding they could not keep it, they raſed it to the ground, and after that, returned home with great booty to Dynefawr, and repaired the fortifications of the caſtle there. About the ſame time alſo, Howel, Prince Owen Gwynedh's ſon, fortified Humphry's caſtle in the valley of Caletwr.

A D. 1151.   But the following year, prince Owen did a very barbarous action to Cunetha, his brother Cadwalhon's ſon, for fearing leſt that this young man ſhould lay claim to any part of his eſtate as his father's right, he firſt pulled out his eyes, and afterwards caſtrated him, for fear he ſhould beget any children, who might ſome time or other renew their claim, and right to Cadwalhon's eſtate. This inhuman ſeverity was ſucceeded by another of no ſmall remark ; Lhewelyn ſon to Madoc ap Meredith having watched a convenient opportunity, ſet upon, and ſlew Stephen the ſon of Baldwin. But Cadwalader, Prince Owen's

brother

I

brother, after a tedious imprifonment which he had fuftained through the malice and rancour of his nephew Howel, at length made his efcape, and flying to the Ifle of Anglefey, brought a confiderable part of that ifland under his fubjection. But prince Owen hearing how that his brother had got loofe from cuftody, and that he was in actual poffeffion of a great part of Anglefey, he prefently difpatched an army over, which proving too formidable to Cadwalader's party, he was conftrained to efcape to England, and to defire fuccour from his wife's relations, who was the daughter of Gilbert Earl of Clare. This year Galfrede Arthur, commonly called Geffrey of Monmouth, was made bifhop of St. Afaph, and at the fame time Simon Archdeacon of Cyfeilioc, a man of great worth and efteem in his country died.

But the year following, Meredith and Rhys the fons A.D. 1152; of Gruffydh ap Rhys, Prince of South-Wales, laid fiege to Penwedic caftle, which belonged to Howel Prince Owen's fon, and after great pains and confiderable lofs of men of their fide, at laft made themfelves mafters of it. From thence they marched by night to Tenby, and unexpectedly falling upon the caftle, of which one William Fitzgerald was governor, they fcaled the walls before the garrifon were aware of any danger, and fo poffeffing themfelves of the caftle, they fell foul upon the garrifon, in revenge of the mifchief they had done, and further defigned to their brother Cadelh. For Cadelh at this time was gone upon a pilgrimage, and during his abfence had committed his whole inheritance and all other concerns in Wales, to the care of his brethren Meredith and Rhys. But after the taking Tenby caftle, they divided their army into two parties, with one of which Rhys marched to Yftratcongen, and after great havock and wafte committed there, he paffed to Cyfeilioc, which fared in like manner with Yftratcongen. Meredith, with the other party, fat before Aberavan caftle, and after a fhort fiege won and got poffeffion of it, and then returned home with very confiderable booty, and many rich fpoils. About the fame time

time Rondel, earl of Chester, who had lived in continual enmity and frequent hostility with prince Owen of North-Wales, departed this life, leaving his son Hugh to enjoy both his titles and estate in England, and to prosecute the feuds and hostilities against the Welch.

A. D. 1153.   And shortly after died Meredith, son to Gruffydh ap Rhys, prince of South-Wales, who was Lord of Cardigan, Ystratywy, and Dyfed, being not passed the twenty-fifth year of his age; a person of incomparable valor and audacity, and in all his warlike attempts and achievements very fortunate. He was presently followed by Geoffrey Bishop of Llandaf, a man as famous for learning and a good life, as the other was for masculine bravery and martial prowess. In England the face of things looked very lowering, Henry, surnamed Shortmantel, the empress' son, landed in England, and in his progress through the country took several castles, among which were Malmesbury, Wallingford, and Shrewsbury. But his fury was quickly appeased by the death of Eustace, king Stephen's son, so that the sole obstacle for his succeeding to the crown, being now removed, we willingly concluded a peace with king Stephen, permitting him to enjoy the crown peaceably for his life, upon con-

1154. dition that himself was declared his successor. But king Stephen did not long survive this treaty; and then Henry Plantagenet, the empress's son, was crowned

1155. in his stead.   Towards the beginning of King Henry's reign, Rhys Gruffydh ap Rhys, king of South-Wales, upon apprehension that Owen Gwynedh had raised an army for the conquest of South-Wales, drew together all his strength, and marched to Aberdyfi to face the enemy upon their own borders. But finding the rumor to be false, and that the prince of North-Wales had no such design in hand, having built a castle at Abedyfi, which might defend the frontiers from any future design of his country, he returned back without attempting any thing farther. At the same time, Madoc ap Meredith built a castle at Caereneon near Cymer, and then Eglwys Fair in Myfot,

was

was founded.   About this time alfo, Meyric, nephew to prince Madoc ap Meredith, made his efcape out of prifon, wherein he had been detained by his uncle for a confiderable time.

The fame year king Henry being difpleafed with the Flemings, whom his predeceffor King Stephen had brought over into England, iffued out a proclamation, charging the greateft part of them to depart his dominions, and to retire to their countrymen in Weft-Wales, where his grandfather, Henry the firft the Baftard's fon had planted them.   And thus that part of Wales, called Pembrokefhire, was over-run with thefe ftrangers, who being better befriended by the Kings of England, than the Welch could well expect to be, made fure footing in that country, where they have ever fince continued firm.   It was the Englifh policy of thofe times to accept of any opportunity to curb and keep under the Welch, whom they experienced to be none of the fafeft neighbours, and therefore the kings of England did grant any lands and privileges in Wales to any that would accept of them, which, honeftly, they had no power to beftow.

But this was not enough in detriment to the Welch, A. D. 1156. for the year following, King Henry raifed a very great army, which he gathered from all parts of England, with purpofe to fubdue all North-Wales, being principally moved hereto, by the inftigation of Cadwalader the prince's brother, whom Owen Gwynedh, for what reafons not known, deprived of his eftate, and banifhed the country.   Alfo Madoc ap Meredith, prince of Powis, who maligned the liberty and privilege of the princes of North-Wales, who owned fubjection to no other than the king of England, whereas thofe of Powis were obliged to do homage to the prince of North-Wales, did jointly confent to this invitation.   The king of England accepted of their propofals, led his army to Weft-Chefter, and encamped upon the marfh called Saltney, in Welch, Morfa-Caer-Lleon.   Prince Owen, all this while, was not ignorant of this intended invafion; and therefore having

having made all possible preparations to confront the
enemy, he marched his army to the frontiers of
England, and encamping at Basingwerk, resolved to
give the English battle. King Henry understanding
of the prince's resolution, detached some of the
chiefest troops out of the main-body, under the
command of several earls and other lords, and
sent them towards the prince's camp. But after
they had advanced some little way, and were passing
through a wood, called Coed-Eulo, David and Conon,
prince Owen's sons, unexpectedly set upon them, and
what by the advantage of the ground, and the sud-
denness of the action, the English were born down
with a great slaughter, and those who survived narrowly escaped to the king's camp. This was a very
unwelcome beginning to king Henry; but however,
in order to prosper better hereafter, he thought it adviseable to decamp from Saltney, and to rank his
troops along the sea-coast, thinking thereby to get
betwixt prince Owen and his country, which if he
could effect, he was sure to reduce the Welch to a
very great inconveniency. But the prince, foresee-
ing the danger of this, retired with his army to a
place called Cil Owen, that is, Owen's Retreat, which
when King Henry perceived, he let fall his design,
and came to Ruthlan. W. Parnus writes, that in
this expedition against the Welch, King Henry was
in great danger of his life, in passing through a
strait at Counsylth near Flint, where Henry Earl of
Essex, who by inheritance enjoyed the office of bearing
the standard of England, being over-charged by the
enemy, cast down the same and fled, This accident
so encouraged the Welch, that they bore on so violently, that the king himself narrowly escaped, having
of his party Eustace Fitz-John, and Robert Curcie,
two valiant knights, together with several others of
his nobility and gentry slain in the action.

After this prince Owen decamped from Cil Owen,
and intrenched himself upon Bryn y Pin, where little of moment passed between the two armies, only
some slight skirmishes happened frequently. King
Henry

Lib. 2.
cap. 5.

Henry in the mean time fortified the caftle of Ruthlan,
and during his ftay there, Madoc ap Meredith prince
of Powis, failed with the Englifh fleet to Anglefey,
and having put fome men on fhore, they burnt two
churches, and ravaged part of the country about.
But they paid very dear for it, for all the ftrength of
the ifland being met together, they fet upon them in
their return to their fhips, and cut them off in fuch a
manner, that not one remained to bring tidings to
the fleet of what had befel them. But they on
board quickly perceived what had happened, and
therefore thought it not very fafe harbouring upon
that coaft, but judging it more advifeable to weigh
anchor, they prefently fet fail for Chefter; when
they were arrived thither, they found that a peace
was actually concluded betwixt King Henry and
prince Owen upon this article; That Cadwalader
fhould have all his lands reftored to him, and he received to the favour and friendfhip of his brother.
Then king Henry leaving the caftles of Ruthlan and
Bafingwerk well manned and fortified, and having
near the latter founded a public ftructure for the
order of Knights Templars, returned to England.
But the troubles of Wales did not end with him,
for Iorwerdh Goch ap Meredith who had taken part
with the king of England during this war, laid fiege
to the caftle of Yale, which was built by prince Owen,
and making himfelf mafter of it, rafed it to the
ground.

The next year commenced with a very unfortu-A.D. 1157.
nate action, Ifor ap Meyric having long before caft
a very wifhful eye upon the land and eftate of
Morgan ap Owen, was now refolved to put in execution what he had before contrived; and as covetoufnefs feldom bears any regard to virtue or
honour, he treacheroufly fet upon him, and flew
him; and with him fell Gurgan ap Rhys, the moft
famous Britifh poet of his time. Morgan's eftate
Ifor beftowed upon his brother Iorwerth, who about
the fame time got alfo poffeffion of the town of
Caer-Lheon. But thefe inward and home-bred diſturbances

. sturbances were quickly mitigated by a general peace, which was presently after this concluded, betwixt the king of England and all the princes and lords of Wales, Rhys ab Gruffydh ap Rhys, prince of South-Wales, only excepted. For this prince Rhys, who probably would not rely too far upon the king of England's fidelity, refused to consent to a peace; but however, to secure himself the best he could from the English, whom he had no small reason to be afraid of, he thought it his best prudence to issue out his orders, commanding his subjects to remove their cattel and other effects to the wilderness of Tywy, where they were like to remain securest from the eyes and reach of the enemies. But he had not continued there long, when he received a more positive express from King Henry, commanding him to appear forthwith at his court, and to accept of the proposals of peace, before the joint forces of England and Wales were sent to fetch him up. Prince Rhys, having received such a threatning message, thought it now high time to repent of what he had afore so rashly resolved upon, and therefore after long consultation, he judged it his wisest way to accept of the king's proposals and to appear at court. There it was agreed upon, that Rhys, whose lands heretofore lay scattered about, and were intermixed with other person's estates, should enjoy Cantref Mawr, and any other Cantref which the king should be pleased to bestow upon him. But contrary to this article, the king assigned him several lordships and other lands far remote from each other, and particularly intermixed them with the estates of Englishmen, whom. he was sure would be a watch and a curb to all the motions of prince Rhys. This was indeed a very politick contrivance of king Henry to keep under the high and restless spirit of Rhys; but the justice of the action does not so evidently appear in breaking one of the chiefest articles of the peace, and chopping and bestowing that which was not justly in his power to give. But it is manifestly apparent that the English of these times were mainly concerned right

or

or wrong to opprefs and keep under the Welch, of whofe mortal hatred to fubjection they had fo frequently and fo cruelly felt. Prince Rhys was not at all ignorant of thefe wrongful and deceitful dealings of king Henry, but knowing himfelf to be unable to redrefs thefe grievances, he thought it more advifeable for a time to live quietly with a little, than rafhly to hazard all. But in a fhort time he had opportunity either to demand redrefs from the king, or elfe to endeavour it himfelf by force of arms. For as foon as Roger earl of Clare was informed of the diftribution which the king of England had granted to prince Rhys, he came to king Henry, requefting of his majefty, that he would grant him fuch lands in Wales, as he could win by force of arms. The king readily complied with his requeft, being always very forward to grant any thing which feemed to curb and difcommode the Welch, and therefore the earl of Clare marched with a great army into Cardigan, and having fortified the caftles of Yftrat-Meyric, Humphrey, Dyfi, Dynerth and Lhanrhyftyd, he made feveral incurfions into the country. In the fame manner, Walter Clyfford who was governor of Lhanymdhyfri caftle, made inroads into the territories of prince Rhys, and after he had flain feveral of the Welch, and made great wafte in the country, returned with confiderable booty.

Prince Rhys as he was unable to bear thefe outrages, fo he was refolved either to have immediate redrefs, or elfe to proclaim open war againft the Englifh, and therefore he fent an exprefs to king Henry, complaining of the hoftilities which his fubjects the earl of Clare and Walter Clyfford had committed in his country. But finding the king to put him ftill off with only fmooth words and fair promifes, and that he always winked at the faults of the Englifh and Normans, without any farther confultation about the matter, he laid fiege to the caftle of Lhanymdhyfri, and in fhort time made himfelf mafter of it. Alfo Eineon the fon of Anarawd, Rhys's brother's fon, and a perfon of great valour, being defirous to

N   free

free his country from that miferable fervitude they
now groaned under, and judging withal that his uncle
was now difcharged from the oath he had lately fworn
to the King of England fat before the caftle of Humphrey, and having forcibly made his entrance into
it, he put all the garrifon to the fword, where he
found a gieat number of horfes and armour, enough
to arm a confiderable body of men.   And whilft
Eineon was thus engaged at Humphrey's caftle,
Prince Rhys perceiving that he could not enjoy any
part of his inheritance but what he afterwards got
by the fword, drew all his power together and entered Cardigan, where like a moft violent torrent, he
over-run the country, that he left not one caftle
ftanding of thofe which his enemies had fortified,
and fo brought all the country to his fubjection.
King Henry being fore offended at the progrefs which
Prince Rhys fo fuddenly made againft him, returned
with a great army into South Wales, but finding it to
no purpofe to attempt any thing againft the Prince,
he thought it more advifeable to permit him to enjoy all that he had gotten, and only to take hoftages
for his obferving of peace during his abfence out of
the kingdom, which Prince Rhys promifing to do,
he forthwith returned to England, and foon after
went for Normandy, where he concluded a peace with
the French King.

A.D. 1158.   But the year following, Prince Rhys of South Wales
without any refpect to his promife to King Henry laft
year, led his forces to Dyfed, and deftroyed all the
caftles that the Normans had fortified in that country,
and then laid fiege to Caermardhyn.   But Reynold
Earl of Briftol, the king's bafe fon, being informed
of it, called together the Earl of Clare, his brother-
in-law Cadwalader, Prince Owen of North Wales's
brother, Howel and Conan Owen's fons, with two
Earls more, who with their joint forces marched to
raife the fiege.   But Prince Rhys was wifer than to
abide their coming, and therefore upon the firft
intimation of fuch great oppofition, he retired to the
mountains called Cefn Refter, and there encamped
being

being sufficiently secure from any enemy, by the natural fortification of the place. The confederate army lay at Dynwylhir; and there built a caftle, but finding no news or tidings of Prince Rhys, they returned home without effecting any thing of note. King Henry was ftill in Normandy, and there made war againft the Earl of St. Giles, for the city and earldom of Tholoufe.

Towards the beginning of this year, Madoc ap Meredith ap Blethyn Prince of Powis died at Winchefter, whence his body was honourably conveyed to Powis, and buried at Myfod. He was a Prince very much affected to piety and religion, very charitable to the neceffitous, and good to the diftreffed ; but his great fault was, that he ftickled too hard for the intereft of the Englifh, and was always in confederacy with King Henry againft the good fuccefs of his native country. He had iffue by his wife Sufanna, the daughter of Gruffydh ap Conan Prince of North Wales, three fons, Gruffydh Maylor, Owen and Elis, and a daughter named Marred. He had alfo three natural fons, Owen Brogynton, Cynwric Efelh, and Eineon Efelh, who though bafe born, yet according to the cuftom of Wales, co-inherited with their brethren who were legitimate.

And here it will not be amifs, once for all, to give a particular account of the principality, afterwards the lordfhips of Powis, how it came to be divided into many fhares and portions, and by that means became fo irrecoverably broken and weakened, that it was made fubject to the Normans before the reft of Wales. For Powis before King Offa's time, reached eaftwards to the rivers of Severn and Dee, in a right line from the end of Broxon hills to Salop, and comprehended all the country between the Wye and Severn, which was antiently the eftate of Brochwel Yfcithroc, of whom mention is made before. But after the making of Offa's dike, Powis was contracted into a narrower compafs, the plain country towards Salop being inhabited by Saxons and Normans, fo that the length of it reached north-eaft from Pul-

ford bridge to Lhangiric, parifh on the confines of
Cardiganfhire, to the fouth-weft, and the breadth
from the fartheft part of Cyfeilioc weftward, to Elfmere on the eaft-fide. This principality, Roderic the
Great gave to his youngeft fon Merfyn, in whofe pofterity it remained entire, till the death of Blethyn ap
Confyn, who though he had divided it betwixt his
fons Meredith and Cadwgan; yet it came again whole
and entire to the poffeffion of Meredith ap Blethyn.
But he again broke the union, and left it between his
two fons Madawc and Gruffydh; the firft of which
was married to Sufanna the daughter of Gruffydh ap
Conan Prince of North Wales, and had with her that
part, afterward called by his name, Powis Fadoc.
After his death, this lordfhip was divided alfo betwixt his fons Gruffydh Maelor, Owen ap Madawc,
and Owen Brogynton, which laft, though bafely
born, had however, for his incomparable valour and
courage, a fhare of his father's eftate, namely, Edeyrneon and Dinmael, which he left to his fons Gruffydh,
Blethyn and Iorwerth. Owen Madawc had to his portion Mechain-is-Coed, and had iffue Lhewelyn and
Owen Fychan. But Gruffydh Maelor the eldeft fon,
lord of Bromfield, had to his part, both the Maelors
with Mochnant-is-Raydar, and married Angharad the
daughter of Owen Gwynedh Prince of North Wales, by
whom he had iffue one fon named Madawc, who held
his father's inheritance entirely, and left it fo to his
only fon Gruffydh, who was called Lord of Dinas
Bran, becaufe he lived in that caftle: he married Emma the daughter of James Lord Audley, by whom he
had iffue Madawc, Lhewelyn, Gruffydh and Owen.
This Gruffydh ap Madawc took part with King Henry
the Third and Edward the Firft againft the Prince of
North Wales; and therefore for fear of the faid prince,
he was forced to keep himfelf fecure within his caftle
of Dinas Bran, which being fituated upon the fum-
mit of a very fteep hill, feemed impregnable to all
the daring efforts that could be ufed againft it. After his death, Edward the Firft dealt very unkindly
with his children, who were of age to manage their

own

own concerns; and making two of them privately
away, beſtowed the wardſhip of Madoc his eldeſt ſon,
who had by his father's will, the lordſhips of Bromfield and Yale, with the reverſion of Maelor Saeſnec
Hopeſdale and Mouldſdale his mother's jointure, on
John Earl Warren; and the wardſhip of Lhewelyn,
to whoſe ſhare fell the lordſhips of Chirke and Nanheudwy, to Roger Mortimer, third ſon to Roger Mortimer the ſon of Ralph Mortimer, Lord Mortimer of
Wigmor. But Emma, Gruffydh's wife, having in her
poſſeſſion for her dowry, Maelor Saeſnec, Hopeſdale,
and Mouldſdale with the preſentation of Bangor rec-
tory; and ſeeing two of her ſons diſinherited and done
away, and the fourth dead without iſſue, and doubting
leſt Gruffydh her only ſurviving child could not long
continue, ſhe conveyed her eſtate to the Audley's,
her own kin, who getting poſſeſſion of it took the
ſame from the king, from whom it came to the
houſe of Derby, where it continued for a long time;
till at length it was ſold to Sir John Glynne, ſerjeant
at law, in whoſe family it ſtill remaineth. But Earl
Warren and Roger Mortimer forgetting what ſignal
ſervice Gruffydh ap Madoc had performed for the
king, guarded their new poſſeſſions with ſuch caution
and ſtrictneſs, that they took eſpecial care they ſhould
never return to any of the poſterity of the legal proprietor; and therefore having obtained the king's patent, they began to ſecure themſelves in the ſaid lordſhips. John Earl Warren began to build Holt caſtle,
which was finiſhed by his ſon William, and ſo the
lordſhips of Bromfield and Yale continued in the
name of the Earls of Warren for three deſcents, viz.
John, William and John, who dying without iſſue;
the ſaid lordſhips, together with the earldom of Warren deſcended to Alice ſiſter and heir to the laſt John
Earl Warren, who was married to Edmond Fitz
Alan Earl of Arundel, in which houſe they remained
for three deſcents, namely, Edmund, Richard, Richard
his ſon, and Thomas Earl of Arundel. But for want
of iſſue to this laſt, Thomas Earl of Arundel and
Warren, the ſaid lordſhips fell to two of his ſiſters,

wh. rec

whereof one named Elizabeth was married to Thomas Mowbray duke of Norfolk, and the other called Joan, to William Beauchamp Lord of Abergavenny: but since they came to the hands of Sir William Stanley knight, who being attainted of High treason, they devolved by forfeiture to the crown, and now are annexed to the principality of Wales. But Roger Mortimer the other sharer in the lands of Gruffydh ap Madoc, was made Justice of North Wales, built the castle of Chirke, and married Lucia the daughter and heir of Sir Robert de Wafre knight, by whom he had issue Roger Mortimer, who was married to Joan Turbervill, by whom he had John Mortimer Lord of Chirke. This John sold the lordship of Chirke to Richard Fitzalan Earl of Arundel, Edmund's son, and so it was again annexed to Bromfield and Yale.

The third son of Gruffydh Lord of Dinas Bran, named also Gruffydh, had for his part Glyn Dwrdwy, which Gruffydh ap Gruffydh had issue Madoc Crupl, who was the father of Madoc Fychan, the father of Gruffydh, the father of Gruffydh Fychan, who was the father of Owen Glyndwr, who rebelling in the days of Henry the Fourth, Glyndwrdwy by confiscation came to the King, of whom it was afterwards purchased by Robert Salisbury of Rug, in whose family it still remaineth. Owen the fourth son of Gruffydh Lord of Dinas Bran had for his share Cynlhaeth with the rights and privileges thereunto belonging. The other part of Powys, comprehending the countries of Aruftly, Cyfeilioc, Lhannerch-hudol, Caereneon, Mochnach uwch Rayadr, Mechan uwch Coed, Moudhwy, Deudhwr, Yftrad Marchelch, and Teir Tref, or the Three Towns, rightfully descended to Gruffydh ap Meredith ap Blethyn, by Henry the First, created Lord Powis, who married Gweyryl or Weyryl the daughter of Urgene ap Howel ap Iefaf ap Cadogan ap Athleftan Glodryth, by whom he had issue Owen surnamed Cyfeilioc. This Owen enjoyed his father's estate entire, and married Gwenlhiam the daugh-

:::ter

ter of Owen Gwynedh Prince of North Wales, who bore him one fon, named Gwenwynwyn or Wenwyn- wyn, from whom that part of Powis was afterwards called Powis Wenwynwyn. He had moreover a bafe brother, called Cafwalhon, upon whom he beftowed the countries of Swydh Lhannerch Hudol, and Brani- arth. Gwenwynwyn fucceeded his father in all his eftate, faving what Cafwalhon enjoyed, and married Margaret the daughter of Rhys ap Theodor Prince of South Wales, by whom he had Gruffydh ap Gwen- wynwyn, who fucceeding his father in all his pof- feffions, had iffue fix fons, by Margaret the daugh- ter of Robert Corbet, brother to Thomas Lord Cor- bet of Cous; and fo the entire eftate of Gruffydh ap Meredith ap Blethyn Lord of Powis, became fhattered, and torn into divers pieces. Owen, Gruf- fydh ap Gwenwynwyn's eldeft fon, had for his part Aruftly, Cyfeilioc, Lhannerch Hudol, and a part of Caereneon; Lhewelyn had Mochnant uwch Rayadr and Mechain uwch Coed; John the third fon, had the fourth part of Caereneon; William had Moud- hwy; Gruffydh Fychan had Deudhwr Yftrat-Mar- chelh, and Teir Tref; and David the fixth and youngeft fon, had the other fourth part of Caere- neon. Owen ap Gruffydh had iffue one only daugh- ter, named Hawys Gadarn, or the Hardy, whom he left his heir; but her uncles Lhewelyn, John, Gruf- fydh Fychan and David, thinking it an eafy matter to difpoffefs an orphan, challenged the lands of their brother Owen, alledging for a cloak to their ufur- pation, that a woman was not capable of holding any lands in that country. But Hawys made fuch friends in England, that her cafe was made known to King Edward the Second, who beftowed her in marr age upon a fervant of his, named John Charleton, termed *Valectus domini. regis,* who was born at Appley rear Wellington, in the county of Salop, *anno* One thou- fand two hundred fixty-eight, and in her right, created him Lord Powis.

This

..This John Charleton Lord Powis, being aided and
fupported by the King of England, quickly broke
all their meafures; and having taken Lhewelyn,
John, and David, his wives uncles, he put them in
fafe cuftody, in the king's caftle of Harlech; and
then obtained a writ from the King to the Sheriff of Shropfhire, and to Sir Roger Mortimer,
Lord of Chirkland, and Juftice of North Wales, for
the apprehenfion of Gruffydh Fychan, with his fons-
in-law, Sir Roger Chamber and Hugh Montgomery,
who were then in actual hoftility againft him and his
wife Hawys. But Gruffydh Fychan and his accomplices fufpecting their own ftrength, and having loft
Thomas Earl of Lancafter, their main fupport, thought
it moft advifeable to fubmit themfelves to the king's
pleafure, touching the difference betwixt them and
Hawys; who finding upon record, how that Gruffydh ap Meredith, anceftor to the faid Hawys, upon
his fubmiffion to King Henry the Firft, became fubject to the King of England, and thereupon was
created Baron of Powis, which barony he and his
pofterity had ever fince held *in capite* from the king;
was of opinion, that Hawys had more right to her father's poffeffions now in their hands, than any pretence
they could lay to her eftate. But to make a final de-
termination of this matter, and to compofe the difference more amicably betwixt them; it was agreed,
that Hawys fhould enjoy her inheritance in fee-fimple
to her and her heirs for ever, after the tenure of England; and that her uncles Lhewelyn, John, David,
and Gruffydh, fhould quietly enjoy their portion,
and the fame to defcend to their heir males perpetually; but in default of fuch heir males, the fame was
to defcend to Hawys and her heirs. But William Lord
of Moudhwy, the fourth brother, called otherwife
Wilcock Mowdhwy, becaufe he did not join with
the reft againft Hawys, had all his lands confirmed
to him, and to all his heirs, both male and female
for ever. He married Elianor, the fifter of Elen,
Owen Glyndwr's mother, who was lineally defcended
from Rhys ap Theodore, Prince of South Wales, by
whom

whom he had iffue John de Mowdhwy; whofe daughter Elizabeth, being heir to his whole eftate, was married to one Sir Hugh Burgh, knight. His fon Sir John Burgh, Lord of Moudhwy, married Jane the daughter of Sir William Clapton of Glocefterfhire, by whom he had four daughters, Elizabeth, Ancreda, Ifabel and Elianor; the firft of whom was married to Thomas Newport, the fecond to John Leighton of Stretton; the third to John Lingen; and the younger to Tho. Mytton; who, by equal diftribution, had the lordfhip of Modhwy divided betwixt them.

But John Charleton Lord of Powis had iffue by his wife Hawys, a fon named John, who enjoyed the fame lordfhip for about feven years, and then left it to his fon, of the fame name, who was Lord of Powis fourteen years; and then it defcended to his fon, called alfo John Charelton who enjoyed his father's eftate twenty-feven years; but dying without iffue, the lordfhip of Powis fell to his brother Edward Charleton. This Edward had iffue by his wife Elianor, the daughter and one of the heirs of Thomas Earl of Kent, and the widow of Roger Mortimer Earl of March, two daughters, Jane and Joyce; the firft of which was married to Sir John Gray, knight; and the fecond to John Lord Tiptoft, whofe fon was by King Henry VI. created Earl of Worcefter. But after the death of Elianor, this Edward Lord Powis married Elizabeth the daughter of Sir John Barkley, knight; and fo after his death, which happened in the year 1420, the lordfhip of Powis was divided into three parts, whereof his widow Elizabeth had for her jointure Lhannerch Hudol, Yftrad Marchelh, Deudhwr and Teirtref, and was afterwards married to Lord Dudley. Jane his eldeft daughter had Caereneon, Mechain, Mochnant, and Plafdinas; and Joyce had Cyfeilioc, and Aruftly. But the lordfhip of Powis continued in the family of Sir John Gray, for five defcents, in right of his wife Jane; the laft of whom, Edward Gray, Lord Powis, married Anne, one of the daughters and co-heirs of Charles Brandon, duke of Suffolk, and died without any lawful iffue.

Dugdale Bar. Engl. tom. II. p. 284.

issue. This Edward Lord Powys, in 15 Henry VIII. accompanied the Duke of Suffolk in the expedition then made into France, and was at the taking of Bray, and other places then won from the French. And in 36 Henry VIII. being again ready to march in the King's service, he made his last testament, whereby he settled the succession of his whole barony and lordship of Powys, his castle and manor of Pool, with divers other lordships in the county of Montgomery, and all the rest of his estate in the county of Salop, upon the heirs of his own body lawfully begotten, or to be begotten; and in default of such issue, his castle and manor of Charlton and Pontisbury in Shropshire, upon Jane Orwell, daughter of Sir Lewis Orwell, knight, and her assigns, during her natural life. And in case he should die without any issue of his own body lawfully begotten, that then Edward Grey, his illegitimate son by the same Jane Orwell, should have and enjoy his said barony and manor of Powis, his castle and manor of Pool, and all other his lordships in the county of Montgomery; with the reversion of the castle and manor of Charlton and Pontisbury, to him and his heirs lawfully begotten; and for lack of such issue, to remain to that child, in case it should be a son, wherewith the same Jane Orwell was then great by him, and to the heirs of his body lawfully begotten. But if it should not prove a son, or if the son die without issue, then that the whole barony of Powis and all the premises before-mentioned, should come to Jane Grey his daughter, and to the heirs of her body lawfully begotten; and for lack of such issue, to Anne Grey, his other daughter, and heirs of her body lawfully begotten; and lastly for default of such issue, to such woman-child as should be born of the body of the said Jane Orwell. But after Edward Grey, the title of Lord of Powis lay extinct to the fifth year of King Charles I. when Sir William Herbert son of Sir Edward Herbert of Redcastle (antiently called Pool-castle, now Powis castle) in the county of Montgomery, second son to William Earl of of Pembrock, was advanced to the dignity of a Baron of the realm, by the title of Lord Powis of Powis, in the marches of Wales; in whose family it still continues, though the title has been changed from a Baron to an Earl, and since to a Marquifs.

About the same time that the Prince of Powis died, Cadwalhon ap Madawc ap Ednerth, who had been for some considerable time at variance with his brother Eineon Clyd, was taken prisoner by him; who delivered him up to Owen Prince of North Wales. But the Prince being willing to gratify the king of England, whose interest Cadwalhon has as much as in him lay oppofed, sent him to the king's officers to be imprisoned at Winchester; from whence he quickly found a way to escape: and by the advice of the rest of his brethren he returned home to his country. King Henry continued all this while in Normandy, and during his stay there, a match was concluded upon betwixt his son Henry and Margaret daughter to Lewis king of France. But this new alliance could A.D.1160. not prevent these two monarchs from falling at variance with each other, which happened the year following; and thereupon King Henry marched with his army into Gascoyne, to quell certain rebels, who upon first notice of this breach between both kings, were up in arms against the English. But the next year, a 1161. peace was again concluded, and so all things returned to their former state of amity and quietness.

But it was not fo in Wales; for Howel the son of Ievaf ap Cadwgan ap Athleftan Glodryth, having got into his hand the castle of Walwern in Cyfeilioc, rafed it to the ground, which fo incensed Prince Owen, who was owner of it, that nothing could lay his fury, till he had drawn his forces together, and made an incursion into Lhandhinam in Aruftly, Howel's country; which he cruelly harraffed, and carried away considerable booty. The people of the country perceiving these devaftations of the North Wales men, came together to the number of three hundred men, offering their service to their natural Lord, Howel ap Iefaf;

who

who upon this addition of strength, followed the enemy to the banks of Sevérn, where they were encamped. Prince Owen finding them to march after
him, was glad of the opportunity to be further revenged upon Howel; and so turning suddenly upon
them, he slew about two hundred men; the rest narrowly escaping with Howel to the woods and rocks.
Owen being more joyful for the revenge he had taken
of Howel, than for any victory he had gained, rebuilt Walwern castle, and having well fortified and
manned it, returned home to North Wales.

A. D. 1162. The year following, the like thing happened;
Owen the son of Gruffydh ap Meredith, commonly
called Owen Cyfeilioc o Wynedh, together with Owen
ap Madawc ap Meredith, and Meredith ap Howel,
set upon Carrechofa castle near Ofweftry, and having
over-powered the garrison, committed great waste
and destruction therein. But about the same time,
a pleasant passage happened in England; Robert
Mountford and Henry de Effex, who had both fought
against the Welch upon the marches, and both run,
began now to impeach each other, as being the first
occasion of flying. The dispute was to be tried by
combat, in which being engaged, Henry was overcome; and for his false accusing of Robert, he was
sentenced to have his estate forfeited, and then having
his crown shorn, he was entered a monk at Redding.
Within a little after, King Henry calling to mind
what Prince Rhys had committed during his absence
out of the kingdom, drew up a great army against
South Wales, and having marched as far as Pencadyr
near Brecknock, Rhys met him, and did his homage;
and having delivered up hostages for his future behaviour, stopped the king's farther progress, so that
thence he returned to England. But after the king's
departure, two very unlucky accidents happened in
Wales; Eineon the son of Anarawd ap Gruffydh, nephew to Prince Rhys, being villainously murdered in
his bed by his own servant, called Walter ap Lhywarch; as also Cadwgan ap Meredith in like manner,

ner, by one Walter, ap Riccart. But the lofs of his nephew Prince Rhys made up, by poffeffing himfelf of that large country called Cantref Mawr, and the land of Dynefowr, which he afterwards enjoyed. Of men of learning there died this year, Cadifor ap Daniel, archdeacon of Cardigan; and Henry ap Arthen, the greateft fcholar that had flourifhed in Wales for many years.

The next year, a total rupture broke forth betwixt A.D. 1163. the Englifh and Welch; Prince Rhys, a man of an active and uncontroulable fpirit, being now experimentally fenfible he could never carry on the greatnefs and grandeur of his quality, with fuch lands as the king of England had allotted him, made an invafion into the lordfhip of Roger de Acre Earl of Glocefter; being moved thereto in a great meafure, by reafon that his nephew Anarawd ap Gruffydh was murdered by his motive and inftigation. Being advanced with a ftrong army into the Earl of Glocefter's eftate, without any great oppofition he took Aberheidol caftle, with thofe belonging to the fons of Wyhyaon; all which he rafed to the ground. Thence he marched to Cardigan, bringing all that country under his fubjection; and from thence he marched againft the Flemings, whofe country he cruelly harraffed with fire and fword. The reft of the eftates of Wales, perceiving Prince Rhys to profper fo fuccefsfully againft the Englifh, thought they might equally fucceed, and fhake off the Englifh yoke, which fo unreafonably oppreffed them. And therefore they unanimoufly agreed to caft off their fubjection to the Englifh, whofe tyranny they could no longer bear, and to put over them princes of their own nation, whofe fuperiority they could better tolerate. And fo this year concluded with making fuitable preparations for the following campaign.

And therefore as foon as the time of year for action 1164. was advanced, David fon of Owen Prince of North-Wales fell upon Flintfhire, which pertained to the king of England; and carrying off all the people and cattle with him, brought them to Dyffryn Ciwyd, other-

otherwife Ruthyn land. King Henry underftanding
this, gathered together his forces, and with all fpeed
marched to defend both his fubjects and towns from
the incurfions and depredations of the Welch. Being
come to Ruthlan, and encamped there three days, he
quickly perceived he could do no great matter, by
reafon that his army was not fufficiently numerous ;
and therefore he thought it more advifeable to return
back to England, and to augment his forces, before
he fhould attempt any thing againft the Welch. And
accordingly he levied the moft chofen men throughout
all his dominions of England, Normandy, Anjou, Gaf-
coin and Gwien ; befides thofe fuccours from Flanders
and Britain ; and then fet forward for North Wales,
purpofing to deftroy without mercy every living thing
he could poffibly meet with ; and being advanced as
far as Croes-Ofwalt, called Ofweftry, he encamped
there. On the other fide, Prince Owen and his brother Cadwalader, with all the ftrength of North Wales ;
Prince Rhys with thofe of South Wales ; Owen Cyfeilioc and Madawc ap Meredith with all the power of
Powis ; the two fons of Madawc ap Ednerth, with
the people living betwixt the rivers of Severn and
Wye, met together, and pitched their camp at Corwen
in Edeyrneon, intending unanimoufly to defend their
country againft the king of England. King Henry,
underftanding that they were fo near, was very defirous to come to battle ; and to that end he removed to the banks of the river Ceireoc, caufing all
the woods thereabouts to be cut down, for fear of
any ambufhment lurking therein, and for a more
clear profpect of the enemy. But fome of the Welch
took advantage of this opportunity, who being well
acquainted with the paffage, without the knowledge
of their officers, fell upon the king's guard, where all
the pikemen were pofted ; and after a hot skirmifh,
feveral were flain on both fides. But in fine, the king
won the paffage, and fo marched on to the mountain
of Berwyn, where he lay fometime without any hoftility on either fide, both armies ftanding in fear of
each other. The Englifh kept the open plains, and
                                    were

were afraid to be entrapped in the ftreights and narrow paffages; and the Welch on the other hand watched the advantage of the place, and obferved the Englifh fo narrowly, that neither forage or victuals could pafs to the king's camp. And what augmented the mifery of the Englifh army, there happened to fall fuch a rain, that mightily difturbed their encampment, in fo much that the foldiers could fcarcely ftand, for the difadvantage of thofe flippery hills. But in the end King Henry was forced to decamp, and after a very confiderable lofs of men and ammunition, befides the great charges of this expedition, was compelled to return back to England. But to exprefs the great diffatisfaction he entertained of this enterprize, in a great fury he plucked out the eyes of the hoftages, which he had fome time afore received from the Welch; which were Rhys and Cadwalhon the fons of Owen Prince of North Wales, and Cynric and Meredith the fons of Rhys of South Wales. Some write, that in affailing of a bridge, the king was in no fmall danger of his life; one of the Welch having aimed directly at him, was like to pierce him through the body, had not Hubert de Clare, Conftable of Colchefter, who perceived the arrow a-coming thruft himfelf betwixt the king and it, though to the lofs of his own life.

But though King Henry was fhamefully forced to return to England, yet he did not give over the thoughts of fubduing the Welch; and therefore after a long confultation, he made a third expedition into Wales, conveying his army by fea, as far as Chefter. There he ftaid for fome time, till all his fleet, as well thofe fhips that he had hired out of Ireland, as his own, were all arrived. But when they were all come together, and got fafely to Chefter, his mind was altered; and inftead of a defign againft Wales, he unexpectedly difmiffed his whole army. Prince Rhys was glad of this opportunity, and therefore withdrawing his forces from the confederate army, he marched to the fiege of Aberteifi caftle, which being furrendered to him, he rafed to the gr und. For the he got before Cilgerran, which he used after the same manner, and therein took prisoner Robert the son of Stephen his cousin-german, who was the son of Nest his aunt, who after the death of Gerald, had married Stephen Constable. The joy of these happy successes on the part of the Welch, was somewhat clouded by the death of Lhewelyn, son of Owen Prince of North Wales, a person of great worth and exceedingly well beloved of all his country.

A. D. 1165. And now the Welch being something secure from any invasion from the English; there rose up another enemy to create them disturbance; the Flemings and Normans finding the English to fail in their attempt against the Welch, thought they might with better success quell and subdue them. And therefore they came to West Wales with a great army, and laid siege to the castle of Cilgerran, which Rhys had lately fortified; but after two different assaults, they were manfully beat back, and forced to depart home again. But what the Flemings could not affect against the Welch in South Wales, the Welch easily brought about against the English in North Wales; for Prince Owen having besieged Basingwerk castle, then in the possession of the king of England, without much time spent, made himself master of it. But it was always the misfortune of the Welch, that when they found themselves secure from any enemy abroad, they were sure to quarrel and fall out at home; though indeed it could not be well otherwise expected, where so many petty states endeavoured still to surmount and out-vie one another. And now when all things went very successfully of their sides, in opposition to the English; two ambitious persons began to kindle a flame in their own bosoms; Owen Cyfeilioc the son of Gruffydh ap Meredith Lord of Powis, and Owen Fychan second son to Madawc ap Meredith, forcibly dispossessed Iorwerth Goch of his estate in Powis, which they divided betwixt themselves; Mochnant uwch Rayadr to Owen Cyfeilioc, and Mochnant is Rayadr to Owen Fychan.

But

But the reſt of the princes of Wales could not A. D. 1166. brook this injury done to Iorwerth Goch; and therefore Owen Prince of North Wales, with his brother Cadwalader; and Rhys Prince of South Wales, went with an army into Powis againſt Owen Cyfeilioc, and having chaſed him out of the country, they beſtowed Caereneon upon Owen Fychan, to hold it of Prince Owen; and Rhys had Walwern, by reaſon that it lay near his own territories. But within a while after, Owen Cyfeilioc returned with a numerous band of Normans and Engliſh along with him, and laid ſiege to the caſtle of Caereneon, which he burnt to the ground. But the loſs of this place was made up by the taking of Ruthlan caſtle, which Owen, Rhys, and Cadwalader jointly beſieged; and which was ſo ſtrongly fortified, and ſo manfully defended, that it coſt them three months before they could make themſelves maſters of the place. Afterwards they won the caſtle of Preſtatyn, and reduced the whole country of Tegengl, ſubject to Prince Owen; and then returned home to their reſpective dominions. And from henceforward nothing of moment was tranſ- 1167. acted, during the remainder of Prince Owen's reign, only his ſon Conan moſt unmercifully ſlew Urgeney abbot of Lhwythlawr, together with his nephew Lhawthen. But a little after, Prince Rhys of South 1168. Wales releaſed out of priſon his nephew Robert, ſon to Stephen Conſtable, whom as is ſaid before, he had taken at the ſiege of Cilgarran caſtle, and ſent him to Ireland to the aid of Dermot the ſon of Murchart king of Linſter, who was then in actual war with the king of Leimſter. With him and his brother Morris Fitz-Gerald, and their nephews Robert Meyler and Raymond, went over a ſtrong detachment of Welchmen, under the command of Richard Strongbow Earl of Strigule, who were the chief motive of the conqueſt of Ireland, when it was firſt brought in ſubjection to the crown of England.

But the next year, Owen Gwynedh ſon of Gruf- 1169. fydh ap Conan prince of North Wales, departed this life in the two and thirtieth year of his reign.

O   He

A.D. 1169. He was a wise and valourous prince, ever fortunate and victorious in all his undertakings, insomuch, as he never undertook any design but what he accomplished. He had by different women several issues, who got themselves greater esteem by their valour, than by their birth and parentage. He had by Gwaldus the daughter of Lhywarch ap Trahaern ap Caradoc, Iorwerth Drwyndwn, or the Broken Nose, Conan Maelgon, and Gwenlhian; by Christian the daughter of Grono ap Owen ap Edwyn, he had David, Roderic, Cadwalhon abbot of Bardsey and Angharad, afterwards married to Gruffydh Maylor. He had by other women several other children, as Conan, Lhewelyn, Meredith, Edwal, Rhun, Howel, Cadelh, Madawc, Eineon, Cynwric, Philip, and Ryrid Lord of Clochran in Ireland. Of these, Run, Lhewelyn, and Cynwric died before their father; and the rest will be mentioned in the sequel of this history.

DAVID AP OWEN.

PRINCE Owen Gwynedh being dead, the succession was of right to descend to his eldest legitimate son, Iorwerth Drwyndwn, otherwise called Edward with the Broken Nose; but by reason of that blemish upon his face, he was laid aside as unfit to take upon him the government of North Wales, Therefore his younger brothers began every one to aspire, 1170 in hopes of succeeding their father; but Howel, who was of all the eldest, but base born, begotten of an Irish woman, finding they could not agree, stept in himself and took upon him the government. But David, who was legitimately born, could not brook that a bastard should ascend his father's throne; and

3　　　　　　　　　　　　　　　therefore

therefore he made all the preparations possible to pull
him down.   Howel on the other hand was as resolute
to maintain his ground, and was not willing so quickly to deliver up, what he had not very long got possession of; and so both brothers meeting together in
the field, were resolved to try their title by the point
of the sword.   The battle had not lasted long, but
Howel was slain; and then David was unanimously
proclaimed and saluted Prince of North Wales, which
principality he enjoyed without any molestation, till
Lhewelyn, Iorwerth Drwyndwn's son came of age, as
will hereafter appear.   But Madawc, another of Owen
Gwynedh's sons, finding how his brothers contended for
the principality, and that his native country was like
to be turmoiled in a civil war, did think it his better
prudence to try his fortune abroad;   and therefore
leaving North Wales in a very unsettled condition,
sailed with a small fleet of ships which he had rigged
and manned for that purpose, to the westward; and
leaving Ireland on the north, he came at length to an
unknown country, where most things appeared to him
new and uncustomary, and the manner of the natives
far different from what he had seen in Europe.   This
country, says the learned H. Lhoyd, must of necessity be some part of that vast tract of ground, of which
the Spaniards, since Hanno's time, boast themselves to
be the first discoverers; and which by order of Cos-
mography, seems to be some part of Nova Hispania
or Florida; whereby it is manifest, that this country
was discovered by the Britains, long before either Co-
lumbus or Americus Vesputius sailed thither.   But
concerning Madawc's voyage to this country, and
afterwards his return from thence; there be many fabulous stories and idle tales invented by the vulgar,
who are sure never to diminish from what they hear,
but will add to and increase any fable as far as their
invention will prompt them.   However says the same
author, it is certain that Madawc arrived in this country,
and after he had viewed the fertility and pleasantness of
it, he thought it expedient to invite more of his countrymen out of Britain; and therefore leaving most of

those

thofe he had brought with him already behind, he returned for Wales. Being arrived there, he began to acquaint his friends with what a fair and extenfive land he
had met with, void of any inhabitants, whilft they employed all their fkill to fupplant one another, only for
a ragged portion of rocks and mountains; and therefore he would perfuade them to change their prefent
ftate of danger and continual clafhings for a more
quiet being of eafe and enjoyment. And fo having
got a confiderable number of Welch together, he bid
his final adieu to his native country, and failed with
ten fhips back to them he had left behind. It is therefore to be fuppofed, fays our author, that Madawc
and his people inhabited part of that country, fince
called Florida, by reafon that it appears from Francis
Loves, an author of no fmall reputation, that in A-
cufanus and other places, the people honoured and
worfhipped the crofs; whence it may be naturally concluded, that chriftians had been there before the coming of the Spaniards; and who thefe chriftians might
be, unlefs it were this colony of Madawc's cannot be
eafily imagined. But by reafon that the Welch who
came over, were not many, they intermixt in a few
years with the natives of the country, and fo following
their manners and ufing their language, they became
at length undiftinguifhable from the barbarians. But
the country which Madawc landed in, is by the learned
Dr. Powel fuppofed to be part of Mexico; for which
conjecture he lays down thefe following reafons; firft,
as it is recorded in the Spanifh chronicles of the conqueft of the Weft Indies, the inhabitants and natives
of that country affirm by tradition, that their rulers
defcended from a ftrange nation, which came thither
from a ftrange country; as it was confeffed by King
Montezuma, in a fpeech at his fubmiffion to the king
of Caftile, before Hernando Cortez the Spanifh general. And then the Britifh words and names of
places ufed in that country, even at this day do undoubtedly argue the fame; as when they fpeak and
confabulate together, they ufe this Britifh word
                                                    Gwrando,

Gwrando, which fignifies to hearken or liften ; and a
certain bird with a white head, they call Pengwyn,
which fignifies the fame in Welch. But for a more
complete confirmation of this, the ifland of Corroefo,
the cape of Bryton, the river of Gwyndor, and the
white rock of Pengwyn, which are all Britifh words
do manifeftly fhew, that it was that country which
Madawc and his people inhabited.

As foon as the troubles of North Wales were over, A D. 1117.
and Prince David fecurely fettled in his throne, the
ftorm fell prefently upon Powis : for Owen Cyfeilioc
the lord of the country, had always, as much as in
him lay, oppofed the intereft and advantage of Rhys
Prince of South Wales ; upon which account Prince
Rhys came with a great army againft Powis, and
having fubdued Owen Cyfeilioc his enemy, he was
for all that fo favourable to him, that upon his delivering him pledges for his future behaviour, he
prefently departed out of Powis, and returned with
much honour to South Wales.   And now all the
ftates of Britain being at perfect reft and amity with
one another, the whole tide and fcene of action returned to Ireland ; for Henry king of England having called together all his nobility, began to confult
about the Irifh expedition, which had already been
determined to be taken in hand.   To this confultation there came fome meffengers from Richard Strongbow Earl of Strigule Marfhal of England, to deliver
up to the king's hands the city of Dublin, the town
of Waterford, with all fuch towns and caftles as he
got in right of his wife ; whereupon the king reftored
to him all his lands both in England and Normandy,
and created him Lord Steward of Ireland.   For this
Earl Strigule had lately, without the king's permiffion,
gone over to Ireland, and had married the daughter
of Dermott king of Dublin ; which King Henry
took in fuch indignation, that he prefently feized
upon all his lands in England and Normandy. Therefore the king having now fome footing in Ireland,
the expedition was unanimoufly concluded upon ; and

O 3   fo

so the king set upon his journey, and coming towards Wales was received by Prince Rhys, whose submission, the king liked so well, that he presently confirmed to him all his lands in South Wales. To return the king's favour, Rhys promised to his Majesty three hundred horses and four thousand oxen toward the conquest of Ireland; for the sure payment of which he delivered fourteen pledges. Then King Henry marching forward, came to Caerlheon upon Uske, and entering the town, he dispossessed the right owner Iorwerth ap Owen ap Caradoc, and kept it for his own proper use, placing a garrison of his own men therein.

But Iorwerth was not so easy-mouthed, as to be so unreasonably curbed by the king; and therefore departing in a great fury from the king's presence, he called to him his two sons Owen and Howel, whom he had by Angharad the daughter of Uchtryd bishop of Llandaf, and his sister's son Morgan ap Sitsyhlt ap Dyfnwal; and bringing together all the forces they were able, upon the king's departure they entered the country, and committing all the waste and destruction as they came along, they at last came before Caerlheon, which when they took, they used in the like manner, spoiling and destroying whatever they could meet with; so that nothing escaped their fury, excepting the castle, which they could not win. The king was in the mean time upon his journey to Pembrock, where being accompanied by Prince Rhys, he gave him a grant of all Cardigan, Ystratywy, Arustly, and Eluel; in recompence of all the civilities and honour he paid him. And so Rhys returned to Aberteifi, a town he had lately won from the Earl of Glocester, and there having prepared his present, about the beginning of October he returned again to Pembrock, having ordered eighty-six horses to follow him; which being presented to the king, he accepted of thirty-six of the choicest, and returned the rest with great thanks. The same day King Henry went to St. David's, and after he had offered to the memory of that saint, he dined with the bishop, who was the

son

fon of Gerald, coufin-german to Rhys; whither Richard Strongbow Earl of Strygule came from Ireland to confer with the king. Within a while after, King Henry being entertained by Rhys at the White-Houfe, reftored to him his fon Howel, who had been for a confiderable time detained as a pledge, and appointed him a certain day for payment of his tribute, at which time, all the reft of the pledges fhould be fet at liberty. The day following, being the next after the feaft of St. Luke, the king went on board, and the wind blowing very favourably, fet fail for Ireland; and being fafely arrived upon thofe coafts, he landed at Dublin; where he refted for that whole winter, in order to make greater preparations againft the following campaign.

But the change of the air and climate occafioned fuch a raging diftemper and infection among the foldiers, that to prevent the perifhing of his whole army, A. D. 1172. the king was forced to return with what fpeed he could back for England; and fo having fhipped off all his army and effects, he loofed anchor, and landed in Wales in the Paffion-week next year, and coming to Pembrock, he ftaid there on Eafter-day, and then proceeded upon his journey towards England. Rhys hearing of the king's return, was very officious to pay him his devotion, and would gladly feign to be one of the firft who fhould welcome him over; and fo meeting with him at Talachan, he expreffed all the ceremonies of duty and allegiance. Then the king paffed on, and as he came from Caerdyf by the new caftle upon Ufk, meaning to leave Wales in a peaceable condition, he fent for Iorwerth ap Owen ap Caradoc, who was the only perfon in open enmity againft him, and that upon very juft ground, willing him to come and treat about a peace, and affuring him of a fafe conduct for himfelf, his fons, and all the reft of his affociates. Iorwerth was willing to accept of the propofal, and thereupon fet forward to meet the king, having fent an exprefs to his fon Owen, a valourous young gentleman, to meet him by the way. Owen, according to his father's orders, fet forward on his journey, with a fmall retinue, without any thing of arms or weapons of war, as thinking it folly to clog himself with such needless carriage, when the king had promised a safe conduct. But he did not find it so safe; for as he passed the new castle upon Uske, the Earl of Bristol's men, who were garrisoned therein, laid in wait for him as he came along, and setting cowardly upon him, slew him, with most of his company. But some few escaped to acquaint his father Iorwerth of such a treacherous action; who hearing that his son was so basely murdered, contrary to the king's absolute promise of a safe passage; without any farther consultation about the matter, presently returned home with Howel his son, and all his friends, and would no longer put any trust or confidence in any thing that the king of England, or any of his subjects, promised to do. But on the other side to avenge the death of his son, who was so cowardly cut off; he presently raised all the forces that himself and the rest of his friends were able to do; and so entering into England, he destroyed with fire and sword all the country, to the gates of Hereford and Glocester. But the king was so intent upon his return, that he seemed to take no great notice of what Iorwerth was doing; and therefore having by commission constituted Lord Rhys Chief Justice of all South Wales, he forthwith took his journey to Normandy. About this time died Cadwalader ap Gruffydh, the son of Gruffydh ap Conan, sometime Prince of North Wales; who by his wife, Alice the daughter of Richard Clare Earl of Glocester, had issue, Cunetha, Radulph, and Richard; and by other women, Cadfan, Cadwalader, Eineon, Meredith Goch, and Cadwalhon. Towards the end of this year Sitsylht ap Dyfnwal, and Iefan ap Sitsyhlt ap Riryd, surprised the castle of Abergavenny, which belonged to the king of England, and having made themselves masters of it, they took the whole garrison prisoners.

A.D. 1173.   But the following year, there happened a very great difference, and a falling out betwixt King Henry and his son of the same name; this latter being upholden by the queen his mother, his brethren Geffrey and Richard,

Richard, the French King, the Earl of Flanders, together with the Earl of Chester, William Patrick, with
several other valiant knights and gentlemen. But the
old King having a stout and faithful army, consisting
of Almanes and Brabanters, was not in the least dis-
mayed or discouraged at such a seeming storm; and
which made him more bold and adventurous, he was
joined by a strong party of Welchmen, which Lord
Rhys had sent him, under the command of his son
Howel. King Henry overthrew his enemies in divers
encounters, and having either killed or taken prisoners
most of them who were rose up against him, he easily
dissipated the cloud which at first seemed so black and
threatening. Iorwerth ap Owen was not very sorry
to see the English clash, and fall into civil dissentions
among themselves; and therefore taking advantage of
such a seasonable opportunity, he drew his army against
Caerlheon, which stood out very stiffly against him. But
after many warm disputes of both sides, Iorwerth at
length prevailed, and entering the town by force, he
took most of the inhabitants prisoners; and then laying siege to the castle, it was surrendered up in exchange for the prisoners he had taken in the town.
Howel his son at the same time was busy in Gwent is
Coed; and having reduced all that country, excepting
the castle, to subjection, he took pledges of the inhabitants, to be true and faithful to him, and to withdraw their allegiance from the King of England. At
the same time, something of action passed in North-
Wales; for David ap Owen Gwynedh, Prince of North-
Wales, bringing an army over the river Menai into
Anglesey, against his brother Maelgon who kept that
island from him, forced him to make his escape to
Ireland; in his return from whence the following
year, he was accidentally discovered and seized upon,
and then by his brother's orders committed to close
prison. Prince David having brought the isle of Anglesey to its pristine state of subjection to him, was resolved to move all manner of obstacles which might at
any time for the future endanger its falling off from
him; and these he judged to be his own next relations,
                                                      and

1174. and therefore he expelled and banished all his brethren and coufins out of his territories of North-Wales. But before this fentence was put in execution, his brother Conan died, and fo efcaped the ignominy of being banifhed his native country, for no other reafon but the jealoufy of an ambitious brother.

About the fame time, Howel the fon of Iorwerth ap Owen of Caerlheon, took prifoner his uncle Owen Pencarn, who was right heir of Caerlheon and Gwent; and now having him fecure, and to prevent his getting any children to inherit thofe places which himfelf was next heir to, he firft pulled out his eyes, and then very inhumanly cut off his tefticles. But vengeance did not permit fuch a bafe action to go unpunifhed; for upon the Saturday following, a great army of Normans and Englifhmen came unexpectedly before the town, and won both it and the caftle, notwithftanding all the oppofition which Howel and his father Iorwerth made; though this laft was not privy to his fon's action. About the fame time King Henry came over to England, a little after whofe arrival, William king of Scots, and Roger de Moubray, were taken prifoners at Alnewike by the Barons of the north, as they came to deftroy the northern part of the country in the quarrel of the young King. But old King Henry having committed them to the fafe cuftody of the Earl of Leicefter, and received Hugh Bygod Earl of Chefter to his mercy, returned to Normandy with a very confiderable army of Welchmen, which David prince of North-Wales had fent him; in return of which, he gave him his fifter Emme in marriage. When he was arrived in Normandy, he fent a detachment of the Welch to cut off fome provifions which were going to the enemies camp; but in the mean time the French King came to a treaty of peace, which was fhortly afterwards concluded upon; fo that all the brethren, who had all this time maintained fuch an unnatural rebellion againft their father, were forced to beg the old King's forgivenefs and pardon for all their former mifdemeanours. David Prince of

North

North Wales began to grow very bold and assuming, by reason of his new alliance with the King of England; and nothing would serve his turn, but he must put his brother Roderic in prison, and secure him with fetters; for no other account, than because he demanded his share of his father's lands. It was the custom of Wales, as is said before, to make an equal division of the father's inheritance between all the children; and therefore David had no colour of reason or pretence to deal so severely with his brother; unless it were to verify that proverb; *Might overcomes right.* But though Prince David might depend much upon his affinity with the King of England; yet Rhys Prince of South-Wales gained his favour and countenance the more, by reason that he let slip no opportunity to further the King's interest and affairs in Wales, and by that means was a very necessary and useful instrument to keep under the Welch; and to promote the surer settlement of the English in the country. Not that he bore any love or affection to either King Henry or his subjects; but because he was sufficiently rewarded for former services, and was still in expectation of receiving more favours at the King's hands, he was resolved to play the politician so far, as to have regard to his own interest, more than the good of his native country. And what did ingratiate him to King Henry most of all, upon the feast of St. James he brought all such lords of South Wales as were at enmity with the King, to do him homage at Glocester; namely, Cadwalhon ap Madawc of Melyenyth, his cousin-german; Eineon Clyt of Eluel, and Eineon ap Rhys of Gwerthrynion, his sons-in-law; Morgan ap Caradoc ap Iestyn of Glamorgan; Gruffydh ap Ifor ap Meiric of Sengennyth, and Sitsylht ap Dyfnwal of Higher Gwent, all three his brothers-in-law, who had married his sisters; together with Iorwerth ap Owen of Caerlheon. King Henry was so well pleased with this stratagem of Rhys, that notwithstanding these persons had been his implacable enemies, he readily granted them their pardon, and received them to favour; and restored to Iorwerth ap Owen the town and castle of Caerlheon, which he had unjustly taken from him.

This

This reconciliation betwixt King Henry and thefe Welch lords; fome of the Englifh in Wales took advantage of, and more particularly William de Bruce Lord of Brecnock, who having for a long time a great longing to Gwentland, could not bring about his defign, by reafon that Sitfylht ap Dyfnwal, the perfon of greateft fway and power in the country, was an inveterate enemy to all the Englifh. But being now reconciled to the King, William de Bruce, under pretence of congratulating this new peace and agreement between the Englifh and Welch, invited Sitfylht and Geffrey his fon, with feveral others of the perfons of chiefeft note in Gwentland, to a feaft in his caftle of Abergavenny, which by compofition he had lately received from them. Sitfylht, with the reft, came according to appointment, and without the leaft fufpicion of any treafonable defigns; but after they had been civilly entertained for fome time, William Bruce, to move a quarrel againft them, began at laft to propound certain articles to them, to be by them kept and performed; and among other unreafonable conditions, they were to fwear, that none of them fhould at any time carry with them bow or fword. The Welch refufing to confent to and fign fuch improper articles as thefe; William Bruce prefently calls out his men, who were ready for that purpofe, and bidding them fall to their bufinefs, they moft treacheroufly fell upon and flew the innocent and naked Welch; and as if it did not fufficiently exprefs their cruelty and inhumanity, they immediately went to Sitfylht's houfe, which ftood not far from Abergavenny, and taking hold of Gwladus his wife, they flew her fon Cadwalader before her face, and then fetting fire to the houfe, they packed her away to the caftle. This execrable murder being thus moft barbaroufly, and which was worft of all, under pretence of friendfhip and kindnefs, committed; William Bruce, to cloak his treafon with fome reafonable excufe, and to make the world believe it was not for any private intereft or expeftation he had done fuch an act, as he knew would be by all men abhorred; caufed it to be reported

ported abroad, that he had done such a thing in revenge of the death of his uncle Henry of Hereford, whom the Welch on the Eastern-Even before had slain. But whilst these things passed in South-Wales, Roderic, David Prince of North-Wales's brother, made his escape by some means or other out of prison, and fleeing to Anglesey, he was received and acknowledged by all the country on the other side the river Conwey, for their Lord and Prince; which they were the more willing to do, by reason that they conceived an utter abhorrence of Prince David, who contrary to all rules of equity, and almost nature, had disinherited all his brethren and cousins; as boldly relying upon his affinity and relation to the King of England. But David perceiving the storm to grow very violent, and that the country did numerously flock and adhere to his brother Cadwalader, thought it his best way to stay a while, till the storm was abated; and so retired over the river Conwey. Towards the end of this year, Cadelh the son of Gruffydh ap Rhys, and brother to Lord Rhys, after a tedious fit of sickness. and taken upon him the Monkish order, departed this life, whose body was very honourably interred at Stratflur.

In the spring of the following year, died also David 1176. Fitz-Gerald Bishop of Menevia, or S. Davids, whose see was supplied by one Piers, being nominated thereunto by the King of England. But what happened most remarkable this year; the Lord Rhys Prince of South-Wales made a very great feast at Christmas in his castle of Aberteifi, which he caused to be proclaimed through all Britain, Ireland, and the islands adjacent, some considerable time before; and according to their invitation, many hundreds of English, Normans, and others coming to Aberteifi, were very honourably received, and courteously entertained by Prince Rhys. But among other tokens of their welcome and entertainment, Rhys caused all the bards or poets throughout all Wales to come thither; and for a better diversion to the company, he provided chairs to be set in the hall, in which the bards being seated, they were to answer each other in rhyme; and to the

that acquitted themselves most handsomely, and overcame the rest, were promised great rewards and rich
presents. In this poetical disceptation, the North-
Wales bards obtained the victory, with the applause
and approbation of the whole company; and among
the professors of musick, between whom there was no
A.D. 1177. small strife, Prince Rhys's own servants were accounted the most expert. But for all this civil and
obliging treatment of Prince Rhys, the Normans upon
the marches fell to their accustomed manner of treacherous way-laying, and privately assaulting the harm-
less and undesigning Welch; and therefore Eineon Clyt
Rhys his son-in-law, and Morgan ap Meredith, falling
into the net which the Normans had deceitfully laid
for them, were treacherously murdered. Therefore,
to keep the Normans under greater fear and awe for the
future, Prince Rhys built a castle at Rhayadr Gwy,
being a place where the river Wye falls with a very
great noise and precipitation down a great rock. But
1178. this castle was like to stand him in a double stead;
for it was not long after he had perfectly finished it,
that the sons of Conan ap Owen Gwynedh made war
against him; but finding upon trial that their design
against Rhys was impracticable, they thought it more
adviseable to retire back to North-Wales.

1179. The next year, Cadwalhon, brother to Owen Gwynedh, an uncle to David and Roderic, who for fear
of his brother had some time ago fled for refuge to
the King of England; as he was conveyed home by
some of the King's servants, to enjoy his patrimonial
Estate in Wales, was by those barbarous and treacherous villains murdered in his journey. This year the
sepulchre of that famous and noble British King Arthur, with his wife Gwenhofar (by the means of some
Welch bard, whom King Henry had heard at Pembrock relate in a song the worthy and mighty acts of
that great Prince, and the place where he was buried)
was found in the isle of Afalon, without the Abbey of
Glastenbury; their bodies being laid in a hollow elder tree, buried fifteen foot in the earth. The bones
of King Arthur were of marvelous and almost incredible

dible bigneſs, having ten wounds in the ſkull, whereof
one being conſiderably larger than the reſt, ſeemed to
be his death-blow; and the Queen's hair ſeemed to the
ſight to be fair and yellow, but when touched crumbled
preſently to duſt.   Over the bones was laid a ſtone, with
a croſs of lead, upon the lower ſide of which ſtone were
engraven theſe words :

HIC JACET SEPULTUS INCLYTUS REX
ARTHURUS IN INSULA AVALONIA.

Here lies buried the famous King ARTHUR *in the
iſle of* Aſalon.

No action of moment had paſſed in Wales this
long time, and the Welch were in perfect amity and
concord with the King of England; but ſome unlucky accident fell out at laſt to diſſolve this happy
union and agreement.   One Ranulph de Poer, who was 1182.
ſheriff of Gloceſterſhire, or rather as Giraldus Cambrenſis obſerves, of Herefordſhire, being a cruel and
unreaſonable oppreſſor of the Welch, put the Lord of
Gwentland to death; in revenge of whom a certain
young perſon of that country, ſet upon Ranulph with
ſeveral other gentlemen his companions, and ſlew
them to a man.   King Henry was implacably enraged
at this news, and ſo cruelly incenſed, that he preſently raiſed and drew together all his power, and
came to Worceſter, intending to march forward to
Wales, and to invade the enemies country.   But the
Lord Rhys ap Gruffydh, a ſubtile and a politick Prince,
thinking it impoſſible to withſtand the Engliſh army,
and fearing the King's puiſſance, which he perceived
to be ſo implacably bent againſt the Welch, went in
perſon to Worceſter, and ſwearing fealty to the King,
became his perpetual liege-man; and for the due ob-
ſervance of this contract, he promiſed to ſend his
ſons and nephews for pledges.   But when he would
have perſuaded them to anſwer his requeſt, the young
men conſidering with themſelves, how former pledges
had not been very genteely treated by the Engliſh,
refuſed

refufed to go; and fo the whole matter refted for that time. What became of the matter afterwards we know not; but probable it is, that King Henry returned to England fatisfied with Rhys's fubmiffion; for we hear no more of his coming to Wales. And fo the country remained quiet and undifturbed for a long time; till at length the Welch began to fall to their wonted method of killing and murdering one another. Cad-

A.D.1186. walader Prince Rhys's fon was privately murdered in Weft-Wales, and buried in the Ty Gwyn. And the

1187. year following, Owen Fychan the fon of Madawc ap Meredith, was flain by night in the caftle of Car-rergova near Ofweftry, by Gwenwynwyn and Cadwal-hon the fons of Owen Cyfeilioc. But what was moft un-natural of all, Lhewelyn, whofe father Cadwalhon ap Gruffydh ap Conan was lately murdered by the Englifh-men, was taken by his own brothers, who very barba-roufly put out his eyes. About the fame time, Baldwyn, Archbifhop of Canterbury, being attended by Giraldus Cambrenfis, took a progrefs into Wales, being the firft Archbifhop of Canterbury that vifited that country; whofe authority the clergy of Wales in vain oppofed, though they ftifly alledged the liberties and priviledges of their metropolitan church of S Davids. In this vifitation, defcribed by Giraldus in his Itinerarium Cambriæ, he perfuaded many of the nobility of Wales to go to the Holy Land againft thofe prevailing enemies of chriftianity, the Saracens; to whofe prevailing greatnefs, Jerufalem itfelf was now in great danger

1188. to become fubject. The Archbifhop having left the country, Malegon the fon of Lord Rhys brought all his power againft Tenbigh, and having by force made himfelf maiter of it, burnt the whole town to the ground, and fo carried away very confiderable fpoil. He was a perfon of fuch civil behaviour and eafy ac-cefs, of fo comely perfonage, and honefty in all his ac-tions, that he attracted the moft earneft love and affec-tion of all his friends; by which means he became very terrible and formidable to his enemies, efpecially the Flemings, of whom he obtained divers victories and conquefts.

The

The next year, being the year of Chrift 1189, A.D. 1189. Henry the Second, furnamed Courtmantel, king of England died, and was buried at Fonteverard; after whom, his fon Richard, called Curdelyon, was by the unanimous confent of all the peers and nobility of England, crowned in his place. Prince Rhys being thus deprived of his greateft friend, thought it his wifeft way to make the beft provifion he could for himfelf, by enlarging his dominions, and extending the bounds of his prefent territories; and therefore having raifed all the ftrength he could, he won the caftles of Seynclere, Abercorran, and Lhanftephan; and having taken and committed to prifon Maelgwn his fon, who was the greateft thorn in his fide, as one that was moft paffionately beloved by the South Wales men, he brought the whole country to his fub-jection. Then he built the caftle of Cydwely; but 1190 what took away from him the joy of all this good for-tune, he loft his daughter Gwenlhian, a woman of fuch incomparable beauty, and exceeding in all femi-nine qualifications, that fhe was accounted the faireft and beft accomplifhed lady in all the country. And 1191 not long after her died Gruffydh Maylor, lord of Brom-field, a man of great prudence and experience, and one that excelled all the nobility of his time in hof-pitality, and all other acts of generofity and libera-lity. His corps was carried to Myfod, and honour-ably interred there, being attended by moft of the per-fons of quality throughout the whole country. He had iffue by his wife Angharad daughter of Owen Gwynedh prince of North Wales, a fon called Ma-dawc, who fucceeded his father in that part of Powys, called from him Powys Fadawc. Rhys, prince of South Wales, was growing very powerful, and had made himfelf mafter of the greateft part of South Wales, only with fome few places more, Dynefawr held out ftill; which however, upon the firft affault he made againft it, was delivered up to him. But as he increafed in the number of towns and caftles, he had the misfortune to have that of his children diminifhed; for his daughter Gwenlhian was lately deceafed; and

P.

now

now he had no sooner got Dynefawr castle into his possession, but his son Owen died at Strata Florida, or Yftratflur. King Richard was gone to the Holy Land against the Saracens; but on his return to England, he won the kingdom of Cyprus, and gave it to Gwido king of Jerusalem, upon condition he would resign his former title to him: during his stay in this island, he married Berengaria the daughter of the king of Navarre.

A.D. 1192. Maelgon, Prince Rhy's son had been now detained a long time in prison, where his father had shut him up; but being at last utterly weary of such a close confinement, he found some means or other, to get out, and to make his escape. His father, Prince Rhys was not so troubled at his being broke out, and that he had got his liberty, as to give over the conquest, which all this while he had gone so furiously on with; but laying siege to Lhanhayaden castle he took it without any great opposition, and brought all the country about to his subjection. And what favoured him more in his attempts against the English, King Richard having most bravely signalized himself against the infidels, in his return home through Austria, was taken 1192. prisoner by Duke Leopold, who presented him to the Emperor Henry, who demanded 200,000 marks for his ranfom; laying to his charge, that he had spoiled and plundered the island of Sicily in his voyage, to the Holy Land. And as Rhys took the advantage of King Richard's absence to subject South Wales; so Roderic brother to David Prince of North Wales, made use of Gothrike's the king of Man's help, to get the principality of North Wales to himself, and eject his brother. And therefore entering into Anglefey, he quickly reduced the whole island to his subjection. But he did not enjoy it long; for before the year was over, the sons of his brother Conan came with an army against him, and forcing him together with the king of Man to fly the island, they took present possession of it themselves. And while these things were done in North Wales, Maelgon, Prince Rhys of South Wales his son, who was lately escaped from prison, besieged Yftratmic the castle, and after some small

oppo-

oppofition got into his own hands upon Chriftmas night; which encouraged him to farther attempts. And at the fame time, his brother Howel, furnamed Says, or the Englifhman, by reafon that he had ferved for fome time under the king of England, another fon of Prince Rhys, got by furprife the caftle of Gwys, and having fecured Philip de Gwys the owner, with his wife and two fons, he made them all prifoners of war. Then the two brothers Howel and Maelgon joined their forces; but fearing that they had more caftles than what they were able to defend, they thought it convenient to rafe Lhanhayaden caftle; which the Flemings having notice of, they gathered all their power together, and coming to Lhanhayaden at the day appointed, they unexpectedly fet upon the Welch, and flew a great number of them. But notwithftanding this fudden and unhappy accident, they thought it neceffary to deftroy the caftle; and fo coming to Lhanhayaden the fecond time, they rafed it to the ground, without any moleftation from, or appearance of any enemy to difturb them. But when Anarawd, another fon of Prince Rhys, faw how profperoufly his brothers fucceeded, he thought to make himfelf as rich as they, and by a fhorter and an eafier method; and therefore having under a fmooth pretence of friendfhip and love got his brothers Howel and Madawc in private, being moved with ambition and covetoufnefs to enjoy their eftates, he firft made them prifoners, and then very unnaturally pulled out their eyes. But Maelgon efcaped this fnare, and hearing what a foul action was committed, he promifed his brother Anarawd the caftle of Yftratmeyric, for the liberty and releafement of his two brothers, which Anarawd granted. But it is no wonder that thofe brothers could be unnatural and cruel to one another, who could join and agree to rebel againft their father; and now Prince Rhys having rebuilt the caftle of Rhayadr Gwy, was laid wait for, and taken prifoner by his own fons, who were afraid, that in cafe their father had them once in his power, he would feverely revenge their cruel and unnatural deeds. But Howel proved more kind and dutiful than the reft;

A. D. 1194.

P 2   who,

who, though blind, found a way to let his father escape
out of Maelgon's prison, and so Prince Rhys being set
at liberty, he took and destroyed the castle of Dynefowr, which belonged to his son Maelgon. But tho'
he succeeded in this attempt, yet he lost another castle elsewhere; for the sons of Cadwalhon ap Madawc
of Melyenydh being informed that Prince Rhys was
detained prisoner by his son Maelgon, they besieged
Rhayadr Gwy castle, which being surrendered up to
them, they fortified for their own use.

But whilst these unhappy differences, and unnatural clashings betwixt Prince Rhys and his sons,
continue and rage in South Wales, a new revolution
of affairs happened in North Wales. Prince David
had now enjoyed the sceptre of North Wales for above
twenty-four years; and one would think, that so long
a possession would secure him in his throne, that it
could not be very easy to pull him down. But possession is not always the surest card, which proved very
true in Prince David's case at this time; for Lhewelyn
the son of Iorwerth Drwyndwn, who was the eldest
son of Owen Gwynedh prince of North Wales, being
now arrived to years of maturity, and having sense
enough to understand what a just title and claim he
had to the principality of North Wales, of which his
uncle David had so unjustly kept him out; he thought
it high time to endeavour to recover what was lawfully
his own, which however he was well persuaded his
uncle David would never easily part with. And therefore being well assured that the justness of his title
would never mount him up to the throne, without he
had an army at his heels to help him on; he called
together all his friends and relations by his mother's
side, who was Marred the daughter of Madawc ap
Meredith prince of Powys, and having drawn to his
side his cousins the sons of Conon ap Owen Gwynedh,
and Rhodri ap Owen, he came into North Wales,
proclaiming how against all justice his uncle David
had first disinherited his father Iorwerth, and then
had kept the government from him who was the right
heir. And the son his father Iorwerth had been incap-

able

able of taking upon him the government by reason of some infirmity; yet there was no reason that his father's weakness should exclude and turn him out; and therefore, being now sensible of what he was not capable to understand in his youth, he laid claim to the principality, which was justly his own. But there was no great need of conjuring to understand his claim, nor of much rhetorick to persuade the people to own him for their prince; whose affection was cooled, and almost worn off from David, ever since he had dealt so unnaturally with his brothers, whom after he had deprived of their estates, he banished out of the country. And therefore before Lhewelyn could expect to have any sure footing, the whole country of North Wales was at his devotion, excepting only three castles, which David by the help of the English, in whom, by reason of his affinity with the late King Henry, he depends much upon, kept to himself. And thus David being deprived of almost all that he formerly possessed, we shall reckon him no more among the princes of North Wales, but restore the principality to the true heir Lhewelyn ap Iorwerth.

LHEWELYN AP IORWERTH.

LHEWELYN ap Iorwerth the son of Owen Gwynedh, having thus successfully carried on his just claim to the dominion of North Wales, and being quietly settled in the government of it, Roger Mortimer marches with a strong body to Melyenith, and built the castle of Cymaron, whereby he reduced that country to his subjection, and forced thence the two sons of Cadwalhon ap Madawc that were governors thereof. About this time Rhys and Meredith, two valiant, but undutiful sons of Prince Rhys, having got together a body of hot-headed, daring soldiers, came before Dynefawr, and took the castle that was garrisoned by their father, and thence they proceeded to Cantre-Bychan, and the country civil

P

received them, and furrendered up the caftle to them. At this their father was juftly incenfed, and therefore to put a ftop to their farther proceedings, he endeavoured by all means to take them, which not long after happened; for their adherents now began to be touched with the fenfe as well of their treafon againft, as of their allegiance due to their lawful lord Prince Rhys; and therefore to atone for their paft faults, and to procure his future favour, they betrayed their rebellious leaders to their offended father, who immediately committed them to fafe cuftody.

A.D. 1196. The enfuing year Prince Rhys levies a great army, whofe firft attempt was upon the town and caftle of Caermadthyn, both which he took in a fhort time and deftroyed, and then returned with confiderable booty. Not long after he led the faid army to the marches, and invefted the caftle of Clun, which was not fo eafily taken as the former; for this coft him a long fiege, and many a fierce affault; and therefore to be revenged of it, when he took it he laid it in afhes; thence he proceeded to the caftle of Radnor, which he likewife won; but immediately after it coft him a bloody battle; for he was no fooner mafter of the caftle, but Roger Mortimer and Hugh de Say came with a numerous and well-difciplined army, confifting of Normans and Englifh, to the relief of it. Whereupon Prince Rhys thinking it not his beft courfe to confine his men within the walls, led them up into a champaign ground hard by, and there, like a valiant prince, refolved to give his enemies battle, though they had much the advantage of him; for his men were neither fo well armed, nor fo much accuftomed to battle as the others were; however, their courage made amends for their arms; and their leader's prudence and conduct fupplied the defects of their difcipline; for they chofe rather to die honourably in the defence of their country, than fhamefully to furvive the lofs of it: and therefore they attacked their enemies fo valiantly, that they were not long able to withftand their force, but quitted the field in great diforder, leaving a great number of their men behind
them

them flain upon the fpot; and Prince Rhys purfued them fo warmly, that they were glad of the fhelter of the night to protect them from his fury. After this victory, he befieged the caftle of Payne in Elfel, which he eafily took, and kept in his own hands, till William de Bruce, the owner thereof, came to him, and humbly defired peace of him, which he granted him, and withal delivered him up his caftle again. Not long after, the archbifhop of Canterbury (whom King Richard had fubftituted his lieutenant in England) marches with a powerful army towards Wales, and befieges the caftle of Gwenwynwyn, at the pool; but the garrifon made fuch a vigorous defence, that he loft a great many of his men, and all his attempts proved ineffectual; therefore he fent for fome pioneers, whom he ordered to undermine the walls; which when the befieged underftood, they bethought of fecuring themfelves on the moft honourable terms they could; they were not willing to put themfelves to the hazard of a battle, for their enemies were thrice their number; therefore they propofed to furrender up the caftle, on condition they fhould carry off all their arms along with them: which offer the archbifhop accepted of, and fo permitted the garrifon to march out quietly. Then fortifying the caftle for the king's ufe, and putting a ftrong garrifon in it for its defence, he returned again to England. But Gwenwynwyn was not fo willing to part from his caftle, as never to attempt the recovery of it; therefore as foon as he underftood that the archbifhop was gone back, he immediately befieged it, and fhortly after received it on the fame terms that his men had delivered it up, and afterwords kept it for his own ufe.

The following year there broke out a terrible plague, which fpread over all Britain and France, and carried off a great number of the nobility, befides common people. This year likewife died the valiant Rhys, Prince of South Wales; the only ftay and defence of that part of Wales; for he it was that got them their liberty, and fecured it to them. He often very readily expofed his own life for the defence of

A. D. 1197. theirs and their country; generally he got the better of his enemies, and at laſt either brought them entirely under his ſubjection, or forced them to quit their country. He was no leſs illuſtrious for his virtuous endowments, than for his valour and extraction; ſo that it was with good reaſon that the Britiſh bards and others wrote ſo honourably of him, and ſo mightily deplored his death.

To this prince were born many ſons and daughters, whereof his eldeſt ſon Gruffydh ſucceeded him: the others were Cadwalhon, Maelgon, Meredith, and Rhys. Of his daughters, one called Gwenlhian was married to Ednyfed Fychan, anceſtor to Owen Tudor that married Katharine queen-dowager to King Henry the Fifth: and the reſt were very well matched with ſome of the nobility of the country. Prince Gruffydh being ſettled in the government of his country, did not long enjoy it peaceably; for his troubleſome brother Maelgon thought it now a fit time to endeavour the recovery of the inheritance his father had deprived him of. To this purpoſe he makes a league with Gwenwynwyn, the ſon of Owen Cyfeilioc, lord of Powys, and by their joint intereſt got together a conſiderable body of men, wherewith they ſurpriſed Prince Gruffydh at Aberyſtwyth, whom, after they had ſlain a great many of his men, they took priſoner. Thus Maelgon effectually accompliſhed his deſign in the recovery of the caſtle, and the whole country of Cardigan. His unfortunate brother he committed to the cuſtody of his ſpiteful confederate Gwenwynwyn, who immediately out of malice delivered him up to the mercy of his inveterate enemies the Engliſh. After this Gwenwynwyn having got together an army entered Aruſtly, and brought it to his ſubjection.

David ap Owen, whom Prince Lhewelyn had forced to quit his uſurpation of the principality of North Wales, had hitherto lived quietly and peaceably, not ſo much out of kindneſs to his nephew, as becauſe he knew not how to redreſs himſelf; but now having got a great army of Engliſh and Welch, he uſed his utmoſt efforts to recover his principality. Whereupon Prince

Lhewelyn

Lhewelyn, who was the right heir, and in possession
of it, came on boldly to meet him, and gave him battle, wherein he shamefully routed his army, and took
his uncle David prisoner, whom he delivered into safe
custody, whereby he secured to himself and his country peace and quietness. Towards the close of this
year Owen Cyfeilioc lord of the Higher Powys departed this life, and left his estate to Gwenwynwyn
his son; after whom that part of Powys was called
Powys-Wenwynwyn, to distinguish it from the other
called Powys-Fadoc, the inheritance of the lords of
Bromfield. Much about this time Trahaern Fychan,
a man of great power and authority in the county of
Brecknock, was suddenly seized upon as he was going
to Llancors to confer about some business with William de Bruce lord thereof, and by an order of the
lords, tied to an horse's tail and dragged through the
streets of Brecknock to the gallows, where he was beheaded, and his body hung up by the feet for three
days. Which barbarity inflicted on him for no known
just cause, so frightened his brother's wife and children,
that they fled their country for fear of the same usage.
The year following Maelgon, who had before routed A. D. 1198.
his brother Prince Gruffydh's army, and taken him
prisoner, begins now to enlarge his territories, and
takes in his brother's castles of Aberteifi and Ystratmeyric. Also the youngest son of Prince Rhys about
this time recovered the castle of Dynefowr from the
Normans.

' The same summer, Gwenwynwyn took up a resolution of attempting to extend Wales to its antient limits; and for this purpose he raises a powerful army,
with which he first designs to be avenged of William
de Bruce for the inhuman death of his cousin Trahaern
Fychan, and therefore he besiegeth his castle of Payn
in Elfel, where he makes a protestation, that as soon
as he had taken it, for a farther satisfaction to his revenge, he would unmercifully ravage the whole country as far as Severn. But these mighty menaces were
soon blown over; for he had neither battering engines nor pioneers, so that he was forced to lay before

the

the caftle for three weeks without effecting any thing;
whereby the murderers had time enough to apply
themfelves to England for fuccours, which they obtained. For upon this Geoffrey Fitz-Peter, Lord
Chief Juftice of England levies a confiderable army,
to which he joins all the Lords Marchers, and comes
in all hafte to the relief of the place, where he meets
Gwenwynwyn; with whom before he would hazard
a battle, he was defirous to have a treaty of peace,
to which Gwenwynwyn and his adherents would in no-
wife hearken or condefcend, but returned in anfwer,
that their bufinefs there was to be revenged of old injuries done them. Hereupon the Englifh lords refolved to enlarge Prince Gruffydh of South Wales, whom
they knew to be an inveterate enemy of Gwenwynwyn,
as he that delivered him up to their hands ; and likewife to be a man of great authority in his country,
therefore they rightly concluded he might be more fer-
viceable to them when at liberty than under confinement, wherein they were not difappointed ; for he immediately got together a ftrong body of his countrymen, and joining with the Englifh advanced towards
the caftle, where they furioufly attacked Gwenwynwyn, who made no lefs vigorous defence ; hereupon
there enfued a bloody battle, with a great flaughter
on both fides, but at length the Englifh got the victory, and Gwenwynwyn loft a great number of common foldiers (if we believe Matthew Paris, 3700 men)
befides a great many of his beft commanders, among
whom were Anarawd, fon of Eineon, Owen ap Cadwalhon, Richard ap Ieftyn, and Robert ap Howel.
Meredith ap Conan was likewife taken prifoner, with
many more. After this the Englifh returned home
triumphantly, and requited Prince Gruffydh's fervice
with a perfect liberty, who immediately, partly by
his own force, partly by the affection of his people,
repoffeffed himfelf of all his dominions, fave the caftles of Aberteifi and Yftratmeyric, which his ufurping
brother Maelgon, by the affiftance of Gwenwynwyn,
had, during his confinement by the Englifh, taken
from him, and ftill unjuftly detained. Hereupon,

fome

some of Prince Gruffydh's prime nobility and clergy came to him, and offered him their endeavours of reconciling him to his brother, and made him so apprehensive of his just displeasure at him, that he took a solemn oath before them, that in case his brother would give him hostages for the security of his own person, he would deliver him up his castle of Aberteifi by a day appointed; which proposals Prince Gruffydh accepted of, and accordingly sent him his demands: but it was the least of Maelgon's intention to make good his part, or else he was very inconstant in his resolution; for he had no sooner received the hostages, but instead of delivering up the castle, he fortifies it, and puts in a garrison for his own use, and commits the hostages to the custody of Gwenwynwyn, Prince Gruffydh's mortal enemy; but not long after, their innocency procured them an opportunity of an escape.

In the year 1199, Maelgon still pursuing his hatred A. D. 1199. of his brother Prince Gruffydh, gets an army, wherewith he besiegeth his castle of Dynerth, which he was master of in a short time, and then put all the garrison to the sword. But about the same time Prince Gruffydh in lieu of this, won the castle of Cilgerran, and strongly fortified it. This year Richard the First of England, as he was besieging the castle of Chalons in France, was shot from the walls with an arrow, whereof he not long after died, and left his kingdom to his brother John, who thereupon was with great solemnity crowned at Westminster. But he could not expect to enjoy this kingdom peaceably; for his elder brother Geoffrey Plantagenet had left a son behind him named Arthur, whose right to the crown of England was by lineal descent; which now therefore he justly lays claim to, and by the assistance of King Philip of France (who espoused his quarrel) endeavours to recover. But before Prince Arthur had made sufficient preparations to carry on his design, he was unexpectedly set upon by his uncle, his army routed, and he himself taken prisoner, and committed to

safe

safe custody; not long after which, he died, and so King John was rid of his competitor.

The following year, Gruffydh ap Conan ap Owen Gwynedh died, and was buried in a monk's cawl in the abbey of Conway, which way of burying was very much practised (especially by the better sort) in those days; for the monks and friars had deluded the people into a strong conceit of the merits of it, and had firmly persuaded them it was highly conducive to their future happiness to be thus interred. But this superstition, together with the propagators of it, they had lately received from England: for the first abbey or monastery we read of in Wales, since the destruction of that famous house of Bangor, which favoured of Romish dregs, was the Ty-Gwyn built in the year 1146, after which they mightily increased and spread over all the country; and now the fountain head began to be corrupted; for the clergy maintained a doctrine, which their ancestors abhorred, as may easily be gathered from the writings of that worthy divine Ambrosius Telesinus, who flourished in the year 540, when the christian faith (which we suppose to be delivered at the isle of Afalon by Joseph of Arimathea) flowed in this land in a pure and uncorrupted stream, before it was infected and polluted by that proud and blood-thirsty monk Augustine. I say, he then wrote and left behind him as his own opinion, and the opinion of those days, these following verses:

Gwae'r offeiriad byd
Nys angreifftia gwyd
Ac ny phregetha:
Gwae ny cheidw ei gail
Ac ef yn figail
Ac nys areilia;
Gwae ni cheidw ei dhefaid
Rhae bleidhie Rhufeniaid
A'i ffon gnwppa.

i. e. Woe be to the bishop who does not rebuke vice, and give good example; and who does not preach.

preach. Woe be to him, if he does not keep well
his fold : and he a shepherd. And does not keep
together and guard his sheep from popish wolves,
with his pastoral staff.

From whence it is apparent, that the Church of
Rome was then corrupt, and that the British churches
persevered in the primitive and truly apostolical
profession of christianity; as it was at first planted
in the island; and that no Roman innovations had
crept in among them, which afterwards mightily increased, when they were once introduced by Augustine the monk.

This year likewise we find the spiteful and turbulent Maelgon, choosing rather to persist still in his
rebellion, than to return to his allegiance, and to pre-
fer a small lucre to the love and safety of his country. For now finding that the castle of Aberteifi was
not tenable by his own power and force, yet rather
than deliver it up to his brother Prince Gruffydh, and
thereby procure his favour, he chose to sell it to his
bitter enemies the English, for an inconsiderable sum
of money, whereby he opened them a free passage into
all Wales; this being reckoned one of its chief de-
fences and bulwarks. About this time Madawc son
of Gruffydh Maylor lord of Bromfield built the abbey of Lanegwest, commonly known by the English
by the name of Vale Crucii.

In the year 1201, the valiant Lhewelyn ap Ior- A. D. 1201,
werth, prince of North Wales banished out of his
territories his cousin Meredith the son of Conan ap
Owen Gwynedh, whom he suspected of treasonable
practices, and therefore confiscated his lands which
were the Cantref of Lhyn and Efyonyth. Much
about the same time Meredith the son of Prince
Rhys was slain at Carnwilhion by treason, whereupon his elder brother Gruffydh possessed himself
of his castle in Lhanymdhyfri and all his lands.
This Gruffydh was a valiant and discreet prince,
and one that was like to bring all South Wales

to

to good order and obedience; for in all things he
trod in his father's steps, and made it his bufinefs to
fucceed him as well in his valour and virtuous endowments, as in his government. But the vaft hopes
A. D. P202. conceived of him foon proved abortive; for in the
enfuing year, on St. James's day, he died, to the great
grief and lofs of his country, and fhortly after was
buried at Yftratflur with great pomp and folemnity.
He left behind him for a fucceffor a fon called Rhys,
which Maud the daughter of William de Bruce had
bore him. The following year fome of the Welch
nobility marched with an army towards the caftle of
Gwerthrynion, which belonged to Roger Mortimer,
and after a fhort fiege they took it and levelled it
with the ground.

This year Lhewelyn ap Iorwerth calling to mind his
eftate, and title, and how all the Welch princes were
obliged both by the laws of Roderic the Great, and
thofe of Howel Dha to acknowledge the king or prince
of North Wales for their fovereign lord, and to do
homage to him for their dominions; yet notwithftanding that they knew this to be their duty, and
that they formerly had readily performed it; yet becaufe of late years his predeceffors, had neglected to
call them to their duty, they now began to imagine
themfelves exempted from it; and fome thought themfelves accountable to no fuperior prince; others de-
nied fubjection to Prince Lhewelyn, and held their
dominions of the king of England. To put a ftop
therefore to the further growth of this contempt, and
to affert his own right, Prince Lhewelyn fummons
all the Welch lords, who for the moft part appeared
and fwore allegiance to him. But Gwenwynwyn lord
of Powys, neither came to this meeting, nor would
own the prince's fupremacy; which ftubbornefs and
difobedience the prince acquainted his lords with,
whereupon they delivered their opinion, that it was
but reafonable, that Gwenwynwyn fhould be compelled to his duty, or elfe forfeit his eftate: this all
the lords confented to, but Elis ap Madawc, who was
an intimate friend of Gwenwynwyn, and therefore
would

would not consent to the enacting any thing that might be prejudicial to him, but broke off from the meeting much diffatisfied with their proceedings. Notwithftanding which, Prince Lhewelyn, purfuant to the advice of the reft of his lords, raifes an army, and marches towards Powys; but before he made any ufe of it, he was by the mediation of fome learned and able men reconciled to Gwenwynwyn, and fo Gwenwynwyn became his dutiful fubject; which he confirmed both by oath and writing: and indeed it was not without good reafon, that Prince Lhewelyn ufed all the caution imaginable to bind this man; for he had fworn allegiance before to the king of England. Lhewelyn having thus fubjected Gwenwynwyn, he thought it now convenient to fhew likewife fome marks of his refentments againft his adherent Elis ap Madawc, and therefore he ftript him of all his lands; whereupon Elis fled the country, but not long after, yielding himfelf to the prince's mercy, he received of him the caftle of Crogen, and feven townfhips befides. And now having mentioned Crogen, it will not be improper to ftep a little out of the way, and here take notice of the reafon why the Englifh formerly, when they had a mind to reproach the Welch, called them Crogens. The firft occafion of it was this, King Henry the Second in his expedition againft the Welch to the mountains of Berwin, lay a while at Ofweftre, during which time he detached a number of his men to try the paffages into Wales, who as they would have paffed Offa's ditch at the caftle of Crogen, at which place there was a narrow way through the fame ditch, which appears now very deep through all that country, and bears its old name; thefe men, I fay, as they would have paffed this ftreight, were met by a party of Welch, and a great many of them flain and buried in that ditch, as appears by their graves there to be feen; and the name of the ftreight imports as much, being called in Welch *Adwy'r bedhaw.* The Englifh therefore bearing in mind this flaughter, whenever they got any of the Welch into their clutches, upbraided them with the name of Crogen, intimating

thereby

thereby that they fhould expect no more favour or
mercy at their hands, than they fhewed them in the
fkirmifh. But this word, which at firft was rather a
badge of reputation than difgrace to the Welch, came
afterwards to be ufed in a bad fenfe, and only then
applied when they defigned to reproach and abufe
them. But to return to Prince Lhewelyn, whom we
find returning home after he had fuccefsfully afferted
his fovereignty over all Wales, and fet all things in
good order: And by the way he fortifies the caftle of
Bala in Penlhyn. About this time Rhys the fon of
Gruffydh ap Rhys the right prince of South-Wales
took the caftle of Lhanymdhyfry upon Michaelmas-
day. This year Lhewelyn Prince of Wales took to
wife Joan the daughter of king John, which Agatha
daughter of Robert Ferrers Earl of Derby bore him,
with whom he gave the Prince for a dowry the lordfhip of Elfmere in the marches of Wales.

A. D. 1203. Prince Rhys whom we mentioned the year before
to have taken the caftle of Lhanymdhyfri, wins likewife the caftle of Llangadoc, and puts a garrifon
therein; but he enjoyed neither of them long; for
fhortly after, his uncle Maelgon, with his friend
Gwenwynwyn, levied a powerful army, and with it
befieged and took the caftle of Lhanymdhyfri; thence
they removed to Llangadoc, and wan the caftle likewife, upon this condition, that the garrifon be permitted to march out quietly. When they had taken
thefe two caftles, they went to Dinerth, where Maelgon finifhed the caftle he had formerly begun there.
This year likewife Prince Lhewelyn fet at liberty his
uncle David ap Owen Gwynedh, who made but a
forry return to his kindnefs; for inftead of living
peaceably at home, and enjoying that liberty that was
granted him, he flees to England, and there gets an
army, wherewith he attempts to reftore himfelf to
his antient eftate of North-Wales; but he miffed his
mark; for his prudent nephew immediately met him
on his march, and gave him a fhameful overthrow,
wherewith David was fo mightily difheartened, that
he

he-prefently returned for England, and fhortly after
died for meer forrow. The next year Howel, a blind _{A. D. 1204.}
fon of Prince Rhys was flain at Camaes by his bro-
ther Maelgon's men, and buried juft by his brother
Gruffydh at Yftratflur. But notwithftanding that,
Maelgon in thofe days ufurped all the rule and government of South Wales; yet his brother Gruffydh's
fons, Rhys and his brethren, won from him the chief
defence of all that country, to wit, the caftles of
Dynefowr and Lhanymdhyfri. About this time William Marfhal Earl of Pembrock, befieged the caftle
of Cilgerran, and took it; and not long after, Mael- _{1205.}
gon hired an Irifhman to kill Gadifor ap Griffri; after
which horrid fact, Maelgon feized upon his four fons,
and put them to death; thefe were forward promifing
young gentlemen, and defcended from a noble ftock;
for their mother Sufanna was a daughter of the faid
Howel ap Rhys, by a daughter of Madawc ap Mere-
dith Prince of Powis. In the year 1206, Maelgon _{1206.}
built a caftle at Abereneon. At which time there
was fuch abundance of fifh feen at Aberyftwyth, that
the like number was never known to have come there
in the memory of man before.

This year the king of England banifhed the realm _{1207.}
William de Bruce and his wife, on the account of a
grudge that he bore his fon, and then feized upon all
his lands; whereupon, William with his wife and fon
fled to Ireland, and there continued for fome time.
And this hardfhip he now underwent was the lefs
pitied, becaufed he exercifed the great power he had
in the marches of Wales with extreme cruelty and
injuftice. The fame year Gwenwynwyn came to
Shrewfbury to fpeak with the king's council, where he
was detained prifoner: Whereupon Prince Lhewelyn
conquered all his country, took all his towns and caftles, and garrifoned them for his own ufe. This expedition of Prince Lhewelyn mightily alarmed the
ufurping Maelgon, and the more, becaufe he had intelligence that Lhewelyn was on his march towards
South W.... .. .. puts him?'f in the
beft poftu ... . re.. re h.a; but finding
                                                        h..

self not able to abide the Prince's coming, and to withstand his forces, he demolisheth his castles of Aberystwyth, Ystratmeyric, and Dinerth, which before he had fortified. Notwithstanding which, the Prince comes to Aberystwyth, and rebuildeth the castle and puts a garrison therein; after this he seized upon the Cantref of Penwedic and the land betwixt Dyfi and Aeron which he gave to Maelgon's nephews the sons of Gruffydh ap Rhys, and then returned home with great joy and triumph. Not long after Rhys Fychan, son to Prince Rhys, besieged the castle Lhangadoc, and took it, contrary to the promise and league he had made with his nephews, forgetting likewise how freely and readily they had administered to him in his necessity; therefore to be revenged of this ingratitude and breach of promise, Rhys and Owen no sooner heard of it, but they furiously attacked the castle, and took it by assault, and put to the sword, or took prisoners all the garrison, and then burnt the castle to the ground.

A. D. 1209. This year King John levied a powerful army with which he made a voyage to Ireland; but as he was on the borders of Wales on his journey thitherwards, there was a criminal brought before him who had murdered a priest. The officer desired to know the king's pleasure, how he would have the delinquent punished; but the king, instead of ordering any punishment to be inflicted upon him suitable to the heinousness of his crime discharged him with a *Well done* thou *good* servant, thou hast slain mine enemy; for such he reckoned the clergy of those days, who were very ill-affected to his usurped, arbitrary government, and therefore he slightly regarded any injuries that were done them, nay, thought those did him good service who did them wrong. He had not been long in Ireland, but he got into his clutches the unfortunate William de Bruce the younger, and his mother Mawd de Saint Valerike, whom we have mentioned before to have quitted England for fear of him, and to have fled her for shelter. Upon his return to England he brought his in the arms with him, and committed

mitted them to Windfor caftle, where, by his orders, not long after they were inhumanly famifhed. The reafon of King John's difpleafure againft William de Bruce Lord of Brecknock, Matthew Paris delivers, to Page 303. be this;

When the Pope had excommunicated the realm of England, the king, to prevent any inconveniencies that might enfue thereupon, took pledges of fuch of his nobles as he thought were difaffected to him, and would be like, if occafion offered, to countenance and promote a rebellion. Amongft others, he fends meffengers to William de Bruce to demand his fons for pledges, to whom Mawd, de Bruce's wife, being the readier fpeaker, anfwered, (though what fhe faid was no lefs her hufband's fentiment than her own) That the king, who had proved fo bafe a guardian to his nephew Prince Arthur, whom inftead of fetting in, he deprived of his right, fhould have none of her children. This anfwer the meffengers delivered to the king, whereat he was fo highly difpleafed, that he ordered fome foldiers fhould be fent to feize this lord; but he having timely intelligence of this order, fled into Ireland with his wife and children, where now his wife Mawd, with her fon, were unfortunately taken by King John, but he himfelf efcaped, and fled into France, where not long after he died.

This year the Earl of Chefter rebuilt the caftle of Dyganwy, fituate on the fea-fhore, eaft of the river Conway, which Prince Lhewelyn had before demolifhed. He likewife fortifies the caftle of Treffynon or St. Wenefrid. Upon this Lhewelyn enters into the Earl's land, which when he had ravaged fufficiently, he returns home with confiderable booty. About this time, Rhys Fychan fon to Prince Rhys, fearing left Prince Lhewelyn fhould fall upon him for the wrong he had done to his nephews, whom he, Prince Lhewelyn, ftiffly defended in their right; made his application to the king of England, who readily granted him what fuccours he defired; and with thefe he befieged the caftle of Lhanymdhwri; the garrifon for fome time made a vigorous defence, but having

no hopes of any relief, they thought it their wifeſt courſe to capitulate, and ſo they defired they might march out with their arms, bag and baggage, and all that belonged to them, which was granted them. About this time likewiſe Gwenwynwyn was ſet at liberty, whom the king had hitherto detained priſoner, and withal lends him ſome forces to attempt the recovery of his country which Prince Lhewelyn had ſeized upon during his impriſonment ; and though by his own ſtrength he was not able to cope with the Prince, yet by this aſſiſtance granted him by the king, he ſoon re-poſſeſſed himſelf of his dominions. This ſucceſs of Gwenwynwyn encouraged Maelgon likewiſe to endeavour the recovery of that part of his country which the Prince had taken from him in the ſame expedition. Now he makes his application to the king of England, and ſwears allegiance to him. Hereupon the king grants him a confiderable army as well Engliſh as Normans ; to theſe he joins what forces he could raiſe in Wales, and then contrary to the oath and agreement he had made with his nephews Rhys and Owen, he in an hoſtile manner enters their country ; when he was come to Cantred Penwedic, he encamped at Cilcenny where he ſtaid ſome time to take meaſures for the better accompliſhment of his deſigns ; by this time his nephews had got together about 300 choſen well diſciplined men, but with ſo ſmall a number durſt not oppoſe their uncle's numerous army in open field ; therefore they were to endeavour to overthrow thoſe by a ſtratagem which they could not do by main force. Herein they proved very ſucceſsful, for coming as near their enemies as they could without being diſcovered, they ſent out their ſpies that night for intelligence, who brought back the good news, that all was quiet in Maelgon's camp, and that they kept no ſtrict watch, being not aware of an approaching enemy. This intelligence mightily encouraged the brothers to proſecute their deſigns, and now they march as ſilently as they can towards their enemies camp, where they met with no oppoſition, being not diſcovered becauſe all were faſt
aſleep.

afleep. When they were advanced as they thought
as far as Maelgon's tent, they furioufly fell on, and
flew a great number of his men before they awaked;
the reft being frightened with the noife and fhouts of
their enemies, and withal thinking their numbers to
be far greater than it was, were glad to make ufe of
the darknefs of the night to quit the field, only Maelgon's guard valiantly kept their poft, and defended
their lord till he had time and opportunity to efcape.
But Maelgon's army fuffered very much in this action,
his nephew Conan ap Howel with his chief counfellor
Gruffydh ap Cadwgan were both taken prifoners, and
Eineon ap Caradoc with a great number more were
flain upon the fpot. About the fame time Gilbert
Earl of Glocefter fortified the caftle of Buelht, where
a little before he had loft a confiderable number of
his men, by reafon that the place was not very ftrong
and tenable. And towards the conclufion of this year,
Mallt or Mawd de Bruce, the wife of Gruffydh ap
Rhys departed this life, and was interred by her hufband in a monk's coul in Yftratflur.

But the following year a great ftorm threatened
North Wales, by reafon that the Marchers made frequent and grievous complaints to King John how
that Prince Lhewelyn perpetually molefted their country, flew their men, and committed all the wafte
and deftruction poffible as he paffed along. The king
hearing of fuch intolerable depredations continually
exercifed by the North Wales men, thought it high
time to redrefs his fubjects, and therefore he raifed a
mighty army throughout all England, and called to
him all the lords and princes of Wales as held their
lands and patents from him, as Howel ap Gruffydh
ap Conan ap Owen Gwynedh, whom Prince Lhewelyn had banifhed out of North Wales: Madoc ap
Gruffydh Maylor lord of Bromfield, Chirke and Yale,
Meredith ap Rotpert Lord of Cydewen, Gwenwynwyn
Lord of Powis, Maelgon and Rhys the fons of Prince
Rhys and governors of South Wales. With this formidable army he came to Chefter, intending to enter

Q 3

in

into North Wales by that way, and being fully refolved to execute the fevereft vengeance upon the
inhabitants, and not to let one living foul remain
alive throughout the whole country. But matters
of this nature are eafier refolved upon, than accomplifhed ; Prince Lhewelyn was no fooner informed of thefe mighty preparations againft him,
comprehending the whole ftrength of the Englifh
nation, and what was worft of all, being affifted
by his own countrymen, but he iffued forth his orders, commanding all his fubjects of the inland
counties of Denbigh and Flint, together with them
of the ifland of Anglefey, to remove for a time all
their cattle and other effects to Snowden-hills, where
they were fure to remain fecureft from their enemies. But King John marched his army along the
fea-coaft to Ruthlan, and there paffing the river
Clwyd, he came to the caftle of Teganwy, where he
encamped for fome time to refrefh and recreate his
army, which by reafon of the long marches they
made, was in a great meafure weary and fatigued.
But what the more augmented their mifery, Lhewelyn getting behind them, cut off all their hopes of
provifion from England, and the Welch by the advantage of being acquainted with the ftraits and narrow paffages, cut off all that ftraggled from the Englifh camp, fo that in time, they were glad to take up
with horfe-flefh, and any thing were it never fo mean,
which might fill up their greedy and empty ftomachs.
At laft King John finding no other remedy, and perceiving it impoffible to continue longer there fo hun-
gry and faintly, thought it his wifeft way to march
for England, and leave the Welch to themfelves, and
fo he decamped in a great fury, leaving Lhewelyn to
bury that great number of dead, which had ftarved
in this fuccefslefs expedition. But to recover the honour he had now loft, he was refolved to try another
touch with the Welch, but poffibly not with the fame
confidence and affurance of victory. And therefore
returning to Wales in the next Auguft, he entered with
fuch another trouble . . . of . . . . . . was affifted

lifted by the fame Welch lords, at Blanch monaftery, now Ofweftry, being in the lordfhip of John the fon of William Fitzalan. In this expedition, King John paffing the river Conwey, and encamping at the other fide towards Snowden hills, fent part of his army conducted by guides who were acquainted with the country, to burn Bangor, which they effectually did; and taking Rotpert bifhop of that fee out of church, they carried him prifoner to the Englifh camp, where he continued for fome time, till he obtained his ranfom for a prefent of two hundred hawks. But Prince Lhewelyn finding the whole ftrength of England and almoft Wales to fight againft him, and judging it impoffible for himfelf alone, to withftand fo great a multitude, thought it his beft way to endeavour to find out fome method or other, to reconcile himfelf to the king. And no better meafures could poffibly be thought of, than to fend Joan his wife, King John's daughter, to intreat with her father about a peace, and a ceffation of all hoftilities; who being a prudent, fly woman, fo prevailed upon the king, that he granted Prince Lhewelyn her hufband, a fafe conduct to come to him, and to renew the former peace and amity that was betwixt them. And fo Lhewelyn having done homage, promifed the king towards his expences in this expadition, 20,000 head of cattle and 40 horfes, and what was more than all, he granted all the inland countries of Wales, with the appurtenances, to him and his heirs for ever. And then King John having received better fuccefs in this, than the former expedition, returned to England in great triumph, having fubdued all Wales, excepting that part which Rhys and Owen the fons of Gruffydh ap Rhys, ftill kept and maintained againft the Englifh. But having no leifure to march againft them himfelf at his departure out of the country, he gave ftrict charge to Foulke Vifcount of Caerdyff, warden of the marches, a cruel tyrant, though well beloved and favoured by the king, to take an army with him, and fo joining with Maelgon and Rhys Fvchin, to compel the fons

Q 4

of Gruffydh ap Rhys to acknowledge him for their
fovereign, and to do him homage. Foulke having
received fo pofitive a command, prefently raifed his
forces, and calling Maelgon and Rhys, came to the
Cantref of Penwedic; which when the young lords
Rhys and Owen heard of, and being affured that this
blow was levelled againft them, which they knew they
were not able to bear, before the ftroke was ftruck, they
fent to Foulke to fue for peace, and a fafe conduct
for them to pafs to the court of England. . This being granted, they came to London, and making their
fubmiffion to the king, and requefting his pardon for
all former mifdemeanors, they gave up all pretence to
their lands betwixt Aeron and Dyfi; and fo paying
their homage, they were difmiffed very gracioufly.
But Foulke before his departure out of the country,
fortified the caftle of Aberyftwyth, and placing a
ftrong garrifon therein, kept it for the king's ufe.
But Maelgon and Rhys Fychan, a couple of head-
ftrong, inconftant people, quickly repented them of
the peace they had made with the king of England,
and thereupon, without the leaft reafon or provocation, they laid fiege to Aberyftwyth caftle, and with
much ado having made themfelves mafters of it, they
deftroyed thofe fortifications, which Foulke had lately
erected, and defaced the caftle to the ground. But
they paid fauce for this another way, for as foon as
Rhys and Owen had heard that their uncles had
broken and violated the king's peace, they made in-
roads into Ifaeron, which was Maelgon's country,
and having flain a confiderable number of his men,
among whom was one brave and lufty youth called
Bachglas, they returned with very rich booty.

A. D. 1211.
Maelgon and Rhys Fychan were quickly followed
by the North Wales men in their revolt from the
king of England, for Prince Lhewelyn being not able
to endure any longer the tyranny and oppreffion which
the king's garrifons exercifed in his country; called
together Gwenwynwyn from Powis, Maelgon ap Rhys
from South Wales, Madoc ap Gruffydh Maylor from
Bromfield, and Meredith ap Robert from Cydewen, and

I   plainly

plainly declared before them the pride and infolency of the Englifh, and how that they who were always ufed to have a prince of their own nation, were now by their own wilfulnefs and neglect become fubject to ftrangers. However, it was not too late to recover their antient liberty, and if they did but unanimoufly agree among themfelves, they might eafily caft off that yoke which was fo intolerably burdenfome to them. Then the lords being fenfible of the truth and reafonablenefs of what Prince Lhewelyn delivered, and being confcious to themfelves that their prefent flavery and fubjection to the Englifh, was wholly owing to their own fear and cowardice, fwore fealty to Prince Lhewelyn, and fwore to be true and faithful to him, and to ftick by each other to the utmoft of their lives and fortunes. And fo joining their forces together, they took all the caftles in North Wales which were in the hands of the Englifh, excepting Ruthlan and Dyganwy; and then going to Powis, they laid fiege to the caftle which Robert Ufpont had built at Mathrafal. But King John being informed how the Welch had confpired againft him, and that they had taken and feized upon almoft all his caftles in North Wales, and how that they were now in actual befiegement of Mathrafal, prefently drew up his army, and coming to Mathrafal, quickly raifed the fiege, and to prevent the Welch from coming any more againft it, he burnt it to the ground and fo returned to England, having no time to ftay any longer in Wales, by reafon of the differences that happened betwixt him and his nobility. But being afterwards at Nottingham, and hearing how that Prince Lhewelyn crue!ly harraffed and deftroyed the marches, he caufed all the Welch pledges which he had received the laft year to be hanged, among whom were Howel the fon of Cadwalhon, and Madoc the fon of Maelgon, with many others of the nobility's fons, to the number of twenty-eight. And about the fame time Robert Vepont caufed Rhys the fon of Maelgon to be hanged at Shrewfbury, being a youth of about feventeen years

of

of age, and fo cruelly murdered the innocent child to revenge the crimes and offences committed by his father and others.

But though King John was fo fevere to the Welch, yet the Princefs of North Wales was more dutiful and favourable to him, for whilft he ftaid at Nottingham, fhe fent him an exprefs, declaring how that the barons had entered into a confpiracy with the French king againft him, and that the latter was preparing and raifing an army to come over to England, upon pretence that the king was a rebel, and bid open defiance to the Holy Church, in as much as he would not condefcend nor yield to the Bifhop of Rome's requeft. And in confirmation of all this, fhe told him that Robert Fitzwalter, Euftace de Vefcy and Stephen Redell, were fecretly fled into France, to promote and carry on this intrigue. And that this defign againft King John was no feigned furmife, the next A.D. 1212. year Pope Innocent the Third detached one of his nuncios to Wales, who abfolved Prince Lhewelyn, Gwenwynwyn and Maelgon from their oaths of allegiance to King John, and withal gave them a ftrict command under the penalty of excommunication, to moleft and annoy him with all their endeavours, as an open enemy to the church of God. Prince Lhewelyn, you may be fure, was not in the leaft troubled at this, for now he gained the fitteft opportunity imaginable, to reftore fuch lands as he had formerly much againft his mind delivered up to the king, being in the inland country of Denbigh and Flint, which Lhewelyn at this time repoffeffed himfelf of. And well it was he was fo quick, for within a little while after, King John by the perfuafions of Pandulph the Pope's legate, granted his Holinefs all his requeft, and fo obtained abfolution at Pandulph's hands, and upon performance of his promifes, an affurance of a releafement from that Ecclefiaftical Bull, which had fo formidably roared againft him.

1213   South Wales had now been quiet for a confiderable time, and they that ufed to be commonly very turbu̶ ͏ ͏ ͏ ͏ ͏ ͏ ͏ ͏ ͏ ͏ ͏ ͏ ͏ were now very peaceable and amicable.

amicable. But it was impoſſible that ſuch a peaceable courſe of life ſhould hold long, where injuſtice
and oppreſſion had ſo much liberty, and where people
were wrongfully kept out of their juſt and rightful inheritance. And this was the occaſion of the breach of
that quietneſs, which for the two or three years laſt paſt
they had ſo ſatisfactorily enjoyed. For Rhys the ſon
of Gruffydh ap Rhys, who was right heir to Prince
Rhys, finding he could have no ſhare of his father's
eſtate, but that his uncles forcibly kept all from him,
thought it his beſt way to make his caſe known to the
king of England, and to deſire a remedy and redreſs
from him. King John in compaſſion of the young
man's hard condition, ſent to his deputy Foulke Viſ-
count of Caerdyff warden of the marches, and to the
Steward of Hereford, commanding them to take away
all Yſtratywy from Rhys Fychan, by ſome called
Rhys Grig, unleſs he would permit his nephews to
enjoy Lhanymdhyfry caſtle, with all the lands and priviledges thereunto belonging. Foulke having received
ſuch orders from his maſter the king of England, ſent
to acquaint Rhys of the propoſals, and ſo demand
of him whether or no he would deliver up Lhanymdhyfry to his nephews, according to the king's command; who returned anſwer, that he did not know of
any ſuch obligation due from him to the king of England as to part with his lands at his command, and
therefore aſſured him peremptorily and in plain terms,
that he would not willingly part with one foot of what
he was in preſent poſſeſſion of. Foulke therefore having received this reſolute anſwer, was likewiſe as reſolute to get that by force which he could not obtain
by fair means ; and ſo having raiſed a great army, he
marched to Talhwynelgain to meet with young Rhys,
who was to come thither with all the forces he could
raiſe in Brecknock ; and from thence they marched in
three battles towards Dynefawr, the firſt being commanded by young Rhys, the ſecond by Foulke and
Owen brother to Rhys led the third, Rhys Fychan
was not in it. being rallied at their marching, that

thinking it more adviseable to meet them in the field,
rather than suffer them to block him up at Dynefawr,
came out very boldly, and gave them battle, but
after a warm engagement on both sides, Rhys Fychan
in the end got the worse, and after a loss of a great
number of his men, he was glad at last to make his
escape by flight. And so retiring to Dynefawr, he
doubled the garrison of that place, but thinking the
town of Lhandeilo-fawr not to be tenable, he burnt
it to the ground, and then kept himself private in the
woods and other desart places. But young Rhys and
Foulke laid siege to Dynefawr, and in the first assault
came on so fiercely, that they forced the garrison to
retire to the castle, which for some time they defended
very manfully. But the besiegers began to play so
violently with their battering engines, and to undermine the wall in such a manner, that the governor after a short defence began to capitulate, giving three
pledges for security, that if they received no relief by
the morrow at noon, the castle should be surrendered
up, conditionally that the garrison should march out
with all the tokens of honour, and carry their arms
and all other implements of war along with them.
No relief being arrived, the castle the next day was
accordingly surrendered, and all the articles of the capitulation observed; and so young Rhys being possessed of Dynefawr, in a little time afterward, brought
all Cantreffawr to his subjection. When Rhys Fychan was sensible how the stream run violently against
him, he thought it his wisest way to remove his wife
and children, and all his other effects, to his brother
Maelgon's country, and so leaving Lhanymdhyfry
castle well manned and fortified, he departed towards
Aberystwyth. But as soon as Foulke was returned to
the marches, young Rhys came with an army consisting of Welch and Normans before Lhanymdhyfry,
intending to besiege that place, but before they were
encamped before the town, the governor thought it
his best way to surrender, upon condition only, that
the garrison should depart away with their lives. And
shortly

shortly afterwards, Rhys Fychan was taken at Caermardhyn, and committed to the king's prison, and so all the disturbances and troubles of South Wales came to a peaceable issue. But it was not so in North Wales, for Prince Lhewelyn being desirous to rid his country from the insupportable tyranny and oppression of the English garrisons, laid siege to the castles of Dyganwy and Ruthlan, the only places now remaining in the hands of the English, which he took without any great opposition, and so freed his country from any title or pretence the king of England might claim in North Wales. King John indeed was engaged another way, and consequently in no good condition to help himself, for having repented of all the indignities and stubbornness he expressed against Pope Innocent; at this time he received penance at the hands of the Archbishop of Canterbury, to atone for all the severities he had practised against the church. And to restore himself the more to his Holiness's favour he made the kingdom of England tributary to the church of Rome, to be holden of the Pope, in paying him the sum of 1000 marks yearly for ever; and withal recalled and restored to their former preferments and places all such as had been banished, or had voluntarily fled the kingdom upon the account of their strict adherence and submission to the Pope of Rome.

Nor was this all, for the next year King John with two of his nobility, the Earls of Chester and Derby, was resolved upon a voyage to the Holy Land, but was unfortunately prevented of his journey, by the rebellion of his barons, which now broke forth violently by reason that the king would not grant them some antient laws and privileges, such as their forefathers always enjoyed. Therefore the barons entered into a confederacy with Prince Lhewelyn of North Wales, desiring him to make what diversion he could on his part, which they were resolved to do on theirs; and so having raised an army, they appointed Robert Fitzwalter their general. Coming to

A. D. 1215.

Lead d

Bedford, they were honourably received into the caftle by William Beauchamp, and from thence marching to London, they were entertained with all the ex-
preffions and tokens of joy. King John perceiving
how powerful they were like to prove, and how that
the country did in a great meafure favour their caufe,
thought it his wifeft way to nip them in the bud,
and to fall upon them before they grew too ftrong ;
and therefore having levied his forces, he marched together with William Marfhal Earl of Pembroke, towards the caftle of Rochefter. Being arrived there,
he laid clofe fiege to the caftle, but the governor William de Abbineto fo bravely defended it, that it could
hardly be taken after three months fiege, but at length
the king's men bore on fo violently, that they took
it by ftorm, where befides William de Abbineto, the
king took feveral of the barons prifoners. This was
an ill beginning to the defign of the confederates, and
what did not add a little to their misfortune, the Pope
prefently iffues out his Bull of Excommunication
againft Lhewelyn Prince of Wales, and all the Englifh barons as made war againft King John, who
was under the protection of the Church of Rome.
But Prince Lhewelyn did not regard his threatening
anathemas, and therefore having raifed an army, he
came to Shrewfbury, which was delivered up to him
without any refiftance. And whilft Lhewelyn remained there, Giles de Bruce bifhop of Hereford, one
of the chief of this confpiracy, fent his brother Reynold to Brecknock, whom all the people readily
owned for their lord ; and fo without the leaft grum-
bling or oppofition he received the caftles of Aber-
gefenny and Pencelhy, the Caftelh Gwyn, or the
White Caftle, together with Grofmont caftle and the
ifland of Cynuric. But when the bifhop came thither in perfon, he had the caftles of Aberhondhy,
Hay, Buelht, and Blaenlhyfny, delivered up to him ;
but thinking he had enough himfelf, and being rather
defirous to fecure his intereft, and to ftrengthen his
party in the country, then to heap more upon his
own Lord as i an ic yus vell bie ic fupurt, he

                                              beftowed

bestowed Payn castle, Clune and all Eluel upon Walter Fychan, the son of Eineon Clyd.

In the mean time, young Rhys the son of Gruffydh ap Rhys, and his uncle Maelgon were reconciled and made friends, and so coming both to Dyfed, they destroyed Arbeith and Maenclochoc castles, and recovered all such lands as formerly belonged to them, excepting Cemais. But Rhys's brothers Maelgon and Owen went to North Wales, and did homage and fealty to Prince Lhewelyn, whilst their brother Prince Rhys marched forward to Cydwely, and having rased the castles of Cainwylheon and Lhychwr, brought all the country about under his subjection. But this was not enough to satisfy the ambitious humour of that young prince, for having once tasted the pleasure of victory, and the taking and demolishing of towns, he was resolved to prosecute his conquest whilst Fortune seemed to favour his undertakings; and therefore he led his army against Talybont castle, which belonged to Hugh de Miles, and forcing his entrance into the same, he put a great number of the garrison to the sword. The next day he marched to Sengennyth castle, but the garrison which kept it, thinking it fruitless and to no purpose to oppose him, burnt the place and departed to Yftymlhwynarth. But he followed them at the heels, and the next day took it, and rased it to the ground, and over-ran the country in such a violent manner, that in three days time, he became master of all the castles and fortresses in all Gowerland and Morgannwc, and so returned home with great victory and triumph. At the same time Rhys Fychan, otherwise Rhys Gryg, young Prince Rhys's uncle obtained his liberty from the king of England, leaving his son with two more for pledges for his modest and peaceable behaviour towards his subjects, whom at other times he was wont to molest and oppress. About this time the abbots of Tal y Llecheu and Tuy Gwyn, were consecrated bishops, the former of St. David's, and the other of Bangor. But the bishop of Hereford

againſt King John, and was otherwiſe unwilling to part with what he had got in Wales, could not for all that refuſe the injunction of the Pope, by whoſe expreſs command he was conſtrained to make peace with the king, which being concluded, in his return homeward, he died at Gloceſter, leaving his eſtate to his brother Reginald, who had married the daughter of Prince Lhewelyn.

But for all that, Giles de Bruce biſhop of Hereford was fallen off, and reconciled to King John, yet Prince Lhewelyn did not think it convenient to follow his example, and therefore with his whole army he marched againſt Carmardhyn, and took the caſtle in five days, having raſed it to the ground, he ſucceſſively laid ſiege to the caſtles of Lhanſtephan, St. Cleare, and Talacharn, which he uſed after the ſame manner. From thence he went to Cardigan, and winning Emlyn caſtle, he ſubdued Cemaes, and then laying ſiege to Trefdaeth caſtle, in Engliſh called Newport, he quickly took it, and afterwards raſed it to the ground. His next deſign was upon Aberteifi and Cilgerran caſtles, but the garriſons which defended them, finding it to no purpoſe to wait his coming, and ſo to withſtand all his attempts againſt thoſe places voluntarily ſurrendered, and by that means prevented all the miſchief, which in oppoſing him, would in all probability unavoidably attend them. And ſo Prince Lhewelyn having ſucceſsfully over-run and ſubdued all Carmardhyn and Cardigan, triumphantly returned to North Wales, being attended by ſeveral of the Welch nobility, ſuch as Howel ap Gruffydh ap Conan, Lhewelyn ap Meredith, Gwenwynwyn Lord of Powis, Meredith ap Rotpert, Maelgon and Rhys Fychan the ſons of Prince Rhys of South Wales, Rhys and Owen the ſons of Gruffydh ap Rhys, together with all the power of Madoc ap Gruffydh Maylor Lord of Bromfield.

A. D. 1216. But the next year Prince Lhewelyn returned to Aberteifi to compoſe a difference, which ſince his departure, had happened betwixt Maelgon and Rhys Fychan, Prince Rhys's ſons on the one ſide, and Rhys and Owen, Gruffydh ap Rhys's ſons, on the other. There-

Therefore to make up this quarrel, and to reduce all matters to a quiet and amicable issue, Prince Lhewelyn made an equal distribution of South Wales betwixt them, alloting to Maelgon, three Cantrefs in Dyfed, viz. Gwarthaf, Penlhwynoc, Cemaes, and Emlyn with Cilgerran castle; to young Rhys, two castles in Yftratywy, Hiruryn and Maelhaen, Maenor Bydfey, with the castle of Lhanymdhyfry, and two in Cardigan Gwynionyth and Mahwyneon. His brother Owen had to his fhare the castles of Aberteifi and Nant yr Arian, with three Cantrefs in Cardigan; and Rhys Fychan, otherwife called Rhys Gryc, had Dynefawr caftle, the Cantref Mawr, the Cantref Bychan, excepting Hiruryn and Midhfey, together with the Comotes of Cydwely and Carnwylhion. This division being accomplifhed to every one's fatisfaction, and all the lords of South Wales being amicably reconciled, Prince Lhewelyn took his journey for North Wales; but he had not advanced very far, when news was brought him that Gwenwynwyn lord of Powis was revolted, and was become again the king of England's fubject. This unwelcome news ftruck very deep in the prince's mind, by reafon that Gwenwynwyn was a man of great power and ftrength in the country, and went a great way to repel the incurfions of the Englifh upon the marches, which now he being gone off, could not, he feared, be fo well effected. But however, to make the beft of a bad market, he endeavoured to take him off from the Englifh, and to reftore him to his former allegiance due to himfelf as his natural prince; and to that end, he fent to him fome bifhops and abbots to put him in mind of his oath and promife, how that he with the reft of the lords of Wales, had obliged himfelf to oppofe the Englifh to the utmoft of his power, and had delivered pledges for the fure performance of what he had then by oath engaged in; and left he fhould have forgot what he had then promifed, he was defired to read his own hand writing, whereby it was apparent that he had very unjuftly violated both his oath and promife. But all the rhetorick the bifhops could make ufe of, was not

R

of

of force enough to work Gwenwynwyn to a reconciliation with the Prince, and an averfion to the king of England; and therefore feeing nothing would do, Prince Lhewelyn was refolved to make him incapable of ferving the Englifh, and fo entering Powis with a ftrong army, he fubdued the whole country to himfelf, Gwenwynwyn being forced to fly for fuccour to the Earl of Chefter.

Whilft thefe things paffed in Wales, Lewis the Dauphin of France being invited by the Englifh barons againft King John, landed in the ifland of Thanet, and marching forward to London, he there received homage of all the barons, that were in actual war againft the king. And then fetting forward to Winchefter, where King John then lay, he took in his way the caftles of Rygat, Guildford and Farnham, and coming to Winchefter, had the town prefently furrendered to him. King John did not think fit to abide his coming, but removing to Hereford, in the marches of Wales, he fent to Prince Lhewelyn and Reynald Bruce, defiring their friendfhip, and imploring their aid and affiftance againft the French. But they refufing to hearken to his propofals, he deftroyed Radnor and Hay caftles, and marching forward to Ofweftry, which belonged to John Fitzalan, he burnt it to the ground, and then departed towards the North. But after that he had fettled his affairs there, and appointed governors in all the towns and places of ftrength; whilft he was making all neceffary preparations at Newark to confront the barons, he fell fick, and in a fhort time died, and was buried at Worcefter.

After his death his fon Henry was by feveral of the Englifh nobility proclaimed king, and in a little while, moft of the barons, who upon their hatred to King John, had maintained an open war againft him, came in, and owned their allegiance to his fon Henry, though contrary to their oath to Lewis the Dauphin. A. D. 1217. But what was moft pernicious to the Welch, Reynald de Bruce who had all this while maintained a confederacy with Prince Lhewelyn his father in law againft

King

King John, underhand made his peace with King Henry. But he fuffered feverely for his treachery; for young Rhys, and Owen his nephew by his fifter, feeing that he in whom they put their greateft confidence, had deceitfully forfaken them, came upon him with all their power, and took from him all Buelht, excepting only the caftle. Prince Lhewelyn was prefently made acquainted with Bruce's revolt, but as foon as he was informed that his fon-in-law was gone over to the king of England, he went in great fury to Brecknoc, and laying fiege to the town of Aberhondhy, he was with much ado prevailed upon by young Rhys to raife the fiege for the fum of a hundred marks; and then croffing the mountainous part of Glamorgan, called the Black Mountains, where his carriages fuffered very much, he came to Gwyr, and encamping at Lhangruc, Reynald Bruce with fix knights in his company, came to meet him, defiring his pardon for his paft offence, affuring him that for the future, he would be true and faithful to him, and would do his endeavour to affift him againft the King of England. Prince Lhewelyn was too good natured to rejeft his fubmiffion, and fo did not only receive him to his favour, but beftowed upon him alfo the caftle of Senghennyth, which Reynald committed to the cuftody of Rhys Fychan.

Prince Lhewelyn having fettled all things in good order in Gwyr, marched to Dyfed and being at Cefn Cynwarchon, the Flemings fent their agents to him to defire peace, which the Prince, by reafon that they always adhered to the Englifh intereft, would not grant them. And fo young Rhys, being the firft man, paffed the river Cledeu to ftorm the town, Iorwerth bifhop of St. David's, with the reft of his clergy came to the prince to intreat for a peace for the Flemings, which after a long debate, was granted, and concluded upon thefe terms; firft, That all the inhabitants of Rhos, and the country of Pembroke fhould from thence forward fwear allegiance to Prince Lhewelyn, and ever after acknowledge his fovereignty : to him, That towards the defraying of

charges in this expedition, they fhould pay one thoufand marks to be delivered to him before the enfuing
feaft of St. Michael; thirdly, That for the fure performance of thefe articles they fhould deliver up
twenty hoftages, who were to be fome of the moft
principal perfons in their country. Then Prince Lhewelyn having now brought all Wales fubject to himfelf, and put matters in a fettled pofture in South
Wales, returned to North Wales, having purchafed
very confiderable honour and efteem for his martial
atchievements in this expedition.

And now all matters of differences being adjufted,
and the Welch in good hopes of a durable freedom
from all troubles and hoftilities; another accident unhappily fell out to crofs their expectation. Lewis the
Dauphin perceiving the Englifh barons to flight and
forfake him, concluded a peace with King Henry, and
returned to France; and then the barons, the king
promifing to anfwer all their requefts, and to redrefs
their grievances, made their fubmiffion, without in-
cluding the Welch in their articles. They had all this
while gladly embraced the friendfhip and aid of the
Prince of Wales; but now upon their reconciliation
to the king, thinking they had no farther need of him,
they very bafely forfook him, who had been the principal fupport and fuccour of their caufe. And not
only fo, but they confpired together to convert their
arms againft Wales, thinking they could without any
breach of equity or confcience, take away the lands of
the Welch, to make addition to what fome of them
had already unjuftly poffeffed themfelves of. William
Marfhal Earl of Pembroke opened the fcene, and
coming unexpectedly upon the Welch, took the town
of Caerlheon. But he got nothing by this, for Rhys
Fychan perceiving what he would fain be at, rafed
Senghennyth caftle, and all the reft in his cuftody in
that country, and banifhing the Englifh with their
wives and children, divided the country betwixt the
A. D.1218. Welch, who kept fure poffeffion of it. Prince Lhewelyn alfo finding thofe to become his focs, who had
but

but lately courted his friendſhip, and fearing leſt that
the Engliſh being now in arms ſhould make any attempt upon his caſtles, augmented the garriſons of
Carmardhyn and Aberteifi, to make them capable of
withſtanding the Engliſh, in caſe they ſhould come
againſt them. But though the Welch and Engliſh
were at open variance and in actual hoſtility one a-
gainſt another, yet young Rhys with Prince Lhewelyn's approbation and conſent, thought it adviſeable
to go and do homage to the king of England, for
his lands in Wales. This might be thought a matter of ſupererogation, to make courtſhip to one who
was declared enemy to all the Welch, and one that
would not in all probability, ſuffer him to enjoy a
quiet poſſeſſion of his eſtate, in caſe he had ability
and opportunity to eject him. But the Welch inte- A. D. 1219.
reſt was in a great meaſure augmented by a new alliance with ſome of the moſt powerful among the
Engliſh; Rhys Gryc, Prince Rhys's ſon, being married to the Earl of Clare's daughter; and Marret,
Prince Lhewelyn's daughter, to John Bruce.

The Prince of Wales had quickly an occaſion to 1220.
experience his power, for the Flemings in Dyfed, who
had lately ſworn allegiance to him, began now to repent of what they had but a little time ago gladly
ſubmitted to, and contrary to their oaths, and the
league they had ſworn to obſerve, they fell upon A-
berteifi caſtle, which they took. Prince Lhewelyn
being highly diſpleaſed with the treacherous practices of theſe perjured Flemings, marched with all
ſpeed to Aberteifi, and having recovered the caſtle,
which he afterwards raſed, he put all the garriſon
to the ſword. Gwys was ſerved in the ſame manner,
and the town of Haverford was burnt to the ground,
and overrunning Rhos and Daugledhau, he committed
a lamentable deſtruction throughout the whole country. This the Flemings received as the due reward
of their finiſtrous dealing, which made them quickly
apprehenſive of their folly, and their imprudeut behaviour towards the Prince of Wales; and therefore

　　being

being forrowfully fenfible how unable they were to put a ftop to his farther progrefs by force of arms, they made overtures for ceffation of all hoftilities till the May following, which being granted them upon ftrict conditions, Prince Lhewelyn returned to North Wales. In the mean time fome Welch lords befieged Buelht caftle, which was in the poffeffion of Reynald Bruce, but before they could take it, King Henry brought an army to the marches and raifed the fiege, and then marching forward to Montgomery, built a new caftle in that town.

A D. 1221. The next year an unhappy diffention fell out betwixt Prince Lhewelyn and his fon Gruffydh this latter having kept himfelf in poffeffion of the Cantref of Merionyth, contrary to the confent and well-liking of his father. The Prince therefore having now no great matter of moment abroad, was refolved to curb the infolency of his fon, and therefore fent to him to command his appearance, and to wifh him to deliver up the Cantref quietly, left he fhould be forced to take it violently out of his hands. Gruffydh was not in the leaft difmayed at his threatenings, but being refolved to keep what at prefent he enjoyed, would neither go to his father, nor deliver up the Cantref to him. The Prince being enraged that he fhould be fo flighted by his fon, made a vehement proteftation, that he would be feverely revenged both of him and all his accomplices; and therefore coming to Merionyth with a great army, was refolved to drive his fon out of the country. But Gruffydh made all poffible preparations to oppofe his father, and drew up his forces to give him battle, but when both armies were ready to join, the differences betwixt them was happily compofed, and Gruffydh prevailed upon to make his fubmiffion to his father. But the Prince, though he forgave his fon his offence, and received him to favour, would not however, permit him to enjoy Merionyth and Ardydwy; but taking them away from him, and building a caftle in the latter, returned home. But he had not continued long at his palace at Aberffraw, when another occafion

occasion called him abroad; for young Rhys being
disappointed of Aberteifi, which in the division of
South Wales was allotted to his share, forsook the
prince, and put himself under the protection of William Marshal Earl of Pembroke. Prince Lhewelyn
hearing this, marched in great haste to Aberystwyth,
and being desirous to punish Rhys for his desertion
from his allegiance due to him, seized to his own use
that castle, together with all the domain and lands belonging to it. When Rhys understood what the prince
had done, he presently made his complaint to the king
of England, who coming to Shrewsbury, and sending
for Prince Lhewelyn, adjusted matters so betwixt
them, that the Prince promised to treat with Rhys
for Aberteifi, after the same manner as he had done
with Maelgon for Caermardhyn. And towards the
close of the year, John Bruce, Prince Lhewelyn's son-
in-law, obtained leave to fortify Senghennyth castle,
which in right to the prince's grant to Reynald Bruce,
belonged to him. But young Rhys did not long survive the agreement betwixt him and Prince Lhewelyn;
for he died the following year, and was buried at
Yftratflur; after whose death, the prince divided his
estate betwixt his brother Owen and his uncle Maelgon.

William Marshal Earl of Pembroke was now in A.D. 121
Ireland, and very busy in prosecuting the war against
the king of England's enemies in that kingdom; the
opportunity of whose absence Prince Lhewelyn taking
advantage of, won the castles of Aberteifi and Caermardhyn, belonging to the Earl; and putting both
the garrisons to the sword, placed in their room a
strong party of his own men. But when the Earl was
informed of what the Prince of Wales had done, he
presently left Ireland, and landed at St. David's with
a great army, and having recovered his castles, he
treated the Welch after the same manner, as Prince
Lhewelyn had used his garrisons, and passing forward
into the prince's country, destroyed all before him as
he went along. The Prince understanding how violently l. c. . . . . rward, s. . . . . .
R

confiderable body of men to check his fury;
who coming to Cydwely, and receiving intelligence
that the magiftrates of that place, had a private defign to betray him to the enemy, he put the whole
town in flames, and burnt it to the ground, without
fparing either churches, or other religious houfes.
The Earl of Pembroke had paffed the river Tywy at
Caermardhyn, where Gruffydh met him, and gave
him battle; but the victory proved fo uncertain, that
the night was forced to part them; and fo the Englifh
retired over the river. Matthew Paris writes, that the
Earl obtained a very fignal victory, and that of the
Welch there were nine thoufand flain and taken;
though the Welch account, which in this cafe is in
all likelihood the beft, makes the whole army of the
Welch to confift but of that number. But both armies
having lain for certain days in that pofture, and the
river Tywy being betwixt them; Gruffydh, by reafon
that provifion began to grow fcarce in his camp, returned back; and then the Earl decamped, and marched to
Cilgerran, where he began to build a very ftrong caftle. But before he could have time to finifh it, he
received an exprefs from the king, with orders to
come to him; and fo he went by fea to London, leaving his army at Cilgerran, to continue the work which
he had begun. Shortly after, the king, together with
the Archbifhop of Canterbury, came to Ludlow, and
fending for Prince Lhewelyn thither, they had good
hopes to adjuft all differences, and to make an amicable compofition betwixt him and the Earl. But
when this could not be effected, both parties fticking
clofe to their private intereft; the Earl being affifted
by the Earl of Derby and Henry Pyggot Lord of
Ewyas, defigned to pafs by land to Pembroke; but
his purpofe being difcovered to the prince, he detached his fon to fecure the paffage of Carnwylhion,
and came in perfon to Mahedryd; which when the
Earl underftood, finding it dangerous to profecute his
defign any further, he returned to England; and then
the prince marched to North Wales. The next action

tion that paſſed in Wales, was ſomewhat rare, and A. D. 1227.
not redounding much to the credit and eſteem of the
Welch; for Rhys Fychan, having by ſome ſiniſtrous
means or other, taken his father Rhys Gryc, contrary
to all filial affection and duty, detained him priſoner,
and would not ſet him at liberty, till he had delivered
up Lhanymdhyfri caſtle to him. About the ſame time,
Meredith Archdeacon of Cardigan, Prince Rhys's ſon,
departed this life, and was honourably interred at St.
David's, by his father.

But a while after, a great ſtorm threatened the 1228.
Welch; King Henry having raiſed a great army, was
reſolved to make a violent proſecution of the Earl of
Pembroke's quarrel againſt the Prince of Wales, and
if poſſible, to make all that country, for ever ſubject
to the crown of England; and ſo being advanced
into the marches, he encamped at Ceri. Prince Lhewelyn on the other hand, being informed of theſe
mighty preparations in England, and underſtanding
that they were intended againſt him, did uſe all the
endeavours poſſible, to make a vigorous reſiſtance;
and having drawn together all the forces he was able
to levy, thought it his wiſeſt way to meet the Engliſh
upon the marches, and not to permit the enemy to
enter his country. Both armies being come in ſight of
each other, frequent ſkirmiſhes happened betwixt
them; but one day, almoſt the whole armies engaged,
and after a vigorous attack of both ſides, the Engliſh
at laſt got the worſt, and were forced to retire, having
a great number of men ſlain and taken priſoners.
Among the latter, was William Bruce, Reynald's
ſon, who offered for his ranſom all Buelht, together with a conſiderable ſum of money, which the
prince would not accept of. But King Henry finding
that his army was worſted in this rencounter, thought
it beſt to make peace with the prince of Wales, which
being concluded, Lhewelyn came to the king, and
having paid him all other reſpects, beſides that of ſubmiſſion and allegiance, he returned in great honour
to North Wales. But this action is ſomewhat other-
-wiſe

wife laid down by Matthew Paris, who writes, that
this fkirmifh betwixt the Englifh and Welch happened upon another account; for the garrifon of
Montgomery iffuing out of the caftle, to enlarge a
certain paffage leading through a wood, where the
Welch were wont to rob and kill all paffengers; began to fell the timber, and cut down all the bufhes
which leffened the road, thereby to make the paffage
more clear and fecure. The Welch receiving intelligence of this, came prefently upon him in great numbers, and furprifing the enemies, being bufy at their
labour, forced as many as could efcape, to betake
themfelves for refuge into the caftle, which afterwards,
having firft caft a deep trench about it, they fmartly
invefted. Hubert de Burgh, Lord Chief Juftice of
England, and owner of the caftle, having notice of
this, fent prefently to King Henry, defiring his fpeedy
help againft the Welch, who thereupon came in perfon with part of his army, and raifed the fiege. Then,
the reft of his forces being arrived, he marched into
the wood, which was five miles in length, and by reafon of the thicknefs of the growth, impaffable; and
for an eafy paffage through it, caufed it to be burnt
down. After that, he led his army farther into the
country, and coming to an abbey called Cridia, which
the Welch were wont to take for refuge, he caufed it
to be burnt down; but finding it a very convenient
place for a fortrefs, he granted leave to Hubert de
Burgh to build a caftle there. But whilft the work
was going on, the Welchmen gauled the Englifh, and
fkirmifhed with them frequently, fo that many were
flain on both fides; but at laft William de Bruce
with many others that went abroad to fetch provifion,
was intercepted by the Welch, and taken prifoner,
and moft of his company were flain, among whom,
one who was knighted a few days before, feeing fome
of his fellows in great danger, rufhed boldly into
the midft of his enemies, and after a manful defence,
bravely loft his life. Several of King Henry's men
were corrupted by Prince Lhewelyn, and upon that
account took no great pains to repulfe the enemy;
which

which when the king perceived, and finding withal
that provifion was grown very fcarce in his camp,
he was forced to conclude a difhonourable peace
with the Welch, confenting to demolifh that caftle,
which with fo great an expence both of men and
money was now almoft finifhed, upon his own
charges, Prince Lhewelyn paying only three thoufand pounds towards it. Then both armies feparated, Prince Lhewelyn marching to North Wales,
and the king leaving William Bruce prifoner with the
Welch, returned to England, having purchafed no
fmall difcredit in this expedition.

William Bruce was brought to Wales, and there A. D. 1230.
had an honourable confinement in the prince's palace;
but he had not continued there very long, when he
began to be fufpected of being too familiar with the
princefs, King Henry's fifter; and as the report went,
was taken in the very act of adultery; for which the
prince caufed him to be hanged forthwith. About the
fame time, Lhewelyn, Maelgon's fon died in North
Wales, and was buried at Conwey: and Maelgon,
Prince Rhys's fon in South Wales, and was buried at
Yftratflur; whofe eftate defcended to his fon Maelgon.
And a little after, William Marfhal Earl of Pembroke 1231.
died, one that ever entertained an inveterate enmity to
the Welch, and upon whofe account King Henry had
chiefly brought his army into Wales. He was fucceeded both in his title and eftate by his brother Richard, who was much more favourably inclined towards the Welch, and never attempted any thing a-
gainft them. But the king of England was refolved
to retrieve the honour he had loft in the late expedition againft the Welch; and therefore being returned
from France, whither he had made a defcent, to recover what his father had loft in that kingdom, he
came to Wales; and having remained fome time in
the marches, he returned again to England, leaving
his army under the command of Hubert Burgh Earl
of Kent, to defend the marches againft any in-road
which the Welch might attempt. And he had not
remained there long when he received intelligence,

that a party of Welch had entered the marches near
Montgomery, whom he forthwith pursued, and setting
upon them surprisedly, he put a great number of
them to the sword. Prince Lhewelyn hearing this,
came in person with a great army to the marches,
and sitting before Montgomery castle, he forced Hubert to withdraw, and then making himself master of
the place, he burnt it to the ground, and put the
garrison to the sword; the like fate attended the castles
of Radnor, Aberhondhy, Rhayadr Gwy, Caerlheon,
Neth, and Cydwely; though Caerlheon held out very
stubbornly, and the prince had several of his men destroyed before the place. King Henry being informed of
what miserable desolation the Prince of Wales so successfully committed upon his subjects in these countries, had him presently excommunicated; and then
coming to Hereford with a mighty army, he detached
the greatest part of it, with a great number of his
nobility to Wales. These by the direction of a friar
of Cymer, unexpectedly as they thought, fell upon a
party of Welch; who at the first encounter seemed to
fly, till they had allured the English to pursue them
to a place where a greater party of Welch lay in ambuscade; who rushing of a sudden upon the English,
put them in such a confusion, that the greatest part of
them was cut off. The king being sensible, that this
was a treacherous insinuation of the friar, was resolved
to be revenged, by burning the abbey of Cymer; but
the prior, for three hundred marks, prevented it; and
so the king returned to England, having effected nothing in this expedition, besides the building of Mawd
castle. In the mean time, Maelgon, son of Maelgon
ap Rhys, laid siege to Aberteifi, and having by force
got entry into the town, he put all the inhabitants to
the sword, then destroyed all before him to the castle
gates, which were so strongly fortified, that it seemed
almost impracticable to take it in any short time. But
Maelgon, being joined by his cousin Owen, Gruffydh
ap Rhys's son, was resolved to try the utmost that
could be effected; and therefore taking with him
some of Prince Lhewelyn's most experienced officers,
he

he broke down the bridge upon the river Teifi, and then invefting the caftle more clofely, he fo battered and undermined it, that he became in a little time mafter of it.

The year following, Prince Lhewelyn made a de-A. D. 1232. fcent upon England, and having committed very confiderable wafte and deftruction upon the borders, he returned to North Wales with a rich booty both of men and cattle. King Henry, to correct the Welch for thefe grievous devaftations, and to prevent their further incurfions into England, demanded a very great fubfidy of his fubjects to carry on the war againft the Welch; which being granted him, he made all poffible preparations for his expedition to Wales. In the mean time, Randulph Earl of Chefter died, and was fucceeded in that honour by John his fifter's fon, who was afterwards married to Prince Lhewelyn's daughter. But the Englifh in Wales being in expectation of King Henry's coming thither, began to repair and fortify their caftles; and particularly, Ri- 1233. chard Earl of Cornwal rebuilt Radnor caftle, which the prince had lately deftroyed. Prince Lhewelyn was fufficiently fenfible, that the king of England intended an invafion, and therefore to be before hand with him, he came with an army to Brecknock, deftroyed all the towns and caftles throughout the country, excepting Brecknock caftle, which held out fo manfully, that after a month's fitting before it, he was at laft conftrained to raife the fiege. In his return to North Wales, he burnt the town of Clun, recovered all that country called Dyffryn Tefeidiat, in the poffeffion of John Fitzalan, deftroyed Red caftle in Powis, and burnt Ofweftry. But what happened very fortunately to the Welch, Richard Marfhal Earl of Pembroke being fallen at variance with King Henry, took part with Prince Lhewelyn; with whom joined Hubert de Burgh, who had lately made his efcape out of the caftle of Devizes, where the king, upon fome articles of information brought againft him, had committed him to prifon. But the Earl of Pembroke, attended by Owen ap Gruffydh ap Rhys, came to St. David's;
and

and being very glad of an opportunity to revenge himfelf upon the king, flew every one that owned any dependance upon the crown of England. Maelgon and Rhys Gryc, with all the forces of Prince Lhewelyn, quickly joined the Earl; who in their march through the country, took the caftles of Cardyff, Abergevenny, Pencelhy, Blaenlhefyni, and Bwlch y Ddinas, which all, excepting Cardyff, they burnt to the ground. The king receiving intelligence, that the Earl of Pembroke had entered into a confederacy with the Prince of Wales, and that he was now in open hoftility againft his fubjects in that country, gathered a very formidable army, confifting, befides Englifh, of Flemings, Normans, and Gafcoigns; and coming to Wales, he encamped at Grofmont, where the Earl, with the Welch army met him. But when the Englifh would have endeavoured to advance further into the country, the Welch oppofed them, and fo a battle enfued, wherein the Englifh loft five hundred horfe, befides a far greater number of their infantry. The Welch having gained a confiderable victory in this action, the king was advifed to withdraw his forces, for fear left that the Welch fhould again fet upon them, and fo fuftain a greater lofs, which counfel the king willingly hearkened unto, and fo he returned for England. The Englifh being withdrawn, the Earl likewife decamped, and marched to Caermardhyn, which he befieged; but after three months vain affault, the garrifon moft bravely defending the place; and the Englifh fleet, having thrown in new provifions, he thought it moft advifeable to raife the fiege. Shortly after, Rhys Gryc, fon to Prince Rhys died at Lhandeilo Fawr, and was honourably interred by his father at St. David's. About the fame time, Maelgon Fychan, Maelgon ap Rhys's fon, finifhed Trefilean caftle, which was begun in his father's time.

A.D. 1234. King Henry was not willing to hazard any more campaigns in Wales, and therefore he appointed John of Monmouth, a great foldier and general of the Englifh forces, warden of the marches of Wales; who thinking

thinking to get to himſelf an eternal name in conquering the Welch, raiſed all the power he could;
and imagining that the Welch could not be privy to
his purpoſe, he apprehended he could fall upon the
Earl Marſhal unexpected. But in this, he was to his
ſorrow moſt widely miſtaken; for the Earl having received private intimation of his deſign, hid himſelf in
a certain wood, by which the Engliſh were to march;
and when they were come ſo far, the Welch of a ſudden gave a great ſhout, and leaping out of the place
they had abſconded themſelves in, they fell upon the
Engliſh, being unprovided; and putting their whole
army to flight, they ſlew an infinite number both of
the Engliſh and their auxiliaries. John of Monmouth
himſelf made his eſcape by flight; but the Earl Marſhal entering his country, deſtroyed it with fire and
ſword. And what added to the miſery of the Engliſh, Prince Lhewelyn in the week after Epiphany,
joining the Earl Marſhal, made an incurſion into the
king's territories, deſtroying all before them, from the
confines of Wales to Shrewſbury; a great part of which
they laid in aſhes. King Henry was all this while
with the biſhop of Wincheſter at Gloceſter, and for
want of ſufficient power or courage to confront the
enemy, durſt not take the field; of which being at
length perfectly aſhamed, he removed to Wincheſter,
leaving the marches naked to the mercy of the enemy.
And now, there being no apprehenſion of fear from
the Engliſh, the Earl of Pembroke, by the counſel
of Geoffrey de Mariſco, tranſported his army into
Ireland, thinking to obtain a conqueſt in that kingdom; but in the firſt encounter with the Iriſh, he was
unfortunately ſlain through the treachery of his own
men: and ſo his eſtate and title deſcended to his brother Gilbert.

But King Henry finding it impracticable to force
the Welch to a ſubmiſſion, and being in a great meaſure weary of continual wars and inceſſant hoſtilities,
thought it his beſt prudence to make ſome honourable
agreement with the Prince of Wales; and therefore
he deputed i.   a   .· : i .   ·. Canterbury, the

biſhops

bishops of Rochester, Coventry, Litchfield and Chester, to treat with Prince Lhewelyn about a peace. When the king came to meet with them in their return from this negociation, being at Woodstock, he was certified of the death of the Earl of Pembroke, which he took so much to heart, that he presently melted into tears, being afflicted for the death of so great a person, whom he openly declared had not left his second in all his kingdom. Going from thence to Glocester, he met with the archbishop and bishops, who delivered to him the * form of the treaty of peace with Prince Lhewelyn, which he would not conclude, unless upon this condition; That all the English nobility who were confederated with him, and by evil counsel were exiled, should be recalled, and restored to the king's favour. The Archbishop further acquainted his Majesty with what difficulty he had brought the matter to this conclusion, being sometimes forced to add threatenings on the king's behalf, with his clergy; to which menaces the prince is said to have answered; That he bore more regard to the king's charity and piety, than he did fear his arms, or dread his clergy. But the king, who was very desirous of a peace, readily consented to what the prince required; and therefore he issued out his letters, recalling all the nobles who were outlawed, or otherwise exiled, requiring them to appear at Glocester, upon Sunday next before Ascension-day, where they should receive their pardons, and be restored to their estates, which the king had taken into his own hands.

* See the Appendix.

The peace being thus concluded betwixt the English and Welch, Prince Lhewelyn set his son Gruffydh at liberty, whom for his disobedient and restless humour he had detained in close prison for the space of six years. About the same time, Cadwalhon ap Maelgon of Melienydh, departed this life, who was quickly followed by Owen, Gruffydh ap Rhys's son, a person of great worth, and exceedingly beloved, and was buried at Yftratflur, by his brother Rhys. And the year following died Owen ap Meredith ap Rotpert

A.D. 1235.

of

of Cydewen; and not long after him, Madawc the A.D.1236. son of Gruffydh Mayelor, Lord of Bromfield, Chirk, and Yale, who was buried at the abbey of Lhan Eg-weit, of Vale Crucis, which he had built; leaving iffue behind him one son, called Gruffydh, who fucceeded into the possession of all these lordships. A little after, Gilbert Earl of Pembroke, got by treachery Marchen castle, which belonged to Morgan ap Howel, and fortified the same very strongly, for fear of Prince Lhewelyn. The next spring Joan, King John's daugh- 1237. ter, and Princess of Wales, departed this life, and was buried, according to her own defire, upon the fea-fhore, at a place called Lhanfaes; in the isle of An-glefey; where the Prince, in memory of her, afterwards founded a religious house, for the order of mendicant friars. About the same time also died John Scot, Earl of Chester, without any issue, upon which account the king feized that earldom into his own hands. Hugh Lupus was the first that enjoyed this honour, who coming over to England with the Conqueror, was by him created Earl of Chester, and fword-bearer of England; *Habendum & tenendum dictum comitatum Cestriæ, sibi & hæredibus suis, ita libere ad gladium, ficut ipse rex totam tenebat Angliam ad coronam*: To have and to hold the said county of Chester, to him and his heirs by right of the fword, so freely and fecurely as the king held the realm of England in the right of the crown. After five defcents, Randulph Bohun came to be Earl of Chester, who was uncle to this John, the last Earl. This Randulph had feveral encounters with Prince Lhewelyn, and was in continual agitation against him; but once more particularly, meeting with the Prince, and being fenfible of his inability to withstand him, he was obliged to retire for refuge to the castle of Ruthlan, which the prince presently befieged. Randulph perceiving himfelf to be in danger, fent to Roger Lacy, constable of Chester, requesting him to raife what strength he could possible, and come to fuccour him in this extremity. Wherefore Lacy having received this express, called to him prefently all his friends, craving aid, and to this

all the endeavours imaginable to refcue the Earl from
that imminent danger which fo feverely threatened
him: at whofe requeft, Ralph Dutton, his fon-in-law,
a valourous youth, affembled together all the players
and muficians, and fuch as then, being fair-time, had
met to make merry ; and prefenting them to the conftable, he forthwith marched to Ruthlan, raifed the
fiege, and delivered the Earl from all his fear.   In recompence of this fervice, the Earl granted the conftable feveral freedoms and privileges ; and to Dutton
the ruling and ordering all players and muficians within the faid country, to be enjoyed by his heirs for ever.

A. D. 1238. In the year 1238, Prince Lhewelyn being difcom-
pofed in body, called unto him all the lords and barons
of Wales to Yftratflur, where each of them fwore
to remain true and faithful fubjects, and did homage
to David, Lhewelyn's fon, whom he had named to
fucceed him.   Matthew Paris writes, That Prince
Lhewelyn being impotent by reafon of a palfy, and
fore difquieted by his fon Gruffydh, fent ambaffadors
to the king of England, fignifying to him, that for as
much as he could not expect to live long, by reafon
of his age, he was defirous to lead the remainder of
his days in peace and tranquility : and therefore now
purpofed to fubmit himfelf to the government and
protection of the king, and would hold his lands of
him ; promifing withal, that whenever the king fhould
ftand in need of his help, he would ferve him both
with men and money, to the utmoft of his power.
The bifhops of Hereford and Chefter were fent me-
diators in this behalf, though fome of the nobility of
Wales openly and peremptorily withftood it, and upon
no condition whatfoever would accept of fuch a peace.
But David being declared fucceffor to the principality,
began to plague his brother Gruffydh, who though elder, was yet bafe-born ; and took from him Aruftly,
Ceri, Cyfeilioc, Mowahwy, Mochnant, and Careneon;
and let him only enjoy the Cantref of Lhyn.   But a
little afterwards he difpoffeffed him of all, and contrary to his oath to the bifhop of Bangor, in whofe
protection Gruffydh then remained, took him prifoner;
having

having upon promife of no violence, obtained to fpeak with him, and fent him to Cricieth caftle. But whilft thefe two brothers continued to entertain an irreconcileable odium one to another, their father Prince Lhewelyn ap Iorwerth, to the great grief and diffatisfaction of all the Welch, departed this life, and was very honourably interred in the abbey of Conwey, after he had reigned fix and fifty years. He was a prince of great courage and audacity, and had no lefs prudence in contriving, than boldnefs in executing any martial adventure; he was a great fupport to the Welch, and no lefs a plague to the Englifh; he made very confiderable conquefts upon the borders, and extended the frontiers of Wales, much beyond their former limits. He had iffue by his only wife Joan, daughter to King John of England, one fon called David, who afterwards fucceeded in the principality of Wales; and a daughter named Gladys, who was married to Sir Ralph Mortimer. He had alfo a bafe fon, named Gruffydh, whom his brother David kept a clofe prifoner to his dying day.

DAVID AP LHEWELYN.

PRINCE Lhewelyn ap Iorwerth being deceafed, his only legitimate fon David, whom all the barons of Wales had, as is faid, in his father's life-time fworn to obey, legally fucceeded in the government; wherein being actually confirmed, he went to the king of England to Glocefter, and there did him homage * for his principality. Then all the barons, both Englifh and Welch who held any lands in Wales in like manner did homage and fealty for the fame. But the Englifh could not long refrain from their wonted hoftilites towards the Welch;

taking advantage of this revolution, before matters
were thoroughly fettled, b ought an army before the
caftle of Aberteifi, which being delivered up to him,
he fortified with a ftrong garrifon. Prince David was
as yet too weak to appear in the field; and indeed the
more, by reafon that feveral of his nobility and others,
could not affectionately love him, for that unnatural
fpleen he fhewed to his brother Gruffydh, whom, for
no vifible reafon, he detained in clofe cuftody. But
above the reft, Richard bifhop of Bangor, ftormed at
the Prince, and finding that he violated his promife,
in fetting his brother at liberty, whom under pretence
of an amicable confultation he had fraudulently feized
upon in the bifhop's prefence, without more ado excommunicated him; and then retiring to England,
made a very querimonious relation of the whole matter to the king, defiring to releafe Gruffydh out of
prifon, before the rumour of fo heinous a fact fhould
reach the court of Rome, and fo reflect upon his Majefty's reputation. King Henry thereupon fent to his
nephew Prince David, blaming him highly for fuch
a treacherous action, and dealing fo feverely with his
brother; and then earneftly requefted him to deliver
Gruffydh out of cuftody, both to fave himfelf from
perpetual defamation, and to deferve an abfolution
from the fevere fentence pronounced againft him.
But David abfolutely refufed to comply to the king's
defire, affuring him, that Wales could never enjoy a
peaceable time, as long as his brother Gruffydh had
his liberty.

Gruffydh being acquainted with his brother's refolution, and thinking that thereby he had unavoidably
difpleafed the king of England, privately fent to King
Henry, affuring him, that if by force he would deliver him out of prifon, he would not only hold his
lands for ever from him, but alfo pay him the yea ly
acknowledgment of three hundred marks; offering
both to give his corporal oath, and deliver up fufficient pledges for the performance of it; and withal
to affift the king with all his power in bringing in
the

the reft of the Welch to his fubjection. Moreover, Gruffydh ap Madawc, Lord of Bromfield, pofitively affured the king, that in cafe he would lead an army into Wales, to revenge the falfity and injurious practices of David, he would give him all poffible aid and affiftance. Indeed, King Henry, befides this folemn invitation, had no weak pretence to come to Wales; for Richard, bifhop of Bangor, a fiery man, had profecuted the matter fo warmly at Rome, that he obtained of the Pope alfo to excommunicate David, which excommunication being denounced againft him, his lands were pretendedly forfeited. But the king being chiefly allured with the promifes of the Welch in the behalf of Gruffydh, levied a very formidable army to lead to Wales; ftrictly commanding by proclamation, all the Englifh, who owed him any martial fervice, to repair armed to Glocefter, by the beginning of Autumn. This rendezvous being accordingly performed, the king came thither in perfon at the time appointed, and having regulated his troops, and put all matters in convenient order, he marched to Shrewfbury, where he remained fifteen days to refrefh his army. During his ftay there feveral of the nobility became fuitors unto him on behalf of Gruffydh, whofe condition they defired he would commiferate; among whom were, Ralph Lord Mortimer of Wigmore, Walter Clifford, Roger de Monte Alto, Steward of Chefter, Maelgon ap Maelgon, Meredith ap Rotpert Lord of Cydewen, Gruffydh ap Madawc of Bromfield, Howel and Meredith the fons of Conan ap Owen Gwynedh, and Gruffydh ap Gwenwynwyn Lord of Powis. Thefe noblemen prevailed fo far with King Henry, that a league was concluded between him and Senena the wife of Gruffydh. For the performance of thefe articles, the aforefaid noblemen offered to be fecurities, *See Appendix.* and bound themfelves by their feveral writings. But *See Appendix.* as if all things had confpired together againft Prince David, feveral perfons that had been at continual variance and enmity among themfelves to this time, were now, by reafon that they equally favoured Gruffydh's caufe,

made

made friends among one another: Morgan ap Howel
Lord of Cery, made his reconciliation to Sir Ralph
Mortimer, and his submission to King Henry, in a
See Ap-very solemn manner: in the same form several others
pendix.of the nobility, submitted to the king; as, Owen ap
Howel, Maelgon ap Maelgon, Meredith ap Meredith,
Howel ap Cadwalhon, and Cadwalhon ap Howel.
David finding himself thus relinquished by the greatest
part of his nobility, and particularly by Gruffydh ap
Madawc, Lord of Bromfield, whom he chiefly feared,
by reason of his great wisdom and power, and that he
was much esteemed by the king of England, could
not easily conclude how to carry himself in this per-
plexity of affairs. But in fine, considering with
himself what a puissant army King Henry brought
against him, and how himself was considerably weakened by the defection of his subjects, he thought it
most adviseable to truckle to the king; and therefore
with all speed sent him his submission.

See Ap-   Prince David having given a plenary submission
pendix.to the king, desired, that being his nephew, and the
lawful heir and successor of his father Prince Lhewelyn, he should enjoy the principality of Wales, rather than Gruffydh, who was illegitimate, and in no
wise related to the king; assuring him further, that
the war would never be at an end, if he was set at
liberty. King Henry knowing well the truth of all
this, and withal being assured that Gruffydh was not
only valiant himself, but had likewise very powerful
abettors and promoters of his cause, was very inclinable to assent to David's request, and to prevent
any farther troubles, willingly granted it. Therefore David in a while after sent his brother Gruffydh
to the king, together with the pledges promised for
the performance of the articles lately agreed upon;
who were all sent to the tower of London to be kept
in safe custody; Gruffydh being allowed a noble a-
day to provide himself with necessaries. Shortly after, David came himself to London, and after he had
done his homage, and sworn fealty to the king of
England, returned to Wales, being honourably and
                                        peaceably

peaceably difmiffed. But as foon as Gruffydh found out King Henry's mind, and that it was the leaft part of his defign to fet him at liberty, having flatly de-nied the bifhop of Bangor his requeft therein ; he be-gan to fet his brains a-working, and to devife means whereby he might make his efcape out of the tower. Whereupon, having one night deceived his keepers, he let himfelf down from the top of the building, by a line which he had compofed out of the fheets and hangings of the room ; which being too weak to bear his weight, being a heavy corpulent perfon, let him down headlong to the ground ; by the greatnefs of which fall he was crufhed to pieces, and fo prefently expired. King Henry being informed of this unhap-py accident, feverely punifhed the officers for their inexcufable carelefffnefs ; and ordered that his fon, who was kept prifoner with him in the tower, fhould be more narrowly obferved.

After this King Henry fortified the caftle of Dy-ferth in Flintfhire ; and for their paft fervice, or rather to oblige them to the like after, granted to Gruffydh ap Gwenwynwyn all his eftate in Powis, and to the fons of Conan ap Owen Gwynedh their lands in Me-rioneth. And the next year Maelgon Fychan forti- A. D. 1242. fied the caftle of Garthgrugyn, John de Mynoc the caftle of Buelht, and Roger Mortimer that of Mely- 1243. enyth. But all thefe preparations were to no pur-pofe ; for the following year early, King Henry came with an army into Wales, and began very unreafon-ably to moleft the Welch, and without any juft pre-tence forcibly to feize upon their lands and eftates. Indeed, after the death of Gruffydh, he had a mind no longer to keep his promife to David, and there-fore entitled his eldeft fon Edward to the principality of Wales, whom he thought to oblige the Welch to obey. But Prince David underftanding his defign, levied all his power for the defence of his juft right ; yet finding himfelf unable to withftand the army of the Englifh, purpofed to effect that by policy which he could not attain by force. He fent therefore to

S 4   the

the Pope, complaining how that King Henry of England compelled him unjuftly to hold his lands of him, and that upon no legal pretence he feized the eftates of the Welch at his pleafure; telling him moreover, that Prince Lhewelyn his father had left him and the principality of Wales to the protection of the fee of Rome, to which he was willing to pay the yearly fum of five hundred marks, obliging himfelf and his fucceffors by oath, for the due performance of this payment, The Pope (you may be fure) gladly accepted of the offer, and thereupon gave commiffion to the two abbots of Aberconwey and Cymer, to abfolve David from his oath of allegiance to the king of England, and having enquired into the whole ftate of the quarrel, to tranfmit an account of it to him. The abbots according to their commiffion, directed a very pofitive mandate to the king of England. King Henry admiring the ftrange prefumption and confidence of thefe abbots, or more the unfatiable avarice and greedinefs of the Pope, fent alfo to Rome; and with a greater fum of money, eafily adjufted all matters: his Holinefs being very defirous to make the beft advantage of both parties.

See Append?.

But Prince David finding that the Pope minded his own gain, more than to juftify his complaints againft the king of England, thought it to no purpofe to rely upon his faith, but judged it more advifeable to vindicate himfelf by force of arms. Having therefore gathered his forces together, (being now reconciled to, and followed by all the nobility of Wales, excepting Gruffydh ap Gwenwynwyn and Morgan ap Howel, who alfo fhortly after fubmitted to him,) he drew up his army to the marches, intending to be revenged upon the Earls of Clare and Hereford, John de Monmouth, Roger de Monte Alto, and others, who injured and oppreffed his people; with whom he A.D. 1245 fought divers times, and with various fuccefs. But in the Lent-time next year, the Marchers and the Welch met near Montgomery, between whom was fought a very fevere battle; the governor of that caftle being general of the Englifh, and having cunningly placed

an

an ambuscade of men, pretended, after some short engagement, to flee, whom the Welch daringly pursued, not thinking of any treachery. But as soon as they were past the ambushment, up rises an unexpected party of men, who falling upon the backs of the Welch, put them to a very great disorder, and killed about three hundred men, not without a considerable loss of their own side, among whom was slain a valiant knight called Hubert Fitz-Matthew. But King Henry being weary of these perpetual skirmishes and daily clashings between the English and Welch, thought to put an end to the whole with one stroke; and therefore raised a very great army of English and Gascoigns, and entered into North Wales, purposing to waste and destroy the country. But before he could advance very far, Prince David intercepted him in a narrow pass, and so violently set upon him, that a great number of his nobility and bravest soldiers, and in a manner all the Gascoigns were slain. The king finding he could effect nothing against the Welch, invited over the Irish, who landing in Anglesey, began to pillage and waste the country; but the inhabitants gathering themselves together in a body, quickly forced them to their ships: after which, King Henry having victualled and manned all his castles, returned dissatisfied to England.

But concerning this expedition to Wales, and the continuance of the English army therein, a certain person in the camp, wrote to this effect to his friends Mat. Paris. in England: 'The king with his army is encamped at Gannock, and is busy in fortifying that place, sufficiently strong already, about which we lay in our tents, in watching, fasting, praying, and freezing. We watch for fear of the Welch, who were used to come suddenly upon us in the night-time: we fast for want of provision, the halfpenny loaf being now risen and advanced to five pence: we pray that we may speedily return safe and scot-free home: and we freeze for want of winter-garments, having but a thin linen shirt to keep us from the wind. There is a fmall arm of the fea under the caftle where we lye, which the tide reached, by the conveniency of which, many fhips bring us provifion and victuals from Ireland and Chefter : this arm lies betwixt us and Snowden, where the Welch are encamped, and is in breadth, when the tide is in, about a bow-fhot. Now it happened, that upon the Monday before Michaelmas-day, an Irifh veffel came up to the mouth of the haven, with provifion to be fold to our camp, which being negligently looked to by the mariners, was upon the low ebb ftranded on the other fide of the caftle, near the Welch. The enemy perceiving this, defcended from the mountains, and laid fiege to the fhip, which was faft upon the dry fands ; whereupon we detached in boats three hundred Welch of the borders of Chefhire and Shropfhire, with fome archers and armed men, to refcue the fhip : but the Welch, upon the approach of our men, withdrew themfelves to their ufual retirements in the rocks and woods, and were purfued for about two miles by our men afoot, who flew a great number of them. But in their return back, our foldiers being too covetous and greedy of plunder, among other facrilegious and profane actions ; fpoiled the abbey of Aberconwey, and burnt all the books and other choice utenfils belonging to it. The Welch being diftracted at thefe irreligious practices, got together in great number, and in a defperate manner fetting upon the Englifh, killing a great number of them, and following the reft to the water-fide, forced as many as could not make their efcape into the boats, to commit themfelves to the mercy of the waves. Thofe they took prifoners they thought to referve for exchange ; but hearing how we put fome of their captive nobility to death, they altered their minds, and in a revengeful manner fcattered their dilacerated carcaffes along the furface of the water. In this conflict, we loft a confiderable number of our men, and chiefly thofe under the command of Richard Earl of Cornwal ; as Sir Alan Bufcell, Sir Adam de Maio, Sir

Geoffry-

Geoffry Eftuemy, and one Raimond a Gafcoign, with about an hundred common foldiers. In the mean time, Sir Walter Biffet ftoutly defended the fhip till midnight, when the tide returned; whereupon the Welch, who affailed us of all fides were forced to with-draw, being much concerned that we had fo happily efcaped their hands. The cargo of this fhip, was three hundred hogfheads of wine, with a plenty of other provifion for the army, which at that time it ftood in very great need of. But the next morning, when the fea was returned, the Welch came merrily down again to the fhip, thinking to furprife our men; but as luck would have it, they had at full fea the night before relinquifhed the fhip, and returned fafe to the camp. The enemy miffing of our men, fet upon the cargo of the fhip, carried away all the wine and other provifions; and then when the fea began to flow, they put fire to the veffel, and returned to the reft of the army. And thus we lay encamped in great mifery and diftrefs for want of neceffaries, expofed to great and frequent dangers, and in great fear of the pri-vate affaults and fudden incurfions of our enemies. Oftentimes we fet upon and affailed the Welch, and in one conflict we carried away an hundred head of cattle, which very triumphantly we conveyed to our camp. For the fcarcity of provifion was then fo great, that there remained but one hogfhead of wine in the whole army; a bufhel of corn being fold for twenty fhillings; a fed ox for three or four marks; and an hen for eight pence; fo that there happened a very lamentable mortality both of man and horfe, for want of neceffary fuftenance of life.'

The Englifh army having undergone fuch mife-ries as are here defcribed, and King Henry, as is faid, perceiving it was in vain for him to continue any longer in Wales, where he was fure to gain no great credit, he returned with his army into England, being not very defirous to make another expedition into Wales. Then all the nobility and barons of Wales, and thofe that had favoured and maintained

G ffydd

Gruffydh's caufe, were made friends and reconciled to Prince David, to whom they vowed true and perpetual allegiance. But the Prince did not long furvive this amity and agreement between him and his fubjects: for falling fick toward the beginning of this year, he died in March, at his palace in Aber, and was buried at Conwey, leaving no iffue to fucceed.

A.D. 1246. The only thing unpardonable in this prince, was his over jealoufy and feverity againft his brother Gruffydh, a perfon fo well beloved of the Welch, that upon his account their affection was much cooled, and in fome entirely alienated from their prince. Indeed thus much may be faid for David, that Gruffydh was a valourous and an afpiring man, and if fet at liberty, would bid fair to eject him out of his principality; which King Henry of England too (who thought he might bring over David, a milder man, to what terms he pleafed,) was fenfible of, when he would by no perfuafion difmifs him from cuftody in the tower of London. But this occafioned all the difturbances that happened in his time, the Welch themfelves, for the love they bore to Gruffydh, inviting the king of England to come to invade their country, and to correct the unnatural enmity their Prince expreffed to his brother. But when all differences were over, the king of England returned with his army fhamefully back, and the Prince and his nobility reconciled; the Welch might have expected a very happy time of it, had not death taken the Prince fo unnaturally away, before he had well known what a peaceful reign was.

LHEWELYN

LHEWELYN ap GRUFFYDH.

PRINCE David being dead, the principality of North Wales legally defcended to Sir Ralph Mortimer, in right of his wife Gladys, daughter to Lhewelyn ap Iorwerth. But the Welch nobility being affembled together for the electing and nominating a fucceffor, thought it by no means advifeable to admit a ftranger to the crown, though his title was never fo lawful; and efpecially an Englifhman, by whofe obligations to the crown of England, they muft of neceffity expect to become fubjects, or rather flaves to the Englifh government. Wherefore they unanimoufly agreed to fet up Lhewelyn and Owen Goch, the fons of Gruffydh, a bafe fon of Lhewelyn ap Iorwerth, and brother to Prince David; who being fent for, and appearing before the affembly, all the nobles and barons then prefent, did them homage, and received them for their fovereigns. But as foon as the king of England underftood of the death of the Prince of Wales; he thought the country being in an unfettled and wavering condition, he might effect great matters there; and therefore he fent one Nicholas de Miles to South Wales, with the title of Juftice of that country, with whom he joined in commiffion Meredith ap Rhys Gryc, and Meredith ap Owen ap Gruffydh; to eject and difinherit Maelgon Fychan of all his lands and eftate in South Wales. The like injurious practices were committed againft Howel ap Meredith, who was forcibly robbed of all his eftate in Glamorgan by the Earl of Clare. Thefe unreafonable extortions being infupportable; Maelgon and Howel made known their grievances to the Princes of North Wales, defiring their fuccour and affiftance for the recovery of their lawful inheritance from the ufur-

ments of the English. But the king of England understanding their defign, led his army into Wales;
upon whofe arrival, the Welch withdrew themfelves
to Snowden hills, where they fo tired the Englifh
army, that the king finding he could do no good,
after fome ftay there returned back to England. Within a while after, Ralph Mortimer, the hufband of
Gladys Dhu died; leaving his whole eftate, and with
it a lawful title to the principality of North Wales,
to his fon Sir Roger Mortimer.

A. D. 1247.   The next year nothing memorable paffed between
M. Par's,   the Englifh and the Welch, only the difmal effects of
page 739.   the laft year's expedition, were not worn off; the ground
being uncapable of cultivation, and the cattle being
in great meafure deftroyed by the Englifh, occafioned
great poverty and want in the country.   But the
greateft calamity befel the bifhops; St. Afaph and
Bangor being deftroyed and burnt by the Englifh,
the bifhops thereof were reduced to that utmoft extremity, as to get their fubfiftence by other mens
charity; the bifhop alfo of St. David's deceafed, and
he of Landaff had the misfortune to fall blind.   In
the bifhoprick of St. David's fucceeded Thomas, furnamed Wallenfis, by reafon that he was born in Wales;
who thinking himfelf obliged to benefit his own country what lay in his power, defired to be advanced from
the archdeaconry of Lincoln to that fee: which the
king eafily granted, and confirmed him in it.   The
1248   next fummer proved fomewhat more favourable to
the Welch; Rhys Fychan fon to Rhys Mechyl, won
from the Englifh the caftle of Carrec Cynnen, which
his unkind mother, out of malice, or fome ill opinion entertained of him, had fome time before privately delivered up to them.   And about the fame
time the body of Gruffydh ap Lhewelyn bafe fon to
Lhewelyn ap Iorwerth, was recovered from the king
of England, by the earneft follicitations of the abbots of Conwey and Yftratflur; who conveying it
to Conwey, beftowed upon it a very pompous and
honourable interment.

After

After this, the affairs of the Welch proceeded A.D. 1255. peaceably for a long while, and the country had sufficient opportunity to recover its former plenty ; but at laft, to make good the proverb, that *Plenty begets War* ; they began, for want of a foreign enemy, to quarrel and fall out among themfelves. Owen was too high and ambitious to be fatisfied with half the principality, and therefore muft needs have a fling at the whole ; wherein fortune fo far deceived him, that he loft his own ftake, as will afterwards appear. But the better to encompafs his defign, by fly infinuations he perfuaded David his younger brother to fecond his caufe ; and they with joint intereft levied their power, with intention to dethrone their elder brother Lhewelyn, But that was no eafy matter ; for Lhewelyn was prepared to receive them, and with a puiffant army met them in the field, and fo was refolved to venture all upon the fortune of a battle. It was ftrange and grievous to behold this unnatural civil war ; and the more grievous now, by reafon that it fo manifeftly weakened the ftrength of the Welch to withftand the incurfions of the Englifh, who were extremely pleafed with fo fair an opportunity to fall upon them. But they were too far engaged, to confider of future inconveniencies ; and a trial of war they muft have, though the Englifh were ready to fall upon both armies. The battle being joined, the day proved bloody on both fides, and which was like to conquer was not prefently difcovered ; till at length Owen began to give ground, and in fine was overthrown, himfelf and his brother David being taken prifoners. Lhewelyn, though he had fufficient reafon, would not put his brothers to death ; but committing them into clofe prifon, feized all their eftates into his own hands, and fo enjoyed the whole principality of Wales.

The Englifh feeing the Welch at this rate opprefs and deftroy one another, thought they had full liberty to deal with them as they pleafed ; and thereupon began to exercife all manner of wrong and injuftice againft them ; infomuch that the next year, all 1256.

I   the

the lords of Wales came in a body to Prince Lhewelyn, and declared their grievances, how unmercifully Prince Edward (whom his father had fent to
Wales) and others of the nobility of England dealt
with them, how without any colour of juftice they
feized upon their eftates, without any room for appeal ; whereas, if themfelves offended in the leaft,
they were punifhed to the utmoft extremity. In fine,
they folemnly declared, that they preferred to die honourably in the field, before to be fo unmercifully en-
flaved to the will and pleafure of ftrangers. Prince
Lhewelyn was not a ftranger to all this ; and now
having happily difcovered the bent and inclination
of his fubjects, was refolved to profecute, if poffible,
the expulfion of the Englifh, and to be revenged upon them for their moft cruel, and almoft inhuman
practices towards the Welch. Having therefore drawn
all his power together, being accompanied by Meredith ap Rhys Gryc, in the fpace of one week he recovered out of the hands of the Englifh all the inland country of North Wales, and then all Merionyth with fuch lands as Prince Edward had ufurped
in Cardigan, which he beftowed upon Meredith the
fon of Owen ap Gruffydh. Having alfo forced Rhys
Fychan out of Buelht, he conferred it upon Meredith ap Rhys ; and in like manner beftowed all the
lands which he recovered, between his nobles ; referving nothing to his own ufe, befides Gwerthryncon,
A. D. 1257. the eftate of Sir Roger Mortimer. The next fummer, he entered into Powis, and made war againft
Gruffydh ap Gwenwynwyn, who always had taken
part with, and owned fubjection to the king of England, which he totally overcame, excepting the caftle
of Poole, fome fmall part of Caerneon, and the country lying upon the banks of the Severn.

But Rhys Fychan was not fatisfied with the lofs of
Buelht, and therefore was refolved to try to recover
it ; to which end, he went to the king of England,
of whom he obtained a very ftrong army, commanded by one Stephen Bacon, which being fent by
fea, landed at Caermarthyn in the Whitfun-week.

From

From thence the Englifh marched to Dynefawr, and laid fiege to the caftle, which valiantly held out, until Lhewelyn's army came to its relief. Upon the arrival of the Welch, the Englifh decamped from before the caftle, and put themfelves in pofture of battle, which the Welch perceiving, they made all hafte to anfwer and oppofe them. Whereupon there enfued a very terrible engagement which lafted a very long while; this being for number of men the greateft battle that had been fought between the Englifh and the Welch. But the victory favoured the Welch, the Englifhmen being at length forced to fly, having loft above two thoufand men, befides feveral barons and knights who were taken prifoners. After this the prince's army paffed to Dyfed, where having burnt all the country, and deftroyed the caftles of Abercorran, Lhanftephan, Maenclochoc and Arberth, with all the towns thereunto belonging, returned to North Wales with much fpoil. But as foon as he was arrived, great complaints were exhibited to Prince Lhewelyn againft Jeffrey Langley lieutenant to Edward Earl of Chefter, who without any regard to equity and confcience, moft wrongfully oppreffed the inhabitants of Wales under his jurifdiction. Whereupon the prince to punifh the mafter for the fervant's fault, entered with fome part of his army into the Earl's eftate, burnt and deftroyed all his country on both fides the river Dee, to the gates of Chefter. Edward had no power at prefent to oppofe him, but being refolved to be revenged upon the Welch with the firft opportunity, he defired aid of his uncle, then chofe king of the Romans, who fent him a ftrong detachment, with which he purpofed to give Prince Lhewelyn battle. But finding him too ftrong, he thought it more advifeable to defift from hoftility, the prince's army confifting of ten thoufand experienced men, who were obliged by oath, rather all to die in the field, than fuffer the Englifh to gain any advantage over the Welch. But Gruffydh ap Madoc Maelor, Lord of Dinas Bran, a perfon of notorious reputation for injuftice and oppreffion, bethi i-

T　　　　　　　　　　　　look

fook the Welch his countrymen, and with all his forces went over to the Earl of Chester.

A.D. 1258. The next year Prince Lhewelyn paffed to South Wales, and feized into his hands the land of Cemaes, and having reconciled the difference betwixt Rhys Gryg and Rhys Fychan, he won the caftle of Trefdraeth, with the whole country of Rhos, excepting Haverford. There he marched in an hoftile manner toward Glamorgan, and rafed to the ground the caftle of Lhangymwch, and then returning to North Wales, he met by the way with Edward Earl of Chefter, whom he forced precipitoufly to return back. But before he would put an end to this expedition, he muft needs be revenged upon that ungrateful fugitive Gruffydh ap Madoc Maelor, and thereupon paffing through Bromfield, he miferably laid wafte the whole country. Upon this the kings of England and Scotland fent to Lhewelyn requiring him to ceafe from hoftility, and after that unmerciful manner to devour, and forcibly to take away other mens eftates. The prince was not over follicitous to hearken to their requeft, but finding the time of the year very feafonable for action againft the Englifh, he divided his army into two battles, each of thefe confifting of 1500 foot and 500 horfe, with which he purpofed to enlarge his conqueft. Edward Earl of Chefter, to prevent the blow which fo defperately hung over his head, fent over for fuccours from Ireland, of whofe coming Prince Lhewelyn being certified, manned out a fleet to intercept them, which meeting with the Irifh at fea, after a fharp difpute, forced them to return back with lofs. King Henry being acquainted with the mifcarriage of the Irifh, refolved to come in perfon againft the Welch, and having drawn together the whole ftrength of England, even from St. Michael's mount in Cornwal to the river Tweed; marched with his fon Edward in a great rage to North Wales, and without any oppofition advanced as far as Teganwy. But the Prince had ftopped his farther progrefs and prevented any long ftay he could make in Wales, having before hand caufed all manner

of

of provision and forage to be carried over the river, and then securing the strait and narrow passages whereby the English might get farther into the country; the army was in a short time so mortally fatigued, that the king for want of necessary subsistence was forced to retire in haste to England with considerable loss.

The prince after that sending for all the forces in South Wales, came to the marches, where Gruffydh Lord of Bromfield finding that the king of England was not able to defend his estate yielded himself up, and then passing to Powis, he banished Gruffydh ap Gwenwynwyn, and took all the lands in the country into his hands. Proceeding farther, he was encountered with by Gilbert de Clare Earl of Glocester, who with a choice party of English gave him battle. But Lhewelyn's army exceeding both in number and courage, easily vanquished and overcame the English, and so the victory being quickly obtained, the prince presently reduced to his power all the castles belonging to the Earl of Glocester. King Henry hearing of the Earl's overthrow, was much concerned at the loss of so many brave soldiers, in whose valour and experience he always put a very great confidence, and therefore to revenge their deaths, he was again resolved to march against the Welch. Having called his forces together, and received supply from Gascoign and Ireland he came to Wales, but not daring to venture far into the country, for fear of being forced to make another shameful retreat, he only destroyed the corn near the borders, it being harvest time, and so returned to England. But Lord James Audley, whose daughter was married to Gruffydh, Lord of Bromfield, did more mischief and hurt to the Welch, who having brought over a great number of horsemen from Germany to serve against the Welch, so terrified them with the unusual largeness of the horses, and the unaccustomed manner of fighting, that in the first encounter the Welch were easily overcome. But minding to revenge this disgrace, and withal being better acquainted with their method of arms,

T 2   the

the Welch in a little time after made in-roads into the
Lord Audley's lands, where the Germans prefently fet
upon them, and purfued them to certain ftraits, which
the Welch difcovered for a politick retreat. The
Germans thinking they had entirely drove the Welch
away, returned careleſsly back, but being fet upon of
the fudden, without any thought of an enemy behind,
they were all in a manner flain by the rallying Welch.
This year a very great fcarcity of beefs and horfes
happened in England, whereof feveral thoufands yearly were fupplied out of Wales, by reafon of which,
the marches were perfectly robbed of all their breed,
and not fo much as a beaft to be feen in all the borders.

A. D. 1259   The next fpring all the nobility of Wales convened
together and took their mutual oaths to defend their
country to death, againft the oppreffing invafions of
the Englifh, and not to relinquifh and forfake one
another upon pain of perjury; though notwithftanding, Meredith ap Rhys of South Wales violated this
agreement, and put himfelf in the fervice of the king
of England. King Henry was ready to fall upon
the Welch, to which purpofe he fummoned a parliament, wherein he propofed to raife a fubfidy towards the conqueft of Wales, being not able of himfelf to bear the expences of this war, by reafon of
feveral loffes he had already received, the country of
Pembroke being lately deftroyed and taken by the
Welch, where they found plenty of falt, which before they were in great neceffity of. But William
de Valentia accufing the Earls of Leicefter and Glocefter as the authors of all this mifchief quite broke
all their meafures, fo the king was forced to prorogue
the parliament for a time without any grant of a
fubfidy. But within a while after, it fat at Oxford,
where King Henry and Edward his fon took a folemn oath to obferve the laws and ftatutes of the
realm, and the fame being tendered to Guy and
William the king's brothers, and to Henry fon to
the king of Almain, and to Earl Warren, they
refufed to take it, and fo departed. In this parliament

liament the lords of Wales fairly proffered to be tried by the laws for any offence they had unjuftly
committed againft the king, which was mainly oppofed by Edward, who caufed one Patrick de Canton
(to whom the lordfhip of Cydwely was given, in cafe
he could win and keep the fame) to be fent to Caermardhyn as lieutenant for the king with whom Meredith ap Rhys was joined in commiffion. Being arrived at Carmardhyn, Patrick fent to the Prince, to
defire him to appoint commiffioners to treat with him
concerning a peace, which he confented to, and without any fufpicion of treachery, fent Meredith ap
Owen, and Rhys ap Rhys to Emlyn, if poffible,
to conclude the fame. But Patrick meaning no fuch
thing, laid an ambufcade for the Welch, who coming
honeftly forward, were by the way villainoufly fet upon
by the Englifh, and a great many flain ; but thofe
that happily efcaped, calling up the country, prefently gave chafe to Patrick and his accomplices, who
being at length overtaken, were almoft all put to
the fword. But Prince Lhewelyn was now altogether bent upon a peace, and did not only defire it,
but was willing to purchafe it for a fum of money,
to which purpofe he offered to give the king 4000
marks, to his fon 300, and 200 to the queen, which
the king utterly refufed, replying, That it was not a
fufficient recompence for all the damages he had fuffered by the Welch. Matthew of Weftminfter reporteth, that about Michaelmas this year, the bifhop
of Bangor was commiffioned by the prince and nobility of Wales to treat with the king of England a-
bout a peace, and to offer him 16,000 pounds for the
fame, upon thefe conditions, that according to their
antient cuftom, the Welch fhould have all caufes tried
and determined at Chefter, and that they fhould freely
enjoy the laws and cuftoms of their own country ; but
what was the refult of this treaty, my author does not
mention.

There being no hopes of a peace, Prince Lhewelyn A.D. 126.
early next year appeared in the field, and paffed to
South Wales, and firft fell foul upon Sir Roger Mortimer,

timer, who contrary to his oath, maintained the king of England's quarrel. Having forcibly dispossessed him of all Buelht, and without any opposition taken the castle, where was found a plentiful magazine, he marched through all South Wales, confirming his con-

A.D. 1261. quest, and afterwards returned to his palace at Aber, 1262. betwixt Bangor and Conwey. The year following, Owen ap Meredith Lord of Cydewen died. But the next summer was somewhat more noted for action, a party of Prince Lhewelyn's men took by surprise the castle of Melienyth, belonging to Sir Roger Mortimer, and having put the rest of the garrison to the sword, they took Howel ap Meyric the governor with his wife and children prisoners; and after that, the castle was demolished by the prince's order. Sir Roger Mortimer hearing of this, with a great body of lords and knights came to Melienyth, where Prince Lhewelyn met him, but Sir Roger not daring to hazard a battle, planted himself within the ruins, and finding he could do no good, desired leave of the prince to retire peaceably. The Prince upon the account of relation and near consanguinity betwixt them, and withal because he would not be so mean spirited as to fall upon an enemy, who had no power to resist him, let him safely depart with his forces, and then passing on himself to Brecknock at the request of the people of that country, who swore fidelity unto him; so passed on and returned to North Wales. And now being confederate with the barons against King Henry, he was resolved to practise something in the prejudice of the English, and so set upon the earldom of Chester, destroyed the castles of Tygannmy and Diserth belonging to Edward, who coming thither, was yet not able to prevent the mischief done to him by the Welch.

1263. The next year John Strange junior, constable of Montgomery with a great number of marchers, came a little before Easter by night, through Ceri to Cydewen, intending to surprise the castle, which when the people of the country understood, they gathered together, and setting upon them, slew two hundred of his men, but Strange with a few got safely back.

4

Within

Within a while after, the marchers and the Welch met again near a place called Clun, where a hot engagement happened between them, in which the Welch were worfted, and had a great number of their men flain. After this, nothing remarkable fell out for a confiderable time, unlefs it were, that David being releafed out of prifon by Prince Lhewelyn his brother, moft ungratefully forfook him, and with all his might, fided with his enemies the Englifh; alfo Gruffydh ap Gwenwynwyn having taken the caftle of Mold, demolifhed it to the ground. During this quiet and unactive interval in Wales, Meredith ap Owen, the main fupport and defender of South Wales died, to the great difadvantage of the affairs of that country. And A. D. 1268. now indeed, the Welch were like to be made fenfible of the lofs of fo confiderable a perfon, for King Henry was refolved once more to lead an army into Wales, and to fee if he could have better fuccefs than he had hitherto againft the Welch. But when he was prepared to undertake this expedition, Ottobonus, Pope Clement's legate in England, interpofed and meditated a peace, which was concluded upon at the caftle of Montgomery, wherein it was articled, that Prince Lhewelyn fhould give the king thirty thoufand marks, and the king was to grant the prince a charter, from thenceforth to receive homage and fealty of all the nobility and barons of Wales, befides one, fo that they could hold their lands of no other but himfelf, and from thence forward he was to be lawfully ftiled Prince of Wales. This charter being ratified and confirmed as well by the authority of the pope, as the king's feal; Prince Lhewelyn defifted from any farther acts of hoftility, and punctually obferved all the articles of the agreement betwixt him and King Henry, fo that nothing more was outrageoufly tranfacted between the Englifh and Welch, during the remainder of this king's reign. Within that fpace, died Grono ap Ednyfed Fychan one of the chief lords of the prince's council, and fhortly after him Gruffydh Lord of Bromfield, who lies buried at Vale Crucis.

T 4

But

A D. 1272. But the death of King Henry put an end to the ob-
servations of the peace betwixt the Englifh and Welch,
who dying on the fixteenth day of November this year,
left this kingdom to his fon Edward. Prince Edward
was then in the Holy Land, and very active againſt
thoſe enemies of chriſtianity, the Turks, where he had
already continued above an year; but underſtanding of
his father's death, and that in his abfence he was proclaimed king of England, he made all haſte to return
to receive the folemnity of coronation. But what by
the tediouſnefs of the journey, and what by being honourably detained at princes' courts in his way, it was
two years before he could get into England, then
upon the fiftcenth of Auguſt, and in the year 1274, he
was crowned at Weſtminſter. Prince Lhewelyn was
fummoned to attend at his coronation, but he flatly
refuſed to appear, unlefs upon fure terms of fafe conduct, for having offended feveral of the Englſh nobility, he could not in fafety pafs through their country
without the danger of expoſing his peiſon to the inveterate malice and acceptable revenge of fome of them.
And therefore without the king's brother, the Earl of
Gloceſter, and Robert Burnell Lord Chief Juſtice of
England, were delivered up as pledges for his fafe conduct, he would not come to do his homage and fealty
at his coronation, according to the writ directed to
him. And indeed, feeing King Edward had broke the
peace lately concluded upon before the Pope's legate,
and did receive, and honourably entertain ſuch noblemen of Wales, as for their difloyalty were banifhed
by Prince Lhewelyn, by whom he feared fome treachery; there was no reaſon that the prince fhould pay
him any fubjection, but by the breach of peace was
exempted from all homage. However, Prince Lhewelyn to fhew that it was not out of any ſtubbornnefs or
difrefpect to the king of England, that he refuſed to
come, fent up his reaſons by the abbots of Yſtrat-
flur and Conwey to Robert Kilwarby archbiſhop of
Canterbury, and the reſt of the biſhops then fitting
in convocation in the New Temple at London, which
were to this eſſect.

To

To the moſt Reverend Fathers in God, Robert, Archbiſhop of Canterbury, and Metropolitan of all England, the Archbiſhop of York, and the reſt of the Biſhops in Convocation; Lhewelyn Prince of Wales and Lord of Snowden, ſendeth greeting.

WE would have your Lordſhips to underſtand, that whereas formerly moſt terrible and inceſſant wars were continually managed betwixt Henry king of England and Ourſelf; the ſame were at laſt compoſed, and all matters of differences were adjuſted by the means of his Excellency Cardinal Ottobonus, the Pope's legate, who having drawn the articles and conditions of the peace agreed upon, they were ſigned and ſwore to, not only by the king, but alſo the prince his ſon, now king of England. Among theſe articles were comprehended, that We and our ſucceſſors ſhould hold of the king and his ſucceſſor, the principality of Wales, ſo that all the Welch lords, one baron excepted, ſhould hold their baronies and eſtates *in capite* of Us, and ſhould pay their homage and fealty for the ſame to Us; We in like manner doing homage to the king of England and his ſucceſſors. And beſides, that the king and his ſucceſſors ſhould never offer to receive and entertain any of Our enemies, nor any ſuch of Our own ſubjects as were lawfully baniſhed and excluded our dominions of Wales, nor by any means defend and uphold ſuch againſt Us. Contrary to which articles, King Edward has forcibly ſeized upon the eſtates of certain barons of Wales, of which they and their anceſtors have been immemorably poſſeſſed of and detains a barony, which by the form of peace ſhould have been delivered to us; and moreover, has hitherto entertained David ap Gruffydh our brother, and Gruffydh ap Gwenwyn-

1   wyn,

wyn, with feveral other of Our enemies who are outlaws
and fugitives of Our country, and though We have often exhibited Our grievances and complaints againft
them, for deftroying and pillaging our country, yet We
could never obtain of the king any relief or redrefs for the
feveral wrongs and injuries we received at their hands ;
but on the contrary they ftill perfift to commit waftes
and other outrages in Our dominions. And for all
this, he fummons Us to do him homage at a place
which is altogether dangerous to Our perfon, where
Our inveterate enemies, and which is worfe, Our own
unnatural fubjects, bear the greateft fway and refpect
with the king. And though we have alledged feveral
reafons to the king and his council, why the place by
him affigned, is not fafe and indifferent for Us to come,
and defire him to appoint another, whereto we might
with more fafety refort, or elfe that he would fend commiffioners to receive Our oath and homage, till he could
more opportunely receive them in perfon ; yet he would
not affent to Our juft and reafonable requeft, nor be fatisfied with the reafons We exhibited for Our non-appearance. Therefore We defire your lordfhips earneftly to weigh the difmal effects that will happen to the
fubjects both of England and Wales upon the breach
of the articles of peace, and that you would be pleafed
to inform the king of the fad confequence of another
war, which can no way be prevented, but by ufing
Us according to the conditions of the former peace,
which for Our part, We will in no meafure tranfgrefs.
But if the king will not hearken to your counfel, We
hope that you will hold Us excufed, if the nation be
difquieted and troubled thereupon, which as much
as in Us lieth We endeavour to prevent.

King Edward would admit of no excufe, nor
hearken to any manner of reafon in the cafe, but
was unmercifully enraged, and conceived an unpardonable difpleafure againft Prince Lhewelyn, which
yet he thought convenient to conceal and diffemble
for a time. Indeed, he could never abide Lhewelyn,
                                                    fince

since the time that he was vanquished and put to flight by him at the marches, so that the chief cause of King Edward's anger, originally proceeded from a point of honour, which this refusal of homage served sufficiently to increase. But to prosecute his revenge, which upon this score is in princes very fierce and unforgetful, in a short time he came to Chester, meaning to recover by force what he could not obtain by fair means. From hence he sent to the Prince of Wales, requiring him to come over and do him homage, which Lhewelyn either absolutely refusing or willingly detracting to do, King Edward made ready his army to force him to it. But there happened an accident A. D. 1277. which took off a great part of Prince Lhewelyn's stubbornness; for at this time the countess of Leicester the widow of Simon Montfort who lived at Montargis a nunnery in France sent over for Wales her daughter, the Lady Eleanor, (whom Lhewelyn extremely loved) with her brother Aemerike, to be married to the prince, according to the agreement made in her father, Earl Montfort's time. But Aemerike fearing to touch upon the coast of England, steered his course towards the islands of Scilly, where by the way they were all taken by four Bristol ships, and brought to King Edward, who received the lady very honourably, but committed her brother prisoner to the castle of Coff, whence he was afterward removed to the castle of Shirburne. The king having obtained this unexpected advantage over Lhewelyn, began boldly to fall upon him, and so dividing his army into two battalions, led one himself into North Wales, and advanced as far as Ruthlan, where he strongly fortified the castle. The other he committed to Paganus de Camutiis, a great soldier, who entering into West Wales, burned and destroyed a great part of the country. But the people of South Wales, fearing that his next expedition was levelled against them voluntarily submitted themselves to the king, and did him homage, and then delivered up the castle of Ystratywy to Paganus.

Prince

Prince Lhewelyn hearing of this and finding his own subjects to forsake him, but more especially being desirous to recover his espouse the Lady Eleanor, thought it likewise adviseable to submit, and therefore sued to King Edward for a peace, who granted it, but upon very severe conditions upon Lhewelyn's side. The agreement consisted of ten articles, which were, I. That the prince should set at liberty all manner of prisoners, that upon the king's account were detained in custody. II. That for the king's favour and good-will, he should pay 50,000 marks, to be received at the king's pleasure. III. That these four cantreds or hundreds, viz. Cantref Rós, where the king's castle of Teganwy stands; Ryfonioc, where Denbigh; Tegengl, where Ruthlan; Dyffryn Clwyd, where Rhuthyn stands, should remain in the king's hands. IV. That the Lords Marchers should quietly enjoy all the lands they had conquered within Wales, excepting in the isle of Anglesey, which was wholly granted to the Prince. V. That in consideration of this island, the prince should pay 5000 marks in hand, with the reserve of a 1000 marks yearly to begin at Michaelmas; and in case the prince died without issue, the whole island should return to the king. VI. That the prince should come every year to England to pay his homage to the king for all his lands. VII. That all the barons of Wales, excepting five in Snowden, should hold their lands and estates of the king, and no other. VIII. That the title of Prince should remain only for his life, and not descend to his successors, and after his death, the five lords of Snowden should hold their lands only from the king. IX. That for the performance of these articles, the prince should deliver up for hostages ten persons of the best quality in the country, without imprisoning, disinheriting, and any time of redemption determined. And farther, that the king should chuse twenty persons in North Wales, who besides the prince should take their oaths for the due performance of these articles, and in case the prince should swerve and recede from them, and upon admonition thereof not repent,

they

they should forsake him, and become his enemies. X. The Prince was obliged to suffer his brethren quietly to enjoy their lands in Wales, whereof David for his service was dubbed knight by the king, and had the Earl of Derby's widow given in matrimony, and with her as a portion, the castle of Denbigh in North Wales, besides a 1000 pounds in lands. His other brother Roderic was lately escaped out of prison into England, and the younger called Owen, was upon his composition delivered out of prison.

King Edward having imposed these severe and unmerciful conditions upon Prince Lhewelyn, and for a better security for the performance of them, built a castle at Aberystwyth, returned very honourably into England; upon whose arrival, the people willingly granted him a subsidy of the twentieth part of their estates towards his charges in this war. But it seems very probable that Prince Lhewelyn submitted to these intolerable conditions, more upon the account of his amours, and to regain the Lady Eleanora out of the king of England's hand, than that he was apprehensive of any considerable danger he might receive by the English troops. For it is hardly conceiveable, that a prince of such notorious conduct and valour, would so easily accept of such hard terms, and in a measure deliver up his principality, when there was no necessity so to do, without resisting an enemy, whom he had frequently overcome, and forced to retire back with greater inequality than the English had at present over him. But the force of love worked wonders, and in this case proved most irresistible, which to obtain, Lhewelyn did not think hard to forfeit his proper right to his inveterate enemies, and for ever to exclude his posterity from succeeding in their lawful inheritance. The next year A.D.1278 therefore, he had his wish accomplished, and was married to Eleanora at Worcester, the king and queen, with all the nobility and persons of quality in England, honouring the wedding with their presence.

But

But this specious amity, and the peace lately concluded betwixt them did not last long, the English governors in the marches and in-land countries of Wales, presuming upon the prince's submission to the king, grievously oppressed the inhabitants of the country, with new and unheard of exactions, and with intolerable partiality openly encouraged the English to defraud and oppress the Welch. These insupportable practices moved the Welch to go in a body to David Lord of Denbigh, to endeavour a reconciliation between him and his brother the prince, that they both being at unity, might easily deliver themselves and their country from the unmerciful tyranny of the English. David was not ignorant of the miseries of his countrymen, and therefore gladly submitted to be reconciled to his brother, with promise never to side again with the king of England, but to become his utter enemy. This happy union being thus effected, David was chose general of the army, with which he presently marched to Hawarden, and surprising the castle slew all that opposed him, and took Roger Clifford prisoner, who had been sent by King Edward, Justitiar into those parts. From thence, being joined by the prince, he passed to Ruthlan, and laid siege to the castle; but upon notice given that the king was marching to raise the siege, he thought convenient to withdraw, and to retire back. At the same time Rhys ap Maelgon and Gruffydh ap Meredith ap Owen, with other lords of South Wales, took from the English the castle of Aberystwyth, with divers others in that country, and spoiled all the people thereabouts, who owned subjection to the crown of England. In the mean while, John Peckham, archbishop of Canterbury, perceiving how matters were like to proceed between the king and the prince; and how the kingdom was effectually involved in a war, of his own proper motion came to Prince Lhewelyn, to endeavour a re-submission from him and his brother David to King Edward, and so to put a stop to any farther hostilities.

A. D. 1281.

But

But he fent before-hand to the prince and people of Wales, intimating to them, ' That for the love he bore to the Welch nation, he undertook this arbitration, without the knowledge, and contrary to the king's liking; and therefore earneftly defired, that they would fubmit to a peace with the Englifh, which himfelf would endeavour to bring to pafs. And becaufe he could make no long continuance in thofe parts, he wifhed them to confider, how that if he fhould be forced to depart before any thing was brought to a conclufion, they could hardly find another who would fo heartily efpoufe their caufe; and farther threatened, that in cafe they contemned and derided his endeavours, he would not only inftigate the Englifh army, now greatly ftrengthened and increafed, 'to fall upon them, but alfo fignify their ftubbornnefs to the court and bifhop of Rome, who efteemed and honoured England, beyond any other kingdom in the world. Moreover, he much lamented to hear of the exceflive cruelty of the Welch, even beyond that of the Saracens and other infidels, who never refufed to permit flaves and captives to be ranfomed; which the Welch were fo far from practifing, that even fome time they flew thofe for whofe redemption they received money. And whereas they were wont to efteem and reverence holy and ecclefiaftical perfons, they are now, fo far degenerated from devotion and fanctity, that nothing is more acceptable to them than war and fedition, which they had now great need to forfake and repent of. Laftly, he propofed, that they would fignify to him, wherein, and what laws and conftitutions of their's was violated by the Englifh, and by what means a firm and a lafting peace might be eftablifhed; which, if they rejected, they muft expect to incur the decree and cenfure of the church, as well as endure the violent in-roads and depredations of a powerful army.'

To thefe, partly admonitions, and partly threatenings of the archbifhop, Prince Lhewelyn returned an
answer:

answer: 'That he humbly thanked his Grace for the
pains and trouble he undertook in his, and his subjects' behalf; and more particularly, because he would
venture to come to Wales, contrary to the pleasure
and good liking of the king. And as for concluding
a peace with him, he would not have his Grace be
ignorant, that with all readiness he was willing to
submit to it, upon condition that the king would duly
and sincerely observe the same. And though he would
A.D.1281. be glad of his longer continuance in Wales, yet he
hoped that no obstructions would happen of his side,
why a peace (which of all things he most desired)
might not be forthwith concluded, and rather by his
Grace's procuring than any others; so that there
would be no farther need of acquainting the Pope
with his obstinacy, nor moving the king of England
to use any force against him. And though the kingdom of England be under the immediate protection
of the see of Rome, yet when his Holiness comes to
understand of the great and unsufferable wrongs done
to him by the English; how the articles of peace were
broken, churches and all other religious houses in
Wales were burned down and destroyed, and religious
persons unchristianly murdered, he hoped he would
rather pity and lament his condition, than with addition of punishment encrease and augment his sorrow. Neither shall the kingdom of England be any-
wise disquieted and molested by his means, in case
the peace be religiously observed towards him and
his subjects. But who they are that delight themselves with war and bloodshed, manifestly appears
by their actions and behaviour; the Welch being
glad to live quietly upon their own, if they
might be permitted by the English, who coming
to the country, utterly destroy whatever comes in
their way, without regard either to sex, age, or religious places. But he was extreme sorry that any
one should be slain, having paid his ransom; the
author of which unworthy action he did not pretend
to maintain, but would inflict upon him his condign
punishment,

punifhment, in cafe he could be got out of the woods
and defarts, where as an outlaw, he lives undifcovered.
But as to commencing a war in a feafon inconvenient,
he protefted he knew nothing of that till now; yet
thofe that did fo, do folemnly atteft that to be the
only meafure they had to fave themfelves, and that
they had no other fecurity for their lives and fortunes, than to keep themfelves in arms. Concerning
his fins and trefpaffes againft God, with the affiftance
of his Grace, he would endeavour to repent of, neither fhould the war be willingly continued by him, in
cafe he might fave himfelf harmlefs; but before he
would be unjuftly difpoffeffed of his legal property,
he thought it but reafonable, by all poffible meafures
to defend himfelf. And he was very willing, upon
due examination of the trefpaffes committed, to make
fatisfaction and retribution of all wrongs committed
by him and his fubjects; fo that the Englifh would
obferve the fame on their fide; and likewife was ready
to conclude a peace, which he thought was impoffible to be eftablifhed, as long as the Englifh had
no regard to articles, and ftill opprefs his people with
new and unwarrantable exactions. Therefore feeing
his fubjects were unchriftianly abufed by the king's
officers, and all his country moft tyrannically harraffed,
he faw no reafon why the Englifh, upon any fault of
his fide, fhould threaten to bring a formidable army to
his country, nor the church pretend to cenfure him:
feeing alfo, he was very willing upon the aforefaid
conditions, to fubmit to a peace. And laftly, he defired his Grace, that he would not give the more credit to his enemies, becaufe they were near his perfon,
and could deliver their complaints frequently, and by
word of mouth; for they who made no confcience of
oppreffing, would not in all probability, ftick to de-
fame, and make falfe accufations; and therefore his
Grace would make a better eftimation of the whole,
matter, by examining their actions, rather than be-
lieving their words.'

U   Prince

Prince Lhewelyn having to this purpose replied in general to the archbishop's articles, presented him with a copy of the several grievances, which himself and others of his subjects had wrongfully and unjustly received at the hands of the English, and these, though somewhat tedious, are thought necessary to be particularly inserted in the appendix, by reason that they demonstrably vindicate the Welch nation, from the unreasonable aspersions which the English of these times cast upon it. For, the breach of peace, and the occasion of those dismal disturbances in the kingdom, are, by the English writers of those times wholly attributed to the restless and rebellious humour and unconstant temper of the Welch : whereas, had they looked at home, they might have found the original of all these troubles, to have proceeded from the intolerable extortions and insupportable oppressions of their own nation. For whoever considers these unmerciful grievances, and the manifold wrongs the Welch endured, it cannot in reason be expected, but that they would endeavour to vindicate themselves, and repel force by force. For had the English the liberty of dispossessing them wrongfully of their proper inheritance and estates, and it was not lawful for the Welch to endeavour the defending and keeping of their own ? and must they be reckoned disobedient, and promoters of sedition, upon the account that they would not be trampled under, and enslaved by the English ? these measures were too hard and intolerable, and scarce allowable in an infidel nation ; to oppress, (and what in them lay) eradicate a people, for no other reason, than because they were weaker and more helpless than themselves ; and then, what is worse, to accuse them of being authors of sedition, because they would not suffer themselves to be peaceably enslaved, but endeavoured to vindicate their right by main force. But it is highly probable, that King Edward had no inclination to observe, what articles of agreement soever were concluded upon ; and therefore encouraged his deputies in the marches and inland country of Wales, in all their oppressions and

sinistrous

finiftrous dealings towards the Welch. This was the beft method, and the moft expedient means to reduce the country of Wales to fubjection to the crown of England, which the king had long ago intentionally effected ; and to accufe the Welch of not obferving the conditions of peace, was a fpecious pretence to bring that actually to pafs, and to lead an army into the country. But whatever the Englifh might pretend, it is evident the Welch had the greater occafion to complain, as appears from the grievances committed as well againft the prince himfelf, as others of his fub-jects.

See the Appendix.

The archbifhop having read over thefe grievances, and finding the Welch to be upon good reafon guilt-lefs of that fevere character, which by the malicious infinuations of the Englifh, he had conceived of them, went to King Edward ; requefting him to take into confideration the unjuft wrongs and injuries done to the Welch ; which if he would not redrefs, at leaft he might excufe them from any breach of obedience to him, feeing they had fo juft a reafon for what they did. The king replied, That he willingly forgave them, and would make reafonable fatisfaction for any wrong done; fo that they had free accefs to declare their grievances before him ; and then might fafely depart, in cafe it would appear juft and lawful they fhould. The arch-bifhop upon this thought he had obtained his purpofe, and therefore, without any ftay, pofted it to Snowden, where the prince and his brother David refided ; and having acquainted them with the king's mind, ear-neftly defired that they, and the reft of the nobility of Wales, would fubmit themfelves, and by him be introduced to the king's prefence. Prince Lhewelyn, after fome times conference and debate, declared that he was ready to fubmit to the king, with the referve only of two particulars; namely, his confcience, whereby he was obliged to regard the fafety and liberties of his peo-ple ; and then the decency of his own ftate and quality. But the king underftanding by the archbifhop, how

U 2

that

that the prince stood upon terms, posititvely refused to
consent to any more treaty of peace, than that he should
simply submit without any farther conditions. The
archbishop had experience enough, that the Welch
would never agree to such proposals; and therefore desired of his Majesty, that he would give him leave,
with the rest of the English nobility present, to confer and conclude upon the matter; which being
granted, they unanimously resolved upon the following articles, and sent them to the prince by John
Wallensis, bishop of St. David's.

I. The king will have no treaty of the four cantreds, and other lands which he has bestowed upon
his nobles; nor of the isle of Anglesey.

II. In case the tenants of the four cantreds submit themselves, the king purposeth to deal kindly
and honourably with them; which we are sufficiently
satisfied of, and will, what in us lies, endeavour to
further.

III. We will do the like touching Prince Lhewelyn, concerning whom we can return no other
answer, than that he must barely submit himself to
the king, without hopes of any other conditions.

These were the publick articles agreed upon by
the English nobility, and sent to Prince Lhewelyn;
besides which, they sent some private measures of
agreement, relating both to him and his brother David; promising, that in case he would submit, and
put the king in quiet possession of Snowden, his Majesty would bestow an English county upon him,
with the yearly revenue of a thousand pound sterling. And moreover, his daughter should be provided for, suitable to her birth and quality, and all
his subjects according to their estate and condition;
and in case he should have male issue by a second
wife, the aforesaid county and a thousand pound should
remain to his posterity for ever. As for David, the

prince's brother, if he would consent to go to the
Holy Land, upon condition not to return but upon
the king's pleasure, all things should be honourably
prepared for his journey with respect to his quality;
and his child maintained and provided for by the
king. To thefe the archbishop added his threats;
That in cafe they did not comply, and submit themfelves to the king's mercy, there were very fevere
and imminent dangers hanging over their heads; a
formidable army was ready to make an in-road into
their country, which would not only gaul and opprefs them, but in all probability totally eradicate
the whole nation: befides which, they were to expect the fevereft cenfure and punifhment of the
church.

But all this could not force fo unlimited a fubmiflion from the prince, but that he would ftick
upon fome certain conditions; and therefore by letter he acquainted the achbifhop, ' That he was with
all willingnefs defirous to fubmit himfelf to the king;
but withal, that he could not do it but in fuch a manner as was fafe and honeft for him. And becaufe the
form of fubmiflion contained in the articles fent to
him, were by himfelf and his council thought pernicious and illegal for him to confent to, as tending rather to the deftruction, than the fecurity of himfelf
and his fubjects, he could in no wife agree to it;
and in cafe himfelf fhould be willing, the reft of his
nobility and people would never admit of it, as knowing for certain the mifchief and inconveniency that
would enfue thereby. Therefore he defired his lordfhip, that for a confirmation of an honeft and a durable peace, which he had all this while earneftly laboured for, he would manage matters circumfpectly,
and with due regard to the following articles. For it
was much more honourable for the king, and far more
confonant to reafon, that he fhould hold his lands
in the country where he was born and dwelt in, than
that by difpoffeffing of him, his eftate fhould be beftowed upon ftrangers.' With this was fent the ge-

U 3 neral

neral anſwer of the Welch to the archbiſhop's articles, viz.

I. ·Though the king would not conſent to treat of
the four cantreds, nor of the iſle of Angleſey; yet
unleſs theſe be comprehended in the treaty, the prince's
council will not conclude a peace; by reaſon that
theſe cantreds have ever, ſince the time of Camber the
ſon of Brutus, properly and legally belonged to the
Princes of Wales; beſides the confirmation which the
preſent prince obtained by the conſent of the king and
his father, at the treaty before Cardinal Ottobonus, the
Pope's legate, whoſe letters patent do ſtill appear.
And more, the juſtice of the thing itſelf is plainly
evident, that it is more reaſonable for our heirs to
hold the ſaid cantreds for money, and other ſervices
due to the king, than that ſtrangers enjoy the ſame,
who will forcibly abuſe and oppreſs the people.

II. All the tenants of the cantreds of Wales do
unanimouſly declare, that they dare not ſubmit themſelves to the king's pleaſure; by reaſon that he never from the beginning took care to obſerve either
covenant, oath, or any other grant to the prince and
his people; and becauſe his ſubjects have no regard
to religion, but moſt cruelly and unchriſtianly tyran-
nize over churches and religious perſons; and then,
for that we do not underſtand ourſelves any way
obliged thereunto, ſeeing we be the prince's tenants,
who is willing to pay the king all uſual and accuſtomed
ſervices.

III. As to what is required, that the prince ſhould
ſimply commit himſelf to the king's will, we all declare, that for the aforeſaid reaſons, none of us dare
come, neither will we permit our prince to come to
him upon thoſe conditions.

IV. That ſome of the Engliſh nobility will endeavour to procure a proviſion of a thouſand pounds
a-year in England; we would let them know, that
we can accept of no ſuch penſion; becauſe it is
procured for no other end, than that the prince

4   being

being difinherited, themfelves may obtain his lands in Wales.

V. The prince cannot in honefty refign his paternal inheritance, which has for many ages been enjoyed by his predeceffors, and accept of other lands among the Englifh, of whofe cuftoms and language he is ignorant; and upon that fcore, may at length be fraudulently deprived of all, by his malicious and inveterate enemies.

VI. Seeing the king intends to deprive him of his antient inheritance in Wales, where the land is more barren and untilled; it is not very probable that he will beftow upon him, a more fruitful and an arable eftate in England.

VII. As to the claufe, that the prince fhould give the king a perpetual poffeffion of Snowden; we only affirm, that feeing Snowden effentially belongs to the principality of Wales, which the prince and his predeceffors have enjoyed fince Brute, the prince's council will not permit him to renounce it, and accept another eftate in England, to which he has not equal right.

VIII. The people of Snowden declare, That though the prince fhould give the king poffeffion of it, they would never own, and pay fubmiffion to ftrangers; for in fo doirg, they would bring upon themfelves the fame mifery, that the people of the four cantreds have for a long time groaned under; being moft rudely handled and unjuftly oppreffed by the king's officers; as woefully appears by their feveral grievances.

IX. As for David, the prince's brother, we fee no reafon, why againft his will he fhould be compelled to take a journey to the Holy Land; which if he happens to undertake hereafter upon the account of religion, it is no caufe that his iffue fhould be difinherited, but rather encouraged.

Now feeing neither the prince nor any of his fubjects upon any account whatfoever, have moved and

   begun

begun this ·war, but only defended themfelves, their
properties, laws, and liberties from the encroachments
of other perfons; and fince the Englifh, for either
malice or covetoufnefs to obtain our eftates, have
unjuftly occafioned all thefe troubles and broils in
the kingdom, we are affured that our defence is juft
and lawful, and therein depend upon the aid and affiftance of heaven; which will be moft cruelly revenged upon our facrilegious and inhuman enemies,
who have left no manner of enormities, in relation to
God and man, uncommitted. Therefore your Grace
would more juftly threaten your ecclefiaftical cenfures,
againft the authors and abettors of fuch unparallelled
villanies, than the innocent fufferers. And befides,
we much admire, that you fhould advife us to part
with our own eftates, and to live among our enemies ;
as if, when we cannot peaceably enjoy what is our
own unqueftionable right, we might expect to have
quiet poffeffion of another man's : and though, as you
fay, it be hard to live in war and perpetual danger;
yet much harder it is, to be utterly deftroyed and reduced to nothing ; efpecially, when we feek but the
defence of our own liberties from the infatiable ambition of our enemies. And feeing your Grace has promifed to fulminate fentence againft all them that either for malice or profit would hinder and obftruct the
peace; it is evident who in this refpect are tranfgref-
fors and delinquents ; the fear and apprehenfion of
imprifonment and ejection out of our eftates, the fenfe
of oppreffion and tyrannical government; having compelled us to take up arms for the fecurity of our lives
and fortune. Therefore as the Englifh are not difpoffeffed of their eftates, for their offences againft the
king, fo we are willing to be punifhed, or make other
fatisfaction for our crimes, without being difinherited ;
and as to the breach of the peace, it is notorious that
they were the authors, who never regarded either promife or covenant, never made amends for trefpaffes,
nor remedy for our complaints.

2   When

When the archbishop saw there was no likelihood
of a mediation, and that a peace was impossible to
be concluded as long as the Welch stuck upon conditions; he presently relinquished his pretended affection towards them, and denounced a sentence of
excommunication against the prince and all his adherents. It was a subject of no little wonder, that
a person of so reputed a sanctity, who esteemed the
several grievances done to the Welch to be intolerable,
should now condemn them for refusal of unlimited
submission to the king of England; whereas he had
already owned it to be unreasonable. But this ecclesiastical censure was only a prologue to a more me-
lancholy scene; King Edward immediately upon it,
sending an army by sea to Anglesey, without any great
opposition, conquered the island, and without any
mercy, put all that withstood him to the sword. From
thence designing to pass over to the continent, he
caused a bridge of boats covered with planks to be
built over the Menay (being an arm of the sea which
parteth the isle from the main land) at a place called
Moel y don, not far from Bangor, where the water
is narrowest. The bridge being finished, which was
so broad as that threescore men might pass in a breast,
William Latimer, with a strong party of the best experienced soldiers, and Sir Lucas Thany, commander
of the Gascoigns and Spaniards, whereof a great number served the king, passed over, but could discover
no sign, or any the least intimation of an enemy. But
as soon as the tide began to appear, and the sea had
overflown beside the bridge, down come the Welch
fiercely out of the mountains, and setting upon the
disheartened English, killed or drowned their whole
number, excepting Latimer, who by the swimming
of his horse got safe to the bridge. In this action,
several worthy soldiers of the English side were lost;
among whom were Sir Lucas Thany, Robert Clifford,
Sir Walter Lyndsey, two brothers of Robert Burnel
bishop of Bath, with many others; in all to the
number of thirteen knights, seventeen young gentle-

Lu

men, and two hundred common foldiers. A little
after, or as fome fay before, another engagement paffed
between the Englifh and the Welch, wherein the former loft fourteen colours, the Lords Audley and Clifford the younger being flain, and the king himfelf
forced to retreat for fafety to the caftle of Hope.

And while thefe things paffed in North Wales, the
Earl of Glocefter and Sir Edmund Mortimer acted
vigoroufly with their forces in South Wales; and
fighting the Welch at ,Lhandeilo Fawr, overthrew
them with the lofs of no confiderable perfon, faving
William de Valence the king's coufin-german, and
four knights befides. Prince Lhewelyn was all this
while in Cardigan, wafting and deftroying all the country, and principally the lands of Rhys ap Meredith,
who very unnaturally held with the king of England
in all thefe wars. But being at length tired with action, with a few men privately feparated himfelf from
his army, and came to Buelht, thinking to eafe and refpite himfelf there undifcovered. But coming to the
river Wye, he met with Edmund Mortimer and John
Gifford, with a confiderable party of the people of
that country which Mortimer was lord of. But neither
party venturing to affail the other, Prince Lhewelyn with
one only fervant retired to a private grove in a neighbouring valley, there to confult with certain lords of
the country, who had appointed to meet him. In the
mean time Mortimer defcends from the hill, with intention to fall upon Lhewelyn's men; which they perceiving, betook themfelves to the bridge called Pont
Orewyn, and manfully defended the paffage he was
to crofs. Mortimer could effect nothing againft them,
till he had gained the bridge, the river being impaffable; and to force them to quit it, feemed altogether
impracticable. But at laft, the river was difcovered to
be fordable a little below, and fo Helias Walwyn was
detached with a party through the river, who unexpectedly falling upon the backs of the defendants,
eafily forced them to leave the bridge, and fave themfelves by flight. Prince Lhewelyn all this while in
vain

vain expected the lords of Buelht, and in fine continued to wait so long, till Mortimer having passed over the bridge, surrounded the wood he was in with armed men. The prince perceiving himself to be betrayed, thought to make his escape to his men; but the English so closely pursued him, that before he could come in, one Adam Francton, not knowing who he was, run him through with his sword, being unarmed. The Welch still expected the arrival of their prince, and though but a few in number, so gallantly maintained their ground, that in spite of the far greater number of the English, they were at length with much ado put to flight. The battle being over, Francton returned to plunder his dead; but perceiving him to be the prince of Wales, he thought himself to have obtained a sufficient prize, and thereupon presently chopt off his head, and sent it to King Edward at Conwey, who very joyfully caused it to be placed upon the highest pinnacle of the tower of London. And thus fell this worthy prince, the greatest, though the last of the British blood, betrayed most basely by the lords of Buelht, and being dead, most unworthily dealt with by the king of England; who, contrary to all precedents, treated a lawful prince like a traitor, and exposed his crowned head to the derision of the multitude.

Not long after, David the prince's brother was delivered up by the Welch themselves, and in a parliament for that purpose assembled at Shrewsbury, was condemned to die; his head to be sent to accompany his brother's upon the tower of London, and his four quarters to the four cities of Bristol, Northampton, York, and Winchester. Then the king for the easier keeping the Welch in due subjection, built two strong castles in North Wales; the one at Conwey and the other at Caernarvon. There was none that now stood out besides Rhys Fychan of Ystratywy; and he finding David was gone, and himself like to do nothing to purpose, fairly yielded himself up to the Earl of Hereford, who by the king's orders committed him
prisoner

prifoner to the tower of London; and fo all the country of Wales became ever fince fubject to the crown of England.

The PRINCES of WALES of ENGLISH BLOOD.

PRINCE Lhewelyn and his brother David being fo bafely taken off, and leaving no body to lay any fpecious claim to the principality of Wales; King Edward by a ftatute made at Ruthlan, incorporated and annexed it to the crown of England; conftituting feveral new and wholefome laws; as concerning the divifion of Wales into feveral counties, the form and manner of writs and proceedings in trials, with many others not very unlike the laws and conftitutions of the Englifh nation. But all this could never win the affection of the Welch toward him; who by no means would own him as their fovereign, unlefs he would condefcend and agree to live and reign among them. They had not forgot the cruel oppreffions and intolerable infolencies of Englifh officers; and therefore they flatly told him, they would never yield obedience to any other, than a prince of their own nation, of their own language, and whofe life and converfation was fpotlefs and unblameable. King Edward perceiving the Welch to be refolute and inflexible, and abfolutely bent againft any other prince, than one of their own country, happily thought of this politic, though dangerous expedient. Queen Eleanor was now quick with child, and ready to be delivered; and though the feafon was very fevere, it being the depth of winter, the king fent for her from England, and removed her to Caernarvon caftle, the place defigned for her to lye in. When the
time

Anno 11. Edw. I.

time of her delivery was come, King Edward called
to him all the barons and chief persons throughout all
Wales to Ruthlan, there to consult about the publick
good and safety of their country: And being informed
that his queen was delivered of a son, he told the Welch
nobility, that whereas they had oftentimes intreated him
to appoint them a prince, he having at this time occasion to depart out of the country, with their request,
upon condition they would allow of, would comply and
obey him whom he should name. The Welch readily
agreed to the motion only with the same reserve, that
he should appoint them a prince of their own nation.
King Edward assured them, he would name such an
one as was born in Wales, could speak no English,
and whose life and conversation no body could stain ;
whom the Welch agreeing to own and obey, he named
his own son Edward, but little before born in Caernarvon castle.

King Edward having by these means deluded the
Welch, and reduced the whole country of Wales to
his own devotion, began to reward his followers with
other mens properties, and bestowed whole lordships
and towns in the midst of the country upon English
lords, among whom Henry Lacy Earl of Lincoln obtained the lordship of Denbigh ; Reginald Grey, second
son to John Lord Grey of Wilton, the lordship of
Ruthyn. This Henry Lacy was son to Edmund
Lacy, the son of John Lacy, Lord of Halton Pomfret, and constable of Chester, who married Margaret the eldest daughter, and one of the heirs of Robert
Quincy Earl of Lincoln. This Henry Lacy lord of
Denbigh married the daughter and sole heir of William Longspear Earl of Salisbury, by whom he had
issue two sons, Edmund and John, who both died
young, one by a fall into a very deep well within
the castle of Denbigh ; and a daughter named Alicia,
who was married to Thomas Plantagenet Earl of Lancaster, who in right of his wife was Earl of Lincoln
and Sarum, Lord of Denbigh, Halton Pomfret, and
constable of Chester. After his death, King E l

ward II. beftowed the faid lordfhip of Denbigh upon
Hugh Lord Spencer Earl of Winchefter, upon whofe
deceafe, King Edward III. gave it, together with
many other lordfhips in the marches, to Roger Mortimer Earl of March, in performance of a promife he
had made, whilft he remained with his mother in
France, that as foon as he fhould come to the poffeffion of the crown of England, he would beftow
upon the faid Earl of March, to the value of a thoufand pound yearly in lands. But within few years after, Mortimer being attainted of high treafon, King
Edward beftowed the faid lordfhip of Denbigh upon
Montague Earl of Salifbury; but it was quickly reftored again to the Mortimers, in which houfe it continued, till the whole eftate of the Earls of March,
came with a daughter to the houfe of York, and fo
to the crown, Richard Duke of York, grandfather to
Edward the fourth, having married the fole daughter
and heir of the houfe of the Mortimers. And fo it
continued in the crown to Queen Elizabeth's time,
who in the fixth year of her reign, beftowed the
faid lordfhip upon her great favourite Robert Earl
of Leicefter, who was then created Baron of Denbigh. After him it returned again to the crown, where
it has continued to this prefent year 1696, when his
prefent Majefty granted a patent under the Great Seal
to William Earl of Portland, for the lordfhips of
Denbigh, Bromfield, and Yale. Some of the Welch
reprefentatives, perceiving how far fuch a grant en-
croached upon the properties and privileges of the
fubject, difclofed their grievances to the honourable
Houfe of Commons, who after fome confideration,
refolved (*nemine contradicente*) that a petition fhould
be prefented to his Majefty by the body of the whole
Houfe, to requeft him ro recall his grant to the faid
Earl of Portland; which was accordingly done in the
manner following:

May

May it pleafe Your Moft Excellent Majefty,

WE Your Majefty's moft dutiful and loyal fubjects, the knights, citizens, and burgeffes in
parliament affembled; humbly lay before Your Majefty, That whereas there is a grant paffing to William Earl of Portland, and his heirs, of the manors
of Denbigh, Bromfield, and Yale, and divers other
lands in the principality of Wales; together with feveral eftates of inheritance, enjoyed by many of Your
Majefty's fubjects by virtue of antient grants from the
crown :

That the faid manors, with the large and extenfive
royalties, powers, and jurifdictions to the fame belonging, are of great concern to Your Majefty and the
crown of this realm : and that the fame have been
ufually annexed to the principality of Wales, and
fettled on the Princes of Wales for their fupport :
and that a great number of Your Majefty's fubjects,
in thofe parts, hold their eftates by royal tenure, under
great and valuable compofitions, rents, royal payments,
and fervices to the crown and princes of Wales ; and
have by fuch tenure great dependance on Your Majefty and the crown of England; and have enjoyed
great privileges and advantages with their eftates, under fuch tenure.

We therefore moft humbly befeech Your Majefty,
to put a ftop to the paffing this grant to the Earl of
Portland, of the faid manors and lands; and that the
fame may not be difpofed from the crown, but by
confent of parliament : for that fuch grant, is in diminution of the honour and intereft of the crown, by
placing in a fubject, fuch large and extenfive royalties, powers, and jurifdictions, which ought only to be
in the crown ; and will fever that dependance, which
fo great a number of Your Majefty's fubjects in thofe
parts, have on Your Majefty and the crown, by reafon of their tenure; and may be to their great oppreffion in thofe rights which they have purchafed, and
hitherto enjoyed with their eftates : and alfo, on occa-

fion

fion of great vexation to many of Your Majefty's
fubjects, who have long had the abfolute inheritance
of feveral lands (comprehended in the faid grant to
the Earl of Portland) by antient grants from the
crown.

His MAJESTY's Anfwer.

Gentlemen,

I Have a kindnefs for my Lord Portland; which he
has deferved of Me, by long and faithful fervices;
but I fhould not have given him thefe lands, if I had
imagined the Houfe of Commons could have been
concerned; I will therefore recall the grant, and find
fome other way of fhewing My favour to him.

The lordfhip of Ruthyn continued in the poffeffion of the Greys, till the reign of Henry VII. when
George Grey Earl of Kent, and Lord of Ruthyn, upon
fome bargain, paffed the fame over to the king, fince
which it has been in the poffeffion of fome of the
Earls of Warwick, and afterwards came to the Mid-
dletons of Chirk caftle in the county of Denbigh,
where it ftill continues; being now enjoyed by the
right worfhipful Sir Richard Middleton, baronet.
But befides Henry Lacy and Reginald Grey, feveral
other gentlemen of quality came at this time with
King Edward to North Wales, who in fome time became to be men of great poffeffions and fway in
the country, whofe pofterity enjoy the fame to this
time. But he that expected to fare beft in the diftribution of thefe lordfhips and eftates in Wales,
was one Rhys ap Meredith a Welchman, and one
that, contrary to the allegiance fworn to his prince,
and his duty to his native country, had ferved the
king of England, in all thefe wars, and done the
greateft hurt of any man to the intereft of Prince
Lhewelyn. For thefe great fervices done to King
Edward, Rhys expected to be fure to be promoted

to the higheft preferments; whom the king after the Prince of Wales's overthrow firft dubbed knight, and afterwards fed him with fair words and great promifes.

But when he, and all his neighbours and country-men had fubmitted themfelves to the government of the king of England; it happened that the Lord Pain Tiptoft, warden of the king's caftles which joined to Rhys's country, and the Lord Alan Plucknet, the king's fteward in Wales, cited Sir Rhys ap Mere-dith, with all the reft of the country, to the king's court; which he refufing to do, alledging his antient pri-vileges and liberties, together with the king's promifes to him, the aforefaid officers proceeded againft him according to law. Whereupon Sir Rhys being greatly A. D. 1283. vexed to be thus ferved by thofe whofe intereft he had all this while fo warmly efpoufed, thought to be re-venged of Pain Tiptoft, and the reft of the En-glifh. And to that end, having drawn together fome of his tenants and countrymen, he fell upon the faid Pain Tiptoft; between whom feveral fkirmifhes after-wards happened, and feveral men were flain on both fides. King Edward was now at Arragon to compofe the differences betwixt the kings of Arragon and Naples; but being informed of the difturbances which had hap-pened in Wales, betwixt his minifters there, and Sir Rhys ap Meredith; he wrote to his latter, requiring him to keep the peace, till his return; at what time he would redrefs all grievances, and reduce matters to a good and reafonable order. But Sir Rhys hav-ing already waited fufficiently upon the king's pro-mifes, and being now in a good condition to offend his enemies by force of arms, would not give over the enterprize he faw fo promifing, but marching with his forces to his enemies' lands, burnt and fpoiled feveral towns belonging to the Englifh. Upon this, the king fent to the Earl of Cornwal, whom he had appointed his deputy during his ab-fence, to march with an army into Wales, to reprefs the infolencies, and to prevent any farther diforderly attempts of the Welfh. The Earl accordingly mar-

pared an army and went againſt Sir Rhys's, whoſe
army he quickly diſperſed, and overthrew his caſtle
of Dreſolan, but not without the loſs of ſome of his
chief men. For as they beſieged and undermined the
ſaid caſtle, the walls unexpectedly fell down, by which
unlucky accident, ſeveral of the Engliſh were oppreſ-
ſed and bruiſed to death, among whom were the
Lord Strafford, and the Lord William de Monchency.
But within a while after, Robert Tiptoft Lord Deputy
of Wales, raiſed a very powerful army againſt Sir
Rhys, and after a ſlaughter of 4000 of the Welch,
took him priſoner, who the Michaelmas following,
at the king's going to Scotland, was condemned and
executed at York.

A.D.1293.   But the death of Sir Rhys did not put a final period to all the quarrels betwixt the Engliſh and
Welch, for in a ſhort time after, there happened a
new occaſion for the Welch to murmur againſt, and
upbraid the government of the Engliſh over them.
King Edward was now in actual enmity and war with
the king of France; for the carrying on of which, he
wanted a liberal ſubſidy and ſupply from his ſubjects. This tax was with a great deal of paſſion and
reluctancy levied in divers places of the kingdom,
but more eſpecially in Wales, the Welch being never
acquainted with ſuch large contributions before, vio-
1294. lently ſtormed and exclaimed againſt it. But not
being ſatisfied with villifying the king's command,
they took their own captain Roger de Puleſdon, who
was appointed collector of the ſaid ſubſidy, and hanged
him up, together with divers others who abettted the
collecting of the tax. Then the Weſt Wales men
choſe Maelgon Fychan for their captain, and ſo entering into Caermardhyn and Pembroke ſhires, they cruelly harraſſed all the lands that belonged to the En-
liſh, and then returned laden with conſiderable booty.
The Glamorganſhire men, and they towards the ſouth
parts, choſe one Morgan for their leader and ſet upon
the Earl of Gloceſter, whom they forced to make his
eſcape out of the country ; and ſo Morgan was put
in poſſeſſion of thoſe lands which the anceſtors of the

Earl

Earl of Glocefter had forcibly taken away from Morgan's forefathers. On the other fide, the North Wales
men fet up one Madoc related to the laft Lhewelyn
flain at Buelht, who having drawn together a great
number of men, came to Caernarvon, and fetting upon
the Englifh who in great multitudes had then reforted
thither to a fair, flew a great many, and afterwards fpoiled
and ranfacked the whole town. King Edward being
acquainted with thefe different infurrections and re-
bellions in Wales, and defirous to quell the pride and
ftubbornefs of the Welch, but moft of all to revenge
the death of his great favourite Roger de Pulefdon,
recalled his brother Edmund Earl of Lancafter, and
Henry Lacy Earl of Lincoln and lord of Denbigh,
who with a confiderable army were ready to embark
for Gafcoign, and countermanded them into Wales.
Being arrived there, they paffed quietly forward, till
they came to Denbigh, and as foon as they drew near
unto the caftle, upon St. Martin's day the Welch with
great fury and courage faced them, and joining battle, forced them back with a very confiderable lofs.
Polydore Virgil fays, (but upon what authority is not
known) that the Welch obtained this victory rather
upon the account that the Englifh army was hired
with fuch money as had been wrongfully taken out
of the abbies and other religious places, fo that it was
a judgment from above, more than the force of the
Welch, that overcame the Englifh army. But be the
caufe of it what it will, it is certain the Englifh were
vanquifhed, upon which account King Edward came
in perfon to Wales, and kept his Chriftmas at Aberconwey, where Robert Winchelfey archbifhop of Canterbury being returned from Rome, came to him, and
having done homage, returned honourably again to
England: But as the king advanced farther into the
country, having but one part of his army with him,
the Welch fet upon and took moft of his carriages,
which contained a great quantity of victuals and provifion, fo that the king with all his followers were conftrained to endure a great deal of hardfhips, in fo
much that at laft water mixed with honey, and very

coarfe

coarfe and ordinary bread with-the falteft meat, were
accounted the greateft delicacies for his Majefty's own
table. But their mifery was like to be greater, had
not the other part of the army come in time, becaufe
the Welch had encompaffed the king round, in hopes
to reduce him to the utmoft diftrefs, by reafon that
the water was fo rifen, that the reft of the army could
not get to him. But the water within fome time after abating, the remainder of the army came in, whereupon the Welch prefently retired, and made their
efcape. One thing is very, remarkable of King Edward during his diftrefs at Snowden, that when the
army was reduced to very great extremity, a fmall
quantity of wine was found, which they thought to
referve for the king's own ufe. But he to prevent
any difcontent, which might thereupon be raifed in
his foldiers abfolutely refufed to tafte thereof, telling
them, ' That.in time of neceffity all things fhould be
common, and as he was the caufe and author of their
diftrefs, he would not be preferred before them in his
diet.'

But whilft the king remained in Snowden, the Earl
of Warwick being informed that a great number of
Welch were affembled, and had lodged themfelves in
a certain valley betwixt two woods, chofe out a troop
of horfe, together with fome crofs-bows and archers,
and fet upon them in the night-time. The Welch
being thus furprifed and unexpectedly encompaffed
about by their enemies, made the beft hafte they could
to oppofe them, and fo pitching their fpears in the
ground, and directing the points towards their enemies, endeavoured by fuch means to keep, off the
horfe. But the Earl of Warwick having ordered his
battle fo, as that between every two horfes there ftood
a crofs-bow, fo gauled the Welch with the fhot of the
quarrels, that the fpear-men fell apace, and then the
horfe breaking eafily in upon the reft, bare them
down with fo great a flaughter, as the Welch had
never received before. After this, King Edward to
prevent any more rebellious attempts of the Welch,
cut

cut down all the woods in Wales, wherein, in any time of danger, they were wont to hide and save themselves. And for a farther security, he repaired and fortified all the castles and places of strength in Wales, and built the castle of Bewmoris in the isle of Anglesey, and so having put all things in a settled posture, and punished those that had been the occasion of the death of Roger de Pulesdon, he returned with his army into England. But as soon as the king had left the Welch, Madoc, who, as it is said before, was chosen captain by the North Wales men gathered some forces together, and came to Ofweftry, which presently yielded to him. And then meeting with the Lord Strange near Knookine, who with a detachment of the marchers came to oppose him, gave him battle, vanquished his forces, and miserably ravaged his country. The like success he obtained a second time against the marchers, but at last they brought together a very great number of men, and met Madoc marching towards Shrewsbury, upon the hills of Cefn Digolh, not far from Camrs castle, where after a bloody fight on both sides, Madoc was taken prisoner, and his army vanquished and put to flight. Then he was sent to London, and there sentenced to remain in perpetual imprisonment in the Tower, though others affirm, that Madoc was never taken, but that after several adventures and severe conflicts, whereby the Welch were reduced to great extremities, he came in and submitted himself to the king, who received him upon condition he would not defist to pursue Morgan captain of the Glamorganshire men, till he brought him prisoner before him. Madoc having performed this, and the whole country being peaceable and undisturbed, several hostages from the chiefest nobility of Wales for their orderly and quiet behaviour were delivered to the king, who disposed of them into divers castles in England, where they continued in safe custody till the end of the war, which was presently commenced with Scotland.

In the 29th year of King Edward's reign, the prince of Wales came down to Chester, and received homage of all the free holders in Wales as follows, Henry

A. D. 1301

X

Earl of Lancaster for Monmouth; Reginald Gray for
Ruthyn; Foulke Fitzwarren for his lands; the Lord
William Martyn for his lands in Cemaes; Roger Mortimer for his lands in Wales; Henry Lacy Earl of
Lincoln for Rhos and Rhyfoncioc; Robert Lord Mon-
talt, for his lands, and Gruffydh Lord of Poole, for
the lordship of Powys, at the same time paid their homage Tudor ap Grono of Anglesey, Madoc ap Tudor
archdeacon of Anglesey, Eineon ap Howel of Caernarvon, Tudor ap Gruffydh, Lhewelyn ap Ednyfed, Gruffydh Fychan son of Gruffydh ap Iorwerth, Madoc Fychan Denglfield, Lhewelyn bishop of St. Asaph, and
Richard de Pulesdon. This last in the twelfth year
of King Edward was constituted sheriff of Caernarvon for life, with the stipend of forty pounds sterling
yearly. At the same place, Gruffydh ap Tudor, Ithel
Fychan, Ithel ap Blethyn, with many more did their
homage. Then the prince came to Ruthlan, where
the Lord Richard de Sutton Baron of Malpas, paid
homage and fealty for the said barony of Malpas.
Thence the prince removed to Conwey, where Eineon
bishop of Bangor, and David abbot of Maynan did
their homage; as did Lewis de Felton son of Richard
Felton, for the lands which his father held of the
prince in Maelor Saesneg, or English Maelor. John
Earl Warren swore homage for the lordships of Bromfield and Yale, and his lands in Hope-Dale, at London in the chapel of the Lord John de Kirkby sometime bishop of Ely; as also a while after, Edmund
Mortimer for his lands of Cery and Cydewen.

But besides all these, there paid homage to the
prince of Wales at Chester, Sir Gruffydh Llwyd son
of Rhys ap Gruffydh ap Ednyfed Fychan, a stout and
a valiant gentleman, though not very fortunate, and
as Florus says of Sertorius, he was *magnæ quidem, sed
calamitosæ virtutis.* He was knighted by King Edward
the First, upon his bringing the first news of the
queen's safe delivery of a son at Caernarvon castle,
the king holding then a parliament at Ruthlan. This
Sir Gruffydh continued for some time very gracious
.with

3

with the king of England, but obferving at length
the intolerable oppreffion and tyranny exercifed by the
Englifh officers, efpecially by Sir Roger Mortimer
Lord of Chirke and Juftice of North Wales, towards
his countrymen the Welch, became fo far concerned
and difcontented with fuch unwarrantable practices,
that he prefently brake out into open rebellion
againft the Englifh. And the better to effect what
he purpofed, he treated with Sir Edward Bruce
brother to Robert then king of Scotland, who had
conquered Ireland, to bring or fend over fome forces
to affift him in his defign againft the Englifh, upon
which account he fent him the following letter.

Nobili in Chrifto conqueftori domino
EDVARDO, illuftriffimo regi Hiberniæ,
fuus, fi placet, GRIFFINUS LLWYD in
North-Wall: reverentiam debitam in
honore.

AUDITA nobis veftri in terrarum conquifitione
fama egregia in partibus noftris præcipue debel-
land. æmulos noftros & veftros, qui tam vos quam
nos ab hæreditatibus vi injufte expellendo deftruxerunt,
& nomen noftrum memoriamque in terris delere conati
fuerunt, ab initio fupra modum applaudimus, ut merito debemus, omnes unanimiter in partibus noftris,
unde vobis ex parte Wallenfium nobilium fignifico per
præfentes, quod fi ad Walliam cum hominibus veftris
dignemini venire, vel fi vos in propria perfona accedere
illuc non poteritis, aliquem nobilem Albanen. comitem,
baronem vel militem, cum paucis, fi plurimi nequeant
adeffe, ad dictas partes noftras volueritis mandare. Parati erimus omnes unanimiter . . . . dicem eo
quod nomen veftrum celebre ubique publicetur expug-
nat; fi quid Saxonibus in Albania, per illuftrem regem
fratrem veftrum ultim. per vos in Hibernia, per vos
& nos in Wallia ftatum veftrum priftinum per Brutum
conquifitum recuperabimus, ipfifque fuppeditatis, con-

X 4   fufis

fusis & difperfis, Britannia juxta difcretam veftræ do
minationis ordinationem inter Britones & Albaneos in
pofterum divifa cohæreditabitur.   Valeat dominatio
veftra regia per cuncta fæcula.

To this letter of Sir Gruffydh Llwyd's, Sir Edward Bruce returned the following anfwer.

OMNIBUS defiderantibus a fervitute liberari
falutem in eo.   Qui defiderant in fe releavat. &
liberat. ab anguftiis, temporibus opportunis, quia quilibet chriftianus obligatur fuo proximo in omni anguftia fubvenire, & præcipue illis qui ex una radice originis five parentelæ & patriæ primitus proceferunt,
ideo compatientes veftræ fervituti & anguftiæ, jam
. . . . . . Anglicana moleftia indigenti decrevimus
(auxiliante altiffimo) veftro gravamini occurrere, &
innaturalem & barbaricam totis viribus Anglicanam de
veftris finibus expellere fervitutem, ut fic ficut a principio Albanicus et Britannicus populus expulfis hofti-
bus in perpetuum fiet unus.   Et quia nullus inimicus
faciliter relevatur libenter præcipimus, fi jugum Angli-
canum in tantum vos deprimit, quantum nuper de-
prefferat populum Scotianum, ut fic ex veftro concordi
conamine, & noftro fuperveniente (juvamine difponente
femper divino) pofitis jura veftra & juftitiam recupe-
rare & proprietatem . . . . hæreditatem pacifice
poffidere.   Veruntamen dei cum omnia ferviunt in ifto
propofito filium invocamus, quod non ex præfumpti-
one & ambitione injufti dominii talia attemptamus,
fed ex mera compaffione effufionis innocentis veftri fanguinis & fubjectionis intollerabilis & fignant: ad hoc
quod vellemus inimicorum veftrorum & noftrorum vi-
res reprimere, qui nec pacem nec concordiam defiderant.   Imo veftram & noftram finalem deftructionem,
ficut a principio ingreffionis eorum in Britanniam incef-
fanter diebus ac noctibus molientur, & quia nullo modo eft noftræ confcientiæ quemquam decipere, nec
etiam decipi a quocunque, noftram intentionem &
propofit. fine tergiverfatione aliqua declaramus quod
libenter fciremus veftram voluntatem, fi rationem noftri
laboris

laboris & conaminis intuitu revelationis veſtræ acceptare decrement. nobis committere proſecutionem que-
relæ veſtræ & juſtitiæ nec non capitale dominium veſtri
pro ut alius hactenus princeps veſter liberius habere
conſuevit. Ita quod vos omnes & ſinguli cujuſcunque
extiteritis conditionis priſtinis hæreditatibus, terris, libertatibus, poſſeſſionibus conſuetis, & omnibus condi-
tionibus ad vos expectantibus integre & finaliter gau-
deatis. Veſtram igitur voluntatem ſuper hiis & qui-
buſcunque aliis in quibus vos conſolari poterimus, ſi
videatur expediens caute & celeriter nobis remandetis.
Valete domini in domino.

But for all that theſe letters paſſed betwixt them
whether by reaſon that Bruce's terms were conceived
unreaſonable, nothing however was concluded upon,
and the whole treaty came to nothing. But Sir Gruffydh, though without any hopes of aſſiſtance from the
Scots, would not lay aſide what he had once under-
taken, and therefore having gathered all the forces he
could, deſperately ſet upon, and almoſt in an inſtant
over-ran all North Wales and the Marches, ſeizing
upon all the caſtles and ſtrong holds through the country. But all to no purpoſe, for as the moſt violent
ſtream is quickly over, ſo Sir Gruffydh's army was
preſently ſpent, and then being met with by a ſtrong
detachment of Engliſh, his party was eaſily diſcom-
fited, and himſelf taken priſoner.

The ſame year being the 15th of the reign of King A. D. 1322.
Edward the Second, his eldeſt ſon Edward born at
Windſor, in a parliament holden at York, was created
Prince of Wales, Duke of Aquitaine, and Earl of
Cheſter. This prince ſucceeded his father in the
kingdom of England, by the name of Edward the
Third, one of the greateſt and moſt powerful mo-
narchs that ever ſat upon the Engliſh throne.

Edward born at Woodſtock, eldeſt ſon and heir to 1343.
King Edward the Third, was created prince of Wales,
upon the 12th day of May in the 17th year of his
father's reign, being then about fourteen years of age.

H5

He was a prince of incomparable qualifications, but
fo fignally famous in martial affairs, that upon the
account of the feveral actions he was engaged in,
he received the name of Black Prince. He took
John the French king prifoner at the battle of Poic-
tiers, and fhamefully vanquifhed the French army
in the battle of Creffy. He did not live to enjoy
the crown, but died one year before his father in the
forty-fixth year of his age; no prince was in his life-
time better beloved, and after his death more lamented by the Englifh nation, who had he lived
to fit at the helm, no one doubted but that he would
have exceeded as to all qualifications, the moft glorious renown of the greateft of his anceftors.

In the time of Edward the Third, lived Sir Tudor
Vaughan ap Grono, defcended lineally from Ednyfed
Vaughan, a perfon as to eftate, power and intereft,
one of the chiefeft in North Wales. Upon fome
motive, either of ambition or fancy, he affumed to
himfelf the honour of knighthood, requiring all people to call and ftile him Sir Tudor ap Grono, as
if he did prognofticate and forefee, that out of his
loins fhould arife thofe that fhould have power to
confer that honour. King Edward being informed of
fuch unparalleled prefumption, fent for Sir Tudor, and afked him, with what confidence he durft
invade his prerogative, by affuming the degree of
knighthood, without his authority, Sir Tudor replied,
That by the laws and conftitution of King Arthur, he
had the liberty of taking upon himfelf that title, in
regard he had thofe three qualifications, which who-
foever was endued with, could by thofe laws claim
the honour of a knight. Firft, he was a gentleman.
Second, he had a fufficient eftate. And thirdly, he
was valiant and adventurous; adding this withal, If
my valour and hardinefs be doubted of, lo, here I
throw down my glove; and for due proof of my courage, I am ready to fight with any man, whatever he
be. The king approving and liking well the man's
forwardnefs and refolution, was eafily perfuaded to
confirm the honour of knighthood upon him. From
this

this Sir Tudor lineally defcended Henry the Seventh, king of England, who was the fon of Edmund Earl of Richmond, the fon of Sir Owen Tudor, fon to Meredith, the fon of this Sir Tudor ap Grono.

After the death of the Black Prince, his fon Richard born at Bourdeaux in France, being but ten years of age, was created prince of Wales at Havering at Boure, on the twentieth day of November, and in the fiftieth year of Edward the Third, his grandfather's reign, whom he fucceeded in the crown of England. A. D. 1377.

Henry born at Monmouth, fon and heir to Henry the Fourth, king of England, upon the fifteenth of October, in the firft year of his father's reign, was created prince of Wales at Weftminfter, who fucceeded his father in the Englifh crown by the name of Henry the Fifth.

Whilft Richard the Second reigned, one Owen ap Gruffydh Fychan, defcended of a younger fon of Gruffydh ap Madoc Lord of Bromfield, was not a little famous. This Owen had his education in one of the Inns of Court, where he became barrifter at law, and afterwards in very great favour and credit ferved King Richard, and continued with him at Flint Caftle, till at length the king was taken by Henry Duke of Lancafter. Betwixt this Owen and Reginald Lord Gray of Rhuthyn, there happened no fmall difference touching a common lying between the lordfhip of Rhuthyn, whereof Reginald was owner, and the lordfhip of Glendowrdwy in the poffeffion of Owen, whence he borrowed the name of Glyndwr. During the reign of Richard the Second, Owen as being a courtier, and in no mean efteem with the king, did overpower Reginald, who was neither fo well befriended at court, nor beloved in the country as Owen was. But after King Richard's depofal, the fcene was altered, and Reginald as then better befriended than Owen, entered upon the common, which occafioned Owen in the firft year of Henry the Fourth to make his complaint in parliament againft him, for thus divefting him of his right. No redrefs being

being found, the bishop of St. Asaph wished the lords to take care, that by thus slighting his complaint, they did not irritate and provoke the Welch to an insurrection, to which some of the lords replied, That they did not fear those rascally barefooted people. Glyndwr therefore perceiving how his petition was slighted in parliament, and finding no other method to redress himself having several friends and followers, put himself in arms against Reginald, and meeting him in the field, overcame and took him prisoner, and spoiled his lordship of Rhuthyn. Upon this many resorted to him from all parts of Wales, some thinking him to be in as great favour now, as in King Richard's days, others putting in his head, that now the time was come when the Britains by his means might again recover the honour and liberties of their ancestors. But Reginald being thus kept prisoner, and very severely handled by Owen, to terrify him into compliance with him in his rebellious actings, and not permitted to have his liberty, under ten thousand marks for his ransom, whereof six thousand to be paid upon the feast of St. Martyn, in the fourth year of Henry the Fourth, and to deliver up his eldest son with some other persons of quality as hostages for the remainder; the king at the humble suit of Reginald, seeing no other way for his enlargement, gave way thereto, authorising Sir William de Roos, Sir Richard de Grey, Sir William de Willoughby, Sir William le Zouche, Sir Hugh Huls, as also, John Harvey, William Vaus, John Lee, John Langford, Thomas Payne, and John Elnestow, to treat with Owen and his council, and to conclude in what they should conceive most expedient and necessary to be done for his redemption. Whereupon they consenting to give the sum demanded by Glyndwr for his deliverance, the king gave licence to Robert Braybroke bishop of London, as also to Sir Gerard Braybroke the father, and Sir Gerard the son, then feoffees of divers lordships for this Reginald, to sell the manor of Hertelegh in the county of Kent, towards the raising of that money. And for the better enabling him to pay so great

a fine

a fine, the king was pleafed to grant, that whereas it was enacted, that fuch perfons who were owners of lands in Ireland, and did not there refide, fhould for fuch their neglect, forfeit two parts of the profits of them to the king; that notwithftanding this act, he fhould forfeit nothing for non-refidence there, during the term of fix years next enfuing.

This good fuccefs over the Lord Gray, together with the numerous refort of the Welch to him, and the favourable interpretation of the prophecies of Merdhyn, which fome conftrued very advantageoufly, made the fwelling mind of Glyndwr overflow its banks, and gave him fome hopes of reftoring this ifland back to the Britains. Wherefore he fet upon the Earl of March, who met him with a numerous party of Herefordfhire men, but when they came to clofe, the Welchmen proved too powerful, and having killed above a thoufand men of the Englifh, they took the Earl of March prifoner. King Henry upon this was frequently requefted to ranfom the Earl but to no purpofe, for whether by reafon that Mortimer had a jufter title to the crown than himfelf he being the next heir in blood after King Richard who was as yet living, or becaufe of fome other private odium, the king would never hearken to his redemption, alledging that he wilfully threw himfelf into the hands of Glyndwr. But about the midft of Auguft, to correct the prefumptuous attempts of the Welch, the king went in perfon with a great army into Wales; but by reafon of extraordinary excefs of weather, which fome attributed to the magic of Glyndwr, he was glad to return fafe.

But the Earl of March perceiving that he was not like to obtain his liberty by King Henry's means, whether out of compliance, by reafon of his tedious captivity, or affection to the young lady, he agreed to take part with Owen againft the king of England, and to marry his daughter; with them joined the Earl of Worcefter, and his brother the Earl of Northumberland, with his fon the valiant Lord Percy, who confpiring to depofe the king of England, in the houfe of the r . . .

the realm amongſt them, cauſing a tripartite indenture
to be made, and to be ſealed with every one's ſeal: by
which covenant all that country lying betwixt the
Severn and the Trent, ſouthward, was aſſigned to the
Earl of March; all Wales, and the lands beyond the
Severn, weſtward, were appointed to Glyndwr; and all
from the Trent, northward to the Lord Percy. This
was done (as ſome ſaid) through a fooliſh credit
they gave to a vain prophecy, as though King
Henry was the execrable moldwarp, and they three
the dragon, the lion, and the wolf which ſhould pull
him down, and diſtribute his kingdom among themſelves: After that they had exhibited articles of their
grievances to King Henry, and divulged their reaſons for taking up arms; at length they marched
with all their power towards Shrewſbury to fight the
king, depending mainly upon the arrival of Glyndwr
and his Welchmen. But the matter was gone ſo far,
that whether he came in or no, they muſt fight, and
ſo both armies being joined, the king's party prevailed, young Percy being ſlain upon the ſpot, and
Douglas, beſides moſt of the Engliſh of quality,
who with a party of Scotch had come to the aid of
the confederates, was taken priſoner, but afterwards
honourably ſet at liberty by the interceſſion of the
prince of Wales. In the mean time the Earl of
Northumberland was marching forward with a great
party from the North, but the king having ſettled
matters about Shrewſbury, coming to York, and
ſending to him to lay down his arms, he voluntarily ſubmitted and diſmiſſed his forces. Then the
king returning from Yorkſhire, determined to paſs
over to North Wales, to chaſtiſe the preſumptuous
practices of the immorigerous Welch, who after
his departure from Shrewſbury, had made in-roads
into the marches, and done much hurt to his Engliſh ſubjects. But other buſineſs of greater conſequence intervening, he detached his ſon the prince
of Wales, who took the caſtle of Aberyſtwyth,
which was quickly again retaken by Owen Glyndwr,

who

who thruſt into it a ſtrong garriſon of Welch. But in the battle of Huſke fought upon the fifteenth of March, the Welch received a very conſiderable blow from the prince's men, Glyndwr's ſon being taken priſoner, beſides fifteen hundred more taken and ſlain. After this, we hear little of Glyndwr, excepting that he continued and perſiſted to vex and plague the Engliſh upon the marches, to the tenth year of King Henry's reign, when he miſerably ended his life ; being as Hol-Hollinſh. lingſhed reporteth towards his latter days driven to that extremity, that deſpairing of all comfort, he fled and lurked in caves and other the moſt ſolitary places, fearing to ſhew his face to any creature, till at length being ſtarved for hunger and lack of ſuſtenance, he miſerably ended his life.

But theſe rebellious practices of Glyndwr, highly exaſperated King Henry againſt the Welch, inſomuch that ſeveral rigorous and unmerciful laws were en-acted, relating to Wales, which in effect deſtroyed all the liberties of the Welch ſubject. They were made incapable of purchaſing any lands, or to be elected members of any county or borough, and to undertake any office, whether civil or military in any town incorporated. If any ſuit at law happened betwixt an Engliſhman and a Welchman, the for-mer could not be convicted, but by the ſentence of an Engliſh judge, and the verdict of an Engliſh jury; beſides that any Engliſhman who married a Welch-woman was thereby forthwith disfranchiſed from all the liberties of an Engliſh ſubject. It was further enacted, that no Welchman ſhould be in poſſeſſion of any caſtle, or other place of ſtrength, and that no victuals or armour ſhould be brought into Wales, without a ſpecial warrant from the king or his coun-cil; and farther, that no Welchman was capable of undertaking the office of juſtice, chamberlain, ſheriff or any other place of truſt in any part of Wales, notwithſtanding any patent or licenſe heretofore given to the contrary. Theſe, with many others moſt ri-gorous and unjuſt laws, particularly that forbidding

any

any Welchman to bring up his children to learning,
or to bind them apprentices to any trade or occu-
pation, were enacted by the king against the Welch; so
that nothing could cool his displeasure, but that a whole
nation should be wrongfully oppressed, for the fault
and miscarriage of one person.   But one might think,
that this was no politic method to secure a nation in
its allegiance, which upon lighter affronts was used
to defend its privileges; and therefore we may well
attribute the quiet disposition of the Welch towards
this time, to the moderation of Henry the Fifth, who
within a little time succeeded his father in the crown
of England.

Contemporary with Glyndwr was Sir David Gam,
so called by reason he had but one eye, the son of
Lhewelyn ap Howel Vaughan of Brecknock, by
Mawd the daughter of Iefan ap Rhys ap Ifor of
Eluel.   He was a great stickler for the Duke of
Lancaster, and for that reason became a mortal enemy to Glyndwr, who having his education as is said
before, at one of the Inns of Court, got to be preferred to the service of King Richard the Second, who,
as Walsingham, says, made him his *Scutifer*, or shield-
bearer.   But being informed that his master Richard
was deposed and murdered, and withal being provoked by several wrongs and affronts done him by
his neighbour the Lord Gray of Rhuthyn, whom
King Henry greatly countenanced, and looking upon
Henry as an usurper, he caused himself to be proclaimed Prince of Wales.   And for a better grace
of the matter he feigned himself to be descended
by a daughter from Lhewelyn ap Gruffydh the
last prince; whereas in truth, he came paternally
but from a younger brother of the house of Powys.
But as ambition has no moderation, so Glyndwr
for a time acted the part of a prince, and sum-
moned a parliament to meet at Machynlleth, whither the nobility and gentry of Wales appeared,
and among the rest Sir David Gam, but not upon
the same design with the rest, having an intention in

this

this meeting to murder Glyndyfwr. But the plot being difcovered, and Sir David fecured, he had liked to undergo prefent execution, had not Glyn-dyfwr's beft friends, and the greateft upholders of his caufe, pleaded in his behalf, by whofe intercef-fion he was prevailed with to grant Sir David both his life and liberty upon condition he would ever after continue true and loyal to him. Sir David promifed very loudly, but with the refervation never to perform; for as foon as he came to his own coun-try, where he was a perfon of very confiderable fway and intereft, he did exceedingly annoy and moleft thofe that any way favoured or adhered to Glyn-dyfwr. While Sir David lay in prifon at Mach-ynlleth, for his attempt againft Owen's life, this Englyn was made upon him.

Dafydd Gam dryglam dreigl, iti yn wan frwydr,
    Fradwr Riffiart Bhrenin,
Llwyr y rhoes Diawl (hawn hwyl Flin
    Y fath yftad) ei fys ith Din.

i. e. David Gam thou wilt be a wanderer and an ill end will come to thee. Thou wilt be weak in battle, thou traitor to King Richard. So eagerly vexatious in thy ftation that the devil wholly entered thy heart.

But Glyndyfwr receiving information how that Sir David Gam contrary to the promife he had made at his releafement, endeavoured all he could to deftroy his intereft among the Welch, entered the marches, and among other tokens of his in-dignation, burned the houfe of Sir David, and as the report goes, calling to him one of Sir Da-vid's tenants, fpake to him thus merrily in verfe;

O Gweli di wr côch Cam
Yn ymofyn y Girnigwen
Dywed ei bôd hi Tan y Lan
A nôd y glo ar ei Phenn.

i. e. If thou feeft a red-haired, fquint-eyed * man
looking for the loft fheep, tell him fhe is below the
hill, and he may know her as fhe is marked with
fire.

But Sir David had the luck to efcape his reach,
and was conftrained to retire to England, where
he lived for the moft part at court, till the death of
Glyndyfwr.

When King Henry the Fifth went with an army
to France againft the French king, Sir David Gam
brought into his fervice a numerous party of ftout
and valourous Welchmen, who upon all occafions
expreffed their courage and refolution. In the battle of Agincourt, news being brought to the king
that the French army was advancing towards him,
and that they were exceeding numerous, he detached
Captain Gam, to obferve their motions, and to re-
view their number. The Captain having narrowly
eyed the French, found them twice to exceed the
Englifh, but not being in the leaft daunted at fuch
a multitude, he returned to the king, who enquiring of
him what the number of the French might be, he made
anfwer, An't pleafe you my liege, they are enough
to be killed, enough to run away, and enough to
be taken prifoners. King Henry was well pleafed,
and much encouraged with this refolute and undaunted anfwer of Sir David's, whofe tongue did
not exprefs more valour than his hands performed.
For in the heat of battle, the king's perfon being
in danger, Sir David charged the enemy with that
eagernefs and mafculine bravery, that they were glad to

---

* *Squint-eyed* is *Gam* in Welch, from which he took his name,
and his family continue it to this day, and all fquint with one
eye Si David C. was the perfon who is here defcribed
in the charater of Captain Fluellin.

give ground, and so secured the king, though with
the loss of much blood, and also his life, himself and
his son-in-law Roger Vaughan, and his kinsman Walter Llwyd of Brecknock, having received their mortal wounds in that encounter. When the king heard
of their condition, how that they were past all hopes
of recovery, he came to them, and in recompence of
their good services, knighted them all three in the
field, where they soon after died; and so ended the
life, but not the fame of the signally valiant Sir David Gam.

Edward of Westminster, the sole issue of that unfortunate prince King Henry the Sixth, by Margaret
the daughter of Rayner duke of Anjou, and titular
king of Jerusalem, Sicily, and Arragon; was created
Prince of Wales, in a parliament held at Westminster,
on the fifteenth day of March, in the thirty-second
year of his father's reign. When the day was lost
at Tewkesbury, this young prince thought to make
his escape by flight, but being unfortunately taken,
and brought to the presence of King Edward the
Fourth, who then sat upon the helm, made such resolute and unexpected replies, that he put the king into
such a passion, that he smote him on the mouth with
his gauntlet; and then his brother Richard the Crouch-
back, ran him into the heart with his dagger.

Edward, born in the Sanctuary at Westminster, the
eldest son of King Edward the Fourth, was, after his
father's expulsion out of England, in the forty-ninth
year of King Henry the Sixth, created Prince of Wales
and Earl of Chester, in the eleventh year of his father's
reign. Upon the death of Edward the Fourth, this
young prince being then at Ludlow in the marches
of Wales, was presently sent for to London, and proclaimed king of England, but never lived to be
crowned; for his uncle Richard duke of Glocester,
who was appointed his protector, most villainously
made him away, together with his brother the duke of
York; and afterwards was himself proclaimed and
crowned king.

Edw i

Edward the Fourth, in his wars againſt Henry the Sixth, was very much aſſiſted by the Welch; in re-compence of which ſervice, he deſigned to reform matters ſo in Wales, as that intolerable oppreſſion which they had hitherto endured, ſhould be regulated and taken off. And to that end, he meant to eſta-bliſh a court within the ſaid principality, and con-ſtituted John biſhop of Worceſter preſident of the prince's council in the marches; who, together with Anthony Earl of Rivers, ſat in the town-hall of Shrewſbury, and conſtituted certain ordinances for the public good and tranquility of that place. But the matter proceeded no farther; for the troubles and diſquietneſs of his kingdom, coming heavy upon him, and the ſhortneſs of his reign after his eſtabliſh-ment not permitting, he was forced to leave that to others, which himſelf thought once to bring about.

Edward, born at Middleham near Richmond in the county of York, the only ſon of King Richard the Third, was at ten years of age created by his father Prince of Wales, and died ſoon after.

Arthur, the eldeſt ſon of King Henry the Seventh, born at Wincheſter, was in the ſeventh year of his father's reign created Prince of Wales. About the fifteenth year of his age, being then newly married to Katherine the Infanta of Spain, he was ſent by his father into Wales, that by his preſence he might keep that country in better awe. With him King Henry ſent Dr. William Smith, afterwards made bi-ſhop of Lincoln, as preſident of his council; toge-ther with Sir Richard Pool, his chamberlain, Sir Henry Vernon, Sir Richard Crofts, Sir David Philip, Sir William Udal, Sir Thomas Englefield, Sir Peter New-ton, and others, to be his counſellors and directors in his management of affairs. But the prince had not continued long there, but he fell ſick at his caſtle at Ludlow, of which indiſpoſition he ſhortly after died, and was buried with great ſolemnity in the cathe-dral church of Worceſter. But the creating of his brother Henry duke of York Prince of Wales in his

ſtead,

Wokins
p. 789.

ftead, was deferred for about the fpace of a month, to difcover whether the Lady Katherine was with child by Prince Arthur. But when it appeared for certain, fhe had not conceived; on the eighteenth day of February, in the nineteenth year of his father King Henry the Seventh's reign, Henry duke of York was created Prince of Wales.

King Henry the Seventh, being by his grandfather Owen Tudor defcended out of Wales, and having fufficiently experienced the affection of the Welch towards him; firft of thofe, who upon his firft landing, opportunely joined him under Sir Rhys ap Thomas, and then of thofe, who under the command of Sir William Stanley, Lord of Bromfield, Yale, and Chirkland, aided him in Bofworth-field; could not in honour and equity, but bear fome regard to the miferable ftate and condition of the Welch, under the Englifh government. And therefore this prudent prince, finding the calamities of the Welch to be infupportable, and feeing what grievous and unmerciful laws were enacted againft them by his predeceffors, he took occafion to redrefs and reform the fame, and granted to the Welch a charter of liberty and immunity, whereby they were releafed from the cruel oppreffion, which fince their fubjection to the Englifh government, they had moft cruelly fuftained. And feeing the birth and quality of his grandfather Owen Tudor was called in queftion, and that he was by many upbraided of being of a mean and ignoble parentage; King Henry directed a commiffion to the abbot of Lhan Egweft, Dr. Owen Pool canon of Hereford, and John King herald at arms, to make inquifition concerning the pedigree of the faid Owen; who coming to Wales, made a diligent enquiry into this matter; and by the affiftance of Sir John Leyaf, Guttyn Owen Bardh, Gruffydh ap Lhewelyn ap Efan Fychan, and others, in the confultation of the Britifh books of pedigrees, they drew up an exact genealogy of Owen Tudor, which upon their return they prefented to the king.

Vide Appendix.

Edward, son to Henry the Eighth, by the Lady Jane Seymour, his third wife, was born at Hampton Court, on the twelfth of October; and upon the eighteenth of the said month, was created Prince of Wales, Duke of Cornwal, and Earl of Chester.

King Henry the Seventh, had already abrogated those unreasonable and intolerable laws, which the former kings of England, particularly Henry the Fourth, had made against the Welch; and now, King Henry the Eighth, willing to make a plenary reformation of what his father had wisely begun, thought it necessary towards the good and tranquility of both nations, to make the Welch subject to the same laws, and the same government with the English. He understood that the usual hostilities and depredations were still continued and kept up by both sides upon the borders; and though his father had eased the yoke of the Welch, yet he perceived, that it did contribute but little towards the disannulling of that inveterate and implacable envy and animosity which raged in the marches. Therefore to remedy this, otherwise unavoidable, distemper, he concluded that it was the only effectual method, to incorporate the Welch with the English, that they being subject to the same laws, might equally fear the vio-

A. D. 1536. lation of them. And accordingly, in the twenty-seventh year of his reign, an act of parliament passed to that purpose, which together with another act in the thirty-fifth year of his reign, made a plenary incorporation of the Welch with the English, which union has had that blessed effect, that it has dispelled all those unnatural differences which heretofore were so rife and irreconcilable.

When the Reformation was first established in Wales, it was a mighty inconveniency to the vulgar people, such as were unacquainted with the English tongue, that the bible was not translated into their native language. Queen Elizabeth was quickly apprehensive of the inconveniency which the Welch incurred, for the want of such a translation; and there-

fore

fore in the eighth year of her reign, an act of parliament was passed, whereby the bishops of Hereford, St. David's, St. Asaph, Bangor, and Landaff, were ordered to take care that the Bible containing the Old and New Testaments, with the Book of Common Prayer, and Administration of the Sacraments, be truly and exactly translated into the British or Welch tongue, and that the same so translated, being by them perused and approved, be printed to such a number at least; as that every cathedral, collegiate and pachurch and chapel-of-ease within the said diocese where that tongue is vulgarly spoken, might be supplied before the first of March, anno 1566. And from that time forward, the Welch divine service should be used in the British tongue, in all places throughout those dioceses, where the Welch is commonly spoke, after the same manner as it was used in the English tongue; and that the charge of procuring the said Bible and Common Prayer, should equally depend betwixt the parson and the parish: the former being obliged to pay one half of the expence; and that the price of the book should be set by the aforesaid bishops, or by three of them at the least. But this act of parliament was not punctually observed; for the Old Testament was wholly omitted, and only the New, with the Book of Common Prayer and Administration of the Sacraments, then translated, which translation was chiefly owing to Richard bishop of St. David's, who was assisted by William Salusbury, a perfect critick in the Welch tongue, and one excellently conversant in all British antiquities. But in the year 1588, Dr. William Morgan, first bishop of Landaff, and then of St. Asaph, undertook the translation of the whole Bible; and by the help of the bishops of St. Asaph and Bangor, Gabriel Goodman, dean of Westminster, David Powel, D. D. Edmund Price archdeacon of Merionyth, and Richard Vaughan, he effectually finished it. This was of singular profit and advantage to the Welch, to have the whole Scripture read and perused in their own native tongue; by which means they received a clearer

demonstration of the corruptions of the church of
Rome, when they saw many of their principles appa-
rently contradicting, and others not very firmly founded
upon the Holy Scriptures. And on the other hand
they perceived the necessity and advantage of the Reformation, they easily discovered that the whole doctrine
of the church of England was sound and orthodox,
and that they were now happily delivered from that
popish slavery which their forefathers ignorantly adored;
and therefore being convinced of the truth of their religion, they became, and continued generally, very strict
adherents and firm observers of the doctrine and difcipline of this church.

And here by the bye, I cannot but observe what a
reverend writer has lately insinuated, relating to the
christian religion planted in Wales. For that learned
person in his funeral sermon upon Mr. Gouge, would
fain induce the world to believe, that christianity was
very corrupt and imperfect among the Welch, before
it was purified by that, whom he terms apostolical man.
Whereas it is notoriously evident, that since the Reformation was settled in that country, and the
Bible, with the Book of Common Prayer, translated
into the Welch tongue, no place has been more exact, in keeping to the strict rubrick and constitution
of the Church of England, both as to the substance
and form of worship. But what may more truly be
attributed to Mr. Gouge, is that since his travels into
Wales, and the propagating of his doctrine among the
ignorant of that country, presbytery, which before had
scarce taken root, has daily increased, and grown to a
head.

Henry, eldest son of King James the First, being
arrived to the age of seventeen years, was created prince
of Wales, on the 30th of May, anno 1610, but he dying of a malignant fever, about two years after; his
brother Charles being fifteen years of age, was created
prince of Wales in his room, anno 1615. For joy of
this new creation the town of Ludlow, and city of
London, performed very great triumphs; and the
more

more to honour this folemnity, the king made twenty-five knights of the Bath, all lords' or barons' fons; and the Inns of Court, to exprefs their joy, elected out of their body forty choice gentlemen, to perform folemn jufts and barriers.

Charles, eldeft fon of King Charles the Firft, by Henrietta Maria, daughter to King Henry the Fourth of France, was born May 29, 1630, and afterwards created prince of Wales.

Since the happy incorporation of the Welch with the Englifh, the hiftory of both nations, as well as the people is united; and therefore I fhall not repeat that which is fo copioufly and frequently delivered by the Englifh hiftorians; but fhall conclude with Dr. Heylyn, ' That fince the Welch have been in-corporated with the Englifh, they have fhewed them-felves moft loyal, hearty and affectionate fubjects of the ftate; cordially devoted to their king, and zealous in defence of their laws, liberties and religion, as well as any of the beft of their fellow-fubjects.'

APPENDIX

APPENDIX.

The return of a Commiſſion ſent into Wales by King Henry the Seventh, to ſearch out the Pedigrees of Owen Tudor.

HENRY the Seventh, king of England, &c. ſon of Edmund Earl of Richmond, ſon of Owen ap Meredith, and of Queen Catherine his wife, daughter to Charles the Sixth, king of France. This Owen was ſon of Meredith ap Tudor ap Gronw ap Tudor, ap Gronw, ap Ednyfed Fychan, baron of Brinſeingle in Denbigh-land, Lord of Kriceth, Chief Juſtice and chief of council to Lhewelyn ap Iorwerth Drwyndwn prince of all Wales. And in the time of Prince Llewelyn grew a variance between King John of England and the ſaid prince; whereupon Ednyfed came with the prince's hoſt, and men of war, and alſo a number of his own people, and met theſe Engliſh lords in a morning, at what time theſe Engliſh lords were hoſtied and ſlain; and immediately brought their heads, being yet bloody, to the ſaid Prince Llewelyn. The prince, ſeeing the ſame, cauſed Ednyfed Fychan, from thenceforth to bear in his arms or ſhield, three bloody heads in token of his victory, where he had born in his arms before a Saracen's head; and ſo

ever

ever after this Ednyfed bore the said arms, his son, and his son's son, unto the time of Tudor ap Gronw, ap Tudor ap Gronw, ap Ednyfed Fychan. And after this Ednyfed wedded one Gwenllian daughter to Rhys prince of South Wales, and had issue by her Gronw: which Ednyfed Fychan had in Wales divers goodly houses, royally adorned with turrets and garrets; some in Anglesey, some other Caernarvonshire, and some in Denbigh-land; but his chiefest manor-house was in the commot of Crythin in Caernarvonshire, which was a royal palace, now decayed for want of reparations. Also he builded there a chapel in the worship of our lady, and had licence of the pope for evermore to sing divine service therein for his soul, and his ancestors' and progenitors' souls always; and had authority to give his tythes and offerings to his chaplain there * starving; which Ednyfed Fychan was son to Kyner ap Iers ap Gwgan, ap Marchudd, which was one of the fifteen tribes of North Wales, and son to Kynan ap Elfyn, ap Mor, ap Mynan, ap Isbwis Newintyrche, ap Isbwis ap Cadrod Calch Efynydd, Earl of Dunstable and Lord of Northampton, ap Cywyd Cindion, ap Cynfelyn ap Arthuys, ap Morydd ap Cynnaw, ap Coel Godeboc king of Britain, of whom King Henry the Seventh descended lineally by issue-male, and is son to the said Coel in the thirty-first degree, as it is approved by old chronicles in Wales. Which Coel was son of Tegfan ap Deheufraint, ap Tudbwyl, ap Urban, ap Gradd, ap Rhyfedel, ap Rhydeirne, ap Endigant, ap Endeyrn, ap Enid, ap Endos, ap Enddolaw, ap Afalach, ap Aflech, ap Beli mawr king of Britain, of whom King Henry the Seventh descendeth by issue-male, and is son to him in forty-one degree. Which Beli was son to Monnogon king, ap King Kaxor, ap King Pyr, ap King Sawl Benniffel, ap Rhytherch king, ap Rydion king, ap Eidol king, ap Arthafel king, ap Seisfilt king, ap Owen king, ap Caxho king, ap Bleuddyd king, ap Meirion king, ap Gwrguft king, ap Elydno king, ap Clydawc king, ap Ithel king, ap Urien king,

* Vide an serving.

king, ap Andrew king, ap Kereni king, ap Porrex
king, ap Coel king, ap Cadell king, ap Geraint king,
ap Elidr king, ap Morydd king, ap Dan king, ap
Seiffilt king, ap Cyhelyn king, ap Gwrgan king (alias)
Farfdrwch, ap Beli king, ap Dyfnwal king, ap Do-
dion king, ap Enyd, ap Kwrwyd, ap Cyrdon ap Dy-
fufarth Prydain, ap Aedd mawr, ap Antonius ap Seif-
ilt king, ap Rhegaw daughter and heir of King Lyr,
and wife of Henwin prince of Cornwall. This Lyr
was fon of Bleuddyd, ap Rhunbaladr brâs, ap Lleon,
ap Brutus darian làs, ap Effroc Cadarn, ap Mymbyr, ap
Madoc, ap Locrine, ap Brutus which inherited firft this
land, and after his name was called Britain, and had three
fons Locrine, Kamber, and Albanaétus. Locrine the
eldeft, parted the ifle with his brethren, and kept half
the land for himfelf, and called it Leogria. Kamber
fecond fon had the land beyond Severn, and named
it Kambria, in Englifh, Wales. Albanaétus had Scotland, which he then called Albania after his own name.
Of which Brute King Henry the Seventh is lineally
defcended by iffue-male, faving one woman, and is fon
to Brute in fivefcore degrees.

How Owen grandfire to King Henry the Seventh,
cometh of Beli mawr by Angharad, mother to
Ednyfed by iffue-female, by Gittin, Owen, and
Sir John Leiaf's books.

T H E mother of Ednyfed was Angharad, daughter of Hwfa, ap Cyner, ap Rhywallon, ap Dinged,
ap Tudor Trefor, ap Mymbyr, ap Cadfarch, ap Gwr-
genaw, ap Gwaethiawc, ap Bywyn, ap Biordderch,
ap Gwriawn, ap Gwnnan, ap Gwnfiw frych, ap Cadell
Dehurnlluc, ap Pafgan, ap Rhydwf, ap Rhudd Fedel
frych, ap Cyndeirn, ap Gwrtheirn Gwrthenau, called
in Englifh Vortiger, by whom King Henry the Seventh, by the aforefaid Angharad, mother to Ednyfed
Fychan, and wife to Cyner ap Iers, ap Gwgon, is fon
to

to the faid Vortiger in thirty degrees. Which Vortiger was fon to Rhydeyrn ap Deheufraint, ap Eidi-
gant, ap Endeirn, ap Enid, ap Endos, ap Enddolau,
ap Afallach, ap Afflech, ap Beli mawr, to whom King
Henry the Seventh is fon by Angharad, mother to
Ednyfed Fychan in forty degrees.

*How King Henry the Seventh cometh of Beli mawr
by Gwenllian wife to Ednyfed Fychan, and daughter to the Lord Rhys, called Arglwydd Rhys, by
iffue-female.*

Owen ap Meredith ap Tudor ap Gronw, ap Tudor,
ap Gronw, ap Gwenllian, daughter to Rhys prince of
South-Wales, ap Gruffydh prince, ap Rhys prince, ap
Tudor mawr prince, ap Cadell prince, ap Rodri
mawr, prince of all Wales. This Rodri had three
fons, and divided the principality of Wales between
them in three parts; to Merfyn his firft fon, prince
of North Wales, all North Wales, who died without
iffue; and Anarawd prince of Powys, and Cadell
prince of South Wales, of whom King Henry the
Seventh defcendeth, by Gwenllian daughter to Prince
Rhys, called Arglwydd Rhys, wife to Ednyfed Fychan; and the faid King Henry the Seventh is fon to
Rodri mawr in the feventeenth degree; which Rodri mawr was fon to Merfyn firft king of Man,
which wedded Effilt daughter and heir to Cynan Dyndaethwy.

This Merfyn frych was fon to Gwriad ap Elidur,
ap Handdear Alcwn, ap Tegid, ap Gwiar, ap Dwywc,
ap Llywarch hên, ap Elidur Lydanwin, ap Meirchion,
ap Grwft, ap Cenaw, ap Coel Godeboc king of Britain as before. This Coel was king of Britain and
Earl of Colchefter, a right worthy king, to whom
King Henry the Seventh is fon, by the faid Gwenllian wife to Ednyfed Fychan, in the thirty-firft degree, by the faid Gittin Owen, and Sir John Leiaf's
books.

A

How Owen Grandsire to King Henry the Seventh cometh of Beli mawr, by Essillt daughter to Cynan Dyndaethwy.

Owen ap Meredith ap Tudor ap Gronw, ap Tudor ap Gronw, ap Gwenllian daughter of Prince Rhys, ap Gruffydh ap Rhys, ap Tudor mawr, ap Engion, ap Owen, ap Howell Dda, ap Cadell, ap Rodri mawr, ap Essillt daughter of Cynan Dyndaethwy and heir, Prince of Wales, ap Rodri Moelwynoc, ap Idwal jwrch, ap Cadwalader Fendigaid King of all Britain, to whom King Henry the Seventh is son in the twenty second degree. Cadwalader was son to Cadwallan King, ap Cadfan King, ap Iago, ap Beli, ap Rhun, ap Maelgwn Gwynedd King, ap Casswallan Lawhir, ap Eincon irth, ap Cynnedda weledig, ap Edeirn, which wedded Gwawl, Ferch Coel Godeboc King, which Edeirn was son to Padarn Peisrydd, ap Tegid, ap Iago, ap Genedawc, ap Cain, ap Gwrgain, ap Doli, ap Gwrtholi, ap Dufu, ap Gorddufu, ap Amwerid, ap Omwedd, ap Duve Brichwain, ap Owen, ap Affallach, ap Afflech, ap Beli mawr, to whom King Henry the Seventh is son by the said Gwenllian in the fiftieth degree.

Owen ap Meredith ap Tudor ap Gronw, ap Tudor ap Gronw, ap Gwenllian, daughter to Arglwydd Rhys, son to Gwenllian daughter of Gruffydh Prince, ap Cynan Prince of North Wales, son of Iago Prince, ap Idwall Prince, ap Meuric Prince, ap Idwall Foel Prince, ap Anarawd Prince, ap Rodri mawr Prince of all Wales, to whom King Henry the Seventh is son by Gwenllian mother to the Arglwydd Rhys in the seventeenth degree.

Owen ap Meredith ap Tudor ap Gronw, ap Tudor, ap Gronw, ap Gwenllian, Ferch Arglwydd Rhys, ap Gwladis, Ferch Rhywallon ap Cynfyn Prince of Powys, and Angharad wife to Cynfyn, daughter and heir to Meredith Prince of Powys, son of Owen Prince of Powys and South-Wales, son to Cadell Prince there. Which Owen ap Howell Dda, had two sons, Meredith and Eineon, and Owen their father gave the

principality

principality of South Wales, to Eineon his fon, and the Principality of Powys to Meredith his other fon. Which Meredith had iffue Angharad, that wedded Cynfyn, by whom he was Prince of Powys, which Cadell was fon to Rodri mawr Prince of all Wales, fon to Merfyn frych, &c. to Beli mawr, as above written by Guttin Owen's book.

Owen ap Meredith ap Tudor ap Gronw, ap Tudor, ap Gronw, ap Gwenllian, Ferch Arglwydd Rhys, ap Gruffydh, ap Rhys, ap Tudor, ap Eineon, ap Howell Dda, ap Cadell, ap Angharad, wife to Rodri mawr, daughter to Meyric ap Dyfnwal, ap Arthen, ap Seiffillt, ap Clydawc, ap Artholes, ap Arnothen, ap Brothan, ap Seirwell, ap Uffa, ap Carédic, ap Cwnedda weledic, ap Edeirn, ap Padarn Peifrydd, which Edeirn wedded Gwawl ferch Coel Godeboc, Mother to Cwnedda weledyc, &c.

How Owen cometh of Meuryc Lord of Gwent, by Morfydd's daughter, wife to Gronw ap Ednyfed Fychan.

Owen ap Meredith ap Tudor ap Gronw, ap Tudor, ap Morfydd, Ferch Meuryc L. of Gwent.

How Owen cometh of Rodri mawr, by Angharad, daughter to Ithel Fychan, ap Ithel Llwyd, and wife of Tudor ap Gronw, ap Ednyfed Fychan.

Owen ap Meredith ap Tudor ap Gronw, ap Angharad, ferch Ithel Fychan, ap Ithel Llwyd, ap Ithel Gam, ap Meredith ap Vchdrud, ap Edwin King of Tegengle in Flintfhire.

How Owen cometh of Rodri mawr by Adleïs, wife to Ithel Fychan, daughter to Ricart.

Owen ap Meredith ap Tudor ap Gronw, ap Angharad Ferch Adleis wife to Ithel Fychan, daughter to Ri..., ap C.. I..ler, ap Gru..y.h. ap Kynan

Prince

Prince of North-Wales, ap Iago, ap Idwal Foel, ap Anarawd, ap Rodri Mawr, &c. all this by Gyttin Owen's book.

How Owen cometh of Beli Mawr by Gwerfill Ferch Madawc, o'r hen dwr, wife to Gronw ap Tudor, ap Gronw, ap Ednyfed Fychan.

Owen ap Meredith ap Tudor ap Gwerfill Ferch Madawc o'r hen dwr, ap Iers, ap Madawc, ap Meredith, ap Bleddyn, ap Kynfin prince of Powis, &c. and so to Beli Mawr.

How Owen cometh to Beli Mawr by the mother of the said Gwerfill Ferch Madawc.

Owen ap Meredith, ap Tudor, ap Gwerfill Ferch Madawc o'r hen dwr, ap Lleucu Ferch Angharad, Ferch Meredith, ap Madawc, ap Gruffudh Maelor prince of Powis. This Madawc ap Gruffudh Maelor, built the abbey of Valacrucis, in Welch, Manachlog Llan Egweftl, the year of our Lord 1200, and lieth there buried, and this Gruffudh Maelor was son to Madawc, ap Meredith, ap Bleddin, ap Cynfin, ap Gweriftan, ap Gwalthfoed, ap Gwrydor, ap Caradawc, ap Lles Llaw Ddeawc, ap Edwal, ap Gwnnan, ap Gwnnawc Farf Sych, ap Keidic, ap Corf, ap Cadnawc, ap Tegonwy, ap Teon, ap Gwinaf Daufreuddwyd, ap Powyr lew, ap Bywdec, ap Rhun rhudd baladr, ap Llary, ap Casfar Wledic, ap Lludd, ap Beli Mawr king of all England and Wales, to whom King Henry the Seventh is son this way by Ludd in thirty-six degrees.

How Owen cometh to Beli Mawr by the mother's side of Gwerfill Ferch Madawc.

Owen ap Meredith, ap Tudor, ap Gwerfill Ferch Eva, Ferch Llewelyn ap Gruffydh, ap Gwenwynwin, ap Owen Cyfeiliac ap Gruffydh ap Madawc, ap

Meredith of Powis, ap Bleddyn, ap Cynfin, &c. to Beli Mawr.

Owen ap Meredith ap Tudor ap Gwerfill Ferch Eva, Ferch Margret, Ferch Meredith gôch, ap Meredith, ap Iers Fychan, ap Iers gôch, ap Meredith ap Bleddyn, ap Cynfin, &c. to Beli.

Owen ap Meredith ap Tudor, ap Gwerfyll, Ferch Eva, Ferch Margret, Ferch Meredith gôch, ap Chriftin, ap Bledrws, ap Edwal Owen Bendew one of the fifteen tribes of North Wales, fon to Cynan Fieniard ap Gwalthfoed, ap Gwlyddien, ap Gwridor, ap Caradawc, ap Lles Llaw ddeawc, ap Edwal, ap Gwnnan, ap Gwannawc Farf fvch, ap Ceidio, ap Corf, ap Cadnawc, ap Tegonwy, ap Teon, ap Gwinan dau Freuddwyd, &c. and fo to Beli.

Owen ap Meredith, ap Marget Ferch Tomas, ap Lhewelin, ap Owen ap Meredith Lord Ifcoed, ap Owen, ap Gruffydh, ap Rhys prince of South Wales, fo to Rodri Mawr.

Owen ap Meredith, ap Margret, Ferch Tomas ap Llewelyn, ap Angharad, Ferch Arglwydd Sion, John of Haffon by William ap David ap Gruffydh. Dubium.

Owen ap Meredith, ap Margret, Ferch Tomas ap Llewelyn, ap Angharad Ferch Margret, Ferch Philip, ap Ifor Lord Ifcoed by William ap Gruffydh. Dubium.

Owen ap Meredith, ap Margret, Ferch Tomas ap Llewelyn, ap Angharad, Ferch Margret, Ferch Angharad, Ferch Llewelyn ap Iers drwyndwn prince of all Wales. This Llewelyn wedded Inet daughter of King John, who was fon to Henry the Second, fon to Mawd the emprefs, daughter to Henry the Firft, fon to William the Conqueror, fon to Robert duke of Normandy.

Owen ap Meredith, ap Margret, Ferch Tomas ap Elinor Ferch. . . . . Lord Barre by Gyttin Owen, by information of Dr. Owen Pool, and Mr. Lingam's wife by an old pedigree.

Owen

;Owen ap Meredith, ap Margret, Ferch Tomas, ap Elinor, Ferch Elinor, Ferch Edward Longſhanks king of England.

Owen ap Meredith, ap Margret, Ferch Tomas ap Elinor Ferch Elinor, Ferch Elinor ſecond to King Edward abovefaid. Dubium.

Owen ap Meredith, ap Margret, Ferch Elinor Ferch Meredith, ap Owen, ap Gruffydh, ap Rhys prince of South Wales, by Madawc ap Llewelyn ap Howel his books.

Owen ap Meredith, ap Margret, Ferch Elinor, Ferch Catrin, Ferch Llewelyn ap Gruffydh laſt prince of Wales.

Owen ap Meredith, ap Margret, Ferch Elinor, Ferch Llewelyn ap Gruffydh, ap Tangwiſtl, Ferch Llywarch gôch, ap Lhowarch ap Pyll, ap Cynan, ap Einion ap Gwridor gôch, ap Helic, ap Glannawc, ap Gwgon Gleddyfrudd, ap Cariadawc Freichfas, ap Llir Merini, ap Einion irth, ap Cunedda wledic.

Owen ap Meredith, ap Margret, Ferch Elinor, Ferch Caterin, Ferch Elinor ap Gruffydh ap Tangwiſtl, Ferch Tangwiſtl, Ferch Llowarch, ap Bran, ap Dinawal, ap Efnydd, ap Alawe, Alſer, ap Tudwal, ap Rodri mawr: ap Gyttin Owen.

Gwen ap Meredith, ap Margret, Ferch Elinor Fychan. Ferch Simon Montford earl of Leiceſter: by Gyttin Owen.

Owen ap Meredith, ap Margret, Ferch Elinor, Ferch Caterin, Ferch Elinor Fychan, Ferch Elenor, Ferch John king of England.

Hereafter followeth the ancient lineage of the ſaid Owen's mother Margaret wife to Meredith ap Tudor.

Owen ap Margret, Ferch Dafydd Fychan, ap Dafydd Llwyd, ap Cyner, ap Gronw, ap Cyner, ap Iers, ap Hwfa, ap Cwmus, ap Cillin, ap Maeloc dda, ap Gredel, ap Kwmus du, ap Cillin Ynad, ap Predur

Teirnée, ap Meilir Eryr, gwyr gorfedd, ap Tiday, ap Tyfodde, ap Gwybfyw, ap Marchwin, ap Branap Pill, ap Cerfyr, ap Meilir Meilirion, ap Goron, ap Cunedda wledic, ap Gwawl Ferch Coel Godeboc as before.

Owen ap Margret, Ferch Dafydd Fychan, ap Dafydd Llwyd, ap Ceyner, ap Gronw, ap Cyner, ap Iers, ap Hwfa, ap Generis Ferch Ednowain, Bendew, ap Cynon Finiaid, ap Gwarthfoed, ap Gwridr ap Cradoc, ap Lles llaw ddeuawc, ap Edwal, ap Gwynnan; and fo to Ludd, ap Beli mawr, as before by Gyttin Owen.

Owen ap Margret, Ferch Dafydd Fychan, ap Dafydd Lhwyd ap Cyner, ap Llayfedd daughter to Sir William Twychet, knight, by William. Indub.

Owen ap Margret, Ferch Dafydd Fychan, ap Dafydd Lhwyd, ap Alis, Ferch Robert, ap Turftan Holland captain of Harlech: by William.

Owen ap Margret, Ferch Dafydd Fychan, ap Dafydd Lhwyd, ap Alis, Ferch Margret, Ferch Alan Norris, knight, by William. Indub.

Owen ap Margret, Ferch Dafydd Fychan, ap Angharad, Ferch Howell ap Meredith, ap Iers, ap Cadwgan, ap Llywarch, ap Bran, as before, &c.

Owen ap Margaret, Ferch Dafydd Fychan, ap Angharad Ferch Howell ap Meredith, ap Iers, ap Gwenllian, Ferch Cynan ap Owen Gwynedd, ap Gruffydh ap Cynan, &c.

Owen ap Margret, Ferch Dafydd Fychan, ap Angharad, Ferch Owen ap Bleddin, ap Owen Brogennwn, ap Madawc, ap Meredith, ap Bleddin, ap Cynfin prince of Powis; thefe three by Gyttin Owen.

Owen ap Margret, Ferch Dafydd Fychan, ap Angharad, Ferch Gwladis, Ferch Llewelin gethni, ap Edwal, ap Gruffydh, ap Meuric, ap Cadhayarn, ap Gwrydd, ap Rhys goch one of the fifteen tribes of North Wales; which was fon to Sandwr ap Iarddwr, ap Mor, ap Tegerin, ap Aelaw, ap Gredres, ap Cwmus du, ap Cillin Ynad, &c. to Coel Godeboc.

Owen ap Margret, Ferch Dafydd Fychan, ap Angharad, Ferch Gwladus, Ferch Mall Llwyd, Ferch
Iers

Iers ap Engion, ap Geraint, ap Tegwared, ap Cyn-
fawr, ap Madawc diffaeth, which were rulers and great
men in Pentraeth.

Owen ap Margret, Ferch Neft, Ferch Jermy, ap
Gruffjdh, ap Howell, ap Meredith, ap Engion, ap
Gwgon, ap Merwvdd, ap Golwyn, one of the fifteen
tribes of North Wales, fon to Tangno, ap Cadfael,
ap Lludd, ap Llen, ap Llaminod Angel, ap Pafgen,
ap Urien Rheged, ap Meirchion, ap Grwft, ap Cen-
naf, ap Coel Godeboc king as before,

Owen ap Margret, Ferch Neft, Ferch Jermy, ap
Gweifill, Ferch Gwladus, Ferch Edwal Fychan as
before.

Owen ap Margret, Ferch Neft, Ferch Angharad,
Ferch Gruffydh, ap Dafydd goch, ap Gruffydh, ap
Llewelyn prince of Wales.

Owen ap Margret Ferch Neft, Ferch Angharad,
Ferch Gruffydh ap Dafydd goch, ap Dafydd, ap Gruffydh, ap Tangwiftl, Ferch Llowarch goch, ap Llowarch Holbwrch, ap Pill, ap Cynan, ap Gwridor
goch, ap Helic, ap Glannoc as before.

Owen ap Margret Ferch Neft, Ferch Angharad,
Ferch Gruffydh, ap Dafydd goch, ap Rhanullt, Ferch
Rheinalt king of Man.

Owen ap Margret Ferch Neft, Ferch Angharad,
Ferch Gruffydh, ap Angharad, Ferch Heylyn, ap Tudor, ap Ednyfed Fychan.

Owen ap Margret Ferch Neft, Ferch Angharad,
Ferch Gruffydh, ap Angharad, Ferch Heylyn, ap Ad-
leir, Ferch Ricart, ap Cadwalader, ap Gruffydh, ap
Cynan prince. Thefe four by Gyttin Owen.

Owen ap Margret Ferch Neft, Ferch Angharad,
Ferch Gruffydh, ap Angharad, Ferch Heylyn, ap
Adleis, Ferch Ricart, ap Cadwalader, ap Gruffydh, ap
Cynan, ap Afandrec wife to Iago, daughter to Gwayr,
ap Pill, ap Cynan, ap Cynddelw gam, ap Elgudi,
ap Grwyfnad, ap Diwgludd, ap Tegawc, ap Cyfnerth, ap Madoc Madogion, ap Sauddl bryd An-
rrf, ap Llylwarch hên, ap Elidor Ludanwin, ap Me-

irchon

irchion gûl, ap Erwſt galedlwm, ap Cenaw, ap Cola Godeboc king as before.

Owen ap Margret Ferch Neſt, Ferch Angharad, Ferch Marret, Ferch Tudor, ap Iers, ap Ewrgwnon, ap Cyfnerth, ap Rhuon, ap Nefydd hardd, one of the fifteen tribes of North Wales.

Owen ap Margret Ferch Neſt, Ferch Angharad, Ferch Margret, Ferch Tangwiſtl, Ferch Madawc, ap Cyfnerth, ap Cyhelyn, ap Llywarch Fychan, ap Lly-warch gôch, ap Llowarch Holbwrch, ap Pill, ap Cynon, ap Gwrydr gôch, ap Helic ap Glannoc, ap Gwgon gleddyfrud, ap Cariadoc freich frâs, ap Glir Meirini, ap Engion yrth, ap Cynedda wledic, by Gyttin Owen.

Abſtracted out of the old Chronicles of Wales, by Sir John Leiaſ, prieſt, Gut-tin Owen, Gruffydh ap Llewelyn ap Jermy, Fychan, Madawc ap Llewelyn ap Howell, Robert ap Howel ap Tho-mas, John King, with many others, at the King's Majeſty's coſts and charges. The abbot of Llanegweſtle, and Dr. Owen Pool, canon of Harſ, overſeers.

APPENDIX.

Rex omnibus, &c.

SCIATIS quod cum Lewelinus princeps de A-
berfíraw & dominus Snawerden, nobis conceíferit &
firmiter promiferit, quod ftabit provifioni venerabilium
patrum Redulphi Ciceftrenfis epifcopi & cancellarii
noftri, & Alexandri Conventrenfis & Lichfield epifcopi, & dilectorum & fidelium noftrorum Richardi
Marefchalli comitis Pembroch, Joannis de Lafcy comitis Lincolniæ & conftabularri Ceftriæ, Stephani de
Segrave Jufticiarii noftri Angliæ, & Radulphi filii Nicholai Senefchalli noftri, una cum Idnevet Senefchallo
ipfius Lewelini & Werrenoc fratre ejus, Infano Vachan
& David Clerico, quam ipfi facturi funt fuper congruis
emendis nobis faciendis, de omnibus exceffibus nobis
& noftris, ab eo & fuis factis & de reftitutione nobis
& hominibus noftris faciendâ de omnibus terris &
poffeffionibus noftris & noftrorum per ipfum Lewelli-
num & Wallenfes occupatis, occafione Werræ inter
nos & ipfum motæ; fimul etiam de recipienda reftitutione a nobis & noftris, de omnibus terris ipfius Lewelini & hominum fuerum per nos & noftros occupatis, occafione Werræ prædictæ, & de affignando David filio ipfius Lewelini & Ifabellæ uxori ejus primo-
genitæ filiæ & hæreredis. Gullielmi de Breus, rationa-
bili portione ipfam Ifabellam contingente, de terris quæ
fuerunt prædicti Gullielmi partis fui, & de refufione
pecuniæ nobis, faciendâ, pro prædictis exceffibus con-

grue emendandis & portione prædicta affignanda; pro-
visa tamen fuper hoc ab eisdem fufficiente fecuritate de
fideli feruitio nobis præftando & de tranquilitate nobis
& regno noftro Angliæ, obfervanda.　Ita quod damp-
num vel periculum, nec nobis nec regno noftro inde
poffit evenire.　Et fi pendente provifione prædicta,
aliquid de novo emerferit emandandum, idem Lewelinus voluerit & conceffirit, quod per prædictos pro-
vifores emendetur.　Nos provifionem eorundem quam
facturi funt fuper omnibus præmiffis, gratam habemus & acceptam pro nobis, & noftris ficut præfatus
Lewelinus pro fe & fuis & in hujus rei reftimonium
has literas patentes inde fieri fecimus.　Tefte me ipfo
apud Salop feptimo die Decembris & decimo feptimo
anno regni noftri.

Rex, &c.

LEWELINO principi de Aberfraw falutem.
Sciatis quod recipimus in gratiam noftram, Gilbertum
Marefchallum & omnes qui fuerunt impriffi Richardi
Marefchalli tam de Anglia quam de Wallia qui ad pacem noftram venire voluerunt & eis reddidimus omnes
terras & tenementa fua quæ de nobis tenuerunt, & de
quibus diffeffiti fuerunt occafione guerræ motæ inter
nos & prædictum comitem, & nobis remanent quieta
quæcunque fuper nos & noftros per prædictum comitem, vel fuos impriffios occupata fuerunt quæ vobis
duximus fignificanda.　Volentes quod vobis innotef-
cant quæ penes nos acta funt in hac parte, & quia per
venerabilem patrem Edmundum Cantuarienfem archiepifcopum & co-epifcopos fuos captæ funt treugæ
inter nos & vos fub firma fpe tractandi de pace inter nos
& vos formanda & fortius firmanda.　Mittimus propter
hoc prædictum archiepifcopum & venerabiles patres
Alexandrum Coventrenfem & Lichfieldenfem & Henricum Roffenfem co-epifcopos fuos ad partes marchiæ;
ita quod erunt apud Salop die Lunæ in craftino fanctæ
trinitatis;

trinitatis: et rogamus vos quatenus ficut noſtram deſideratis amicitiam non omittatis quin in craſtino die Martis loco tuto & competenti, quem prædictus archiepifcopus vobis ſignificabit ipſi archiepiſcopo & coepiſcopus ſuis occuratis ad tractatum cum eis habendum ſuper præmiſſis. In quorum etiam ore quædam quæ non duximus ſcripto commendanda poſuimus vobis plenius exponenda; rogantes quatinus ſicut decet taliter ea quæ reformationem pacis reſpiciunt & quæ ipſi plenius in hac parte vobis explicabunt audire cum effectu & eiſdem adquieſcere velitis, quod non ſtet per vos quin firmum & ſtabile pacis vinculum inter nos & vos roboretur ad noſtrum pariter & veſtrum commodum & honorem.

Rex, &c.

DILECTO & fideli ſuo Richardo comiti Cornubiæ & Pictaviæ ſalutem. Sciatis quod treugæ captæ ſunt inter nos & Lewelinum principem de Aberfraw per venerabilem patrem Edmundum archiepiſcopum Cantuarienſem & epiſcopos ſecum adjunctos & quoſdam alios fideles noſtros propter hoc ad partes Walliæ deſtinatos duraturæ a feſto Sancti Jacobi anno regni noſtri decimo octavo uſque in duos annos ſequentes in hac forma. Quod omnes injuriæ & damnæ hinc inde facta infra ultimam treugam captam per venerabilem patrem Henricum Roffenſem epiſcopum in media quadregiſſima proximo præterita per dictatores ejuſdem treugæ emendabuntur, quod omnes terræ hinc inde occupatæ per ultimam guerram motam, reſtituentur his quibus poſtea ſint oblatæ, homines etiam illi qui hinc inde receſſerint a fidelitate dominorum ſuorum & ſe tenuerunt ex parte adverſa libere revertantur. Ita quidem quod durantibus treugis prædictis in nullo occaſionabuntur nec aliquid dampni vel mali eis fiet occaſione prædicta. Adjectum eſt etiam in eadem proviſione treugarum; quod ſi vos & dilectus & fidelis

noſter

noster Radulphus de Thorny nolueritis sub eisdem
treugis comprehendi bene placebit eidem Lewelino.
Sin autem nihilominus, quod ad nos & alios fideles
nostros eas firmiter observabit.   Et sub tali conditione
quod si forte tenere non velletis contra vos se defendet.
Ita quod contra ipsum & defensionem suam nullum
vobis faciemus nec facere poterimus per nos vel per
aliquem de marchia vel alium interim consilium vel
auxilium ad ipsum gravandum, & taliter sunt treugæ
prædictæ ex parte ipsius Lewelini juratæ & assecuratæ
& in adventu prædicti archiepiscopi ad nos similiter ex
parte nostra eas jurari faciemus & assecurari, & ideo
vobis mandamus firmiter injungentes, quatinus prædictis treugis sine difficultate aliquâ adguiescentes eas
teneatis & ex parte vestra eas teneri faciatis.   Quia
modis omnibus volumus quod eas teneatis & firmiter
observetis.   Quid autem inde facere proposueritis aperte responsum vestrum nobis sub festinatione scire faciatis.   Teste rege apud Westmonasterium tricesimo die
Junii.

   Radolphus Herefordensis episcopus, decanus Here-
fordiæ, Walterus de Clifford & Walterus de Bello
Campo iterum constituti sunt dictatores emendarum,
faciendarum & recipiendarum de interceptionibus factis, ut dicitur Lewelino principi de Aberfraw, &c. et
Morganô de Carleon quoad castrum Carleon & eisdem
dictatoribus associati sunt prior de Wenloc & Joannes
extraneus & debent convenire in crastino clausi Paschæ
apud vadum de Montgomery ad consequendum quod
priore die ad hoc constituto debuisset fuisse executum.
Teste rege apud Northamton sexto die Martii.

REX

REX omnibus ad quod præfentes literæ perve-
nerint. Sciatis quod conceffimus bona fide & fine
malo ingenio & ratas habemus et gratas treugas captas
apud Theokfburiam die Veneris in fefto Sancti Bene-
dicti, anno regni noftri vicefimo per venerabilem patrem Edmundum Cantuarienfem archiepifcopum inter
nos et omnes homines et imprifios noftros apertos ex
una parte, et Lewelinum principem de Aberfraw et
dominum de Snaudan et omnes homines et imprifios
fuos apertos tam Wallenfes quam alios ex alia parte
duraturos a fefto Sancti Jacobi, anno eodem ufque in
unum annum completum. Ita fcilicet quod tam nos
et noftri quam prædictus Lewelinus et fui fimus in
eifdem terris et tenementis, hominibus et homagiis in
quibus fuimus prædicto die captionis treugarum ifta-
rum. Salva Morgano de Carleon reftitutione fua tam
de terris quam de bonis et mobilibus fuis quæ comes
Gilbertus Marefchallus occuparerat, fuper eum infra
treugas alias inter nos et ipfum Lewelinum ultimo captas. Siquid autem interim fuerit foris factum per captionem terrarum vel caftrorum vel bonorum mobilium
et manifeftum de captione terrarum vel caftrorum illorum terræ; et caftra ftatim reddantur non expectata
aliqua correctione emendatorum treugæ, fed de bonis
mobilibus ita captis per ipfos correctores fiant emendæ,
treugis nihilominus durantibus in fuâ firmitate in forma prædicta. Ita quod hinc inde nulla namia capi-
antur pro aliqua interceptione facta infra treugas iftas
de bonis mobilibus, nec pro aliqua contentione ante
captionem hujus treugæ orta, fed per ipfos correctores
fiant. Nullus etiam receptet in poteftate fuâ imprifios alterius inde emendæ ficut prædictum eft durantibus treugis. Nullum etiam caftrum novum firme-
tur in marchia vel dirutum reficiatur durantibus treugis, et terræ fint communes fecundum formam treugarum quæ ultimo captæ fuerunt inter nos et ipfum

L .ntii. lni

Lewelinum. Juraverunt autem in animam noftram ex
parte noftra in hanc treugam bona fide, et fine malo
ingenio fideliter obfervandam ufque ad prædictum terminum dilicti et fideles noftri Henricus de Aldithely.
Joannes Leftrange et Henricus de Stafford, in cujus.
&c. Tefte me ipfo apud Theokefburiam, undecimo
die Julii, anno regni noftri vicefimo.

Sciant præfentes et futuri, quod ita convenit inter
dominum Henricum regem Angliæ illuftrem ex una
parte, et David filium Lewelini quondam principis
Norwalliæ et dominum de Aberfraw ex altera, apud
Glouceftriam die Martis proximo ante feftum Sancti
Dunftanni, anno regni ipfius regis vicefimo quarto, de
homagio ipfius David quod ipfe offerrebat eidem domino regi pro jure fuo Norwalliæ et de terris quas barones ipfius domini regis fcilicet Griffinus filius Wen-
nuwan et alii barones domini regis petebant verfus ipfum David ut jura fua excepta de monte alto fecundum
quod continetur in fcripto nuper confecto apud crucem Griffini per Senefchallos domini regis, quæ ad
præfens excipitur ab arbitrio, falvo tamen in pofterum
jure fenefchalli Ceftriæ in terra illa fi quod habent.
Scilicet, quod prædictus dominus rex cepit homagium præfati David de prædicto jure fuo Norwalliæ, et
quod tam idem dominus rex pro præfatis baronibus
fuis de confcenfu eorundem quam præfatus David pro
fe et fuis et hæredibus eorum fuper omnibus terris
prædictis fe fubmiferunt, arbitrio venerabilium patrum
Ottonis Sancti Nicolai in carcere Tulliano diaconi, cardinalis apoftolici fedis legati ; Wigorniæ et Noriveci
epifcoporum, et nobilis viri Richardi comitis Pictaviæ
et Cornubiæ, fratris ipfius domini regis et Joannis de
Monemue ex parte ipfius domini regis, et venerabilis
patris epifcopi de Sancto Afaph Idnevet Vaghan, Eyn-
guan Vaghan ex parte præfati David. Ita quod quomodo libet ab ipfis omnibus vel à majori parte eorundem,fuper præmiffiis fuerit arbitratum, utraque pars ipforum ftabit arbitrio et illud in perpetuum firmiter obfervabit ; et ad hæc fideliter fine fraude fervanda Gu-
l. 'mus

lielmus de Cantelupo de præcepto regis juravit in animam ipsius regis et idem David in propria persona sua
corporate præstitit sacramentum. Et insuper se submiserunt jurisdictioni et inordinationi præfati domini
legati quamdiu in Anglia legationis fungatur officio,
ut partem contra præmissa venientem per censuram ec-
clesiasticam modis omnibus quibus melius viderit expedire, tam ad prædictum arbitrium observandum quam
ad transgressionem contra illud perpetratam emendan-
dam valeat coercere, ordine juris observato. Dum tamen idem David vel sui, si forsitan contra prædicta venire presumpserint prius coram dicto domino legato
vel aliquibus aliis ad hoc ab ipso deputandis et partibus merito non suspectis in confinio marchiæ loco eidem David et suis tuto legitime communicantur, si ad
hoc vocati venirent : vel si legitimè vocati non venerint pro contumacibus habeantur nisi rationabile et suf-
ficiens habeant impedimentum, finito vero prædictæ
legationis officio sub forma prescripta et cohercioni et
jurisdictioni domini Cantuariensi archiepiscopi et suc-
cessorum suorum et ecclesiæ Cantuariensis se partes
prædictæ submiserunt. Et sciendum quod per hanc
pacem remanent domino regi et hæredibus suis omnia
homagia baronum Walliæ quieta, et remittuntur omnia
incendia, homicidia, et alia mala tam ex parte Anglicorum quam Wallensium perpetrata; ita quod ad in-
vicem plene reconcilientur. Salvo præfati David jure
suo, si quod habet in aliis terris. Et si forte aliquis
prædictorum arbitrorum ante hoc arbitrium completum
in fata decesserit, vel per impedimentum rationabile
prædicto arbitrio faciendo non possit interesse: alius
loco suo substituetur qui neutri partium merito suspec-
tus habeatur: ad hoc præfati episcopus de Sancto A-
saph Idnevet et Ignan et Griffinus filius Rotherich
præstiterunt sacramentum, quod quantum in eis est,
prædicta fideliter observabunt et ab ipso David et suis
modis omnibus quibus poterunt, facient observari: ad
majorem autem hujus rei securitatem factum est hoc
scriptum inter ipsos regem et David in modo chirogra-
phi. Ita quod parti remanenti penes ipsum dominum
regem a.. .... ipsius .... cum .. ...
. ...

prædictorum epiſcopi de Sancto Aſapho Idnevet, Ignan et Griffini, et parti penes ipſum David remanenti
appoſitum eſt ſigilum domini regis: his teſtibus ve-
nerabilibus patribus Ottone Sancti Nicolai in carcere
Tulliano diacono, cardinali apoſtolicæ ſedis legato;
Waltero Eboracenſi archiepiſcopo, Waltero Careleo-
lenſi, Waltero Wygornenſi et Gulielmo Norwicenſi
epiſcopis; Richardo comite Pictaviæ et Cornubiæ fratre domini regis, venerabili patre epiſcopo de Sancto
Antando; ſeneſchallis noſtris Joanne extraneo. Ede-
nyfet Watham, Griffino filio Rotherich, David archi-
diacon de Sancto Aſaph et aliis.

Rex, &c.

David filio Lewelini ſalutem. Bene recoli-
mus qualiter nos vobis nuper in mandatis dedimus,
quod coram nobis apud Wigorniam compareretis ad
providendum arbitros qui loco eorum qui primo ad
hoc electi fuerint et qui ad partes receſſerunt tranſmarinas, juſtitiam ſecundum formam pacis inter et vos
proviſe ſingulis conquerentibus exhiberent; et in arbitrio prædicto ſecundum formam debitam procederent
et ſimiliter ad juſtitiam recipiendam de portione uxorem veſtram contingente de hæreditate ſuâ: et ſimili-
tar ad ſtandum recto ſuper his de quibus ſeneſchallus
de monte alto et aliis de vobis ſunt conqueſti. Et
quia ad diem et locum vobis præfixos non acceſſiſtis,
ſed literas veſtras nobis miſiſtis; continentes quod tres
ex veſtris ad nos loco veſtro deſtinaſtis, ex quibus tantum unus ad nos acceſſit qui ad præmiſſa adimplenda
nullam poteſtatem habuit; unde quibuſdam ex noſtris
viſum fuerat quod hoc malitioſe et ut ſubterfugium
quæreretis per vos factum fuit. Nos tamen hoc non
credentes ſed fidelitatem veſtram adhuc magis probare
volentes, vobis mandamus in fide qua nobis tenemini,
præcipiendo quatinus omni occaſione poſtpoſita perſo-

3　　　　　　　　　　　naliter

naliter compareatis apud Salop, die dominica ante domi-
nicam palmarum coram fidelibus noſtris quos iiluc dux-
erimus tranſmittendos ad conſentiendum in perſonas
certas, ad procedendum in arbitrio prædicto loco eorum qui ad partes tranſmarinas receſſerunt et ad faciendum in eodem arbitrio id quod adhuc reſtat faciendum ; et ad recipiendum juſtitiam de portione uxorem
veſtram de hæreditate ſua contingente et ad ſtandum
recto ſeneſchallo Ceſtriæ et aliis de vobis conquerentibus, Quod ſi perſonaliter ad hoc faciendum venire
non poſſitis tales loco veſtro mittatis qui plenam poteſtatem habeant hæc omnia nomine veſtro faciendi.
Nos enim vobis et veſtris per eos quos ibidem mittimus aut per noſmet ipſos ſalvum et ſecurum provideri
faciemus conductum. Teſte rege apud Wudeſtock
decimo nono die Februarii.

Anno domini milleſimo ducenteſimo quadrageſimo
primo, die dominica proxima ante inventionem ſanctæ
crucis aſſignata, David filio Lewelini quondam principis Norwalliæ et marchionibus ad conſentiendum in
arbitros ſuſtituendos loco abſentium et ad faciendam et
recipiendam juſtitiam ſecundum formam pacis conven-
tæ inter dominum regem et dictum David comparuit
Thudius ſeneſchallus ipſius David, cancellarius et
Phillippus filius Ibor clericus ex parte David procuratores ; oſtendentes literas ipſius David, in quibus
dictus David promittebat ſe ratum habiturum quicquid per ipſos fieret ſecundum formam pacis ſupra-
dictæ. Radulphus vero de mortuo mari et Rogerus
ſeneſchallus Ceſtriæ et Griffinus pro ſe et aliis marchionibus comparuerunt ; petentes inſtanter quod ſecundum dicta teſtium productorum coram domino Ste-
phano de Segrave, et conjudicibus ſuis vicem domini
regis gerentibus apud Salop eiſdem exhiberetur juſtitiæ
complementum. Sed contra procuratores præfati David aſſerebant dictos reſtes non eſſe receptos ſecundum
formam pacis. Quare ſecundum dicta eorum non dicebat nec poterat judicari. Tandam continuata die et
altercatione magna ſuper hoc et aliis habitata inter

partes,

partes, forma pacis prædictæ producta in medio visa-
que et perfecta loco absentium arbitrorum scilicet domini Ottonis Sancti Nicholai in carcere Tulliano diaconi cardinalis, domini Papæ quondam legati in Anglia Wigornensis et Norwicensis episcoporum subrogati
sunt per dominum regem de consensu dictorum procu-
ratorum episcopus Coventrensis, Joannes filius Galfridi
et Herebertus filius Matthæi, et Walterus de Clifford :
quibus data est eadem potestas quam haberent absentes
si præsentes essent secundum formam pacis prædictæ
et assignata est dies partibus à die Pentecostes proximo
in unum mensem apud pontem de Maneford ultra Salop ad probanda hinc inde sive per productos testes ;
non obstante productione jam facta per alios et quoli-
bet probationis genere sive per instrumenta, sive alio
modo quæ voluerunt et sibi noverint expedienda ; et
illa die dabitur alia ad judicium audiendum secundum
probata coram eisdem arbitris juxta formam pacis su-
perius prælibatæ.

Rex, &c.

DAVID filio Lewelini quondam principis Norwalliæ salutem. Ex certâ quorundam relatione didi-
cimus quod vos contra juramentum nobis præstitum
quosdam fratres Griffini filii Madoc et etiam quosdam
homines nostros de Keri, qui homagia nobis fecerunt
vobis confœderatis et ab obsequio et fidelitate nostra
subtraxistis et fratres prædicti Griffini contra nos in
terra vestra receptatis. Tres quidem seneschallis
vestris in succurium eorum qui expugnant dilectum et
fidelem nostrum Radulphum de mortuo mari destinas-
tis cædes et incendia per vos et vestros in terra sua et
terris aliorum fidelium committendo, terras etiam quæ
in curia nostra abjudicatæ fuerunt Oweno Vaghan et
nepotibus suis, eis contra justitiam deforciatis, non per-
mi........ q..d ex...tio fi.t de i.s que in curia nostra

ſtra ſunt conſiderata. Quandam etiam navem Ceſtriæ
quæ in poteſtate veſtra applicuit cartata blado et aliis
victualibus areſtari feciſtis per vos et gentem veſtram,
in .nullo his quorum bladum et victualia fuerint inde
ſatisfacientes ſuper quibus non modicum admiramur et
movemur; et multo fortius quod cum nuper miſiſſe-
mus nuntios veſtros ſolempnes uſque Salop, utpote venerabilem patrem Henricum Coventrenſem et Lich-
fieldenſem epiſcopum, et dilectos et fideles noſtros Joannem filium Galfridi, et Henricum de Aditheleg pa-
ratos ad emendas faciendas et recipiendas de interceptionibus factis, tam ex parte noſtra, quam ex parte
veſtra, vos tanquam in contemptum noſtrum prædictis fidelibus noſtris non occurriſtis, nec per aliquos de
veſtris in eorum occurſum mittere curâſtis, quod quidem ægre nos movet cum tot et tantas injurias quas
longum eſſet enumerare contra nos et noſtros nullo
modo attemptare debuiſtis: et ideo vobis mandamus
quod prædictos fideles noſtros tam fratres prædicti
Griffini quam homines noſtros de Keri quos a fidelitate
noſtra ſubtruxiſtis ad fidem noſtram redire faciatis.
Non impedientes quin prædictus Owenus Vaghan et
nepotes ſui ſecundum abjudicatum eſt in curia noſtra
terris ſuis gaudere poſſint et eas pacificè poſſidere. Id
etiam quod contra dilectum et fidelem noſtrum Radul-
phnm de mortuo mari et alios fideles noſtros et etiam
quod de navi illa Ceſtrenſi attemptaſtis, ſic emendari
faciatis; quod nobis non relinquatur materia injurias
prædictas gravius ulciſcendi quod nollemus. Nec
omitatis quin citra feſtum Sancti Petri ad vincula nobis ſignificetis qualiter dampna et injurias prædictas,
quæ nullo modo diſſimulare poterimus nobis emendare
volueritis. Teſte rege apud Merlebergh, quarto decimo die Julii.

Sciant præſentes et futuri quod ita convenit inter
dominum Henricum regem Angliæ illuſtrem ex una
parte et ſenanam uxorem Griffini filii Lewelini quondam principis Norwalliæ, quem David frater ejus tenet carcèri mancipatum cum Owen filio ſuo nomine

A a

ejufdem Griffini ex altera; fcilicet quod praedicta Senana manucepit pro praedicto Griffino viro fuo quo dabit domino regi fexcentas marcas, ut rex eum et praedictum Owen filium fuum liberari faciat a carcere deti-
neri. Et ut rex poftea judicio Curiae fuae fecundum
legem Walenfem ei et haeredibus fuis habere faciat
fuper portione quae eum continget de haereditate quae
fuit praedicti Lewelini, patris fui et quam praedictus
David ipfi Griffino deforciavit. Ita fi quod idem
Griffinus vel haeredes fui per confiderationem curiae
domini regis reciperent portionem quam fe dicunt contingere de haereditate praedicta, eadem Senana manucepit
pro praedicto Griffino et haeredibus fuis quod ipfe et
haeredes fui imperpetuum inde reddent domino regi et
haeredibus fuis trecentas marcas annuas. Scilicet tertiam partem in denariis et tertiam partem in bobus
et vaccis, et tertiam partem in equis per aeftimati-
onem legalium hominum liberandas vicecomiti Salop, apud Salop, et per manum ipfius vicecomitis ad
faccarium regis deferendas et ibidem liberandas fcilicet unam medietatem ad feftum Sancti Michaelis et
aliam medietatem ad pafcham. Eadem etiam Senana
manucepit pro praedicto Griffino viro fuo et haeredibus
fuis quod firmam pacem tenebunt cum praefato David fuper portione quae eidem David remanebit de
haereditate praedicta; manucepit etiam Senana pro
praefato Griffino et haeredibus fuis, quod fi aliquis
Walenfis aliquo tempore regi vel haeredibus fuis re-
bellis extiterit, praefatus Griffinus et haeredes fui ad
cuftum fuum proprium ipfum compellent ad fatisfaci-
endum domino regi et haeredibus fuis. Et de his omnibus fupradictis obfervandis, dicta Senana dabit domino regi David et Rothery filios fuos obfides: Ita tamen
quod fi de praefato Griffino et Oweno filio fuo qui cum
eo eft in carcere humanitus contingat antequam inde
deliberentur; alter praedictorum filiorum eidem Senanae reddetur reliquo obfide remanente: juravit infuper
Senana tactis facro-fanctis evangeliis pro fe et praefato
Griffino et haeredibus fuis quod haec omnia firmiter
obfervabunt. Et manucepit quod praefatus Griffinus
idem

idem jurabit cum à carcere liberatus fuerit, et super
praemiffis fe fubmifit nomine dicti Griffini jurifdictioni
Herefordenfis et Conventrenfis epifcoporum. Ita quod
praefati epifcopi, vel alter eorum quem dominus rex
elegerit ad requifitionem ipfius regis per fententias excommunicationis in perfonas et interdicti in terras eorum coherceant ad omnia praedicta et fingula obfervanda. Haec omnia manucepit praedicta Senana et
bona fide promifit fe facturam et curaturam quod omnia impleantur, et quod praefatus Griffinus cum liberatus fuerit, et haeredes fui hac omnia grata habebunt et
complebunt et inftrumentum fuum inde dabunt domino regi in forma praedicta. Ad majorem fiquidem hujus
rei fecuritatem factum eft hoc fcriptum inter ipfum
dominum regem et praefatam Senanam nomine praefati
Griffini viri fui. Ita quod parti remanenti penes ipfum
dominum regem appofitum eft figillum praefati Griffini per manum praefatae Senanae uxoris fuae una cum
figillo ipfius Senanae; et parti remanenti penes ipfam
Senanam nomine praefati Griffini appofitum eft figillum ipfius domini regis: de fupradictis etiam omnibus
complendis et firmiter obfervandis dedit praedicta Senana nomine praefati Griffini domino regi plegios fub-
fcriptos, viz. Radulphum de Mortuo Mari, Walterum
de Clifford, Rogerum de Monte alto fenefcallum Ceftriae, Mailgun filium Mailgwn, Mereduc filium Roberti, Griffinum filium Maddoc de Baunfeld, Howel et
Mereduc fratres ejus, Griffinum filium Wennwen, qui
haec omnia pro praefata Senana manuceperunt, et cartas fuas ipfi domino regi inde fecerunt. Actum apud
Salop die Lunae proxima ante affumptionem beatae
Mariae anno ipfius regis vicefimo quinto.

OMNIBUS hoc fcriptum vifuris Rogerus de
Monte Alto fenefchallus Ceftriae falutem. Sciatis quod
ego me conftituti plegium Senanae uxoris Griffini filii
Leolini quondam principis Norwalliae, et manu cepi

pro

pro eâ ergâ dominum meum Henricum regem Angliae illuftrem, quod omnia quae conventionavit eidem domino meo nomine praefati viri fui a carcere in quo David frater ejus eos detinet et pro portione quae ipfum Griffinum contingit de haereditate quae fuit praedicti Leolini patris fuis et quam praefatus David frater ejus ei deforciat, domino regi firmiter obfervabit. In cujus rei teftimonium huic fcripto figillum meum appofui. Actum apud Salopefbury die Lunae ante affumptionem Beatae Mariae, anno regni ipfius vicefimo quinto.

Sub eadem forma fecerunt finguli plegii praefcripti.

Sciant praefentes et futuri quod ego Mereducus filius Howel, tactis facro-fanctis juravi quod ab ifto die in antea omnibus diebus vitae meae ero ad fidelitatem domini regis Angliae, et ferviam ei fideliter et devote cum omnibus viribus meis et toto poffe meo quandocunque indiguerit fervitio meo, et treugam inter dominum Radulphum de Mortuo Mari et me initam ufque ad feftum S. Michaelis anno regni regis Henrici vigefimo quinto ex parte mea fideliter obfervabo : et tam ad fidelitatem domino regi in perpetuum obfervandum quatu ad treugas praedictas obfervandas ufque ad terminum praedictum fuppofui me jurifdictioni domini Herefordenfis epifcopi, et domini Coventrenfis et Lichfieldenfis epifcopi, vel alterius eorum, quem dominus rex ad hoc elegerit, ut fi in aliquo contra praedictam fidelitatem domini regis, vel contra obfervantiam praedictarum treugarum venerit, liceat eis vel eorum alteri quem dominus rex ad hoc elegerit perfonam meam et omnes meos excommunicare et terram meam interdicere, donec de tranfgieffione ipfam fatisfecero ad plenum. Et fi forfitan infra praedictum feftum S. Michaeli inter praedictum Radulphum de Mortuo Mari et me nulla pax fuerit formata, licet poft feftum illud bellum moveant praedicto Radulpho, non obligabit me praedictum juramentum dum tamen erga dominum regem fidelitatem obfervam continuam, ficut

praedictum

praedictum eſt., Etſi bellum poſt praedictum termi-
.num inter nos moveatur, nihilominus dominus re-
fuſtinebit quod ego et mei receptemur in terra ſua ſicut alii fideles ſui. Ad praedicta autem obſervanda
domino regi et haeredibus ſuis obligo me per juramentum praedictum, et per ſigilli mei appoſitionem
quod huic ſcripto appoſui, ad majorem confirmationem praedictorum. Actum in craſtino aſſumptionis
Beatae Mariae, anno regni regis Henrici vigeſimo
quinto.

Sub eiſdem verbis fecerunt domino regi chartas ſuas,
   Owen filius Howell.   Mailgon filius Mailgun.
   Mereduc filius Mereduc. Howel filius Cadwach-
   lan, et Cadwachlan filius Howel.

OMNIBUS Chriſti fidelibus ad quos praeſentes
literae pervenerunt, David, filius Leolini, ſalutem.
Sciatis quod conceſſi domino meo Henrico regi Angliae illuſtri filio domino Joannis regis : quod delibe-
rabo Griffinum fratrem meum quem teneo incarcera-
tum una cum filio ſuo primogenito et aliis qui occaſione praedicti Griffini ſunt in parte mea incarcerati,
et ipſos eidem domino meo regi tradam. Et poſtea
ſtabo juri curiae ipſius domini regis tam ſuper eo, u-
trum idem Griffinus debeat teneri captus quam ſuper
portione terrae quae fuit praedicti Leolini patris mei,
ſi qua ipſum Griffinum contingere debeat, ſecundam
conſuetidinem Walenſium. Ita quod pax ſervetur
inter me et praedictum Griffinum fratrem meum quod
caveatur de ipſa tenenda ſecundum conſiderationem curiae ipſius domini regis, et quod tam ego quam praedictus Griffinus portiones noſtras que nos contingent
de praedictis terris tenebimus in capite de praedicto domino rege. Et quod reddam Rogero de Monte Alto
ſeneſchallo Ceſtriae terram ſuam de Monthaut cum
pertinentiis : et ſibi et aliis baronibus et fidelibus domini regis ſeiſinas terrarum ſuarum occupata... a tem

pore belli orti inter ipfum dominum Johannem reg m et
praedictum' Leolinum 'patrem meum, falvo jure pro-
prietatis cujuflibet pacti et inftrumenti fuper quo fta-
bitur juri hinc inde in curia ipfius domini regis: et
quod reddam ipfi domino regi omnes expenfas quas
ipfe et fui fecerunt occafione exercitus iftius. Et quod
fatisfaciam de damnis et injuriis illatis fibi et fuis fecundum confiderationem praedictae curiae vel malefactores ipfos, ipfi domino regi reddam omnia homagia quae dominus Johannes rex pater ejus habuit,
et quae dominus rex de jure habere debet ; et fpe-
cialiter omnium nobilium Wallenfium. Et quod idem
dominus rex non dimittit aliquem de fuis captivis
quin ipfi domino regi et fuis remaneant feifinae fuae.
Et quod terra de Engufmere cum pertinentiis fuis in
perpetuum remanebit domino regi, vel haeredibus fuis,
et quod de caetero non receptabo vilagas vel foris
banniatos ipfius domini regis, vel baronum fuorum de
marchia in terra mea, nec permittam receptari; et de
omnibus articulis fupradictis, et fingulis firmiter et in
perpetuum obfervandis, domino regi, et haeredibus
tuis, pro me et haeredibus meis cavebo per obfides et
pignora et aliis modis quibus dominus rex dicere voluit vel dictate. Et in his et in omnibus aliis ftabo voluntati, et mandatis ipfius domini regis et juri parebo
omnibus in curia fua. In cujus rei teftimonium,
praefenti fcripto figillum meum appendi. Actum apud
Atrieum juxta fluvium Elvey de S. Afapho in fefto
decollationis S. Johanni Baptiftae, anno praedicti domi-
regis Henrici vigefimo quinto.

Sciendum quod illi qui capti detinentur cum praedicto Griffino, eodem modo tradentur domino regi
donec per curiam fuam confideratum fuerit, utrum et
quomodo debeant deliberari. Et ad omnia firmiter
tenenda, ego David juravi fuper crucem fanctam
quam coram me feci deportari. Venerabilis etiam
pater Howelus epifcopus de S. Afaph ad petitionem
meam firmiter promifit in ordine fuo, quod haec omnia praedicta faciet, et procurabit modis quibus poterit, obfervari. Ednevet fiquidem Waugam per prae-
. ti um meum, illud dem juravit fuper crucem praedictam,

dictam. Actum ut supra. Præterea concessi pro me et hæredibus meis quod si ego, vel hæredes mei contra pacem domini regis, vel hæredium suorum, vel contra articulos prædictos, aliquid attentaverimus tota hæreditas nostra domino regi, et hæredibus suis incurratur. De quibus omnibus et singulis supposui me, et hæredes meos, jurisdictioni archiepiscopi Cantuariensis, et episcoporum Londinensis, Herefordensis, et Coventrensis, qui pro tempore præerunt, quod omnes, vel unus eorum quem dominus rex ad hoc elegerit, possit nos excommunicare, et terram nostram interdicere, si aliquid contra prædicta attentaverimus. Et procuravi quod episcopi de Bangor et de S. Asaph chartas suas domino regi fecerunt per quas concesserunt, quod omnes sententias tum excommunicationis quam interdicti à prædictis archiepiscopo, episcopis, vel aliquo eorum, ferendas, ad mandatum eorum exequentur.

Rex omnibus, &c.

DAVID filius Lewelini quondam principis Norwalliæ, Salutem. Noverint universitas vestræ me spontanea voluntate mea pepegisse domino meo Henrico Dei gratia Angliæ, quod ego et hæredes mei eidem domino regi, et hæredibus suis omnibus diebus vitæ nostræ constanter et fideliter serviemus, nec aliquo tempore contra eos erimus: quod si forte evenerit, quod à fideli servicio suo, vel hæredum suorum, quod absit, recesserimus, tota terra nostra erga ipsum dominum regem et hæredes suos incurratur, et in usus eorum perpetuis cedat temporibus. Hanc autem pactionem et concessionem sigilli mei appositione roboravi, et ad majorem hujus rei declarationem venerabiles patres Bangorensem, et de S. Asaph episcopi, ad petitionem meam præsenti scripto sigilla sua apposuerunt. Actum apud Rothetan tricesimo primo die Augusti.

ILLUSTRI viro domino Henrico Dei gratia regi Anglorum, &c. abbates Haberconwiæ, et de Kemere Ciftercienfis ordinis inquifitores dati a domino, Papâ, falutem in domino. Mandatum domini Papæ recipimus in hæc verba, 'Innocentius Epifcopus, fervus fervorum Dei, dilectis filiis abbatibus de Haberconwiæ, & de Kemere Ciftercienfis ordinis Bangorum diocefis falutem et apoftolicam benedictionem. Ex parte dilecti filii noftri nobilis viri David principis Norwalliæ fuit propofitum coram nobis, quod cum inter ipfum, quem parentes ejus in alumnum Romanæ ecclefiæ donaverunt, et chariffimum in Chrifto filium noftrum regem Anglorum illuftrem bellum longo tempore perduraffet, tandem poftquam fuit in venerabilem fratrem noftrum epifcopum de S. Afaph et collegas ipfius de ftando hinc inde eorum arbitrio fuper omnibus querelis juramento a partibus præftito concorditer bonis viris mediantibus conpromiffum. Idem rex, non attendens quod pendente illorum arbitrio, fibi fuper hoc aliquid attentare non licebit in prædictum principem ex infperato hoftiliter iruit ad præftandum, quod fuper prædictis de quibus conpromiffum fuerit & juratum, ac aliis ipfius regis, mandare per vim computit, & metum qui cadere poterat in conftantem.

Cum igitur ea quæ vi & metu fiant, carere debeant robore firmitatis, difcretioni veftræ per apoftolica fcripta mandamus, quatenus inquifita fuper hoc diligentius veritate, fi rem inveneritis ita effe, auctoritate noftra prædictum principem ab obfervatione fic extorti juramenti penitus abfolventes, fententia, fi qua occafione ejufmodi in ejus perfonam, vel terram ab aliquo forfan tota fuerit, juxta formam ecclefiæ fine difficultate qualibet, ficut juftum fuerit relaxetis. Teftes vero, &c. Datum Januæ feptimo calendas Augufti pontificatús noftri anno fecundo. Hujus igitur autoritate muniti vobis mandamus quatenus in vigilia S. Agnetis Virginis, apud Keyrus in ecclefia Guftefend coram vobis compareatis, fuper contentis in autentico dicto principi refponfuri, fi vobis videritis expedire.

Ifti

Ifti funt ARTICULI intimati Domino LEOLINO Principi WALLIÆ, et
populo ejufdem loci, ex parte Archi-
epifcopi fupra dicti.

PRIMO, Quod propter falutem eorum fpiritu-
alem, et temporalem ad partes iftas venimus, quas
femper dileximus, ut plures eorum noverunt.

Secundo, Quia venimus contra domini regis voluntatem, cui etiam adventus nofter dicitur plurimum
difplicere.

Tertiò, Quia rogamus eos et fupplicamus eis pro
fanguine Jefu Chrifti, quatenus venire velint ad uni-
tatem] cum gente Anglorum, et ad pacem domini
regis, quam eis intendimus, quanto melius poterimus
procurare.

Quarto, Volumus eos fcire quod in his partibus
domini non poterimus remanere.

Quinto, Volumus eos attendere quod poft receffum
noftrum non invenient aliquem, qui ita velit fua am-
plecti negotia promovenda, qui vellemus, fi placeret.
Altiffima vita noftra temporali corporum pacem ho-
neftam et ftabilem perpetuo procuraffe.

Sexto, Quia fi noftras preces fpreverint et labores,
ftatim intendimus eorum pertinaciam fcribere fummo
pontifici et curiae Romanae, propter peccata mor-
talia, quae multiplicantur occafione difcordiae omni die.

Septimo, Noverint quod nifi citius ad pacem venerint aggravabitur eis bellum, quod non poterunt fufti-
nere, quia crefcit regia potentia omni die.

Octavo, Noverint quod regnum Angliae eft fub
fpeciali protectione fedis apoftolicae, et quod Romana
curia plus inter regna caetera diligere confuevit.

Nono, Quod eadem curia nullo modo volet permittere ſtatum regni Angliae vacillare, quod ſibi ſpecialibus obſequiis eſt devotum.

Decimo, Amariſſimè plangimus hoc quod dicitur. Wallenſes crudeliores exiſtere Saracenis; quia cum Saraceni capiunt Chriſtianos, eos ſervant pecunia redimendos, quos Wallenſes captos dicuntur illico jugulare quaſi ſolo ſanguine delectentur; immo quod eſt deterius, quos promittunt redimi, tradunt accepta pecunia jugulandos.

Undecimo, Quod cum conſueverit deum et perſonas eccleſiaſticas revereri, a devotione hominum videntur multipliciter receſſiſſe, qui in tempore ſanctiſſimo in redemptoris injuriam moverunt ſeditionem, homicidia et incendia perpetrantes, in quo eos nullus poterit excuſare.

Duodecimo, Petimus ut tanquam veri Chriſtiani ad cor redeant pœnitentes, quia cœptam diſcordiam non poſſent continuare etiam ſi juraſſent.

Tertiodecimo, Petimus ut nobis ſignificent quibus modis velint et valeant turbationem pacis regiae, laeſionem reipublicae, te mala alia emendare.

Quartodecimo, Ut ſignificent nobis qualiter valeat ipſa concordia ſtabiliri, fruſtra enim pax firmari videbitur quae tam aſſidue violatur.

Quintodecimo, Ut ſi dicant leges ſuas vel fœdera ex pacto inito non ſervari, nobis ſignificent quae ſunt illa.

Sextodecimo, Noverint quod etiam poſito quod eis derogatum fuiſſet, quod neſcimus, nullo modo licebit eis quaſi eſſent judices in cauſa ſuà taliter majeſtatem regiam impugnare.

Septimodecimo, Quod niſi modo pax fiat proceditur contra eos forſitan ex decreto militiae, ſacerdoti, et populi convocati.

Reveren-

REverendiſſimo patri in Chriſto domino J. de gratia
cantuarienſi archiepiſcopo totius Angliæ primati, ſuus
humilis et devotus filius Leolinus princeps Walliæ,
dominus Snaudon, ſalutem et filialem dilectionem cum
omnimoda reverentia, ſubjectione et honore, ſanctæ
paternitati veſtræ pro labore vobis quaſi intolerabile
quem aſſumpſiſtis ad præſens pro dilectione quam erga
nos et noſtram nationem geritis, omni qua poſſumus
devotione regratiantes vobis aſſurgimus; et eo amplius
quod contra domini regis voluntatem veniſtis prout
nobis intimaſtis. Cæterum quod nos rogaſtis ut ad
pacem domini regis veniamus, ſcire debet veſtra
ſanctitas quod ad hoc prompti ſumus, dummodo idem
dominus rex pacem debitam et veram nobis et noſtris
velit obſervare. Ad hoc licet gauderemus de mora
veſtra facienda in Wallia, tamen per nos non eritis
impediti quin pax fiat, quantum in nobis eſt, quam
optamus per veſtram induſtriam magis quam alicujus
alterius roborari. Et ſperamus nec per Dei gratiam
erit opportunum propter noſtram pertinaciam aliquid
ſcribere domino Papæ. Nec veſtras paternas preces
ac graves labores ſpernemus, ſed eas amplectimur
omni cordis affectu ut tenemur. Nec erit opus quod
dominus rex aggravet contra nos manum, cum prompti
ſumus ſibi obedire juribus noſtris et legibus nobis ut
præmittatur reſervatis.

Et licet regnum Angliæ ſit Curiæ Romanæ ſpecia-
liter ſubjectum et dilectum, tamen cum dominus Papa,
necnon et Curia Romana audiverint quanta nobis
per Anglicos mala ſunt illata, videlicet quod pax prius
formata non fuit nobis ſervata nec pacta; deinde
devaſtationes, combuſtiones, et eccleſiaſticarum perſonarum interfectiones, ſacerdotum videlicet et in-
cluſorum, et aliarum religioſarum perſonarum paſſim
mulierum et infantium ſuggentium ubera et in utero
portantium, combuſtiones etiam hoſpitalium et aliarum
domorum religioſarum, homicidiorum in coemiteriis,
eccleſiis, et ſuper altaria, et aliorum ſacrilegiorum et
flagiciorum et aliorum ...

rum ficut expreffius in aliis rotulis confcripta vobis tranfmittimus infpicienda.

Speramus imprimis, quod veftra pia et fancta paternitas clementer nobis compatietur, nec non et curia fuper dicta, nec per nos regnum Angliæ vacillabit, dum, ut promiffum eft, pax debita nobis fiat et fervetur. Qui vero fanguinis effufione delectantur manifeftum eft factis. Nam Anglici hactenus nulli fexui vel ætati, feu languori, pepercerunt, nulla ecclefiæ vel loco facro detulerunt, qualia vel confimilia Wallenfes non facerunt. Super eo autem quod unus redemptus fuit interfectus, multum dolemus, nec occiforem manu tenemus, fed in fylvis uti latro vagatur. De eo vero quod inceperunt guerram aliqui in tempore indebito, illud ignoravimus ufque poft factum, et tamen ipfi afferunt quod nifi eo tempore hoc feciffent mortes et captiones eis imminebunt, nec audebunt in domibus refidere, nec nifi armati incedere, et fic præ timore tali tempore id fecerunt. De eis vero quæ fecimus contra dominum, ut veri chriftiani per Dei gratiam pœnitebimus, nec erit ex parte noftra quod bellum continuetur, dum fumus indemnes ut debemus. Ne tamen exhæredemur et paffim occidemur, oportet nos defendere ut valemus. Cum vero injuria et damna hinc inde confiderentur et ponderentur parati fumus emendare pro viribus quæ ex parte noftra funt commiffa, dum de prædictis injuriis et damnis nobis factis et aliis emenda nobis fiat. Et ad pacem firmandam et ftabiliendam fimiliter fumus prompti debitis modis.

Quando tamen regales chartæ et pacta inita nobis non fervatur, ficut nec hucufque funt obfervata, non poteft pax ftabiliri, nec quando novæ exactiones et inauditæ contra nos et noftros omni die adveniunt. Vobis autem tranfmittimus in rotulis damna nobis illata et fœdera non fervata fecundum formam pacis prius factam. Quod vero guerravimus quafi neceffitas nos cogebat; nam nos et omnes Wallenfes eramus adeo oppreffi et fuppeditati et fpoliati et in fervitutem redacti per regales Jufticianos et Ballivos contra fo . . . . iam amplius quam fi
                                         Saraceni

Saraceni effemus vel Judæi, ficut credimus et fæpe
denunciavimus domino regi, nec aliquam emendâm
habere potuimus. Sed femper mittebantur jufticiarii
et ballivi ferociores et crudeliores, et quando illi erant
faturati per fuas injuftas exactiones, alii de novo mittebantur and populum excoriandum in tantum quod
populus mallebat mori quam vivere. Nec oportet mi-
litiam ampliorem convocare, vel contra nos moveri
facerdotium dum nobis fiat pax et fervetur modis debitis ut fuperius eft expreffum. Nec debitis fancte pater
omnibus verbis credere noftrorum adverfariorum ; ficut
enim nos factis oppresferunt et opprimunt, ita et vobis
diffamant, nobis imponentes quæ volunt.

Ipfi enim vobis funt præfentes et nos abfentes, ipfi
oprimentes et nos oppreffi. Et ideò propter Deum
fidem eis in omnibus non exhibeatis; fed facta potius
examinetis. Valeat fanctitas veftre ad regimen ecclefiæ
per tempora longa.

Primus Articulus eft talis, cum in forma pacis fic
contineatur ut fequitur. Si vero idem Leolinus jus
vendicaverit in aliquibus terris quas alii præter dictum dominum regem occupaverint extra quatuor
cantredos prædictos, pleniariam fibi juftitiam exhibe-
bit præfatus dominus rex fecundum leges et confuetudines partium illarum in quibus terræ illæ confiftunt :
qui articulus non fuit obfervatus fuper terris Arwyft-
ley et inter Dyvy et ductus fluviorum, pro eo quod
cum dominus Leolinus dictas terras vendicaffet coram domino rege apud Ruthlan, et rex fibi con-
ceffiffet caufam examinare fecundum leges et confuetudines Walliæ ac advocati pretium fuiffent intro-
ducti coram rege ut judicarent de dictis terris fecundum leges Wallicanas ; parte rea comparente et re-
fpondente adeò quod eo die deberet finaliter terminari ex præfixione domini regis qui apud Glover-
niam exiftens diem prædictum partibus affignavit, licet fæpius in diverfis locis coram jufticiariis fuiffet
dicta caufa examinata, et terræ ipfæ effent in pura
Wallia. Nec unquam judicata fuit fuper eis nifi fecundum leges Wallicanas , nec dominus rex poffet

vel deberet prorogare nisi secundum leges Walliæ; diem tamen ipsum motu proprio prorogavit, et contra leges antedictas, et ad ultimo fuit vocatus ad loca varia ad quæ non debuit evocari, nec justitiam obtinere potuit, nisi secundum leges Angliæ contra illud quod in dicto articulo continetur. Et idem factum fuit coram justiciariis apud Montgomery, cum partes essent in judicio constitutæ et firmatæ, et dies datus ad sententiam audiendam, diem prorogaverunt leges memoratas. Demum apud Londinum post multos labores et expensas varias rex ipse justitiam sibi denegavit, nisi vellet secundum leges Angliæ subire, judicium in causa memorata.

Secundus articulus non servatus est talis. Et omnes transgressiones injuriæ et excelsus hinc inde factæ pœnitus remittuntur usque in diem hodiernum Ille articulus non fuit observatus quia dominus Regnialdus de Grey statim cum fuit factus justiciarius, movit varias quæstiones et innumerabiles contra homines de Tegengl, et nos super transgressis quæ factæ fuerunt in tempore domini Henrici regis, et dicti domini Leolini dum dominum in partibus illis obtinebat unde dicti homines multum timentes non audebant in domibus suis permanere.

Tertius articulus, Ubi dictus Rys Vachan filius Nefi filii Maelgon cum terra quam nunc tenet et cum post pacem initam fuit spoliatus de terra de Geneverglyn, quam tunc tenebat cum hominibus et Averiis eorundem.

Quartus articulus, Item concedit dominus rex quod omnes terras tenentes in quatuor Cantredis, et in aliis terris quas dominus rex retinet in manu sua, teneant eas adeo libere et plenarie sicut ante guerram tenere consueverint, et eisdem libertatibus et consuetudinibus gaudeant quibus prius gaudere solebant, et cum contra istum articulum dictus Reginaldus consuetudines varias de novo introduxit, et hoc contra pacis formam supradictam.

Item quintus articulus, Controversiæ et contentiones motæ vel movendae inter principem et quoscunque teriu . . . . secundum leges

Marchiae

Marchiæ de his quæ emergunt in Marchia, et fecundum leges Walliæ de rebus contentiofis quæ in Wallia orientur. Contra iftum articulum venit dominus rex mittendo jufticiarios ufque ad Montgomery, qui ibidem judicare præfumpferunt homines dicti Leolini, vindictum ponendo fuper illos contra leges Walliæ, cum hoc vel aliud fimile nunquam factum fuiffet ibidem temporibus retroactis, quofdam incarcerando, alios in exilium mittendo, cum ipfe idem princeps paratus effet de eifdem hominibus fuis exhibere juftitiæ complementum omnibus quærelantibus de eifdem.

Item fextus articulus. Item cum fit contentum in dicta pacis forma, quod Griffinus Vachan homagium faceret domino regi, de terra, de Yâl, et principi de terra de Edeyrnahu jufticiarii domini introduxerunt, in totam terram prædictam de Edeyrnahu cujus cognitio caufæ ad principem pertinebat fimpliciter, et non ad illos Jufticiarios; et tamen pro bono pacis princeps hoc tolerabat cum ipfe princeps paratus effet eidem dominæ fuper hoc juftitiam exhibere.

Septimus articulus, ubi dicitur et licet idem princeps fe noftræ ut dictum eft fuppofuerit voluntati, nos tamen concedimus et volumus quod voluntas noftra . . . . . ultra dictos articulos fe in aliquo non extendant. Contra iftum articulum exigebatur aurum ad opus reginæ in qualibet folutione facta regi cum . . . . . Aurum nunquam fuit exactum Wallenfibus, nec in tempore domini Henrici, vel alicujus alterius regis Angliæ; quod aurum exfolvit pro bono pacis, cum tamen nihil de hoc tactum fuit in forma pacis vel excogitatum: et nunc infuper exigitur à principe aurum ad opus reginæ fenioris matris videlicet domini Edvardi nunc regis Angliæ, pro pace facta in tempore domini Henrici nunc regis Angliæ, cum nihil de hoc tunc fuerat dictum vel quoquomodo excogitatum, videlicet duo millia Marcarum et dimidium, et nifi dictæ Marcæ folverentur, minabatur dicta regina quod bona ejufdem Leolini occuparet quæ invenire poterat in domino regis, et

3   homines

homines fuos capere vel venundare quoufque dictam
fummam haberet ad plenum. Item cum invitaffet
dominus rex dictum principem adfectum Wiggor-
nienfem verbis blandiffimis promittendo ei quod daret
tunc confanguineam fuam fibi in uxorem, et multis di-
taret honoribus; nihilominus cum illuc véniffet in die
defponfationis, ante miffam petiit dominus rex unam
literam confignari à princepe continentem inter cæ-
tera, quod idem princeps nullum omnino honorem in
terra fua teneret contra regis voluntatem, vel manu
teneret ex quo poffit contingerc quod omnes fideles
principis ab eo commoverentur. Quam quidem lite-
iam fibi figillatam tradidit, computans per metum qui
cadere poffet in conftantem virum, cum tamen in forma pacis, ut præmiffum eft, contineatur quod nihil
ab eo deberet exigi, ultra quod in dicta forma continetur.

Item, cum fecundum eandem pacis formam confuetudines eidem principi confirmentur quibus ufus fuerat ab antiquo ; ac idem princeps et anteceffores fui,
ex confuetudine diutina et obtenta bona de naufra-
gis in terris fuis provenientia confueverant recipere,
et in fuos ufus convertere ad libitum : Jufticiarius
Ceftrenfis namium recepit fupcr principem pro bonis
quæ recepit de naufragiis ante guerram contra dictam
pacis formam per quam hinc inde erant remiffa, et
contra confuetudines ante dictas. Dato etiam quod
hoc effet foris factum namium recepit tale, videlicet
quindecem libratas mellis et plures equos ac homines
fuos incarceravit, et hoc ex propriis bonis principis
antedicti. Preterea, accipit fcaphas de Banweys quæ
venerant apud Liverpol cum mercandiis per niercato-
res, et eas numquam deliberavit donec pecuniam pro
eis accepit quantum volebat.

Item, cum quidam homines de Geneurglyn quædam
bona abftuliffent ab aliis vicinis fuis de Geneurglyn,
dum effent in domino principis de Merpyreton homines regis de Llanbadarn prœdam fecerunt, et acce-
perunt de terra principis de Merpyreton, et cum homines fui veniffent illuc ad quærendum quare dictam
prædam recep uait enim de eis interiecerunt, et
alios

alios vulneraverunt, & quofdam incarceraverunt. Et
cum in dicta pacis forma contineatur quod in marchia
deberent emendari quæ in Marchia committebantur,
tamen dicti homines regis homines principis audire no-
luerunt alibi quam in caftro de Llanbadarn, & hoc
contra pacis formam antedictam, fuper quo hactenus
nullam juftitiam habere potuerunt. In iftis articulis
injuriatus dominus rex principi & fuis, & etiam in multis aliis : et licet princeps tam per fe quam per fuos
petiviffet fæpius a domino rege quod pacis formam fu-
pradictam erga fe & fuos faceret obfervari, in nullo tamen extitit obfervata fed omni die de novo jufticiarii
& ballivi domini regis in partibus illis injurias injuriis,
& varia gravamina cumulaverunt : propter quod mi-
rum non debet videri alicui fi princeps præfatus af-
fenfum præftitit illis qui guerrare cœperunt, cum in
his fides quam in animam domini regis, fibi dominus
Robertus Tibetot juraverat in nullo fervabatur, &
maxima & principaliter cum princeps fuiffet præmunitus a perfonis fide dignis quod princeps foret a rege
capiendus in fuo primo acceffu apud Ruthlan, &
etiam fuiffet captus fi rex illuc acceffiffet poft Natale
ficut propofuerat.

Nec gravamina & alia quafi innumerabilia, fancte
pater, confiderantes, nobis affectu paterno compacia-
mini, et pro falute animæ domini regis, et noftræ, et
etiam multorum aliorum, ad pacem bonam utriufque
populi laboretis fructuofe.

Cum dominus David primo veniffet ad dominum
Edwardum tunc comitem Ceftriæ, ac homagium fibi
feciffet, idem dominus Edwardus eidem Davidi duas
cantredas, videlicet de dyffryn-Clwyd et Cywonant
cum omnibus fuis pertinentiis dedit plenarie, et literas
fuas patentes fuper hoc fieri fecit, tandem etiam donationem eidem invocavit, poftquam creatus eft in regem, et etiam illum Davidem in poffeffionem illarum
cantredarum induxit corporalem.

Demum domina Gwenlhian de 'Lacy mortua, tres
villas quas in dictis cantredis tenuit quoad vitam quæ
ad ipfum Davidem fpectabant ratione donationis fu-

B b   pradictæ

pradictæ dominus rex fibi abstulit minus juste contra
tenorem chartæ fuæ.

Item, Cum dictus David ex donatione domini regis
prædicti villas de Hope et Eston obtineret in Wallia,
de quibus nulli respondere tenebatur nisi secundum leges Wallicanas ; tandem justiciarius Cestriensis fecit
ipsum ad instantiam cujusdam Anglici Willh. de Va-
nabel nomine ad comitatum Cestriensem super dictis
vilulis ad judicium evocari. Et licet dictus dominus
David petivisset multoties quod injuriose contra eundem non procederetur in dicto comitatu, pro eo quod
ibidem respondere nullatenus tenebatur super villis
prædictis quæ sitæ erant in Wallia, sed potius tracta-
retur, hoc sibi plene denegavit.

Item, Idem justiciarius Cestriensis in gravamen dicti
domini Davidis nemus suum de Lleweni et Sylvas
suas de Hope fecit succidi tam per villanos de Ruthlan, quam per alios, cum idem justiciarius in terris
prædicti domini Davidis nullam omnino haberet juris-
dictionem, et non contenti quod meremium ibidem
quærerent ad ædificia exigenda tam apud Rodelanum
quam alibi in patria, sed nemus destruendo meremium
ibidem sectum ad vendendum in Hiberniam transtu-
lerunt.

Item, Cum idem dominus David quosdam Fortani-
cos de terra domini regis qui in nemoribus latitabant
cepisset, ac suspendio tradidisset, idem tamen justiciarius ipsum Davidem penes regem accusabat, ac si ipse
dictos malefactores defenderet et manuteneret, quod
verisimile non erat cum ipse David dictos latrones
suspendi faceret et occidi.

Item, Cum esset cautum in forma pacis quod Wallenses deberent in causis suis tractari secundum leges
Wallicanas, istud tamen circa dictum Davidem et
suos homines in nullo extitit observatum.

De premissis vero gravaminibus et aliis petiit idem
David aliquam emendationem vel secundum leges Walliæ, vel consuetudines, vel etiam ex gratia speciali ;
et hoc etiam petiit a domino rege, quorum neutrum
potuit aliquatenus obtinere : et cum hoc præmunitus
fuit a qui idam a curia domini regis, quod in primo
regressu

regreſſu domini Reginaldi de Gray de euria idem Das vid eſſet capiendus ut filii ſui capiendi pro obſedibu eſſet, inſuper ſpoliandus caſtro ſuo de Hope, et etiam ſylva ſua ibidem ſuccidenda. Ideo cum idem David multum laboraſſet pro domino rege prædicto in diverſis guerris tam in Anglia quam in Wallia, et expoſuiſſet ſe et ſuos variis periculis et injuriis, ac amiſiſſet nobiliores de ſuis et fortiores, ac multos nimis, nihilominus de dictis graviminibus et aliis nullam omnino juſtitiam, emendationem, ſeu gratiam potuit obtinere. Propter quæ gravamina et pericula, timens mortem propriam aut filiorum ſuorum, vel incarcerationem perpetuam, vel ſaltem diutinam, quaſi coactus et invitus incepit prout potuit ſe et ſuos defenſare.

Hæc eſt forma quam dominus rex Angliæ promiſit hominibus de Ros, antequam ipſi fecerunt ſibi homagium, & illam formam eis promiſit inviolabiliter obſervare, videlicet,

Quod ipſe dominus rex concederet unicuique eorum jus ſuum, et juriſdictionem ſuam, et etiam dominium, bonæ memoriæ domini Henrici quondam regis Angliæ, ſecundum quod prædicti homines de Ros referent ipſos haberent temporibus prædicti Henrici.

Item, Promſit prædictus dominus rex ſupradictis hominibus quod non darentur nec ad firmam ponerentur; quibus articulis conceſſis præfatis hominibus homagium fecerunt domino regi, et ipſe eis promiſit ore proprio dictos articulos obſervare. Hoc non obſtante quidam cementarii redeuntes ad villam de Ruthlan, de loco ubi ipſi operabantur, obviaverunt cuidam nobili tranſeunti cum uxore ſua per viam regiam ſuper pace domini regis, qui cementarii per vim propoſuerunt auferre a prædicto nobili ſuam uxorem, et quia ipſe nobilis defendit ſuam uxorem ne ab ipſo auferetur, prædicti cementarii prædictum nobilem interfecerunt. Ille autem cui plus opponebatur dictum homicidium perpetraſſe, cum quibuſdam ſociis ſuis capti fuerunt: et cum pare ...

domino jufticiario Ceftrienfi de morte confanguinii
eorum, illi de parentela ipfius interfecti fuerunt incarcerati, et interfectores fuerunt a carcere liberati. . .

Item, Quidam homo interfecit quendam nobilem,
qui videlicet filium Goronu de Heylyn nutriverat, et
interfector captus fuit: et cum quidam de parentela
prædicti interfecti peterent juftitiam de eorum confan-
guineo a domino jufticiario Ceftrienfi, quidam eorum
capti fuerunt, et interfector fuit in caftello domini
regis liberatus, et adhuc eft ibi, denegata juftitia prædictæ parentelæ.

Item, Quidam nobiles vindicaverunt jus in quibufdam terris, et de mobilibus fuis obtulerunt domino
regi magnam fummam pecuniæ pro juftitia habenda
per rationem et veredictum proborum et legalium hominum de patria ; quæ quidem terræ adjudicatæ fuerunt, prædictis vendicantibus totam terram prædictam
cum omnibus ædificiis biadis, et aliis bonis in ipfis
contentis. Dominus Reginaldus de Grey; et fic amife-
runt primo pecuniam quam pro terra pacaverunt, et
poftea terram.

Item, Jurifdictionis noftræ eft quod nullus extraneus
extirparet fylvas noftras, nifi prius habita licentia noftra; hoc non obftante, proclamatum fuit apud Rodolanum quod liceret unicuique Anglicano extirpare fylvas noftras fine noftra licentia ad libitum eorum vo-
luntatis, et quod nobis fuit prohibitum dictas fylvas
noftras extirpare.

Item, Terras quas probi homines a domino Davide
filio Leolini bonæ memoriæ habuerunt per donationem
prædicti Davidis abftulit prædictus jufticiarius a prædictis probis hominibus.

Item, Quando aliquis ad villam de Ruthlan veniret
cum mercandiis fuis, fi refutaret illud quod Anglicus
eidem, offerret pro fuis mercandiis, ftatim duceretur
ille Wallenfis ad caftrum, et emptor ibidem haberet
rem quam larginaverat, et dominus rex haberet pretium dictæ rei, tunc caftellam dictum Wallenfem fpo-
liatum et atrociter verberatum deliberabant, pacatis
prius portario caftri quatuor denariis. Si vero aliquis
Wallenfis emeret aliquam rem in villa de Ruthlan,

4   Anglicus

Anglicus qualiſcunque ſuperveniret, et rem venditam dicto Wallenſi auferet ab ipſo pro minori pretio quam dictus Wallenſis ſolverat pro eadem.

Item, Contra promiſſionem domini regis prædictis hominibus de Ros, ipſe dedit territoriam villæ de Maenam in Penmayn et Lhysfaen.

Item, Taurus cujuſdam probi hominis deprehenſus fuit in pratis domini regis apud Ros, et captus, et dominus ejus vocatis fuit ad placitum uſque Rodolanum, et fuit condemnatus in quinque libris occaſione dicti tauri; bis adivit Londinium pro juſtitia petenda, et nullam fuit aſſecutus, et in illis duabus vicibus expendidit prædictus homo tres libras.

Item, Quidam nobiles de cantreda de Ros emerunt officia pro certa ſumma pecuniæ; pacata pecunia, meritis ſuis non exigentibus, dominus juſticiarius Ceſtrenſis abſtulit ab eis eorum officia.

Item, Quidam ruſticus Goronow ab Heylyn condemnatus fuit in 17 l. bonæ et legalis monetæ juris, ordine non ſervato.

Item, Goronow filius Heylyn accipit ad firmam territorium de Pennmaen et Lhysfaen a magiſtro Godfrido M. pro certa pecuniæ ſumma, uſque ad finem quatuor annorum, quo facto dominus Robertus de C. cum equis et armis, et cum viginti quatuor equitibus venit ad inequitandum prædictum Goronow, occaſione dictæ terræ, ita quod ſic non fuit ſecurus tranſitus nec uſque Rodolanum, nec uſque ad juſticiarios niſi cum forti Warniſtura de ſua parentela et etiam de ſuis amicis.

Item. In reformationem pacis ultro factæ et firmatæ inter dominum regem, et ſuos ex una parte, et dominum principem et ſuos ex altera expreſſe continebatur; quod omnes injuriæ et tranſgreſſiones factæ ex utraque parte penitus remitterentur; hoc non obſtante, oppoſitum fuit contra quoſdam nobiles quoddam fore factum tempore guerræ, et ſtatim capti fuerunt, nec potuerunt a carcere liberari antequam ipſi pacarent ſedecem marcas.

Item, Cum cauſæ debent tractari et terminari ſecundum legem et conſuetudinem terræ noſtræ compellun tur homines cantredæ noftræ ad jurandum in caufis prædictis contra fuam confcientiam, nec aliter jurare patiuntur.

Præ nos couftavimus trecentas marcas eundo ad dominum regem pro juftitia petenda in prædictis articulis, ibidem morando, et ad propria redeundo; et cum nos credebamus habere plenam juftitiam de fingulis articulis prædictis; dominus rex tranfmifit ad partes noftras dominum Reginaldum de Grey, cui dictus dominus rex totam terram ad firmam conceffit, ad tractandos homines prædictæ cantredæ prout fuæ placeret voluntati; qui compulfit nos jurare per manum fuam cum deberemus jurare per manum domini regis, et ubi crux domini regis levari deberet, quod crux prædicti Reginaldi levaretur, in fignum quod ipfe erat verus dominus. Dictus vero Reginaldus in fuo avdentu ad partes Walliæ vendidit quibufdam fervientibus domini regis officia fua, quæ prædicti fervientes prius emerant a dom. rege pro 23 Marcis, et illa officia non deberent vendi nifi cum dominium dominorum mutaretur.

Item, Dominus rex dedit Maredudo filio Madoc magifterium fatellitum pro fuo fervitio, dominus Reginaldus de Grey abftulit ab eo fuum officium, nec a domino rege affequi potuit aliquam juftitiam.

Item, Unus de confilio prædicti Reginaldi nobis dixit ore tenus, fcilicet Cynwricus Fychan, quod in adventu prædicti Reginald ad partes Walliæ, viginti quatuor homines de probioribus hominibus cujuflibet cantredæ caperet ad incarcerandos ipfos perpetuo vel decapitandos: propter ifta gravimina, et alia quæ dictus Reginaldus nobis fecit, et etiam propter minas quas ipfe nobis intulit, videlicet quod fi mitteremus aliquos nuncios ad curiam domini regis pro juftitia petenda decapitarentur. Multa alia damna nobis allata, et injuriæ factæ; et quando mittebamus ad curiam domini regis, nuntii non permittebantur nec aufi fueiunt intrare, fed expendebant multa inutiliter; ob ifta gravamina æftimabamus nos effe liberos a juramento facto domino regis coram deo.

Item, Bledyn Seis et Anjanus filius Genaf de Ros c. . . . . D. . id filii
                                                          welini

Lewelini, & Henrici regis, de homicidiis factis tunc satisfactionem et emendam satisfacere monstraverunt; et modo de novo Reginaldus de Grey vellet et cogetet illam emendam renovare, donec oportuit ipsos terram proprias relinquere.

Item, Census et obventiones quos solvimus de veteri moneta per medietatem unius anni ante adventum novæ monetæ, cogerunt nos reddere eis novas monetas pro veteri et hoc sub eodam numero.

Ista sunt gravamina per dominum regem & suos justiciarios illata Rheso parvo de Yystrad Tywy.

Primum est, Postquam dictus Rhys dedit et concessit domino regi castrum suum apud Dynefowr post ultimam pacis formam : qui dictus Rhesus tunc temporis erat in tentilio domini Payn de Gadfry, eodem tempore interfecti fuerunt sex nobiles viri domini Rhys, de quibus satisfactionem nec justitiam unquam habuit quod fuit eis damnum et gravamen.

· Item, Johannes Giffard calumniavit cum Rhesum super hæreditatem propriam apud Hirwryn, quicquid Rhesus inquisivit a domino rege legem patriæ suæ, aut legem comitatus Caermardden, in quo comitatu antecessores dicti Rhys solebant habere leges, quando fierent in unitatem Anglicorum, et sub eorum dominis; quod idem Rhys nullas leges habuit, et suam terram prædictam totaliter amisit; vellent ipsum instringere in comitatu Herefordiensi, ubi numquam antecessores ejus responderunt.

Præterea in tertis præfati Rhesi talia gravamina fuerunt per Anglicos facta, maxime pertinent ad ecclesiasticos, videlicet in ecclesia Sancti Davidis quæ vocatur Llangadawc fecerunt stabula, et meretrices collocaverunt, et omnia bona quæ in ea continebantur omnino asportaverunt atque totos domos combusserunt; et in eadem ecclesia juxta aram percusserunt capellanum cum gladio ad caput ejus et eum reliquerunt semivivum.

Item, in eadem patria ecclesiam Dyngad et ecclesiam Llantreda spoliaverunt et combusserunt; cæterasque ecclesias ex partibus illis omnino spoliaverunt calcibus, et libris, ac omnibus aliis ornamentis et rebus.

Gravamina Lewelini filii Rhys, & Howeli fratris ejus per dominum regem illata sunt hæc.

Postquam in formam pacis inter dominum Henricum tunc temporis regem Angliæ et dominumprincipem apud Rhydchwnna, tunc præfatus rex concessit, et per cartas suas confirmavit præfato principi homagium prædictorum nobibium *exos*. Prædicti nobiles fuerunt fideles et constantes cum præfato principe, juxta eorum donationem et cartarum suarum confirmationem : Edwardus nunc rex Angliæ prædictos nobiles dehæreditavit, denegando eisdem omnes leges et consuetudines Walliæ; ita quod non habuerunt terras suas nec per legem, nec per gratiam.

So long as. (margin)

Ista sunt gravimina, damna, seu molestia per Anglicos illata filiis Maredudi, filii Oweni.

Primum est quamquam dominus rex concessit prædictis nobilibus suas proprias hæreditates post pacis formam, videlicet Geneur'glyn et Creudhyn ; præfatus vero rex, contra suam donationem et pacis formam, terris supradictis antedictos nobiles dehæreditavit, denegando eidem omnes leges et consuetudines Walliæ, et Angliæ, atque comitatus Caermardhyn.

Secundum est, Quod præfatus rex in suo comitatu de Cardigan, per suos justiciarios antedictos nobiles compellit, ut ipsi traderent judicium super ignobiles ac subditos patriæ, et quod tales homines e comisso judicium super ipsos opponerent, ubi numquam antecessores eorum ab Anglicis talia sustinuerunt.

Tertium est, Quod justiciarii domini regis curiam eorum nobilium abstulerunt, compellendo homines suos proprios coram eis satisfacere quia de jure coram prædictis nobilibus deberent satisfacere.

Quartum est, Quod quoddam naufragium in terris antedictorum nobilium fuit, qui quidem nobiles bona naufragii receperunt, sicut antecessores eorum fecerunt, et hoc non fuit eis prohibitum per aliquos

ex

ex parte regis : antedictus vero rex contra eorum confuetudinem et legem, occafione illius Naufragii eofdem
damnavit in octoginta Marcis fterlingorum; atque
bona quæ in Naufragio continebantur omnino afporta-
verunt.

Quintum eft, quod nullus noftrum in comitatu
Uftegd de Cardigan aufus effet venire inter Anglicos
propter timorem carceris et nifi fuiffet propter periculum Nobilibus Metrop. nihil contra honoram domini
regis moverent.

Significant vero quod omnes Chriftiani habent leges
et confuetudines in eorum propriis terris; Judæi vero
inter Anglicos habent leges, ipfi vero in terris fuis, et
eorum anteceffores habuerunt leges immutabiles et confuetudines, donec Anglia poft ultimam guerram ab eis
leges fuas abftulerunt.

Memorandum de quærelis omnium nobilium virorum
de Yftradatuy eifdem latis ac factis per Rogerum
de Clyfford, & Rogerum Crofcil vicem domini
Rogeri de Clyfford gerentem contra privilegium,
juftitiam, et confuetudinem prædictorum virorum
de Yftratuy, ut dicunt et probant.

Primus articulus eft quod cum dicti Rogeri cogerunt dictos homines de Yftradatuy reddere fibi pro confuetudinibus fuis viginti Marcas fterlingorum, et poft
folutionem dictæ pecuniæ cito fregerunt in hunc modum, quod pofuerunt fuper 17 viros judicantes fecundum jus Angliæ; quod nunquam fuit confuetudo
nec privilegium dictæ patriæ.

Item. Madecus filius Bledyn condemnatus fuit in
quatuor Marcio injuftè.

Item. Lewelinus Rufus condemnatus fuit in quinque Marcis et 17 averiis contra privilegium et confuetudinem patriæ.

Item. Quod ipfi Rogeri fecerunt foreftam fuper
terram propriam virorum patriæ: et propter pedem
unius cervi inventum id ore canis alicujus, tres homines fuerunt fpoliati omnino.

Item.

Item. Michael ab Yguſtyl condemnatus fuit in decem ſolidis pro facto patris ſui, quadraginta annis elapſis.

Item. Cogerunt parentes Ennii à Strabonis ad red-dendum ſuum relevagum in vita ſua.

Item. Quod ipſi poſuerunt ſuper nos omnes ſatelli-tos de Anglicis, quod nunquam fuit noſtra dimidietas.

Item. Dati fuimus domino Mauritio de Crumy, et vinditi fuimus domino Rogero de Clyfford, quod nunqnam fuit ſuper parentes noſtros.

Item. Roberti de Monte alto petiit, à domino rege tertiam partem terræ de Monte alto in Ward, et dijudicata fuit coram domino rege quod numquam dic-ta terra fuit in Ward data.

Hi ſunt articuli quæſtionum illati ab hominibus de Penlhyn, injuſte per conſtabularium Albi Mona-ſterii & ſuos cives.

Primo. Cynwric filius Madoci fuit ſpoliatus ab eis tempore pacis octo libris, et quatuor bobus, et blado laboris unius aratri, per duos annos et valore trium librarum à tribus hominibns ejuſdem; affirmat etiam quod ſolvit 16 libras per octo in valore, et majorem habuit injuriam imponendo manus in ipſum quam totum quod amiſit, quia tunc erat conſtabularius do-mini principis apud Penllyn: non fuit alia cauſa dictæ ſpoliationis niſi quia dicebatur invenire 24 garbàs de decimis in domo cujuſdam hominis dicti Cynwrici.

Item. Adam Preco condemnatus fuit in ſeptem ſo-lidis & octo denariis, et equa valoris unius libræ, im-ponendo manus in ipſum et liberando latronem dictæ equæ, quia ipſe venerat ibidem cum dicto latrone capto.

Item. Endevot ab Gruffydh condemnatus fuit in 27 s. nec fuit cauſa niſi quia vendidit equam unam ad unum miliare citra villam, ſicut ſolebant à tempore quo non extat memoria, quando veniebant ad nun-dinas.

Item. Adaf Ddu condemnatus fuit in 30 s. eo quod duo boves quos propoſuerat vendere in foro Albi i. n ſterii

Monaſterii exibant villam ipſo conveniente, et captus
fuit et detentus uſque ad ſolutionem 30 s. nec ipſi boves exierant niſi da Plateo qua ſtabant uſque ad aliam
Plateam.

Item. Biryt filius Gwyn, condemnatus fuit in quinque ſolidis, et in carcerem ductus ; eo quod percuſ-
ſit unum bovem indomitum ipſum calcantem in
foro.

Item. Yorwerch ab Gorgonon condemnatus fuit
7 s. eo quod evaſerat quondam de carcere eorum
tempore guerræ, et in tempore pacis inventus fuit in
dicta villa, et hoc contra formam pacis initæ inter dominum regem, et dominum principem.

Item. Duo famuli Kenwric ap Gruffydh condem-
nati fuerunt in duabus Marcis, eo quod dicebant ipſos
non ſolviſſe toletum poſtquam ſolverant.

Item. Caducanus Niger famulus conſtabularii de
Penlyhyn captus fuit et condemnatus in 6 s. et 4 d. eo
quod nolebat recipere veterem monetam pro nova.

Item. Gruffydh ap Goronow *tercinarius* domini A Servant.
Principis ſpoliatus fuit uno bove valoris 11 s. et 8 d.
et poſtquam arraveret conſtabularius cum dicto bove
per ſeptem menſes, ſolvit dictus Gruffynus pro dicto
bove, 40 d.

Item. Howel ap David ſpoliatus fuit per ſatellites albi Monaſterii duobus ſolidis extra villam, eo
quod denegaverat prius munera ut ſolent ſatellites petere.

Item. David ab Gronow ab Eynion ſpoliatus fuit
30 s. eo quod quidam cives albi monaſterii dixit, quod
quidam de Penlhyn, qui mortuus fuerat, denegabatur
ei in quibuſdam rebus.

Item. Duo famuli Y bongam capti fuerunt et con-
demnati in duabus libris, eo quod poſuerunt manum
in quendam latronem qui ſpoliabat eos in villa per noc-
tem, et liberaverunt latronem.

Item. Eneyon filius Ichael captus et verberatus fuit,
et ſpoliatus duobus bobus valoris, 24 s. et 6 d. nulla
alia de cauſa, niſi quod boves ipſo connivente moverunt
ſe de platea ad iliam plateam.

Item.

Item. Adaf ap Ychael condemnatus fuit in duabus libris pro una libra, et ipfe pofuerat in juramento cujufdam civis de albo monafterio quod non tenebatur nifi in una libra pro principe, nec voluit jurare, et ideo fpoliatus fuit una libra.

Item. Guyan Maeftran fpoliatus fuit 5 s. eo quod dicebat quod quidam Mercator de Ardydwy tenebatur eis in quibufdam rebus, cum ipfe nec erat de dicta Balliva : item condemnatus fuit in 8 d. quia dicebant ipfum vendere quafdam oves extra villam cum ipfe non vendiderat.

Item. Famulus Lewelini ab Gwyn fpoliatus fuit feptem ovibus, et 5 s. et fuo pallio, eo quod dicebant ipfum effe de domino Griffydh ab Gwyn cum ipfe non erat.

Item. Iorwerch ab Meylir captus fuit et condemnatus in 15 s. cum pallio, eo quod denegavit dare munus fatellitibus quod petebant, ipfi finxerunt eum in villa pernoctare.

Item. Cives albi monafterii rapuerunt à Madoco Rufo filio Ychael unum bovem valoris, 11 s. et 6 d.

Ifta omnia facta fuerunt per Henricum Gamber dicti loci conftabularium, cum aliis innumerabilibus articulis.

Item. Ybicre captus fuit in negotio domini principis, et condemnatus in 5 s. abfque aliqua caufa.

Hæc funt gravamina Goronow filii Heylyn, viz.

Quod quidem Villanus dictus Coronon vocatus fuit ad curiam domini regis occafione indebitæ caufæ. Tunc dictus Goronow venit ad fuum villanum defendendum, et petiit pro ipfo veritatem à domino jufticiario, aut legem qua utuntur homines fuæ patriæ; omnibus autem his eidem denegatis, dictus villanus condemnatus fuit in 27 libris, et tribus obolis : tunc dictus Goronow adivit Londonium pro juftitia habenda, et expendit quinque Marcas et quatuor Solidos, et promiffa fuit fibi juftitia, et nullam fuit affecutus.

Item. Quidam nobilis fuit interfectus, videlicet, qui nutrverat filium dicti Goronow, et ille interfector

fector captus fuit et deportatus fuit apud caſtrum de
Ruthlan : tunc dictus Goronow et quidem de parentela
interfecti petierunt juſtitiam de interfectore : tunc denegata eis juſtititia, quidam fuerunt incarcerati, et ille
interfector fuit in Caſtello liberatus. Tunc dictus Goronow interum adivit Londonium propter ſupradicta
gravamina ad juſtitiam petendam, et expendit, 20
Marcas, 3 s. 4 d. Et dominus rex promiſit eidem
plenariam juſtititiam, et nullam fuit adeptus cum per-
venit ad patriam ſuam.

Item. Tertio ex defectu juſtitiæ oportuit dictum
Goronow adire Londonium occaſionibus ſupradictis
pro juſtitia petenda, et expendit illa vice 18 Marcas,
6 s. 8 d. bonæ et legalis Monetæ ; et tunc ſimpliciter
promiſit dominus rex eidem juſtitiam perhibere ; et
quando credebat habere juſtitiam, tunc venit Reginaldus de Grey, et dixit aperte quod ipſe deberit trac-
tare totam patriam per chartas domini regis, et abſtulit
totam Ballivam à dicto Goronow ; quam ſibi dominus
rex conceſſit, et vendidit illam Ballivam ad voluntatem
ſuam, et tunc petiit dictus Goronow juſtitiam à domino
Reginaldo de gravaminibus ſupradictis, et nullam fuit
adeptus.

Item. Dictus Goronow recepit terram, videlicet,
Penmaen et Llysfaen ad firmam de Godfrido Merlyn,
uſque ad finem quatuor annorum pro certa pecuniæ
ſumma. Tunc Robertus de Cruquer venit cum equis
ſuis et armis ad quærendum dictam terram per vim,
et quia dictus Goronow non permitteret auferre dictam terram ab eodem uſque terminum præſignatum,
tunc vocatus fuit ad curiam dictus Goronow illa
occaſione ; tunc venit Reginaldus de Grey, cum
viginti quatuor equitibus armatis ad proponendum
capere dictum Goronow, vel ad eundem decapi-
tandum ; et quia viderunt quod non poſſent implere
ſuum propoſitum illo die, vocaverunt dictum Goronow craſtino die apud Ruthlan, et tunc dictus Goronow habuit conſilium ita quod non deberent adire
dictam curiam : iterum dictus Goronow vocatus fuit
adplacitum apud Caerwys, et non auſus fuit adire dictum placitum niſi per conductum domini epiſcopi
Aſaphenſis,

Afaphenfis, quia dictus Reginaldus et fui compfures ibidem erant armati.

Item. Propter ista gravamina de quibus nullam habuit juftitiam nifi laborare et expendere duas libr. quatuor Marcas, et 9 d; et quia non aufus fuit in propria perfona adire curiam, mifit quendam nuncium deportantem duas literas, unam ad dominum regem, et aliam ad fratrem Lewelinum, ad fignandum domino regi quod amitteret totam patriam, et dictum Goronow quia non obfervavit illud quod eifdem promifit; et quia nullam poffent homines de Ros et Arglifeld affequi juftitiam, et quia noluit corrigere five emendare ifta gravamina propter hoc amifit totam patriam.

Supplicant fanctitati veftræ, domine archipiefcope Cantuarienfis totius Angliæ primas, nobiles viri de Tegengyl, et vobis demonftrant quod cum prædicti nobiles fecerunt homagium domino Edwardo regi Angliæ, ipfe rex eifdem promifit quod eofdem immunes obfervaret et indemnes, tam in bonis, libertatibus, juribus, jurifdictionibus, privilegiis quibus ufi fuerunt tempore Henrici regis per fuum obtentum privilegium; ex quibus privilegiis fuerunt poftmodo fpoliati.

Imprimis. Juribus et confuetudinibus partiæ fuerunt fpoliati, viz. prædictus Edwardus compellendo quod ipfi procederent in caufis fecundum legem Anglicanam, cum fecundum tenorem privilegii fui fecundum legem Wallicanam procedere debuiffent, viz. apud Tref Edwyn, et apud Ruthlan, et apud Caerwys; et optimati de patria fuerunt manu capti quia ipfi provocabant quod ipfi procederent in caufa apud Tref Edwyn fecundum legem et confuetudinem Wallicanam fecundum tenorem privilegii.

Secundo. Quia unus jufticiarius duceret in caufis peragendis, alius fuus prædeceffor in irritum revocaret, viz. in caufa Davidis Reginaldus de Grey recitavit proceffum quem fuus anteceffor ratum habuit, et etiam approbavit.

Tertio

. Tertio. Quod fi unus nobilis de patria fuiffet propter calumniam fibi impofitam captus, quod non re-
mitterent eundem pro *cautione fideviſſoria* evadere, quod Surety.
facere debuiffent.

Quarto. Quod tres unius nobilis dedu&ti ad caftrum
fuerunt de Flynt, propter parvam accufationem, una
cum averiis fuis, nec potuerunt de caftro devenire, nec
dilationem obtinere donec unufquifque dedit unum
bovem conftabulario de Flynt, et donec folverunt tres
libras Kynwrico Seis pro dilatione habenda.

Quinto. iReginaldus de Grey terras virorum de Merton dedit et conceffit abbati de Bafingwerk ordinis Ci-
fterciend. contra legem Wallicanam, et patræ confue-
tudim; et contra formam pacis initæ inter dominum
Lewelinum principem et dominum regem, viz. 16 can-
tatas terræ.

Sexto. Mirantur nobiles et optimati patriæ pro eo
quod dominus rex fecit ædificare caftrum fuper terram
et poffeffionem magnatum, et mandavit dominus rex
jufticiario fuo quod ipfe folveret eque bonam terram illis fpoliatis et adhuc aliquam terram, nec fuæ
terræ æftimationem funt confecuti in Flynt.

Septimo. Reginaldus de Grey non permitteret poſ-
feffores fylvarum uti fylvis fuis, donec ab eifdem pretium
et præmium fuiffet confecutus, et aliis rufticis gratis
permitteret fylvam prædi&torum abfcidere, cum non
debuiffent fecundum patriæ confuetudinem et legem
Wallicanam.

O&tavo. Cum homines de Cyrchynan fecerunt pactum cum domino rege, quod cum ipſi concederent di-
midietatem cujufdam prati, ad hoc quod dominus rex
non permitteret fylvam prædi&torum abfcidere Howelo
filio Gruffydd præfente, et poftmodum Reginaldus
de Grey prædi&tum pratum infirmavit, viz. conce-
dendo aliis quod abfciderent fylvam prædi&torum, et
eofdem dimidietate prati fui fpoliando.

Nono. Filius Kynwrici ab Goronow fuit captus
apud Ruthlan culpa fua minime præcedente, nifi vellet pignus fuum *acquietare* a quoddam muliere, et con- Redeem the
ftabularius de Ruthlan fecit eundem detradi in car- gage.

ccr m.

cerem injuriofe, nec potuit exinde deliberari donec
prædictus fuit condemnatus ultra fuorum bonorum
Velua. *hypotheca.*

Decimo. Cum ballivus de Ruthlan erat in convivio
apud villam Four Hutmus de Limayl quendam virum
nobilem crudeliter vulneravit in præfentia ballivi fu-
pradicti; cujus vulneris occafione prædictus Hutmus
fuit in octo libris condemnatus; et quum ille cui injuria fuiffet facta petere voluiffet prædictas libras, eundem fecit detrudi in carcerem una.

Undecimo, Nuntii Reginaldi de Grey propofuerunt
facere illud quod erat abfurdum et diffonum juris fecundum canonicas fanctiones; videlicet petere ab eifdem quod ipfi ararent Reginaldo de Grey, et quod
ipfi feminarent illam araturam; et illi fuerunt nuntii,
viz. Kynwricus Seis et Hutmus de Limayl, quod
prædictus vero Kynwricus in præfentia omnium de
patria juravit, nifi omnes de patria ararent quod ipfi
infra tempus pœniterent, et ipfi multum timuerunt
metu qui potuit cadere in conftantem virum.

Duodecimo. Quod præcones de Tegeyngl emerunt
officium præconiæ pro 30 marcis a domino rege, et
poftmodum Reginaldus de Grey prædictos præcones
tam pecunia quam præconia fpoliavit contra legem et
confuetudinem Anglicanam.

Tertiodecimo. Septem nobiles fuerunt interfecti
minus jufte ab Anglicis, et adhuc parentes prædictorum aliquam fatisfactionem non habuerunt, cum illi
malefactores fuerunt capti; et poftmodum prædictos
malefactores remiferunt prædicti conftabularii impu-
nitos.

Quartodecimo. Conftabularius unus de Ruthlan de-
tradit duos Satellites domini regis in carcere, pro eo
quod ipfi tenuerunt aliquem Anglicum qui grave
delictum commifit hominem alium vulnerando,

Ifti omnes articuli in præmiffis nominati, fuerunt
perpetrati contra prædictorum virorum libertatem,
jurifdictionem, et privilegium et contre legem et confuetudinem Wallicanam; videlicet, quod non erant
aufi eorum quærelas domino regi per fuos nuncios
denun-

denuntiare, propter metum Reginaldi et timorem, qui
metus potuit cadere in conſt antem virum : ' quia prædictus Reginaldus ſua voce Dilvada fuit proteſtatus ; Openly.
quod ſin inveniret nuntios prædictorum quod eoſdem
decapitaret prout nobis ex parte unius ex conſilio ſuo
fuit certive intimatum. In tantum quod lingua non
poteſt proferre, nec penna ſcribere in quantum prædicti homines de Tegeyngl fuerunt aggravati.

Conqueritur vobis, domine archiepiſcope Cantuari-
enſis totius Angliæ primas, Lewelinus filius Griffini filii
Madoci de conſtabulario de cruce Oſwaldi regis, et
de hominibus ejuſdem villae, qui prædictum Lewelinum tertia parte cujuſdam villae quae vocatur Ledrot,
et curia patris ſui, ſine obſervatione juris patriae ſuae
vel conſuetudine inequiter ſpoliarunt.

Praeterea. Praedictus conſtabularius et ſui, com-
plures eundem Lewelinum communi paſtura, qua
praedictus Lewelinus uſus fuit temporibus retroactis,
ordine juris patriae minime obſervaro, ſpoliarunt, et in
70 libris occaſione praedictae paſturae condemnaverint.
Cæterum dominu rex Angliae conceſſit quaſdam literas
cuidam Baſtardo, ſcilicet Griffino Fychan ab Cynlhaeth, ad litigandum contra eundem Lewelinum pro toto
dominio ſuo obtinendo, quarum literarum occaſione
idem Lewelinus expendit cc l. ſterlingorum legalis
uſualiſæ monetæ.

Iterum. Prædictus conſtabularius, compulſit prædictum Lewelinum ad mittendum duos ſuos nobiles
ad eos ſuſpendendos ad prædictum cónſtabularium
quicquid viri nobiles ſuſpendi minime debuiſſent,
quam ſuſpenſionem nollent parentes prædictorum hominum ſuſtinuiſſe pro ccc libris ſterlingorum. Poſt-
midum, prædictus, conſtabularius incacerravit bis 60
homines prædicti Lewelini nulla præmiſſa ratione, niſi
quod quidam gareo emiſit quandam vocem, nec potuerunt evadere ſuum carcerem donec quilibet eorum
ſolvit decem ſolidos pro ſua deliberatione.

Item. Quando homines prædicti Lewelini yeni-
rent ad forum ad ſuos boves vendendos, prædictus
conſtabularius faceret boves deduci ad caſtrum, nec
poſtmodum boves reſtituerit, nec pretium ſolveret

C c   venditori ;

venditori : præfertim idem conftabularius et fui cepe-
runt jumenta præd icti Lewelini ad terram fuam propriam, et de eifdem jumentis fecerunt fuam voluntatem.

Præterea. Jufticiarii domini regis compulferunt
prædictum Lewelinum ad tradendum quandam villam filiis Eneoni filii Griffini; qui quidem prædictam
villam, nec a fe, nec a prædecefforibus fuerunt confecuti, ordine juris patriæ fuæ in hac parte minime
obfervato.

Idem. Prædictus conftabularius abftulit equum
ballivi prædicti Lewelini fine aliqua ratione, nec fibi
aliquid debebatur; nec adhuc prædictus ballivus fatisfactionem aliquam eft confecutus.

Cæterum. Quando prædictus Lewelinus volebat
adire villam quæ vocatur Caerlleon cum literis domini regis ad comperiendum ibidem in die fibi affig-
nata; filii Griffini filii Gwenynny et armigeri domini Rogeri Starainge ex confilio Rogeri eundem Lewelinum et fuos incarcerarunt in fui injuriam et fuorum non modicam læfionem ; quam injuriam et læfionem nollet prædictus Lewelinus et fui fuftinuiffe
pro ccc marcis fterlingorum; hec ab eifdem potuit
evadere donec invenit pro fe fufficientem cautionem.

His et aliis receptis in fcriptis acceffit, archiepifcopus ad dominum regem ; fupplicans ei humiliter ut
gravamina fuppradicta dignetur avertere, et ea correctione debita terminare : et faltem pro tanto habere ex-
ceffus Wallenfium excufatos : qui refpondit Wallenfes
injuriis fibi illatis effe excufabiles, quia omni tempore
potatus extiterat omni facere juftitiam conquerenti:
quo audito, archiepifcopus regi iterum fupplicavit ut
permitteret Wallenfes pro fuis gravaminibus expo-
nendis et remediis afferendiis ap ipfum habere acceffum
liberum et regreffum: qui refpondit quod libere permitteret eos ad fe accedere fed et redira; fi fecundum
juftitiam regreffus eorum meritis refponderet. Quibus auditis acceffit archiepifcopus ad principem Walliæ in Snawdoniam ut tam ipfum quam Davidem fratrem fuum et cæteros Wallenfes ad aliquam humili-
tatis regulam ipforum animos inclinaret ; per quam
poffet qui ipforum nuntius regiam clementiam ad
ipfos admittendos in gratiam inclinare. Poft varios
autem

autem tractatus respondit princeps : quod paratus erat
voluntati regiæ se supponere duobus præsuppositis,
salva scilicet conscientia sua qua populo suo assistere
tenebatur; salva etiam condescentia status sui. Quæ
cum archiepiscopus retulisset domino regi, respondit
dominus rex quod nullum alium de · pace volebat
cum principe ac subditis suis habere tractatum, nisi
quod ipsi supponerent se in omnibus regiæ voluntati :
et cum constaret archiepiscopo Wallenses nullo modo
velle se regiæ voluntati supponere, nisi præcite in forma eis tolerabili et accepta, tractatum habuit ex per-
missioni domini regis cum magnatibus tunc præsen-
tibus, qui omnes consenserunt in articulos infra scrip-
tos, quos per fratrem Joannem Wallensem inscriptos
principi et suis archiepiscopus destinavit.

Primo. Quod dominus rex de quatuor cantredis et
terris ab eo datis, magnatibus suis nullum vult habere tractatum, nec etiam de insula Anglesey.

Idem. De tenentibus eorum cantredorum si ad
suam pacem venerint, proponit facere prout condecet
regiam majestatem, credimus tamen quod aget cum
eis misericorditer si ad pacem venerint, et ad hoc
proponimus una cum cæteris amicis efficaciter laborare, sperantes efficaciter exaudiri.

Item. De facto domini Lewelini nullum potuimus
aliud habere responsum nisi quod simpliciter et absolute conformet ad domini regis voluntatem, ut credimus firmiter quod dominus rex cum eo aget mise-
recorditer, et ad hoc intendimus cum totis viribus laborare cum cæteris amicis exaudiendis ut confidimus
cum effectu.

Primo. Quod proceres hanc formam gratiæ regiæ
conceperunt; ut videlicet domino Lewelino se regiae
gratiae submittente, provideatur ei per regem honorifice in mille libratis sterlingorum de aliquo honori-
fico comitatu, in aliquo loco Angliae; ita tamen quod
praedictus Lewelinus ponat dominum regem in Sey-
sina Snaudonum absolute, perpetue et quiete. Et ipse
rex filiae principis secundum condiceftiam sui proprii
sanguinis providebit, et ad hoc sperant se posse regis
animum inclinare.

Item.

Item. Si contingat Lewelinum ducere uxorem et
habere de ea puellam mafculam, intendunt impetrare
proceres a domino rege, ut proles illa fuccedat perpetuo hæreditario Lewelini in terra. mafculorum li-
berorum videlicet comitatu.

Item. De populo principi immediate fubjecto tam
in Snaudon quam alibi providebitur fecundum deum
prout complete faluti ejufdem populi et honori ; et ad
hoc eft regia clementia fatis prona, populo defiderans
confolabiliter providere.

Primo. Quod fi ad honorem Dei et fuum juxta
crucis affumptae debitum velit in terrae fanctae fub-
fidium proficifci, providebitur ei honorifice fecundum condefcentiam ftatus fui, ita tamen quod non
redeat nifi per regiam clementiam vocatus : rogabi-
mus etiam dominum regem, et fperamus efficaciter
exaudiri, ut provideat proli fuae.

His omnibus motu noftro fubjungimus Wallenfibus omnia pericula imminere longe gravius quam eis
diximus oraculo vivae vocis : fcribimus dure valde fed
longe durius eft obrui.vi et armis, et in fine totaliter
extirpari, quoniam omni die pericula nobis imminen-
tia aggravantur.

Item. Longe difficilius eft omni tempore in guerra effe in anguftia cordis et corporis vivere, et femper in infidiis malignari, et cum hoc vivere et mori
in peccato mortali continuo et rancore.

Item. De quo doleremus valde fi ad pacem minime veniatis, indubitanter timemus contra vos de-
bere fententiam ecclefiafticam intolerabiliter aggra-
vari pro exceffibus veftris; de quibus non poteritis
vos aliquatenus excufare in quibus invenietis mifericordiam, fi ad pacem veniatis et de his nobis refpon-
deatur in fcriptis.

Reveren-

Reverendiffimo in Chriflo patri ac domino J. Dei
gratia Archiepifcopo Cantuarienfi ac totius An-
gliæ primati fuus in Chriflo devotus filius
Lewelinus princeps Walliæ, dominus Snaudon,
falutem cum defideriis benevolentiæ filialis ac re-
verentiis multimodis et honoribus,

SANCTE pater, ficut vofmet confuluiftis, ad gratiam regiam parati fumus venire fub forma tamen
nobis fecura et honefta: fed quia forma contenta in
articulis nobis miffis minime fecura eft et honefta prout
nobis et confilio noftro videtur; et de qua multum
admirantur omnes audientes, eo quod plus tendit ad
deftruétionem et ruinam populi noftri ac noftram, quam
ad noftram honeftatem et fecuritatem, nullo modo permittit confilium noftrum nos in ea confentire fi vellemus;
alii quoque nobiles et populus nobis fubjeétus nullo
modo confentirent in eandem ob indubitatam deftructionem et diffipationem quæ inde eis poffent evenire.

Tamen fupplicamus veftræ fanétæ parternitati quatenus ad reformationem pacis debitæ, honeftæ, et fe-
cutæ, ob quam tot labores affumpfiftis, proinde laboretis, collatiónem habentes ad articulos quos vobis
mittimus in fcriptis: honorabilius enim eft et rationi
magis confonum ut de domino rege teneamus terras in
quibus jus habemus, quam nos exhæredare et eas tradere
alienis. Datum apud Garthcelyn.

Primo. Quod licet dominus rex de quatuor Cantredis et aliis terris ab eo datis magnatibus fuis, ac
de Infula Anglefey nullum voluerit habere traétatum,
tamen confilium principis non permittit, fi còntingat
aliquam pacem fieri, quin traétètur de premiffis; eo
quod ifti Cantredi funt de puro principis tenemento,
in quibus merum jus habuerunt principes et præde-
ceffores fui à temporibus Cambri filii Bruti, tum quia
funt de principatu, cujus confirmationem princeps

obtinet pro bonæ memoriæ Octobonum fedis *Apoftolicæ*
legatum in Anglia, confenfu domini regis et fui patris ad hoc intervenienti, ficut pater Chartas eorum
infpicienti, tum quia etiam equius eft quod veri hæredes teneant dictos Cantredos de domino rege pro pecunia et fervitiis confuetis, quam eos dari extraneis et
Advenis, qui et fi fuerunt regere aliquam tamen per
vim et potentiam.

Dicunt etiam comiter omnes tenentes de omnibus
Cantredis Walliæ quod non funt aufi venire ad voluntatem regis ut de eis difponat fecundum regiam ma-
jeftatem.

Primo. Quod dominus rex nec pacta, nec juramenta, nec Chartas fervavit ab initio verfus dominum
fuum principem et ipfos.

Secundo. Quia regales in ecclefias et ecclefiafticas
perfonas inivit crudeliffimam tyrannidem.

Tertio. Quod non tenentur ad prædicta, cum fint
homines principis qui etiam paratus eft de dictis tenementis domino regi obedire per fervitia confueta. Ad
id quod dicit quod princeps veniet fimpliciter et abfolute
ad voluntatem domini regis: refpondetur quod cum
nulli de dictis Cantredis aufi fint venire ad talem voluntatem propter caufas prædictas, nec comitas eorum
permittat principem venire ad dictam voluntatem modo
prædicto.

Item. Quod proceres regni procurent ut domino
principi provideatur in mille libratis in aliquo loco
Angliæ; dicatur quod illam provifionem non debet
acceptare cum fit procurata per dictos proceres, qui
nituntur ad exhæreditationem principis, ut habeant
terras fuas in Wallia. Item idem princeps non tene-
tur dimittere hæreditatem fuam et progenitorum fuorum in Wallia à tempore Bruti, et etiam fibi confir-
matam per Romanæ fedis legatum, ut dictum eft;
et terram in Anglia acceptare, unde linguam, mores et
leges ac confuetudines ignorat; ubi poffent etiam fibi
quædam malitiori imponi ex odio inveterato à vicinis Anglicis quibus terra illa privaretur in perpetuum.

4   Item.

Item. Ex quo rex proponit privare principem fua
priftina hæreditate, non videtur probabile quod rex permitteret ei habere terram in Anglia ubi nullum jus videtur habere. Et fi etiam non permitteretur principi
terra fterilis et inculta jure hæreditario ab antiquo et
debita in Wallia; nullatenus permitteretur eidem in
Anglia terra fertilis culta et habundans.

Item. Quod dictus princeps ponat dominum regem
in Seyfino Snawdon abfolute, perpetue et quiete: dicatur quod cum Snawdon fit de appendiciis principatus
Walliæ, quem ipfe et antecefforcs fui tenuerunt à tempore Bruti, ut dictum eft; confilium fuum non permittit
eum renuntiare dicto loco, et locum nimis fibi debitum
in Anglia receptare.

Item. Populus Snawdon dicit, quod licet princeps
vellet dare regi Seyfinam eorundem, ipfi tamen nollent homagium facere alicui extraneo, cujus linguam,
mores, legefque penitus ignorant. Quia fic poffet
contingere eos in perpetuum captivari, ac crudeliter
tractari, ficut alii Cantredi circumquaque per Ballivos regis ac alios regales alias tractati fuerunt, cru-
delius quam Saraceni; prout patet in rotulis quos vobis miferunt fancte pater. Ifta funt dicenda pro Davide fratre principis. Quod cum voluerit terram
fanctam adire hoc faciet voluntarie et ex voto pro Deo
non pro homine, unde invitus non peregrinabitur Deo
dante; qui coacta fervitia Deo novit difplicere. Et
fi contingat ipfum in pofterum terram fanctam adire
bona ductus voluntate, non propter hoc deberent
ipfe et hæredes fui in perpetuum exhæreditari;
immò potius præmium obtinere. Præterea quia
princeps, et fui caufa odii, ad aliquos concipiendi, vel
lucri captandi non moverunt guerram alienas terras in-
vadendo; fed fuam propriam hæreditatem jura li-
bertatefque, necnon fuorum defendendo; dominuf-
que rex et fui odio inveterato, et caufa lucrandi terras noftras guerram fecit: credimus in hoc juftam
guerram nos fovere, et fperamus in hac Deum nos
velle juvare, ac in ecclefiarum devaftatores divinam
ultionem convertere, qui ecclefias funditus deftruxerunt ac combufferunt, facra ex eis rapuerunt, Sacer-

dotes, Clericos religiosos, claudos, surdos, mutos, infantes; ubera lactentes, ac debiles et miserabiles personas, ut usque sexu occiderunt; et alia enormia perpetrarunt, sicut in dictis rotulis vobis transmissis contineatur: unde absit à sancta paternitate vestra sententiam aliquam fulminare in alios quàm in illos qui prædicta perpetrârunt. Nòs enim qui regalibus prædicta passi fuimus, speramus à vobis super praemissis paternum solatium, et remedium obtinere; et in prædictos sacrilegos eorumque fautores, qui nullo super his privilegio defenduntur, animadvertere; ne prae defectu dignæ correctionis seu ultionis in eos exercendo prædicta mala in perpetuum per alios trahantur in exemplum.

Mirantur etiam quamplures in terra nostra, quod consuluistis nobis dimittere terram nostram propriam, et alienam adire inter hostes nostros conversando; quia ex quo non possumus pacem habere in terra quæ nostra est ipso jure nostro, minime poterimus in aliena terra inter hostes nostros pacifice conservari: et licet durum sit in guerra et insidiis vitam ducere; durius tamen est funditus destrui, et ad nihilum, nisi Deus avertat, deduci populum Christianum qui nihil aliud quærit nisi sua jura defendere; unde necessitas ad hoc nos cogit, et inimicorum cupiditas non offendit; et vos, sancte pater, coram nobis dixistis, quod vos sententiastis in omnes qui impediunt pacem causa odii vel lucri; sed manifestum est qui sunt illi qui guerrant istis causis.

Timor enim mortis, et incarcerationis, vel perpetuæ exhæreditationis, nulla observatio fœderum pactorum vel chartarum, tyrannica dominatio, vel multa alia consimilia cogunt nos esse in guerris; et hoc Deo et vobis ostendimus, et petimus à vobis paternum adjutorium, ut patet in literis nostris.

Ad hoc multi alii in regno Angliæ offenderunt regem et tamen nullos exhæredavit in perpetuum, ut dicitur; unde si aliqui ex nostris ipsum offenderunt injuste, dignum est ut satisfaciant prout possint sine exhæredatione; et sicut in vobis confidimus, supplicamus quod ad hoc laboretis sancte pater: nam etsi nobis imponatur quod fregimus pacem, tamen illi verius fregerunt qui nullum fœdus vel pactum nobis servaverunt;

vaverunt; qui nullam emendam de quærimoniis nobis
fecerunt, ut patet in rotulis.

*Primo auditis refcripfit Archiepifcopus Wallenfibus
in hæc verba :*

IN nomine domini, Amen. Cum nos frater J. per-
miffione divina Cantuarienfis ecclefiæ minifter humilis totius Angliæ primas; fcientes noftro incumbere
officio, pro vobis domine Leweline princeps Walliæ
ac fubditis veftris exponere nos et noftra fpretis viarum
incommodis et periculis, veftram adjuverimus præfen-
tiam oves erroneas reducturi; et fpeculatoris fungentis
officio vobis myfteriæ vivæ vocis diximus pericula quæ
genti veftræ videbamus luce clarius imminere, fubjunctis
remediis eorundem; tefte optantes altiffimo juxta pon-
tificale debitum cuilibet veftrum ecclefiam minimo de
corpore noftro pontem facere ad falutis littora redu-
cendo. Tandem veftris auditis precibus et anguftiis
eas ut neceffitatis veftræ nuntius præfentavimus regiæ
majeftati, quem ab olim ad pœnitentes adverfarios in-
troitum fcimus effe propitium; ut quidam de veftris
et aliis ut nobis certis conftat indiciis ipfius clementia
abutantur. Tractavimus infuper cum magnatibus
et proceribus Angliæ præfentibus de modificatione gratiæ regiæ ipforum affiftentia noftris vobis fupplicationi-
bus impretranda, cujus modificationis feriem per fer-
vum Dei fratrem Johannem Wallenfem vobis mifimus
in fcriptum, una cum confilio noftro quod vobis fecundum deum falubrius videbatur; vos autem deli-
berationem veftram nobis in quadam remififtis cedula
per eundem, cujus cedulæ pernitiofas latebras vobis
paterno affectu præfentibus aperimus. Primò igitur
dictis vos juri nolle cedere quatuor Cantredarum, quia
progenitores veftri à temporibus Cambri filii Bruti in
eifdem juris plenitudinem habuerunt; fed ne fimplici-
ores in vobis de fucceffu hujufmodi gloriantur, falva in
omnibus pace veftra; vobis licet inviti ipfius radicem
originis ex geftis Britonum et Anglorum ad memoriam
revocamus. Difperfis enim olim Trojanis pro eo quod
Paridis adulterium defenfarunt; fatemur progenitores

V A---

veſtræ multitudinis interpoſitis quibuſdam ſeditionibus
fugæ ſibi præſidium aſſumpſiſſe; et utinam non
maneat in eis hujuſmodi contagii memoria qui ſic
libera matrimonia parvipendunt ut ſpurios et inceſtu
genitos à ſucceſſione hæreditaria ut dicitur non repel-
lunt, quin potius uxores legitimæ Howeli da patro-
ciniæ, contra Evangelium dato repudio fama teſte, vel
potius infamia, repelluntur; qualiter demum Brutus
Dianæ præſagiis non ſine diaboli præſtigiis per ido-
latriam immolato Cervæ Venatitiæ obtentis, inſulam Britannicam pervaſerit per famoſas hiſtorias de-
claratur; pervaſerit inquam inhabitatam inſulam,
agentibus ſtatura proceris quarum peremit fortiſſimum
Corineus. Gentibus inquam, de boreali praſapia quæ
non ſolum . . . . verum etiam Scythiam trans
Danubium ab occidente noſtro per Aquilonis latera
uſque in Orientales terminos occupavit. Quam ergo
quæſumus fecerunt vobis injuriam Angli et Saxones
ejuſdem generis, ſi vos proceſſu temporis ab uſurpato
dominio perturbarunt: cum ſcriptum eſſe noveritis,
vae qui prædaris in omne prædaberis. Non oportet
autem ſimplices in radice adulterina proceſſu idololatriæ,
et uſurpationis ſpoliis gloriari. Progenitores inſuper
veſtri moderniores, cum enervati deliciis ſibi non
ſufficerent defenlandis, obruentibus eos Scotis et
Pictis, denegato etiam eis Romani imperii præſidio
poſtulato, ad Germanorum refugium convolârunt, qui
venientes repudiarunt, hoſtes uſque in praeſentem diem
ſuarum labores manuum manducantes. Ex his cauſis
quum ſedet ſola à vobis inſula olim populo plenâ, veſtro
proſcribente Jeremia, quia prophetae tui viderunt
tibi vana et ſtulta; item prædictorum juribus Cantredorum confirmationem legati frivole allegatis, cum
non fuerit intentionis ſuae jura regia, ſeu etiam jura
civilia et Canonica, ſicut nec potuit enervare: pro
crimine enim leſæ majeſtatis, in quod vos incidiſſe
dicimini, juxta quod ſcribitur ſexta quaeſtione. Se-
cunda paragrapho; *Si quis cum militibus*, et 22.
Quæſt. *ultima capitulo* de forma fidelitatis. Omne
perit jus haereditarium et expirat: in Cantredis igitur
prædictis in quibus ab olim domino regi jus dicitur
adquiſitum, et in Snawdon ac caeteris quae teneris
                                                      jure

jure haereditario, nihil poteftis ficut nec fubditi veftri, ut ex praeallegatis videtur, nifi ex fola regia clementia praeftolari. Dicitur demum quod populus non vult ad gratiam regiam convolare, quia dominus rex, nec pacta, nec juramenta, nec chartarum fœdera principi confervavit. Et nos quaerimus ex cujus vel quorum iftud fit judicio declaratum, nifi per vos qui in caufa propria judicium ufurpatis, et per fingulas luftrales periodos pacem infringitis, innocentes jugulatis, incendia facitis, munitiones regias pro viribus vaftatis; ac domini Howell da quitalia injuriarum remedia in lege fua quam vidimus inftituit, autoritate quam ei diabolus delegavit. Praeterea in regem impungitis, dicentes, quod regales ecclefias et perfonas ecclefiafticas crudeli vaftavit tyrannide, et confumunt; ad quod taliter refpondemus, quod, dominus rex praedicta mala nec fieri mandavit, nec rata habuit, quin potius nobis obtulit ultronei, quod quam citò aderit oportunitas ecclefiarum proponit difpendia refacire; quod differt ufque ad fedatam guerrae tempeftatem, ne fi prius fieret deftruerentur iterum per latrones. Praeterea timetis in Anglia honorem fufcipere, ne confequenter vobis occafionata malitia auferatur, cum tamen fateamini quod dominus re nullum fuum exhæredaverit inimicum; quod fruftra vos timere credimus, fi legaliter vivere vos et veftri didiceritis, et non a parti cum domino veftro contendere vel certare. Mores vobis et populo veftro caufamini incognitos; et nos è contrario opinamur quod expediret vobis omnibus in modum alium et mores penitus transformari. Cum enim fitis ficut cæteri homines donis Dei gratuitis adornati, fed in veftro Anglo devoramini: ut nec ecclefiam juvetis contra hoftes fidei militando; nec Clerum ftudio fapientiae, exceptis pauciffimis, decoretis; quin potius major pars veftrum torpet otio et lafciviis, ut pene nefciat mundus vos effe populum, nifi per paucos ex vobis qui videntur ut plurimum in — mendicare. Deinde fcribitis quod creditis altiffimum vos juvare pro juftitia decretantes; utinam inquam altiffimus juvet vos falubriter et dirigat ad falutem. Sed ne ruinas aliquas Anglorum ex inconfideratione fua provenientes veftris

velitis

velitis meritis arrogare curetis advertere qualiter qui in
cœlis habitat fatuos fublimat et elevat ad modicum ut
perpetuo allidat ; fic certe olium populus Dei electus
ante harum repertam civitatem pro unius Anathemate
confortis, verfus in fugam quofdam fuorum perdidit
bellatorum : fic certe quater centena millia bellatorum
duodecim tribuum Ifrael in fuo numero et fortitudine
confidentes ab unius tribus modico populo, occifis ex
40 millibus bellatorum, per vices varias funt confufi :
cum tamen purgato unius Anathemate, prædicta Civi-
tas finaliter deleleta fuerit per illos, qui prius confufi
fuerant, et per lacrymas placato domino cum jejuniis,
oblatis facrificiis, tribus illa quæ praevaluerat prius, per
prius confufos quafi totaliter fit deleta ; fic certe aliter flagellat dominus filios quos recipit, et aliter quos
decernit ut arbores ftériles extirpare. Ista vobis fcribimus in cordis amaritudine ab his partibus recedentes,
nec prenidicare intendimus falubriori confilio, fi vobis
cœlitus deftinetur, nec latre vos volumus quod nullum
per vos invenimus excufationis fufficiens remedium, quo
obftante minime. debeatis in excors Irnam incidiffe
pernuntiari : dudum laret in Oxon confilio contra pacis règiæ turbatores, viam autem pacis aliam invenire
non poffumus, nec adhuc in fpe fumus aliud obtinendi.
Sed fi nobis aliquid confultius videatur agendum, vobis
numquam claudemus grémium, nec auxilium denega-
bimus opportunum. Dat. apud Ruthelan 18 Calend.
Decemb. Ann. Dom. 1282.

Lewelinus autem princeps Walliæ prædictus fpretis
omnibus oblationibus et pacis formis poft fcriptis, in-
vafit hoftiliter terram domini regis Angliæ deftruendo
eam incendio et rapina, nec non homines terræ illius
ad fe trahendo, et à bonitate pacis regiæ feparando.
Qui tamen princeps infra menfem illum ignominofa
morte primus de exercitu fuo occifus eft, per familiam
domini Cadmundi de mortuo mari, filii domini Rogeri
de mortuo mari ; et totus exercitus fuus vel occilus, vel
in fugam converfus in partibus Montis Gomerici die
Veneris proximo, ante Feftum S. Lucæ, videlicet 3.
Id. Decemb. fub Anno. Dom. 1282. In —— decima
litera dominicali D. currente.

A TABLE

A

T A B L E

OF THE

Moſt Remarkable Things in this
B O O K.

A.

ABerffraw deſtroyed by the Iriſh, Page 57.
Adelred King of the Weſt Saxons vanquiſhed by the
Britains, 15.
Adelred married Emma daughter of the duke of Normandy,
and the reaſons of it, 70. The conſequence of the Marriage, 71. Flies with his wife and children into Normandy, 75. Returns, ibid. His death, 78.
Aedan ap Blegorad having ſlain his competitor Conan, is proclaimed Prince of North-Wales, 69. Is ſlain with his four
ſons in battle, 79.
Alan the 2d. King of Little Britain aſſiſted Cadwalader, 9.
Adviſed him to obey the viſion, 11.
Alfred King, an encourager of learning, and founder of the
univerſity of Oxford, 32. Routs the Danes, ibid. Makes
them forſwear the ſight of Engliſh ground, 33. He cauſed
the laws of Dyſnwal Moelmut and queen Marſia to be
tranſlated into Engliſh, &c. 43.
Alfred propoſed to be ſent for to be king over the Engliſh, 85.
Oppoſed by earl Goodwyn, 68. Had his eyes put out,
ibid.
Anarawd prince of North-Wales ſucceeds his father Rodri,
37. Dies, his iſſue, 45.

Angleſey

The T A B L E.

Anglesey destroyed by the men of Dublin, 46. Ravaged by Madoc ap Meredith prince of Powys, but all his men were cut off, 175.

Arthur King of Britain, his sepulchre found in the isle of Asalon, 206. The inscription upon it., 207.

Arthur eldest son to king Henry the seventh, created prince of Wales, and dies at Ludlow, 324.

Athelstane, tho' a Bastard, the worthiest prince of the Saxon blood, 48. His victory over the Danes, Scots and Normans, ibid. Removes the Britains to Cornwal, dies, 49.

Aulafe and all his Danes received baptism, 49. Swears never to molest England, 66.

B.

BAldwin archbishop of Canterbury, the first that made his visitation in Wales, 208.

Bede his education and writings, 16.

Bible, how, when, and by whom translated into Welch, 326.

Blethyn and Rhywalhon princes of North-Wales assist Edric against the king of England, 101. A rebellion formed against them by Meredith, and Ithel ap Gruffydh, ibid. Battle wherein Rhywalhon and Ithel were slain, Blethyn murdered Rich. 104.

Britain, how and when forsaken by the Roman forces, 1. Invaded by the Scots and Picts, ibid.

Britains, their sad complaints to Ætios thrice consul, 2. The reasons of their weakness, 3 and 4. Their message to the Saxons, 5. The Britains of Stratclwyd and Cumberland settle in North-Wales, 38.

Brochwel once prince of Powys, a great defender of the Monks of Bangor, 23.

Bruce de William, Lord of Brecknock under pretence of friendship, barbarously murders Sitsylht ap Dysnwal, his son and followers, 204.

Bruce Sir Edward, his letter to sir Griffydh Llwyd, 312, and 313.

C.

CAdelh prince of South-Wales dies, his issue, 44. Cadelh takes Caermardhyn, and beats the Normans and Flemings, 165. Like to be murdered, 170. Gone upon pilgrimage, 171.

Cadwgan murdered by Madawc, 138.

Cadwalader the last king of Britain of the British race, 8. Retires to Alan king of Little Britain, ibid. Learned in a vision to go to Rome, and there shorn a Monk, 10.

Cadwalader with his brother Owen Gwynedh from North-Wales

Wales In conjunction with several South-Wales lords made an horrible slaughter of the Normans and Flemings, and drove them out of South-Wales, 157, 158.

Cadwalader forced to flee from his brother Owen to Ireland, 163. Returns with Irish forces, concludes a peace with his brother, made prisoner by the Irish, rescued by his brother, 164. Escapes out of prison, 171. Flies to England, ibid. His death and issue, 200.

Canterbury redeemed by the citizens from being burnt by the Danes, for 3000 l. 73. Betrayed afterwards to them and burnt, 74.

Caradoc king of North-Wales fights and is slain by the Saxons, 21. His pedigree, ibid.

Celibacy enjoined to the clergy in a synod held at London, 127.

Christian faith pure in the British church, 221.

Charles duke of York created prince of Wales, 328.

Charles eldest son of king Charles the First created prince of Wales, 318.

Civil war in Wales, and Edwal son of Meyric the indisputable heir set up in North-Wales, 67.

Clare, earl of, possessed himself of divers strong-holds in Cardigan, 177.

Clynnoc fawr an abby in Arfon, 11. When and by whom built, 12. Endowed by prince Anarawd, 39.

Cnute the Dane chosen king, and his cruelty to the English Hostages, 75. Returns to England, ibid. The Northumbers submit to him, 76. Besieges London, is routed by Edmund, ibid. Combats Edmund, agree and divide England between them, 78. Generously punishes Edmund Ironside's murder, ibid. Marries Emma Edelred's widow, 80. Requires a subsidy of the English, ibid. Made a pompous journey to Rome, 82. Makes the Scots do him homage, ibid. Dies, and is succeeded by his son Harold Harefoot, 83.

Conel prognosticating the Norman invasion, and success, 100.

Commotions in England, 158.

Conan, War between him and his brother Howel, 22. Dies, 23. His pedigree, ibid.

Conspiracy against William the conqueror by the English and the Welch detected, and the conspirators executed, 104.

Constable, Walter, marries Nest's daughter, and has the lordship of Brecknock, 116. A strange passage related by him to Henry the First, concerning Gruffydh ap Rhys, ibid.

Crogens, used as a term of reproach by the English to the Welch, 123. No reason for it, 224.

Cynric, prince Owen's son, slain 162.

Danes

D.

DAnes begin to difturb England, 20, 21. They prevail and winter in England, 28. They take and deftroy Winchefter, 30. Kill Ofbright and Elba kings of Northumberland 31. Slew Edmund king of the Angles, ibid. Fought five battles with Ethelred, ibid. They win London and Redding, 33. Routed by the Weft-Saxons, 34. Are defeated by Alfred and received the Chriftian faith, 37. They harrafs North-Wales, 39. Defeated by the Armonican Britains, ibid. Forced to rife from before Exeter, and fpoil the fea-coaft of Wales, 41. Receive a great overthrow, 42. They grow powerful, not only in England but alfo in Ireland, 44. Thrice overthrown by the Englifh, 45. Cruelly overthrown by Tottenhale, 46. Routed by king Edward, 48 Driven out of the kingdom by king Edmund, 52. Force the Englifh to pay the Dane-Gelt, 65. Make a terrible havock in Wales, and had tribute paid them, 66. Make frefh deveftations in Wales and England, 70. They are maffacred by the Englifh, 71. Force the Englifh nobility to buy their peace for 30,000 l. 72. They beat Wolf kettel, 73. Slew Ethelftan and ranfacked the country, 74.

Dafydh ap Owen killed his brother Howel in battle, and gets to be prince of North-Wales, 195. Secures his brother Maelgon, reduces Anglefey, and banifhes his brethren, 202. Sends a band of Welch to accompany king Henry into Normandy, ibid. Is difpoffeft by his eldeft brother's fon Lhewelyn ap Iorwerth, 213. Ungrateful to prince Lhewelyn for his liberty, 224.

Dafydh ap Lhewelyn prince of Wales did homage at Glocefter to the king of England, 259. Is excommunicated by the bifhop of Bangor for detaining his brother Gruffydh in prifon, whom he refufed to deliver at the king's requeft, 260. Submits to the king of England, 262. Cajols the king to detain his brother Gruffydh prifoner, ibid. Engages the Pope on his fide againft the king, but he proves falfe, 264. Fights the Englifh often with various fuccefs, ibid. Dies without iffue, 268.

Davids, St. burnt by the Weft-Saxons, 21. Deftroyed by the Danes, 45 Again by the Danes 69. Deftroyed by ftrangers, 107. The cathedral facrilegioufly robbed, 111. Made fubject to the fee of Canterbury, 125.

Dunftan, St. bifhop of Canterbury, his prediction and death, 61.

The T A B L E.

E.

EASTER, the Britains and Saxons quarrel about the obfervation of it, 18, 19.

Edgar, advanced to the kingdom in his brother Edwin's room, 56. He waftes North-Wales, and agrees for a yearly tribute of 300 wolves, ibid. Regulates drinking veffels becaufe of the Danes excefs, 57. Rowed in his barge by fix kings on the river Dee, 59.

Edgar Edeling proclaimed king, forced into Scotland, 101. Received to king William's mercy, 103.

Edmund king of England's death, and the uncertain manner of it, 53.

Edmund Ironfide flain by Edric's fon, 78.

Edwal Foel and his his brother Elis fight the Englifh, and are flain, 49. Their iffue, ibid.

Edward fent for from Normandy and made king, 86. The Confeffor's death, 98.

Edward I. king of England invades Wales, and prevails, 283. Infifts upon prince Lhewelyn's fubmiffion without referve, 292. Sets prince Lhewelyn's head upon the Tower of London, and puts his brother David to death, 299. Subdues all Wales, ibid. Kept his Chriftmas at Aber-Conwey, 307. In neceffity, would tafte no wine for the fatisfaction of his foldiers, 308. Cuts down all the woods in Wales, and builds Beaumaris-caftle, 309.

Edward of Caernarvon firft prince of Wales of the Englifh Blood, 301. Received homage at Chefter of all the Freeholders of Wales, 310. Goes farther into the country to the fame purpofe, ibid.

Edward eldeft fon to king Edward II. created prince of Wales 313.

Edward eldeft fon to king Edward III. created prince of Wales 313. His character and death, 314.

Edward fon to Henry VI. created prince of Wales, 323. Murdered, ibid.

Edward eldeft fon to king Edward VI. created prince of Wales, murdered, 223.

Edward VI. inclined to favour the Welch, 323.

Edward fon to Richard III. created prince of Wales, 324.

Edward fon to Henry VIII. created prince of Wales, 325.

Edwyn king of England vitious, difpoffeffed and dies, 56.

Egbert fole monarch in Britain, 25. Calls the country England, ibid. He fights the Danes, 26.

Eineon invites the Normans into Wales, and perfuades them to ftay, 112.

Elfleda, Mercian queen, her valiant acts both againft the

D d   Danes

The T A B L E.

Danes and Welch, 46. Her death, 47. Left a daughter
Alfwyden difinherited by king Edward, ibid.
Ethelwulph king of the Weft-Saxons paid Peter-pence to
Rome, 29. Learned and devout, ibid.
Eyes of feveral plucked out, a barbarous cuftom, 155.
Ethelbald king of Mercia invades Wales, 16. - In conjunc-
tion with Adelred, overthrow the Britains, ibid.

F.

FLanders, a part of it drowned prejudicial to the Welch,
128.
Flemings fettled in part of Wales, 128.

G.

GAllio routs the Scots and Picts, 2. Builds a wall crofs
the land, ibid.
Gam, Sir David, imprifoned by Owen Glyndyfwr, and releafed, 321. Revolts from Owen, ibid His anfwer in
France to Henry V. concerning the French army, mor-
tally wounded at Agincourt, knighted and died, 322.
Gavelkind, that cuftom in Wales, 22.
Geoffrey of Monmouth made bifhop of St. Davids, 171.
Glamorgan, lordfhip defcribed, 314. The beft of it Fitzha-
mon the chief of the Normans kept to himfelf, 115.
Godwyn, earl, rebels againft king Edward, 89. Invades the
land, and is reconciled to the king, 90. Dies fuddenly
fitting at the king's table, 91.
Gray, Reginald, lord of Ruthyn taken prifoner by Owen
Glyndyfwr and ranfomed, 316, 317.
Gruffydh ap Lhewelyn declared prince of North-Wales, 84.
His country invaded by the Englifh and Danes, and routed
by him, 85. Reduced all Wales under his fubjection, ibid.
Routs Howel prince of South-Wales at Pencader, ibid.
Taken prifoner by the Irifh under the command of Iago
ap Edwal, and recovered by his own men, 87. Overcomes and flays Gruffydh ap Rhyderch and his army, &c.
ibid. Concludes a peace with Harold king Edward's general, 94. His palace at Ruthlan burnt by the Englifh,
ibid. Prince Gruffydh murdered by Harold's contrivance
after he had reigned 30 years, 95.
Gruffydh ap Conan confirmed in the principality of Wales,
109 Refufed at firft an accommodation with king Henry,
at laft fues and obtains peace, 141. Careffed by the king,
and promifed to deliver up Gruffydh ap Rhys, 143. Dies
158. His iffue, 159.
Gruffydh the fon of Rhys ap Tudor laid claim to South-
Wales, 143. Flies to North Wales, 143. Wifhed with
his

his brother Howel to withdraw into South-Wales, 144.
Forced to bid open defiance to the king of England, ibid.
The Flemings and Welch lords join together to oppose
him, 145. He takes Caermardhyn, 146. Invited to the
government of Cardigan-shire, ibid. Succeeds, 147. War
at Aberystwyth, 148. Invidiously dispossessed of his estate,
154. Dies, 158.

Gruffydh son to the lord Rhys succeeded his father, 116.
Plagued with his brother Maelgon, 219. A hopeful prince,
dies, 222.

Gruffydh ap Conan ap Owen ap Gwynedh buried in a
Monk's Cowl, the superstition of it, 221.

Gruffydh prince David's brother endeavouring to make his
escape out of the Tower of London, breaks his neck,
263. His body recovered and conveyed to Conway and
honourably buried, 270.

Gruffydh Llwyd knighted by king Edward I. rebels, 311.
Treats with Sir Robert Bruce for succours against the
English with his letter to him, ibid. Over-runs North-
Wales and the Marches, and is taken prisoner, 313.

Gurmundus a Norwegian from Ireland, invades Britain, 7.

Gwenwynwyn worsted by the English, 218. Refuses ho-
mages to prince Lhewelyn, 222. At last consents to it,
223. Detained prisoner at Shrewsbury, 225. Set at
liberty, regains his country, 228. Revolts from prince
Lhewelyn and is dispossest, 242.

H.

HArold succeeds Canute his brother in England, 83.
Dies, and is succeeded by Hardi Canute his brother, 85.

Harold's favour with the king, envied by his brother Tosty
who barbarously murdered his men at his house in Hereford, and his saying, 7. Made king, 98. Slain, 100.

Hasting a Dane invades France, 40. His policy to obtain
Limogis, 41. His cruelty, ibid.

Henry I. his partiality in favour of the Normans, 127. Makes
his brother Robert prisoner, and puts out his eyes, 128.
Kind to Cadwgan the father of Owen, 132. Invades
Wales with three armies, 140. Overcomes the French
king, 151. Lost his children at sea, and marries, 152.
Invades Wales, in danger, ibid. Agrees with Meredith
ap Blethyn and returns, 153. His death and Successor,
156.

Henry II. sends the Flemings into West-Wales, 173. Invited to the conquest of Wales, ibid. Repulsed and in
danger of his life, 174. Concludes a peace with prince

 Owen,

Owen, 175. Quarrels and concludes a peace with France, 187. Invades Wales and brings prince Rhys to do him homage, 188. Invades Wales again with a most potent army, 190. Returns without any thing memorable, and for revenge puts out the eyes of the hostages, 191. Makes a third expedition into Wales to as little purpose, ibid. Passes through Wales, receiving homage of prince Rhys in his way to the conquest of Ireland, 198, 199. Returns through Wales and inclined to leave it in a peaceable condition, 199, 200. Engaged in a civil war against his son Henry, 201. Makes a peace with France, and his children forced to submit, 202. Dies, 209.

Henry III. king of England invades Wales, and is worsted, 251. Invades Wales again, 254. Makes Henry of Monmouth his general against the Welch, but with ill success, 255. Laments the death of the earl of Pembrock, 256. Invades Wales, and makes prince David to submit, 261, 262. Invades Wales, 263. Fights the Welch with no success, and invites the Irish into Anglesey, 265. Oppresses Wales, and returns dissatisfied, 269, 270. Item, 274. Wastes the borders, 275. Requires a subsidy to subdue Wales, 276. Dies, 280.

Henry, eldest son to Henry IV. created prince of W. 318.

Henry IV. makes unmerciful laws against the Welch, 319.

Henry duke of York created prince of Wales, 324.

Henry VII. grants the Welch a charter of liberty, and directed a commission to enquire into the birth and quality of his grandfather Owen Tudor, 325.

Henry VIII. incorporates the Welch with the English, 326.

Henry eldest son to king James created prince of Wales, 328.

Howel Dha preferred to be prince of all Wales, 50. His laws, ibid. Goes to Rome to have them confirmed, 51. His death and issue, 53.

Howel ap Ievan expelled his uncle Iago, and took the government of Wales upon him, 59. At last agree, 60. Kills Edwal Fychan, and the reasons of it ibid. Overthrows the Danes, 61. Invades England, and is slain, 62. He is succeeded by his brother Cadwalhan, who was quickly slain, 63.

Howel and Meredith, prince Lhewelyn's murderers invite the Irish Scots into South Wales, 82. Slew Rhydderch, and take the government, 83 Meredith slain by the fons of Conan ap Sitfylht, ibid. Howel attempts the recovery of South-Wales, is overcome and slain by prince Gruffydh near Tywy-Head, 87.

Howel ap Grono driven out of Rydcors castle by the Normans,

mans, 126. Bafely betrayed to them, and murdered, 127.

Howel ap Owen Gwynedh won the caftle of Ewyas, 167. with his brother Conan quarrel with their uncle Cadwalader, befiege and take the caftle of Cynfael from him, 168. Makes Cadwalader his prifoner, and poffeffes his land, ib. He loft all his country to Cadelh, Meredith, and Rhys ap Gruffydh, who put the garifon of Llanrhyftyd to the fword, 169.

I.

IAgo ap Edwal recovers his right to North-Wales, 82. Slain in battle againft Gruffydh ap Lhewelyn, 84.

Ifor fent into Britain with an army, by his father Alan, 13. Routs the Saxons, ibid. Marries Ethelburga, Kentwyn's coufin, and fucceeded him in the Weft-Saxon kingdom, 14. Founded Glaftenbury Abby, ib. Died at Rome, 15.

John, Arch-deacon of Llanbadarn dies, and is canonized, 160.

John, K. of England in his way to Ireland through Wales, difcharged a criminal that murdered a prieft, 226. Famifhed Will de Bruce, and Maud his aunt at Windfor after his return, 227. The reafon of his cruelty and difaffection to priefts, ib. Marches with a great army into Wales, and returns without fuccefs, 229, 230. Makes a fecond expedition, ib. Orders Foulk vifcount Cardyff to fubdue thofe that oppofe in South-Wales, and they at laft do him homage, but quickly revolt, 231, 232. Makes an expedition into Wales, 229. Makes a fecond and third, and hangs the Welch pledges, reconciles himfelf to Rome, and engages in a civil war with his barons, 237. Dies, and is fucceeded by his fon Henry, 242.

Iorwerth ap Blethyn revolts from the earl of Salop, 124. Bafely ufed by king Henry for it, the reafon of it, 125. Delivered out of prifon, 133. Forbids Owen and Madawc to retire to his eftate, 134. Befet and flain by Madawc and Llywarch ap Trahern, 137.

Jofeph bifhop of Landaff dies at Rome, 88.

Ireland molefted with Locufts, 42.

Ithel king of Gwent flain, 28.

L.

LHewelyn ap Sytfylht makes himfelf prince of all Wales, 79. His good government, ib. Slays Meuric that rebelled againft him with his own hand, 80. Suppreffes another rebellion, 81. Bafely flain, ibid.

Lhewelyn

Lhewelyn prince of North Wales takes David ap Owen pri-.
foner, 217. Receives homage of moſt of the Welch lords,
222. Conquers Gwenwynwyn's country, ¹225.⁷· Makes
an expedition into South Wales, and Maelgon flees, 225,
226. Marries Joan King John's daughter, 224. ·Sues
and obtains peace of the king by the means of his wife,
231. Animates the lords of North Wales to join with
him in a revolt againſt the king, 233. Diſpoſſeſſes the
Engliſh of all their holds in his country, 237. Takes
Shrewſbury, though excommunicated by the Pope, 238.
Subdues Cardigan and Carmarthen, 240. Reconciles the
the lords in South Wales, 241. Subdues Powis, 242.
Refuſes aſſiſtance to King John againſt the Dauphine,
ibid. Makes Rynald Bruce, who had revolted, ſubmit to
him, 243. Receives the ſubmiſſion and allegiance of the
Flemings in Dyfed, ibid. Subdues the revolted Flemings
again, 246. Makes his ſon Gruffydh ſubmit, ib. Complained of to the king of England by young Rhys, adjuſts
matters with him, 247. Seizes the caſtle of William
Marſhal Earl of Pembroke in Wales, and occaſions a war
between them, 247, 248. Worſts the Engliſh army, pays
homage to Henry III. 249. Deſtroys the marches, 252.
Makes a deſcent upon England, 253. Being joined by
the earl of Pembroke againſt King Henry, routs his army,
254. Makes an incurſion into the king's territories, 255. Makes peace with the king, 256. Sets
his ſon Gruffydh at liberty, ibid. Buries his princeſs
Joan, 257. Forced to quit the ſiege of Ruthlan, 258.
Makes the Welch do homage to his ſon David ibid. Dies,
his character and iſſue, 259.
Llewelyn ap Gruffydh, and Owen Goch his brother, declared princes of North Wales, 269. Quarrel, and Owen
with his brother David made cloſe priſoners, 271. Recovers
the inland country of North Wales from the Engliſh, 272.
Waſtes Cheſhire, ibid. Beats the Iriſh by ſea, 273. De-
ſires peace with the king, but fails, 277. Kind to Sir Roger Mortimer, 278. Makes a peace by the Pope's mediation
with the king, 289. Refuſes to attend upon K. Edward's co-
roronation, 280. The reaſons for his refuſal, 281. An accident made him pliable, 283, Severe conditions of peace im-
poſed upon him, 284. Married to Elianor Earl Montford's
daughter at Worceſter, 215. Reconciled with his brother David and join againſt the Engliſh, 286. Offers to ſubmit to the
king conditionally, 292. Sends a letter to the archbiſhop of
Canterbury, and the general anſwer of the Welch to his
propoſals,

3

proposals, 293, 294, 295.   Betrayed in Buelht and killed, 297.

London besieged by the Danes, 65.

M.

MAhael dispossest of his inheritance by his unnatural mother Nest's means, and how, 115.

Madoc ap Meredith prince of Powis sticks to the English interest, 173.

Madawc reconciled to King Henry, 138.   Taken prisoner by Meredith ap Blethin, 139.   Has his eyes pulled out by Owen, ibid.

Madawc ap Owen Gwynedh sails into America, 196.   Plants a colony there, ibid.

Maelgon disturbs South Wales, 228.   Beaten by his nephews, Rhys and Owen, 229.

March, earl of, marries Owen Glyndwr's daughter, 318.   Consented by indenture to divide England between Owen, Piercy, and himself, 318.

Maud, the empress, lands in England, and is received at Arundel, 162.

Meredith ap Owen possest of all Wales, 64.   Dispossest of North Wales, 67.   And routed by Edwal ap Meuric their new prince, 68.   Died without issue-male, 69.

Meredith ap Owen made prince of South Wales, 96.   Slain in battle against Caradoc ap Gruffydh, 102.

Meredith and Rhys ap Gruffydh prevails in South Wales, 171.   Meredith's death and character, 172.

Merfyn Frych is made king of Wales, 24.   Is slain, 27.

Merlyn, Ambrose, and Sylvester, their time, country, and prophesies, 10, 11.

Morgan Hen dies, an hundred years old; his marriage, estate, and issue, 58.

Morgan ap Owen kills Robert Fitz-Gilbert and his son, 157.   Slain, 175.

Morgan ap Cadogan repents of his murder committed, 156.

Murders committed, 156.   Item, 163.

N

NEwmarch, a Norman, obtains the lordship of Brecknock, and marries Nest, daughter to Llewelyn ap Gruffydh, 115.

Normans twice decimated and put to death in England, 86.   They waste and plunder Dyfed, 103.   They seize upon The lordship of Glamorgan, 113.   The names of the adventurers, ibid.   They possess themselves of several lordships in Wales, 117.   Divers of them slain in Cardigan, ibid.

: ibid. Routed again by Cadwgan ap Blethyn prince of
South Wales, and their castles destroyed, 118. Slaugh-
tered divers times by the Welch, and forced to quit the
country, 119, 120.
Northumberland invaded by the Scots, 109.

O.

OFfa king of Mercia makes a ditch from sea to sea, 20.
His death, 21.
Owen ap Edwyn a traitor to his country, 121. Made prince
of Wales by the English, but soon lost it, 122 . His
death and pedigree, 126.
Owen the son of Cadwgan enamoured of Nest the wife of
Gerald, King Henry's lieutenant in Wales, 122. Steals
her away, ibid. Flies into Ireland, 135. Returns and
wastes the country, in conjunction with Maradoc ap Ri-
ryd, 133. His men slay an English bishop the cause of
Cadwgan, his father, being dispossessed of his estate, 135.
Forced to flee into Ireland with Madawc, ibid. Returns,
and is reconciled to the king, 138. Divides Madawc's
estate between himself and Meredith ap Blethyn, 139.
Flees for fear of King Henry into North Wales, 140.
Reconciled to to the king 141. Owen is brave and knighted in Normandy 142. Employed by King Henry against
Gruffydh ap Rhys, 148. Slain by Gerald, 149.
Owen Gwynedh succeeds prince of North Wales, 160.
mightily concerned at the death of his son Run, 165. takes
and rases the castle of Mould, 166. Pulls out his nephew Cunedah's eyes, and castrates him, 170. Being provoked invades Llandhinam, 193. Dies, his character and
issue, 194.
Owen Cyfeilioc and Owen Fychan dispossess Iorwerth Goch
of his estate in Powis, 192. Cyfeilioc dies, leaving his
estate to Gwenwynwyn his son, 217.
Owen Glendwr, his family, education, and employment,
315. Opposed by the Lord Ruthyn without redress, takes
up arms, and makes him prisoner, 316. Prevails, takes the
earl of March prisoner, 317. Retakes Aberystwyth castle, 319. Summons a parliament at Machynlleth, 320.
Secures David Gam upon a suspicion of a design he had to
murder him, 321. Burnt his house, and his verse upon
it, ibid.

P.

PAtent of lands granted in Wales to the earl of Portland,
302. Commons address upon it, 303. King's answer, 304.

Peckham

Peckham, John, archbiſhop of Canterbury endeavours a
  reconciliation of Prince Llewelyn, and his brother, with
  the king, 286. His remonſtrance to the prince and people, 287, 288, 289, 290. Solicits the king on behalf
  of the Welch, 291. Sends articles to the Welch, 292,
  Excommunicates the prince of Wales and his adherents.
  297.
Peace in general between England and Wales, except with
  Prince Rhys, who was forced to comply with the king,
  176. Unjuſtly dealt with, 177.
Powis, prince of, removes his ſeat from Pengwern to Mathraval, 20. An account of it while a principality and a
  lordſhip, with the ſeveral diviſions and poſſeſſors thereof,
  whether of Britiſh or Engliſh blood, 175, to 185.

R.

REbellion in the North, cauſed by Earl Toſty's inſolence,
  97. Appeaſed, 89.
Rhydderch ſeizes upon South Wales, 82.
Rhydderch and Rhys the ſons of Rhydderch ap Ieſtyn put in
  their claim to South Wales, 88.
Rhys brother to Prince Gruffydh taken by the Engliſh, and
  put to death at Bulendun, 91.
Rhys ap Owen and Rhydderch ap Caradoc jointly govern
  South Wales, 105. The latter dies. 106. A rebellion
  againſt the other, ibid. Invaded alſo from North Wales,
  flies, purſued, and ſlain, 187.
Rhys ap Theodor allowed prince of South Wales, as lawful heir, 107. A rebellion formed againſt him, flies into
  Ireland, returns and defeats his enemy, 110. Suppreſſes
  another rebellion, 111. Slain near Brecknock in a fight
  againſt the invading Normans and his own rebellious ſubjects, 112.
Rhys ap Gruffydh prince of South Wales takes Llanymd-
  dyfri caſtle, 177. Subdues Cardigan, 178. Gives Hen. II,
  hoſtages to obſerve the peace made between them,
  ibid. Beſieges Carmarthen, then forced to quit it, 179.
  Poſſeſſed himſelf of divers lands belonging to foreigners in
  Wales, as did others according to his example, 189. Takes
  Aberteifi caſtle and raſes it, 191. Subdues Owen Cyfeilioc, 197. Brings the lords of South Wales at enmity with
  King Henry to do him homage, 203. Makes a great feaſt
  at Chriſtmas at Aberteifi, where the bards of North Wales
  and South Wales ſtrive for the maſtery, 205, 206. Takes
  advantage upon King Henry's death to enlarge his country,
  209. His family diminiſhes, 210. Made priſoner by his
  own ſons, 211. Eſcapes, 212. Takes two of his ſons
  priſoners, 212. Dies, ...

English and Normans, 214, 215. Dies, his character and issue, 216.

Rhys Fychan takes Lhanymdhyfri castle, 257.

Rhys ap Gruffydh ap Rhys prevails in South Wales, 239. Does homage to Henry III. 145. Dies, 147.

Rhys ap Meredith unfaithful to his country, 304. Knighted by King Edward; revolts, 305. Defeated, taken prisoner, and executed 306.

Rhythmarch, archbishop of St. David's dies, 122.

Richard king of England's feasts in the Holy Land, 210. Taken prisoner in Austria, ibid. Died of his wounds received at Chalons in France, 219.

Richard of Bourdeaux created prince of Wales, 315.

Robert Cyrthois rebels against his father in Normandy, 110.

Robert earl of Salop rebels against Henry I. 122. Engages the Welch in the quarrel, 123. Seeks aid of Magnus, Harold's son, and fails; banished with his brother Arnulph into Normandy, 124.

Robert de Belissimo a great disturber of the Welch committed to perpetual imprisonment by King Henry, 139.

Roderic Molwynoc succeeded Isor, anno 720, 15. Driven by the Saxons out of the western countries to his inheritance in North Wales, 17 Died soon after, 18.

Roderic the Great, prince of Wales, 27. Beats the Danes out of his country, 33. Fights the English, and with his brother Gwyriad is slain, 34. His pedigree and division of Wales between his three sons, ibid. His imprudence herein, 36.

S.

Saxons, their answer to the British message, 5. They first repel the Scots and Picts, 6. Enter into league with the Scots ibid. They encroach upon the Britains, 19.

Scots and Picts invade Britain, 1.

Siward, Earl, his saying upon his sons being slain in battle, 19. His soldierly temper at his death, 92.

South Wales invaded twice in one year by Ievaf and Iago, princes of North Wales, 55. They quarrel, and the consequence of it, 57. Embroiled in war between Rhys ap Gruffydh and Rhys Fychan, and the former supported by the English, 235, 236.

Stephen king of England agrees with the king of Scots, 157. Ravages Scotland, 160. Suppresses insurrections at home, and routs the Scots by his lieutenants, 161, Besieges Arundel castle in vain, 162. Takes Lincoln, is defeated ... ..., and overthrown

overthrown a fecond time at Wilton, 163. Wins the battle of Farendon, agrees with Henry the Emprefs's fon, and dies, 172.

Stewards, the family, and their original, 91, 92.

Sulien, archbifhop of St. David's dies, 111.

Sulien, a learned man of Llanbadarn dies, 165.

Swane the Dane waftes the ifle of Man. Lands in North Wales, 68. Kills Edwal prince of the country, ibid. His fuccefs in England, and efteemed king hereof, 74, 75.

Swane king of Denmark invades England; and takes York, 102. Forced to fly, ibid.

T.

TRahaern Fychan ftrangely hanged, 217.
    Trahaern ap Caradoc made prince of North Wales, 105. His country invaded from Ireland by Gruffydh ap Conan the right heir, ibid. They fight, and Trahern with his coufins worfted and all flain, 108.

Tribute paid by the prince of Wales to the kings of England, 48.

Tudor Vaughan ap Grono, his family, would be ftiled knight and his reafons for it to King Edward III. who confirmed the honour of it, 314.

V.

VOrtigern invites the Saxons into Britain, 5.
    Vortimer repels the Saxons, 7.

W.

WAles wafted by the Mercians, 24. By King Egbert, ibid. Divided into three provinces, 27. Invaded by the Englifh, 52. Forcibly managed by Ievaf and Iago princes of North Wales only, 56. Afflicted by the Danes, and a murrain, 65. Gives hoftages to pay the antient tribute, 95. Seldom governed by the right heir, 109. Wafted by the Englifh as far as Anglefey, 121. Embroiled with civil divifions, 151. Item, 153, 154. In great fcarcity, 276. Annexed to the crown of England, 300.

Walwey, King Arthur's nephew, his tomb found, whofe body was of a prodigious length, 110.

Welch quarrel amongft themfelves, 22. Ibid. 23. They defeat the Mercians at Conwey, and call it Dial Rhodri, 38. Difable the Danes and Englifh that invaded them, then fall out among themfelves, 61. Too late, fee the folly of foreign aid, 114. Miferably flaughtered, 130, 131. Being at peace from abroad, they fall to their wonted method of   in

The T A B L E.

prince of their oppreffion from the Englifh, 272. Beaten by the Englifh, 279. Worft the Englifh, 297, 298. Beaten in Buelht, ibid. Revolt becaufe of an heavy tax from Edward I. every where, 306. Beat the Englifh, 307. Take the king's carriages, ibid. Routed by the Earl of Warwick, 308. Beat the marchers, but are at loft overcome, and their leader Madoc made prifoner, 309.

Welch minftrels reformed, whereof were three forts, 159.

William duke of Normandy claims the crown of England, 98. Lands at Haftings, and defeats the Englifh, 100.

William I. goes with an army on pilgrimage to St. David's, 110.

William Rufus invades the Welch without fuccefs, 118. Idem, 120. Killed, 122.

F I N I S.

CPSIA information can be obtained
at www.ICGtesting.com
Printed in the USA
BVHW041452171219
566853BV00010B/148/P